The Russian
Provisional Government
1917

VOLUME III

HOOVER INSTITUTION

PUBLICATIONS

HOOVER INSTITUTION PUBLICATIONS

The Russian Provisional Government 1917

DOCUMENTS

Selected and edited by
ROBERT PAUL BROWDER
and
ALEXANDER F. KERENSKY

VOLUME III

STANFORD UNIVERSITY PRESS
STANFORD, CALIFORNIA
1961

STANFORD UNIVERSITY PRESS
STANFORD, CALIFORNIA
© 1961 by the Board of Trustees of the Leland Stanford Junior University
Library of Congress Catalog Card Number: 60-9052
Printed in the United States of America

Contents

OF VOLUMES I, II, AND III

Volume I

Volume II

Volume III

Documents in Volume III

Chapter 22. *The April Crisis and the Formation of a
Coalition Government*

Chapter 23. *The First Coalition Government*

THE FIRST ALL-RUSSIAN CONGRESS OF PEASANTS' SOVIETS

THE EIGHTH CONGRESS OF THE PARTY OF THE
PEOPLE'S FREEDOM (KADETS)

THE RESIGNATION OF KONOVALOV

KRONSTADT

MUNICIPAL DUMA ELECTIONS

THE FIRST ALL-RUSSIAN CONGRESS OF SOVIETS OF WORKERS' AND
SOLDIERS' DEPUTIES AND THE JUNE DEMONSTRATIONS

PART VII. *THE JULY DAYS AND SUBSEQUENT EFFORTS TO STABILIZE THE REGIME*

Chapter 24. *The July Uprising*

THE ARMED DEMONSTRATIONS OF JULY 3–5 AND THEIR SUPPRESSION

Chapter 25. *The Political Crisis*

THE END OF THE FIRST COALITION

THE RECONSTRUCTION OF THE GOVERNMENT

ATTEMPTS TO STRENGTHEN GOVERNMENTAL POWER
AND RESTORE REVOLUTIONARY ORDER

Chapter 26. *The Moscow Conference*

PART VIII. *FROM KORNILOV TO OCTOBER*

Chapter 27. *The Kornilov Affair*

BACKGROUND AND PREPARATION

THE REVOLT

Chapter 28. *Military and Civil Demoralization*

THE ARMY AND NAVY

Chapter 29. *The Dissolution of the Democratic Coalition*

DISSENSION IN THE RANKS OF THE DEMOCRACY,
THE FORMATION OF THE COUNCIL OF FIVE,
AND THE PROCLAMATION OF A REPUBLIC

Chapter 30. *October*

THE FORMATION OF THE LAST MINISTRY

THE PROVISIONAL COUNCIL OF THE RUSSIAN REPUBLIC

THE CONGRESS OF PUBLIC LEADERS AND THE
TENTH CONGRESS OF THE KADET PARTY

THE BOLSHEVIK SEIZURE OF POWER
AND THE LAST STAND OF THE PROVISIONAL GOVERNMENT

The Russian
Provisional Government
1917

VOLUME III

PART VI

The Provisional Government and Political Forces to July

The first weeks following the February revolution passed with a minimum of political controversy, but in an atmosphere of unrestrained liberty and jurisdictional confusion. The Petrograd Soviet and its Executive Committee supported the Provisional Government on the basis of the principles established during the conferences of March 2 between their representatives and those of the Temporary Committee of the State Duma. The various liberal and socialist parties also voiced their individual acceptance of the new regime. Even the small Bolshevik group in Petrograd, temporarily under the leadership of Stalin, advised cautious cooperation. In the Soviet, factionalism was as yet subordinated to common aims.[1] Viewing the Government as an organ of the bourgeoisie, it assumed its self-appointed task as the "watchdog" of the revolution, to control the activities of the Government and ensure faithful adherence to the obligations undertaken. The establishment of this unusual relationship was difficult for both sides.

The disappearance or disorganization of civil and military administrative and enforcement agencies and the disruption of economic and social life had provoked a wave of arbitrary actions throughout the country and in the capital, especially in the army, the factories, and the villages. New spontaneously organized committees and soviets sprang up everywhere. In Petrograd, the Soviet gave invaluable support to the Duma and later the Provisional Government in the restoration of order and the regulation of food supply. But, at the same time, it became the political center for hundreds of thousands of workers and soldiers in the city who were, not unnaturally, disoriented by their sudden complete freedom and concomitant fears of a counterrevolutionary movement. Under these conditions of urgency, uncertainty, and hasty organization, the Soviet often found its course confused and the name of its Executive Committee and its agencies used by the most diverse and frequently irresponsible elements.[2] As a result, serious misunderstandings often developed between it and the Government. To remedy this situation and facilitate relations, the Executive Committee, with the approval of the ministers, appointed a Liaison Committee to meet regularly with members of the Government.

Changes in personnel, as the exiled leaders of the left returned, also affected attitudes and policies. To the benefit of continued cooperation between the Government and the Soviet, Irakli Tsereteli, who arrived from Siberia in March, as-

[1] N. N. Sukhanov, *Zapiski o revoliutsii*, II, 121–22.
[2] See Doc. 1054.

sumed a pre-eminent position in the Soviet, promoting order in its work and advocating that constant vigilance be tempered with restraint and efforts at a *modus vivendi.* To the detriment of concord, Lenin, back in early April from Switzerland via Germany, preached a program calling for no confidence in the Government and the transfer of all power to the Soviets. Although the reaction to these and others of his drastic proposals was in the beginning overwhelmingly antagonistic or amused, undeterred, he set about converting his party and recruiting new supporters.

By the beginning of April, the initial period of popular license had passed, a semblance of order was restored, and political parties began to define their aims more precisely and to work for their accomplishment more forcefully. Political life quickened. So, too, did Soviet demands upon the Government. On the other hand, the Temporary Committee of the State Duma, representing moderate public opinion, showed growing anxiety over the influence of the Soviet, a concern shared by some members of the Provisional Government, principally from the Kadet Party. Still, the leaders of the Soviet refused to recognize that their interference in many of the Government's important political decisions, without complete knowledge of the points at issue or any responsibility for the consequences, reduced the effectiveness of the Government and undermined its authority, which they sought to maintain. Only with the crisis over foreign policy and its accompanying political impasse, precipitated by Miliukov's Note of April 18, did the socialist parties agree to participation in the Government.

On March 27, the Provisional Government had issued an internationally important declaration on the new war aims of free and democratic Russia. But Foreign Minister Miliukov did not officially notify the Allied governments of its publication and contents, leading to speculation in foreign journals that it was only for domestic consumption. Meanwhile, Miliukov's contemporaneous statements, often incompatible with the assertions of the Declaration, caused widespread suspicion of his motives. Finally, the Declaration was transmitted by Miliukov to the Allies with an accompanying Note. When the Note appeared in the press on April 20, a storm of protest rose from the Soviet and left circles in general, who viewed it as a nullification of the Declaration. Strong action was advocated by extremist deputies, but more moderate voices prevailed in the decision to confer with the Government and, simultaneously, appeal to the populace to remain calm and refrain from violence. Nevertheless, the Finland Guard Reserve Regiment, led by a leftist intellectual, F. F. Linde, came into the streets, where it was joined by fellow soldiers and workers, spurred on by Bolshevik and other agitators.

Direct negotiations between the Soviet leaders and members of the Government led to a solution satisfactory to both sides, in the form of a supplementary explanation signed by Miliukov, and to the termination of the unauthorized action of the crowds. It was abundantly clear, however, that beneath the ostensible foreign policy issue in the April Crisis lay the real problem of the moment: the refusal of the left parties to participate in the Government and share responsibility for the direction of the nation.

Thus, immediately following the settlement of the crisis, the Provisional Government, in its Declaration of April 26, after reviewing its accomplishments of the previous two months, gave warning of potential dangers and called for the active support and cooperation of all the progressive elements in the country. "Before Russia rises the terrible apparition of civil war and anarchy, carrying destruction to freedom. There is a somber and grievous course of peoples, a course well known in history, leading from freedom through civil war and anarchy to reaction and the return of despotism. This course must not be the course of the Russian people. . . . The Government, on its part, will be particularly persistent in renewing its efforts directed at expanding its composition by drawing into responsible government work representatives of those active creative forces of the country who have not previously taken direct . . . part in the government of the state."

On the same day, the newspapers published a letter from Kerensky addressed to the Executive Committees of the State Duma and the Petrograd Soviet and to the Central Committees of the Socialist Revolutionary Party and the Trudovik faction. In it, the Minister of Justice insisted that participation of the left parties in the Government was indispensable and implied that he could not otherwise continue in his present post. Two days later, a letter to Chkheidze and Rodzianko from Prince L'vov, also made public, advanced the same appeal and asked Chkheidze to bring the matter before the Soviet Executive Committee. Accordingly, that evening, April 28, the Committee met, only to reject the proposal, after considerable debate, by an inconclusive majority of 23 to 22 votes, with 8 abstentions. The second session on the question took place during the night of May 1–2. Under continued pressure from the Government and growing public criticism of its actions, reinforced by the resignation of Guchkov, a decided change of heart had taken place. The vote was 44 to 19, with two abstentions, to permit representatives of left parties to accept ministerial posts.

The reorganization of the Government on a coalition basis began almost at once. It was immediately preceded by the resignation of Miliukov, following his refusal to accept the proffered portfolio of Education in place of Foreign Affairs, which a majority of his colleagues were convinced he should relinquish. By May 5, the expansion of the Government had been accomplished and a declaration issued outlining its aims and policies. The approval of the Temporary Committee of the Duma and the Executive Committee of the Petrograd Soviet was quickly forthcoming.

For the moment there was a considerable improvement in the political climate. Enjoying more broadly based public confidence, the Government appeared stronger and better prepared to deal with current problems in both domestic and international affairs. But some of the old and new ministers, and the groups they represented, harbored reservations, for contrary reasons, regarding the efficiency of the new structure. Reflecting these doubts, Minister of Trade and Industry Konovalov[3] resigned his post at the end of May with the suggestion that it would be more logical to organize a homogeneous socialist cabinet. Such a proposal was, however, no more acceptable than Miliukov's insistence, at the beginning of the crisis, on continuing the first, almost completely bourgeois ministry.[4] Despite all their divergence of doctrine, the liberals and socialists were agreed on the necessity for cooperation in the defense of the country, at the front against the external enemy and in the rear against the increasing attacks from the Bolshevik Party. The consequences of this disposition of political forces were evident in the Kronstadt episode in the middle of May and the mass demonstration of June 18.

The convocation of the First All-Russian Congress of Soviets of Workers' and Soldiers' Deputies, in May, brought both manifestations of support for the Gov-

[3] At this time Konovalov was still a Progressist. He joined the Kadet Party in the summer.
[4] P. N. Miliukov, *Istoriia vtoroi russkoi revoliutsii*, I, vypusk 1, 103.

ernment and disturbing evidences of dissatisfaction encouraged by Bolshevik propaganda and agitation. In a surprise move on May 31, the Workers' Section voted
for the transfer of all power to the Soviets. Shortly thereafter, the Bolsheviks issued
a call for a demonstration on June 10, but the angry opposition of the Congress persuaded the Party to cancel its appeal, which had been prepared without the knowledge of the Congress.[5] When, after condemning the Bolshevik attempt, the Central
Executive Committee decided to authorize its own demonstration on June 18 to
proclaim the people's confidence in the Congress, the majority was badly shaken
by the prevalence of Bolshevik slogans among the marchers. The news which
reached Petrograd that evening of the successful launching of an offensive tended
to check the anti-Government manifestation in the Capital, but continued Bolshevik activity among the confused and impatient workers and soldiers presaged new
blows against the regime.

[5] On the attitudes and activities of the Congress toward the June 10 demonstration, see I.
Tseretelli, "Nakanune iiul'skogo vosstaniia," *Novyi Zhurnal*, L(1957), 198–219.

CHAPTER 21

Political Parties and the Soviet

PARTY ATTITUDES TOWARD THE FIRST
PROVISIONAL GOVERNMENT

1033. An Appeal from the Party of the People's Freedom (Kadets)

[*"Izvestiia"* Revoliutsionni Nedeli, No. 7, March 3, 1917, p. 1.]

The old government has disappeared. The State Duma, ignoring the differences
in the views of parties, has united in the name of saving our native land and has
taken upon itself the formation of a new government.

Citizens, trust this government, combine your efforts, each one of you to the
last man; let the government which was created by the State Duma perform its
great work of liberating Russia from the external foe and of establishing internal
peace within the country based on the principles of justice, equality, and freedom.

Our valiant army and navy, which have carried the heaviest burden of the disorganization brought into the country by the former government—the army and
the navy which, until now, silently performed their majestic feat on the field of
battle—have performed their civil duty in this most arduous moment for our
native land; they have formed an invincible wall around the representatives of the
people and, together with them, are laying the foundations for a new free Russia.

Let all the differences of party, class, estate, and nationality likewise be forgotten within the country. Let the united Russian people rise in a burst of enthusiasm and create the conditions for the peaceful existence of all citizens. Let the
system be strengthened under which every class, every estate, and every nationality
will be able freely to express its opinions and work for the achievements of its
desires. Now the principal slogan is "Organization and Unity"; organization and
unity for victory over the external foe; organization and unity for internal construction. And let hope kindle in the hearts of all that this time we will succeed
in avoiding fatal disunity.

The dawn of freedom blazes over our native land at a time of gravest ordeals.
These ordeals make it incumbent upon us to exhibit the highest degree of self-
discipline and, fixing our eyes on the immediate goal—the consolidation of the
new power, to preserve peace and order in every way and to prevent the old
power from taking advantage of possible confusion within our ranks.

Citizens, the Party of the People's Freedom calls upon all of you, each one in
his place, to exert every effort for the protection of the new order. Let each one
bring a sacrifice within his powers to his reborn native land. Let every peasant,
cultivator, and *pomeshchik* bring grain for the army and the urban population,
with a feeling of assurance that the grain will be used for feeding the truly hungry
and will not fall into evil hands. Let the merchant open up his storehouses with
the assurance that there will no longer be extortion and mercenary acts, which
used to leave some unpunished and others burdened by requisitions impossible

to fill. Let the working people go to work with redoubled energy, with the assurance that the foremost concern of the new government will be to provide for those
who are facilitating the prosecution of the war by their labor and are staunchly
repelling the enemy, and for the peasants who are obtaining the bread for them.
Let all the old offenses be forgotten in the general enthusiasm and may they never
revive. May our native land emerge from these grave ordeals happy, free, and
united by the bonds of love and universal brotherhood.

CENTRAL COMMITTEE OF THE PARTY OF THE PEOPLE'S FREEDOM

1034. THE VOTE OF THE SEVENTH CONGRESS OF THE PARTY OF THE PEOPLE'S FREEDOM IN FAVOR OF A DEMOCRATIC PARLIAMENTARY REPUBLIC

[*Rech'*, No. 72, March 26, 1917, pp. 3–4.]

The business part of the Congress was opened [on March 25] by the address of
F. F. Kokoshkin on the revision of Section II of the party program on the state
regime in Russia. M. M. Vinaver presided.

. . .

The formula about the democratic republic is on the lips of everyone, said
Prof. Kokoshkin. This formula should be well defined. Eleven years ago the program of the party included a point on the desirability of a parliamentary monarchy as the form of government for Russia. However, we could not be called
monarchists in the true sense of the word. Most of us never regarded monarchy,
even a parliamentary one, as the best form of government. To us monarchy was
never that supreme principle which guided our entire political program. To us
monarchy was at that time not a question of principle but a political expediency.
On the question of the state regime we always differentiated between the question
of form and the question of substance and content. The second question was always
the most essential and basic for us.

Our conception of a state regime is based on three principles—the principle
of the inviolability of civil liberty and civil equality, the principle of the guaranty
of complete rule by popular will, and the principle of realizing the bases of social
justice.

The implementation of these principles was the aim of the party. Everything
else serves merely as a means to this aim. From this point of view, when eleven
years ago the question of the form of government was being decided, the party
proceeded in the light of the political conditions of the time. At that time monarchy had just accepted the principle of representative institutions, and naturally
to talk of a republic seemed inexpedient. We knew that constitutional monarchy
was nothing more than a compromise between the beginning of popular rule and
absolutism. But this compromise was for the majority a historic transitory step.
History shows that leaps from absolutism to popular rule seldom occurred quite
happily. On the contrary they frequently resulted in a dangerous relapse to personal rule. In our opinion parliamentary monarchy was the best means of forestalling such undesirable consequences. Moreover, we had in mind the fact that
parliamentary monarchy in actual practice reduces the difference between this
form of government and the republican form to an insignificant minimum. We
also had in mind the fact that England, at any rate, is no less free than France

and is infinitely more free than Mexico or any republic of South or Central America. Moreover, the attitude of the population toward monarchy eleven years ago was quite different from what it is now. We took into consideration, therefore, the people's habit of embodying the conception of the state only in a living symbol. Conditions today have changed radically. These eleven years did not pass in vain for Russia. During these eleven years Russia made tremendous strides in her political development.

The Russian people passed that stage of political development where a conception of the state is impossible without a personal symbol. They no longer need this symbol now.

Parallel with this, another process also occurred in the life of the country which culminated in the Great War. During this war the old formula "For the Tsar and the Fatherland" was shattered. It seemed that one could not be for the Tsar and the fatherland because monarchy was against the fatherland. (*Applause*.) One could be either for the Tsar or for the fatherland. The people had no choice. The army and the people rose for the fatherland and against the Tsar. The war was a test both for the monarch and the people. The people passed that test; the monarchy failed.

The whole force of the monarchy resided in the continuity of traditions, but this succession no longer exists now. The question is not the continuation of monarchy, but its restoration, and of course no party in any way aligned with democratic principles can set itself the aim of restoring what no longer exists. Now in order to restore monarchy blood would have to be shed, just as heretofore blood had to be shed to bring about a republic, because as a matter of fact the republic is already in existence.

·   ·   ·

Resolution of the Congress on the Democratic Republic

The Congress took the vote. Accompanied by tempestuous applause, the following resolution proposed by F. F. Kokoshkin was accepted unanimously.

"Russia must be a democratic parliamentary republic. Legislative power must belong to the national representatives. At the head of the executive power must be a president of the republic elected for a definite period of time by the national representatives and governing with the aid of a ministry responsible to the people."

·   ·   ·

1035. THE POLITICAL PLATFORM OF THE COOPERATIVE MOVEMENT
[*Russkiia Vedomosti*, No. 71, March 30, 1917, p. 3.]

One of the most significant political events of recent days is undoubtedly the all-Russian Cooperative Congress which met in Moscow from the 25th to the 28th of March. To the Congress came representatives of an army of cooperative workers many millions strong, the best organized, or, to tell the truth, the only really organized part of the population, and in the course of four days they kept providing answers to the whole series of urgent questions which face the country. Among the questions were those that demand imperative solution without any delay and that can be solved at all satisfactorily only by the united efforts of the entire Russian cooperative movement. Such a question, first of all, is the problem of food supply. Having inherited in this respect an extremely heavy burden from the old regime, the Provisional Government chose a perfectly correct way out in turning for help to the cooperatives, and calling on them with an appeal to "hold up their wide powerful shoulders," to take upon them this "heavy burden" and to "engage the whole nation in this task, everybody who can provide bread." This appeal did not go unheeded. The cooperative movement had even before that delegated some of its most prominent workers to the staffs of central organs of the rejuvenated Ministry of Agriculture for managing the food-supply matters. Now, the Congress sanctioned the readiness of the cooperatives to take this matter into their own hands. Of course, the cooperative workers who gathered at the Congress realized the full difficulty and responsibility of the task imposed upon them, but they refused to be frightened either by work or by responsibility. An appeal was put forth at the Congress for stern, everyday work to prevent a food-supply collapse, with a slogan "To the hold!" to staunch the leak in the Ship of State. At a difficult moment, and in perhaps the most responsible matter, the Cooperative Congress gave its support to the Provisional Government, and the latter is now truly leaning on the powerful shoulders of the Russian cooperative movement.

But this is only one side of the matter. . . . The cooperative workers, according to a picturesque expression of one of the orators who spoke at the Congress, "are imbedded deep in the very heart of the population," and, with their degree of organization and numerical strength, we might expect to hear the true voice of the whole country and its hopes and moods precisely at the Cooperative Congress rather than at some other assemblage, no matter how numerous. Remaining on a strictly democratic platform, the Congress gave a proper rebuff to the attacks against the Provisional Government emanating from certain democratic circles, and it placed itself in a truly statesmanlike position in regard to the war.

. . . At the Cooperative Congress the appeals to Germany met with no sympathy, and the cooperative workers proved not to be frightened by the idea of the possibility of correcting the geographic borders in favor of Russia; they bring such amendments to the formula "peace without annexations" as would hardly please the authors of this formula.

Despite the revolution that has been achieved, despite the time of transition through which we are living, the broad masses of people still maintain their emotional balance and judge quite soberly the state problems which face Russia. This frame of mind, which was clearly shown in all of the activities of the Cooperative Congress, imparts to it an especially great significance. It enhances our faith that the healthy instincts of the people will lead the country onto the right road.

1036. An Appeal from the Trudoviks

[*Izvestiia*, No. 5, March 4, 1917, p. 4.]

By your courageous efforts and your heroic perseverance you were able in the very first days to capture the most fortified and the most prominent, frontal positions of the old regime. Remain strong and persevering to the end.

The struggle has not ended. Our enemies will still be grasping at every opportunity to shoot from behind every corner. They will not stop at cruel bloodshed in order to replace the sovereign will of the people by the interests of people who are masters of every shade of treachery and deceit and who crave exclusive right to power and wealth.

Be capable of countering this irresponsible stubbornness of the old regime with *adamant courage* and counter its belief in traditional blind obedience with your discipline, which stems from inner freedom.

Counter the far-from-depleted material resources of the old regime with your high degree of *organization*.

In the name of this discipline, in the name of organization, in the name of final victory, *there is no place—nor must there be any place—for party strife and misunderstanding in the ranks of the revolutionary people.*

Everyone sympathizing with the cause of national emancipation must march arm in arm, shoulder to shoulder, to storm the last strongholds of the regime, subordinating themselves completely to the Provisional Government, organized by the State Duma.

Among the members of the new government are persons who have the reputation of being staunch and courageous defenders of the interests of the people; the new government has established a close relationship with the Soviet of Workers' Deputies, which was created for the purpose of representing the interests of the working people.

Submission to the new center of power, endurance and discipline, are the absolutely essential conditions for assuring the quick and inevitable victory of the people.

We believe that the victorious people will be able to cope with the heavy burden of the legacy of the old regime and will do everything possible to overcome the disorder in the matter of food supplies and put an end to the anarchy of street violence and looting.

The working people and our people's army will then emerge from the struggle with minimum losses.

Comrades-Citizens, especially you, workers, who suffered more than anyone else under the old regime, remember that the future of our country is in your hands.

Be staunch, self-denying, and enduring to the end.

THE TRUDOVIKS

1037. SOCIALIST REVOLUTIONARY SUPPORT FOR THE PROVISIONAL GOVERNMENT
[Leading editorial in *Delo Naroda*, No. 1, March 15, 1917, p. 1.]

The political program of the new government is promulgated. The party is confronted with the questions: how to treat it and, accordingly, what position to assume toward the Provisional Government—to support it or to combat it?

The answer to these questions has already been given in the resolutions of the Petrograd and regional conferences of the Socialist Revolutionaries.[1] It declares: "The Conference considers it most necessary to support the Provisional Government in so far as it fulfills the political program which it has announced" ...

But it would be a grave error to think that this decision is dictated only by purely negative motives of fear of splitting the ranks and of possible counterrevolution. Such compromise and political fear were always foreign to the tactics of genuine socialism. . . .

. . . .

[1] For a description of these conferences and other contemporary events in the Party, see Oliver H. Radkey, *The Agrarian Foes of Bolshevism*, p. 140 ff., and all of Chap. V.

In the declaration of the Provisional Government we read, on the contrary, that "it has not the slightest intention of taking advantage of the military situation to delay in any way the realization of reforms and legislation."[2]

Such a declaration, speaking for the sincerity of the new government, forces us to admit that our fatherland possesses a degree of political freedom which is at the present moment greater than the political freedom of any of the Allied or enemy states. More than that: the same declaration contains some points which are not taken into consideration in any of the belligerent countries of Europe. Such a point is paragraph seven of the declaration, which declares: "While preserving strict military discipline on duty and during military service, the soldiers are to be free from all restrictions in the exercise of those civil rights to which all other citizens are entitled." This condition, which has already begun to be implemented by means of various orders of the War Minister, represents a concept unknown to the armies of the most advanced democracies.

On the strength of the above it cannot but be admitted that the political program of the government is quite broad.

Consequently, in accepting it, the Party accepts in this respect its own program. By defending it, it defends its demands. By supporting the Provisional Government it realizes through it its own aims.

Such are the purely positive motives which conditioned the acceptance of the above-mentioned resolution.

Needless to say, this decision in no way obligates the Party to support the new authority under all circumstances.

The Party "reserves the right to change its attitude toward the Provisional Government should it deviate from the fulfillment of its outlined program." This, to be sure, self-evident qualification is not devoid of deep meaning and content.

The declaration of the government so far only outlines the area of inalienable civil rights. As yet we have no concrete measures for the realization of freedom of speech, press, unions, etc.

If, in implementing the freedoms, deviations from the proclaimed principles should occur, we shall naturally have to replace our tactics of active support of the government with a tactic of direct struggle against it.

1038. A MENSHEVIK STATEMENT ON THE PROVISIONAL GOVERNMENT
[Editorial in *Rabochaia Gazeta*, No. 1, March 7, 1917, p. 1.]

It is *temporary*, i.e., it exists only until the time when the Constituent Assembly creates a permanent one. It is *revolutionary*, i.e., it was created by a revolution in order finally to consolidate its gains and to cast down the old regime. It is a *government*, i.e., it possesses the full power which is supported by the revolutionary army and the people.

Its tasks are clear and simple: with the support of the people and the army, to destroy swiftly and decisively *everything* that remains of the old order and that interferes with the new one, and to create, just as swiftly and decisively, everything without which the new order cannot exist. The Soviet of Workers' and Soldiers' Deputies has already exercised its influence, at the formation of the Provisional Government, to the effect that the program of the Government contains all the measures that are necessary for the establishment of democratic Russia.

[2] Volume I, Doc. 112.

The workers and the army are ready—while preserving their independence—to march together, and they say: act, demolish, and build! Without delay, for delay is like unto death.

Arrest the entire Imperial family. Appoint new officials and replace the old, unfit ones. Introduce by decree a democratic organization in the army and abolish there the hated system of bondage. Establish civil equality before the law, legalize all freedoms, abolish all discriminations. The decrees must be brief, simple, and intelligible to everyone: "Class privileges for upper classes and class discriminations against lower ones are hereby abolished. All citizens are equal before the law." This decree, consisting of a few words, would tear out by the roots, to the very foundation, the disfranchisement of the peasant class, on the one hand, and the unlimited privileges of the gentry, on the other. Or: "Local self-government is established on the basis of universal franchise." Out of a few words, a new free Russia emerges. In order to destroy the master-slave relations in the army, all Guchkov has to do is to issue immediately a number of orders abolishing all former measures which humiliated the human dignity of the soldiers and deprived them of all civic rights.

If the Provisional Government fulfills its duty, *if* it begins to act, without reservation and delay, in the way that the interests of democratic Russia demand, if it carries *to the end* the struggle against the old regime, then it inevitably will enjoy the confidence of the people, and the struggle will be carried on on a single front: against the common foe—the remnants of the old regime.

The proletariat and the revolutionary army showed by their entire demeanor, during the first and most difficult week of the revolution, their readiness not to split, and to conduct the cause of the liberation of Russia together with the liberal bourgeoisie. Now it is up to the Provisional Government to show by its *actions* that it deserves the support accorded it.

Members of the Provisional Government! The proletariat and the army await immediate orders from you concerning the consolidation of the revolution and the democratization of Russia. Our support is contingent on *your* actions. The sooner and the more decisively you act, the sooner and more thoroughly will preparations be made for the Constituent Assembly, whose decisions will determine the subsequent fate of Russia. Let us get down to work, and destroy the old and preserve the new Russia! We demand from you the immediate realization of your program!

1039. LENIN'S APRIL THESES

[*Collected Works of V. I. Lenin: The Revolution of 1917*, XX, Bk. I, 95–103, 106–10. Lenin arrived in Petrograd on the night of April 3. The following day, he read and commented upon these Theses first to a meeting of his fellow Bolsheviks and then to a joint conference of Bolsheviks and Mensheviks called to discuss the possible union of all the Social Democratic factions. They were then published in *Pravda* on April 7. At the conference, Lenin also vigorously opposed unification, called for a re-examination of the whole program of the Party, recommended the change of its name to the Communist Party, and, in general, laid to rest the attempts at unity. *Izvestiia*, No. 36, April 9, 1917, pp. 3–4.

Previous to Lenin's return, the party line in Petrograd, as expressed in *Pravda*, had moved from attacks on the Provisional Government in the first days, during the editorship of Molotov and Shliapnikov, to conditional support of the Government and a more conciliatory attitude toward other socialist parties, under the direction of Stalin,

Kamenev, and Muranov after March 15, following their return from Siberia. Meantime, Lenin, in Switzerland, was developing the program which he publicized in the Theses. See David Shub, *Lenin*, pp. 176–79.]

1. In our attitude toward the war not the slightest concession must be made to "revolutionary defencism," for under the new government of Lvov and Co., owing to the capitalist nature of this government, the war on Russia's part remains a predatory imperialist war.

The class-conscious proletariat may give its consent to a revolutionary war actually justifying revolutionary defencism, only on condition (a) that all power be transferred to the proletariat and its ally, the poorest section of the peasantry; (b) that all annexations be renounced in deeds, not merely in words; (c) that there be a complete break, in practice, with all interests of capital.

In view of the undoubted honesty of the mass of rank and file representatives of revolutionary defencism who accept the war only as a necessity and not as a means of conquest, in view of their being deceived by the bourgeoisie, it is necessary most thoroughly, persistently, patiently to explain to them their error, to explain the inseparable connection between capital and the imperialist war, to prove that without the overthrow of capital it is *impossible* to conclude the war with a really democratic, non-oppressive peace.

This view is to be widely propagated among the army units in the field. Fraternisation.

2. The peculiarity of the present situation in Russia is that it represents a *transition* from the first stage of the revolution, which, because of the inadequate organisation and insufficient class-consciousness of the proletariat, led to the assumption of power by the bourgeoisie,—to its second stage which is to place power in the hands of the proletariat and the poorest strata of the peasantry.

This transition is characterised, on the one hand, by a maximum of legality (Russia is now the freest of all the belligerent countries of the world); on the other, by the absence of oppression of the masses, and, finally, by the trustingly ignorant attitude of the masses toward the capitalist government, the worst enemy of peace and Socialism.

This peculiar situation demands of us an ability to adapt ourselves to the specific conditions of party work amidst vast masses of the proletariat just awakened to political life.

3. No support to the Provisional Government; exposure of the utter falsity of all of its promises, particularly those relating to the renunciation of annexations. Unmasking, instead of admitting, the illusion-breeding "demand" that *this* government, a government of capitalists, cease being imperialistic.

4. Recognition of the fact that in most of the Soviets of Workers' Deputies our party constitutes a minority, and a small one at that, in the face of the *bloc* of all the petty-bourgeois opportunist elements, from the People's Socialists, Socialists-Revolutionists, down to the Organisation Committee (Chkheidze, Tsereteli, etc., Steklov, etc.), who have yielded to the influence of the bourgeoisie and have been extending this influence to the proletariat as well.

It must be explained to the masses that the Soviet of Workers' Deputies is the only possible form of revolutionary government and that, therefore, our task is, while this government is submitting to the influence of the bourgeoisie, to present a patient, systematic, and persistent analysis of its errors and tactics, an analysis especially adapted to the practical needs of the masses.

While we are in the minority, we carry on the work of criticism and of exposing errors, advocating all along the necessity of transferring the entire power of state to the Soviets of Workers' Deputies, so that the masses might learn from experience how to rid themselves of errors.

5. Not a parliamentary republic,—a return to it from the Soviet of Workers' Deputies would be a step backward—but a republic of Soviets of Workers', Agricultural Labourers' and Peasants' Deputies throughout the land, from top to bottom.

Abolition of the police, the army, the bureaucracy.*

All officers to be elected and to be subject to recall at any time, their salaries not to exceed the average wage of a competent worker.

6. In the agrarian programme, the emphasis must be shifted to the Soviets of Agricultural Labourers' Deputies.

Confiscation of all private lands.

Nationalisation of all lands in the country, and management of such lands by local Soviets of Agricultural Labourers' and Peasants' Deputies. A separate organisation of Soviets of Deputies of the poorest peasants. Creation of model agricultural establishments out of large estates (from one hundred to three hundred *desiatinas,* in accordance with local and other conditions and with the estimates of local institutions) under the control of the Soviet of Agricultural Labourers' Deputies, and at public expense.

7. Immediate merger of all the banks in the country into one general national bank, over which the Soviet of Workers' Deputies should have control.

. . .

8. Not the "introduction" of Socialism as an immediate task, but the immediate placing of the Soviet of Workers' Deputies in control of social production and distribution of goods.

9. Party tasks:

    A. Immediate calling of a party convention.

    B. Changing the party programme, mainly:

        1. Concerning imperialism and the imperialist war.

        2. Concerning our attitude toward the state, and our demand for a "commune state."†

        3. Amending our antiquated minimum programme.

    C. Changing the name of the party.‡

10. Rebuilding the International.

    Taking the initiative in the creation of a revolutionary International, an International against the social-chauvinists and against the "centre."§

---

* Substituting for the standing army the universal arming of the people.

† A state the model for which was given by the Paris Commune.

‡ Instead of "Social-Democracy," whose official leaders throughout the world have betrayed Socialism, by going over to the bourgeoisie (defencists and vacillating Kautskians), we must call ourselves the *Communist Party.*

§ The "centre" in the international Social-Democracy is the tendency vacillating between chauvinists ("defencists") and internationalists, *i.e.,* Kautsky and Co. in Germany, Longuet and Co. in France, Chkheidze and Co. in Russia, Turati and Co. in Italy, MacDonald and Co. in England, etc.

1040. *Rabochaia Gazeta* ON LENIN'S PROGRAM
[No. 24, April 6, 1917, p. 1.]

When Lenin, just returned from exile, was reading his report at the conference on unification of the Social Democrats, many of his listeners felt the touch of a real, genuine tragedy, the tragedy which is concealed in every revolution, the tragedy of revolution's transformation into reaction. The developing revolution is always menaced by danger not only from the right, but from the left as well. The revolution can successfully struggle against reaction and force it out of its position only so long as it is able to remain within the limits which are predetermined by the objective necessity (the state of productive forces, the level of mentality of the masses of people corresponding to it, etc.). One cannot render a better service to reaction than by disregarding those limits and by making attempts at breaking them.

Lenin arrived in our midst in order to render this service to reaction. After his speech, we can say that each significant success of Lenin will be a success of reaction, and all struggle against counterrevolutionary aspirations and intrigues will be hopeless until we secure our left flank, until we render politically harmless, by a decisive rebuff, the current which Lenin heads. . . .

. . . It is imperative, by active struggle and propaganda, to render the revolution safe from this stab in the back which is being prepared for it.

People who call to their aid the best, the most cherished aspirations of the proletariat are coming to the aid of reaction. Basing themselves on those aspirations and on the illusory possibility of putting them into effect, they will arouse against the revolution the backward majority of the population of the country, and thereby pave the sure road to reaction.

An undoubted danger threatens the revolution. Before it is too late, Lenin and his supporters must be given a most decisive rebuff.

1041. CHERNOV ON LENIN
[*Delo Naroda*, No. 26, April 16, 1917, p. 1.]

The average man is always inclined to be panicky. The average man is always inclined to expect all sorts of horrors. The average man always expects the coming of antichrist.

Such an antichrist has now appeared. This antichrist is Lenin. Avid for sensation, some popular and semipopular newspapers artlessly reflected the panic of the average man, others exploited it in the interest of sales, and a third group supported it simply because it is easier to talk about people than about ideas. And the latest "legend about antichrist" grows like a snowball. . . .

.   .   .

I think that Lenin can only thank his enemies for this assiduity. I think that it is in the interests of Lenin to become a "bugaboo" to the bourgeoisie, to play upon its imagination as a living embodiment of the specter of social war with a head of Medusa, with the blazing wind-blown hair and an arsonist's torch in hand. He can only rejoice at the hatred of the bourgeoisie. It is only to his advantage to have daily all the mongrels, foaming at the mouth, rush at him through the literary back door. And when he is attacked by the enemies of his ideas from the camp of the socialists, he will attempt to irritate them in a haughty and rude fashion to such an extent that they will lose all balance and resort to polemic excesses. Then he has them in his hand. They can easily be dumped into one pile with the heroes of the bourgeois, baited by the leader of the Social Democrats, who has renamed himself a "communist."

For Lenin is a typical outcome—I would say more—a victim of those abnormal political conditions that have existed in Russia up to this time. . . .

By his endowments Lenin is an outstanding figure, cruelly shallowed, distorted by the abnormal conditions of that time.

Lenin possesses an imposing wholeness. He seems to be made of one chunk of granite. And he is all round and polished like a billiard ball. There is nothing you can get hold of him by. He rolls with irrepressible speed. But he could repeat to himself the well-known phrase: *"Je ne sais pas où je vais, mais j'y vais résolument"*—"I don't know where I am going, but I am going there resolutely."

Lenin possesses a devotion to the revolutionary cause which permeates his entire being. But to him revolution is embodied in his person . . .

Lenin possesses an outstanding mind, but it is a mind that embraces things not with three dimensions; it is a *mind of one dimension*—more than that, a unilinear mind. . . .

Lenin is unquestionably a pure man, and all filthy insinuation of the narrow-minded press to German money in connection with his passing through Germany must be once and for all kicked aside with disgust. But he is a man of one-sided will and consequently a man with a stunned moral sensitivity. He marches toward his chief aim. All that is important for him is the correctness of the basic direction. Everything else is unimportant. As for the choice of methods, this is sheer particulars and details. I am convinced that he never gave a thought to the fact that to petition the government of Wilhelm through Platten for the right to travel is something not too far removed from addressing a petition to his imperial majesty in the good old days. . . .

As is known, Lenin was never distinguished by excessive moral sensitivity or by inordinate tact. He substituted inflexibility for them.

Lenin has a great militant temperament and a tremendous reserve of energy. But up to this time he has been condemned to shallowness in microscopic class squabbles. Deprived of an arena to pour out his energy in great political actions, he poured it out in great polemic words. He has elaborated a jargon capable of offending the most insensitive ear. His settling of accounts with opponents screeches crunchingly like iron over glass. He loves to fence, but he fences with a heavy shaft, its weight and energy dominating his sweeping movements, and not vice versa. His entire socialism is a sort of uncouth socialism, for Lenin employs a clumsy axe where a sharp and fine scalpel is called for.

At the bottom of his volitional impulses there is in Lenin almost always some grain of unquestionably vital and political truth. But, good God, what does he not contrive to do with this poor little truth that falls into his hands! . . . He supports it strongly and firmly as a rope supports a hangman.

Such is this curious political figure. The new Russian life must break it. I am amused by the fears that the reverse will occur, that he will destroy the new Russian life. Mice squeak about them for whom "there is no stronger beast than a cat." I am amused also that Lenin should hypnotize the attention of such newspapers as *Edinstvo*, and one wonders what would become of them should Lenin suddenly die by the will of God or should he have not been born.[2] Everything should be reduced to true, real and not fantastic, proportions. We shall analyze point by point the Lenin program and shall attempt first of all to grasp his starting point and the basic motives that inspire him. But is it not clear at first sight that, perhaps more than anything else, it expresses an intoxication with the air of the revolution and dizziness from the extreme heights to which events raised us? Is it not clear that we deal here with the absence of a feeling of responsibility gained through life for one's "words and gestures," an absence so understandable in the past when these "words and gestures" had no particular consequences and were evaluated only from the point of view of how they appeared outwardly?

Let us, therefore, not be unduly frightened by Lenin's political excesses, just because their derivation and character are too clear. The extent of their influence, and consequently also their dangers, will be extremely limited and "localized." We, socialists, can localize it. And we shall do it the sooner the less we are disturbed by the senseless uproar of the timid souls who are frightened to death.

VICTOR CHERNOV

THE SOVIET AND THE QUESTION OF DUAL POWER

1042. *Izvestiia* ON THE DEGREE OF SOVIET PARTICIPATION IN OR COLLABORATION WITH THE PROVISIONAL GOVERNMENT

[Leading editorial, No. 3, March 2, 1917, p. 2. A similar stand was taken in *Rabochaia Gazeta*, No. 1, March 7, 1917, p. 1. See also Volume I, Docs. 104, 113, and 119.]

The bourgeois parties that have currently joined the Temporary Committee of the State Duma are by no means burning with desire to consummate the revolution and to realize the complete triumph of democracy. The most attractive outcome for them would be a compromise with the old regime, the return to power of Nicholas II in the role of a "constitutional monarch." However, the vitality and the solidarity of the revolutionary democracy have already compelled the bourgeoisie to take a few steps beyond the limits of the position that the ruling class was unwilling to abandon. The Temporary Committee had to become the Provisional Government, to sanction the arrests of ministers and other agents of the old regime, and to establish a new power by revolutionary means. But in order to prevent the transformation of the revolution into a counterrevolution, the democratic forces must participate with unbounded energy in the further reorganization of the country; they must become an organic part of the Provisional Government, preventing it from stopping at midpoint, driving it further and further until the Constituent Assembly, elected on the basis of universal, equal, direct, and secret suffrage, consolidates the new republic on firm and unshakable foundations. The realization of this goal requires, of course, not only collaboration with the bourgeoisie in the ranks of the Provisional Government, but also the existence of

---

[2] *Edinstvo* was the organ of G. V. Plekhanov.

a powerful and independent organization of democratic forces such as the Soviet of Workers' and Soldiers' Deputies, since it is only by drawing on the strength of the latter that the democratic members of the Provisional Government will be able to command the respect of their bourgois colleagues. But while the real strength of the democratic forces springs exclusively from its own solidarity in the revolutionary struggle, it would be a very serious mistake to arrive at the conclusion that participation in the Provisional Government carries no vital significance to the representatives of workers, peasants, and soldiers, or that the goals of democracy can be realized only by the efforts of a union of strictly democratic forces.

Should the revolutionary Soviets of Workers' Deputies sever all connections with the Provisional Government, the bourgeoisie will inevitably view them as the mainspring of a democratic as well as a socialist coup d'état. The fear of this "red phantom," of course, will reinforce and intensify the [counterrevolutionary?][3] tendencies of the bourgeoisie, and in this manner, instead of pushing the bourgeoisie ahead, we will throw it a long way back and force it to dream of the restoration of autocracy as the only bulwark against socialism. There would be no disaster in such a change of front by the ruling classes if the democratic forces could build the entire state apparatus, relying solely on their own forces and drawing on organizers solely from their own midst.

But, comrades, no matter how great are the capabilities, the energy, and the courage of the revolutionary elements of Russian democracy, it must be admitted that the democratic forces, by themselves, in a struggle against a coalition of all the bourgeois elements, are not as yet capable of fulfilling a task of such enormous complexity as the establishment of a state system.

In the meantime, the reactionaries would skillfully exploit every mistake on the part of a government created by the Soviet of Workers' and Soldiers' Deputies; they would have no difficulty in stirring up discontent among the backward elements of the military and civilian population and, in this way, lay the groundwork for creating cadres of a counterrevolutionary army.

Regardless of the dauntless courage with which our revolutionary soldiers would throw themselves into the struggle against this black army, when abandoned at a crucial moment by the officers they would inevitably fall victims to it.

The tactics of total isolation promise us nothing but a quick and certain collapse of the national revolution. The adoption of such tactics would be a fatal mistake, bordering on suicide.

1043. THE APPOINTMENT OF A COMMISSION FOR LIAISON WITH THE GOVERNMENT BY THE EXECUTIVE COMMITTEE OF THE SOVIET

[Session of March 8. *Protokoly*, pp. 26–27. The Commission remained very active until after the formation of the first coalition government. See N. N. Sukhanov, *The Russian Revolution, 1917*, Joel Carmichael, ed. and trans., *passim*.]

After a lively exchange of opinions, the following propositions were accepted:

1. Pursuant to the decision of the Soviet of Workers' and Soldiers' Deputies[4] and in line with the general policy laid down by it, the Executive Committee of

---

[3] Illegible in text.
[4] On March 2. See Volume I, Doc. 104.

the Soviet of Workers' and Soldiers' Deputies finds it necessary to adopt immediate measures for keeping the Soviet informed of the intentions and actions of the Government; to keep the latter informed of the demands of the revolutionary people; to bring influence to bear upon the Government for the purpose of satisfying these demands; and to exercise vigilant control over the realization of these demands.

2. In order to carry out this resolution, the Executive Committee of the Soviet of Workers' and Soldiers' Deputies is selecting a delegation composed of the following comrades: Skobelev, Steklov, Sukhanov, Filipovskii, and Chkheidze; and is instructing them to enter at once into negotiations with the Provisional Government.

3. Upon establishing the results of these negotiations, a delegation shall be selected for the establishment of permanent relations with the Council of Ministers, with the individual ministries and departments for the purpose of realizing the demands of the revolutionary people.

1044. The Selection of a Delegation from the Provisional Government to Meet with the Liaison Commission
[Proposed by Kerensky, *Zhurnaly*, No. 14, March 10, 1917.]

Resolved:

To select for negotiations with the Soviet of Workers' and Soldiers' Deputies, regarding the establishment of mutual relations between the Provisional Government and the aforesaid Soviet, a delegation consisting of three representatives of the Provisional Government: Minister-President Prince Georgii Evgen'evich L'vov, Minister of Transport Nikolai Vissarionovich Nekrasov, and the Minister of Finance Mikhail Ivanovich Tereshchenko.

1045. *Den'* on the Liaison Commission
[No. 7, March 12, 1917, p. 1.]

The decision of the Soviet of Workers' and Soldiers' Deputies to form a five-member commission for preliminary agreement on and control over the most essential measures of the Provisional Government is an act of great political importance. In this way the degree of coordination between the Government and the revolutionary forces will be greatly enhanced and the work of the two organs of the revolution, which differ in political composition, will reach the necessary degree of unity.

As is known, the question of two representatives of the Soviet of Deputies joining the membership of the Provisional Government has been resolved in the negative. A. F. Kerensky received an unofficial but sufficiently emphatic approval for his decision to enter the cabinet after his decision was made.[5] In a general way, further relations between the Soviet of Deputies and the Provisional Government have progressed in a most satisfactory manner. On all the more or less serious questions complete agreement has been reached.

At every important balloting of the Soviet of Deputies the Bolshevik and anarchic elements received a pitifully insignificant number of votes. It became

[5] Volume I, Docs. 105, 106.

the practice that more than 1,000 members voted for and an insignificant group of 20–40 persons voted against the Executive Committee's proposals, which were dictated by the necessity to maintain unity between the people and the Government.

As a result, the Provisional Government itself, which naturally was inclined to exaggerate the danger of a split, has begun to show in this matter a desirable measure of equanimity.

. . .

The Provisional Government should hasten to accept the decision of the Soviet of Deputies not only for the sake of the revolution, but also for the sake of con- solidating its own authority in the eyes of the Russian masses at large. As a matter of fact, they are the same thing. By accepting the proposal of the Soviet of Deputies, the Provisional Government will avoid a number of partial misunder- standings and, instead of undergoing the consequent and therefore inevitably sharpened criticisms, will be able to carry out its orders in the absolute certainty that they have the support of the Soviet of Deputies. For, by sending the com- mission, [the Soviet] assumes, for the time being, its part in the responsibility for these orders.

When the decision of the Soviet of Deputies is put into practice, the present panicky whisperings, on the one hand, and the anarchic ventures of the advocates of the Dictatorship of the Proletariat, on the other, will have to disappear under the pressure of organized public opinion, of broad groups of the population.

1046. GENERAL KORNILOV AND THE SOVIET

[Session of the Executive Committee, March 10. *Protokoly*, pp. 34, 36. General Korni- lov had been appointed Commander of the Petrograd Military District. Following the April Days, he was relieved at his request and transferred to the front.]

Pal'chinskii had a conversation with Kornilov. Kornilov wished to keep in contact with the Executive Committee and the Military Committee. He offered to confirm by orders to the Military District [the appointment] of persons who had been approved for office by the Military Committee. Kornilov advised that he is dismissing persons who have not been approved because of their hostile attitude toward the revolution; he will approve all instructions regarding the movement of troops, etc. Pal'chinskii believes that General Kornilov has fully grasped the state of affairs and can be retained as Commander of the Military District.

. . .

A report on the necessity of being circumspect with him [Kornilov], that he is a general of the old vintage who wants to put an end to the revolution:

Steklov is pressing for the realization of all our demands in the rear, for the promise to revise the regulations in the active army, for the refusal to withdraw the garrison.

Sokolovskii believes that the fighting capacity of the army can be restored by appointing commanders who are acceptable to the people and the soldiers and by carrying out a minimum of democratic reforms in the active army.

One of the members of the Executive Committee proposed that a neutral posi- tion be maintained on the question of strengthening the authority of Kornilov.

The only units of the local garrison that can be withdrawn are those that are still untrained and did not participate in the movement.

Skobelev pointed out the doubts that we have about him [Kornilov].

Pavlovich proposed insistance on the elective principle for Petrograd;* also for the army with respect to the lower posts.

1047. REPORT TO THE EXECUTIVE COMMITTEE BY THE LIAISON COMMISSION
[Session of March 11. *Protokoly*, p. 43.]

Chkheidze reported on the delegation's visit to the Provisional Government. L'vov, Maniulov, Tereshchenko, Nekrasov, and some others were present. Our representatives pointed out to the Provisional Government that it is not fulfilling its promise to inform the Executive Committee of all the important measures of the Government. The Provisional Government denied this fact. It considers that it has always been mindful of the Executive Committee, but that the fault lies in the absence of a flexible organ through which [the Executive Committee] can be notified in time. In general, it is not the Provisional Government that ignores the Executive Committee, but, on the contrary, the Executive Committee that often takes action without communicating with the Provisional Government. (Order No. 1, arrest,† etc.)

The question was raised of controlling the activities of the Government and the way in which this control should be conceived. The representative of the Executive Committee explained how important it was to be always well informed on all the measures of the Government. The Provisional Government expressed its complete willingness on this point and declared itself in favor of forming an organ of the Executive Committee which could eventually be included in the Provisional Government. As concerns the demands of General Alekseev, it is his own wish to resign; Nikolai Nikolaevich has already been replaced. There can be no question but that the Constituent Assembly will be convoked in Moscow.

1048. THE DECISION OF THE EXECUTIVE COMMISSION TO ESTABLISH A SPECIAL INFORMATION SECTION FOR RELATIONS WITH OTHER COUNTRIES
[Session of March 20. *Protokoly*, pp. 65–66.]

At the session of March 20 of this year the Executive Committee of the Soviet of Workers' and Soldiers' Deputies resolved to form a special Information Section for relations with other countries.

The following instructions were accepted:

THE INFORMATION SECTION OF THE SOVIET OF WORKERS' AND SOLDIERS' DEPUTIES

1. The Section of International Relations under the Soviet of Workers' and Soldiers' Deputies shall have its commissar in the Petrograd Telegraph Agency, which transmits news to the foreign press on the activities and resolutions of the Soviet of Workers' and Soldiers' Deputies and on other of the more important information and material published in the official organ of the Soviet of Workers' and Soldiers' Deputies (in *Izvestiia*).

---

* Evidently for the Petrograd garrison.

† In all probability, the reference is to the arrest of Nicholas II.

2. All telegrams designated by the Section for the foreign press shall be reported beforehand to the representative of the Provisional Government in the Petrograd Telegraphic Agency, Deputy Gronskii. All other telegrams to be sent abroad through the Petrograd Agency shall be reported beforehand by Deputy Gronskii to the commissar of the Section.

3. If Deputy Gronskii objects to the text of any telegram from the Section and if the commissar of the Section objects to the text of any other telegram, the disagreement shall be referred for examination to the Council of Representatives of the Provisional Government and the Soviet of Workers' and Soldiers' Deputies.

4. The Section of International Relations shall have the right to establish its business agency in Stockholm.

5. The Section of International Relations shall receive uncensored all telegrams and letters which its agency abroad sends to the address: Petrograd, Tauride Palace, Sovdep. The Provisional Government shall issue telegraphic instructions to the Ministries of War, Foreign Affairs, and Interior on permitting letters and telegrams addressed to the Sovdep to go through uncensored.

6. The Section has the right to send letters and telegrams to its agency abroad without [subjecting them] to customary censorship, [but] having them looked over only by a commissar appointed for this purpose to the Soviet by the Provisional Government.

7. When authorized by the Executive Committee of the Soviet of Workers' and Soldiers' Deputies, the Section has the right to send its couriers abroad. The Provisional Government shall give instructions to appropriate authorities to issue exit and re-entry permits to the couriers, and the documents entrusted to the courier shall be examined not by the customary [channels of] censorship, but by the commissar of the Provisional Government (referred to in article 6).

8. The Section of International Relations shall have the right to communicate by post or telegraph without censorship but with the knowledge of the Commissar of the Provisional Government with all persons, organizations, and institutions abroad which it may find necessary in the interest of [obtaining] information for the public or for the Soviet of Workers' and Soldiers' Deputies.

9. The Section shall publish in *Izvestiia* reports on the basis of information received from abroad and twice a week it shall give a report on the foreign socialist press to the Executive Committee.

10. The Section shall function under the control and supervision of the Executive Committee of the Soviet of Workers' and Soldiers' Deputies.

The organization of this Section has been assigned to Comrades Chkhenkeli and Skobelev, who must present a list of collaborators for this Section for the approval of the Executive Committee.

1049. *Izvestiia* ON THE RELEASE OF GENERAL IVANOV
[No. 24, March 24, 1917, p. 5.]

Russkaia Volia reports:

The Minister of Justice, A. F. Kerensky, arrived at noon at the Tauride Palace and proceeded to the Ministers' Pavilion. There, in the presence of the Minister, General N. I. Ivanov gave a written guarantee not to leave Petrograd, and signed a statement of loyalty to the Provisional Government. Following this, the Minister, accompanied by General Ivanov, left the Tauride Palace.

General Ivanov will remain on liberty under the personal supervision of the Minister of Justice.

FROM THE EDITOR: If the cited report is true, then we cannot but express our complete amazement. General Ivanov was accused of the gravest crime against the people. According to the information we have, General Ivanov was going to Petrograd in the role of a dictator in order to crush an uprising and to restore the power of the Tsar. To his good fortune, the Cavaliers of St. George, whom he deceived into accompanying him, refused to march against the people—otherwise General Ivanov would have been subject to shooting without a trial. After this unsuccessful campaign, General Ivanov very calmly returned to Stavka and remained there for some time, and it was only in Kiev that he was arrested.

Granting freedom to such a dangerous enemy of the people is utterly incomprehensible. And what has the "personal supervision of the Minister of Justice" got to do with it?

Such matters must not be decided "within the family." Before freeing General Ivanov, it was the duty of the Government to publish a report on this case, and, in any event, it should inform the Executive Committee of the Soviet of Workers' and Soldiers' Deputies about it.

We firmly protest against such strange lenience to a notorious criminal and a dangerous enemy of the people.

1050. *Novoe Vremia* ON THE RELATIONS BETWEEN THE GOVERNMENT
AND THE SOVIET

[No. 14737, March 28, 1917, p. 5.]

The great Russian revolution is the result of the efforts of the whole Russian people; moreover, not only of the present generation but also of our ancestors who struggled for freedom and who laid down their lives for it.

In the brief skirmish which finally overthrew the old regime, a prominent role was played by workers and the Soviet of Workers' and Soldiers' Deputies. Its energy served as a support and as a living, moving force for the Executive Committee of the State Duma, which became during the first few days of the revolution the center of the popular and military movement. This service of the Soviet will be credited to it by the grateful people.

We consider the existence of the Soviet necessary also for the final triumph of the revolution and the consolidation of the free regime. It enjoys the trust of the workers and has within its grasp an opportunity to impart sensible organized forms to the chaos that has developed among the workers. It will probably retain the leadership of the socialist movement in the future also. At the same time, the Soviet of Workers' Deputies, in yielding to suggestions that are foreign to its true position in the state, may cause innumerable troubles to the cause of freedom.

The present article has as its subject one such aberration.

The Soviet of Workers' Deputies has proposed a new theory of state power. It insists that the authority of the Provisional Government is determined by the agreement between the Committee of the State Duma and the Soviet of Workers' and Soldiers' Deputies. Therefore, the Soviet, as the true embodiment of the revolution, has the right of supervision over the actions of the Government, and even a higher right of suspending the orders of the Government which run contrary to the views of the Soviet. At the same time, the Soviet insists that it has no intention of undermining the power of the Provisional Government.

It is hardly possible that anyone would agree with the outlined views.

The Provisional Government holds governmental power not at all because it was handed to it by random organizations. After the overthrow of the autocratic regime, the supreme power in the country was fully restored to the hands of the people. Not to the hands of revolutionary organizations, but to the hands of the revolutionary nation as a whole.

After the former Emperor was deposed and after Mikhail Aleksandrovich renounced claims to the vacant throne, we recognized only one sovereign. This sovereign is not the population of the Capital, nor its garrison and workers, nor yet their hastily and accidentally gathered representatives, but a nation consisting of 180 millions of competent and free citizens who, in their totality, are the only and indisputable bearers of governmental sovereignty.

Here is where the source of the power of the Provisional Government resides: in the sovereignty of the people. . . .

. . . . .

1051. ARTICLE IN *Den'* ON THE RELATIONS BETWEEN THE GOVERNMENT
AND THE SOVIET
[No. 15, March 22, 1917, p. 1.]

. . .

. . . The Soviet exists first of all as an organ representing the revolutionary working class and the army; second, as an organ of supervision over the Government. The first condition determines the second, because the success of the supervision and the measure of influence over the Government are in direct proportion to the degree of organization of the Soviet and of the masses upon which it rests. An excessive expansion of membership, lack of order, extreme centralization, lack of planning for the work of the commissions, and much else show a picture of organizational build-up which can hardly be called satisfactory.

As for Soviet control, what precisely is its character? Is it an administrative or a public control? Unfortunately it is evident that the executive committee does not distinguish between the two concepts. This confusion breeds chaos in the minds of the people, leads the Blanquist elements in the Soviet into temptation, and leads directly toward a disorganization of the revolutionary forces.

An administrative control can be exercised only by organs of authority, established not only in fact but officially. As an administrative organ the Soviet becomes a power which seems to stand above the Provisional Government, i.e., in fact, the only real power. Such an authority should alone bear responsibility before the nation. What is resulting is not a dual power, of which people speak with anxiety in all corners of awakened Russia, but rather a single power, namely, the single power of the Soviet, and not of the Provisional Government. While in the first days of the revolution such a state of affairs was required by the course and the very essence of the revolutionary struggle, it now stands in sharp contradiction to the logic of the revolutionary movement. The Soviet of Workers' and Soldiers' Deputies cannot and should not turn into a government. The laws of history which determine the course of Russia's social development rebel against it; the relationship of the forces which are consolidating the conquests of the bourgeois revolution argue against it.

The Soviet should be exclusively an organ of public control. Like all public organizations, and in this case a very influential one, it stands on guard over the revolution with more persistence than any other. The fact of its existence alone is sufficient to regulate the whole political activity of the Provisional Government. Thanks to its revolutionary authority, the Soviet of Deputies organizes and directs public opinion. Only in this way can it exercise control over the provisional authority which it itself recognizes.

Those who are leading the Soviet along another path are either making an unconscious mistake and, their compasses lost, are wandering about or are quite consciously "deepening" the revolution down to a social upheaval, which is illusory at the present time. Both cases are pregnant with danger. The revolution is in peril of losing its organizing center if the Soviet does not follow the right tactical course.

1052. *Izvestiia* ON THE QUESTION OF DUAL POWER
[No. 27, March 29, 1917, p. 2.]

The campaign against the Soviet of Workers' and Soldiers' Deputies continues.

Bourgeois newspapers and bourgeois congresses are advancing a series of grave charges against the Soviet.

The Soviet is undermining the prestige of the Government.

The Soviet is creating dual power in the country.

The Soviet, having a large diversified membership, brought together by fortuitous circumstances, is unable to govern the country.

These charges remind us of those good old times when the Octobrist–Black Hundred State Duma was in session at the Tauride Palace.

In those "dark" days the country was governed by an "irresponsible" bureaucracy—in reality, by the Romanov family and a small group of the most prominent landed nobility. The bourgeoisie and part of the *pomeshchiki* protested against this order and attempted to subordinate the Government to its control, in the same way as the Soviet is establishing its control over the Provisional Government at the present time. Let us recall what the Black Hundred had to say about these attempts on the part of the State Duma.

They were saying:

"The Duma is undermining the prestige of the Government. The Duma is creating a dual power. The Duma, having a large diversified membership brought together by fortuitous circumstances is unable to govern the country." In short, all the charges that were once advanced against the State Duma are now being advanced against the Soviet of Workers' and Soldiers' Deputies.

This is no accident.

The groups that are in power are always striving to become the sole possessors of power. It has always been that the ruling groups tend to interpret every attempt on the part of the larger segments of the population to gain control over them as an encroachment on their rights. And they always counter these attempts by instilling fear of dual power and anarchy.

Empty fears! For without control, there can be no confidence. Control does not undermine the prestige of the Government. Control may weaken and diminish the importance of individual persons empowered by the Government, or of individual rulers, but it improves the very process of governing the country.

The representatives of the bourgeoisie understood this very well as long as they were in the opposition. But as soon as the power fell into their hands, they were quick to forget these simple truths.

They forgot where they got this power.

They forgot that the Provisional Government was created by the revolution and that they assumed their offices in the Government with the consent of the Petrograd workers and soldiers. They forgot that the people remain the highest source of any power and that the people, represented by their elected bodies, are endowed with the right to control any government.

The proletariat remembers this.

Life has changed.

In the Peter and Paul Fortress, where formerly the champions of freedom languished, sit now the old ministers. The Tauride Palace, where formerly the representatives of the *pomeshchiki* and the capitalists were in session, is now the site of workers' and soldiers' meetings.

In the Mariinskii Palace the seats of the old ministers are now occupied by members of the bourgeois Provisional Government.

The changes are enormous!

But even greater changes await us in the future. Meeting these changes headlong and boldly, the proletariat will not let its banner out of its hands. The Soviet of Workers' and Soldiers' Deputies will not refuse to control the activities of the Government—it is its duty and its right to do so.

1053. TSERETELLI'S SPEECH UPON HIS RETURN FROM SIBERIAN EXILE
[*Izvestiia*, No. 20, March 21, 1917, pp. 2–3.]

Comrades-workers, on behalf of your faction in the State Duma,[6] which was liberated by you, I want to express my deep gratitude to you for the welcome [you have given us] . . . We came here to join your ranks, and, comrades, before we take our place once again in the kindred ranks of the working class, we would like to share with you our reactions to this victory and our understanding of the tasks that now confront the revolutionary working class and all the popular movements as a result of recent events. It is in the name of these tasks that we are ready to fight together with you until victory or death. Thus we have a natural need to share with you everything that we have experienced during these days and to outline together with you the tasks for which we will fight and the paths which we will follow. Comrades-workers, it was arm in arm with all the living forces of the country that you cast the autocracy into oblivion; it was together with the revolutionary army, the peasantry, and all the progressive bourgeoisie. Your achievement is great, comrades-workers, but the greatness of this achievement is equaled by your other achievement; having overthrown the old regime, you weighed the circumstances from the point of view of the interests of the great people, you understood that the time has not yet come for achieving the ultimate aims of the proletariat, the class aims which have nowhere as yet been achieved, but [you under-

---

[6] Tseretelli was arrested and exiled in November 1907, along with other members of the Social Democratic faction in the Second Duma who were accused by Stolypin of treasonable activities.

stood] that the hour had struck for the complete triumph of democracy, the triumph which the working class and all the living forces of the country are interested in. And you, having no opportunity fully to realize all those lofty ideals which will be realized by the combined efforts of the world proletariat, you did not want to assume the responsibility for the collapse of the movement [which would have occurred] had you in a desperate attempt decided to force your will on the events at that time. You understood that a bourgeois revolution is taking place, that it represents a stage of the social revolution, and that, first of all, you must strengthen your position at this stage in order to accelerate the progress of all Russia, the progress of all mankind toward the bright ideals of socialism. The power is in the hands of the bourgeoisie. You transferred this power to the bourgeoisie, but at the same time you have stood guard over the newly gained freedom—you control the actions of the bourgeoisie, you push it into the fight, you support its resolute measures in the fight against the old order. And in order to fulfill this task, you, together with the revolutionary army, have created a powerful bulwark of freedom, standing guard over new Russia.

· · ·

. . . The Provisional Government must have full executive power in so far as this power strengthens the revolution, in so far as it is overthrowing and breaking down the old order. The proletariat represents the prime moving force behind these decisions; the proletariat dictates these decisions; the proletariat supports them with all its strength. But in order to apply its revolutionary tactics it is imperative to have organization and strict discipline in the ranks of the proletariat itself. I know, comrades, that at the present moment you are occupied with the problem of improving your organization in view of the fact that the Petrograd Soviet of Workers' and Soldiers' Deputies, having assumed the leadership of the all-Russian revolutionary movement, has now expanded to such an extent that it technically cannot cope with all the tasks that confront it. We believe that the question of reorganizing the revolutionary vanguard of Russia is a basic, cardinal question: will[7] we succeed in organizing a workers' representation and a representation of the revolutionary army on such principles as would enable them actually to subject the bourgeoisie to their control, actually to dictate revolutionary measures to the bourgeoisie, and at the same time to exert all their authority in support of those actions of the executive power which are essential to free Russia?

· · ·

But should the moment arrive when this government renounces the revolutionary path and chooses the path of negotiations, the path of compromises, then you and we together, comrades, will march dauntlessly against this government and together we will cast it into oblivion in the same way as we did the old regime. But as long as this government, under the impact of revolutionary events, is following the revolutionary path, as long as the interests of the bourgeoisie are embodied in acts which coincide with the common national interests of the democracy, as long as the Provisional Government carries the banner of the Constituent Assembly . . . , and as long as its measures are directed toward the liquidation of the old order, we, together with you, will support it. . . .

Comrades, allow me to close my speech with that national cry with which all

---

[7] In text: "*if* we."

speeches at public meetings are brought to a close: "Long Live Free Russia! Long Live the Constituent Assembly! Long Live the Democratic Republic!" (*Stormy applause.*)

Following Tseretelli, other Social Democratic comrades returning from exile delivered speeches. When the speeches were over, the soldiers' deputies stood up and sang "Eternal Glory" to the fallen fighters.

1054. STANKEVICH'S DESCRIPTION OF THE EXECUTIVE COMMITTEE IN MARCH AND APRIL

[V. B. Stankevich, *Vospominaniia, 1914–1919*, pp. 80, 87–90.]

Early in March, I joined the membership of the Executive Committee, to the half-serious, half-jocular indignation of Sukhanov, who thought this was no place for "geometry and fortification specialists." In the Committee I represented the most extreme right group tolerated there—the Trudoviks. All through the months of March and April, I was one of the most assiduous and constant of those who attended the sessions, after abandoning, not without some hesitation, my work on fortification. Actually I limited myself to the role of observer, since political work seemed quite foreign and strange to me after a three-year interruption.

At that time the Executive Committee enjoyed an extraordinary influence and importance. Officially it represented only Petrograd. In reality, however, it was a revolutionary representation for all of Russia, a supreme authoritative organ, eagerly listened to everywhere as the champion and leader of the rising people. But it was a complete delusion. No leadership of any kind existed, nor could it exist there.

. . .

On the whole, the history of the Committee, from the point of view of its organization and membership, could be divided into two periods, one prior to and the other following the arrival of Tseretelli. The first was a period replete with hazards, vacillations, and vagueness, when anyone who wished could use the name and the organization of the Committee. More successful than anybody else in this respect was Steklov, the most talented, assiduous, and stable member of the Committee. That was a period of confusion, when Committee meetings, on unimportant questions to be sure, were possible with a membership composed entirely of Internationalists and Bolsheviks, under the chairmanship of Steklov. Both the left and the right wings felt equally that the Committee was an institution of their own, or alien to them. They used it as much as possible, but assumed no responsibility for it.

As a result, some "amusing" incidents resulted. For example, on one occasion, perhaps thanks to the zeal of a young woman registrar, a communication was somehow retrieved, written on the letterhead of the Committee, with the official seal. It was addressed to the peasants of a village who were given authority to "socialize" the adjoining *pomeshchik* estate. In spite of its radical views on social questions, the incident provoked profound indignation on the part of the entire Committee. A special investigation was launched, and it was revealed that the letter was issued by a member of the agrarian commission, Aleksandrovskii, a Socialist Revolutionary, who thought he had the right to advocate his opinions and views in the name of the Committee. But why take such a trivial example? Actually the *Iz-*

vestiia of the Soviet itself was nothing less than a letter by Aleksandrovskii.[8] The general tone of the articles, the selection of editorials, the decision of what should or should not be published, and even the misprints—everything revealed the hand of the editor and his assistants who advocated views of their own and not at all those of the Committee. *Izvestiia* was regarded by an overwhelming majority of the members of the Committee as something foreign and outrageous. But there was nobody to do anything about it, to find a way out. Yet when I prepared an official statement protesting against the entire policy of *Izvestiia*, all the leaders of the Committee, down to Sukhanov, inclusive, signed it immediately. And Steklov was replaced with no regrets.[9] Such a state of affairs led to the situation that, although officially the Committee supported the Government, and the majority always insisted on the firmness of this position, nevertheless the Committee itself undermined the authority of the Government by its peculiar measures and thoughtless steps. To forestall misunderstandings a special delegation of the Committee was formed. Approximately twice a week it called at the Mariinskii Palace to chat with members of the Government . . . But what could this delegation accomplish if, while it chatted in complete harmony with the ministers, scores of Aleksandrovskii's mailed letters, printed articles in *Izvestiia*, traveled in the name of the Committee as delegates throughout the provinces and in the army, and received representatives from the villages in the Tauride Palace, each one acting independently, disregarding any talks, instructions, laws, or resolutions? In the final analysis, anything could be gained from the Committee if only one insisted stubbornly. In this respect the Committee was guided and determined not by those who sat in it and passed on issues, but by those who appealed to it.

With the appearance of Tseretelli the character of the Committee changed radically. He joined it as a member of the Second Duma, with a deliberative vote only. The first day he modestly declined to express his opinion since he was as yet unfamiliar with the general situation. The following day he delivered a long speech, seemingly groping for firm ground. He did not please the left because he obviously was inclined toward compromise and solidarity with the Government. Nor did he please the right element because his speech in many respects was still breathing the untouched "Siberian" Internationalism.[10] On the third day Tseretelli arrived as a self-confident leader of the Committee and the Soviet. While preserving in principle the international tendencies, in practice he pursued sharply the policy of defensism and one of organic collaboration with and support of the Government. Frequently losing his voice because of his chest ailment, with his face flushed feverishly and his eyes blazing, he led the Committee boldly. And the latter at once changed from a medley of all sorts of people into an institution, into an organ. But the remarkable thing was that just at the moment when the Committee was being organized, when it formed departments which began to function, when the bureau, elected only of parties who favored defensive war, assumed responsibility

---

[8] He is here using Aleksandrovskii simply as a symbol of irresponsible action, in this case with reference to the Editor of *Izvestiia*, Steklov.

[9] See Doc. 1059.

[10] Social Democrats and Socialist Revolutionaries of moderate internationalist views who had developed close ties, regardless of party, during their Siberian exile in and around Irkutsk. Prominent among them were Tseretelli and Gotz. See Radkey, *The Agrarian Foes of Bolshevism*, pp. 167–68, for a discussion of the influence of this relationship on the collaboration of the S.D.'s and S.R.'s during 1917.

for the work—in a word, when the Committee learned how to administer itself—it was precisely at that moment that it let slip through its fingers the leadership of the masses, who abandoned it.

1055. Speech of Steklov on Dual Power Before the All-Russian Conference of Soviets

[Session of March 30. *Izvestiia*, No. 32, April 4, 1917, pp. 2–6.]

. . .

You know, comrades, that the Provisional Government did not come into being right at the very moment of the revolution, according to the classical pattern of the past. . . . In those two or three uncertain days the revolutionary forces of Petrograd, which were scattered in various districts, were gradually drawn on the one hand to the Soviet Workers' Deputies and on the other hand to the Temporary Committee of the Duma. Somehow, during these first days neither the bourgeoisie nor we gave any thought to creating a government, a power; we were trying to group our own forces and gather together all the forces which were flowing to us from all sides. A few days after the beginning of the insurrection, when it began to become sufficiently clear that the insurrection was victorious beyond a doubt, that it was leading to the establishment of a new regime, at that moment emerged the question of forming a Provisional Government, a more or less permanent organ, at least until such time as the Constituent Assembly voiced its decision. At that moment, I repeat, we were engaged in grouping our forces and arranging those new forces which, by that time, had concentrated around us. At the same time the Temporary Committee of the Duma (which was formed during the same fateful night, almost simultaneously with the Soviet of Workers' Deputies—perhaps a few hours earlier or later, I don't remember exactly) invited the Soviet of Workers' Deputies to send its representatives to a conference on . . .[11] program of the Provisional Government. It was only at that moment that this question was no longer posed in a theoretical, abstract manner, but assumed a completely definite and concrete outline.

. . .

Why is it that at that moment we did not consider the question of taking power into our hands? I will attempt to answer this. As I said, this question was not considered by us in its theoretical aspect for two reasons: first, at the time when this agreement [with the Temporary Committee of the Duma] was contemplated, it was not at all clear as to whether the revolution would emerge victorious, either in a revolutionary-democratic form or even in a moderate-bourgeois form. Those of you, comrades, who were not here in Petrograd and did not experience this revolutionary fever cannot imagine how we lived: the Duma was surrounded by soldiers' platoons that did not even have any noncommissioned officers; we did not have time even to formulate any political program for the movement and at the same time we learned that the ministers were at large and were convening somewhere, either in the Admiralty, or in the Mariinskii Palace. We were not informed on the general attitude of the troops or the attitude of the Tsarskoe Selo garrison,

[11] Line omitted in text: typographical error.

and it was reported that they were marching on us. There were rumors that five regiments were marching from the north, that General Ivanov was leading 26 echelons: shooting resounded through the streets, and we had grounds to assume that this weak group that was surrounding the palace would be routed. We expected from minute to minute that they would arrive, and, if they did not shoot us, they would take us away. However, we sat proudly, like ancient Romans, and conferred, but there was no complete conviction whatsoever in the success of the revolution.

This was one aspect; but the other, more basic aspect . . . was the political . . . and even had we consciously considered the possibility of resolving the question in this way, this political aspect gave us many cues in the sense that at that moment we could not have assumed full power. This political aspect was broken down into two parts. You understand that the attempt on the part of the extreme revolutionary democratic forces to take the power into their own hands can have a historical basis and can rely on the support of the broad national masses only in the event that moderate liberalism becomes bankrupt while carrying its program into effect. And it stands to reason that when this moment arrives, when the liberal bourgeoisie turns out to be politically incapable of carrying out its own political program and not simply satisfying the demands of the national masses, and if it meets with decisive opposition in carrying out its own program and proves to be incapable of realizing the aspirations and demands of the working masses, then at this moment we may be confronted with the question of the revolutionary democratic forces seizing power against the desires and the will of broad sections of the bourgeoisie. Such a situation did not exist at that moment, and it does not exist even now. On the contrary, we have seen that the privileged [*tsensovaia*] bourgeoisie, whose representatives constitute the majority in the Provisional Government, had come to the realization that the time was such and the forces of the revolution were such that it was necessary for them to make broad, democratic concessions. . . .

.   .   .

So here is the main slogan in this campaign of slanders and insinuations, the main theme in bringing dissent into the revolutionary family—*dual power*. What is this dual power? Does it exist in reality? What are its origins? What is its character, its meaning, its historical role? These are the questions that must be answered at this conference, in order to avoid any misunderstandings, and in order that the country may understand the true present-day situation and, in particular, the position of the center in contemporary democracy. Comrades, all those who speak about dual power, and about the dangers of this dual power to Russian freedom, are meanwhile standing on the following position: there exists the generally recognized authority of the Provisional Government, but side by side there exists yet another authority, recognized by only a part of the population: the Soviet of Workers' and Soldiers' Deputies. And now this second power wants to play the same role as the first; it is invading the jurisdiction of the Provisional Government, it is questioning its orders, and it is independently publishing its own orders. In order to substantiate these points they bring up Order No. 1.

. . . The first sign of the terrifying "dual power" is detected in this act: the first attempt on the part of workers' and soldiers' deputies to undermine the authority of the Provisional Government. The extent of their unscrupulous slander can be seen, for example, from the fact that at the time this order was issued, there was no Provisional Government in existence; there existed only the Executive Committee of the Duma. At this point one may raise the question: with whom did the power rest in the country—with the Soviet of Workers' and Soldiers' Deputies or with this Temporary Committee of the Duma? This Temporary Committee of the Duma was selected by a part—and by a very weak part—of the Duma, which was itself convoked on the basis of the electoral law known to you. This Temporary Executive Committee—I do not want to disclaim its merits—which lagged behind events, could not make pretensions to the role of a government against which we should have had no right to issue independent orders. Its only justification as a power was its semblance of tradition, since this Committee of the Duma was, so to speak, a part of the Duma, and therefore, power should have rested with it. It is only on the basis of the Fundamental Laws of the Romanov dynasty that this Duma constituted an inalienable part of the power. This power did not even totally belong to the Duma: it was shared with the State Council and the Tsar; consequently, the Duma Committee could claim no such rights. (*Applause.*) It was also the product of the revolution, but it was a pale and weak creation which emerged from the privileged strata, whereas our Soviet emerged from the healthy, broad masses of hundreds of thousands of people who revolted and established their authority.

I only want to point out that the reference to Order No. 1 is a lie and unscrupulous demagoguery. It might be said that we were interfering with the executive power when, together with the Military Commission, we were organizing military forces and were conducting arrests. But at that time there was no government, and arrests were even conducted by individual persons and, in all probability, by our Soviet as well as by this Military Commission, which was composed partly of our delegates and partly of representatives of the Duma Committee, which to this day remains in an undefined state. It [the Military Commission] is a useful organ to us. There were two attempts on the part of Guchkov to close down our Commission, but we did not allow it to be closed. (*Applause.*)

Of course, the problem assumes a different aspect when we turn to the Provisional Government. Well, from the moment it was formed, did not this dual power become dangerous? Comrades, what are we to understand by dual power? It is only a coexistence of two political forces, each laying claim to equal power, not only [by virtue] of its essence but by virtue of its [legal] form as well; i.e., if our Soviet were issuing laws in the same manner as the Provisional Government is issuing them, if it were convoking a Constituent Assembly in the same way as the Provisional Government anticipates doing—then there might yet be some discussion of dual power. You know perfectly well that nothing of the kind is taking place; the revolutionary democracy is only influencing the bourgeois government in order to force it to take the demands of the revolutionary people into account.

. . . .

. . . The Black Hundred and the liberal bourgeoisie realize the full importance of our Soviet as a center around which [the revolutionary-democratic forces] have rallied. They realize that, inasmuch as the Soviet is expanding its activities in every direction and its influence in the country is spreading, it is preparing [the way] for a regime which these gentlemen will not find to their liking. It is precisely for these reasons that they are now shouting, insinuating, slandering, gossiping, and trying to sow discord. They speak of a dual power which does not formally exist but is present only in the form of the existence of two political aspirations, two political forces. If, even during the tsarist regime, the tsarist government was forced to yield to the pressures of one or another social force—for otherwise a social system is inconceivable; this is a fundamental social law—then it would be scandalous if the Provisional Government, which owes its existence to our support and which emerged during the process of the overthrow of autocracy, permitted itself to speak of dual power, i.e., of the fact that the revolutionary people who made the revolution and gave it [the Provisional Government] the opportunity to exist wants to express its will and assure its influence. Comrades, you must join us in saying that this is inadmissible . . .

1056. Speech of Tseretelli on Relation Between the Soviet and the Government Before the All-Russian Conference of Soviets

[Session of April 3. *Izvestiia*, No. 35, April 8, 1917, pp. 3–4.]

Comrades, the speeches which I heard here have convinced me that the position taken by the Executive Committee in agreement with the Petrograd Soviet of Workers' and Soldiers' Deputies with respect to the Provisional Government has not been presented with sufficient clarity to those present here. I wish to establish the fundamental principle on the basis of which the Soviet of Workers' and Soldiers' Deputies recognized the Provisional Government as the bearer of power in revolutionary Russia. The decision of the Soviet of Workers' and Soldier's Deputies did not stem from a desire to seize power, nor from a desire to place this power in the hands of people who might be far removed from the general popular movement and might pursue a policy which runs counter to this movement, with a view to discussing at a later time the question of the struggle against, and the overthrow of this government.

No, the Soviet of Workers' and Soldiers' Deputies from the very beginning chose the path of agreement with the bourgeoisie which was represented by the Provisional Government. Comrades, nobody here paid attention to a certain part of Steklov's speech which, in my opinion, is the most important part. Steklov said: There was a time, right at the beginning of the revolution, when Rodzianko and Shul'gin were saying to us: "There are no demands that we would not fulfill; there are no solicitations on your part that we would not meet." Comrades, this must be remembered. This situation still holds true to a certain extent. In view of the present balance of power, I think that the Soviet of Workers' and Soldiers' Deputies, should it consider this necessary for the interests of all the people, could even seize the power. I think that under the proper circumstances the proletariat could place its extreme class aims on its order of the day. But the proletariat must base itself not only on considerations of what, at any given moment, we may be capable of accomplishing; no, the proletariat must base itself on considerations of what we may be able to preserve and strengthen and not what we may be able to possess momentarily. (*Applause.*)

It was at this point, comrades, that the wisdom of the revolutionary forces began to tell. Without agreeing to this beforehand, the national masses themselves understood the nature of the immediate task, and when they advanced the democratic republic as the platform on which all the people of Russia agreed, they understood that this republic would be a bourgeois republic, but that, on the other hand, it would also be democratic, and one which, at that given moment, could unite around itself the proletariat, the peasantry, and all the groups of the bourgeoisie who understood the immediate task before the whole nation. (*Applause.*)

Comrades, it was not the proletariat alone or the army alone who adopted this path of agreement; but, I am maintaining, this path of agreement was adopted by an enormous part of the bourgeoisie—otherwise we would not have had the Provisional Government. I think, comrades, that the reproaches which were voiced here against the narrow, self-interested policy of certain bourgeois circles and against the campaign which they launched against the Soviet of Soldiers' and Workers' Deputies are entirely justified. Comrade Steklov gave an excellent account of this aspect of the situation. . . .

Side by side with the attacks directed at us, inciting the unconscious elements of the population against us, we see actions of the Provisional Government which answer to the aspirations of the democracy as a whole. Comrades, there is no realm where it would be more difficult for the democracy to realize its ideals than in the [realm of] foreign policy. Whereas the democratic trend completely prevailed in domestic policy, the realm of foreign policy was still dominated by elements elected under property [*tsenzovykh*] suffrage, the propertied elements of the bourgeoisie. And now in Russia, during the last few days, we have seen how the Provisional Government, the responsible organ of the bourgeoisie, adopted the type of measures which indicated the extent to which the Government, too, was trying to adhere to the general platform of the democracy; and we have seen it make an enormous concession precisely in the realm of foreign policy.

If one were to say that the time is now ripe for us to regard the Provisional Government as a small group of people expressing the self-centered interests of a particular sector of the bourgeoisie that is attempting to fight against the Soviet of Workers' and Soldiers' Deputies, it would mean that one does not see what is occurring. If such was the aim of the Provisional Government, that is, if it was launching such a campaign, it would, of course, have launched it with the very question which we have placed before them, the question of foreign policy. It was precisely in this direction that the Provisional Government was being influenced by the irresponsible circles of the bourgeoisie, like those Kadet orators who had actually advanced such slogans at the Congress of the Kadets, which slogans, were they accepted by the whole bourgeoisie, would have spelled the downfall of the great Russian revolution. But the bourgeoisie as a whole and its responsible organ—the Provisional Government—did not follow this course.

This is what must be established, comrades: as long as there exists a platform which unites around it the enormous nucleus of the working class and the revolutionary army, as long as the responsible circles of the bourgeoisie have not deviated from this platform, we cannot say that our aim is to create another organ of executive power embodied in the Soviet of Workers' and Soldiers' Deputies with a view to leading this power to overthrow the power embodied in the Provisional Government. There must be a unity of will, comrades; without a unity of will we will not emerge victorious. But there must be a unity of national will. And at the very moment, comrades, when the Soviet of Workers' and Soldiers' Deputies announces that they are entering into a conflict with the Provisional Government and it turns out that one part of the people is supporting the Soviets while the other part is supporting the Provisional Government, then at that moment our national cause . . .[12] [will be lost] (*Applause.*)

I think, comrades, that there is no point in touching on the individual reproaches which have been voiced here. In many respects they were justified, inasmuch as some steps taken by the Provisional Government did not point in the direction that we would like. But we do have a Liaison Commission that enters directly into relations with the Provisional Government and informs the democratic elements in the Provisional Government of its will, and there has not been a case yet when the Provisional Government has turned against us on any important question to which we have given the character of an ultimatum. The proletariat turned out to have sufficient awareness of the necessity to place value on the unity of national forces; so far, the bourgeois circles which are represented by the Provisional Government and which are playing the dominant role have been similarly aware of this, and therefore, comrades, we must say this: at the present moment the Soviets of Workers' and Soldiers' Deputies are organs which unify the democratic elements of the population, they are organs of active . . .[13] control over the government which is recognized by us and which is actually expressing the will of the revolutionary people and is realizing it in actions adopted by all the people. This is precisely the position we are taking.

I am not asserting, comrades, that this situation will continue. Perhaps those circles of the bourgeoisie that are forcing the Provisional Government to take irresponsible steps and are pushing it into civil war will succeed in achieving their aims. Perhaps public opinion in those circles on which the Provisional Government relies will undergo a change and will shift foreign policy to different lines. And then, comrades, the moment will come when the Soviets of Workers' and Soldiers' Deputies will enter into conflict with the Provisional Government.

But I firmly believe that they will then enter the struggle in union with all the people, because such acts on the part of the Provisional Government will alienate from it not only the proletariat and a large part of the revolutionary army, but also those elements which now stand behind the Provisional Government. (*Applause.*) That is why this qualification was included in the principal clauses of the resolution which was submitted to you . . . It is precisely when it abandons this path, comrades, when the Provisional Government violates the agreement by its actions, the agreement which was the expression of the will of all the people —it is precisely at this point that the time will have arrived to speak about a conflict. And then the conflict will not be the same as the one into which we are now being pushed; then we will have all the people behind us and there will remain nothing for the Provisional Government to do but leave, and a new organ of national power will be created. (*Applause.*)

1057. RESOLUTION OF SUPPORT TO THE PROVISIONAL GOVERNMENT BY THE ALL-RUSSIAN CONFERENCE OF SOVIETS

[*Izvestiia*, April 6, 1917, p. 2.]

1. In accordance with an agreement with the Petrograd Soviet of Workers' and Soldiers' Deputies, the Provisional Government, formed in the course of the revolution, published a declaration containing a program of government work.

2. The All-Russian Conference of the Soviets of Workers' and Soldiers' Dep-

---

[12] Omission in text.   [13] Omission in text.

uties acknowledges that this program includes the basic political demands of the Russian democracy and that so far the Provisional Government has, as a whole and in general, pursued the course of fulfilling the obligations which it had assumed.

3. The Conference appeals to the whole revolutionary democracy of Russia to rally around the Soviets of Workers' and Soldiers' Deputies as organizational centers of the forces of democracy, created by the revolution. These Soviets, united with other progressive forces, are capable of repelling attempts at a tsarist and bourgeois counterrevolution, and of consolidating and expanding the revolutionary gains.

4. The Conference recognizes the necessity of gradually gaining political control and influence over the Provisional Government and its local organs in order to induce it to pursue the most energetic struggle against counterrevolutionary forces, to take the most resolute steps in the direction of a complete democratization of all walks of Russian life, and to make preparations for universal peace without annexations and indemnities based on the self-determination of nations.

5. The Conference appeals to the democracy to lend its support to the Provisional Government without assuming responsibility for all the work of the government, in so far as the Government is working steadfastly in the direction of regulating and expanding revolutionary gains and in so far as the formulation of its foreign policy is based on the renunciation of ambitions of territorial expansion.

6. At the same time, the Conference appeals to the revolutionary democracy of Russia to be prepared, while organizing and rallying its forces around the Soviets of Workers' and Soldiers' Deputies, to check resolutely all attempts on the part of the Government to escape the control exercised by the democracy, or to evade the fulfillment of the obligations it had assumed.

1058. *Russkiia Vedomosti*'s COMMENT ON THE WORK OF THE CONFERENCE
[No. 75, April 6, 1917, p. 3.]

The well-attended conference of representatives of the Soviets of Workers' and Soldiers' Deputies, which took place in Petrograd, presented an interesting picture of the struggle of two currents, the extreme Bolsheviks and the more moderate Mensheviks. This struggle showed itself both in the question of war and in the question of the Constituent Assembly, as well as in a number of other questions which were on the agenda of the Conference. With this, one interesting peculiarity could be observed: the majority of the most eloquent and at the same time most responsible speeches tended in one direction, but the resolutions adopted tended in the opposite direction. In this regard, there was a characteristic episode in connection with the discussion of the question of the attitude toward the Provisional Government. The speech introducing the resolution on this question was entrusted to the Bolshevik Steklov, who, in place of supporting the resolution, made an impassioned speech of indictment against the Provisional Government; his speech, moreover, not only was prejudiced but contained direct misrepresentations of fact, such, for instance, as the statement that the Provisional Government published the legislative acts on amnesty or on abolition of national restrictions only under the pressure of the Executive Committee of the Soviet of Workers' and Soldiers' Deputies. Steklov was content only to demand especially vigilant watching over the activities of the Provisional Government, but his partisans went even further and proposed that the proletariat directly take power into its own hands. The advocates of the resolution, which was drawn up in a comparatively conciliatory tone and which recognized, even though conditionally, the necessity for supporting the government, spoke at the Conference comparatively little and, with certain exceptions, not at all as eloquently as the opponents of the resolution; nevertheless the resolution was adopted by the Conference.

One may, of course, be puzzled by the fact that the Executive Committee entrusted the introduction and defense of the resolution to its avowed opponent, but that is a trifle, albeit a curious one. Much more characteristic and important is the sharp disparity between the word and the deed, between the vehement accusations against the Provisional Government of preparation of counterrevolution, of connections with Anglo-French capitalist circles, etc., and the resolution which bespoke, even though conditionally, the support of that same Provisional Government. And, again, this discrepancy and this inconsistency interest us chiefly because they manifested themselves not only in one particular case, but in a whole series of other questions, not only at the Petrograd Conference, but at many other meetings. With certain reservations, one may say that the discrepancy between word and deed, between shrieking, ultraradical speeches and more calm and reasonable decisions, is characteristic not only of the Soviets of Workers' and Soldiers' Deputies, but, along with them, of our whole social democracy. Of course, their decisions, too, are not always correct, but still they contain immeasurably more thought, far more common sense and statesmanlike prudence than do the speeches of the orators, even though they may occupy responsible positions. In its mass, the rank and file of the social democracy and the whole working-class mass in general very often are more healthy and wise than their orators and official representatives. Of course, they frequently act under the latter's direct influence, but they have their own opinions, too, for which they can fight.

1059. THE EXECUTIVE COMMITTEE: REPORT OF THE LIAISON COMMISSION AND THE DECISION TO CHANGE THE EDITORIAL DIRECTION OF *Izvestiia*

[Session of April 5. *Protokoly*, pp. 77–82.]

[1.] REPORT OF COMRADE STEKLOV. On the telegram from Stavka and the attacks against the Soviet of Workers' and Soldiers' Deputies, we proposed four measures to the Government: 1) [to conduct] an inquiry for the purpose of discovering the sources of the rumors, 2) to publish a refutation, 3) to prevent the appearance of such rumors and [newspaper] items in the future, 4) to permit the Commissar of the Executive Committee to be present at the time the telegrams of Stavka are composed.

The Provisional Government has found the telegrams tactless and inadmissible. It assured us that they did not originate with it. It promised to take preventive measures. The Government could give no *definite* answers to the rest of the measures until it [takes them up for] consideration.

The next question touched upon the necessity of purging the commanding personnel. The Government assured us that such a purge is already taking place. Guchkov has departed for the Southwestern Front for this purpose.[14]

14 See Chap. 16.

The question of Alekseev's appointment was slurred over. The Government reacted very favorably to dispatching commissars of the Executive Committee to the front.[15]

After the questions on military matters, the question of sending newspapers abroad was raised. The Government assured us that all newspapers without exception will henceforth be permitted to be sent abroad. We received complete satisfaction on the question of Swiss emigrants. The Government promised to communicate with England and France and [request] that henceforth all emigrants regardless of whether their names are on the control lists be permitted to leave for Russia without any obstacles. We refused to speak about the circumstances surrounding the passage of a group of emigrants through Germany. The attitude of the Government on this matter was very clearly established when the conversation turned to the denial of a transit permit to Comrade Platten. The Government did not discuss this, but Miliukov declared that, in his opinion, he regards Platten's actions as hostile to the Russian State. There can be no question of any exchange [of internees or prisoners of war] for the group that has been permitted to depart. The Government does not consider itself bound by obligations assumed without its knowledge or consent.[16]

Now to the question of the 10-million [ruble] fund. According to the report of the Minister of Finance, the Council of Ministers discussed this question and decided to reject it. The motives for the rejection are the insufficiency of funds and the large number of similar requests.[17]

COMRADE TSERETELLI supplemented Comrade Steklov's report.

Misunderstandings in the Caucasus. A number of measures were passed without the knowledge of the Commissars, but everything has been settled now. A telegram from Comrade Chkhenkeli confirmed this.

The question of allocating 500,000 rubles for the transportation needs of a group of persons who were exiled by administrative order, in compliance with their telegraphic request from Irkutsk, has been satisfactorily resolved. The Government, in the person of Kerensky, also gave instructions to release the exiled Adzhars.[18]

COMRADE SUKHANOV. The preceding has made a painful impression on me. The functions of the delegates are reduced to registering what has already been done by the Government. The whole Commission is confronted by facts to which it has to submit. I propose that the work of the delegation be given the widest publicity.

.   .   .

Tseretelli did not share the impressions of Comrade Sukhanov. We received complete satisfaction on a number of questions, for example, in regard to the problem of the emigrants, the allocation of 500,000 rubles for the Adzhars. Our proposal that the oath of allegiance not be administered until the Constituent

---

[15] See *ibid.*

[16] See Chap. 19. Platten, who accompanied the Lenin group, was turned back at the Russian border and his entry visa canceled.

[17] On March 6 and 15 the Executive Committee voted to request this amount from the Government to help meet the needs of the Soviet. It was refused. *Protokoly*, pp. 50, 298.

[18] Moslems of Georgian stock.

Assembly is convoked has been accepted by the Government.[19] The Government has supported us on the necessity of adopting measures for fighting the campaign that has been started against us. It is true that on certain matters we did not receive satisfaction, but we had no definite instructions from you as to how we should act in the event of a refusal, whether we should regard these matters as conflicts, especially in the question of exchanging [Russian political emigrants for German internees or prisoners of war], concerning which you had reached no unanimous decision. But this situation far from justifies our altering the whole system of relations with the Government, as recommended by Comrade Sukhanov.

COMRADE KRASIKOV. The situation is abnormal. Our influence is reduced to a minimum.

There is no organized, public, clear discussion of issues. The refusal of the 10-million ruble fund, for example, puts the Soviets in an impossible position. I protest against the absence of public discussion of the negotiations with the Government. If the conflict comes to a head, our position—a position of secrecy and diplomacy—will put us in an impossible position before the masses.

I propose that the whole character of the negotiations between the Liaison Commission and the Government be changed. I recommend the policy of publicity.

COMRADE YURENEV. The report made the saddest impression on me. I do not see any support on the part of the Government. Everything must be publicized. We are confronted with the general question of relations with the Government. It is coming to a head. We can only rely on the support of the lower classes if our own policy is clear and definite. Specifically, we must insist at once on [obtaining] a passage [permit] for Comrade Platten.

. . .

COMRADE BOGDANOV. It is not the Liaison Commission, or its speeches, that is in question. The question concerns our actual strength. During the past two weeks not so much was said about our prestige as about the struggle. It is possible that Guchkov and L'vov are not maintaining the policy of being a resultant force which they established at the beginning. . . . But we must admit that we are doing many things to weaken ourselves. We have suffered defeat on those points which it would have been disadvantageous for us to contest. Let us even take the question of the oath of allegiance. There was a sharp conflict of opinion on this question. Many considered that this was one of the most controversial questions. We have already suffered defeat in this question although we do not want to admit it. I do not see how we can win in this question. We must find an honorable way out. It must not be forgotten that a section of the army has already been sworn in.

The second question in which we suffered defeat is the question of exchanging [Russian political emigrants for German internees and prisoners of war]. Under the circumstances in which we find ourselves now, the group of comrades who traveled through Germany committed, without doubt, an inadmissible, or at least a political, error. Comrade Lenin and his group did not consider the interests of the Russian revolution—they considered merely their own desires, as revolutionaries, to return to Russia.

---

[19] Session of March 16. *Protokoly*, p. 56.

I was not in favor of trying to obtain the 10-million ruble fund. I do not want to conceal from you that I regard the reasons given by the Government as a simple pretext. There is no doubt that we are being refused as adversaries, but I am still against taking issue on this matter. We are occupied with neither the molding of public opinion nor the organization of the masses—and herein lies the cause of our weakness. The Soviet is inefficient, relations have not been adjusted, there is no over-all campaign and this holds not only for here but for the provinces as well.

. . .

COMRADE CHKHEIDZE. [He] submitted a proposal: to have no direct relations with the Government; to communicate with the Government only in writing and request that the Government reply similarly in writing.

COMRADE BRAMSON. I am very surprised at such a proposal from Comrade Chkheidze, which, essentially, signifies the dissolution of the Liaison Commission. This proposal deprives us of all the advantages of direct personal relations; he proposed that the Liaison Commission itself keep detailed records of the negotiations—records of proceedings—confirmed by the signatures of all the participants of the delegation.

Comrade Krasikov's motion was put to a vote.

It was rejected by 21 votes to 17.

Comrade Bramson's motion was put to a vote.

It was accepted by a majority (Comrade Bramson's proposal to keep records of proceedings, signed by the Liaison Commission itself).

. . .

2. *Izvestiia* of the Soviet of Soldiers' and Workers' Deputies.

REPORT BY COMRADE STANKEVICH. The Soviet has an influential organ in its hands—around 100,000 copies of it are sold, yet we make absolutely no use of this lever. It only serves to undermine our position. It has no properly organized sections. It is overloaded with various resolutions. The situation has reached the point where accounts of meetings in our organ appear in a more chaotic form than in any organ of the bourgeois press. He referred to a number of issues of *Izvestiia*. One must start thinking about a reorganization. It is not a question of lack of space, but of the inadequacies of the editorial staff. It is necessary to reform the *Izvestiia*. This is a burning, urgent matter.

. . .

[A three-man committee consisting of Dan, Stankevich, and Sukhanov was elected and was instructed to present a list of editors within three days and report on the reorganization of the editorial staff.][20]

1060. *Russkiia Vedomosti* ON THE QUESTION OF DUAL POWER
AND THE TASKS OF THE GOVERNMENT
[No. 88, April 21, 1917, p. 3.]

No problem of Russian life is causing so much talk as the problem of relations between the Provisional Government and the organized public groups—in particular, the Soviets of Workers' and Soldiers' Deputies. The members of the

[20] See Doc. 1054.

Provisional Government have declared more than once in public conversations that all talk of dual power, of the pressure exerted on the Provisional Government and of a serious controversy between it and the Soviets of Workers' and Soldiers' Deputies, has no foundation in fact. It is true that, within the Soviets of Workers' and Soldiers' Deputies, the elements which are in an aggressive mood in regard to the Provisional Government, and which call for a direct struggle against it or openly express their lack of confidence in it, have remained thus far invariably in the minority. Still, one could wish for more. Not everything in the relations between the Provisional Government and the Soviets of Workers' and Soldiers' Deputies proceeds as smoothly and felicitously as it should. Of course, the Soviets of Workers' and Soldiers' Deputies have not engaged in a struggle against the Provisional Government, but, at the same time, they have not given it the support that it needs so badly. Whenever the question comes up— for one reason or another—concerning the relations to the Provisional Government, the soviets, it is true, express confidence in the Government in their resolutions, but usually this expression of confidence is accompanied by reservations that weaken or almost destroy its whole moral worth. There are cases, also, when the Soviets take a waiting position in relation to the Provisional Government; perhaps the most nearly correct characterization of the relations of the Soviets of Workers' and Soldiers' Deputies to the Provisional Government would be to call it the policy of neutrality, and watchful neutrality, at that. . . .

The duality of policy on the part of the Soviets of Workers' and Soldiers' Deputies in relation to the Provisional Government is conditioned to a considerable extent by lack of consideration of the fact that this government is only "provisional" (i.e., temporary), and it has a strictly limited program: the convocation of the Constituent Assembly and the carrying on of current work; although it must be admitted that at the present moment this current work, which includes the conduct of the war, the organization of food supply, the ordering of the transport, and the like, is characterized by extreme complexity and difficulty. We are entitled to demand only two things from the Provisional Government: political honesty, i.e., conscientious fulfillment of obligations assumed by it, and businesslike administration; and both of these demands the Government satisfies completely. . . . The attacks against the Provisional Government were made for entirely different considerations. The Government either was subjected to wholesale suspicion of being bourgeois-minded or was accused of failure to do something which it had not undertaken to do in the first place. The Provisional Government, precisely because it is temporary in nature and because there is no correctly organized legislative power alongside it, not only is unable to carry out any broad legislative program, but *has no right* to undertake it. It had to introduce the grain monopoly; otherwise we would have been threatened with famine this very year, and it would have been too late to take measures against it at the Constituent Assembly. It had to introduce a reform of local self-government; otherwise life in the provinces would have been completely disorganized. But all the legislative undertakings that have no such urgency are outside the competence of the Provisional Government. . . .

The present moment places before us strictly limited and comparatively circumscribed tasks. The Provisional Government fulfills *these* tasks completely honestly and conscientiously, but it can solve them only with the unanimous support of the public, in an atmosphere of general good will. Without confidence, there can be neither authority nor firm power, and, lacking these, the Provisional Government will not be able to fulfill its assigned tasks. Because of the extreme seriousness of the situation, it is necessary to forget controversies as much as possible and unite around the Provisional Government to make it really strong. Without this, we risk losing all the attainments of the revolution.

CHAPTER 22

The April Crisis and the Formation of a Coalition Government[1]

MILIUKOV'S NOTE AND THE DEMONSTRATIONS OF APRIL 20–22

1061. *Novoe Vremia* ON THE MILIUKOV NOTE

[No. 14757, April 21, 1917, p. 4.]

This note is not very long; nevertheless, it could be shortened further. Disregarding the usual diplomatic formulas surrounding the substance of this note, we get the following thesis: "It goes without saying that the Provisional Government, while safeguarding the rights of our motherland, will honor in full the obligations assumed in regard to our allies." If Russia, as a nation, has placed its signature under the obligation not to conclude a separate peace, she must keep her word. . . .

If the new regime considers that former treaties are not advantageous to Russia, it can, of course, enter into negotiations with the Allies and effect a change in those treaties in accordance with the changed circumstances. But one cannot tear up the promissory note only because it was signed by the old manager of Russia who has since yielded his place to the new manager of the same Russia. . . .

What would be the practical result of our tearing up the existing treaties and declaring them invalid? Very simple. Our allies would also attain freedom of action: if there is no treaty, no one has to observe it. They would cease to be our allies.

We think that, with the exception of the Bolsheviks, all Russian citizens will consider the basic thesis of yesterday's note a correct one.

---

[1] Miliukov's Note of April 18, which precipitated the internal crisis, and the subsequent explanatory note, which terminated its diplomatic aspect, are found in Volume II, Chapter 19. A detailed account of the April Crisis and the events leading to a coalition government was published by Irakli Tseretelli under the title: "Reminiscences of the February Revolution: The April Crisis," *The Russian Review*, XIV (1955), 93–108, 184–200, 301–21, and XV (1956), 93–108. These articles are excerpts from Chapter 10 of Tseretelli's unpublished manuscript on the revolution, which is on deposit at the Columbia University Archive of Russian and East European History and Culture and at Harvard University's Russian Research Center. See also N. N. Sukhanov, *The Russian Revolution 1917*, Joel Carmichael, ed. and trans., Chaps. 14 and 15; P. N. Miliukov, *Istoriia vtoroi russkoi revoliutsii*, I, vypusk 1, 92–117; A. F. Kerensky, *The Catastrophe*, p. 133 ff.; and Victor Chernov, *The Great Russian Revolution*, pp. 199–209. Attention is also directed to the recently published *Revoliutsionnoe dvizhenie v rossii v aprele 1917: Aprel'skii krizis*, in the important Soviet series *Velikaia oktiabr'skaia sotsialisticheskaia revoliutsiia: Dokumenty i materialy*, and *Khronika sobytii*, of which several volumes have appeared to date.

If there are persons who regard this basic question differently, and if they have enough power in their hands to consider themselves the winning side, let them take the power into their own hands and, together with the power, also the responsibility. The present government cannot and must not take this road.

1062. *Den'* ON THE MILIUKOV NOTE

[No. 39, April 21, 1917, p. 1.]

The note of our Minister of Foreign Affairs to the Allied governments published in yesterday's newspapers cannot but arouse feelings of painful wonder.

. . .

During the three weeks that followed the publication of the Government communication [of March 27] and that preceded the sending of the note to the Allied governments, Mr. Miliukov did everything in his power to weaken the significance of the act of March 27 and to remove all life from this document. In his numerous speeches, in his conversations with the correspondents of the Russian and especially of the foreign press, Mr. Miliukov succeeded, under the pretense of making comments on the act of March 27, in carrying out in full his prerevolutionary military program. From yesterday's issue of *Izvestiia* . . . we learn that, in his capacity as chairman of the section of international relations of the Executive Committee, M. I. Skobelev was obliged to deny the assertions of our Minister of Foreign Affairs that Russia "must obtain domination over the Bosporus and the Dardanelles and the opportunity to fortify them, and that Russia will demand the dismemberment of Austria." Similar declarations regarding Austria and Germany were also made by A. I. Guchkov.

Instead of dissipating the natural perplexity caused by these irresponsible comments, the last diplomatic creation of Mr. Miliukov is bound only to increase our perplexity and alarm.

In the note of April 18 our Minister of Foreign Affairs displayed all the wealth of diplomatic vocabulary which succeeded in gaining in the course of the war the justified hatred of all the world democracy. Here [we find] war "till decisive victory," as well as "guarantees and sanctions," which can be conceived as anything one wishes, but not as genuine democratic guarantees. On the basis of Mr. Miliukov's previous speeches the note published yesterday could easily be interpreted as an attempt to bring to nought the communication of the Government of March 27, and, to be frank, we are far from certain that such an interpretation is wide of the truth . . .

The note of April 18 is particularly difficult to understand in view of the situation that has been created within the country. On April 16, at the plenary session of the S. of W. and S.D., Chkheidze and Tsereteli declared that the Executive Committee made its attitude toward the [Liberty] Loan subject to the step which the Provisional Government was then expected [to take] in the sphere of foreign policy.[2] Actually this step was the note of April 18. Is it possible that Mr. Miliukov did not realize that his note predetermined the answer of the S. of W. and S.D.

[2] On April 22, following the resolution of the question of Miliukov's note, the Soviet voted to support the Liberty Loan. See Volume II, Doc. 437.

in a sense contrary to the interests of the Provisional Government and to the cause of the revolution?

If he really did not understand, then yesterday's note should convince us of the gross political mistake committed by the Provisional Government.

1063. *Rabochaia Gazeta* ON THE MILIUKOV NOTE

[No. 36, April 21, 1917, p. 1.]

On April 18, on the day when the Russian democracy proclaimed the international brotherhood of peoples and called upon the world democracy to unite in a struggle for peace, on that very day it received a stab in the back from the Provisional Government.[3] On the same day the Ministry of Foreign Affairs dispatched a note to the Allied governments through their ambassadors. The Note unequivocally branded as invalid the appeal by the Provisional Government to the citizens on March 27 repudiating all aggressive designs.

The democracy of Russia looked upon the proclamation of March 27 as only the first step. It expected the second step to follow—a proposal to the Allied governments to revise their old Allied treaties in the light of the new principles promulgated on March 27. But now the Ministry of Foreign Affairs declares that no principles were promulgated on March 27. The Ministry maintains that by its pronouncement of March 27 the democracy of Russia merely added "its voice to those of the Allies." And our Government proposes no revision of former treaties. Without equivocation it makes it clear that at no time did it or does it intend to undertake any such revision. The Provisional Government solemnly confirms that it will "fully observe the obligations taken with respect to our allies." In the name of the Russian people it solemnly vows that its blood will continue to be shed until England is firmly entrenched in Asia; until Italy receives the largest share of the Adriatic shore, inhabited by Slavs; until Austria is cut off from the sea, divided between Italy and Serbia; and until Rumania gets Transylvania as its price for participation in the war.

. . .

All peoples are interested in the termination of this slaughter, and the democracy of Russia is interested in it most of all. Her problems are to strengthen the liberty which has been won, to employ it for the rebirth of the country, and not to abandon the country to flood and annihilation in order to please our imperialists and their allies in England, France, and Italy.

Our democracy is of course aware of this task and will undoubtedly meet the new step of the Government with a resolute rebuff.

We were emphatically opposed to the kindling of civil war by the followers of Lenin. But now the signal to civil war is given not by the adherents of Lenin; now it comes from the Provisional Government through the published act which is a mockery of the aspirations of democracy. This is truly a step of madness, and immediate firm actions on the part of the Soviet of Workers' and Soldiers' Deputies are needed to avert its terrible consequences.

[3] April 18, May Day, Old Style.

1064. *Delo Naroda* ON THE MILIUKOV NOTE
[No. 29, April 21, 1917, p. 1.]

Again, during her brief but tempestuous existence the Russian revolution is experiencing a crucial moment.

The Provisional Government and the Soviet of Workers' and Soldiers' Deputies are in conflict. The conflict is over an important question—what course should or should not the Russian revolution take. The fate of youthful freedom and social justice in the east of Europe and of international socialism throughout the world depends on whether or not the toiling democracy of Russia recognizes peace without annexations and contributions.

The Soviet of Workers' and Soldiers' Deputies says yes, it will recognize it. The Provisional Government, confused by the sophism of its Minister of Foreign affairs, says no, it will not recognize it. A fatal clash! The actual executive authority of the requblic and the authority that controls the activity of the toiling masses stand face to face.

How pathetic do the people seem to us who in this historic hour speak about criminal intrigues, about the play of ambitions, about the insane narrowness of revolutionary fanatics, about the fact that the sleep of representatives of the toiling democracy is disturbed by the ministerial laurels of Citizen Miliukov. Either a resolute blow will be struck against war, or war will still torment and destroy mankind for a long time. We are told about the audacity of the proletariat and of the soldier who has designs on the Kadet wisdom of a diplomat . . .

We hope that the great conflict will resolve itself in the interests of revolutionary Russia and world socialism. We want to believe that the Provisional Government will understand the responsibility it assumes by refusing the masses their right to bear the testaments of brotherhood and love to the world which is choking with blood.

1065. *Novaia Zhizn'* ON THE MILIUKOV NOTE
[No. 2, April 20, 1917, p. 1.]

. . . .

Late at night the editorial office received the Note of Mr. Miliukov in which he vows to wage the war to complete victory. He pledges to keep sacred the secret agreements of Nicholas II with the Anglo-French capitalists and finally expresses his approval of the "guarantees" of peace, by which, as is known, is meant annexations and indemnities.

This is an obvious retreat from that program of peace which was declared by the Soviet of Workers' and Soldiers' Deputies and confirmed by the Provisional Government in the famous appeal to the citizens of March 26 [*sic*]. This [Note] is an appeal to the entire Russian democracy, to the entire Russian people—an appeal the more criminal because it is at the same time a threat to the revolutionary movement for peace, which flared up in recent days among the peoples of the German coalition. By these *militant outcries Mr. Miliukov renders a friendly service not only to the imperialists of the Allied countries, but also to the governments of the Hohenzollerns and Hapsburgs, aiding the latter in keeping in check the movement of the German proletariat.*

A champion of the interests of international capital has no place in the ranks of the government of democratic Russia! We have no doubt that the Soviet of Workers' and Soldiers' Deputies will not delay in taking the most energetic measures to make Mr. Miliukov harmless immediately.

1066. *Izvestiia* CALLS FOR CALMNESS
[*Izvestiia*, No. 46, April 21, 1917, p. 1.]

The Provisional Government's Note aroused legitimate indignation on the part of citizens in Petrograd.

Everywhere the streets are filled with crowds of people. They are speaking in agitated tones and discussing the startling issues. These discussions are often so heated that there is danger of being personally insulted.

Comrade-workers and soldiers! In these days of new, heavy trials that befall us, we must remain particularly calm and exercise particular self-restraint.

Our strength lies in our calmness. We will firmly and decisively repulse the counterrevolutionary forces, but we will not allow the triumph of the Black Hundred. It is the Black Hundred that wants to arouse passions and force peaceful citizens to turn from arguing to attacking one another, to insults and derision.

Let everyone bear in mind that the Soviet of Workers' and Soldiers' Deputies stands at the head of the people of Petrograd; it is investigating the newly developed political situation and will give you its decision.

No individual actions must be taken. They will only weaken us. Let us calmly await the decision of the Soviet of Workers' and Soldiers' Deputies; it will show us the way out of the new situation.

Our strength lies in our calmness.

1067. THE SOVIET DECISION TO NEGOTIATE WITH THE GOVERNMENT
[*Izvestiia*, No. 46, April 21, 1917, p. 7. The Executive Committee voted on this course on April 19, and reaffirmed its decision on the 20th, following the Government's agreement. The decision was then taken before the plenary session for ratification.]

A special meeting of the Soviet of Workers' and Soldiers' Deputies was held on April 20. After Comrade Chkheidze's speech in which the purpose of the meeting was made explicit, the plenary session adopted his proposal [which was as follows]: To make no decisions with respect to Miliukov's Note, dated April 18, pending a final clarification of the situation by the Executive Committee in its personal exchange of views with the Council of Ministers [which is] to take place in the evening of April 20 in the Mariinskii Palace.[4] Members of the Soviet of Workers' and Soldiers' Deputies departed for their districts in order to calm [the people] and to appeal for firmness. The speakers of almost all the political parties joined in support of Comrade Chkheidze's views.

1068. KORNILOV IS DENIED PERMISSION BY THE GOVERNMENT TO USE TROOPS AGAINST THE DEMONSTRATORS
[Account of Admiral Kolchak in Elena Varneck and H. H. Fisher, *The Testimony of Kolchak and Other Siberian Materials*, pp. 64–65. On the following day, when Kornilov

---

[4] Tseretelli describes the meeting with the Government at some length in his "Reminiscences of the February Revolution," *The Russian Review*, XIV (1955), 91–98.

attempted to place certain military units before the Mariinskii Palace, the troops turned to the Soviet for confirmation. The Soviet persuaded Kornilov to cancel his order. See Doc. 1069 for the subsequent order or appeal of the Executive Committee to the troops.]

. . . I went direct to the session of the Council of Ministers, which was taking place at Guchkov's house on the Moika [because of Guchkov's illness]. . . .

Sometime toward the end of the session [of April 20] General Kornilov came, I believe from Tsarskoe Selo (this was the first time I saw him). Kornilov said that an armed demonstration of troops against the government was taking place in town; that he had sufficient forces at his disposal to stop this move and in case of need, if there should be an armed clash, he had confidence that it would be possible to suppress the move. He therefore requested the government to sanction this plan and to give him a chance to begin action immediately. This served as a pretext for an exchange of opinions and for debates in which Lvov and Kerensky were especially emphatic in their opposition, the latter declaring: "Our strength lies in moral influence, and to apply armed force would be to adopt the old road of compulsion, which I consider impossible." With this the session closed. But for a long time Kerensky continued to converse with Kornilov. . . .

1069. APPEAL OF THE SOVIET EXECUTIVE COMMITTEE TO THE CITIZENS AND SOLDIERS

[*Izvestiia*, No. 47, April 22, 1917, p. 1, as translated in Golder, pp. 335–36.]

Citizens!

At the moment when the fate of the country is being decided, every rash step is dangerous. The demonstrations against the Government's Note on foreign affairs have led to fights on the streets. There are wounded and dead. In the name of saving the revolution from the trouble that threatens it, we appeal to you and beg you, Be Calm, Keep Order, and Observe Discipline.

The Soviet of Workers' and Soldiers' Deputies is deliberating on the situation. Believe that the Soviet will find a way agreeable to you. In the meantime, let no one disturb the run of peaceable life in free Russia.

Comrade Soldiers!

In these exciting days let no one come out on the street armed, unless called out by the Executive Committee. Only the Executive Committee has the right to give you orders. Every order for the military to come out (except as a matter of routine) should be on a written blank of the Executive Committee, stamped with its seal, and signed by at least two of the seven men herein named: Chkheidze, Skobelev, Binasik, Filipovskii, Skalov, Goldman, Bogdanov.

Confirm every order by telephoning to No. 104-06.

Comrades, Workmen, and Militia!

Your guns are for the protection of the revolution. You do not need them for demonstrations or meetings. On such occasions they are dangerous for the cause of freedom. When you go to meetings or demonstrations, leave your arms behind.

The Executive Committee calls on all organizations to help it in keeping peace and order.

No form of force by one citizen against another can be permitted in free Russia.
Disturbances help only the enemy of the revolution, and he who brings them on is an enemy of the people.

EXECUTIVE COMMITTEE OF THE S.W.S.D.

April 21, 1917

1070. SOVIET ACCEPTANCE OF THE GOVERNMENT'S SUPPLEMENTARY EXPLANATORY NOTE

[Session of the Executive Committee of April 21. *Protokoly*, p. 118. According to Tseretelli, the first draft of the supplemental note was composed by him and Nekrasov at the meeting with the Government the night of the 20th. The final draft, which had shifted the first and second paragraphs to second and third place and added as a first paragraph the statement concerning the unanimity of ministerial approval of the original note, was received by the Executive Committee at 5:00 P.M. on the 21st and approved. Tseretelli, "Reminiscences of the February Revolution," *The Russian Review*, XIV (1955), 198. The supplemental note is published in Volume II as Doc. 966.]

The Executive Committee proceeded to the discussion of Comrade Tseretelli's statement on the clarification issued by the Provisional Government on its Note of April 18.

By a majority of 34 votes to 19 [the Executive Committee] passed a resolution which considered that, following the Government's clarifications, the incident associated with the Note of April 18 was closed. The following principles were accepted for guidance: 1) the Executive Committee considers it necessary to adopt resolute measures at once for increasing its control over the activities of the Provisional Government and, primarily, over the activities of the Minister of Foreign Affairs; 2) no major political act must be published without first notifying the Executive Committee; 3) the personnel of the Russian diplomatic corps abroad must undergo a radical change.

1071. THE REPORT BY THE EXAMINING MAGISTRATE ON THE APRIL DEMONSTRATIONS

[V. Rakhmetov, "Aprel'skie dni 1917 goda v Petrograde," *KA*, XXXIII (1929), 64–81.]

. . .

On the basis of the above data of the preliminary investigation the following general conclusions should be made with regard to the circumstances of the case:

1) The groups of factory workers which participated in the street demonstrations in the day and in the evening of April 21 had been undoubtedly organized in advance: their numerous banners and placards (some [bearing] printed inscriptions or occasionally artistic drawings) were prepared beforehand; the convoying of each group of factory workers demonstrating against the Provisional Government by a detachment of well-armed workers from the factory (people's) militia was obviously planned and systematically worked out not only for the purpose of guarding the banners and the placards, but also for that of deliberately eliminating "the bourgeoisie," i.e., all the ideological opponents of similar demonstrations against the Provisional Government and the continuation of the war.

2) On the contrary, the demonstrations in favor of the Provisional Govern-

ment, and, in particular, the group of these demonstrators which clashed during the day near the Kazan' Cathedral with the workmen of the Vyborgskii district, were not organized in advance, but formed spontaneously; they were composed of the most varied social elements under the influence of the unanimous indignation of casual passersby on the Nevskii Prospekt at the appearance of armed demonstrators against the Provisional Government and the war.

3) Although the demonstration in favor of the Provisional Government, which hastily formed during the day, included a great number of military personnel (soldiers, junkers, and some isolated officers), the latter, being in this instance mere passersby [or] private individuals, did not carry firearms, rifles in particular; only some of them had cold steel, borne according to the regulations by officers and junkers (sabers, dirks, bayonets).

4) Also the individual soldiers from various military units who, after learning of the decision of the Soviet of Workers' Deputies and in compliance with it, started, toward the evening of April 21, to take steps in order to stop all kinds of demonstrations and to clear the Nevskii Prospekt of superfluous persons, possessed no weapons whatsoever.

5) The workers demonstrating against the Provisional Government, who were amply equipped with firearms, are to be held guilty for the firing in the area of the Nevskii Prospekt and Sadovaia Street both during the day and in the evening of April 21; a mitigating circumstance of their guilt should be the fact that their aiming and firing, both during the day and the evening clashes, was due to the attempts of some isolated soldiers and persons from the public, indignant at the inscriptions on some of the placards of the demonstrating workmen, to take the placards away and destroy them.

6) Summarizing the general nature of the testimonies [obtained from] casualties and witnesses, it is possible to conclude that the signs by themselves would hardly have driven the opponents of the demonstration to active deeds, were the procession itself not accompanied by whole detachments of armed men and by threats on their part to get rid of "the bourgeoisie" by force of arms; this could not fail to excite passions on both sides and keep the mood of the public at such a peak of tension that any sharp word, any incautious gesture, was bound to bring about blows or, with one side being armed, shooting.

7) Isolated indications of "provocatory" shooting "at officer's orders" of workers on the part of any kind of military detachment, as well as of firing at demonstrators from house windows (Café Empire, Dagmar Hotel), which have come up during the investigation, should be considered absolutely refuted by all the data [in possession] of the investigation.

8) Owing to the exceptional nature of the events themselves, of their mass character defying attention to detail, it has proved impossible to identify the individuals who directed the armed demonstration of the workers, those who ordered opening fire or whose shots inflicted wounds and death; however, the participation in the armed demonstrations and in the shooting itself of numerous representatives of the factory (people's) militia, whom the onlookers identified under the generic name of "Red Guard," is to be considered an established fact.

It seems useful to add that similar conclusions have been reached meantime by the military authorities, on the basis of an independent investigation of the causes and circumstances of the street shooting on April 21 last. On the other hand, the data gathered by the committee of inquiry of the Soviet of Workers' and Soldiers' Deputies have remained unknown to the examining magistrate. In spite of oral (telephone) and written requests to send them to the investigation, the committee has not forwarded them to this day; this caused a delay of the final discussion and direction of this case, which was actually completed in the beginning of June.

Taking into account the foregoing, and following article 277 of the Regulations on Criminal Proceedings the examining magistrate has decided to submit the present case, through the prosecutor of the Petrograd District Court, to the said court for the purpose of closing the proceedings of the case, the guilty persons having remained undetected.*

> V. SEREDA
> Examining magistrate for especially
> important cases

1072. *Russkiia Vedomosti*'s COMMENT ON THE SIGNIFICANCE OF THE EVENTS OF APRIL 20–21
[No. 89, April 22, 1917, p. 3.]

A governmental crisis has been precipitated in Petrograd. Because of the latest note of the Minister of Foreign Affairs, relations between the Government and the Soviet of Workers' and Soldiers' Deputies became so strained that a question arose concerning the possibility of the resignation of the entire Government. . . . The circumstance, that the crisis arose partly because of an incorrect interpretation of isolated sentences of the Note, testifies better than anything else to the atmosphere of distrust and suspicion of the Provisional Government, which atmosphere constitutes precisely the basic cause of the crisis.

Under such conditions, too much significance should not be attached to the fact that the misunderstanding will be clarified and the incident will be considered closed. It is impossible to carry on work under these conditions, when serious political crises can arise because of a mere misunderstanding of words, and it is clear that something more needs to be done in order to create a really firm government in Russia. At the meeting of the Soviet of Workers' and Soldiers' Deputies on April 20, some speakers pointed to the fact that the Soviet is not sufficiently strong to take power into its own hands, and apparently that opinion is quite widespread among the members of the Soviet. But what does that mean? What is it that gives the strength to the Provisional Government to take power into its hands and denies that strength to the Soviet? The point here is not, of course, that the Petrograd Soviet of Workers' and Soldiers' Deputies is only the Petrograd Soviet and not all-Russian, because the Provisional Government has not even that type of organization behind it. Nor do the personal qualifications or talents matter very much, because it is possible that people could be found with the necessary administrative gifts in circles close to the Soviet. The heart of the matter is that the program of the Provisional Government represents the maximum of what the objective conditions of Russian life permit, and if the Soviet of Workers' Deputies were to take power into its own hands, it would

---

* The decision of the District Court . . . taken only on September 20, 1917, states: "Taking into account the circumstances of the case and seeing no basis for further preliminary investigation, the Court decides in accordance with the conclusion of the prosecutor: . . . to close the investigation, as the guilty persons were not detected . . ."

either continue the policy of the present Provisional Government or push the country into an abyss. Many of the members of the Soviet of Workers' and Soldiers' Deputies do really understand this, and therefore they are sharpening the conflict with the Provisional Government, but, at the same time, they lack the courage to show active support to the policy of the Provisional Government as the only one possible. This perhaps constitutes the main tragedy of the situation, and as long as the majority of the Soviet of Workers' and Soldiers' Deputies fails to take a definite position in regard to the Provisional Government and fails to show it real support, just so long will the crisis remain essentially unresolved.

1073. *Izvestiia* ON THE DEMONSTRATIONS
[No. 47, April 22, 1917, p. 2.]

On April 21, innumerable demonstrations took place in the streets of Petrograd, as a result of the conflict between the Soviet of Workers' and Soldiers' Deputies and the Provisional Government.

The inscriptions on posters and banners testified to the fact that the demonstrators differed in their interpretations of current events.

There were banners expressing complete confidence in the Soviet of Workers' and Soldiers' Deputies. But there were also banners calling for complete confidence in the Provisional Government.

The inscriptions expressing the attitude of the demonstrators toward war were just as divergent. Here were all kinds of slogans ranging from "War until final victory" to the cry "Down with the war!"

The demonstrations varied not only in their slogans, but also in their class composition. There was a sharp contrast between the workers' demonstrations and the demonstrations of the well-to-do classes.

This sharp contrast between the aspirations of the demonstrators revealed the whole acuteness of the conflict between the Soviet of Workers' and Soldiers' Deputies and the Provisional Government.

This issue divided Petrograd into two camps. But the manner in which this division occurred revealed the degree to which Russian citizens were unaccustomed to freedom in political struggle.

At a time when, in full awareness of its responsibility, the Executive Committee of the Soviet of Workers' and Soldiers' Deputies was taking into account the entire gravity of the moment and was trying to find a way out of the situation, many supporters of the Soviet were demonstrating under banners with slogans which did not correspond to the aims of the Soviet.

The Soviet was trying to force the Government to take certain definite steps in the realm of foreign policy. But in fighting the Government on this point the Soviet was not striving to seize power. In the meantime, many banners of the Soviet's supporters bore inscriptions demanding the overthrow of the Government and the transfer of all power to the Soviet.

In the same way, the Provisional Government, realizing that a complete rupture with the Soviet would plunge the country into an abyss of anarchy, was trying to find ways of satisfying the demands of the democratic representatives, even though it considered these demands to be onerous and difficult. Meanwhile, the banners of the supporters of the Soviet often carried inscriptions inflaming the passions and arousing the anger of the workers.

At a time when the responsible policy makers of the bourgeoisie and of the proletariat were exerting every effort to prevent a rupture between the Soviet and the Provisional Government, crowds of demonstrators were making it more and more difficult by the severity of their slogans to resolve the conflict.

But there was another grievous aspect to the demonstrations of April 21.

We do not know the extent to which the bourgeois demonstrations were organized, or the extent to which their actions were governed by a single directing will. But all the proletarian demonstrations of April 21 took place without [the knowledge of] the Soviet of Workers' and Soldiers' Deputies; [the Soviet] took no initiative in [staging] the street demonstrations of its supporters.

But the indignation was too great in the workers' quarters. Indignation against the phantom of a revived tsarist policy of conquest brought the workers out into the streets . . .

Under the conditions of highly aroused passions, the danger arose of a clash between citizens of different parties and different classes. The danger arose of the worst form of civil war.

The danger was increased by one feature of the April 21 demonstrations. Part of the demonstrators were armed. Armed demonstrators were found among Soviet supporters as well as among Government supporters.

As a result, the day of April 21 was darkened by regrettable and disgraceful events. Clashes occurred between workers' demonstrators and bourgeois demonstrators. Firearms were used and in the resulting confusion shots were fired into the crowd.

An investigation of the grievous events of April 21 will throw light on those guilty of this shooting. We will soon discover whose insane or criminal hand was responsible for the killing of workers, soldiers, and citizens who were accidentally present at the time of the clash in the streets of Petrograd. But there is one thing we do know without any investigation: these insane or treasonable shots brought harm to the cause of the revolution. These shots created the danger of sedition, which is fatal to the cause of freedom.

The Soviet of Workers' and Soldiers' Deputies took account of the threatening danger in the current events.

Unanimously it adopted the decisions published in the present issue of *Izvestiia*.[5]

We do not know whether these were traitors or madmen who killed the citizens on April 21. But their wrongdoing played into the hands of the bitterest enemies of freedom. The Soviet rose to the defense of the revolution. Let all the citizens support it.

Anyone who disobeys the decisions of the Soviet which were published today is an enemy of the revolution, an enemy of the people.

1074. Lenin on the "Lessons of the Crisis"

[*Pravda*, No. 39, April 23, 1917, as translated in the *Collected Works of V. I. Lenin: The Revolution of 1917*, XX, Bk. 1, 256–59. All dates in the article are New Style.]

Petrograd and the whole of Russia have gone through a serious political crisis, the first political crisis since the revolution.

On May 1 the Provisional Government issued its notorious note, which con-

[5] Doc. 1069.

firmed the predatory aims of the war with such clarity that it was sufficient to arouse the indignation of the masses who had honestly believed in the desire (and ability) of the capitalists to "renounce the policy of annexations." On May 3 and 4 Petrograd was astir. The streets were crowded with people; meetings of various sizes were held everywhere, day and night; mass manifestations and demonstrations were going on uninterruptedly. Yesterday, May 4, the crisis or, at any rate the first stage of the crisis came to an end: the Executive Committee of the Soviet of Workers' and Soldiers' Deputies, and later the Soviet itself, declared that they were satisfied with the "explanations," amendments to the note and "elucidations" of the government (empty phrases that say absolutely nothing, change nothing, and commit one to nothing), and "the incident was closed."

The future will show whether the masses will regard the "incident as closed." The task before us now is carefully to examine the forces, the classes that revealed themselves in the crisis, and to draw therefrom lessons for the party of the proletariat. For it is the great significance of all crises that they unveil the hidden, cast aside the conventional, the superficial, the petty, sweep away the political rubbish, uncover the secret springs of the true class-struggle that is going on.

As a matter of fact the capitalist government on May 1 merely reiterated its former declarations, which enveloped the imperialist war in a mist of equivocation. The soldier masses grew indignant, because they had honestly believed in the sincerity and pacific intentions of the capitalists. The demonstration started as soldiers' demonstrations under a contradictory, unintelligent, leading-nowhere slogan, "Down with Miliukov" (as if a change in the personnel or cliques could change the essence of their policy).

That means that the broad, unstable, vacillating mass, which is closest to the peasantry and petty-bourgeoisie by scientific class definition, drew away from the capitalists *toward the side* of the revolutionary workers. It was this fluctuation or movement of the mass, whose strength was capable of settling everything, that created the crisis.

Immediately a commotion started, people poured into the streets, and began to organise; but those were not the middle, but the extreme elements; not the in-between petty-bourgeois mass, but the bourgeoisie and the proletariat.

The bourgeoisie occupies the Nevsky—in the expression of one paper, the "Miliukovsky"—Prospect and the adjacent sections of prosperous, bureaucratic, and capitalistic Petrograd. Officers, students, "the middle classes" parade *for* the Provisional Government. Among the slogans on the banners one often sees the inscription, "Down with Lenin."

The proletariat rises in *its own* quarters, in the workers' suburbs, it organises around the slogans and watchwords of the Central Committee of our party. On May 3 and 4, the Central Committee adopts resolutions which through the organisational apparatus are directly passed on to the proletarian masses. The workers' processions fill the poorer and less central sections of the city, and later in separate groups they enter the Nevsky. The proletarian demonstrations are distinguished from the bourgeois ones by greater animation and mass character. Among the inscriptions on the banners—"All Power to the Soviet of Workers' and Soldiers' Deputies."

It comes to a collision on the Nevsky. Banners of "enemy" processions are torn. The Executive Committee receives telephone messages from various points that there is shooting on both sides, that there are killed and wounded; information, however, is exceedingly contradictory and unreliable.

Fearing that the real masses, the actual majority of the people might seize power, the bourgeoisie expresses this fear by shouting about the "spectre of civil war." The petty-bourgeois leaders of the Soviet, the Mensheviks and Narodniks, lacking a definite party programme in the period after the revolution, and particularly in the days of the crisis, allow themselves to be intimidated. In the Executive Committee, which on the eve of the crisis was almost evenly divided between those who were for the Provisional Government and those against it, thirty-four ballots are cast (against nineteen) *for* a return to the policy of confidence in the capitalists and agreement with them.

The "incident" is declared "closed."

What is the essence of the class struggle? The capitalists are for continuing the war, and for concealing their aims behind a smoke-screen of phrases and promises. They have become entangled in the nets of Russian, Anglo-French and American bank capital. The proletariat, through its class-conscious vanguard, stands for taking over of power by the revolutionary class, the working class and semi-proletarians, it stands for the development of a world-wide proletarian revolution which is clearly rising in Germany, it stands for the termination of the war through such a revolution.

The broad mass, of a predominantly petty-bourgeois nature, still trusting its Narodnik and Menshevik leaders, intimidated by the bourgeoisie and actually carrying out the policy of the bourgeoisie, under various pretexts, is swinging now to the right, now to the left.

War is terrible; it is the masses that feel it most keenly; it is among the masses that the realisation, as yet not very clear, is growing that this war is criminal, that it is waged because of the rivalry and the scrambling among capitalists for the division of spoils. The international situation is becoming ever more entangled. There is no escape, except through an international proletarian revolution, which is now sweeping Russia, and which is already developing (strikes, fraternisation) in Germany. The masses fluctuate from faith in the old masters, the capitalists, to bitterness against them; from faith in the new class, the only consistently revolutionary class that is breaking a new path leading to a brighter life for the toilers— the proletariat—to a vague understanding of its world-wide historical rôle.

This is not the first *and not the last* instance of indecision of the petty-bourgeois and the semi-proletarian masses!

The lesson is clear, comrade-workers! Time does not wait. After the first crisis, others will follow. Consecrate *all* your strength to the cause of enlightening those who are lagging behind, creating direct comradely contact (not merely through meetings) with each regiment, with each group of toilers who are still in the dark! Devote *all* your strength to uniting your own forces, organising the workers from the ground up, taking in every borough, every factory, every block in the city and its suburbs! Do not be misled by petty-bourgeois "peace makers" who "reconcile" themselves to the capitalists, by the defencist "supporters" of the Government's policies nor by individuals inclined to be hasty and to shout, "Down with the Provisional Government!" before the majority of the people are strongly united. Crises cannot be overcome by the violence of individuals against other individuals, by partial risings of small groups of armed people, by Blanquist attempts to "seize power," to "arrest" the Provisional Government, etc.

The slogan of the day is: Explain more carefully, more clearly, more broadly the proletarian policy, the proletarian method of terminating the war. Fall in line everywhere, strongly, numerously, fill the proletarian ranks and columns! Rally around your Soviets; use comradely suasion and re-election of individual members inside the Soviets to consolidate a majority around yourselves.

THE CRISIS OF POWER AND THE REORGANIZATION OF THE GOVERNMENT

1075. DECLARATION OF THE PROVISIONAL GOVERNMENT REVIEWING ITS ACCOMPLISHMENTS AND CALLING FOR THE SUPPORT AND COOPERATION OF ALL THE VITAL FORCES IN THE NATION
[*VVP*, No. 40, April 26, 1917, p. 1.]

When the Provisional Government assumed power, after the downfall of the old regime which was overthrown by a powerful outburst of popular will, the members of the Government clearly realized the immeasurable difficulty of the task confronting them and the weight of the burden of the responsibility which fell on them for the fate of Russia. Nevertheless they did not hesitate to accept this burden on their shoulders in the firm belief that the unanimous support of the people would give them the strength and the opportunity to fulfill their duty to the end.

This belief was reinforced by the complete unanimity which followed in the country at that time with regard to the understanding of the immediate tasks confronting liberated Russia. The earliest convocation of the Constituent Assembly for the final determination of Russia's form of government, the immediate realization of the principles of civil liberties and equality, the introduction of democratic local self-government, the extension of all civil rights to army personnel with the preservation of military order and discipline while on duty, the continuation of the fight for the native land in close union with our allies—such were the basic principles in favor of which the will of the people declared itself. The Provisional Government was formed on the basis of this program, uniting representatives of different parties in its milieu, and was unanimously recognized by the country. It pledged itself to fulfill the foregoing demands of the will of the people and sealed this pledge by an oath of its members.

Despite the short time that has elapsed since then, the people have already had an opportunity to judge how the Provisional Government has fulfilled and will fulfill its obligations. In the course of its stay in power, along with its intense activity devoted to the urgent current needs of national life, such as defense of the country against the external enemy, alleviation of the crisis in food supply, improvement of transport, the procurement of funds necessary to the State, it has already achieved a series of reforms reorganizing the national life of Russia along the principles of liberty and justice. Amnesty has been proclaimed. The death penalty has been abolished. National and religious equality has been established. Freedom of assembly and association has been legalized. A radical reorganization of local government and self-government along the broadest democratic principles has been initiated. Of the legislation necessary to achieve this aim, laws on elections to municipal dumas and on the militia have already been issued. As soon as possible laws will be drafted and issued on the volost zemstvo, on reforms in guberniya and uezd zemstvos, on local governmental organs, on local courts, and on administrative justice. A work schedule has been established for drawing up a Statute of Elections to the Constituent Assembly on the basis of universal (without distinction of sex), direct, equal, and secret suffrage, and a special conference is being formed for drafting this statute, which will proceed to work as soon as the representatives of the major political parties and groups, invited to its membership, are nominated by the corresponding organizations.

With respect to the organization of the army and its civil rights status, democratic reforms are being carried out which far surpass everything that has been accomplished in this direction in the freest countries of the world. Applying every effort toward restoring the internal organization of the army, which could not but be shaken during the transition to the new state order, the Government is at the same time steadfastly achieving the recognition of full civil and political rights for army personnel and is working tirelessly on reorganizing military administration and military discipline on a basis that will correspond to the spirit of a free democratic system.

Attending to the matter of providing the army and the country with food supplies, the Government has declared the grain harvested in the current and preceding years to be the property of the state and has established a national procedure for apportioning the grain reserves. For the purpose of preparing a draft for the Constituent Assembly on the resolution of the great land question, a draft that will be just and will correspond to the interests of the people, a Central Land Committee has been formed which shall have the participation of representatives of the major political organizations and parties and local land committees.

The attitude of the Government on the nationality question found clear and definite expression in its acts which uphold the cultural self-determination of nationalities in Russia, by restoring the autonomy of Finland and by recognizing Poland's right to unification and national independence.

At the basis of its foreign policy the Provisional Government has placed the repudiation of encroachments on the freedom of other peoples, or of forceful seizures of their territories, and the fight, in close union with the leading democracies, to attain a lasting peace, based on the self-determination of peoples.

But, in speaking of the tasks that it has fulfilled and is in the process of fulfilling, the Provisional Government cannot conceal from the population those difficulties and obstacles which it is meeting in its work. It also does not consider it possible to pass over the fact that recently these difficulties have been mounting and have given rise to anxious misgivings regarding the future.

The Provisional Government, called into existence by the great popular movement, recognizes itself to be the executor and protector of the will of the people. It believes that the power of a state should be based not on violence and coercion, but on the consent of free citizens to submit to the power which they themselves created. It looks for support not from physical but from moral strength. From the time that the Provisional Government came into power, it has not once retreated from these principles. Not a single drop of the people's blood has been shed through its fault, nor have restrictive measures been set up for a single trend of public thought.

Unfortunately, and to the great danger to freedom, the growth of new social bonds consolidating our country is lagging behind the process of deterioration which was brought about by the downfall of the old regime. Under these conditions, with the repudiation of past coercive methods of government and the artificial external means used for raising the prestige of the power, the difficulties of the tasks which have fallen to the lot of the Provisional Government threaten to become insurmountable. The primordial tendency to fulfill the desires and solicitations of individual groups and strata of the population by means of seizures and by direct action, bypassing legal avenues, and the accompanying transition to the less conscious and less organized strata of the population threaten to destroy the internal civil cohesion and discipline; they are paving the way [on the one hand] for violent acts, thus sowing bitterness and enmity among the victims toward the new order, and [on the other hand] for the development of private ambitions and interests at the expense of the common interest and for the evasion of civic duties.

The Provisional Government considers it its duty to make a forthright and definite declaration that such a state of affairs renders the governing of the state difficult and that a further continuation in the same direction threatens to bring the country to internal disintegration and to defeat at the front. Before Russia rises the terrible apparition of civil war and anarchy, carrying destruction to freedom. There is a somber and grievous course of peoples, a course well known in history, leading from freedom through civil war and anarchy to reaction and the return of despotism. This course must not be the course of the Russian people.

In the name of preserving and strengthening freedom, achieved with the blood and sacrifices of her best native sons, the Provisional Government is appealing to each and everyone for the consolidation of the power which is achieving and protecting freedom. Let everyone who values the freedom of Russia support the state power by obedience and cooperation, by setting an example and by conviction, by participating personally in the common work and the sacrifices, and by appealing to others for the same. The Government, on its part, will be particularly persistent in renewing its efforts directed at expanding its composition by drawing into responsible government work representatives of those active creative forces of the country who have not previously taken direct . . . part in the government of the state.

Citizens of Russia, the fate of our native land is in your hands. The Government is powerless without you. With you it can lead the country boldly and resolutely toward her great future. Remember that freedom cannot be preserved without power and that under the new order the power is created and preserved by you yourselves, your internal discipline and your free submission. By uniting around the power which you created and by assuring it the opportunity to achieve, in practice, its full realization, you will give it the strength to overcome all difficulties and dangers standing in the way of the country and carry the freedom of Russia, in its wholeness and inviolability, to that great day when the people themselves, embodied in the Constituent Assembly elected by them, will stand at the helm of the Government.

1076. LETTER OF KERENSKY ADVOCATING THE ADDITION OF OTHER DEMOCRATIC REPRESENTATIVES TO THE GOVERNMENT

[*Delo Naroda*, No. 33, April 26, 1917, p. 3. In his *The Great Russian Revolution*, p. 205, Victor Chernov asserted that he wrote this letter for Kerensky. Kerensky stated on August 30, 1960: "On his return from abroad Chernov came to me accompanied by

Zenzinov and Avksent'ev. That was our first meeting. It is possible that I did show him an unpublished copy of my letter on the formation of a coalition government. But certainly he did not *write* the letter *for me*, because nobody ever prepared letters for me."]

The Minister of Justice, A. F. Kerensky, sent the following declaration to the Central Committee of the Party of Socialist Revolutionaries, the Petrograd Soviet of Workers' and Soldiers' Deputies, and to the Trudovik faction, as well as to the Executive Committee of the State Duma.

Comrades! At the moment when decisive revolutionary events found the toiling democracy unorganized, bourgeois [*tsenzovaia*] Russia alone took upon itself the organization of power. At that time I had to accept, at my own risk and responsibility, the representation of the interests of this democracy in the Provisional Government and to fulfill the difficult and responsible role of a connecting link between these two basic forces which had gained victory over the old regime. In fulfilling this duty I drew my strength from the confidence shown me by the toiling democracy and the army, personified by the Soviet of Workers' and Soldiers' Deputies.

I carried on this work, perhaps too difficult and responsible for one person, to the best of my strength and ability, always heeding the voice of my socialist and revolutionary conscience.

At present I regard the situation as radically changed. On the one hand, the general state of affairs in the country is becoming increasingly more complicated. On the other hand, however, the strength of the organized toiling democracy has also increased. And perhaps it can no longer stand aside from responsible participation in ruling the state. This participation would add to the [new] order, born of revolution, new strength and the necessary authority to consolidate all the vital forces of the country in order to surmount all barriers that prevent Russia from entering upon the wide road of historic development.

Under these conditions I think that representatives of the toiling democracy have the right to assume the burden of power only through direct election and official authorization by the organizations to which they belong. For the time being, however, and awaiting your decision, I shall continue to bear to the end the brunt of those responsibilities with which I was entrusted.

1077. PRINCE L'VOV ASKS CHKHEIDZE TO BRING THE QUESTION OF
COALITION BEFORE THE SOVIET EXECUTIVE COMMITTEE

[*Izvestiia*, No. 52, April 28, 1917, p. 2.]

[April 27, 1917]

Dear Nikolai Semenovich:

In the statement published by the Provisional Government on April 26, it is pointed out, among other things, that the Government will renew its efforts to widen its circle by asking for the participation in the responsible work of government those actively creative elements of the country who have not until now had a direct part in the government of the state.

In view of this statement, I ask you, in the name of the Provisional Government, to be good enough to bring this matter to the attention of the Executive

Committee of the parties represented in the Soviet of Workers' and Soldiers' Deputies, of which you are President.

I beg you to accept assurances of my sincere respect and devotion.

PRINCE L'VOV
Minister-President

1078. *Novoe Vremia* ON THE GOVERNMENT DECLARATION

[No. 14761, April 26, 1917, p. 5.]

The salvation of Russia is at stake—the very life of the Russian people, the preservation or destruction of the newly won liberty.

The multiple power, created on the ruins of the autocratic regime, threatens us with immediate disintegration. A choice faces us: either, following the example of other revolutions, to come—via anarchy—to the restoration of the old despotism, or immediately to turn the events onto the road which reason, conscience, and duty demand.

The Provisional Government has been created by the people themselves. Its power is based not on compulson but on the conscious choice of the entire nation. It has proved worthy of the trust. Despite all the gravity of daily troubles, it has succeeded in realizing a considerable share of the demands of the revolution. It undertook without delay the preparation for the great Constituent Assembly. It put into practice at once the main principles of political and civic liberty. It extended the rights of man and the citizen to the whole army, from highest ranks to the lowest. It is continuing the struggle for the motherland's independence in close unity with the Allied democracies.

Such a government deserves confidence. It deserves something more. The Government has assumed the burden of power not because of ambition, nor for the sake of selfish aims, but solely in the name of the sacred duty to the most sacred interests of the motherland. It did not capture the power but assumed it by the will of the revolutionary people. It does not do its own will, but the will of the nation. If the instinct of self-preservation has not died in the people, the latter must give to the government chosen by them the full extent of help of which they are capable. . . .

Everyone's effort is indispensable for the salvation of the motherland. The foremost obligation falls, in this infinitely important moment, upon the organized sections of the people; and first of all upon the Soviet of Workers' and Soldiers' Deputies.

If it has not become a plaything in the hands of anarchical impulses, it has an obligation to use all its influence upon the organized workers and soldiers, and to furnish the first example of conscientious obedience to the all-national government.

If worse comes to worst, let it take upon itself the full glory of power but also the full responsibility for the salvation of the motherland and freedom. This power will be handed to it if there is no other way out. But preservation of the present situation is no longer tolerable. Multiple power means the ruin of everything; it means anarchy, the savage riot of dark forces, the falling apart of any sort of order, the disintegration of the army, hunger, the invasion of the enemy into the very heart of the country, the tearing away of the borderlands of the country, the burdening of the Russian people with the total expenditures of the World War, the restoration of the old regime in its most terrifying forms.

The newly won liberty would dissipate like smoke. Land and freedom would prove to be a fleeting mirage. We await, today, a reasonable, firm, and honest answer of the people to the appeal of the Government which they themselves have created.

1079. *Russkiia Vedomosti* ON THE SOVIET ATTITUDE TOWARD COALITION
[No. 94, April 28, 1917, p. 3.]

The question concerning the formation of a coalition government is beginning to assume a practical aspect, and the Provisional Government has already undertaken some steps toward the solution of this problem. The Minister-President, Prince G. E. L'vov, sent letters to the President of the State Duma, M. V. Rodzianko, and the Chairman of the Petrograd Soviet of Workers' and Soldiers' Deputies, N. S. Chkheidze, and in these letters he spoke of the desire of the Provisional Government to broaden its structure . . .

It is usually said that in every undertaking the first step is the most difficult. But in this case this saying does not apply. There has never been any doubt of the readiness of the Provisional Government to broaden its structure by including socialist elements in it, or, if need be, to give up its office altogether to other men. But the plan of a coalition government has met in the past, and is meeting now, great objections precisely in those circles to which the practical suggestion concerning the enlargement of the government is directed. Those circles are the socialist parties and the Soviets of Workers' and Soldiers' Deputies. And such an attitude of those circles to the idea of a coalition government is undoubtedly characteristic of their political psychology. . . .

Rabochaia Gazeta, the organ of the Petrograd Mensheviks, in an article by B. I. Gorev, has expressed itself with rare candor on this question. "The logic of the situation places an obligation," says the article. "Entering the government, socialists would on more than one occasion support certain of its acts that in other cases they would resolutely attack." This would happen, evidently, not always because of the fault of the bourgeoisie, since the author of the article foresees the possibility of the proletariat's presenting claims which "go even beyond the limits of what is generally realizable within a capitalist society." As a result, the socialists would only "compromise themselves in the eyes of the broad masses," and, "despite the best of intentions, they would soon become an object of the most infuriated attacks on the part of anarchy-minded demagogues, and they would lose the influence, the moral authority which they have among the masses. Thus, they would cease to play the leading role in the fortunes of our revolution which has fallen to their lot."

Thus, the decisive role here is played by the fear of compromising themselves, the fear of losing their authority, and, moreover, the fear of compromising themselves by the struggle against *unrealizable* demands of the proletariat, or, at least, by the passive resistance to them. We especially emphasize the word "unrealizable" because the article in *Rabochaia Gazeta* does not speak at all about the difficulty of working out a program on which the bourgeois and the socialist sections of the government would agree; it does not at all foresee cases of disagreement between them on concrete issues, but renders its decision in a general form of principle.

The masses make exaggerated demands on the government. *Rabochaia Gazeta* knows that, and, in order not to compromise themselves by opposing these demands, it recommends that its comrades keep aloof from power, retaining for themselves the less troublesome role of critics. This political psychology is in certain respects even more harmful than the psychology of bolshevism. The latter, at least, is not afraid of responsibility and therefore is definitely striving for power. But the psychology of *Rabochaia Gazeta* rests on fear of responsibility, which no public man and no political group has the right to shun. . . . The question per se of reorganization of the Provisional Government perhaps would have no significance, but if the offer to the socialists to enter it is rejected for approximately the motives that were elaborated in *Rabochaia Gazeta* and uttered in the Moscow organizations of the workers' and soldiers' deputies, our situation will be almost hopeless, because then there will be no way out of the blind alley which will be created. Without the realization of one's own responsibility, there can be no genuine political work. . . .

1080. *Rech'* ON COALITION
[No. 99, April 29, 1917, p. 2.]

. . .

The Provisional Government arose with the event of the revolution. It is a revolutionary government invested with the plenitude of power. It was never conceived as a party government, and only owing to a misunderstanding or to irresistible attachment to a well-known doctrinal terminology may it be called a bourgeois government. It was not created by parties, but by the revolution and by the entire situation of the moment, bringing forward definite individuals, who in part do not even belong to any political party, [but] who are united by a very precisely and very concisely formulated program. This program has been dictated to them by the revolution. All of them together and each of them individually have accepted it and have sworn allegiance to it. This is the foundation of their authority, which is recognized by the revolution and by the whole country. And recognition by the country determined the recognition by foreign states. . . . It is not superfluous to recall that when the revolutionary government originated, the extreme left refused to participate in the government and took the position from which arose the ideas of controlling, observing, and influencing the government in order to induce it to steadfastly fulfill its engagements.

. . . Hence the logical conclusion, that "we enter into a new era of revolutionary Russia's existence," and that "all the *i*'s should be dotted, and all the issues should be put point-blank."

. . .

The Provisional Government has stated [in the declaration of April 26] that it will "renew its efforts directed at expanding its composition by drawing into responsible government work representatives of those active creative forces of the country, who have not previously taken direct . . . part in the government of the State." It has already taken the first steps in this direction, as attested by Prince L'vov's letter to N. S. Chkheidze. But, of course, neither in the declaration of April 26, nor in any other acts, did it imply that the question was to rearrange a government whose composition has proved to be an "outmoded combination."

For, while a period of two months could change the conviction of "the workers' democracy" as to its unpreparedness to assume power, it did not modify the obligation which was taken before the country by the present membership of the Government. Undoubtedly, the Government conceives of any reinforcement only in terms of unity between those reinforcing and those reinforced on the bases established in the first declaration of the Government, because precisely these bases [represent] the obligation which the Government bears.

Thus a far deeper crisis looms ahead of us. The issue is not one of a "coalition cabinet" but one of the "reconstruction of the Provisional Government." This [particular] *i* should be dotted before proceeding any further.

1081. *Volia Naroda* ON COALITION
[No. 1, April 29, 1917, p. 1.]

"Before Russia," says the Provisional Government, "rises the terrible apparition of civil war and anarchy carrying destruction to freedom." In the opinion of the Government the present state of affairs makes the administration of the state extremely difficult and in its progressive development threatens to bring the country to internal collapse and to defeat at the front.

Unfortunately we are forced to admit that the pessimistic conclusions arrived at by the Provisional Government do not represent a deliberate deepening of the dark colors. On the contrary, it is the bitter and stern truth.

During the April Days the people who demonstrated on the streets of Petrograd were sharply divided into two camps. In one camp were those whom the hundred-mouthed goddess simply christened as "Leninists" and whom unfortunately one can find not only in the one party of Leninist communists. These "extremists" vulgarize and simplify even the slogans of *Pravda*. They demand an immediate overthrow of the bourgeois Provisional Government, an immediate cessation of war, an immediate confiscation of lands and expropriation of factories and mills. In other words, they want a communist revolution . . .

The majority of their antagonists were self-determined by the repudiation of "Leninism." The revolutionary-democratic elements could not but protest against the anarchic slogan of immediate overthrow of the Government or against the absurd formula "Down with the war." Sound instinct prompted them to resist the sowers of civil war and defeat at the front. In the overwhelming majority of organs of the socialist press—to be more exact, in all socialist organs, except only *Edinstvo*—they failed to find any foundation for revolutionary defense; they saw no direct and unrelenting desire to protect the country from internal anarchy; they saw no firm will to direct the further development of the Russian revolution into a politically organized course. Instead they read evasive, vague statements about the Liberty Loan; they felt behind each line a badly concealed fear before the demagogy of the anarchy-bound elements.

. . .

The Executive Committee of the Soviet of Workers' and Soldiers' Deputies and, to yet a greater degree, the All-Russian Conference of the Soviets of Workers' and Soldiers' Deputies in their decisions and official speeches took the position of revolutionary defense and the position of immediate support of the Provisional Government.

Following the April events, however, the determined position of the Executive Committee became even more defined, and that was reflected in its decision with regard to the loan.

Now it should take a still more vigorous step. It must face the call of the Provisional Government to "support the state authority."

The Provisional Government points out that on its own side it will renew with particular insistence efforts directed toward expanding its membership by means of attracting representatives of the working democracy. Thus the Government strives to create what is called, now not too correctly, a coalition ministry. A coalition ministry, of course, is possible only under a properly functioning parliamentary order. And in our country the question refers only to the admission of socialists to the membership in the Provisional Government created by the revolution.

. . .

One cannot, in the same breath, greet Comrade Kerensky and declare that socialists cannot be admitted to the coalition ministry. One cannot now support indirectly the anarchy-bound Leninists, who actually remove the ground from under the Provisional Government, from under the organ of authority, born in the fire of the revolution, which must bring the country to the Constituent Assembly.

The socialist parties are forced now to choose openly and definitely between joining the Provisional Government—that is, [rendering] energetic support to the state revolutionary government—and frankly declining—that is, rendering indirect support to Leninism, which distintegrates the country by preparations for civil war and defeat at the front.

There is no doubt that the overwhelming majority of Russian socialists will be able to undertake the responsibility for the future of Russia, will save the country from internal breakdown and from a disgraceful defeat.

1082. *Delo Naroda* on "The Crisis of Power"
[No. 33, April 26, 1917, p. 1.]

We have just been informed about two documents of extreme importance.[6] These documents are signs of the times.

The moment of the crisis of power has arrived—a moment not entirely unexpected and in the progressive course of events hardly avoidable. It has come, at any rate, sooner than the democracy wanted it. Had it depended upon the latter, it would have attempted to postpone it.

What precipitated it was the note of Miliukov. This forced its arrival.

This forced it, but did not create it, because events have their logic.

By whom has this power been created? By bourgeois [*tsensovaia*] Russia of the Duma, that *pays legale* of the old regime. It played an active role in the formation of the new organ of power. The Soviet of Workers' and Soldiers' Deputies, on the contrary, played a passive role. It *recognized* the new power, to be sure, on condition that the new power be guided in its activity by a definite public program. . . .

This distribution of the active and the passive role was understandable. Russia possessed privileges of organization even under the old regime. . . .

[6] The Government's Declaration and Kerensky's letter.

In the case of the toiling democracy it is quite another matter. Deprived under the old regime of an opportunity of genuine party organization, driven into the underground, concentrating on the struggle and not on participation in the government, it was caught unprepared by events. . . .

Under such circumstances the toiling democracy preferred to *withdraw deliberately* from direct participation in the government. It yielded the way to bourgeois Russia after securing a number of general guarantees toward the political program of the government. It concentrated on matters of self-organization. . . .

This process moved forward, of course, quite far. If at the present moment the working democracy is not completely ready to face the problem of implementing a new revolutionary power—for this is a tremendous task, and it is difficult to be *"fully prepared"* for it—it is nevertheless infinitely more prepared now to participate in the solution of this problem than at the time the new power was conceived.

If the old combination—the present composition of the Provisional Government—must be acknowledged as obsolete, if the problem of placing the Provisional Government on a broader basis is urgent, if it is no longer possible to postpone the organization in its name of a fuller and all-round representation of collective forces of the land fit for social and political creative work, this means that we are entering a new era in the life of revolutionary Russia.

Instead of a conditional support based on an agreement of toiling Russia with bourgeois Russia, an infinitely more difficult problem arises—the replacement of the organizational *dualism* with an organizational *monism*. . . .

The question has been raised. It must be answered. The toiling democracy will not, it cannot, decline to solve it. Russia's situation is truly too serious for this. Toiling Russia is not running away from responsibility, no matter how clearly it realizes all the negative sides of replacing the position it has occupied up to this time with a new one. But such a change is possible for her only with definite conditions. And the question of the acceptability of these conditions for the other side is perhaps more complicated than would appear at first sight.

The statements that are being published are the signs of the times. They testify to the new and great shift in Russian life. The revolution continues, and not in its narrow outward and crude sense of the word but in its profound meaning.

1083. THE MEETING OF THE MEMBERS OF THE FOUR STATE DUMAS: THE SPEECH OF PRINCE L'VOV

[*VVP*, No. 42, April 28, 1917, p. 2. On April 27, the eleventh anniversary of the convocation of the First Duma, members of all four Dumas met in the Tauride Palace to commemorate the occasion and the work of the Dumas, and to discuss national issues.]

The great Russian revolution is truly miraculous in its majestic, quiet progress under the red glow of the World War which has been raging now for almost three years. The miraculous thing about it is not the fairylike unbelievableness of the change itself, not the colossal alterations that have taken place, not the force and dash with which the new positions were attained, but the very essence of the guiding spirit of the revolution. The freedom won by the Russian revolution is permeated by elements of a world-wide, universal nature. These ideas, which were sown on the soil of Russia half a century ago in the small seeds of liberty and equality, have grown until they embrace not only the interests of the Russian people but also the interests of all the peoples of the earth. The soul of the Russian democracy has turned out to be, in its very nature, the soul of the world democracy. It is ready not only to merge with the world democracy but also to take a position of leadership and guide the world democracy on the road of human development laid out by the principles of liberty, equality, and fraternity.

A happy lot, gentlemen, has befallen us. It is our lot to live under the influence of great ideas, to participate in the creative labor of popular forces and to cherish and guard the great spiritual blessings attained by that labor.

Gentlemen, we are living through great convulsions. It may be that great trials and dangers await us, but no matter what specters of anarchy and despotism confront us, the task that you, the people's representatives, have begun will be carried through in spite of every hindrance, disillusion, and inimical force. The course of the great revolution is not yet run, and every day that passes renews the belief in the inexhaustible creative power of the Russian people, in its instinct for governing, its greatness of soul, and its tremendous future. We have a right to feel proud of ourselves before the nations of the world that the Russian soul is filled with love and not with pride. Let no one have any fear of Russian freedom.

Let me end my speech of greeting with the words of the bard of liberty—the bard of the great democratic ally who has just joined us in the fight: "Liberty, let others despair of you—I never will despair of you."[7] (*Prolonged applause.*)

1084. THE MEETING OF THE MEMBERS OF THE FOUR STATE DUMAS:
THE SPEECH OF GUCHKOV
[*VVP*, No. 43, April 29, 1917, pp. 1–2.]

· · ·

. . . We are deprived of the right of lawmaking, but we are not deprived of the right—nay, we have the obligation—to take the floor and to give voice to public opinion, and the national conscience, and first of all to that alarming and fright-inspiring feeling which has seized the whole country.

Have a look around, look into your own conscience, and tell me: are we not all of us in the grip of painful anguish, of a dreadful anxiety, bordering upon desperation? Why did the first feeling of bright joy give way to such feelings of anguish and of alarm? The answer to this question will be found in the declaration which the Provisional Government has addressed to the country. The growth of the new social bonds, which are consolidating the country, lags, with great danger to freedom, behind the process of distintegration, resulting from the downfall of the old regime. Thus does the Provisional Government cautiously diagnose the mortal ailment which undermines the very life of the country.

For myself, I would add, destruction precedes construction. Destruction has already touched the foundations of human coexistence and human culture, and also the very notion of the State, without which humanity loses the features of a well-organized cultured society and of an established political organism, and becomes a scattered, formless human mass. Under the conditions of our new life, the vital center which, with the aid of the organized forces of the country, could undertake this great creative task has not yet been formed. Moreover, not only is such a vital center nonexistent; but also nonexistent are the organized

---

[7] From Walt Whitman's "Europe," in *Leaves of Grass*. The poem, which originally appeared in 1850, was inspired by the failure of the 1848 revolution in France.

forces of the country. Will the country pull itself out of this sickly state of fermentation, and when it pulls itself out, will there then emerge those points of stability
around which the new forms of the new life can crystallize? Will these new forms
serve as points of support for erecting the new Government?

On all these questions depends not only the immediate trend of events, not only
the consolidation of the public good achieved at the price of the revolution, but also
the outcome of the war and the fate of the country. The country cannot exist
under conditions of dual power, or even of multiple rule, and, therefore, of
[actual] absence of government, under which it has now been placed. Our ill-
fated country is under torment in the unbelievably hard conditions of an unprecedented war, and an unprecedented internal confusion. Only a strong government,
homogeneous within itself and in union with the nation, which is based upon its
high moral authority and upon the confidence of the nation, and which, therefore,
can freely and boldly avail itself of all the sanctions and all the attributes inherent
in the very nature of government, only such a government can create the mighty
and the vital creative center, in which lies the salvation of the country. (*Shouts*:
"True!" "Right!")

Gentlemen, from the old regime we have received a burdensome heritage.
Lacking ability in matters of peace, it proved even more incapable in matters of
war. The Russian State and the Russian people had to pay a heavy price of innumerable victims for the sins and crimes of the regime. Our incomparable army
carried on the fighting under incredibly hard conditions, standing up for every
inch of Russian soil. Eternal glory to the victims of duty, eternal gratitude of
the fatherland to all those who staunchly and courageously continue this heroic
struggle. And this struggle is far from being hopeless. One more heroic effort,
an effort of the whole country, of both the front and the rear—and the enemy
shall be crushed. (*Shouts*: "Right!") But will we be capable of this effort (*A cry
from the floor*: "We must be capable!"), which might be the last one? One would
like to believe it. For it is bound up with everything that is dear to us, everything for which we live, everything that makes life worth living. (*Cries*: "Right!")
It is bound up not only with the existence of Russia, as a State, not only with the
rights and freedoms, conquered after hard struggle, not only with material wealth
accumulated by the tenacious toil of a number of generations—it is bound up
also with the dignity and honor of Russia (*Cries*: "Right!" *Cheers*), with her good
name among the nations of the world, and with our right to be proud of being
Russian. (*Cries*: "True, bravo!" *Cheers*.)

Both the Army and the Navy have responded with joy to the revolutionary
events, as to an act of salvation for their country. All, as one man, from top to
bottom, joined the new regime, showing a deep and touching faith in its creative
power. Both in the center and locally, work started full swing, aiming at the reconstruction of the whole organization of the Army and of the Navy, and its
adjustment, especially with regard to living conditions, to those new principles
of the concept of the State and of the civic responsibility and obligations of the
citizens which have been laid down by the late events as the foundations of
Russian life.

At one time it seemed that our military might would regenerate with new,
multiplied strength, owing to this unavoidable and salutary process of reconstruction; it seemed that a new sacred enthusiasm would flare up, and that the
will for victory would become as hard as tempered steel; it seemed that under
a new reasonable and conscious discipline the Army would become more united

than it could ever have been under the old, obsolete drill. It seemed that the new, free Army, born of the revolution, would eclipse in its feats the old, freedomless, but nonetheless infinitely cherished and glorious Army of old Russia.

Gentlemen, this has not happened. We must honestly recognize that this has not happened. Our military might is weakening and disintegrating . . . (*A voice from the floor*: "Right!"). The Army is suffering the same ailment as the country: dual power, multiple rule, absence of rule—an identical diagnosis, and identical remedies. Only, for natural reasons, the signs of the disease have appeared in the Army with particular acuteness, and their treatment is required in an especially pressing manner. For the disease carries with it a special danger, a vital danger to the organisms of both State and Nation. Are we now too late with our medical advices and remedies? I do not think so. But would we not be too late if we were to delay even for a short time? I believe that we would be too late.

The pernicious slogan introduced by some people who may or may not realize what they are doing, the pernicious slogan "Peace on the front, and war at home" —this preaching of international peace at any price, and of civil war at any cost—this slogan must be drowned by the imperative call of the great Russian Nation, "War on the front, peace at home." (*Applause*.) Gentlemen, there was a time when the whole country recognized that the fatherland is in danger. Gentlemen, we have advanced one step further, and time does not wait—our fatherland is on the verge of ruin. (*Cries*: "Right!" *General applause*.)

1085. THE MEETING OF THE MEMBERS OF THE FOUR STATE DUMAS: THE SPEECH OF SHUL'GIN

[*Rech'*, No. 98, April 28, 1917, p. 4.]

. . . Two months have passed. It is two months today since the revolution occurred and I cannot hide the fact that many of us have fallen a prey to doubt. It is a question whether these two months which have brought such great conquests to Russia and the various nationalities that live in Russia have not also brought profit to Germany. (*Voices*: "Very much.") It seem to us, at times, that our military situation has greatly deteriorated. In the attempt to get at the causes for this, it seems to me the first thing that strikes the eye is that the Government, now sitting on the benches before you, the Government which we consider honorable and talented and would like to see clothed in the full attributes of power, is under suspicion. Of course it is not in the same position as the government of the old regime, which is imprisoned in the Peter and Paul Fortress, but I would say that it is, so to speak, under "house arrest." (*Voices*: "Right!") It is as if a sentinel had been posted over it and as if the sentinel had been instructed: "Watch them, they are bourgeoisie; keep a close watch on them, and if any thing turns up, you know your duty." Gentlemen, it was plain to all on April 20 that the sentinel performs his duties well, but it is a great question whether those who are responsible for placing the sentry on guard have done well. This question refers to all socialist parties. And I ask them openly: "Are you doing right, gentlemen, when you place a sentry over this government?" Would it not be better to seek other methods of control?

But this is not our only grave fear. Among the socialist parties—fortunately not among all but among several—there are habits and manners that remind one of the historic words that were spoken in this hall on November 1, 1916, when it was asked: "Is this stupidity or is it treason?"[8] When these questions were put to Stürmer, the main accusation against him was that he was seeking to bring about a quarrel between Russia and her allies, especially England. And what is going on now? A few days ago an open and very bitter propaganda battle was being waged in the streets against England. It was pointed out that that country is a nest of all sorts of imperialistic and capitalistic tendencies, and that it is Russia's mission to free the world of this monster. I ask you: "Is this stupidity or is it treason?" (*Voices*: "Treachery!") No, I think it is stupidity. When agitators are sent to the villages and carry anarchy and confusion to the villages—anarchy and confusion, whose only results will be that Petrograd, Moscow, the army, and the northern provinces will be left without bread—I ask you: "What is this?" And I think that after all it is only stupidity. Or when our glorious soldiers are stirred up against their officers—I understand that there are all sorts of misunderstandings and difficulties and that there are officers who are not worthy—when the soldiers are stirred up against all officers as a whole, in the same way that people are being stirred up against the intellectual classes, I ask you: "What is this campaign which may turn our army into a porridge-like mess; what is it, stupidity or treason?" Gentlemen, that, too, is stupidity. But when all three of these things are gathered together and it is said: "You are on the verge of a quarrel with the Allies; you have no army, you have no food; therefore, conclude peace at any price," that is treachery. (*Applause and cries of* "Bravo!" *Mr. Tseretelli, from his seat*: "Who says that?" *A voice from the left*: "Shul'gin says that!")

Gentlemen, let me tell you, go over onto the Petrograd Side[9] and listen to what is being said there. I live on that side and how many times have I heard it with my own ears. Lenin is a trademark, and there is a whole band of people around him who preach anything that comes into their heads. Do not forget that our people are not yet fully ripe for politics and can only pick their way with difficulty in such questions, and that, unfortunately, these doctrines have their effect.

Gentlemen, I am happy that you have allowed me to say these things. I see that this tribune is now as it was before, free and incorruptible.

(*Stormy applause on all benches except those of the Social Democrats and the Trudoviks.*)

1086. The Meeting of the Members of the Four State Dumas: The Speech of Tseretelli

[*Rech'*, No. 98, April 28, 1917, p. 4. See also Volume II, Doc. 801.]

Citizens, members of the four Dumas, I am going to begin by answering all the questions that Deputy Shul'gin asked here. His first question was: "Has the Provisional Government, whose honesty no one questions, complete power or hasn't it?" Are we facing a situation in which this power is being undermined by a sentry placed over the Provisional Government with instructions: "They are bourgeois, watch them." Gentlemen, in answer to this question I can quote the words of a member of the Provisional Government, Mr. N. V. Nekrasov, who said: "The Russian people did not overthrow one autocrat in order to put 12 autocrats in his place." Before bringing his accusation against all those who don't look at the Provisional Government in the light of their being 12 new autocrats, Deputy

---

8 See p. 16.

9 A principal section of the city, where the Bolshevik headquarters were located.

Shul'gin should have asked the Provisional Government what it thinks about its own position. I know, gentlemen, that those circles to which Deputy Shul'gin belongs are bringing forward accusations not only against the Petrograd Side, but also against that body which represents the revolutionary democracy, against the Soviet of Workers' and Soldiers' Deputies. This Soviet demands that the Provisional Government be under control because this Soviet is a powerful democratic organization and expresses the desires of broad classes of the population, of the proletariat, of the revolutionary army and peasants. The position of the Provisional Government would be extremely difficult, and in the moment of the revolution it would not have been equal to the situation, if there had not been that control, if there had not been that contact with the democratic elements. (*Loud applause.*) Deputy Shul'gin said: "You say to the people: 'They are bourgeois, be suspicious of them.'" There is an element of truth in that statement. We do say to the people: "They are bourgeois—the Provisional Government is the responsible organ of the bourgeoisie." But we add: "The Provisional Government represents that part of the bourgeoisie which has agreed upon a general democratic platform and has agreed to defend Russian freedom together with the entire democracy and has decided to go hand in hand with the democracy in that struggle." (*Loud applause.*)

. . .

Deputy Shul'gin recalled the questions that were asked of Stürmer under the old regime, and himself put a number of questions. Deputy Shul'gin asked: "Is it stupidity or is it treason when it is said that England is our enemy, that England is the country that is holding back the development of the Russian revolution?" I have not heard any such propaganda. I have heard the propaganda being waged by the Soviet of Workers' and Soldiers' Deputies. . . . I ask Mr. Shul'gin another question: "When you attempt to identify the whole English people with the [English] imperialistic circles, when you identify the propaganda against the English imperialistic circles with propaganda against the whole English people, what are you committing—a piece of stupidity or treason?" (*Loud applause from the public.*) . . .

Further Deputy Shul'gin said: "Is it stupidity or treason when you send agitators into the villages urging disorderly acts, the confiscation of the land of the estate owners?" I don't know what other horrors are preying on Mr. Shul'gin. But do you know, Mr. Shul'gin, that all your attacks—everything that you say and that your fellow thinkers say—has reference to that solely authoritative democratic organization [The Soviet of Workers' and Soldiers' Deputies] that recently adopted an attitude toward the land question that agrees with the attitude of the entire democracy and especially with the attitude of the entire peasantry? And do you know what kind of agitators are being sent? The agitators that are being sent say: "If the landowners, in this time of terrible trials, have refused to sow and work their land in the fear that it may be taken away from them in the future, you should yourselves create an organization to immediately make use of that land for the good of the whole people, for the army. You should create that organization in accord with the Provisional Government and the organs of the entire democracy and not in opposition to the Provisional Government." That is the kind of agitation that is going on. The question of the liquidation of the great landed estates is a fundamental question which has long kept Russia in uneasiness. It is a question about which Russia has expressed herself, when she could, in free institutions, in the same sense as the working-class deputies in all four Dumas, in the same sense as the Socialist Revolutionaries and the Social Democrats and many other democratic organizations. This system of landholding should be ended in the interests of all Russia, not alone in the interests of the peasantry. This system is leaving Russia a prey to the specter of hunger at a time when Russia is living through a crisis. But the system should be ended in an orderly way, by the Constitutional Assembly, since at the present moment the whole people holds the reins of power and should carry that power into effect. (*Loud applause.*)

You say that unrest is being sown in the army. (*Voice from the gallery*: "Right!") The President of the Duma also spoke of rumors coming from the army to the effect that disintegration is beginning there. What the President of the Duma said is true, but what he added is also true, namely, that he does not believe these rumors. And we do not believe these rumors. (*Loud applause.*)

The question of Russia's relation to the war has now taken such forms that if it were actually true that, with democratic principles having conquered, the army is less able to wage war than when tsarism determined foreign policies imperialistically and in opposition to the interests of the people, then we must count Russia as finished once and for all. But, fortunately, that is not true. (*Stormy applause.*) The Russian democracy, together with the entire revolutionary army, has come to the conclusion that the Provisional Government must announce a break with the imperialistic aims of the Tsar's government. The Provisional Government has openly taken steps in that direction. But the Russian democracy will defend its freedom bravely as long as the imperialistic troops of the invader threaten our country, at the same time making all efforts to reinforce the new democratic policy within the country and also making every effort to arouse a similar movement in other countries. The army cannot hesitate when it has once understood that it is only called upon to remain under arms in the name of the vital interests of the whole people. (*Stormy applause.*) Unfortunately, the words of the President of the Duma aroused the same anxiety in my breast that was aroused by Mr. Shul'gin's. There is one way to sow unrest in the army—that is to tell the army: "Yes, the people have conquered; the people want to defend that liberty, they want to arouse a similar movement in other countries in order to realize their final aims, but we, the Russian bourgeois class, intend to demand that the Provisional Government re-establish the old aims of the war in the same formulas in which the Tsar's government stated its aims, re-establish the old formula that German militarism must be crushed, re-establish the old formula 'everything for the war.' "

Gentlemen of the Duma, the best way to sow imperialism and barbarity in your own country is to crush the militarism of a foreign country by force of arms. The Russian people and the Russian army have had enough experience in that line during the three years of the war. The formula "everything for the war" was the formula of the old regime, to which the war was a means to an end. (*Voice from the hall*: "What about England and France?") In France and England the people are one thing, and the imperialistic circles are another, and very soon you will see the same brilliant proof of that that you have seen in Russia. Wasn't it said abroad at the beginning of the war—and unfortunately the delegates from the Duma sent abroad repeated it—that the [Russian] people and the Tsar are one and the same? What do we see now? Are the Tsar and the people one and the same?

I listened to the speech of Minister-President L'vov with great pleasure. He formulated the problems of the revolution and our foreign policy quite differently.

Prince L'vov said that he does not regard the Russian revolution simply as a national revolution, but that a similar revolutionary movement may be expected in the entire world as a result of the Russian revolution. (*Loud applause.*) I greet these words of the Minister-President, and through them I see the mood of that part of the bourgeoisie which has taken its position on the general democratic platform and on the agreement with the democracy, and I am profoundly convinced that as long as the Provisional Government continues on that road and that as long as it shapes the objects of the war in conformity with the desires of the entire Russian people its position is secure—neither the men from the Petrograd Side that Shul'gin spoke about nor the irresponsible classes of the bourgeoisie who are provoking civil war will be able to shake it. (*Loud applause.*) Deputy Shul'gin mentioned the anxious days we have just passed through. But it was his intention to throw the responsibility for those days onto the men from the Petrograd Side. I shall mention these men separately [later], but I want to say now that the very formulas which Shul'gin proposed here and which, unfortunately, also found expression in the words of the President of the Fourth Duma would act as a signal for civil war. The Provisional Government showed great wisdom and great understanding of the situation when it made its explanation of its note, which removed the possibility of such an interpretation.

Deputy Shul'gin stated that there is a minority in the democracy and he even mentioned Lenin. . . . I must say that I do not agree with Lenin or with his doctrines, but what Shul'gin says is a slander against Lenin. Lenin has never advised action that would infringe on the progress of the revolution. Lenin is carrying on a theoretic and intellectual propaganda and is fed by the irresponsible statements made by Shul'gin and by many of the so-called moderate middle class. This, of course, breeds despair in some parts of the democracy, despair of the possibility of reaching an agreement with the bourgeoisie. Lenin's platform is that, if there are such tendencies in the bourgeoisie, if the bourgeoisie is unable to rise to the national importance of the moment, it must be overthrown and the Soviet of Workers' and Soldiers' Deputies must take the supreme power. It is possible to disagree with Lenin—I myself do disagree with him because I am deeply convinced that the ideas of Shul'gin are not the ideas of the Russian bourgeoisie. But if I believed for one moment that these are your ideas, the ideas of the entire property-owning bourgeoisie, I would say: "There is no salvation for Russia except in the desperate attempt to at once proclaim the dictatorship of the proletariat and the peasantry." These ideas [of Shul'gin's] are the only real menace of civil war, and if they were to gain the upper hand in the ranks of the Provisional Government it would be the signal for civil war.

I do not think the upshot of this meeting should be an impression that there is confusion in the ranks of the bourgeoisie or that there is hesitation in their ranks or a conspiracy to force the Provisional Government to irresponsible steps, since I repeat that that would be the beginning of the end of the Russian revolution, the beginning of the end of the whole country. The Provisional Government should continue on the road it has started, the road of agreement, and it should even more firmly carry out democratic ideals in internal and foreign politics, and if it does so with all the strength of its authority, the democracy will support this revolutionary Provisional Government with all its weight. In this way, with the united strength of all the vital forces of the country, we will carry our revolution to its conclusion and perhaps spread it to the whole world. (*Prolonged applause.*)

1087. *Izvestiia*'s Comment on the Duma Meeting
[No. 53, April 29, 1917, p. 2.]

On April 27, members of the four convoked State Dumas gathered in a solemn meeting held in the Tauride Palace. In the White Hall where, during the course of the past two months, representatives of the revolutionary democracy, soldiers and workers, have been assembling day in and day out, corpses appeared, buried by the revolution. Once again Purishkevich appeared, and Shul'gin, and Rodzianko, and Duma priests, and Duma landowners.

Why did they come to the Tauride Palace? What made them remind the people —who would be glad to forget—about themselves, about the heroes of the June 3 revolution?[10]

The foreign press has recently been conducting a continual campaign against the Soviet of Workers' and Soldiers' Deputies. Bourgeois newspapers declared that the Soviet had willfully seized the power which belonged to the State Duma. They gave kind advice to the Provisional Government: to resume the Duma session. Then, they say, the activities of the Soviet would automatically cease.

On April 27 an attempt was made to bring the Fourth State Duma back to life. In order that this Duma's isolation from the people should not be too conspicuous, the adherents of the idea of resuming the Duma sessions tried to cover up the Fourth Duma by bathing it in the glory of the First and Second Dumas.

The eleventh anniversary of the convocation of the First Duma was used by them to serve this purpose.

But the very first attempt at reviving the corpses buried by the revolution demonstrated that the resumption of a Duma session at the present time is as impossible as the reinstatement of old tsarist ministers to positions of power.

Only those who are strong through commanding the confidence of the people can speak in the name of the people.

. . .

The Fourth State Duma, of course, cannot drown the voice of the Soviet. It cannot even express the views of those classes which stood behind it before the revolution. Under the changed, revolutionary conditions, the Fourth Duma turns out to be too right even for the bourgeoisie.

At the solemn meeting of April 27, not only Shul'gin, but Rodzianko as well, spoke as though they were people who had just waked up from sleep, or who had just risen from their graves. The cautious speech of Prince L'vov, the head of the bourgeois Provisional Government, which has the support of the democratic forces, was an exact antithesis to their speeches.

After the meeting of April 27, the bourgeoisie must have felt that there can be no return to the old, that only in the Constituent Assembly will it have an opportunity to advance its aspirations in opposition to the aspirations of the broad national masses.

The Duma has died forever. This is the lesson to be derived from the meeting of April 27.

And this result of the attempt at resurrecting the State Duma is a new victory for democracy because henceforth it is clear to everybody that, pending the convocation of the Constituent Assembly, the right to speak on behalf of democracy,

---

[10] Date of the dissolution of the Second Duma.

on behalf of the people, belongs solely to the Soviet of Workers' and Soldiers' Deputies.

1088. The First Meeting of the Soviet Executive Committee Concerning the Question of Coalition

[*Russkiia Vedomosti*, No. 96, April 30, 1917, p. 5. The minutes of this meeting, which took place during the night of April 28–29, were so carelessly taken that it was impossible to reproduce them. *Protokoly*, p. 6.]

The question of expanding the membership of the Provisional Government by bringing into it representatives of socialist parties continues to agitate in the most lively fashion the leading circles of democracy. Yesterday, late into the night, the question was discussed in the Executive Committee of the Workers' and Soldiers' Deputies. The debates were heated, and the debaters divided on this issue into two almost equal sides. Advocates of the participation in the Provisional Government of representatives from the socialist parties argued for the necessity of rendering the needed support to the Provisional Government in its present difficult situation, to assure it of the confidence of the wide democratic circles without which it cannot have the necessary power, and they argued for the Soviet to assume openly its share of responsibility for present events. The opponents, however, were motivated chiefly by fear that the presence of representatives from the socialist groups in the Provisional Government would hardly strengthen the position of the latter, but rather, the pulling out of the most authoritative and influential leaders, such as I. G. Tseretelli and V. M. Chernov, from the Soviet of Workers' and Soldiers' Deputies might possibly weaken the Soviet's influence. [It would thus] only strengthen the position of the extreme elements who try in every way to undermine the position of the Provisional Government, to remove it from power, and to transfer power into the hands of the Soviet of Workers' and Soldiers' Deputies.

Those most insistent on the entrance were the Trudoviks, Popular Socialists, and many members of the Socialist Revolutionary and Social Democratic parties. Those who argued against it were principally Bolsheviks, also such prominent leaders of the executive committees as I. G. Tseretelli and M. I. Skobelev.

In its concluding debates yesterday the Executive Committee, by a majority of 23 to 22 votes, with 8 abstaining, expressed itself against sending representatives of the Executive Committee into the Provisional Government. It is possible that, in view of the extremely insignificant majority, the Committee will review, and possibly even reconsider, this question. At any rate, its final decision will depend upon the Soviet of Workers' and Soldiers' Deputies itself.

1089. Guchkov's Letter of Resignation to Prince L'vov
[*Russkiia Vedomosti*, No. 97, May 2, 1917, p. 5.]

[May 1, 1917]

In view of the condition in which the power of the government is now placed, and particularly the authority of the Minister of War and Navy over the Army and Fleet, conditions which I am powerless to alter and which threaten the defense, freedom, and even the existence of Russia with fatal consequences, I can no more conscientiously continue my duties as Minister of War and Navy and share the responsibilities for the grievous sin which is being carried on against the fatherland. I therefore request the Provisional Government to release me from these duties.

1090. STATEMENT OF THE PROVISIONAL GOVERNMENT ON GUCHKOV'S RESIGNATION

[*VVP*, No. 45, May 2, 1917, p. 1.]

On the subject of Minister of War and Navy A. I. Guchkov's announcement of his resignation from the Provisional Government, which also contained the motivation underlying his decision, the Provisional Government notes that its views on the contemporary political situation were set forth in an address to the people, published on April 26 of this year, and that the text of this address was approved at that time with the full agreement of A. I. Guchkov. In this address, the Provisional Government openly declared to the country that the state is in definite danger and that, in order to save it, it is necessary to tax all the vital forces of the country. At that same time, the Government decided unanimously to do everything possible to invite the participation of all those creative forces that have not as yet participated in responsible government work. While anticipating the resolution of this question, it called on the population to maintain peace and order. At the present time, Guchkov has found it necessary, as he [staged] an individual walkout from the Provisional Government, to declare that he could not share the responsibility for the grave harm that is being inflicted on Russia.

The Government, no less than Guchkov, is clearly aware of the dangers that now confront Russia after the shocks she has endured. However, the Provisional Government, true to the dictates of its conscience, does not consider that it has the right to relieve itself of the burden of power and is remaining at its post in the firm belief that the entry into its composition of representatives of democratic elements of the population who have not heretofore participated in the responsible work of the state will assure the unity of power through which the country will be saved.

1091. THE SOVIET DECISION TO ENTER THE GOVERNMENT

[Executive Committee session of May 1. *Protokoly*, pp. 130–31. See Tseretelli's account in his "Reminiscences of the February Revolution: The April Crisis," *The Russian Review*, XV (1956), 45–48. These minutes were also indecipherable, but in view of the importance of the session, the editors of *Protokoly* collated an account of the meeting from the report in *Novaia Zhizn'*, May 3, and Avdeev, II, 95 ff.]

A special meeting of the Executive Committee was held on the night of May 1 into [the morning of] May 2. One question was up for discussion—the situation created by the resignation of Guchkov, and the definite attitude of certain well-known circles of the bourgeoisie toward the Provisional Government and the Soviet of Workers' and Soldiers' Deputies.

Minister of Justice and Vice-President of the Soviet of Workers' and Soldiers' Deputies, A. F. Kerensky, was invited to the meeting in order to acquaint [the members] with the real state of affairs.

From his report and the information of other members of the Executive Committee, it was established that the position of the country is extremely grave and that only with the active participation of the democratic forces will it be possible to form a new government in the country capable of eliminating the economic disorganization, organizing the defenses of the front, and hastening the conclusion of peace on an international scale.

After a thorough discussion of the question, a break was announced in order that individual factions within the Executive Committee could confer among themselves. At the factional conferences all the populist groups and the Mensheviks declared themselves in favor of having democratic representatives enter the Government. The Bolshevik faction was the only one that opposed the entry.

On the final balloting the question of the entry of democratic representatives into the Government was decided affirmatively by a majority of 44 votes to 19, with 2 abstaining. The Bolsheviks, 3 Menshevik-Internationalists, and 4 S.R.'s voted against the participation.

. . .

1092. The Negotiations to Form a Coalition Government

[V. B. Stankevich, *Vospominaniia, 1914–1919*, pp. 128–32.]

A few days after its first decision, the Committee was forced to raise the question of the government for a second time. Even without debates, [but] simply after Tseretelli's declaration, "I declare myself in favor of a coalition government . . ." the question was decided affirmatively.[11] A commission of representatives of all the parties was elected for negotiating with the Government. The negotiations started on the following morning at L'vov's apartment. Representatives of the Committee came with a prepared declaration which set forth their aims. It seemed to me that when the declaration was read to the Government, one could sense a sigh of relief: "Only this." . . . Tereshchenko and Nekrasov did not hide their satisfaction and proposed that they turn at once to the question of membership. But L'vov declared with restraint that the declaration must be discussed in the Government. The representatives of the Committee went to the nearest restaurant on Sadovaia Street to await the reply and discussed their personal candidatures over lunch. Incidentally, it was decided not to insist on Miliukov's resignation, but, on the contrary, to persuade [him], instead, to remain in the cabinet, only not as Minister of Foreign Affairs. After a time Tseretelli was called out by the Government and returned with the Government's corrections to the declaration. After some negotiations the question of editing was straightened out without particular difficulties. But as soon as the question turned to the assignment of portfolios, difficulties began to arise and [the matter] became more embroiled with every hour.

Officially, the negotiations took place in Prince L'vov's study on Teatral'naia Street. But only the final compromises were reached there between decisions that were made elsewhere. Therefore, every stage of the negotiations, every proposal, every correction had to entail a break in the negotiations in order that the members of the Government and the representatives of the Committee could come to an agreement among themselves. Apart from the joint sessions of the Government and the delegation, [and] sessions [held] separately by the Government and

[11] See Tseretelli's comment on this statement in his "Reminiscences of the February Revolution: The April Crisis," *The Russian Review*, XV (1956), 47.

separately by the delegation, there was still the permanent session of the Kadet Central Committee and the [Soviet] Executive Committee. From the very start, the Kadets advanced a series of basic demands: the number of seats that the Kadets [were to receive] in the cabinet must be not less than the number of seats [given to] representatives of the democracy; in addition to the corrected declaration of the Committee, the new Government must approve a declaration condemning anarchy; but the tone of the text of this declaration submitted by the Kadets was obviously unacceptable to the representatives of the [Executive] Committee; furthermore, in discussing the question of personal candidates, the demand was made that the portfolio of the Ministry of Agriculture be in the hands of the Kadets. Contradictory influences came from the Tauride Palace. There the Committee, left without its leaders—all of whom entered the delegation for negotiations—fell under the influence of Steklov and began to formulate its demands and lay down conditions for the entry of its representatives into the Government, insisting also that a whole series of the most important portfolios—of War, Interior, Foreign Affairs, and, of course, Agriculture—be definitely in the hands of the democracy. To these two influences were added auxiliary ones. In the heat of the negotiations, representatives of the Peasants' Congress came with their demands and desires. The Socialist Revolutionaries stated their conditions in terms of an ultimatum: "Chernov [for] Minister of Agriculture." . . . The Popular Socialists [demanded]: "Anyone but Chernov for Minister of Agriculture." The question of Minister of Labor aroused great unrest among the Social Democrats. Chkheidze insisted that Tseretelli should definitely remain in the Soviet, because with his departure to the Government the Committee would lose control over the Soviet . . . The Government insisted precisely on the entry of Tseretelli, considering him to be the only reliable candidate of the democracy. Shingarev did not want to give up the work on food supply for anything, because he wanted to see the results of his measures on supply, which, in his opinion, would begin to tell in a few weeks. Military circles at headquarters were advancing the candidature of Pal'chinskii for Minister of War. Skobelev wanted to be Minister of Navy. The Government insisted that Kerensky be the Minister of War and Navy. Ministers could not be found for some portfolios (Ministry of Justice), [while] portfolios could not be found for some ministers (Tseretelli). To this was added the influence of the fronts, because just in the heat of the negotiations, Alekseev, the Supreme Commander, and all the commanders of the fronts—Dragomirov, Gurko, Brusilov, and Shcherbachev—arrived in Petrograd and, moreover, came out with sharply accusatory speeches. These speeches were evidently intended for the Government, but the Government correctly considered that these speeches were particularly useful to the Committee and proposed to arrange a joint session for hearing the voices from the front.

Meetings after meetings were held, without bringing results. Every day a session of the Plenum of the Soviet was appointed in order to be informed immediately of any results reached. But every day the session had to be canceled. Finally, by the night of May 5, the situation had grown so confused that all hope of reaching an agreement was lost. A delegation from the Committee and the Peasants' Congress was holding a meeting in Prince L'vov's study. In the interior of the apartment, the Government was in conference. Kerensky and Nekrasov were rushing from one room to another in the role of mediators. But the situation was becoming more confused and more hopeless with every minute. All conceivable combinations were exhausted. Every proposal entailed an already familiar cycle of difficulties and objections. Everyone was obviously marking time. The nervous tension had reached its highest limit and gave vent to extreme agitation and irritation. Questions were not even discussed any longer; everyone was simply speaking—or, more precisely, shouting—from his corner. Chernov, disheveled and infuriated, was attacking little Peshekhonov, who was squeezed in a corner. Gvozdev was pronouncing some final words of indignation on the confusion of everything that was going on. . . . Even Tseretelli lost his equilibrium, in spite of my fervent appeals for calm; he was shouting, I think, at Chkheidze . . . when all of a sudden Kerensky rushed in and announced that a solution had been found. The combination announced by Kerensky was, practically speaking, far from new and there was much to be said against it. But all were glad to be swayed by his mood. They no longer wanted to listen to objections; the dissatisfied were forced to stop speaking.

The coalition Government was formed. The war and the power were accepted by the Committee at the same time.

1093. MILIUKOV'S EXPLANATION OF HIS POLICIES AND OF HIS RESIGNATION FROM THE GOVERNMENT

[Speech before the private conference of members of the Duma, May 4. *Rech'*, No. 104, May 5, 1917, p. 3. See also Miliukov's *Istoriia vtoroi russkoi revoliutsii*, I, vypusk 1, 110–11.]

The Causes of His Resignation

I and my companions in the Party of the People's Freedom believed that no one should voluntarily withdraw from the Provisional Government, but that one should only withdraw when forced to do so. You know that my companions in the Party have remained in the Government even after my withdrawal. You can see from that fact that the question was not such that for us, and for our Party, there was any necessity of immediately breaking our connection with the Provisional Government, now the coalition Provisional Government. There is even less reason to take up an attitude of opposition to the Provisional Government.

When I decided that I would only withdraw under threat of violence, I did not take into account that I might have to withdraw, not in obedience to superior force, but in obedience to the desires of my companions—the desires of the large majority of them. I can say with a clear conscience that I did not withdraw but was "ousted." (*Laughter, applause.*) My conscience is clean. I stood at my post until a large majority of my comrades told me that I ought to go because the post I held was needed for other purposes.

Two Divergent Views

You can judge yourselves that my actions in the realm of foreign policy were in accord with what you yourselves believe. (*Cries of* "True, true," *and loud applause.*) My activity was directed along the lines that you considered necessary to the vital interests of Russia. (*Cries of* "True, true.") My opponents said that a revolution, a sharp change, should take place in our foreign policy along with the revolution and a sharp change in our internal politics. They said that our former foreign policy had been the diplomacy of "tsarism" and that now there should be a different diplomacy. I tried to prove that in the domain of foreign politics the situation is completely different from that of internal politics. My fundamental idea was that there are no such things as the "Tsar's diplomacy" and the "Provisional Government's diplomacy," that what exists is a mutual diplomacy of the Allies, a diplomacy which we share along with the Allied countries, along with the leading democracies who came to an agreement with us about the common task. You will recall that we have always developed the idea that the aims of the leading democracies in this war are liberating aims, that these aims look to the self-determination of peoples. We also said that those aims also included certain objects which were necessary for Russia's welfare. We agreed with our allies that if our common efforts were crowned by a common victory we should receive a common reward for our vital needs. During the war we entered into new agreements with countries that only came into the war because these agreements had been reached—Italy and Rumania, for instance. These countries agreed upon the general idea of giving freedom to others, of uniting or completing the unity of their own peoples and the realization of their vital interests. Thus, there was no "Tsar's diplomacy" but only an Allied diplomacy. We were bound to our Allies for better or for worse and were under a moral obligation to stay with them until the end in the mutually pledged troth, in the common fight on a united battlefront. It seemed to us that these ties were sealed by the blood of all those millions belonging to all the Allies in our pledged circle, and that no one could leave that circle on his own initiative. That is why the changes that took place when we changed our internal structure seemed to me to bring about a situation in which we could say with a clean conscience, freely and openly and in the name of the whole country, what formerly a part of the country, represented by the Duma, had said. The part of the country represented by the Duma had taken its position on the heights of those lofty ideas and ideals that had been repeatedly proclaimed by many prominent statesmen in the countries allied with us.

Russia and the Allies

That is the way I understood our problems and it seems to me that that is the way our Allies understood the position of the new government toward them. In my appearance in the Ministry of Foreign Affairs they saw a sign that Russia would not prove false to the treaties she has signed or to the aims she has set herself. I think that this in a measure explains their joyful confidence that the revolution had attained its objects. They believed that under her new freedom Russia would make greater efforts for the attainment of the common object than she had made before. They believed that there would be new enthusiasm in carrying on the war that would multiply the strength of our army tenfold. We constantly said that the old regime was not able to organize the country for victory. It was just that that [organization for victory] was our object in supporting the revolution and it naturally seemed that after the revolution that event would occur which had been to a great extent the cause of the revolution. That is the way I understood my task. The rapid recognition the Allied governments afforded us is a certain sort of proof of what I say.

For a considerable time it seemed to me that I was carrying on our foreign policy in full agreement with my comrades in the Provisional Government, but it was clear, after a while, that new ideas were being introduced from outside. These ideas were based on the views of an insignificant minority of the socialists abroad, who made it their object before the war not to allow the war and, after the start of the war, to stop it because the war is a capitalists' affair, because the objects of the war are imperialistic and the proletariat's duty is to force its governments to stop the war. Their task as formulated was difficult enough because it was only accepted in other countries by an insignificant minority of the social-democratic parties. The majority of socialists in all the Allied countries turned out to be national and not international; that is, they agreed to the idea of defending their country and fighting that German militarism which interfered with the establishment of a stable peace. The bourgeois parties, in an even greater degree, adopted this national idea. And it would seem that nothing has happened in Russia to change those ideas. The socialist minority which tried to realize the ideas I have mentioned was a hopeless minority in other countries. With German help and with the assistance of the Swiss socialists this minority tried to assemble an international congress and in this way to set up the ghost of the International. They were unable to do this in the little Swiss village of Zimmerwald and still less so at Kienthal. But those Zimmerwald and Kienthal ideas, which were the property of a small group only in other countries, flowed into Russia in a broad stream through the same channels and brought us the formulas that were fabricated in Germany and caught up by the Swiss socialists and our Russian exiles. Our own exiles began a vigorous propaganda campaign in favor of the Zimmerwald formulas when they reached Russia. As a result, large sections of our public, which were poorly informed about all these occurrences in other countries, took up the formulas of the western international minority of the Social Democrats. The formula "without annexations and indemnities" is one of these formulas. The representatives of the current of public opinion which holds that the Soviet of Workers' and Soldiers' Deputies should extend its control to questions of foreign policy insist on this formula. I know what this formula means and whence it comes and naturally very energetically protested its adoption. A few of my colleagues supported me in this (but only a few), and I had to agree to the publication of the Declaration of March 27, which is a compromise between my views and the views of the majority [of the Provisional Government]. The majority insisted on the introduction, not of the formula "without annexations and indemnities," but on a statement that we have no aggressive annexationist aims, which is perfectly true. I, and my companions in thought, insisted that a sentence be added to the effect that Russia will be true to her obligations and will maintain the rights of our country. This proved that until others give up their rights we will not give up ours. These statements guaranteed me freedom of action in following the line of policy formerly agreed on. But as this document was a compromise, it did not satisfy the current of opinion which had insisted that such a document be published. This current of opinion demanded that it be broadened in a different direction, in that direction which was not fully satisfied at first. There was, therefore, a choice between two possible courses. One was to consider the compromise a failure and deny the formula accepted by the Government in the Declaration of the 27th of March and the other was to interpret the Declaration in the sense of "without annexations and indemnities." The latter course was wiser and it was accepted and followed. The working-class press raised a chorus of praise in honor of this formula, interpreting it in the sense of "without annexations and indemnities." This was not so, but it was not my duty to begin arguing when I was told that the idea that it was not so was only my personal opinion.

Later another phase developed, when people began to insist that the document which I had purposely made a declaration to the people of Russia and not a diplomatic document should be turned into a diplomatic act, and that the Allies should at once begin negotiations with us to change the contents of the very treaties of alliance that were themselves in accordance with the sense that these people desired to give to the declaration, namely, in the sense of "without annexations and indemnities." I refused flatly. The new discussions led to a new compromise. I agreed to send, not a note, but the document itself, accompanied by a note which should guarantee the Ministry of Foreign Affairs against the evil results of an incorrect understanding of the compromise. In the accompanying note I plainly indicated that we did not advocate a separate peace, that our army should be strengthened, and so on.

The Proposition That Was Refused

All these statements guaranteed our loyalty, so to speak, to our allies. But as you know, this document aroused a frightful storm against me. It was held to be a step backward, and street crowds gathered—which, to be sure, turned into an ovation for the Provisional Government and for me, personally, by the end of the day. This, however, was only a temporary victory. Those who wanted to annul the compromise in favor of the formula "without annexations and indemnities" continued their fight and decided they would themselves carry out the policy which I refused to carry out. This happened to coincide in point of time with the talk about a coalition ministry, and in the unofficial negotiations about such a ministry the first demand made by the socialists was that the Minister of Foreign Affairs should leave his post. Seven members of the Government agreed to that, but demanded, as a counterweight, that I should nevertheless remain in the Ministry but should change my portfolio [to the Ministry of Education]. These propositions were made to me but I could not accept them. You will understand why. (*Storms of applause.*)

A government declaration will probably be printed tomorrow and the objects of our foreign policy will be put in a form to which I do not agree. Although another person may carry out that kind of foreign policy, I cannot accept any responsibility for such a handling of the question. I consider such a handling of the question injurious and dangerous to Russia because it will not attain the object for which it strives and will at the same time disturb our relations with our allies.

It was perfectly plain to me that changing the portfolio of Minister of Foreign Affairs for the portfolio of the Minister of Education would not free me from responsibility for those foreign policies which I have followed during the entire war and which are well known to the whole world. I cannot accept such a responsibility. That is why I resigned.

The Coalition Ministry

In the above explanation I have not touched on the question of the coalition ministry, and my views regarding it. Some of my party comrades, as you know, considered it imperative for them to enter the coalition ministry and to try to bear the burden of government a little further and, by remaining in the ministry, to continue the work they were engaged in.

Personally, I consider the attempt to form such a ministry extremely decisive. It may also turn out to be risky. But without any doubt it will attain two definitely favorable results. The formation of a coalition ministry will give the Government more power and also make it possible for the Provisional Government to be the exclusive organ of government, which it has not so far been. Let the Soviet of Workers' and Soldiers' Deputies send their representatives into the Provisional Government and let the Soviet take the responsibility for actually governing, but at the same time let that government be the only one. That is the first task. I do not know whether it will be accomplished. As you know, there is a fight within the Soviet itself. You know that not all the members of the Soviet considered it possible to send representatives into the Provisional Government. And it is perfectly plain that those who would not enter the Government are going to criticize those who have entered. It is very possible that the socialists who have entered the coalition ministry will fall under the same shower of missiles that were rained on the Government before it contained any socialists. But now, at any rate, we shall have a government that is undoubtedly stronger.

The other task, that of strengthening the army at the front, is even more important. This task consists in changing the mood of the soldiers who imagined that all these pacifist tendencies and manifestoes were equivalent to an armistice and that there was therefore no more need of fighting. They evidently thought, once we have given up fighting for conquests, what is the use of fighting at all? It was not possible to change that mood under the old regime because the confidence felt by the mass of the soldiers was not sufficient. Now, on the other hand, the Soviet of Workers' and Soldiers' Deputies enjoys that confidence fully, and when we were asked how to make it clear to the soldiers that military defense is not limited to defense in the narrow sense but also includes attack, we answered: "Ask the Soviet of Workers' and Soldiers' Deputies to publish a proclamation stating this and the soldiers will believe it." It is perfectly evident that a ministry including members of those parties which are supported by the Soviet can attain the soldiers' confidence. No matter how carefully the Soviet may outline its action toward the war, nevertheless tomorrow's declaration will state that an attack is not out of the question, that a military defeat would be dangerous to the revolution itself, and that the war must be continued, if only for the narrow and limited aims put forward by the current of opinion that is in control. That is the most important thing that we are able to win at the present moment—that is the most important thing that we can achieve. No matter what beautiful formulas of friendship for our allies may be written, we will be actually betraying our allies if the army remains inactive. And again, no matter what terrible formulas of treachery may be written, we will be actually carrying out our obligations to our allies if the army fights. This is justification enough for the effort to form a coalition ministry. Thus I deem the coalition ministry in general a step forward, one that in any case offers hope of attaining what are now our two great goals: strengthening the Government and changing the mood of the army. And in so far as our aims are being achieved, we should support the Provisional Government in its new form.

1094. MAKLAKOV'S REMARKS ON THE COURSE OF THE REVOLUTION

[Speech before the private conference of members of the Duma, May 4, *Rech'*, No. 104, May 5, 1917, p. 3.]

. . .

. . . In whatever form we clothe our fundamental idea, whether we paraphrase, as did A. F. Kerensky, the ancient "anathema" of I[van] Aksakov, who in a moment of grief exclaimed: "You are not the children of freedom, you are [but] rebellious slaves [sic]," whether we use the diplomatic language of the Provisional Government, which has explained that it was easier to destroy societies than to create new ones—whatever language we use, these words conceal one basic thought: "Russia has proved unworthy of the liberty she has achieved." (Voices: "Correct.") . . . We may deeply regret, as I regret, that in its time the Provisional Government failed to realize the support it might have obtained from the State Duma. (Voices: "Correct." Applause.) It may be said that it did not realize the significance of the fact that the State Duma was abolished and replaced by the Soviet of Workers' and Soldiers' Deputies, by the representatives of class [interests]. One may blame those who talked, and even more those who kept silent. . . . The final summing up might turn out to be the following: Russia received on the day of the revolution more liberty than she could take, and the revolution has destroyed Russia. This is what might be said, and when the revolution is cursed, also those who made it will be cursed. . . .

. . .

Gentlemen, I want to tell you the whole truth. From the benches of the left we have often been blamed for not wanting the revolution. Yes, it was true. We did not want revolution during the war. We realized that the task of changing the regime and the social structure connected with it, that the burden of such upheavals and of bringing the war to an end, would be beyond the force of any nation. But there was a moment when it became clear to everybody that under the old regime it was impossible to conclude war, to achieve victory; and for those who believed that a revolution would be ruinous, it was their duty and their task to save Russia from a revolution from below by means of a palace revolution from above. Such was the task which stood before us, but which we did not fulfill. If posterity curses this revolution, then it will also curse those who did not understand the methods which could have forestalled it.

. . .

What is there to do? . . . The Government goes more and more to the left, the country goes more and more to the right, and the Government will remain without the support of the country, and will fall as the old regime fell, when the Nemesis of history makes her appearance. . . .

. . .

If Russia stops [at the brink of the abyss], then yes, Russia is the great Russia, worthy of freedom; if she falls—the people will receive what they deserve.

. . .

1095. THE DECLARATION OF MAY 5 OF THE NEW COALITION GOVERNMENT

[VVP, No. 49, May 6, 1917, p. 1. The composition of the Ministry was as follows: Minister-President and Minister of the Interior, Prince G. E. L'vov; Minister of War and Navy, A. F. Kerensky; Minister of Justice, P. N. Pereverzev; Minister of Foreign Affairs, M. I. Tereshchenko; Minister of Transport, N. V. Nekrasov; Minister of Trade and Industry, A. I. Konovalov; Minister of Education, A. A. Manuilov; Minister of

Finance, A. I. Shingarev; Minister of Agriculture, V. M. Chernov; Minister of Labor, M. I. Skobelev; Minister of Post and Telegraph, I. G. Tseretelli; Minister of Food, A. V. Peshekhonov; Minister of Welfare, Prince D. I. Shakhovskoi; Ober-Procurator of the Holy Synod, V. N. L'vov; State Controller, I. V. Godnev.]

The Provisional Government, reorganized and reinforced by representatives of the revolutionary democracy, declares that it will energetically carry into effect the ideas of liberty, equality, and fraternity, beneath the standards of which the great Russian revolution came to birth.

The Provisional Government is particularly united as to the fundamental lines of its future action, as follows:

(1) In its foreign policy the Provisional Government, rejecting, in concert with all the people, all thought of a separate peace, adopts openly as its aim the re-establishment of a general peace which shall not tend toward either domination over other nations, or the seizure of their national possessions, or the violent usurpation of their territories—a peace without annexations or indemnities, and based on the rights of nations to decide their own affairs.

In the firm conviction that the fall of the regime of tsarism in Russia and the consolidation of democratic principles in our internal and external policy will create in the Allied democracies new aspirations toward a stable peace and the brotherhood of nations, the Provisional Government will take steps toward bringing about an agreement with the Allies on the basis of its declaration of March 27.

(2) Convinced that the defeat of Russia and her allies not only would be a source of the greatest calamities to the people, but would postpone or make impossible the conclusion of a world-wide peace on the basis indicated above, the Provisional Government believes firmly that the Russian revolutionary army will not permit the German troops to destroy our Western Allies and then throw themselves upon us with the full force of their arms.

The strengthening of the principles of democratization in the army and the development of its military power, both offensive and defensive, will constitute the most important task of the Provisional Government.

(3) The Provisional Government will fight resolutely and inflexibly against the economic disorganization of the country by the further systematic establishment of governmental control of the production, transportation, exchange, and distribution of commodities, and in necessary cases it will have recourse also to the organization of production.

(4) Measures for the protection of labor in every possible way will continue to be promoted further with energy.

(5) Leaving it to the Constituent Assembly to deal with the question of transferring land to the toilers, and proceeding with preparatory measures relative thereto, the Provisional Government will take all necessary steps toward ensuring the greatest possible production of grain required by the country and toward furthering the systematic utilization of the land in the interests of the national economy and of the toiling population.

(6) Looking forward to the introduction of a series of reforms of the financial system upon a democratic basis, the Provisional Government will devote particular attention to the increasing of direct taxes on the wealthy classes (inheritance taxes, taxes on excessive war profits, a property tax, etc.).

(7) Efforts to introduce and develop democratic institutions of self-govern-ment will be continued with all possible speed and assiduity.

(8) The Provisional Government will also make all possible efforts to bring about, at the earliest date practicable, the convocation of a Constituent Assembly in Petrograd.

Resolutely adopting as its aim the realization of the program indicated above, the Provisional Government declares categorically that fruitful work is possible only if it has the full and absolute confidence of all the revolutionary people and the opportunity to exercise fully the power essential to the confirmation of the vic-tories of the revolution and to their further development.

Addressing to all citizens a firm and pressing appeal for the safeguarding of the unity of power in the hands of the Provisional Government, the latter declares that, for the safety of the fatherland, it will take the most energetic measures against all attempts at a counterrevolution, as well as against all anarchical, illegal, or violent acts calculated to disorganize the country and to prepare the ground for a counterrevolution.

The Provisional Government believes that, in so proceeding, it will have the firm support of all those to whom the freedom of Russia is dear.

PRINCE L'VOV, Minister-President
[and all other ministers]

May 5, 1917

1096. SOVIET APPROVAL OF THE DECLARATION AND THE COALITION
[*Izvestiia*, No. 59, May 6, 1917, p. 4.]

A meeting of the Soviet of Workers' and Soldiers' Deputies took place on May 5 in the hall of the Naval School.

After opening the meeting, M. I. Skobelev reported to the comrades on the course of the negotiations between representatives of the Executive Committee and representatives of the Provisional Government. Next, the question as to whether the Soviet of Workers' and Soldiers' Deputies approves of the actions taken by its representatives was submitted for discussion by the meeting.

Comrades Trotsky, Dan, Tseretelli, Chernov, and others took part in the debates.

After the debates the meeting adopted the [following] resolution by an over-whelming majority of votes:

"Recognizing that the declaration of the Provisional Government, which has been transformed and strengthened by the new representatives of the revolutionary democracy, conforms to the will of the democracy and to the tasks of consoli-dating the gains of the revolution and developing the revolution further, the Soviet of Workers' and Soldiers' Deputies resolves:

"1) Representatives of the Soviet of Workers' and Soldiers' Deputies must enter the Provisional Government.

"2) On entering the Government prior to the establishment of the all-Russian organ of the Soviets of Workers' and Soldiers' Deputies, the representatives of the Soviet of Workers' and Soldiers' Deputies must consider themselves responsible to the Petrograd Soviet of Workers' and Soldiers' Deputies and commit themselves to render full account to it for their actions.

"3) The Soviet of Workers' and Soldiers' Deputies expresses its full confidence in the new Provisional Government and calls on the democracy to give active support to this Government, assuring it the plenary authority it requires in order to consolidate the gains of the revolution and to develop the revolution further."

1097. STATEMENT OF PRINCE L'VOV
[Reports to the Department of State, No. 310, May 29 (N.S.), 1917, Enclosure.]

. . .

The Temporary [*sic*] Government (before the formation of the coalition ministry) had to take account of orders which it did not itself issue. Parties that did not want to take over the formal responsibility for the management of the country actually replaced, in many instances, the formal government. Power without responsibility and responsibility without power was what the country was coming to.

. . .

Now representatives of all major political tendencies have entered the government. Having taken these representatives into its midst the government now expects to receive complete support for all its measures, obedience to all its acts and to all the acts of its agents. If it does not receive this support and confidence it will not be a government. There can be no half-confidence and half-obedience now.

1098. STATEMENT OF TSERETELLI
[Reports to the Department of State, No. 310, May 29 (N.S.), 1917, Enclosure.]

If we (socialists) had not hoped that our entrance into the government would render it the sole organ of government and make it strong we would not have entered.

We are convinced that the masses of the people will follow us. All the conscious elements appraise the situation correctly and understand that the new government has announced a platform on which all the living forces of the country should, and will, unite.

Some people are making the mistake of supposing that the socialists who have agreed to undertake to govern the country together with the representatives of the bourgeoisie have made some concessions to the bourgeoisie. No concessions have been made. What has happened is that the revolution is moving forward on the road to the realization of democratic ideals. The present moment is one of the most striking moments of that progress.

When the revolution occurred it was found possible for the bourgeois and democratic elements to work together.

This was the first stage of the revolution, during which all efforts were concentrated to break the remnants of power of the old regime, and to establish the foundations of democracy in our internal politics. At this time those middle-class elements, which had consented to the revolution only because they had despaired of ever realizing their imperialistic aims under the old regime, acted in accord with the democracy.

But now the true soul of the revolution has become evident. The unbreakable bond between democratic principles in internal politics and democratic principles in foreign politics and the genuine democratic yearnings of the masses have been revealed.

This was the cause of that crisis which resulted in the withdrawal from the government of the whole people of those bourgeois elements which were unable to give up their narrow class interests for the sake of the whole people's democratic platform. We believe that in the case of the bourgeois elements, at least in the case of the majority of them, their imperialistic tendencies do not make up the entirety of their very existence. The limitless internal market of Russia when its reconstruction arrives opens such perspectives for the bourgeoisie that only the most bred-in-the-bone and hopelessly doctrinaire imperialists can risk Russia's very existence on the attempt to inculcate democratic Russia with their dreams of Constantinople and so forth. When they do this they are [endangering] . . . the powerful effort the whole people is making to save Russia from the approaching internal and external danger.

The Declaration of the new Temporary [sic] Government can unite the democracy and all the living forces of the country for the strengthening of revolutionary Russia and the saving of the country.

This platform conforms to the essential vital interests of democracy and in order to call forth that heroic effort which is needed in order to save the country the Temporary [sic] Government must realize it, in practice. This is the only way it can call forth into being the creative powers of the revolution. Both in internal and in foreign politics there must be an unambiguous recognition of democratic principles and a practical realization of those principles. Only under these conditions will there be that popular enthusiasm which alone can work the salvation of the country.

1099. *Russkiia Vedomosti* on the Coalition
[No. 101, May 6, 1917, p. 3.]

The ministerial crisis is over, and before us is the cabinet in its new form.

Of the new ministers, all, except Prince D. I. Shakhovskoi, belong to socialist parties, and thus the essence of the changes that have taken place consists of the considerable increase of the representatives of socialist parties within the cabinet. . . . However, these changes must not be understood as denoting a radical change in the program of the Provisional Government. Even in its former composition it never put forth a "bourgeois" program, just as the new Provisional Government does not put forth a "socialist" program, and it is acting that way not only because the socialists still remain in the minority in the new cabinet, but mainly because they themselves admit the objective impossibility of the immediate realization of the socialist program. In substance, the program of the new cabinet will remain the same as was that of the old one, inasmuch as the Provisional Government still remains a "provisional" government which has at its disposal no regular apparatus of legislative power, and which cannot take many of the decisions upon its own responsibility.

The new cabinet will, as did the former one, have to pay chief attention to the current organizational work. . . . However, there are other problems also which were not formulated so sharply and distinctly before the former Provisional Government at the moment of its formation, but which kept appearing, and became fully tangible only gradually, as events developed. These problems are: the creation of a really strong and firm governmental power; the establishment of a durable order—based on law—inside the country; and the rejuvenation of the army. . . . During the past two months, general disorganization made great strides, and we must not close our eyes to the threatening anarchy inside the country, and the collapse of the army. The struggle against this danger presents not only one of the chief problems, but literally the most pressing problem for the new cabinet, and the actual presence of this problem must first of all determine our attitude toward the reorganized cabinet. . . .

It must be stated straight and firmly: we are not concerned now with the realization of our party programs, but only with the salvation of Russia, and the reorganization of the cabinet which has taken place perhaps represents the final attempt at such a salvation. If it fails, there is no discernible way out ahead. That is precisely why, right now, our Provisional Government has a right to demand the most undivided support on the part of everyone, and this support must be given to it by everyone without reservation, unconditionally. V. A. Maklakov is right when he says that "we have no moral right to treat with indifference, let alone with hostility" the undertakings of the Provisional Government. At such responsible moments as the one we are living through now, all of us must closely rally around our unified, firm, and honest government.

1100. *Volia Naroda* ON THE COALITION
[No. 6, May 5, 1917, p. 1.]

The Executive Committee of the Soviet of Workers' and Soldiers' Deputies declares that "the revolutionary authority which Russia expected has been created" and it points out that "as long as socialists remain in the government the country will know that behind each government decree is the authority and all the influence of the Soviet of Workers' and Soldiers' . . . Deputies."

Not so long ago the participation of the socialists in the Provisional Revolutionary Government seemed to many almost a betrayal of all the hopes of international socialism. . . .

At the extraordinary conference of Socialist Revolutionaries, when an agreement had already been reachd between the Government and the Executive Committee, a minority—a small one to be sure—did voice opposition to the S.R.'s participation in the revolutionary government.

Perhaps, of course, this minority was not worth taking into account inasmuch as its resolution was a slavish copy of the Lenin-anarchial models. But undoubtedly some confusion on this question still persists in the socialist camp. Proof of this may be seen in the fact that the resolution on the participation of socialists in the cabinet was approved by an extremely small majority at the Conference of the Petrograd Mensheviks.

In so far as one can get a glimpse of this confusion from the socialist press, many of the socialists have not as yet learned that basic difference which exists between the Provisional Revolutionary Government and any coalition cabinet of a nonrevolutionary period.

A properly organized popular rule does not as yet exist at the present moment in Russia. In the name of democracy and for the sake of its interests spontaneous-revolutionary organizations talk and act.

That is their right, their responsibility.

. . .

The Executive Committee assures us that the entire body of the rejuvenated government is capable of "implementing consistently the democratic program."

And we, Socialist Revolutionaries, have no reason to maintain the former halfway policy of semitrust and semisuspicion toward the government. The Russian socialists must from now on see in the government the sole revolutionary power which is in intimate contact with the Soviet of Workers' and Soldiers' Deputies.

The situation is binding. We have the right to expect of the Provisional Government that it will prove to be the genuine power; that it will vigorously combat tendencies toward anarchy; that it will restore, with the aid of all socialists, civil and military discipline; and that it will create conditions favorable to a planned and organized expression of the people's will in the Constituent Assembly. Have faith in the rejuvenated government to which democracy entrusts all plenary authority!

1101. *Rabochaia Gazeta* ON THE COALITION
[No. 49, May 6, 1917, pp. 1–2.]

The reconstitution of the Government is an accomplished fact. The influence in it of the socialist party is greatly strengthened. P. N. Miliukov, the most brilliant and doctrinairely stubborn champion of the imperialist tendencies among certain strata of our upper bourgeoisie, has withdrawn. It is extremely significant that in the face of all these changes the liberal bourgeoisie remained in power. "The Kadet Fronde," recently talked about, has quieted down. Not only did the Kadets fail to recall their ministers as they threatened to do; they introduced into the Government some of their outstanding members. This should assure the new Provisional Government of complete support from the liberal bourgeoisie and the groups closely allied to it on the right. But what is most important is that by adopting the new course of action the Provisional Government cut itself off completely from imperialist influences. And it quite definitely enters upon the road for the most rapid achievement of universal peace through international means. This, as well as the creative revolutionary work within the country as contemplated by the Government, should assure it active support from the widest strata of democracy. Now [we come to] the question of the attitude of the social democracy toward the new Government.

The Social Democratic organizations of Moscow and Petrograd were against the participation of Social Democrats in the Government. The crux of the matter, however, is not whether the socialists have or have not joined the ministry. The important thing is to determine, first of all, what the Government stands for and what the basis of its activity is. We must take a firm stand that we are obliged to render our most active and wholehearted support to the new government in the course of action it has adopted.

The greatest objection to the participation of Social Democrats in the Government at the present time was that such a government runs the risk of failing to find sufficiently strong popular support from either the right or the left wing, that this would sharpen the class contradiction yet further, and that the forces from the center threatening the downfall of the revolution would gain in strength. But precisely because of this, once the ministry has been formed, every effort should be exerted to strengthen it. And a decisive struggle should be waged against all efforts, no matter where they stem from, to discredit the ministry in advance.

Let us recall that we did favor active support of the former government also. Such was the resolution adopted by the Menshevik delegation of the All-Russian Conference of the Soviets of Workers' and Soldiers' Deputies. There is our reason why we should support the new government because it is new, reconstituted in keeping with the demands of revolutionary democracy, and because its course is extremely difficult and dangerous. And the future course of the new government will determine the destiny of the revolution . . .

It goes without saying that the most active support of the Government does not exclude the right and obligation to criticize it. Moreover, criticism need not necessarily be hostile and destructive. In fact, the Government might profit by such criticism. However, the notorious "in so far as" should be relegated to the archive of history, lest the right use it to their advantage. The Government cannot operate in an atmosphere of halfhearted confidence and in the midst of threats to deprive it of confidence in advance.

There are other questions in connection with the new situation, such as the responsibility of the Social Democratic ministers to the Party for their representation, or the question of mutual relations between the Soviet of Workers' and Soldiers' Deputies and the new government. These questions should be carefully studied. In the meantime, it is necessary *to establish from the very first day* of the existence of the new Provisional Government [that our policy is] *active and wholehearted support of the course of action adopted by it!*

1102. *Izvestiia* ON THE COALITION
[No. 59, May 6, 1917, p. 3.]

Since yesterday Russia has been governed by a new Provisional Government. Socialists, representatives of the Soviet of Workers' and Soldiers' Deputies, have entered its membership.

The Government will base its activities on a program worked out by the revolutionary democratic forces. In the realm of foreign and domestic affairs it has committed itself to carrying out measures which the democratic forces justly consider to be the only means for uniting all the living forces of the country, and for defending the Russian revolution against internal disintegration and against military destruction from without.

. . . Everything will be done to consolidate and increase the gains of the revolution, to bring closer the cherished hour of the coming of a universal peace, without annexations and indemnities, based on the self-determination of peoples.

We know that heavy trials await us on the road to this peace. We know that while the peoples have not as yet awakened and have not risen against their enslavers, our soldiers will have to conduct the hated war with all their energy and courage. But they can now conduct it in the firm belief that their heroic efforts will not be used for evil [ends]. Whether they will be defending themselves at a fortified position, or whether they will be conducting an attack dictated by strategical or tactical considerations, the soldier may now believe that all these military operations are equally serving one and the same goal—the defense of the revolution from destruction and the earliest possible conclusion of universal peace. From now on, they can and must accomplish their military feats in the firm belief that they are acting for a national cause, for the cause of the workers of the whole world.

The revolutionary power must be strong in order to save Russia, and in order to cope with the difficult problem of organizing and maintaining the fighting efficiency of the army, obviating the difficulties in transportation, food supplies, and finances, reconstructing the country along democratic lines, re-placing the old administration, carrying out urgent social reforms and convoking the Constituent Assembly as soon as possible. It alone should possess absolute authority. Its orders should be accepted with absolute confidence and be strictly executed. All the forces of the organized revolutionary democracy should be placed at its disposal. . . . As long as our comrades are in the Government, this is *our* Government. Let us give it all the strength and authority it needs to lead our country out of that terrible impasse into which it was led by the monarchy we have overthrown!

Long live the new Provisional Government!

1103. MENSHEVIK SUPPORT AND BOLSHEVIK OPPOSITION TO THE COALITION
[*Izvestiia*, No. 63, May 11, 1917, pp. 2–3.]

In accordance with the decision of the Soviet of Workers' and Soldiers' Deputies, Comrades Tseretelli, Skobelev, Chernov, and Peshekhonov entered the Government, which, until then, had contained only one socialist — Comrade Kerensky.

Two of the elected representatives of the democracy who assumed the heavy responsibilities of government work—Comrades Tseretelli and Skobelev—belong to the Russian Social Democratic Workers' Party. They belong to the Menshevik faction within the party. For many years they have fought under the banner of this faction. The democracy which sent them to the Provisional Government knows them as representatives of this faction.

The all-Russian Conference of Mensheviks which is taking place at the present time has approved the actions of its representatives.

"Under the present conditions, in spite of all the political dangers connected with the entry of socialists into the bourgeois government, a refusal by the revolutionary Social Democrats to take active part in the Provisional Government on the grounds of their resolute democratic platform in the field of foreign and domestic policies would have threatened the revolution with downfall and would have conflicted with the interests of the working class and the whole revolutionary democracy. The socialists' entry into the government based on a platform of an active policy aimed at the earliest conclusion of universal peace founded on democratic principles should represent a fact of major significance for the cause of abolishing war in the interests of international democracy. Therefore, *the conference considers it imperative to give full and unqualified support to the new Government, which guarantees a firm policy aimed at realizing the demands of the democracy both within the country and in the sphere of international relations, and appeals to the working class and party organizations for active and systematic work in strengthening the power of the new revolutionary government on the central and local levels.* Accepting the responsibility for actions of the party members who entered the government at the request of the Soviet of Workers' and Soldiers' Deputies, the conference considers it necessary that the Social Democratic ministers be responsible not only to the Soviet, but to the party as well."

But on the same day . . . the united Petrograd Conference of Social Democrats [Bolshevik] carried a resolution branding the step taken by our comrades as "an ideological apostasy." This resolution concludes with the following thesis: "The duty of every party worker, therefore, is to explain to the proletarian masses that by joining the bourgeois government Citizens Tseretelli and Skobelev have placed themselves outside the ranks of the revolutionary and social democracy."[12]

But who is it that is assuming the role of judge over the elected representatives of the democracy?

The group that is assuming this role is one that has fought bitterly against our comrades even before they entered the Government. This role is assumed by a group that is doing everything in its power to thwart the organization of a coalition government!

. . .

1104. THE SOVIET EXECUTIVE COMMITTEE'S DECISION TO CLARIFY AND PUBLICIZE ITS REASONS FOR APPROVING A COALITION MINISTRY[13]

[Session of May 12. *Protokoly*, pp. 143–44.]

1. The members of the Executive Committee came to a unanimous decision that it would be desirable to issue a clarification to all the socialist parties and the international proletariat regarding the meaning and motives behind the participation of the Soviet of Workers' and Soldiers' Deputies, through its representatives, in the Provisional Government.

However, Comrade Kamenev's motion—to include the motives of the opposition in the text of the address—. . . was rejected by a majority of votes. . . .

. . .

2. The Executive Committee finds it desirable to hold a series of meetings within the following week with the participation of our comrade ministers as a means of counteracting the campaign that is being conducted against the Soviets, against its decision concerning the coalition ministry.

The arrangement of these meetings is assigned to the Petrograd Section in cooperation with the Agitation Section.

. . .

---

[12] See Lenin's article "Has Dual Power Disappeared?" in *Pravda*, No. 62, May 20, 1917, as translated in the *Collected Works of V. I. Lenin: the Revolution of 1917*, XX, Bk. II, 100–102.

[13] For further political and organizational discussion of the coalition, see Chap. 23.

CHAPTER 23

The First Coalition Government

THE FIRST ALL-RUSSIAN CONGRESS OF PEASANTS' SOVIETS

1105. RESOLUTION ON THE PROVISIONAL GOVERNMENT

[*Delo Naroda*, No. 45, May 10, 1917, p. 2. The Congress convened on May 4. For its resolutions and activities relating to the agrarian question, see Volume I, Docs. 518–22; for its resolution on the war and war aims, see Volume II, Doc. 980.]

The following resolution on the attitude toward the Provisional Government, proposed by the presidium, was adopted at the evening session on May 8:

"The country is in danger. The defense and expansion of the gains made by the revolution call for vigorous measures. One of the conditions for the consolidation of freedom is a stable government that commands the confidence of the working people.

"Therefore, fully aware of the responsibility which the present situation imposes upon it, the All-Russian Congress of Peasants' Soviets believes that the entrance of the socialists in the Provisional Government on the basis of the guarantees given by the latter to the country in the Declaration of May 5 is entirely correct and necessary. It appeals to the country to have implicit confidence in and render full support to the reorganized Provisional Government, bearing in mind that only with this support and the participation of all the working people can it [the Government], while enjoying full power, consolidate the freedom gained and assure the further success of the revolution.

"The Soviet recognizes the socialist ministers as their representatives in the Government, responsible, prior to the Constituent Assembly, to the Soviets of Peasants', Workers' and Soldiers' Deputies."

The resolution was adopted by a majority, with 16 against and 14 abstaining.

1106. *Den'* ON THE CONGRESS
[No. 63, May 19, 1917, p. 1.]

Before our eyes a powerful new organization of revolutionary forces is coming into being. I am speaking of the All-Russian Congress of Peasants' Soviets. The representative strength of this organization is large enough. Its decisive influence will probably be determined in the process of the further development of the revolution. Perhaps we are on the eve of the formation of a mighty petit bourgeois peasant democracy which, after deepening the channel of the revolution, will also strengthen its banks. The revolutionary role of the peasantry is conditioned by its social and economic interests. This constitutes the guarantee for the ideological and political link between the worker and the peasant democracies. The united Soviet of Workers', Soldiers', and Peasants' Deputies is the real and, perhaps, indestructible bulwark of the revolution. Very probably the natural, historically indisputable egocentricism of the proletariat will thereby be neutralized. Hegemony will be shared, or else abandoned completely. This, of course, does not coincide directly with the interests of the worker class, as such. But this should cause no regrets, for the course of history imperiously dictates the self-restriction of the proletariat, which takes part as the master in a bourgeois revolution. "What else could the workers' party do but fight along with the petit bourgeoisie to obtain the rights which would allow it later on to conduct its own battle?" Thus the history of '48 was judged by K. Marx, the founder of scientific socialism.

Of all the political parties, the Socialist Revolutionaries will enjoy the greatest influence within the Congress of Peasants' Soviets. By the will of the revolution they are now being transformed from a small, almost forlorn group of the intelligentsia into a great political party. Before, they had no live contact with the people. The people was being operated upon, as an abstract category, and party thinking could combine in the abstract its socialism with the protection of the interests of the peasantry. Now the ideological populism is being transformed from an abstract doctrine into a political program as the party undergoes in the social struggle its baptism by fire. Through the open doors of the party will enter the cadres of the peasant intelligentsia, bringing with them the genuine ideology of the class of which they have become an integral part. We can say nearly for certain that in the process of the organization's growth, which will be linked to an interchange of ideologies, a unification of various populist tendencies will take place, the mark of socialism will gradually fade away, and a peasant democracy, which is essential for the political and social completion of the revolution, will be formed in Russia.

· · ·

When we now say that only national unity can bring the revolution to victory, one should interpret the notion of "national" in a limited sense. In the course of three months the revolution has wiped out the national unity without which autocracy would not have been eliminated. Now the revolutionary center has been shifted; it is being pushed from two sides. The enemies from the left also pursue various aims, but the Kadets and the "Pravdists" serve the same cause. Both have in mind the seizure of power, and both carry out a work of undermining. With concealed attention, with a feeling of special satisfaction, they watch as new difficulties arise along the path of the revolutionary Government. If the revolution breaks through these obstacles their game will be up. If the exhausted Government falls, they will triumph.

The unification of all the revolutionary forces of democracy for the defense of the revolution—such is the new form of national consolidation. Let the isolated forces of counterrevolution remain beyond the pale of this unification. History, especially Russian history, abounds in paradoxes: *Rech'* and *Pravda* may find a common language.

The organization of the peasant democracy broadens and consolidates the front of the revolution. And we welcome our new ally.

1107. General Statutes on the Organization of Peasants' Soviets
[*Delo Naroda*, No. 54, May 20, 1917, p. 2.]

1. The Soviets of Peasants' Deputies are organs of the peasantry which stand guard over the new order and are to engage in political-revolutionary work.

2. The Soviets of Peasants' Deputies must unite the peasantry from top to

bottom. Consequently, headed by the All-Russian Congress of Peasants' Soviets, the following soviets should be organized: guberniya (oblast where no guberniya division exists), uezd (okrug, otdel), volost (stanitsa) village, and, in case of need, raion and village.

3. The aims of the Soviets of Peasants' Deputies must be: a) clarification of the land question and the implementation of measures which may be realized prior to the Constituent Assembly; b) the preparation of the peasantry for the Constituent Assembly; c) control over the actions of the organs of authority, observing that they do not deviate from democratic principles; d) representation of the interests of the peasantry in all government and public organizations.

4. Wherever peasant organizations have sprung up, the All-Russian Congress of Peasants' Soviets invites them to reorganize immediately into Soviets of Peasants' Deputies lest the unity of the organization be violated and the peasantry divided.

Remark. Inasmuch as classes are abolished, the word peasantry implies not an estate, but the toiling agricultural population in accordance with the type of its occupation.

1108. Resolution on the Future Political Structure of Russia
[*Delo Naroda*, No. 60, May 28, 1917, p. 2.]

At the evening session on May 26, the Soviet . . . adopted the following declaration on the future political structure of Russia:

"The All-Russian Soviet of Peasants' Deputies, the spokesman of the organized will of the toiling peasantry, in the celebrated hour of consolidating and widening the freedom won by the nation's sons, declares:

"Following steadfastly the course of achieving the greatest freedom and complete self-determination of persons as well as of nationalities inhabiting Russia, toiling Russia must create a state order which will guarantee these conditions. With a view to this, the All-Russian Congress of Peasants' Soviets urges the Russian toiling peasantry to insist in the Constituent Assembly on the establishment in Russia of a federated democratic republic in which all the peoples will have complete freedom in organizing their internal life.

"The All-Russian Soviet of Peasants' Deputies is deeply convinced that only under the broadest autonomy of peoples who inhabit Russia, and where no one people oppresses another, can a new Russia be created, strong in a voluntary internal unity of free nations."

1109. *Delo Naroda* on the Work of the Congress
[No. 62, May 31, 1917, p. 1.]

The All-Russian Soviet of Peasants' Deputies adjourned after completing its first session.

The convening of the Soviet and its entire work are an event of tremendous significance in the present circumstances. And primarily [this is true] with respect to solving the problem raised by the revolution of organizing a revolutionary democracy and of organizing the peasantry.

The chief significance of the Soviet resides in the fact that it was the first organ representing the organized peasantry. And in the various localities, in the very depths of life stirred up by the revolution, all the resolutions adopted by the Soviet will find expression as an organized and organizing will of the people.

. . .

All the questions raised by the peasantry were taken up in the Soviet and were decided upon. In all the resolutions approved by the Soviet it was evident that its voice, the voice of the peasantry whom it represented, was decisive. . . .

Let us put aside for the time being the solution of the land question and let us pause on the question of how the Soviet of Peasants' Deputies solved the question of freedom.

. . .

The crowning glory in the building of "freedom" was the declaration of the Soviet on the future political organization of Russia—"the federated democratic republic in which all the peoples will have complete freedom in organizing their internal life."

The organization of internal life the Soviet decided beforehand to interpret as implementing from top to bottom a consistent equality to all peoples.

The question of land was at the center of the Soviet's work. This is understandable because for the first time something that had been a dream was being realized, and, what is more important, the realization of this cherished dream passed into the hands of the peasantry itself.

. . .

Thus the widespread peasant world outlook—the world outlook of the toilers— was victorious. In vain were the efforts of those who attempted to place obstacles on this path, such as introducing private property. The free village did not change its course, the course of the toiling peoples.

On the contrary, in its resolutions, and not on the agrarian question alone, the Soviet of Peasants' Deputies emphasized that the course of the revolutionary peasantry is the course of all toilers. In their ranks the revolutionary peasantry marches toward the common ultimate aim. . . .

THE EIGHTH CONGRESS OF THE PARTY OF THE PEOPLE'S FREEDOM (KADETS)

1110. Miliukov's Speech Before the Congress

[*Rech'*, No. 108, May 10, 1917, p. 3. The Congress opened on May 9.]

. . .

At the proposal of M. M. Vinaver, P. N. Miliukov, whom the Congress greeted with applause, was elected President of the Congress.

The Report of P. N. Miliukov

The Congress began its work with the question of the general political situation. The first report on this issue was made by P. N. Miliukov.

Two Months Ago and Now

Only two months—P. N. Miliukov began—separates the Eighth Congress of the Party of the People's Freedom from the Seventh Congress, with the political situation under which the new Congress is held substantially different from the previous one. Then, two months ago, a wave of enthusiasm which had caught the country after the great upheaval had reached its peak in the important centers and had only just reached the remote corners of the provinces and called forth a unanimous response in the army.

The Provisional Government created by the Committee of the State Duma and consecrated by the forces of the revolution enjoyed high and unopposed authority in the capital and in the provinces. . . . The two months which have passed have considerably altered this picture. During this period the left socialist parties worked energetically at organization and propaganda. The more moderate trends lagged behind them; as a matter of fact, by the very essence of their views, the more radical parties could count upon a speedier growth of their partisans. They gave special attention to the villages and to the army. . . . A wave of agrarian movements, unorganized and elemental, spread over the country. Into the army, together with ideas of civil liberty, penetrated propaganda of freedom from discipline, complicated by obscure interpretations of the democracy's aspiration for an early peace. . . . This picture . . . was further complicated by the arrival of *émigrés* of the Lenin type, who were amiably let through Germany in a sealed car, and who have declared here that the social-democratic ideals were obsolete frippery and emphatically invited everyone under the banner of anarcho-communism and of civil war. This preaching sobered up many and gave a first impulse for uniting the reasonable elements around the Provisional Government created by the revolution. . . . Finally, the extreme excesses of the people who call themselves anarchists but who represent a union of a few fanatics and youths with professional criminals and paid German agents, compelled the Government to think of using means of compulsion. But at that moment the pretension of the Soviet of Workers' and Soldiers' Deputies to give orders to the military forces of the capital became manifest, a pretension which represented a particularly vivid demonstration of the dual power which existed and which deprived the Government of any chance to take any kind of effective measures of compulsion. This situation has forced the Provisional Government to address itself to the country, pointing out the difficulty of its position and inviting into its midst the representatives of the more influential socialist parties united in various organzations.

Three Trends

Analyzing the political frame of mind which all these events have created among the public, one can note in it three main trends, which differ from one another by their attitude toward the revolution. One of them, under the influence of fright or because of encroachments on all established habits and views, would like to turn the revolution back toward its point of departure. This is the counterrevolutionary trend. At first it was silent; its partisans could not find any support and not the slightest sympathy around them. We should not conceal from ourselves that the errors of the revolution give to this trend a broader basis and the hope of getting stronger in the future. However, up to now the forces of counterrevolution cannot be considered to any extent important or organized.

One can observe two different trends in the attitude toward the revolution of all the other public groups besides those counterrevolutionary ones. One of them stands for the preservation and the consolidation of the colossal achievements, both political and social, which the revolution has achieved. With regard to these achievements, this trend is conservative because it stands for their preservation. On this point of view the Provisional Government has to stand, since it has sworn to preserve the conquests of the revolution until the convening of the Constituent Assembly. One can be certain that the huge majority of the reasonably inclined population of the country also stands for it. But this majority is not organized. It manifests itself only in moments of extreme danger to public order and authority, as happened during the events of April 21–22. It expresses its feelings through greetings, telegrams, resolutions. Lately it has started to organize itself mainly around the Party of the People's Freedom. But the process of this organization is not sufficiently rapid to keep up with the demands of the times. The means of propaganda and of agitation, without which any influence on the masses is impossible, are not adapted as yet to the newly created conditions, and their application is an unaccustomed novelty for the party which until now did not have access to the masses, carefully guarded by the old regime against any contact with or influence from the outside. Now the situation has changed, and we witness a fresh flow of forces in the work of spreading sound, statesmanlike notions among the new Russian citizens. But it should be recognized that the old conspirators, who have applied their experience under the new conditions which are extremely favorable for them, are more experienced in the matter of organizing the masses.

Thus a third trend acts and even dominates on the surface of public life. In contrast with the former one, which considers the revolution completed, this trend sharply proclaims the slogan *Let the revolution continue.* As the revolution continues, the creative forces which organize the substance of the results achieved by the revolution become forces of counterrevolution. As a matter of fact, what is the purpose of continuing the revolution?

. . .

In the immediate future, the further course of the destinies of the Russian revolution depends on whether the statesmanlike elements of socialism succeed in organizing around them a majority against the extreme standpoint of socialist utopianism. But one must say that, in order to win, they themselves are compelled to make considerable concessions, if not to the world outlook of their allies, [at least] to the practical requirements deriving from it.

The Position of the Party of the People's Freedom

Such, in very general terms, is the analysis of the situation which has now been created. Then, what should be the place among these three trends, the counterrevolutionary, the creative, and the destructive, in the sense of a further continuation of the revolution; what place should belong to the Party of the People's Freedom? This place, as in 1905, is in the middle. Our place in the struggle of political trends may be called the position of the left center, because in any case we are closer to the groups standing to our left than to those which are [now] completely disorganized, which have disappeared from the field of political struggle, but which in one way or another will get organized and will stand to our right. The Party of the People's Freedom has with full conviction accepted the achievements of the revolution; in the accomplishment of these achievements it played a very important role, and they have allowed it to put forward once again on a broad scale those democratic aims with which it started its political existence in the First State Duma. . . .

.   .   .

1111. NEKRASOV'S SPEECH BEFORE THE CONGRESS
[*Rech'*, No. 108, May 10, 1917, pp. 3–4.]

.   .   .

I acknowledge the classification into three groups, or, more precisely, into three important basic trends, which was given today by P. N. Miliukov; they are, as he has defined them, the counterrevolutionary, the creative, and the destructive trends. I am ready to accept this terminology, and will say frankly: I like its conciseness, its extraordinary precision and accuracy. It outlines the boundaries with such extraordinary sharpness that it leaves no place for misunderstandings. But I regret that I must disagree with P. N. Miliukov. . . .

The Governmental Crisis

Passing to the characteristic of the governmental crisis which has just taken place, N. V. Nekrasov said: I will ask, To whom did the Provisional Government address itself when it appealed for reinforcement; did it appeal to the destroyers or to the creators? You will find the answer to this question in the declaration itself; you will find in it an appeal to the live, creative forces of the country. It means that we addressed ourselves not to the destructive but to the constructive force. And these forces actually did come.

P. N. Miliukov tells us that the destructive trend is that which considers that the revolution continues. When P. N. Miliukov said these words, I thought that I misheard, because who could argue against an evident historical fact. I establish another boundary between the creators and the destroyers. This boundary is where the feeling of national responsibility ends, where people are essentially irresponsible or are ready to take upon themselves the responsibility, not for the destinies of the country, but for the fate of some undefined collective [bodies], of a nonexistent International. I see this boundary there where, instead of national order being promoted, there is the principle of anarchy and impotence; where, instead of the idea of national justice, there is placed the idea of demagogic class interests. But among those who came to us, there are none separated from us by this boundary.

.   .   .

Foreign Policy

During the negotiations for the formation of the coalition cabinet, unity with our Allies was considered, not in a formal sense, not in the sense of preserving and consolidating pacts which may some day be put into effect provided the actual state of things permits it, [for] on the other hand, they might not be put into effect by mutual agreement, without any separate peace or infringement of the confidence which exists between us and the Allies, simply because the actual state of affairs and the practical conditions would not correspond to the conditions under which the agreements had been concluded. I ask myself, as I ask you, what is more precious for us and for our Allies—these pacts whose realization is problematic or that fighting unity which alone can give us a real chance to save the order and dignity of Russia?

The decisive [factor] for me was what I heard from the delegates of the army, among whom was also our party comrade, a man decorated with all the crosses of St. George, who went to the war as a volunteer. And these people told us: If you wish for the army to go and fight, if you want from it its former discipline and its former unity, then give it those war aims which it will be able to understand, which it will be able to see before itself, and which it can really be able to defend, and remember that it is impossible to press on the shoulders of the army, which has already been fighting for three years on the front, a goal which will not be shared by that army. This is the reason that compels me to put to you bluntly the question of our dissent in matters of foreign policy. The unfortunate part of this dissent lies in the fact that there is a constant tendency to clothe it in nebulous forms.

The Declaration of the [Central] Committee

. . .

I want to warn you against a resolution which would be indefinite and unclear. Into the proposed resolution I could introduce all my views on foreign policy and at the same time these views would not correspond to those of P. N. Miliukov. I cannot conceal this and I prefer to say it frankly to all my party comrades. I will ask only one thing: Whatever the decision of the Congress on this matter, let this decision be definite and clear. I am not afraid of putting the issue bluntly, since our Allies, in spite of ominous prophecies, did not back away from the formula proclaimed by the Provisional Government, but took the completely correct way of interpreting it, of [trying to] understand it, and of clarifying some of its controversial points. . . .

. . .

Attitude Toward the Government

Along with striving for an early convocation of the Constituent Assembly, it is essential to specify as early as possible a precise slogan with regard to our attitude toward the Provisional Government. We have protested for a long time against conditional slogans and the formula "in so far as." In the meantime, the resolution which is being proposed to you today by the Central Committee contains such a condition. It is to be found in the concluding words stating that support to the new Provisional Government is promised "in all its initiatives directed to the accomplishment of the goals indicated." Well, it is the same thing as the statements made by the Soviet of Workers' and Soldiers' Deputies in its time. Do not repeat the mistake made by our comrades on the left and do not make your resolution of approval conditional; do not compel us to speculate constantly as to whether we possess those crumbs of confidence without which existence becomes impossible. If there is no confidence, then say it directly. I call upon you to carry out in action what you have demanded and what you have obtained from the Soviet of Workers' and Soldiers' Deputies.

There it is stated: As long as these representatives consider it possible to remain in the Provisional Government, the Government enjoys absolute confidence. State the same thing: Either complete confidence, or that you do not trust us, then recall us. (*Applause.*)

. . .

1112. RESOLUTION OF THE CONGRESS ON THE POLITICAL SITUATION
[*Rech'*, No. 108, May 10, 1917, p. 5.]

On the proposal of the Central Committee, the resolution regarding the general political situation was unanimously approved in the following wording:

"The second period of the revolutionary struggle which was marked by vivid manifestations of dual power, bringing to actual impotence the power of the Provisional Government in the problems of fighting anarchy and the weakening of the army's fighting capacities, ended by the invitation into the membership of the Government of the representatives of the Menshevik group of the S.D., of the S.R., and of the Popular Socialists.

"Having agreed to the idea of such a change in the membership of the Government, the Party of the People's Freedom, in the face of the danger threatening the homeland, owing to the disintegration of the army at the front and to the anarchy within the country, has deemed it its duty, while overcoming inner doubts caused by the painful experiences of the last days, to remain at its post and not to recall its representatives from the cabinet.

"Being the guardian of the principle of statesmanship, without the consolidation of which the liberty conquered by the nation is threatened by unavoidable ruin; convinced that its participation in the Government would be the surest way to preserve the country from counterrevolution; expecting that the participation within the Government of groups more to the left, which are now responsible for the direction of national life, will bring to the Government force and stability and will eliminate the fatal element of dual power both at the front and in the country; welcoming the declaration of the Provisional Government regarding the necessity of offensive operations at the front and regarding its unswerving faithfulness to our allies; the Party of the People's Freedom will render full support to the new Provisional Government in all its initiatives directed toward the accomplishment of the goals indicated."

THE RESIGNATION OF KONOVALOV[1]

1113. *Russkiia Vedomosti* ON KONOVALOV'S RESIGNATION
[No. 113, May 21, 1917, p. 3.]

The resignation of A. I. Konovalov greatly resembles the resignation of A. I. Guchkov. The former War Minister, having reached the conclusion that the de-

---

[1] For the reasons for Konovalov's resignation, namely, his dissatisfaction with prevailing policies in the sphere of trade and industry and his suggestion that under the circumstances the Government should perhaps be replaced by one composed entirely of socialists, see Volume II, Docs. 580 and 581.

fense of the country cannot be guaranteed in the absence of a strong government, decided to undertake a guerrilla action, and by resigning he speeded up the formation of a new revolutionary government. Now, the Minister of Trade and Industry, too, declares that the measures for coping with the impending industrial crisis, which are being planned by the new Government, will not be successful until the Government is in a position to exercise full authority, and until it is able to restore the governmental and public order which is now being disrupted daily. And the extremes meet: A. I. Konovalov, like *Pravda*, thinks that the Russian revolution has to pass a new stage by creating a homogeneous socialist government.

The individual decision of A. I. Guchkov, who elected such an unusual way for the solution of the question concerning the crisis of governmental power, was justly regarded as a guerrilla action. But the resignation of A. I. Konovalov, in connection with his political testament regarding the formation of a homogeneous socialist government, may arouse still greater perplexity. By means of this testament, A. I. Konovalov does a very doubtful service both to the Provisional Government and to those socialists who have to endure an attack from irresponsible anarchical groups which in vain try to cover their anarchism by a banner of socialism. Both the socialist ministers and the authoritative working-class organizations have declared more than once that they do not consider it possible at present to undertake the step that is being recommended by A. I. Konovalov. They do not consider it possible because, in present-day Russia, the objective conditions for going over to the socialist methods of production are lacking. The only persons who can dream of this are the ones who confuse socialism with anarchy, and the socialization of production with the collapse of the economic organism.

Our time, which is the time of a severe test of the economic stability of the new order, advances entirely different tasks.

These tasks are difficult, and perhaps not entirely achievable, but they lie not at all in the realm of unbridled and untimely social experiments: they call for the drawing of all classes toward a public and governmental solution of the economic problem.

But, while the political testament of A. I. Konovalov regarding the formation of a homogeneous socialist government must be categorically rejected, we must not forget at the same time that this declaration, coming from A. I. Konovalov, one of the most influential representatives of our industry, is extremely significant. The very possibility of such a declaration shows how serious and grave is the ailment which eats through our whole social and economic organism.

· · ·

1114. *Rabochaia Gazeta* ON KONOVALOV'S RESIGNATION
[No. 62, May 21, 1917, p. 1.]

Konovalov has left. This means that the "Italian strike" of the upper bourgeoisie, which has for some time been the news of the day in the country, has penetrated into the very center of our public life, into the ranks of the Government. In answer to the anarchical designs of the workers to seize factories and mills, some capitalists politely reply: "Help yourselves!" In answer to the criminal campaign of Leninists, Trotskyists, and other irresponsible demagogues who preach seizure of power, the bourgeoisie as a whole, using Konovalov as its mouthpiece, declares: "Help yourselves!" We must achieve *the next stage in the revolution,* says Konovalov, *and arrive at a homogeneous, that is, socialist ministry.*

Thus Konovalov and Lenin wish for one and the same thing: lockouts, unemployment, famine, civil war; they wish the *destruction of the revolution.* On the ruins of our freedom the bourgeoisie plans to establish its own "strong power," to return with interest all the lost positions. What the Leninists are after and what they are working for we do not know. But we do know one thing, and we must exert superhuman efforts so that the entire democracy understands it; namely, what is profitable to the egotistic group interests of the upper bourgeoisie might be profitable to the Leninists also, but it is not profitable to the proletariat, it is not profitable to the *revolutionary democracy as a whole.*

We must admit that the class-conscious vanguard of the working class is to a considerable degree responsible for the weakness shown by the new Government during the first weeks of its existence, for the absence of civic courage in some of its members, so strikingly demonstrated by the withdrawal of Konovalov. If Konovalov lacked the revolutionary patriotism and revolutionary courage to speak vigorously and with all the authority of an acknowledged leader of large-scale industrialists *against* their excessive appetites, what then did the democracy and its organs do up to this time to back the Government against the abuse and disorganization on the left? What has been done to combat the elemental breakdown of the national economy and of all public life encouraged by the corrupt preaching of *Pravda*? Nothing or practically nothing!

But while it is still not too late, as long as the process of destruction has not gone too far and the work of Leninists of all sorts and trends has not as yet prepared the counterrevolution so passionately craved for by our pillars of home industry and the entire concealed Black Hundreds, the proletariat will not heed the provocations of *Pravda*; it will not be seduced by the attractive offer of Konovalov to achieve the "next stage of the revolution and arrive at a . . . socialist ministry."

KRONSTADT[2]

1115. THE PETROGRAD SOVIET'S RESOLUTION ON THE KRONSTADT DECLARATION

[Izvestiia, No. 76, May 27, 1917, pp. 4–5.]

Having familiarized itself with the events in Kronstadt and all the resolutions

---

[2] From the beginning of the revolution, Kronstadt, the island naval fortress off Petrograd, was a center of extremism. During the February Days, the aroused sailors murdered the Commanding Officer, Admiral Viren, and some other unpopular officers, and incarcerated still others in the island dungeons. Subsequently, a measure of order was restored by the Government and delegates from the Soviet, but the situation remained uneasy, and many of the prisoners continued to be held in close and difficult confinement, despite the efforts of the Minister of Justice to review the validity of the charges against them. *Izvestiia,* No. 17, March 17, 1917, p. 4; *VVP,* No. 24, April 6, 1917, p. 2. Then, on May 16, the Kronstadt Soviet declared that it exercised the sole authority in the fortress, and thus precipitated the episode documented below.

of the Kronstadt Soviet of Workers' and Soldiers' Deputies, the general meeting of the Petrograd Soviet of Workers' and Soldiers' Deputies resolves [that]:

1) The refusal of the Kronstadt Soviet of Workers' and Soldiers' Deputies to recognize the authority of the Provisional Government signifies a rupture with the revolutionary democracy which has sent its representatives into the Government, expressed full confidence in it, and recognized its full power.

2) Such an act on the part of the Kronstadt Soviet of Workers' and Soldiers' Deputies represents a blow to the cause of the revolution and leads to its downfall, while the conflicting decisions [of the Kronstadt Soviet of Workers' and Soldiers' Deputies] testify to its complete inability to resist the anarchical elements which they themselves have encouraged in the past.

3) The incarceration of hundreds [of people] in the worst tsarist dungeons without bringing definite charges [against these persons] and without bringing them to a fair trial is an act of unworthy revenge and reprisal and is a disgrace to the revolution.

Stating that disorganizing acts, which pave the way for a counterrevolution, which contradict the will of the whole revolutionary democracy, and which signify a defection from Russia, became possible only because Kronstadt, being a fortress abounding in wealth, is supplied with food and all the necessities and is, therefore, relieved of the worries and anxieties which beset all Russia; expressing its firm belief that the vast majority of the Kronstadt population, which is loyal to the revolution, will be able to assist arm in arm with the rest of revolutionary Russia in consolidating the strong revolutionary power in the country, the Petrograd Soviet of Workers' and Soldiers' Deputies resolves:

1) To demand that all residents of Kronstadt immediately and unquestioningly execute all the orders which the Provisional Government may deem necessary to issue in the interests of the external security of the revolution.

2) To transmit the present resolution by telegraph to all Kronstadt forts, all fortress and naval commands of the Baltic Fleet, and, also, to all Soviets of Workers' and Soldiers' Deputies.

1116. CONCESSIONS BY THE KRONSTADT SOVIET

[*Izvestiia*, No. 75, May 26, 1917, p. 3. A delegation, composed of the socialist ministers Tseretelli and Skobelev, was sent to Kronstadt, with the approval of the Executive Committee of the Petrograd Soviet, to investigate and, if possible, find a solution to the situation that had developed.]

At the meeting of the Kronstadt Soviet of Workers' and Soldiers' Deputies which I. G. Tseretelli attended, the following resolutions were adopted, in addition to the resolutions transmitted to us yesterday:

All army and navy commanding officers are to follow orders from the Supreme Command. The relationship between the local commanding staff and the organizations of control connected with it is to remain the same.

[The vote was] 213 for, 9 against, 14 abstentions.

On the question of the necessity of immediately introducing democratic organs of local self-government and legal institutions on a basis that is common to all Russia, the Kronstadt Soviet of Workers' and Soldiers' Deputies declares that these laws, being laws for the whole state, cannot be met with resistance on its part.

[The vote was] 203 for, 7 against, 18 abstentions.

On the question of arrested officers, the Soviet of Workers' and Soldiers' Deputies declares that it will lend its assistance to the investigating commission, which is appointed by the Supreme Court. Representatives of the local investigating commission from the Soviet of Workers' and Soldiers' Deputies of the town of Kronstadt will work conjointly with it and will conduct preliminary investigations in Kronstadt providing that those persons whom the commission brings to trial are sent to Petrograd for the trial and that all the representatives of the detachment concerned [in the case] will be summoned from Kronstadt for the trial. Persons who, during the course of the investigations, are found not guilty, will be released in Kronstadt by the designated investigating commission, which fact will be brought to the knowledge of the Executive Committee of the Soviet of Workers' and Soldiers' Deputies and all units of the garrison.

[The vote was] 160 for, 57 against, 16 abstentions.

In view of false reports circulated by certain organs of the press to the effect that arrested officers find themselves under exceptionally oppressive conditions and are being subjected to torture with [resulting] cases of death, the Soviet invites representatives of parties, public organizations, and the press to visit the prisoners and by a personal inspection become convinced of the groundlessness of such rumors. The Executive Committee issues visiting permits without delay at any time, except on holidays. The visitors should carry credentials from a political party or public organization or from the press.

> LAMANOV, Chairman of the Executive Committee
> of the [Kronstadt] Soviet of Workers' and
> Soldiers' Deputies
> PRISELKOV, Secretary

1117. THE RESOLUTION OF THE KRONSTADT EPISODE

[*VVP*, No. 64, May 27, 1917, p. 1. The Soviet Executive Committee also approved this solution at its session of May 25. *Protokoly*, pp. 163, 165.]

Having heard the report of I. G. Tseretelli and M. I. Skobelev on their trip to Kronstadt of May 23–24 as representatives of the Provisional Government and having approved their actions, the Provisional Government has decreed:

1) To permit the Kronstadt Soviet of Workers' and Soldiers' Deputies to nominate a candidate for the office of representative of the Provisional Government for civilian affairs in Kronstadt.

2) To proceed to hold elections of municipal duma members in Kronstadt on the basis of the Provisional Government's law of April 15, 1917, . . .[3]

3) To instruct the Minister of Justice to immediately form an investigating commission consisting of six persons from the justice department, the barristers, and the Executive Committee of the Petrograd Soviet of Workers' and Soldiers' Deputies. To request this commission to include representatives of the investigating commission of the Kronstadt Soviet of Soldiers' and Workers' Deputies in its membership and to proceed to the investigation of cases of persons arrested in Kronstadt. Those persons whom the commission will bring to trial are to be sent under guard to Petrograd and representatives of the detachment concerned

[3] Volume I, Doc. 240.

are to be summoned from Kronstadt for the trial. Those persons, however, against whom there will appear to be insufficient grounds in the process of the investigation for bringing them to trial are to be released from custody, which fact is to be made known to the Executive Committee of the Soviet of Workers' and Soldiers' Deputies and to all units of the garrison.

PRINCE L'VOV, Minister-President

May 24, 1917

MUNICIPAL DUMA ELECTIONS

1118. *Izvestiia* ON THE PETROGRAD MUNICIPAL DISTRICT DUMA ELECTIONS

[No. 80, June 1, 1917, p. 2. The bloc won over half the vote, receiving in ten districts 376,813 votes to the Kadets' 171,400 and the Bolsheviks' 159,500. In the two districts, where the Mensheviks and Socialist Revolutionaries ran separately, the S.R.'s received 16,729 and 43,465 to the Mensheviks' 19,045 and 7,144. In the later elections, on August 20, to the Municipal Duma—which, unlike Moscow, came after the district elections—the S.R.'s received 205,666 votes and the Mensheviks 23,552 to the Bolsheviks' 183,694 and the Kadets' 114,485 and a sprinkling of votes for smaller parties. The total vote in May was approximately 792,865 and in August, 549,379, indicating the prevalence of absenteeism in the later election, a fact widely commented upon in the press. See, for example, *Rabochaia Gazeta*, No. 140, August 23, 1917, p. 1. In both elections the tabulations were incomplete. See Radkey, *The Agrarian Foes of Bolshevism*, pp. 242, 363–65.]

The elections to the [municipal] district dumas have ended.

The list of candidates of the socialist bloc—the Mensheviks of the Social Democrats and the Socialist Revolutionaries—gained a complete victory in all the districts. The Socialist Revolutionaries received the majority [of votes] in the Vasili Ostrovskii district.

Second place, after the bloc of Socialist parties, was taken by the Kadets, and finally, in third place stood the Bolsheviks.

Such are the election results. What do they signify?

First of all, the elections showed that an enormous section of the democracy in Petrograd supports the socialist parties, which uphold the platform of the Soviet of Workers' and Soldiers' Deputies. Soldiers and workers of Petrograd have given a clear and definite expression of their attitude toward the revolution. They did not cast their votes for either the open or veiled reactionaries, nor for those groups within the working class that are systematically fighting the Soviet of Workers' and Soldiers' Deputies and its aspirations to create a single, strong revolutionary power in the country.

The majority of [votes] received by the socialist parties, which uphold the platform of the Soviet, represents an act of political confidence in the policy of the Soviet and an act of decisive condemnation of all the enemies of the Soviet who are undermining it from the right and the left.

Ignoring all the contrivances of the gentlemen Kadets, who imagine themselves to be the only representatives of true statesmanship and who are, in reality, servants of the reactionary and imperialist bourgeoisie; and ignoring the violent agitation of Leninists, who are pushing the Soviet into the path of a coup d' état which would be disastrous to the revolution and who by their actions are paving the way for the growth of anarchy, the Petrograd workers and soldiers cast their votes for the socialist parties that constitute the majority in the Soviet.

Once again the policy of the Soviet gained a decisive victory, an indisputable victory, since this was the first time during the whole period of the revolution that workers and soldiers were able to express their understanding of the problems of the revolution in a properly organized manner.

· · ·

All the congresses of front [organizations], almost all the oblast and raion conferences of the Soviets of Workers' and Soldiers' Deputies, the majority of the Moscow and provincial Soviets, and finally, the election results in district dumas— all these give the same answer on all current issues as does the Petrograd Soviet.

This shows the high degree of political awareness of the Russian democracy and the degree to which the *Pravda* adherents are ineffectual in their attempts to change the course of the Russian revolution.

1119. *Russkiia Vedomosti* ON THE MOSCOW MUNICIPAL DUMA ELECTIONS
[No. 144, June 27, 1917, p. 3. The S.R.'s received 58 per cent of the vote, or 374,885; the Kadets 16.85 per cent, or 108,781; the Mensheviks 11.82 per cent, or 76,407; the Bolsheviks 11.66 per cent, or 75,409; with 1.67 per cent, or 11,086, going to smaller parties. Radkey, *The Agrarian Foes of Bolshevism*, pp. 240–42. *Rech'*, No. 152, July 1, 1917, p. 5 attributed the Kadet failure in their traditional stronghold to their insufficient propaganda activities and to S.R. demagogy.]

The Moscow city elections are of utmost interest, going far beyond the confines of Moscow. Because of their very nature, conditioned by the extraordinary times we are living through, the elections of the members of the Moscow municipal Duma have assumed the importance of an all-Russian political event. These elections were the rehearsal of the elections to the Constituent Assembly, the indicator of the relationship of forces of political parties in that capital city[4] which is the center of public life of the country. That particular significance of the elections puts in the background the municipal nature of the elections of June 25 and their significance for the city economy of Moscow.

The results of the Moscow elections per se, and, in particular, the huge victory in these elections of the Socialist Revolutionary Party, are conditioned by circumstances, the roots of which lie far beyond the limits of Moscow. The Moscow elections have demonstrated once more how strong is the connection between the population of our large urban centers and that of the village, how deeply the thought of land permeates the mass of the urban population of the capital. The cry about the land, and not at all the municipal program of the Socialist Revolutionary Party, caused the success of the latter at the city elections in Moscow. The Russian peasant, while residing in Moscow, has not lost the pull of the land; he did not become a Western urbanite; in his heart he still remains the tiller of the land, always thinking his sacred thoughts of the land. If anyone needed visual

[4] The official capital of Russia at that time was still Petrograd. Moscow was the "second" capital.

proof of the potency of the agrarian question in Russia, it was furnished by the Moscow elections of June 25. At the city ballot boxes a struggle was waged, inspired not by the thought of municipal affairs but by the thought of the land, somewhere out there, far beyond Moscow—in the Orel, Kursk, or Saratov province. . . .

The Moscow elections also demonstrated that the extreme current which is known under the name of bolshevism has no popularity among the masses of the population of urban centers. The feeble showing of ticket No. 5 was a pleasant indication of that fact.

The model order which accompanied the Moscow elections—the first elections conducted on the basis of direct, universal, equal, and secret ballot—testifies to the people's ability to use the newly acquired civil right calmly and reasonably.

1120. MUNICIPAL DUMA ELECTIONS IN OTHER CITIES OF RUSSIA

[*VVP*, No. 124, August 6, 1917, p. 2. See also Radkey, *The Agrarian Foes of Bolshevism*, pp. 243–44.]

According to information received by the Ministry of the Interior from various localities, elections of members to municipal dumas were conducted in 276 cities; elections are scheduled in 278 cities, and electoral lists are prepared in 153 cities.

In guberniya capitals 1,626 members of the municipal duma have already been elected; among them are 105 Mensheviks, 112 Bolsheviks, 299 Socialist Revolutionaries, 626 from the bloc of socialists, 232 from the Party of the People's Freedom, 61 from national groups, and 191 nonparty candidates.

In uezd capitals and small cities 5,679 members of the duma were elected, composed of 338 Mensheviks, 70 Bolsheviks, 426 Socialist Revolutionaries, 1,360 from the bloc of socialists, 307 from the Party of the People's Freedom, 327 from national groups, and 2,851 nonparty candidates.

By per cent the municipal elections gave the following results: a) in guberniya capitals 38.5 per cent were elected from the bloc of socialists, 18.3 per cent Socialist Revolutionaries, 14.3 per cent Party of the People's Freedom, 12 per cent nonparty, 6.8 per cent Bolsheviks, 6.4 per cent Mensheviks, and 3.7 per cent nationalists; b) in uezd capitals and small cities the municipal dumas elected 50.2 per cent nonparty candidates, 23.9 per cent from the bloc of socialists, 7.5 per cent Socialist-Revolutionaries, 6 per cent Mensheviks, 5.7 per cent from national groups, 5.5 per cent from the Party of the People's Freedom, and 1.2 per cent Bolsheviks.

THE FIRST ALL-RUSSIAN CONGRESS OF SOVIETS OF WORKERS' AND SOLDIERS' DEPUTIES AND THE JUNE DEMONSTRATIONS

1121. EXCERPT FROM TSERETELLI'S SPEECH TO THE CONGRESS, JUNE 3

[*Izvestiia*, No. 84, June 6, 1917, pp. 6–9, as translated in Golder, pp. 361–63.]

· · ·

At the present moment, there is not a political party in Russia which would say: Hand the power over to us, resign, and we will take your place. Such a party does not exist in Russia. (Lenin: "It does exist.") . . . They [the Bolsheviks] say: When we have a majority, or when the majority comes over to our point of view, then the power should be seized, Comrade Lenin, you said that. At least the Bolsheviks and you with them say it in their official statements.

Gentlemen, until now, there has not been a single party in Russia which has come out openly for getting for itself all power at once, although there have been such cries by irresponsible groups on the Right and the Left. . . . The Right says, let the Left run the Government, and we and the country will draw our conclusions; and the Left says, let Right take hold, and we and the country will draw our conclusions. . . . Each side hopes that the other will make such a failure, that the country will turn to it for leadership.

But, gentlemen, this is not the time for that kind of a play. . . . In order to solve the problems of the country, we must unite our strength and must have a strong Government . . . strong enough to put an end to experiments dangerous for the fate of the revolution, . . . experiments that may lead to civil war. . . .

This, gentlemen, is our policy. . . .

1122. EXCERPT FROM LENIN'S SPEECH TO THE CONGRESS, JUNE 4

[*Pravda*, Nos. 82, 83, June 15, 16, 1917, as translated in the *Collected Works of V. I. Lenin: The Revolution of 1917*, XX, Bk. II, pp. 195–205. Significantly, the Workers' Section of the Petrograd Soviet voted, on May 31, for a resolution supporting the Bolshevik formula of "all power to the Soviets." Avdeev, II, 241–42.]

Comrades! In the short time allotted to me, I am able—and I deem it more advisable—to dwell only on those questions of fundamental principle that have been brought up by the speaker from the Executive Committee and by the speakers that followed him.

The first fundamental question we have been confronted with is this: *Where are we?* What are these Soviets that have assembled here in an All-Russian Congress? . . .

. . . The Soviets are an institution that does not and cannot exist within, or alongside of, the ordinary bourgeois-parliamentary state. . . .

It is one thing or the other: either we have an ordinary bourgeois government —then there is no need for peasants', workers', soldiers', or any other kind of Soviets, then they will be dispersed by the generals, the counter-revolutionary generals, who control the army, paying no heed whatever to Minister Kerensky's oratory, then they will die an ignominious death otherwise—or we have a real government of the Soviets. There is no other way open for these institutions; they can neither go backward nor remain in the same place if they are to live; they can only exist going forward. Here is a type of state not of the Russians' invention but created by the revolution itself which could not be victorious in any other way. Friction, party struggle for power within the All-Russian Soviet are inevitable. But that will mean that the masses themselves are overcoming possible errors and illusions through their own political experience (*noise*) and not through reports by Ministers who quote what they said yesterday, what they are going to write to-morrow and what they are going to promise the day after to-morrow. This, comrades, is ridiculous, if one looks at things from the point of view of this institution which sprang from the revolution itself and is now facing the question: to be or not to be. The Soviets cannot continue to exist as they exist now. Adult people, workers and peasants, must come together, pass resolutions, listen to reports, without being able to verify them by studying the original documents! Institutions of this kind are a transition to a republic which, in deeds, not in words, will establish a firm power without police, without a standing army—the kind of power that cannot as yet exist in Europe, that is, however, indispensable for a victory of the Russian Revolution if we mean by it a victory over the landowners, a victory over imperialism.

. . .

If you wish to refer to *"revolutionary"* democracy, then please differentiate between this conception and that of *reformist* democracy under a capitalist cabinet, for it is high time we passed from phrases about "revolutionary democracy," from mutual congratulations upon "revolutionary democracy," to a class characterisation as taught by Marxism and scientific Socialism in general. What we are offered is a reformist democracy under a capitalist cabinet. This may be excellent from the point of view of the ordinary patterns of Western Europe. Now, however, a number of countries are on the verge of ruin, and those practical measures, which, according to the preceding orator, citizen-Minister of Posts and Telegraphs, are so complicated that it is difficult to introduce them, that they need special study—those measures are perfectly clear. He said that there is no political party in Russia that would express willingness to take all state power into its hands. I say: "Such a party exists! No party has a right to refuse power, and our party does not refuse it. Our party is ready at any moment to take all power into its hands." (*Applause, laughter.*)

You may laugh, but if the citizen-Minister confronts us with this question side by side with a party of the Right, he will receive the proper reply. No party has a right to refuse power. At the present time while we still have freedom, while the threats of arrest and Siberian exile, made by the counter-revolutionists with whom our near-Socialist Ministers sit in one cabinet, are only threats as yet—at this moment each party should say: give us your confidence, and we shall give you our programme.

. . .

That the revolutionary struggle for peace begun from below may lead to a separate peace is sheer calumny. Our first step, were we in power, would be to arrest the biggest capitalists, to sever all the threads of their intrigues. Unless this is done, all talk about peace without annexations and indemnities is sheer piffle. Our second step would be to address ourselves to all peoples, over the heads of their governments, and to tell them that we consider all capitalists as robbers: both Tereshchenko (who is not a whit better than Miliukov, only a little more foolish) and the capitalists of France, England, and all other countries.

Your own *Izvestia* is off the track, for instead of peace without annexations and indemnities it proposes the *status quo*. No, it is not thus that we understand peace "without annexations." Much nearer the truth in this respect is the Peasant Congress, which speaks of a "federated" republic, thereby expressing the idea that the Russian republic does not wish to oppress any people either in the old or in the new way, that it does not wish to live on a basis of violence either with our own people, or with Finland, or with the Ukraine, with which countries our War Minister quarrels for no reason, creating inadmissible and unforgivable conflicts. We want a single indivisible Russian republic, with a firm government, but firm government can be achieved only through the consent of the peoples. "Revolutionary democracy" are big words, but we are applying them to a government which by petty annoyances is complicating the situation with the Ukraine and Finland, who do not even wish to break away, who merely say: "Do not postpone the application of the ABC of democracy until the Constituent Assembly!"

Peace without annexations and indemnities cannot be concluded unless you yourselves renounce your own annexations. This is simply ridiculous, it is a joke! The workers of Europe laugh at it, they say: "In words they are eloquent, they call upon the nations to overthrow the bankers, but they themselves put their native bankers into the cabinet." Arrest them, expose their tricks, uncover their machinations! You do not do this, although you have the organisations of power which cannot be resisted. You have lived through the years of 1905 and 1917, you know that a revolution is not made to order, that revolutions in other countries have proceeded along the hard and bloody road of insurrection, while in Russia there is no such group, there is no such class that could offer resistance to the authority of the Soviets. In Russia this revolution is possible, by way of exception, as a peaceful revolution. Let our revolution offer this day peace to all the peoples by way of a breach with all the capitalist classes, and within the shortest time we would receive the consent of the peoples of Germany, as well as of France, because these countries are perishing, . . .

. . .

When we seize power we shall curb the capitalists, then the war will be entirely *different* from the one now waged—for the nature of a war is determined by the class that conducts it, and not by what is written on scraps of paper. Anything can be written on scraps of paper. But as long as the capitalist class has a majority in the government, the war will remain an imperialist war, no matter what you write, no matter how eloquent you are, no matter how many near-Socialist Ministers you may have. . . . When the revolution started in Russia, the revolutionary struggle for peace started from below. Were you to take power into your hands, were the revolutionary organisations to seize power for the purpose of waging a struggle upon the Russian capitalists, then the toilers of the other countries would trust you, then you would be able to offer peace. Then our peace would be secure, at least on two flanks, with respect to two peoples, Germany and France, both of which are bleeding to death and are in desperate straits. Should conditions have forced us then into a revolutionary war—nobody knows whether it would be so, nor do we forswear it—our answer would be: "We are no pacifists, we do not refuse to wage war once the revolutionary class is at the helm, once it has actually removed the capitalists from having any influence on the situation, once they cannot aggravate economic ruin which allowed them to make hundreds of millions in profits." The revolutionary power would then proclaim to all the peoples of the world the right of every people to be free; it would make clear that just as the German people has no right to wage war in order to retain Alsace-Lorraine so has the French people no right to wage war in order to retain its colonies. For if France fights for its colonies, then Russia has Khiva and Bokhara, also something in the nature of colonies, and the distribution of colonies begins. But how distribute them? According to what norm? Power. But power has changed; the capitalists find themselves in a situation where they have no way out except war. When you seize revolutionary power, you will have a revolutionary road to peace: you will turn to the peoples with a revolutionary appeal, you will make your tactics understood by your example. By following the revolutionary method of achieving peace, you will forestall the destruction of hundreds of thousands of human lives. Then, you may rest assured that the German and the French people will back you up. And the English, American, and Japanese capitalists, even if they wanted to wage war upon the revolutionary working class which, with the capitalists curbed and removed and with the reins of government in its own hands, would grow ten times as strong—even if the American, English and Japanese capitalists wanted war, there are ninety-nine chances in a hundred that they could not do it. All you would have to do is declare that you were no pacifists, and that you intended to defend your republic, your workingmen's proletarian democracy, against the onslaughts of the German, French, and other capitalists—and this would suffice to make your peace secure.

This is why we consider our declaration on the offensive to be of fundamental significance. The time for a break in the entire history of the Russian Revolution has come. The Russian Revolution began with the aid of the English imperialist bourgeoisie, the latter having thought that Russia was something like China or India. What happened, however, was that by the side of the government composed of a majority of landowners and capitalists there sprang up the Soviets, an unusual representative institution of unprecedented strength which you are now destroying by your participation in the coalition cabinet of the bourgeoisie. What happened, however, was that, in all countries, revolutionary struggle from below against the capitalist governments began to meet with much greater sympathy. To go ahead, or to retreat? this is the question. In times of revolution it is impossible to remain in one place. This is why the offensive is a break in the entire Russian Revolution, not in the strategic meaning of the offensive, but in its political and economic meaning. Objectively, irrespective of the will and consciousness of one particular Minister, an offensive now means the continuation of the imperialist slaughter for the sake of crushing Persia and other weak peoples. The passing of power to the revolutionary proletariat supported by the poorest peasants means passing to as safe and painless a form of revolutionary struggle for peace as the world has ever known, passing to a situation where the power and the victory of the revolutionary workers will be made secure in Russia and throughout the whole world. (*Applause from a part of the audience.*)

1123. EXCERPTS FROM KERENSKY'S SPEECH TO THE CONGRESS, JUNE 4

[*Izvestiia*, No. 85, June 7, 1917, pp. 3–4. The principal part of Kerensky's speech dealt with the situation on the front, the activity of the Germans, and the necessity to reactivate the army.]

Comrades:

You have been told of 1792 and of 1905. How did 1792 end in France? It ended in the fall of the republic and the rise of a dictator. How did 1905 end? With the triumph of reaction. And now, in 1917, we are doing that which we could have done earlier. The problem of the Russian socialist parties and of the Russian democracy is to prevent such an end as was in France—to hold on to the revolutionary conquests already made; to see to it that our comrades who have been released from prison do not return there; that Comrade Lenin, who has been abroad, may have the opportunity to speak here again, and not be obliged to flee back to Switzerland. (*Applause.*)

We must see to it that the historic mistakes do not repeat themselves; that we do not bring on a situation that would make possible the return of the reaction, the victory of force over democracy. Certain methods of fighting have been indicated to us. We have been told that we should not fight with words, not talk of annexation, but should show by deeds that we are fighting against capitalism. What means are recommended for this fight? To arrest Russian capitalists. (*Laughter.*) Comrades, I am not a Social Democrat. I am not a Marxist, but I have the highest respect for Marx, his teaching, and his disciples. But Marxism has never taught such childlike and primitive means. I suspect that Citizen Lenin has forgotten what Marxism is. He cannot call himself a socialist, because socialism nowhere recommends the settling of questions of economic war, of the war of classes in their economic relations, the question of the economic reorganization of the state, by arresting people, as is done by Asiatic despots. . . . Every Marxist who knows his socialism would say that capitalism is international, that the arrest of a few capitalists in a certain state would not affect the iron law of the economic development of a given period. . . . You Bolsheviks recommend childish prescriptions—"arrest, kill, destroy." What are you—socialists or the police of the old regime? (*Uproar.* Lenin: "You should call him to order.")

This gathering of the flower of the Russian democracy understands its problems. Such prescriptions do not excite it, but among the masses such words will be taken seriously. We do not cater to the mob; we are not demagogues. What we say now, we said ten years ago. . . .

. . .

You [Bolsheviks] recommend that we follow the road of the French revolution of 1792. You recommend the way of further disorganization of the country. . . . When you, in alliance with reaction, shall destroy our power, then you will have a real dictator. It is our duty, the duty of the Russian democracy, to say: Don't repeat the historic mistakes. You are asked to follow the road that was once followed by France, and that will lead Russia to a new reaction, to a new shedding of democratic blood.

1124. The Resolution of the Mensheviks and Socialist Revolutionaries Passed by the Congress, June 8
[*Izvestiia*, No. 87, June 9, 1917, p. 10.]

The Congress, having listened to the report of the Executive Committee of the Socialist Revolutionaries and Social Democrats, agrees that:

1. In view of the situation brought about by the first ministerial crisis, it would have been a severe blow to the revolution to have handed over power to the bourgeoisie alone; and

2. It would have greatly weakened and threatened the revolution to have handed over all power, at that time, to the Soviets of Workers' and Soldiers' Deputies, for such an act would have alienated certain elements of the population that are still able to serve the cause of the revolution.

For these reasons, the All-Russian Congress of Soviets of Workers' and Soldiers' Deputies approves the action of the Petrograd Soviet during April 20 and 21, in forming a coalition government on a definite democratic platform, both in foreign and domestic affairs.

Having heard the explanations of the comrade-ministers on the general policy of the Provisional Revolutionary Government, and having expressed full confidence in them, the All-Russian Congress agrees that this policy answers the interests of the revolution.

The Congress calls on the Provisional Government to carry out resolutely and systematically the democratic platform which has been adopted, and, in particular,

a. To strive persistently for the earliest conclusion of a general peace without annexations or indemnities, and on the basis of self-determination;

b. To continue further the democratization of the army, and to increase its fighting power;

c. To undertake, with the direct participation of the toiling masses, the most energetic measures for combating the financial-economic disruption and the disorganization of the food supply, produced by the war and made acute by the policy of the propertied classes;

d. To conduct a systematic and resolute fight against counterrevolutionary attempts;

e. To bring about the speediest realization of the measures affecting the questions of land and labor, in accordance with the demands of the organized toiling masses and dictated by the vital interests of public economy, greatly undermined by the war;

f. To aid in the organization of all forces of the revolutionary democracy, by means of rapid and radical reforms on a democratic basis in local government, and self-government and the speediest introduction of zemstvos and municipal autonomy, where there is none as yet;

g. Particularly the Congress demands the speediest convocation of the All-Russian Constituent Assembly.

The Congress is of the opinion that, in order to carry out the indicated program more speedily and determinedly, and to unite all the strength of the democracy and make its will felt in all state affairs, it is necessary to form one organ with full power to represent all the revolutionary democratic organizations of Russia. This organ should have representatives of the All-Russian Congress of Soviets of Workers' and Soldiers' Deputies and the All-Russian Congress of Peasants' Soviets.

The socialist-ministers should be responsible to such an all-Russian representative organ for all the domestic and foreign politics of the Provisional Government. Such a responsibility will assure the country that as long as the minister-socialists are in the Provisional Government, it carries out the will of the democracy and is therefore entitled to full power and the support of all the democratic strength of the country.

The Congress calls on all the revolutionary democracy of Russia to gather around the Soviets of Workers' and Soldiers' and Peasant Deputies, and to support the Provisional Government energetically in all its efforts to strengthen and broaden the conquests of the revolution.

All resolutions were voted down by an overwhelming majority, with the exception of the last one, proposed by the Mensheviks and Socialist Revolutionaries, which was approved by a vote of 543 to 126, with 52 abstentions.

During the voting, 65 deputies were absent.

1125. *Russkiia Vedomosti*'s Reaction to the Debates in the Congress
[No. 128, June 8, 1917, p. 1.]

The meetings of the All-Russian Congress of Workers' [and Soldiers] Deputies are of great interest both because of the speeches being made and because of the resolutions being adopted. The aims, the problems, and the methods of action of certain political parties become clearer—the positions and aspirations of the majority members of the Congress are being revealed. Perhaps the Bolsheviks spoke their minds more openly than anybody else, clearly presenting to the Congress the methods of administration which they would use if power came into their hands. The declaration made by Mr. Lenin in his speech of reply to Minister Tseretelli leaves no doubt whatsoever concerning the essence of those methods and concerning the interpretation of the word "freedom" by the leader of the Bolsheviks. There is no difference between what had been practiced during the Tsar's regime and what is proposed by Mr. Lenin: the same methods of arrests, restrictions, pressure, and violence which had been practiced by men of the former government, from way back, and to which they attached so many hopes. For the solution of the tangled financial situation of Russia, Mr. Lenin finds no other remedy than arresting a hundred capitalists who, under the influence of this measure, would disclose something unusually beneficial and life-saving. We need not, of course, enlarge too much on the degree of sense and practical worth of such a measure, but the tendency of restriction and violence is clear: arrest, seizure, questioning, pressure. And when Kerensky called this policy the policy of Derzhimordas,[5] the Bolsheviks, as Chairman Gegechkori hinted quite correctly, were offended only because of their meager acquaintance with Russian literature, for there were no reasons for offense: the theory of restriction and slap-in-the-face is precisely the theory of political Derzhimordas. If the experiment with the hundred capitalists proved unsuccessful and the finances of the country did not improve, this would not undermine confidence in the whole theory on the part of the supreme statesmen, led by Mr. Lenin, but would only indicate the numerical insignificance of those arrested. Why not extend this energetic measure to everyone to whom the epithet "bourgeois" is applied? And since this name can be applied to everyone who thinks differently (didn't Mr. Lenin count among petty bourgeois even the chairman of the Soviet of Workers' Deputies, Chkheidze, and some other individuals who are eagerly using that term on their opponents), there is nothing to prevent the use of this old, tried method. Evidently there is no difference between the Lenin "freedom" and the Tsar's regime.

The report of the meeting states that the Congress expressed stormy approval of the ministers who replied to Mr. Lenin, and only an insignificant number of participants applauded Mr. Lenin; and when the question of the offensive at the front was being discussed, the overwhelming part of the meeting voted against the Bolsheviks.

It would appear that the Bolshevist sermon receives no sympathetic audience, that the adherents of that party are forced to preach in the wilderness and hear no sympathetic voice, that Mr. Lenin's doctrine, by its obvious unacceptability, is the harmless play of an exalted but substantially quite peaceful imagination. Many meetings and resolutions apparently confirm such a conclusion: the Bol-

[5] Derzhimorda, a character in Gogol's play *The Inspector-General*, is a personification of arbitrary police rule.

sheviks somehow are always left in the minority; only seldom do their proposals command the majority of votes. By appearances—no matter what attitude one assumes to that group of persons—one cannot ascribe to them anything that has any great influence on the affairs of the country.

And yet, if we really reach such a conclusion, we would hardly be close to the truth. . . .

. . . Even though Bolshevik propaganda is not received favorably at many meetings, even though it is rejected at congresses, nevertheless the mood caused by demagogic exhortations and prospects of easy loot is spreading throughout the land. Who knows what consequences it may lead to if it does not receive counter-action in the form of strong public opinion and firm executive power. Only active struggle against demagogic exhortations — and by "struggle" we do not mean arrests and violence so dear to the hearts of Messrs. Lenins—can rid the country of the growing Bolshevist mood.

1126. *Rabochaia Gazeta* ON THE DEBATES IN THE CONGRESS
[No. 74, June 7, 1917, p. 1.]

The question of the Government is the most militant question of the Congress. It has aroused unusually heated debates which have lasted for the past three days.

· · ·

As to the question on the organization and the forms of governmental author-ity, we have, on the one hand, the proposal of Lenin-Lunacharskii-Trotsky: *the transfer of all power into the hands of the Soviets of Deputies.*

Lunacharskii, outwardly, gave the least fantastic exposition of that proposal: *an immediate formation* from the composition of the present Congress of a *"tem-porary revolutionary parliament,"* whose Executive Committee is to be the actual new government. The deliberate ignoring of the Constituent Assembly in the entire proposal is most glaring. The men who affirm that the majority of the people follow the Soviets seem at the same time to *fear* the Constituent Assembly and *in fact* propose the dictatorship of the proletariat.

On the other hand, we have the line followed by Comrades Martov, Martynov, and others. They maintain that in a bourgeois revolution the government must be purely bourgeois. But it is their opinion also that the bourgeois elements of the *present* government are too much to the right. Even Kerensky pursues a clearly antidemocratic policy. Consequently, they insist on the formation of a new government composed of some sort of *bourgeois-democratic* parties whose position is more to the left than that of Kerensky, although they know perfectly well that, alas! we have no such parties. As a way out of the situation some of the comrades even go so far as to propose the establishment of *"dual power"* as a *nor-mal condition.* And this in *time of war.* In the early weeks of the revolution such duality of authority did prevail, and throughout the multimillion-man army a wail could be heard: Give us any kind of government, but give us *one* government in order that we may know whom to obey.

Both of these extreme positions, in spite of their antithesis in the evaluation of the moving forces and the future of the Russian revolution, have much in com-mon. They are united in their sharp disapproval of the *present* government and particularly in the extreme abstractness and the far-fetched character of all their reasoning. . . .

However, if the *chief* task of the Provisional Revolutionary Government is the convocation of the Constituent Assembly, under the present contradictory internal conditions and existing power relations, the coalition government with the participation of socialists, in spite of all the inconveniences and even dangers threatening the social democracy, is nevertheless the government which can best lead the Russian revolution to the Constituent Assembly with the fewest shocks.

Only on admitting this, only on recognizing that the contradictions, weaknesses, and indecision of this government are the inevitable product of the entire complexity and tragedy of the Russian revolution which erupted at the end of an exhausting three years of world war, only on recognizing all this, can we and should we subject the activity of this government to a thorough criticism. Only then will criticism be fruitful and not demoralize the revolution but force it forward, consolidating the gained positions.

1127. THE DURNOVO VILLA AFFAIR

[*Izvestiia*, No. 87, June 9, 1917, p. 1. The anarchists had seized this villa of the former tsarist minister and were using it as a headquarters, from which they were enjoying some success, especially in the working-class Vyborgskii district itself. When the Provisional Government attempted to evict them, some factories in the district went on strike and demonstrating crowds formed. Later, on June 19, following the anarchists' success, by threatening the warden, in having seven prisoners released from the Kresty Prison, the Government sent troops and arrested some 60 occupants of the villa. *VVP*, No. 84, June 20, 1917, p. 1.]

To all the working population of the Vyborgskii district:

Comrade-workers! Certain individuals who call themselves anarchist-communists have occupied the Durnovo villa, in Vyborgskii district.

The Petrograd Soviet of Workers' and Soldiers' Deputies declared at one time that seizures of private homes, without the owners' consent, are inadmissible and that the Durnovo house must be vacated. The Provisional Government now insists that this house must be immediately vacated. This demand by the Government provoked a section of the working population in the Vyborgskii district; some of these workers for some reason decided that the Government's demand was counterrevolutionary and they announced that they would defend the house of Durnovo with arms. In connection with this a strike has been initiated in some of the plants of the Vyborgskii district.

Comrade-workers! Having discussed the situation that has developed, the Executive Committee of the Soviet of Workers' and Soldiers' Deputies and the Presidium of the All-Russian Congress of Soviets of Workers' and Soldiers' Deputies resolved:

1) To instruct the Executive Committee of the Petrograd Soviet of Workers' and Soldiers' Deputies to adopt immediate measures for safeguarding the rights of the Petrograd residents to the free use of the garden by the Durnovo house.

2) To reaffirm to all the residents of Petrograd that the Soviet prohibits all arbitrary seizures of private or public buildings and considers these to be actions directed against the cause of the Russian revolution. The authorities had insisted

on the evacuation of the printing house of the *Russkaia Volia,* seized by the anarchists. The authorities are now insisting that the Durnovo house be vacated. This is not a counterrevolution; on the contrary, it is the establishment of the revolutionary order.

3) To call on the working population of the Vyborgskii district to resume the interrupted work in the plants immediately; their strike is now playing into the hands of the counterrevolution.

4) To pronounce any organizing for armed demonstrations without an express resolution to that effect by the Petrograd Soviet of Workers' and Soldiers' Deputies completely inadmissible and extremely dangerous to the cause of the revolution.

Comrades! Incoherent actions by individual groups of workers delight the enemies of the revolution. Do not let them rejoice.

. . .

CHKHEIDZE
President of the Petrograd Soviet of Workers' and
Soldiers' Deputies and President of the All-
Russian Congress of Soviets of Workers'
and Soldiers' Deputies

1128. THE BOLSHEVIK CALL FOR A DEMONSTRATION ON JUNE 10

[*Velikaia oktiabr'skaia sotsialisticheskaia revoliutsiia: Revoliutsionnoe dvizhenie v rossii: Iiun'skaia demonstratsiia,* pp. 494–95. Much additional documentation on the planned demonstration will be found in *ibid.,* p. 481 ff. See also Shub, *Lenin,* pp. 202–4, and William Henry Chamberlin, *The Russian Revolution,* I, 160–62.]

June 9, 1917

To all toilers, to all workers and soldiers of Petrograd!

Comrades!

Russia is experiencing heavy trials.

The war, which carries off millions of victims, continues. It is deliberately prolonged by millionaire bankers who grow rich from war.

The industrial collapse brought about by the war leads to the shutdown of factories and to unemployment. The lockout capitalists in their greed for fantastic profits deliberately encourage unemployment.

Shortages of bread and other foodstuffs are felt ever more. High prices strangle the population. And prices continue to rise at the whim of pillagers-speculators.

The sinister specter of famine and ruin hovers over us . . .

At the same time dark clouds of counterrevolution are gathering.

The June 3 Duma which helped the Tsar to strangle the people now demands an immediate offensive at the front—what for? In order to drown in blood the freedom that has been gained.

The State Council which supplied the Tsar with ministers-hangmen is quietly weaving a treacherous noose in the name of law—what for? In order to emerge at the auspicious moment and tighten it around the people's neck.

The Provisional Government, placed between the tsarist Duma and the Soviet of Deputies, with ten bourgeois members, is clearly falling under the influence of *pomeshchiki* and capitalists.

Instead of guaranteeing the rights of the soldiers, the "Declaration" of Kerensky violates these rights at a number of very important points.

Instead of ratifying the freedoms gained by the soldiers in the days of the revolution, new "orders" threaten penal servitude at hard labor.

Instead of consolidating the freedom gained by the citizens of Russia, there are arrests without trials and investigations, new conjectures about article 129, threatening penal servitude at hard labor.[6]

Instead of combating counterrevolution, there is tolerance of revelry and bacchanalia by counterrevolutionaries.

And the ruin grows ever more and no steps are taken against it.

And the war continues and no effective steps are taken to stop it.

And famine is ever closer and no effective steps are taken against it.

Small wonder that the counterrevolutionaries are getting ever more insolent, inciting the Government to repression against soldiers, sailors, workers, and peasants.

Comrades!

We must not continue to endure such things in silence! To be silent after what has been happening is criminal!

Protest is already beginning in the heart of the working masses.

We are free citizens; we have the right to protest, and we must take advantage of this right while it is not too late.

We reserve the right of peaceful demonstration. Let us then stage a peaceful demonstration and make our needs and wishes known!

May the victorious banner rise in the air to frighten the enemies of liberty and socialism!

May our call, the call of the sons of revolution, be heard by all of Russia, to the joy of all who are oppressed and enslaved!

Workers! Join the soldiers and support their just demands. Don't you remember how they supported you in the days of the revolution?

All out in the street, comrades!

Soldiers! Stretch your hand to the workers and support them in their just demands. In the union of the workers and the soldiers is the strength of the revolution. Today not one regiment, not one division should remain in the barracks!

All out in the street, comrades!

March through the streets of the capital in fine order.

State your wishes calmly and with confidence, as befits those who are strong.

Down with the tsarist Duma!

Down with the State Council!

Down with the ten capitalist ministers!

All power to the All-Russian Soviet of Workers,' Soldiers,' and Peasants' Deputies!

[6] On June 4, 1917, the Ministry of Justice announced that it had introduced for the urgent consideration of the Commission for the Revision of the Criminal Code two articles, 129 and 131, dealing with the penalties for public incitement to various grave crimes and unlawful acts. *VVP*, No. 71, June 4, 1917, p. 2. With some editorial changes, they were incorporated in the law of July 6, 1917. See Doc. 1162.

Re-examine the "Declaration of the rights of the soldier"!

Abolish the "orders" against soldiers and sailors!

Down with anarchy in industry and the lockout capitalists!

Hail the control and organization of industry!

Time to end the war! Let the Soviet of Deputies declare just conditions of peace!

Neither separate peace with Wilhelm, nor secret treaties with the French and English capitalists!

Bread! Peace! Liberty!

> THE CENTRAL COMMITTEE OF RSDRP
> THE PETERSBURG COMMITTEE OF RSDRP
> THE MILITARY ORGANIZATION OF THE C.C. AND P.K. OF RSDRP
> THE CENTRAL COUNCIL OF THE FACTORY COMMITTEE OF PETROGRAD
> THE EXECUTIVE COMMISSION OF THE CENTRAL BUREAU OF
> TRADE UNIONS
> THE BOLSHEVIK FACTION IN THE SOVIET OF W. AND S.D. OF
> PETROGRAD
> THE EDITORIAL OFFICE OF *Pravda*
> THE EDITORIAL OFFICE OF *Soldatskaia Pravda*

1129. THE SOVIET PROHIBITION OF THE DEMONSTRATION AND APPEALS TO
THE WORKERS AND SOLDIERS NOT TO HEED THE BOLSHEVIK CALL

[All of the following items appeared in *Izvestiia*, No. 88, June 10, 1917, p. 10, and were issued on June 9, when word of the proposed demonstration reached the Petrograd Soviet, the Congress of Soviets, and party organizations. Between each of these orders and appeals on the page was the admonition: "Do Not Listen to the Appeals of Provocateurs!"]

Comrade soldiers and workers,

The Bolshevik Party is calling on you to go out on the streets.

This appeal is being prepared without the knowledge of the Soviet of Workers' and Soldiers' Deputies, without the knowledge of the Soviet of Peasants' Deputies and all the socialist parties. It was issued exactly in that alarming moment when the All-Russian Congress called on the comrade-workers of the Vyborgskii district to bear in mind that any demonstrations in these days may damage the cause of the revolution [the Durnovo villa affair].

Comrades, on behalf of millions of workers, peasants, and soldiers in the rear and on the front, we are saying to you:

DO NOT DO WHAT YOU ARE BEING CALLED UPON TO DO.

In this alarming moment you are called out into the streets in order to make demands for the overthrow of the Provisional Government, the support of which the All-Russian Congress has just recognized to be essential. Those who are calling on you cannot know that your peaceful demonstrations may give rise to bloody disorders. Knowing your loyalty to the revolutionary cause, we are saying to you:

You are being called upon to demonstrate for the benefit of the revolution.

But we know that the concealed counterrevolutionaries want to profit by your demonstration.

We know that the counterrevolutionaries are avidly waiting for the minute when a civil war in the ranks of the revolutionary democracy would give them the opportunity to crush the revolution.

.   .   .

Comrades:

On behalf of all the Soviets of Workers' and Soldiers' Deputies, on behalf of the Soviet of Peasants' Deputies, the active armies and the socialist parties, we are saying to you:

"There must not be a single company, a single regiment, a single group of workers on the street.

"[There must not be] a single demonstration today.

"A great struggle still lies ahead of us."

When a counterrevolutionary danger really threatens Russian freedom, then we will call upon you.

Disorganizing demonstrations, however, [lead to the] downfall of the revolution.

CONSERVE YOUR STRENGTH, REMAIN IN UNISON WITH ALL REVOLUTIONARY RUSSIA.

> THE ALL-RUSSIAN CONGRESS OF SOVIETS OF WORKERS' AND SOLDIERS' DEPUTIES
>
> THE EXECUTIVE COMMITTEE OF THE PETROGRAD SOVIET OF WORKERS' AND SOLDIERS' DEPUTIES
>
> THE EXECUTIVE COMMITTEE OF THE ALL-RUSSIAN SOVIET OF PEASANTS' DEPUTIES
>
> THE ORGANIZATIONAL COMMITTEE OF THE RUSSIAN SOCIAL DEMOCRATIC WORKERS' PARTY
>
> THE CENTRAL COMMITTEE OF THE SOCIALIST REVOLUTIONARY PARTY
>
> THE CENTRAL COMMITTEE OF THE "BUND"
>
> THE CENTRAL COMMITTEE OF THE LABOR GROUP
>
> THE UKRAINIAN FACTION OF THE ALL-RUSSIAN CONGRESS
>
> THE FACTION OF UNITED INTERNATIONALIST SOCIAL DEMOCRATIC BOLSHEVIKS AND MENSHEVIKS OF THE ALL-RUSSIAN CONGRESS
>
> THE MILITARY SECTION OF THE ORGANIZATIONAL COMMITTEE AND OF THE COMMITTEE OF THE PETROGRAD ORGANIZATION OF THE RUSSIAN SOCIAL DEMOCRATIC WORKERS' PARTY

.   .   .

DO NOT LISTEN TO THE APPEALS OF PROVOCATEURS!

The All-Russian Congress of Soviets of Workers' and Soldiers' Deputies resolved:

All street demonstrations in Petrograd are prohibited for three days (June 10, 11, and 12).

A violation of this resolution is a blow at the revolution.

Whoever calls for the violation of this resolution is an enemy of the revolution.

. . .

DO NOT LISTEN TO THE APPEALS OF PROVOCATEURS!

Resolution of the Soldiers' Section of the Soviet of Workers' and Soldiers' Deputies

Having discussed the "peaceful demonstration" set for June 10, under slogans of the struggle against counterrevolution, the Soldiers' Section of the Soviet of Workers' and Soldiers' Deputies resolved that:

1. The solidarity and organization of the democracy is its only support and defense against all counterrevolutionary attempts.

2. The Soviet of Workers' and Soldiers' Deputies is the leading organ in the democracy's struggle against counterrevolution.

3. The demonstration of June 10, set without the knowledge or consent of the Soviet of Workers' and Soldiers' Deputies and the All-Russian Congress, is a disorganizing action.

4. Under circumstances of exceedingly strained relations, this demonstration may lead to street clashes and provoke a civil war.

Therefore, the Soldiers' Section of the Soviet of Workers' and Soldiers' Deputies considers it necessary to adopt the most resolute measures for preventing the June 10 demonstration from taking place.

1130. THE GOVERNMENT'S APPEAL FOR ORDER AND READINESS TO USE FORCE

[*VVP*, No. 76, June 10, 1917, p. 1. Resolved in the meeting of the Council of Ministers on June 9. *Zhurnaly*, No. 103.]

FROM THE PROVISIONAL GOVERNMENT

In view of the rumors which are being circulated in the city and which are alarming the population, the Provisional Government calls on the population to remain completely calm and announces that any attempts at violence will be suppressed with the full force of government authority.

June 10, 1917

1131. THE BOLSHEVIK DECISION TO CALL OFF THE DEMONSTRATION

[*Izvestiia*, No. 88, June 10, 1917. As a result of the firm opposition of the Soviets, the Bolsheviks decided early in the morning, about 2:00 A.M., of June 10 to cancel the demonstration. At that late hour, they were able to have the call for the demonstration removed from the pages of the June 10 *Pravda*. See *Velikaia oktiabr'skaia sotsialisticheskaia revoliutsiia: Revoliutsionnae dvizhenie v rossii: Iiun'skaia demonstratsiia,* pp. 506–8, for the Bolshevik explanation of their decision. Originally published in *Pravda,* No. 79, June 11, 1917, p. 1. See also Lenin's article in *Pravda,* No. 79, June 11, 1917, as translated in the *Collected Works of V. I. Lenin: The Revolution of 1917,* XX, Bk. II, 238–39.]

*Resolution of the Central Committee of the
Social Democratic Party of the Bolsheviks*

At 3:15 A.M. we received the following resolution of the Central Committee of the Russian Social Democratic Workers' Party [Bolshevik]:

In view of the fact that the Congress of Soviets, in conjunction with the Executive Committee of the Peasants' Soviets, acknowledging the highly exceptional circumstances, resolved to prohibit all, even peaceful demonstrations for three days, the Central Committee of the Russian Social Democratic Workers' Party resolved: to *cancel* the demonstration set by them for 2:00 P.M. Saturday.

The Central Committee calls on all its party members and all its sympathizers to carry out this decision.

CENTRAL COMMITTEE OF THE RUSSIAN
SOCIAL DEMOCRATIC WORKERS' PARTY

1132. THE PETROGRAD SOVIET EXECUTIVE COMMITTEE'S DECISION TO DISCUSS
THE CANCELED DEMONSTRATION WITH THE PRESIDIUM OF THE
CONGRESS OF SOVIETS

[Session of June 10. *Protokoly,* pp. 188–89.]

4. Comrade Bogdanov will make a motion at tomorrow's session of the Congress to sum up politically the events of June 9, to put the question sharply and definitely to the Bolsheviks as to whether they consider themselves obligated, as part of the Congress, to submit to its decisions. Comrade Bogdanov felt that the time had come to dissociate ourselves once and for all from elements that engage in disorganizing activities and bring discord into the common family of the revolutionary democracy. This struggle is necessary and will only serve to restore the Russian revolution to a healthy state. We will undermine our authority among the masses if we continue the policy of halfway measures and indecisiveness in regard to this question.

The majority of the members of the Executive Committee, agreeing in general with the basic principles of Comrade Bogdanov, found, however, that it would be ill-advised to raise this question in its full scope at tomorrow's session of the Congress, when passions have not yet cooled down and the atmosphere was so charged, and recommended that the question be first discussed at the plenary session of the Executive Committee and the Presidium of the Congress tomorrow at 1:00 P.M. Furthermore, some of the members pointed to the overdelicate situation which is conducive to the success of Bolshevik agitation among the masses, and to the failure to satisfy a number of the most vital and urgent needs of proletarian organizations (need for accommodations, printing presses for party publications, etc.) as well as the slow enactment of social legislation by the Government.

1133. THE JOINT SESSION OF THE PETROGRAD EXECUTIVE COMMITTEE
AND THE PRESIDIUM OF THE CONGRESS

[June 11. *Protokoly,* pp. 191–93.]

2. *A brief report from the Commission* (by Dan) on the elaboration of a

resolution in regard to the events of yesterday.[7] Certain general rules regarding street demonstrations.

KAMENEV. We enter the ranks of the demonstration only as a party that is international and [represents] a class. The time may come, ...* on the moods in the country. The Petrograd events are rooted in the Government's slowness in [dealing] with ripe problems. Reports of unrest among the masses have been reaching [us]. At the beginning of last week these reports reached a peak. A conference was called. From the reports it was established that regiments and workers were impatient . . .† At this conference there were comrades who pointed out that this mood could only find an outlet in demonstrations. There was opposition to a demonstration. It was decided to call a new [conference]. This meeting was purely organizational in character. When a vote was taken, the vast majority declared itself in favor of a demonstration. Such was the result. The majority decided that a demonstration was unavoidable, but that [it must be staged] under definite slogans. There was no slogan of "seizure of power"; "All Power to the Soviets" was the only positive slogan. News of the demonstration came in during the Congress. The argument [ran] that the counterrevolutionaries wanted to take advantage of the demonstration, that they wanted to choose the same days, that there existed a counterrevolutionary organization which mingled in with the revolutionary troops and stepped forward under the same flag. It was not easy to call off the demonstration, which is what we did at midnight. The announcement by telephone was received distrustfully in the *Soldatskaia Pravda*. Every step was taken during this night. We gave [the announcement] to *Izvestiia* to be released in a separate issue.

· · ·

TSERETELLI. The answer to the main question has already been given. The main question [was]: "Was there, or was there not, a plot?" (*Cries:* "There was!") If there was no plot, then we have committed an error. Why was it concealed from the Congress? Was it not their duty to inform the Congress? They wanted to take the Congress unawares, to confront them with a fact. It is not surprising that they later took measures, once their plot had been uncovered. There was nothing else for them to do but to disperse [the demonstration], and what we were forbidding was not the demonstration but the possible repetition of plots. We have reached the point beyond which bloodshed begins. The counterrevolution did not rear its head. It proceeds from anarchy—the only road by which the counterrevolution will come to us. By striking at anarchy, we will kill the counterrevolution. We must adopt unavoidable, drastic measures. The physical strength is on the side of the majority of the democracy. We must use our full authority to knock the weapons out [of their hands].

KAMENEV. Mr. Minister, if you are not throwing words around at random, you have no right to limit yourself to a speech. Arrest me and try me for plotting against the revolution.

The Bolsheviks walked out as a form of protest.

· · ·

[7] A resolution of the Congress condemning the attempted demonstration was approved on June 12 and published June 13 in *Izvestiia*, No. 90, pp. 7–8. The wording, however, is completely different from the version in *Protokoly*, pp. 197–98.

* In the original.

† Omission in the original.

CHKHEIDZE. Any lies or slanders from Comrade Tseretelli are out of the question.

. . . .

1134. *Den'* ON THE CANCELED DEMONSTRATION
[No. 82, June 11, 1917, p. 1.]

During the night of June 9–10 the Russian democracy gained an important political victory.

The significance of the historic session of the All-Russian Soviet does not lie only in the fact that during this session the Bolshevik conspiracy against the Soviet was detected and stifled at the roots with an energy and a resoluteness worthy of the revolutionary democracy.

The merit of the Soviet does not lie only in the fact that it has prevented bloodshed and perhaps the beginnings of a fratricidal civil war.

From a political point of view the most important fact is the division which took place at the Congress.

Not in words but in deeds the Congress has split into two sharply opposite, irreconcilable camps, for the victory of one would signify the death of the other: into the camp of the revolution and the camp of anarchy—into the camp of revolution and the camp of counterrevolution.

The fact that the two opposite forces did not cross swords in an oral tournament, but that the air was pregnant with lead and blood, make out of this night an important political stage of the revolution.

Now it is not possible to fill this abyss with words, according to the old revolutionary method of Lassalle;[8] it is essential first of all to state openly what actually exists.

The Congress will not accomplish its duty before the revolutionary democracy if it does not express its attitude toward the Bolshevik attempt in all frankness.

We believe that the Congress should address itself to the whole revolutionary democracy of Russia, both in the rear and at the front, with a proclamation from which the country would learn in an unvarnished exposure the real aspiration of the Bolsheviks and the methods they endeavor to apply in order to carry out their plans for saving Russia.

Let the Congress in this proclamation name them by their real names.

This would be a political act . . .

. . . .

It is essential to bear in mind at all times that we are living through a revolutionary period, where today's words may be answered tomorrow by the echoes of shooting. This circumstance compels the revolutionary democracy to fight against all kinds of anarchic, arbitrary, and disorganizing activities with a maximum of energy, without being stopped by anything.

And first of all, one must look at the danger with open eyes.

The duty of the Congress is to have a clear idea of the mood of revolutionary Petrograd, of its garrison and its workers, and to come to practical conclusions.

It should not be forgotten that the role of Petrograd in the revolution is the role of the leader and that our duty is to take every measure in order that Petrograd not abandon the country, that it reflect the country as a whole.

[8] Ferdinand Lassalle (1825–64), German socialist.

1135. CHERNOV ON THE CANCELED DEMONSTRATION

[*Delo Naroda*, No. 72, June 11, 1917, p. 1.]

. . .

The anarchically inspired elements attempted to inflate the question of their eviction from the villa of Durnovo into a question of the rights of the entire working class to its revolutionary gains. Professing that allegedly all buildings requisitioned after the revolution for educational and social and political purposes were in danger, they spread throughout factories alarm and disorder. In our troubled times it is not hard to find those who are gullible. It appeared that there was danger of some spontaneous, tempestuous movement which threatened to assume unknown forms.

Here a curious thing appeared. It turned out that the work of the Bolsheviks only prepared the ground for anarchism. There is one single district in Petrograd where the Bolsheviks regard themselves with pride as masters of the situation— it is the Vyborgskii district. And now it is revealed that the Bolsheviks held their own there only by maintaining an atmosphere of fury and resorting to incantation of spirits which they themselves could not cope with.

The anarchist propaganda found at once an unusually fertile and prepared ground in the Vyborgskii district. For the anarchists, for the villa of Durnovo, against the counterrevolution headed by the Provisional Government!—such was the call heard throughout the district. The Bolsheviks did try to put on the brakes; no results. Their popularity, based on systematic stirring and instigating, was about to collapse as soon as they attempted to stand in the way of the work "of their own doing." The movement rolled over the heads of the Bolsheviks, throwing them aside as useless and leaving them behind. . . .

The Bolsheviks could find no words to restrain the mob from excesses. These words, this unaccustomed tone, fell badly from their tongues and stuck in their throats. Like one who has just begun to learn a foreign language, they debated, stumbling and stuttering, losing the thread of thought, and shirking. The tongue-tied semiadmonitions were weak and pathetic when confronted with boisterously flaming and direct pressure from the anarchist demogogy. Feeling the ground slipping from under their feet, the Bolsheviks could not hold out and surrendered.

The Bolsheviks of Petrograd were not themselves at once aware of the tragedy of their position. They thought at first that they had simply assumed inadvertently the wrong tone, that they had underestimated the strength of the mood of the masses. And a tempting, a treacherously tempting idea flashed before them: to change the tone, to "seize" the movement, to "head" it and to "guide" it into such channels as would redirect it, the water of the Bolshevik mill, against the "opportunistic" majority of the Soviets of Workers' and Soldiers' Deputies.

Moreover, it seemed that this decision was not what it *actually* was, the result of the cruel *objective logic of events*: a demagogic "heroism of despair." No, they were able—poor people—to convince themselves that it was a brilliant revolutionary improvisation. . . .

Thus, by an "intuitively revolutionary" impulse Lenin engaged bolshevism in a colossal political adventure. "Playing with fire," begun by the anarchists, was picked up by the Bolsheviks. And Lenin's bolshevism sped away full steam . . . whereto? To him, a thoughtful socialist, it was clear whereto. *To political suicide.*

VICTOR CHERNOV

1136. *Izvestiia* WARNS OF CONTINUED BOLSHEVIK AND COUNTERREVOLUTIONARY ACTIVITY

[No. 92, June 15, 1917, p. 2.]

The imminent danger of civil war and counterrevolution has not passed. On the contrary, the threat of this danger is growing with every day, and every hour.

All those who have recently visited regiments that have professed their lack of confidence in the Provisional Government have had the opportunity to become convinced that the agitation of the counterrevolutionaries (the Black Hundred) among the lower, ignorant segments of the population is linking itself to the anarchist-Bolshevik propaganda.

. . .

"Don't trust the socialist ministers!" appeals the speaker.

And sympathetic voices support him from the crowd:

"They are all bourgeois!"

"They have all sold themselves out!"

"They have received 10 million rubles each in bribes."

"The All-Russian Congress of Soviets of Workers' and Soldiers' Deputies is pursuing a hat-in-hand policy toward the bourgeoisie," the Bolshevik enlightens the ignorant masses.

And a chorus of voices supports him from the crowd:

"We don't need any congresses."

"The *zemskie nachal'niki* are holding meetings there."

The Bolshevik speaker, calling for land seizures, blasts the All-Russian Congress of Peasants' Deputies. And the crowd supports [him]:

"The peasants elected priests and *pomeshchiki* to this Congress."

The representative of the "revolutionary" Social Democracy exposes the coalition government:

"What distinguishes this new Government from Miliukov's ministry? In what respects are the political methods of Prince L'vov and Tseretelli any better than those of Nicholas the Bloody? What has the revolution given the people?"

The crowd applauds and voices echo from the audience:

"The revolution has given us nothing! It was better before!"

Thus the counterrevolutionary forces, which have stayed below the surface, are now latching on to Bolshevik slogans. They are trying to erase the dividing line between the anarchist-Bolshevik attitudes and attitudes that have nothing in common with the revolutionary consciousness of the popular masses.

. . .

In addition, [the experience of] recent days has shown with utmost clarity that the slogans leveled at the Soviet of Workers' and Soldiers' Deputies, the All-Russian Congress, and the coalition Provisional Government, which find support among the *minority* of the Petrograd garrison and the proletariat of Petrograd, these same slogans are strongly and *unanimously* denounced in the provinces and at the front. It has become clear that even the remotest possibility of their success poses the question to the provinces and the front of revising the attitudes which they had formed during the revolution toward revolutionary Petrograd . . .

The danger of bloody street clashes has been averted for the time being by the firm action taken by the All-Russian Congress; but it still has not passed.

The awareness of this danger must awaken a feeling of responsibility among all revolutionaries.

1137. RESOLUTION ON THE DUMA AND THE STATE COUNCIL BY THE CONGRESS

[*Izvestiia*, No. 88, June 10, 1917, p. 6.]

By a majority of 491 votes to 216, with 41 abstaining, the Congress adopted the following resolution of the Menshevik faction of the Social Democrats and the Socialist Revolutionaries:

The All-Russian Congress has taken into consideration [the fact] that a group of former members of the State Duma, speaking on behalf of the State Duma and profiting by the position it occupied in the first days of the revolution, has been recently trying, under imperialistic slogans, to become the center for bringing together forces opposing the revolution and the democracy. The All-Russian Congress, considering it necessary to establish that the revolution, having destroyed the foundations of the old regime, thereby (a) abolished the State Duma and the State Council as organs of national representation; and also (b) divested their individual members of titles bestowed on them by the old order,

CONSIDERS

1) that in the future, the Provisional Government must discontinue the allocation of funds for the support and functioning of the State Duma and the State Council as legislative institutions, and

2) that consequently all activities on the part of former members of the State Duma and the State Council are to be regarded as the actions of a private group of citizens in free Russia, invested with no authority.

1138. THE RESPONSE OF THE MEMBERS OF THE DUMA

[*Izvestiia*, No. 93, June 16, 1917, p. 6.]

On June 15, in the office of the President of the State Duma, under the chairmanship of M. V. Rodzianko, a meeting was held of members of the State Duma who belonged to the *Sen'oren konvent*, with the participation of prominent members of the State Duma.

The question concerning the rights of the State Duma in connection with the well-known resolution adopted by the Congress of Soviets of Workers' and Soldiers' Deputies was under discussion.

After a short deliberation the following resolution was unanimously adopted:

"In view of the question that has recently arisen concerning the significance of the State Duma in the revolution and concerning its subsequent activities, the private conference of members of the State Duma, having discussed the question, arrived at the following conclusions:

"Although the victory of the revolution fundamentally altered the position of the State Duma, established by the Fundamental Laws, it remained up until the moment of the downfall of the old regime the only national representative organ, and became the center of the national movement, in the preparation of which it played a prominent role. Having publicized and united this movement around itself, it thereby became the spokesman for the will of the revolutionary people.

"Acting in this capacity, the State Duma, through the mediation of the Temporary Committee which it selected, succeeded in obtaining the abdication of Nicholas II and proclaimed the first revolutionary government of free Russia, selecting it to a significant extent from the ranks of its own progressive majority.

"The immediate recognition of this Government by the whole country, which extremely facilitated the success of the revolution and lessened the number of its victims to an insignificant figure, represented an act of confidence of the people in the authority of the State Duma and, at the same time, sanctioned its existence as a revolutionary institution, independent of its position under the old regime.

"This new significance of the State Duma found expression in the enormous number of declarations of popular sympathy which it received, as well as in the active cooperation of the members of the State Duma in putting into effect and strengthening the new regime in uninterrupted contact with the Provisional Government, as evidenced by numerous governmental acts.

"Regardless of how imperfect the Statute on Elections of June 3, 1907, may have been, until the convocation of the Constituent Assembly the members of the State Duma unavoidably, even against their own will, are forced to maintain their function as national representatives, with all the resulting implications.

"In creating the Provisional Government and endowing it, in view of the exceptional moment, with full governmental authority and in withdrawing, as a consequence of this, from direct legislative activity, the State Duma could not, however, thereby cease to exist as an organ of national representation.

"In view of the foregoing, the private conference of the members of the State Duma deems it its patriotic duty to continue, as previously, to raise its voice in times of difficulty for our native land, to warn of the menacing dangers, and to point to the correct course."

1139. The Soviet-sponsored Demonstration of June 18

[Editorial in *Den'*, No. 87, June 17, 1917, p. 1. Following the June 10 attempt, the Congress of Soviets authorized a peaceful demonstration, with the participation of all parties, for Sunday, June 18, to express confidence in the Soviets.]

The demonstration of June 18 will take place after the All-Russian Congress of Soviets has expressed three times its confidence in the Provisional Government, after the conspiracy of the Bolsheviks against the Provisional Government has been prevented and branded. Also the Bolsheviks will participate in the demonstration with slogans in favor of overthrowing the Provisional Government, and part of the Mensheviks will participate in it with slogans openly directed against the Provisional Government.

Under these conditions, could the initiators of the demonstration of June 18 ignore the issue of the Provisional Government? Do the Congress of the Soviets and the Petrograd Soviet of Deputies have the right to exclude from the slogans of the demonstration the slogan of confidence and support of the Provisional Government?

If the resolution of confidence and support constitutes any kind of obligation, then the obligation of the demonstration's initiators is to manifest this confidence and support, not only during the sessions but also in the street. If the walls of the Kadet school seemed too close for the fight in favor of peace and it became necessary to go out into the street, then these walls should be too narrow also for the fight in favor of consolidating the authority and the prestige of the Provisional Government.

If, with the Bolshevik slogans for the overthrow of the Provisional Government present in the general demonstration, the initiators of the manifestation appeal to the citizens [saying]: "Have respect for the freedom of convictions," then we have the right to address ourselves to the revolutionary parliament of the democracy with the [following] appeal: Respect the freedom of your own convictions.

If the Bolsheviks who believe that it is necessary to overthrow the Provisional Government have the temerity to bring this slogan into the streets, then you who believe that the Provisional Government should be supported and consolidated, you are also obliged to have the courage to bring your slogans out into the streets.

Otherwise, on June 18, Russia will hear with regard to the Provisional Government only one [word]: "Down!" and it will not learn that the ringleaders, that the initiators of the manifestation think completely otherwise, namely, Long live the Provisional Government!

The task of the manifestation of the 18th of June is the fight against counterrevolution. But the fight against counterrevolution is the fight for the Provisional Government. Or could the question of fighting counterrevolution bypass the issue of the Provisional Government?

We consider it impossible. . . .

· · ·

Where are the political groups, where are the revolutionary organizations which have often expressed their confidence in the Provisional Government and have promised their support?

Which political groups and organizations will tomorrow raise the slogan: "Long live the Provisional Government"?

1140. SOVIET APPEAL TO THE SOLDIERS TO PARTICIPATE IN THE JUNE 18 DEMONSTRATION UNARMED

[*Izvestiia*, No. 95, June 18, 1917, p. 4.]

On June 16, the Military Section of the Executive Committee sent the following telegram to all regiment and battalion committees and corresponding committees of independent units in Petrograd, Tsarskoe Selo, Krasnoe Selo, Old and New Peterhof, Oranienbaum, Gatchina, Strel'n, Ligov, Sergiev, and Kronstadt:

"The Military Section of the Executive Committee reminds all the soldiers of all units that the demonstration of June 18, organized in response to a call from the All-Russian Congress of Soviets, must be strictly *peaceful*. [There must not be] a single armed soldier, nor must a single rifle or a single revolver be carried out of the barracks.

"Whoever brings arms is committing a crime against the whole democracy.

"The will of the Congress, embodying the will of the whole organized democracy of Russia, is calling you, comrade soldiers, to a strictly unarmed demonstration.

"SOKOLOV, SKALOV, VERBO, Members of the Executive Committee"

1141. SOVIET RECOMMENDATION FOR SLOGANS TO BE DISPLAYED IN THE DEMONSTRATION

[*Izvestiia*, No. 95, June 18, 1917, p. 1. Sukhanov, in his *The Russian Revolution, 1917*, Joel Carmichael, ed. and trans., pp. 411–12, writes, however, that he didn't "recall that the Ex. Com. made any special preparations for its own official demonstration" except to send members to the factories and barracks "to persuade our hearers not to take arms with them, in order to avoid senseless accidental bloodshed."]

WHAT MUST EVERY PARTICIPANT IN TODAY'S DEMONSTRATION REMEMBER?

1. *That the purpose of the demonstration is to show the unity of the revolutionary forces;*
2. *That it must testify to the aspiration of the revolutionary democracy for universal peace;*
3. *That its slogan must be:*
   Through the constituent assembly toward a democratic republic;
4. *That the demonstration must be peaceful;*
5. *That therefore it is the duty of every citizen on this day to avoid all disorders;*
6. *That it is the duty of everyone, without exception, to come to the demonstration unarmed.*

1142. *Izvestiia* CALLS FOR THE DEMONSTRATION TO BE A MANIFESTATION OF REVOLUTIONARY UNITY
[No. 95, June 18, 1917, p. 10.]

Today in Petrograd and in all large towns of Russia the revolutionary democracy is reviewing its own forces.

Today the eyes of friends and enemies of the Russian revolution, at home and abroad, will be focused on the solemn procession of detachments of the revolutionary proletarian and soldiers' army. Some [will watch] with joyous hope; others—with hidden malice.

. . .

Let the day of June 18 dispel the anxiety of friends and bring to nought the wishes of the enemies of the revolution!

Let this day show that the revolutionary country, while exerting all her strength in a war which was foisted on her and which cannot be eliminated at the present time, is raising higher than ever before her banner of the struggle for *universal peace, the banner of a fraternal union of workers of all countries*!

Let this day show that there can no longer be a return to the past, that the working classes of Russia have attained sufficient political maturity to be clearly aware of the situation, and will be able to lead the country, through the *national Constituent Assembly* which is already close at hand, to a *democratic republic*!

And—above all—let this day show how futile are the calculations of the enemies of the revolution on an internecine dissension in the revolutionary democracy! . . . This fact will show, louder than any words, that in a struggle of ideologies no single faction or group in the revolutionary democracy will ever, under any conditions, attempt to foist its views on the majority; differences of opinion will never take the form of a fratricidal war; any calculations of counter-revolutionaries on splitting the ranks of the revolutionary democracy will be shattered by the *invincible unity of the revolutionary forces!*

This is the profound meaning of today's demonstration. Its success will signify the victory of the revolution and the defeat of all counterrevolutionary schemes.

Comrade workers and soldiers! The eyes of the whole world are upon us!

Let us be worthy of our great cause and of those sacred graves before which our red banners will be lowered today.

1143. BOLSHEVIK PREDOMINANCE IN THE DEMONSTRATION OF JUNE 18

[Editorial in *Den'*, No. 89, June 20, 1917, p. 1. The Bolsheviks dominated the demonstration, using the slogans they had prepared for the June 10 demonstration. See Sukhanov, *The Russian Revolution, 1917*, Joel Carmichael, ed. and trans., pp. 415–19. See also Lenin's article on the demonstration in *Pravda*, No. 86, June 20, as translated in the *Collected Works of V. I. Lenin: The Revolution of 1917*, XX, Bk. II, 268–70.

It should be noted that the offensive began the same day, though the news did not reach Petrograd until that night.]

The Bolsheviks made a demonstration on June 18. It was their day. The Soviet of Workers' and Soldiers' Deputies legalized their manifestation, and many understood that the Soviet of Deputies, having prevented their conspiracy on June 10, made a generous gesture in their direction, saying: If you wish to demonstrate, do so peacefully; we are at your disposal. The Bolsheviks availed themselves of this proposal in full measure. But those representing all the other trends of political thought, apparently realizing that the 18th would be a Bolshevik show, did not see any necessity to enhance or to strengthen by their presence the performance of the Bolsheviks.

All these, except for the Bolsheviks, were passive during this day. Important military units remained in their barracks. The Mensheviks showed the greatest absenteeism. There were a great number of banners, proportionately much too great in comparison with the number of people, for by three o'clock the last sections of the manifestation had passed by.

But after the performance of the Bolsheviks began the performance of their closest companions-in-arms, the anarchists. On the next day the Vyborgskii district, this citadel of bolshevism, offended by the arrest of anarchists, proceeded to their defense. What happened later on is unknown as yet.

But let us turn back. Perhaps at the very time that the Bolshevik performance was going on in Petrograd, over there [at the front] where death was in conflict with death, the Russian regiments rushed to the defense of Russia. When the Bolsheviks waged war against "ten capitalist ministers" the occupation was comparatively innocent.

"But when Stakh[9] went to war," then, from over there came the news: "Some

---

[9] Reference is to the words of a song popularized by Chaliapin which tells with what self-sacrifice and lack of fanfare the common soldier, symbolized by the name Stakh, goes to war.

of our units have suffered severe casualties . . . especially among the officer personnel." We know what is concealed behind those dry words of a military summary. We know that over there blood was shed, that the earth was moaning, and that the ranks of those who have given everything they could were failing, while saving Russia.

Over there, too, there was a manifestation.

And the tragic reflection of that manifestation has eclipsed by its bloody glow the merry lights of the Petrograd manifestation. . . .

. . .

1144. *Rabochaia Gazeta* Deplores Excesses in the June 18 Demonstration and Those Reported Elsewhere in the Country

[No. 87, June 22, 1917, p. 1.]

The wails of the bourgeois press against the "excesses" of our revolution are undoubtedly exaggerated and, unless hypocritical, are based on complete lack of understanding of the depth and significance of the process which is taking place in Russia and on complete unacquaintance with the history of European revolutions.

In a revolution in which the widest and deepest strata of the people participate and which reveals the greatest social conflicts, the so-called excesses in the nature of violation of the principle of private ownership and even constraint of personality are unavoidable.

It should not be forgotten that the great French revolution, which serves as a classic example for all subsequent revolutions, began by the taking of the Bastille on July 14. And when, on the famous night of August 4, the Constituent Assembly abolished the class privileges of the nobility, the entire country was ablaze with the glow of the fire; the castles and country estates of the nobility were burning.

Compared with the French revolution and the revolution of 1905, our agrarian movement bears a much calmer and more organized character. Attacks on personality and private ownership, that is, plunder and violence down to recent times, were comparatively no greater than under the old regime.

But grievous and even terrifying signs of the beginning of a breakdown have recently appeared. [We refer to] the *licentiousness* and *brutality* that have nothing in common with either the social conflicts or the class struggle.

During the past few days the newspapers have pointed out a number of outrages on peaceful citizens committed by soldiers turned beasts. Lynchings, savage arbitrary dealings with those holding different views, the hooligan tearing down of placards bearing slogans of confidence in the Government, . . . drunken pogroms, and mass rapes of women and girls in a number of places—all this . . . reveals our ignorance, savagery, and coarseness, inherited from the old regime, a heritage of century-old slavery and ignorance.

. . .

It is this coarseness, savagery, and ignorance, this bestiality, more than any "excesses" on social grounds, that is threatening the cause of the revolution. For it is upon ignorance and savagery, which prevent the masses from distinguishing a Leninist from a former policeman; upon the universal bitterness among the masses of the people, upon the bestiality, for which the war more than anything else is responsible—upon all these things the actual counterrevolution, and not the one invented by the Leninists, builds all of its plans.

With this bestiality and savagery the revolutionary democracy is destined to wage a vigorous warfare.

And those who disrupt the democratic discipline, who undermine the confidence in the organs of democracy, must remember that they bear a heavy responsibility.

1145. *Den*'s Appraisal of the Work of the Congress
[No. 95, June 25, 1917, p. 1.]

The All-Russian Congress of the Soviet of Workers' and Soldiers' Deputies has ended its labors. This Congress has often been called a revolutionary parliament, but perhaps it would be more correct to call it the Constituent Assembly of the revolutionary democracy. Its resolutions on the more thrilling issues are, in reality, the fundamental laws of the democracy's revolutionary tactics for the next period of our political development, while the Executive Committee which has been created by this constituent assembly may become and should become a legislative body which would direct the struggle of the revolutionary democracy.

The Congress worked for three weeks and in the course of these three weeks a circumstance of great importance became sufficiently obvious for all of Russia: the present Provisional Government is supported by a really overwhelming majority of the genuine revolutionary democracy. During these three weeks too many events have happened which bear witness to the presence of dangerous forces which are disorganizing the revolution and the country. Petrograd alone gave to the delegates which had gathered from all the ends of Russia sufficient material for sorrowful observations and conclusions. Very often the ghost of civil war and of internecine war appeared. The attention of the Congress was often diverted from the problems included in the agenda to the current problems of an old disease —disorganization and anarchy. However, in spite of that, precisely during these days there took root and grew in our conscience a force which is the basic premise of the very existence of Russia—the force of the central authority, the force of the Provisional Government.

The All-Russian Congress did not flatter the Government. On the contrary, it obviously abstained from any words which could have been interpreted as a weakening of its vigilant, even somewhat captious, control of the Government. It was extremely cautious in its resolutions of confidence and support; it did not hesitate to formulate definite accusations. Nevertheless, in spite of this—or, to be more exact, precisely because of this—the central government has received the support which up to now it had been looking for in vain. It may be said boldly that in the history of Russia something unheard of has occurred: the triumph of the ideas and of the organization of the revolutionary democracy was at the same time the triumph of the ideas and of the organization of the central government. Essentially this fact more than any other symbols of the victorious revolution represents for the first time all the depths of the change which we have undergone.

If one has to evaluate the general results of the Congress, then this result that is the consolidation of the Provisional Government, the consolidation of the idea itself of central power, is perhaps the most significant.

. . .

1146. *Izvestiia*'s APPRAISAL OF THE SIGNIFICANCE OF THE CONGRESS

[No. 101, June 25, 1917, p. 6. The resolutions of the Congress on other than strictly political questions are printed in the sections of these volumes on the particular subject involved.]

The All-Russian Congress of Soviets of Workers' and Soldiers' Deputies which ended yesterday opened a new page in the history of the revolutionary democracy of Russia.

For the first time, representatives of all the Soviets, elected properly by apportionment, came together. For the first time, an all-Russian center, closely connected with local organizations, was organized on sound principles. For the first time, firm organic ties have been established with representatives of the peasantry. For the first time, all the forces of the revolutionary democracy of Russia have become concentrated in one mighty organization.

The unification of these forces is urgently required. The mellow days of the revolution, which by its bright rays roused a feeling of unlimited enthusiasm in the hearts of all, were followed by the severe days of trials. War and economic ruin, like cancer growths, are sapping the strength of the revolutionary giant.

The complete concentration of the intellect, will, and energies of the revolutionary democracy is needed in order to cope with this illness. . . .

It is true that with unprecented sharpness the Congress disclosed the divergence between the minority in the Congress and its overwhelming majority. In particular, it disclosed the divergence between a well-known section of the Petrograd proletariat [on the one hand] and the army and the mass of provincial workers-soldiers [on the other]. Contrasting the provinces with Petrograd became the newspapers' favorite theme from the beginning of the Congress.

. . . But whoever closely followed the work of the Congress and the fluctuating moods of Petrograd must admit that the Congress did not participate in these stormy events, which broke out during the course of its session and which threatened to lead the country into catastrophe, without leaving its mark. He must admit that if these events gave the provincial delegates the opportunity to form the most accurate and concrete idea of what is going on in Petrograd, then the weighty voice of the revolutionary country exerted a powerful influence on the residents of Petrograd. This voice reminded them of the concrete correlation of forces existing within the country, of those expectations, hopes, and demands which are being advanced by the revolutionary democracy of Russia; it brought them back to that real revolutionary public which is often forgotten in the feverish environment of the capital. . . .

. . .

Having wholly approved, supported, and developed the point of view which until now was upheld by the revolutionary democracy on questions of war and peace and concerning the organization of revolutionary power, the Congress expressed complete confidence in the socialist ministers and promised the most energetic support to the coalition Provisional Government.

.   .   .

The All-Russian Congress demonstrated the firm determination of the revolutionary democracy to bring the cause of the revolution to a victorious end. It outlined the road—a thorny road—which alone could lead to the desired goal: to peace, and to freedom, and to bread, and to land. It showed that the workers, peasants, and soldiers of revolutionary Russia have the strength and intellect to guide the country through all difficulties along this road to victory.

Then onward, comrades! To revolutionary work!

PART VII

The July Days and Subsequent Efforts to Stabilize the Regime

In the evening of July 3, after a day of meetings and of rising tension in the city, armed units came into the streets of Petrograd, led by the First Machine-Gun Reserve Regiment. On the following morning they were joined by a detachment of sailors from Kronstadt. Both groups were under Bolshevik leadership. Soon other dissident and discontented elements of the population appeared and, with the armed military demonstrators, marched on the Tauride Palace, literally besieging VTsIK and the Executive Committee of the Soviet of Peasants' Deputies and demanding that they take all power into their own hands. The Government, less the immediate object of the uprising than the Soviets, removed its sessions to the district military headquarters for safety. Throughout the capital, soldiers and workers confiscated and armed private cars, set up fortified positions, and engaged in apparently aimless and confused firing that cost the lives of several peaceful citizens.

Certainly the resignation of the Kadet ministers on July 2 played some role in sparking the events of July 3 and 4. But other factors were of far greater significance. Members of the Petrograd Garrison feared transfer to the front for participation in the offensive, and other soldiers resented their recall or retention to strengthen the army during the action. Among the masses, dissatisfaction was growing at the apparent dilatoriness of the coalition government in forwarding land and other reforms and in promoting the cause of peace. But, above all, the previous weeks had witnessed a flood of Bolshevik propaganda and agitation at the front and in the rear, fanning and exploiting every cause of unrest in an effort to destroy the Provisional Government.

During the day of the 3rd, the Bolshevik Central Committee hesitated to take command of the movement openly, as yet unsure of the degree of its success. That evening a conference of the Central Committee, of the Petrograd Committee, of Delegates of the Second Petrograd City Conference of Bolsheviks, and of representatives from the regiments and factories, meeting in the Palace of Kshisinskaia, finally adopted a resolution stating: "The crisis of power which has developed will not be resolved in the interests of the people unless the revolutionary proletariat and the garrison firmly, definitely, and immediately declare that they favor the transfer of power to the Soviets of Workers', Soldiers', and Peasants' Deputies. To this end, it is recommended that workers and soldiers go into the streets immediately to demonstrate the expression of their will."[1] But it was only on July 4, after the reassuring arrival of the Kronstadt sailors, that the Central

[1] *Velikaia oktiabr'skaia sotsialisticheskaia revoliutsiia: Khronika sobytii*, II, 471.

Committee published its proclamation declaring that the All-Russian Soviet "must take power into its own hands" and calling for a *"peaceful* and *organized* demonstration" (though the soldiers and sailors had been instructed to carry rifles)[2] to force the Soviet to accept the demand.

At the Tauride Palace, however, the beleaguered Soviet Central Committees, surrounded by ever more threatening mobs, steadfastly refused to assume the power being thrust upon them. Their reluctance only intensified the frustrated viciousness of the mob. Repeated appeals to the demonstrators to desist and return to their homes and quarters were useless. In the meantime, the Government had hastily ordered troops from the front to quell the uprising. Without military support, repressive efforts were of no avail, and the Petrograd units either were aligned with the demonstrators or maintained neutrality awaiting the course of events.

Then, during the night of the 4th, Minister of Justice Pereverzev permitted the release of part of the material collected by the Government indicating German financial support of the Bolsheviks. As the information spread through the city, even before its premature and unauthorized publication on the 5th, a decided change of atmosphere and attitude became evident. The neutral troops rallied to the support of the Government, while the military and civilian demonstrators hesitated, shaken by the charge of treason against their leadership. The manifestation subsided, and the Government succeeded in restoring order, aided by popular revulsion against the Bolsheviks, the subsequent arrival of front units, and the first rumors of the German counteroffensive. Bolshevik headquarters and the editorial offices of *Pravda* were raided and closed, while the Government moved to arrest the Bolshevik leaders before they could escape in the wake of the charges.

Although the release of the documents was undoubtedly instrumental in the suppression of the uprising, Kerensky, L'vov, Nekrasov, and Tereshchenko were indignant at the disclosure. In April they had received from the French Government through Albert Thomas detailed information pointing to Bolshevik-German collaboration and had secretly been gathering additional materials to support an indictment. In particular, they hoped to seize Ganetskii, one of the principal financial intermediaries between the Bolsheviks and the Germans, who was momentarily expected to cross the Swedish-Finnish border. With the incriminating documents he was presumed to carry, they planned to move decisively against the leading Bolsheviks. Forewarned by the action of the Minister of Justice, Ganetskii remained in Sweden. Pereverzev was dismissed for making public the incomplete documentation in his possession and for violating the Government's instructions that the information be withheld until arrests could be carried out.

Lenin and Zinoviev went into hiding the evening of July 4 and eluded the authorities,[3] but a number of other leaders of the uprising were imprisoned. The Government inquest, according to the announcement of the Prosecutor of the Petrograd Court of Appeals published in the press on July 22, revealed sufficient evidence to establish the guilt of the accused of both armed rebellion and treason.[4]

---

[2] David Shub, *Lenin*, pp. 207-8.

[3] V. D. Bronch-Bruevich, *Na boevykh postakh fevral'skoi i oktiabri'skoi revoliutsii*, pp. 83-85; and Doc. 1171.

[4] The documents from the archives of the German Foreign Ministry that became available after World War II substantiated the charges of German financial support to the Bolsheviks made by the Provisional Government and reiterated later in Germany by Eduard Bernstein and others.

Indeed, the blow to the Bolsheviks' drive for power and the decline in their fortunes and following were severe, forcing Lenin to revise his plans and methods and adopt direct armed action as the only possible road to victory, a tactic which became feasible and was immeasurably and unexpectedly aided in late August by the Kornilov affair and its consequences.[5]

Meantime, the cabinet crisis continued. On July 7 Prince L'vov withdrew from the Government and Kerensky accepted the post of Minister-President. But it was not until July 13, when the remaining ministers and acting ministers put their offices at the disposal of Kerensky, that it was possible to turn to the problem of reconstructing the Government, a delay occasioned by the need to continue the restoration of order and by Kerensky's absence at the front in the face of the German counteroffensive.

Immediately Kerensky encountered grave difficulties in his task. The Temporary Committee of the State Duma showed great reluctance to approve the reorganization because it considered its role to be insufficiently recognized by Kerensky. It was also concerned by the prospect of increased Soviet influence in the new government. Likewise, the independent business and financial groups who were approached for representation hesitated for fear their members would be used only for window dressing. The Kadets, after an exchange of correspondence with Kerensky, declined to serve if the Declaration of July 8 remained as the basis of Government policy. Still other factors complicated the negotiations. The Central Committee of the Socialist Revolutionary Party demanded the retention of Chernov as Minister of Agriculture as a consequence of Kadet and other attacks upon him, which had led him to submit his resignation in order to have a free hand to clear himself of the charges. At the same time, the Kadets insisted upon the inclusion of Kokoshkin. However phrased, these were ultimatums. Finally, on July 21, when Kerensky's efforts seemed to have reached a complete impasse, he resigned as Minister-President, asserting that he found it impossible to form a government.

In this moment of national emergency, the various groups and parties hastily laid their differences to one side and met in the Winter Palace to resolve the crisis. The result was a decision of necessity to ask Kerensky to reassume the Presidency with a free hand in organizing a government of his own choosing. To avoid the possibility of a new conflict, Kerensky accepted both Chernov and Kokoshkin. The Temporary Committee of the Duma as well as the Soviet approved the decision. Kerensky agreed and was able to organize a ministry with relative speed.

In the following weeks, the rapid ebb of Bolshevik influence and the continued measures of the Government to strengthen discipline at the front and promote stability throughout the rest of the country brought hopeful signs of a democratic resurgence. To reinforce these trends, promote unity, and benefit from as broad an expression of public opinion as possible during the period before the convo-

[5] Leon Trotsky, in his *The History of the Russian Revolution*, II, 250 ff., wrote: "In the official soviet histories the opinion has become established . . . that the July attack upon the party—the combination of repression and slander—went by almost without leaving a trace upon the workers' organizations. That is utterly untrue." He then cited convincing evidence of the setback suffered by the Party following the July Days. Leonard Shapiro asserted in his recent *The Communist Party of the Soviet Union*, p. 167, that the "July demonstration . . . seriously altered the whole situation of the bolsheviks. Their popularity waned almost as rapidly as it had waxed." The Bolshevik shift in tactics from an indirect approach, by first forcing the Soviets to take power, to the employment of armed action, was outlined by Lenin in "On Slogans," *Collected Works of V. I. Lenin: Toward the Seizure of Power*, XXI, Bk. I, 43–50.

cation of the Constituent Assembly, the new Government convened a national assembly at Moscow, including representatives of all influential political, social, and economic forces in the country.

The Conference met from August 12 to 15. It heard the reports of members of the Government on the work and problems of their departments; of the Supreme Commander and other military leaders; of soldier and sailor delegates; of representatives of the old and new organs of local self-government; of VTsIK and of the Executive Committee of the Soviets of Peasants' Deputies, including the important declaration of Chkheidze on behalf of both Central Executive Committees and other democratic organizations; of spokesmen of the All-Russian Union of Cooperatives and of various social and economic groups and organizations; and of the national minorities. From it emerged a broad picture of contemporary Russian opinion, organizational development, political alignment, and governmental activity. On occasion cooperation and unity were heralded, notably in the significant on-stage handshake of the industrialist Bublikov and the socialist Tseretelli, signaling the willingness of some members of industrial and financial circles to cooperate with the democracy in the promotion of cardinal political and social reforms.

Yet, the course of the Conference was also accompanied by disturbing developments and events. The opening session was marred by a protest strike in Moscow in several essential services, called by the Bolsheviks, who had refused to participate in the meetings. More immediately portentous, with the weakening of the Bolsheviks, the extreme right came to the forefront of the Government's opposition, supported by some disillusioned liberals and certain commanders at the front, and harboring what proved to be unfounded optimism concerning the strength and extent of its following. Their forthcoming activities were foreshadowed in Moscow by the rallying of the reactionary and conservative elements around General Kornilov as the symbol and leader of their movement.

CHAPTER 24

The July Uprising

THE ARMED DEMONSTRATIONS OF JULY 3–5
AND THEIR SUPPRESSION

1147. The Events of July 3 in Petrograd

[Description in *Russkiia Vedomosti*, No. 150, July 4, 1917, p. 4.]

About 6:00 o'clock in the evening rumors spread through the city that the workers, with the participation of some army units, planned to stage an uprising. Automobiles bearing unknown people appeared on the streets. They stopped in front of the army barracks, informing the soldiers of the forthcoming armed uprising of the people and inviting them to join the rebellion. Some of the army units, as for example the Volynia Regiment, flatly refused to join the rebellion. In those cases the occupants of the automobiles appealed to them not to interfere with the units that agreed to join the revolt. About 7:00 o'clock in the evening a proclamation appeared from the All-Russian Executive Committee of the Soviet of Workers' and Peasants' Deputies, addressed to all soldiers and workers and warning them against the armed rebellion.

However, the rebellion did begin. The signal for it was given on the Vyborgskaia Side. Shortly after 6:00 o'clock in the evening the movement of the Finnish Railway trains from Petrograd stopped. At the Lanskii Station and near the city limits on both sides of the tracks of the Finnish Railway, trucks and armored trucks with machine guns appeared. Having stopped the trains, the occupants of automobiles warned the railway maintenance men that they would be machine-gunned if they attempted to start the trains from Petrograd. About 7:00 o'clock in the evening, hundreds of workers from the Vyborg area began to gather near the Liteinyi Bridge. Separate groups of the so-called "red guard" appeared, and among them, carrying on intensive propaganda, were Bolsheviks and anarchists from the villa of Durnovo. Shortly afterward rows of soldiers appeared, who arrived in several trucks, bearing red posters. The machine-gun regiment also arrived. The soldiers who gathered near the machine-gunners proceeded to drag passengers off the streetcars and send the streetcars into the park. Streetcar movement stopped. Young people appeared on the streets distributing bullets, procured no one knows where, to persons who had arms. On the square near the Finland Station several meetings were taking place, engineered by Bolsheviks and well attended. Appeals to overthrow the bourgeoisie called forth thunderous applause. Several soldiers and disabled servicemen who protested were threatened with blows. On the heels of the machine-gun regiment another group of trucks appeared with soldiers and sailors.

Armed men on horseback appeared. Having crossed the Liteinyi Bridge, the workers and soldiers formed a tremendous crowd into which other soldiers poured,

who were 40-year-old servicemen.[1] Bearing placards, they demanded their discharge for field work. On reaching the Arsenal, the mob removed the night shift
from work. Most of the workers left their places unwillingly. Then several men
on horseback raced over the Liteinyi Bridge, announcing that the Soviet of
Workers' [and Soldiers'] Deputies had taken the power into its hands. The 40-
year-old soldiers were told by the strikers that, in spite of Kerensky's orders, they
would be sent home for field work. The mob carried placards with slogans: "All
power to the Soviets of Workers', Peasants', and Soldiers' Deputies."

1148. CIRCULAR TELEGRAMS OF THE MINISTRY OF THE INTERIOR TO GUBERNIYA, OBLAST, AND MUNICIPAL COMMISSARS DESCRIBING THE EVENTS OF JULY 4

[*VVP*, No. 97, July 6, 1917, p. 2.]

A

On the morning of July 4 the [following] armed units of the army and navy
arrived in Petrograd from Kronstadt: units of the 1st Machine-Gun Reserve Regiment from Oranienbaum and the 3rd Reserve Regiment from Peterhof. At about
12:00 NOON these units and the [following] regiments: 1st Reserve, 176th Reserve, 1st Machine-Gun Reserve, and the Grenadier Guards Reserve battalions,
accompanied by other, partly armed, mobs, set forth toward the Tauride Palace,
where the Central Executive Committee of the Soviets of Workers' and Soldiers'
Deputies, together with the Soviet of Peasants' Deputies, are in permanent session,
in order [to carry out] an armed demonstration under the slogans "Down with
the Provisional Government," "Down with the ten capitalist ministers," "All
power to the Soviets of Workers' and Soldiers' Deputies." The attitude of the
demonstrators toward the leading majority of the Central Committee was obviously hostile. All over the city, armed men were driving trucks and cabs, which
they had seized, with machine guns installed on some of them. During the day,
in many parts of the city, revolver, rifle, and machine-gun firing went on; there
were wounded and dead among the population.

At about 6:00 P.M., during the session at the Tauride Palace of the Executive
Committee with the participation of the socialist ministers, an armed mob of
troops and workmen attempted to arrest the Minister of Post and Telegraph,
Tseretelli, and arrested the Minister of Agriculture, Chernov, who was freed after
a speech by the Bolshevik Trotsky. By that time the Tauride Palace was surrounded from all sides by dense masses of a highly excited armed mob, which was
already penetrating inside the building. During the entire day Minister-President
Prince L'vov and the rest of the members of the Provisional Government were at
the headquarters of the Commander of the Troops of the [Military] District,
where, in accordance with their directions, measures for stopping the disorders
were being planned. The Government summoned from Pavlovsk the Mounted
Guard Artillery, two troops of the 1st and 4th Don Cossack Regiments, and four
companies of the Izmailovskii and two of the Semenovskii [Regiments]. Immediately upon the arrival of the troops, and after receiving extremely alarming news

---

[1] Many soldiers who had reached the age of 40 had been furloughed for agricultural field
work, then called back in preparation for the offensive. Some had protested their recall with
demonstrations and even riots.

from those members of the Provisional Government who were at the Tauride Palace, part of the troops were immediately sent to liberate the Central Committee surrounded in the Tauride Palace. On the way, the Cossacks, who were covering the artillery, were subjected near the Troitskii Bridge to cross-rifle and machine-gun fire, and suffered rather severe casualties. The artillery, having discharged a volley, immediately cleared a way for itself, and the mobs around the Tauride Palace scattered. There was considerable firing on the Liteinyi [Prospekt] and near Ertel Lane.

Prior to the arrival of the troops, the armed mob, led by unknown persons, made an unsuccessful attempt to seize the counterintelligence Bureau on the Voskresenskii Quay. The rebellion has been quelled by the measures taken by the Government, and toward night tangible [signs of] quieting were noticeable in the streets. At various places motorcars and separate groups of armed persons, who quickly discontinued resistance at the appearance of military units, were being stopped and disarmed. The Government has taken all necessary measures for the prevention of similar disorders. Arrests are taking place. This morning the bridges on the Neva were pulled up and the streets are quiet.

PRINCE L'VOV, Minister-President–Minister of the Interior

[No. 2863] July 5, 1917

B

In supplement to No. 2863, the Ministry of the Interior states that on the afternoon of July 4, the Commander of the Troops of the Military District issued the following announcement: "In fulfillment of the order from the Provisional Government to clear Petrograd of people bearing arms, violating order, and endangering the personal security and property of citizens, I enjoin the inhabitants of the capital not to go out on the streets except for urgent reasons, to lock the gates to their homes, and take precautions against possible penetration into their homes of unknown persons. I enjoin the armed units to proceed at once to re-establish order on the streets."

The troops composed of artillery, Cossacks, and infantry proceeded in complete subordination to the orders of the Commander, fulfilling the Government plan—fully approved by the Executive Committees of the Soviets of Workers', Soldiers', and Peasants' Deputies—to suppress decisively the disorders and arrest the participants. The Minister of the Interior has taken into account the possibility of the occurrence of events in various places which would further disrupt the economic life of the country and threaten the entire country with complete ruin in the matter of gathering the harvest and distributing food and fuel, thus weakening the heroic efforts of the glorious army to break down the stubborn resistance of the enemy on the front. He therefore proposes that you take immediate steps to discuss, together with representatives of all the public organizations, means for the most energetic way to avert and stop similar possible actions of the minority which disgrace the revolution. In their appeal the All-Russian Soviets of Workers' and Soldiers' and Peasants' Deputies state: "These actions directed at our revolutionary army, defending at the front the conquests of the revolution, are tantamount to treason. Those in the rear who infringe on the will of the plenary organs of democracy and thereby kindle discord in its ranks stab the revolutionary army in the back."

Informing you of the above-mentioned, the Ministry of the Interior recommends that you immediately widely publicize the events that are taking place and the measures undertaken by the Government, and that you report at once on the situation in the guberniya and state the orders you gave.

LEONTIEV, for the Minister of the Interior
[July 5, 1917, 1:00 P.M.]

1149. TESTIMONY ON THE ORIGINS AND PROGRESS OF THE ARMED UPRISING

[I. Tobolin, "Iiul'skie dni v Petrograde," *KA*, XIII (1927), 13–20, 58–63; XIV (1927), 63–64. The Special Commission of Inquiry into the participation of military units in the events of July 3–5 included a civilian attorney, a military lawyer, a combat officer, a soldier with legal training, two representatives from VTsIK, two representatives from the Executive Committee of the All-Russian Congress of Peasants' Soviets, two representatives from the Executive Committee of the Petrograd Soviet, and one representative from the units which were called in from the front. *Sob. Uzak.*, I, 2, No. 1074.]

A. *The First Machine-Gun Regiment*

On July 18, 1917, the members of the Special Commission of Inquiry, established according to the enactment of the Provisional Government of July 9 of the current year, having discussed the materials gathered with regard to the participation in the uprising of July 3–5 of the personnel of the 1st Machine-Gun Regiment, have found the following:

On July 3, 1917, the members of the regimental committee of the 1st Machine-Gun Regiment met at the Soldiers' Club in order to discuss some questions regarding the internal organization of the Regiment. At the same time in the same club there were already gathered a considerable number of soldiers who were animatedly discussing something. Those gathered soon elected a chairman, the soldier Golovin, who opened the meeting with a speech regarding the contemporary political situation, in which he called upon the soldiers not to send replacements or machine guns to the front, because the offensive at the front was started against the will of the people and sending assistance to the army would merely contribute to the prolongation of the war. The second speaker was Bleichman (on behalf of the Petrograd Federation of Anarchists, [according to] the minutes of the meetings and the testimony of Gibel'), who in an ardent speech called upon the soldiers to protest against the war and to support their claim by a demonstration—not a peaceful demonstration, which would not achieve any goal, but an armed demonstration; he called upon them to take all the power in their own hands, ignoring the Soviet of Workers' and Soldiers' Deputies, of whom the majority was on the side of the bourgeoisie; he demanded the requisition of money and food from the bourgeois, the seizure of the Don Basin mines and of all the plants and factories, the overthrow of the Provisional Government—and all this immediately. (Testified to by the witnesses: Chirikov, Mindrum, Zhigalin, Mikhaveiskii, Shofer, Lobanov, Kurenkov, Grin'kov, Degterev, Karev, Tsar'kov, and others.)

Following the speech by Bleichman, the meeting started to discuss only the question of an immediate demonstration of the Regiment in the streets with arms in hand for the purpose of overthrowing the Provisional Government.

Of the persons outside of the Regiment, the following speakers expressed themselves in favor of such a demonstration: a certain Golubushkin (representative of the Petrograd Federation of Anarchists), a soldier of the 1st Battery of the 110th Artillery Battalion, Pavlov, and a number of other civilians, soldiers, and sailors, who were not identified by the investigation.

Of the soldiers of the Machine-Gun Regiment, only soldiers belonging to the Bolshevik association of the Regiment spoke—Golovin, Kazakov, Romanov, and Il'inskii—who likewise appealed for an armed demonstration for the purpose of seizing power and transferring it to the Soviet of Workers' and Soldiers' Deputies. In their speeches the soldiers mentioned disagreed among themselves as to the moment of the demonstration; some suggested a demonstration immediately, while the others suggested postponing this demonstration until an organized contact would be established with other military units (until the morning of July 4—testimony of Koshelev).

The question of an immediate demonstration of the Regiment was solved unanimously in the affirmative, and the time for the demonstration was set for 5:00 P.M. At the same time, a temporary revolutionary committee to substitute for the regimental committee, with two men from each company, as well as delegates for the purpose of informing other military units and the plants of the action of the 1st Machine-Gun Regiment, was elected (minutes of the meeting). Ensign Semashko took the leadership of the revolutionary committee and of the movement.

The decision of the meeting was put into effect according to the instructions of Ensign Semashko and other members of the Regiment's personnel who were entrusted with the organization and the direction of the action, having for its purpose the overthrow of the Provisional Government. For two days the Regiment, arms in hand, was in the streets of Petrograd for the purpose of accomplishing the aforementioned goals. The consequence of this armed demonstration of the 1st Machine-Gun Regiment and of other military units of the city of Petrograd and its suburbs, which joined it later, was the killing and wounding of a considerable number of persons among the troops which they resisted and which had been summoned by the Government to suppress the rebellion, and also among private individuals.

.   .   .

B

On July 24, 1917, Lieutenant Colonel Ukrainstev, member of the Special Commission of Inquiry established in accordance with the decree of the Provisional Government of July 9 of the current year, interrogated the below-mentioned as a witness, in accordance with article 443 of the Code of Criminal Procedure.

Gregorii Illarionovich Torskii, reservist of the 1st Company of the 1st Infantry Reserve Unit, Orthodox, 30 years old, had never before been on trial.

I am inscribing his testimony in my own hand.

On July 3 at about 5:00 P.M. soldiers, who called themselves the delegation of the 1st Machine-Gun Regiment, came to see me as the president of the regimental committee; several workers from the Lessner, the Metallicheskii, and other plants came with them; in all seven men came: three soldiers, the rest workers. The delegation declared that it was sent by the Machine-Gun Regiment to demand that we should immediately demonstrate, arms in hand, in the streets of Petrograd for the purpose of overthrowing the capitalist ministers and of transferring all power into the hands of the Soviets of Workers', Soldiers', and Peasants' Deputies. The soldiers of the Machine-Gun Regiment and the workers who came with them declared that all the Petrograd garrison and all the workers of the city of Petrograd had decided to get out into the streets at 5:00 o'clock in order to express their protests and therefore they asked us to do the same. Knowing the political attitude of the machine-gunners, I took a very skeptical view of their declaration and asked them to confirm their words by a written document, that is, by the resolution of the meeting of the Machine-Gun Regiment and of the Petrograd garrison. They did not have the latter and only presented their personal identifications [issued] by the committee of the Machine-Gun Regiment. The document presented was signed by the president and the secretary and it had a seal.

They promised to bring me the resolution not later than 7:00 o'clock. To the demand of the delegation I answered: The 1st Regiment is not in sympathy with the anarchists and those who adhere to them, but recognizes the decisions of the central democratic organs.

Ivan Osipov was present at this conversation and left the regimental committee together with the delegation; I do not know where he went. At 9:00 o'clock I left the Regiment and went home. Everything was calm and quiet in the Regiment. I left Shishakin as my deputy. In my presence no one else visited the regimental committee nor called upon us to join the demonstration; the machine-gunners did not bring their resolution. At 10:00 P.M. the member of the regimental committee on duty telephoned me and requested me to come immediately to the Regiment, because the units of the Regiment were going out into the streets with weapons in hand. I asked him to restrain the Regiment from the demonstration at least until my arrival, but received the reply: "Logical arguments do not have any effect; the soldiers are pouring into town; at least they should get out in an organized fashion, so that plundering and violence can be prevented." I immediately went to the Regiment. Armed cars with soldiers and workers were driving in the city. Streetcar traffic stopped. I reached the Regiment on foot only by 11:00 P.M.

On the Okhtenskii Bridge I met soldiers from my regiment, about five or six hundred men; they were carrying rifles and posters: "Down with the counter-revolution, down with party arguments," "All power in the hands of the Soviets of Soldiers', Workers', and Peasants' Deputies," "Down with the capitalist ministers," and "Let us unite around the Soviets." Ensign Sakharov and the Osipovs rode on horseback in front of the procession. I came up to Sakharov and asked him, "Where are you leading the soldiers?" "To the Tauride Palace to greet the Soviet of Soldiers' and Workers' Deputies." To my objections he answered, "This is necessary; you don't understand anything; I have no time to speak with you," and he rode away from me. The soldiers were marching in good enough order.

I went to the Regiment. The men on duty at the committee gave me a telephone message signed by Chkheidze stating that the Regiment should not come out.

With the telephone message, I went to catch the soldiers and met them near the Tauride Palace, where they stood in good order. I drove to Sakharov, gave him the telephone message from Chkheidze. Sakharov read the telephone message and said: "We know well these telephone messages; I know who writes them and who signs them." After this the soldiers elected a delegation from their midst to send to the Executive Committee. Ensign Sakharov, Ivan Osipov, Gavrill Osipov, and Boris Brilliant were elected for the delegation. I do not know where they had been, but when they came from the Tauride Palace, Sakharov told me that now we could return to the barracks. [They said that] the Executive Committee already knew that we had come and that tomorrow again we would surely go out into the streets. I began to admonish the soldiers to go back to the barracks, and this was done. Throughout this day there were no clashes and I again went home.

Having arrived at 9:00 A.M. on the 4th at the Regiment, I learned that during the night, after the soldiers were back in their barracks, Ensign Sakharov and the Osipovs had organized a meeting on the regimental parade grounds, kindling passions with their rebellious speeches and urging a demonstration for the purpose of transferring all the power into the hands of the Soviets. In conclusion they declared that next day there would be a demonstration and the soldiers present gave their consent to it. I was not present at the meeting and know of it from my comrades.

The question of the demonstration was discussed in the regimental committee. Since it did not wish to lose contact with the Executive Committee of the Soviet of Soldiers', Workers', and Peasants' Deputies, a delegation to the Tauride Palace was elected from our regiment and charged to learn whether we should demonstrate or not.

As the most fanatic partisans of the demonstration were Sakharov, the Osipovs, and others, the regimental committee, trusting that these men had not lost their honor and their conscience and would not deceive the committee, sent Sakharov and Gavrill Osipov to the Executive Committee; it was understood that they would let us know from there if the decision of the Executive Committee was to let us demonstrate; if there was no such decision they should themselves propose to the soldiers to postpone the demonstration for which they had agitated so ardently during the previous night.

After the departure of Sakharov and Osipov, two members of the Executive Committee of the Peasants' Deputies came to the committee and, after reporting on the current events, proposed to vote on a resolution, the meaning of which was as follows: The 1st Regiment in principle continues to maintain that the governmental crisis may be resolved only by transferring the power into the hands of the Soviets, but the Regiment abstains from any kind of demonstrations. This resolution was not accepted and another one, whose wording I attach herewith, was adopted. After this the members of the Peasants' Deputies left. Ensign Gavrilov and Master Sergeant Stepanov protested against the resolution proposed by the members of the Executive Committee. Soon I was summoned to the orderly room, where the Commander of the Regiment was and where I saw the First Sergeant of the 2nd Company, Karataev, who declared: "I have come from the Tauride Palace; all the regiments are already there, while our regiment still sits at home; it is necessary to set out immediately."

I remarked to him that Sakharov and Osipov had been sent to the Tauride Palace, and that we could not demonstrate without receiving the authorization from the Executive Committee through those who were sent there. Also the Commander of the Regiment spoke to Karataev, but Karataev insisted and even insulted the Commander. He said: "I know it is to your advantage that we should not demonstrate; you are following the course of the old government." At that moment (it was 1:00 P.M.) a note was received from Gavrill Osipov reading as follows: "It is decided to demonstrate. Call the 4th Battalion to the headquarters of the Regiment and await our arrival. The companies should all be ready.

G. Osipov." It was marked "Tauride Palace, 12:38." The note was brought by First Sergeant Zakoltaev of the 7th Company. I sent this note to the committee and it was decided to leave the matter open until the arrival of Sakharov and Osipov; I was charged to call the 4th Battalion to Regimental Headquarters, which I did. I learned from the Commander that on the 4th a telephone message had been received, signed by General Polovtsev. It stated: "In case of an armed or unarmed demonstration of the Regiment in its full strength or even a part of it, I order that all the officers and committees go with the demonstrators and thus prevent plundering and violence which might take place." This telephone message was not read in the committee for fear that it would be interpreted by the soldiers in a reverse sense. At about 4:00 o'clock the soldiers of the 4th Battalion arrived. At this time a delegation of sailors from the naval artillery firing range came to the regimental committee—one officer and three sailors, all armed; they showed their documents. The purpose of their visit, on the whole, boiled down to a request to give them a company of soldiers, as they expected an attack by the Cossacks. I refused their request; they had no authorization for this detail either from headquarters or from the Executive Committee, and I did not find it possible to satisfy [their demand].

In the meantime they agitated in favor of a demonstration and indicated that Kronstadt had acted quite rightly by taking a whole series of repressive measures. The soldier of the 13th Company, Eliazar Slavkin, who was there, and the soldier of the 15th Company, anarchist Markin, also began to support the sailors and to justify their actions. I must say that during the whole war Slavkin was a deserter and came to the Regiment only after the revolution. At the meetings he delivered speeches which brought disorganization into the Regiment and incited the soldiers to disobey their chiefs.

At that time member Gurevich of the Executive Committee of the Soviet of Soldiers' and Workers' Deputies arrived at the Regiment; coming into the regimental committee, he began to exhort not to demonstrate. He asked me to authorize the holding of a regimental meeting, but I ignored this suggestion, being afraid that Gurevich would be insulted by the soldiers as a representative of the Government. The soldiers began to arrive and a brief meeting ensued. The soldier of the 15th Company, Reshetnikov, spoke at the meeting; his speech boiled down to [asserting that] the demonstration was necessary, because [otherwise] the interests of the masses of soldiers and workers would suffer. He also spoke of the uselessness of the offensive and in general of waging the war.

Sakharov and Gavrill Osipov, back from the Tauride Palace, came into the committee and declared that now the Regiment must get out into the streets and proceed to the Tauride Palace in order to show the Soviet its loyalty and the forces on which the Soviet could rely; he also indicated that the decision was taken unanimously, but, as it turned out later, he concealed intentionally that he had not been in the Executive Committee but at the session of the Workers' Section. Comrade Gurevich opposed him; Sakharov interrupted his speech and rudely declared: "The goal of our demonstration is peaceful, we intend neither to plunder nor to arrest nor to kill; we must only make a show of our force. We take weapons for self-defense; whatever you say or do, we will go; the people demand it and the Regiment decided it yesterday night at the meeting; all conversation is superfluous and I take upon myself the responsibility for the demonstration and for the consequences that might ensue; if the regimental committee refuses to go, I will lead the Regiment myself." After that I summoned Sakharov, Osipov, and some ten members of the regimental committee into another room and asked them not to demonstrate; my proposal was seconded by Ensign Gavrilov, but Sakharov and Osipov protested against it. Then I told them that I would agree only in case the command and the whole authority be transferred to the regimental commander, Lieutenant Colonel Lapinskii, as I knew him to be an honest man who would be able to restrain the demonstrators from undesirable actions. My proposal was accepted and I went to report on it to the regimental commander. The regimental commander ordered me to go to the companies and said that the companies that wanted to go had to form themselves; he told me that the regimental committee must also go with the Regiment. At the same time I received a declaration from the 10th and 9th Companies that they would not go and that they would remain in full strength to carry out their duties; analogous declarations were received from the Composite Working Company and from the noncombatant personnel. Likewise the 1st Battalion, with the exception of a few individuals, took hardly any part in the demonstration. As a result there were not more than 1,200 men in formation on the square. At about 7:00 P.M. we left the Regiment. I personally ordered the soldiers to implicitly obey all the orders of the Commander of the Regiment and to execute them.

When we arrived at the Tauride Palace, a delegation was selected which was comprised of myself, Sakharov, and Osipov. We went to the Tauride Palace, desiring to be admitted to the session of the Executive Committee, but the session was closed and we were not received; then Sakharov led us to the Workers' Section and, having met Volodarskii, asked him to come out and greet us.

Also Mashkevich, a member of the Workers' Section, requested me to give him a company of men in order to guard the food stores from pogroms which might take place. I promised to do so. After this, together with Volodarskii, we went out to the Regiment, and, on behalf of the soldiers who were there, I said: "The soldiers of the 1st Infantry Regiment have come to greet the Soviets of the Soldiers', Workers', and Peasants' Deputies and their executive organs, and they declare themselves ready, at the first call of the Soviet, to place themselves at its disposal." Comrade Volodarskii spoke after me. In his speech he stressed that the Bolsheviks had won, that many ministers had withdrawn from the Government, and that their places would be occupied by people who would lead the country out of the dead end into which the old government had brought it.

Then he greeted the Regiment on behalf of all the Bolshevik organizations and pointed out that the forces of the Bolsheviks were enormous and their victory beyond doubt. In conclusion, he asked the soldiers to return to the barracks and to await further events. His speech was received with tumultuous applause. The regimental commander took advantage of Volodarskii's words and began to admonish [the soldiers] to return to the barracks. At that time I left to organize the detail of soldiers in accordance with Mashkevich's request. I was told that Sakharov had protested vehemently and had begun to exhort the soldiers to go not to the barracks but along the Liteinyi [Prospekt] and the Nevskii [Prospekt] and home, in order to make a show of force to the bourgeois, as he expressed himself. At the same time, Sakharov stressed once again that he was responsible for the demonstration. The regimental commander pointed out that blood might be shed accidentally; then Sakharov replied that he answered also for that blood, but at the same time he declared with assurance that this could not happen, as we were going peacefully, with no intention of killing anyone, and that nobody would fire at us. The Regiment proceeded, and until the Liteinyi Prospekt it went calmly and safely. Turning on the Liteinyi and reaching the arsenal, we heard shots from the side of the Alexander Bridge, on which a group of civilians and military were standing. Others assert that the shots came from the building of the district court. The Regiment took the first shots calmly, but then the shots became more frequent and somewhere machine-gun fire opened up. The soldiers did not resist and in their panicky flight they began to hide themselves wherever they could. Many went behind the guns standing beside the arsenal and opened an aimless fire; they fired upwards and on the bridge but without any definite targets. The regimental commander stood on the Liteinyi and ordered the soldiers to stop firing. This they did. It seemed that everything was ended, but at that moment a troop of Cossacks appeared on the Liteinyi. From the side of the Alexander Bridge, strong rifle and machine-gun fire was opened against them. One could hear three explosions of either gun shells or hand grenades. The fire was directed along the Liteinyi and inflicted casualties among us. Our soldiers, thinking that the Cossacks were firing at them, opened fire against them. Again there was a panicky flight, and heavy firing. Beside me stood a soldier who was wounded by a bullet, and I took him to the arsenal to have the wound dressed. Whether the Cossacks fired or not I did not see, but I saw two Cossacks fall from their horses. Soon after that the shooting stopped and the soldiers returned to the Regiment. The first ranks went in an orderly manner, and a small group walked separately. It turned out that we had five men killed and about twenty wounded; during the firing I did not see Sakharov and the Osipovs and I do not know where they were. Upon return to the Regiment a meeting of the company and of the regimental committees was convened at once. . . .[2]

C

On August 20, 1917, the examining magistrate of the St. Petersburg District Court of the first section of the Tsarskoe Selo uezd, in his room interrogated, in accordance with article 443 of the Code of Criminal Procedure, the person named hereunder as a witness, who testified.

Sergei Aleksandrovich, Count Rebinder, Colonel of the Mounted Guard Artillery, 32 years old, Orthodox, lives in the city of Pavlovsk, has not been tried.

On July 4, 1917, by order of the Commander of the Petrograd Military District, a platoon of the Reserve Mounted Guard Artillery Battery under my command arrived at 7:00 P.M. from Pavlovsk at Dvortsovaia Square in the city of Petrograd. At 8:00 P.M. of the same July 4, the Commander ordered me to take one troop of the 1st and one troop of the 4th Don Cossack Regiments and two artillery pieces from the reserve battery of the Mounted Guard Artillery and to proceed at a trot to Shpalernaia Street toward the State Duma, and there, by all means, including opening fire, to disperse the crowd which was besieging the State Duma. Having received the aforesaid order, I formed my detachment in the following order: a platoon of Cossacks, two horse-drawn artillery pieces, the rest of the Cossacks; I moved the whole detachment at a trot. I chose the following itinerary: Millionnaia Street, Suvorovskaia Square, the Embankment, Voskresenskii Prospekt, Shpalernaia Street. In view of the fact that by moving at a trot the detachment stretched out considerably, I ordered it to slow down when we reached

[2] See Doc. 1159.

the Embankment. In this way and in complete order, the detachment reached the Liteinyi Bridge. Being personally at the head of the detachment when crossing Liteinyi Prospekt near the Liteinyi Bridge, I noticed that an infantry unit in complete order was going from Shpalernaia Street to Liteinyi in the direction of the Nevskii [Prospekt]; a crowd surrounded it. Seeing the vanguard platoon of my detachment, someone from the crowd, or perhaps from the military unit, which was moving from Shpalernaia Street to Liteinyi, shouted "Cossacks!" and at the same time from an armed car on the Liteinyi Bridge a rifle shot was fired; then very strong rifle and machine-gun fire against the vanguard unit of the detachment in my charge started from Liteinyi Prospekt, from the Bridge, from the Embankment, from the neighboring houses, and even from the barges which are located on the Neva. It is impossible to establish precisely from which houses the shots came: the bullets literally showered from all sides. Besides the aforementioned, I testify that not only sailors, soldiers, and civilians fired from the Liteinyi Bridge, but even individuals clothed in convict overalls, who fired at us literally point-blank. The Cossacks and the mounted guns opened fire only when there were already killed and wounded in the detachment. One of the mounted guns was removed from its limber on the Voskresenskaia Quay and fired three times in the direction of the Liteinyi Bridge; the other gun, all its crew and all its horses having been put out of action, remained at the corner of Liteinyi and returned to the platoon at 2:00 A.M. on July 5. The force of the fire directed on the vanguard of the detachment can be judged by the losses which the platoon of the Reserve Guard Mounted Battery suffered: out of 80 soldiers and 60 horses, 3 soldiers were killed and 17 wounded, and 30 horses were killed, which makes 25 per cent of the soldiers and 50 per cent of the horses.

1150. Instructions from the Executive Committee of the Petrograd
Soviet Forbidding Armed Demonstrations
[I. Tobolin, "Iiul'skie dni v Petrograde," *KA*, XIII (1927), 1.]

Telegram

To all troop units:

July 3, 1917, No. 2050. The Executive Committee confirms its previous instructions that demonstrations by the armed forces are not permitted. This order must be strictly obeyed.

Dan, Gots
Members of the Executive Committee's Presidium

1151. Instructions from VTsIK Forbidding Armed Demonstrations
[I. Tobolin, "Iiul'skie dni v Petrograde," *KA*, XIII (1927), 1–2.]

Telegram

Very urgent.

To all the troops, units, headquarters, administrations, military schools of the Petrograd garrison and of the garrisons of Tsarskoe Selo, Krasnoe Selo, Oranienbaum, of the Old and New Peterhof, Ligovo, Strel'na, Sergiev, Pavlovsk, Kronstadt.

July 3, 1917. 8 hours 50 minutes. No. 2056.

Some military units have violated the instructions of the All-Russian Congress, which has prohibited armed demonstrations. Armed groups attempted by threats to impose their will on the plenipotentiary representatives of the majority of the revolutionary democracy of Russia. Drunks appeared on the streets of Petrograd; there were many attempts to break into stores; there was shooting again as on April 20–21; the streets were reddened with blood; there were killed and wounded. At the height of the confusion, Black Hundred agitation was openly conducted in the city; obscure suspect individuals were detected among the agitators who called upon the military units to demonstrate. All these events threatened to create an abyss between the garrison of Petrograd and the front. The rear calls upon the comrade soldiers, while it is not too late, to take measures to save the honor of the Petrograd revolutionary garrison. Comrades, beware of provocateurs. Defend your Soviet of Workers' and Solders' Deputies against the forces of disorganizers who undermine it. Save the unity of the revolutionary forces. The All-Russian Central Executive Committee [VTsIK] of the Soviet of Workers' and Soldiers' Deputies has decided that all the regimental, battalion, company, and command committees and also the members of the Soviet of Workers' and Soldiers' Deputies should be with their units. All these units must maintain contact with the All-Russian Central Executive Committee, advising it of everything. All appeals, except the orders from headquarters, should be checked through the All-Russian Central Executive Committee, telephones 104-05, 104-06, 622-63, 123-68, 48-74.

BOGDANOV, VOITINSKII, BINASIK, SKAALOV
Members of the Committee

1152. ORDER OF THE PROVISIONAL GOVERNMENT FORBIDDING ARMED DEMONSTRATIONS

[*VVP*, No. 95, July 4, 1917, p. 1.]

In view of the actions by some military units which took place on July 4 that resulted in casualties, all armed demonstrations are absolutely forbidden.

July 4, 1917

1153. MEETING OF VTsIK AND THE ALL-RUSSIAN EXECUTIVE COMMITTEE OF PEASANTS' SOVIETS DURING THE NIGHT OF JULY 3–4

[*Izvestiia*, No. 108, July 4, 1917, pp. 3–4, and No. 110, July 6, 1917, pp. 2, 3, 5, 6.]

The meeting opened at 11:40 P.M. [and lasted until 5:00 A.M., July 4].
N. S. Chkheidze was chairman.

DAN. Comrades, we are now going through a difficult and, perhaps, a cruical day. The Central Executive Committee of the Soviets of Workers' and Soldiers' Deputies and the Executive Committee of the All-Russian Soviet of Peasants' Deputies are now faced with carrying out the task that has been placed on them, that of fighting those who are undermining the revolution. Today we face the alternative of fulfilling our duty, or admitting our impotence. We must now demand a definite answer from every participant—is he with us on the path indicated by the Congress, or is he against [us]. On behalf of the Presidium I am inviting to be present only those persons who can assume the responsibility of carrying out the will of the revolutionary democracy, the will of its plenary organ.

SUKHANOV. Taking the gravity of the [present] moment into consideration, I do not thing that there can be any opposition to such a demand. But until some resolution or other [is adopted] by the meeting, no one is in a position to decide whether he should stay or leave the meeting.

CHERNOV. I consider that those people who, at the present moment, are looking in opposite directions—to the decisions of the present meeting or to the decisions of their electors—will have to leave this meeting hall. They will learn from newspapers about the decisions made at this meeting. Then they can decide where to go. But here the only persons who can attend are those consider it imperative to submit to the will of the plenary organ of democracy.

The motion that the decisions of the meeting would be binding for all its participants—binding in the sense that everyone will firmly uphold the decisions of the meeting—was carried, with 21 opposing.

TSERETELLI. Comrades, we must be conscious of what is happening. A particular crisis occurred in the Provisional Government. The Kadets left the Government. The revolutionary democracy is faced with the question of the way in which the Government should be reorganized. . . . The decision which the Central Committee of Soviets of Workers' and Soldiers' Deputies was to carry out tomorrow contained no objections to a government that [represented] the will of the revolutionary democracy. But now they are out in the streets demanding: "All power to the Soviets of Workers', Soldiers', and Peasants' Deputies." . . . Such slogans and actions are fatal to the cause of the revolution. This is the opinion of the All-Russian Congress. We are here for the very purpose of realizing the will of the Russian democracy. Our duty is to defend the unity and integrity of the Russian revolution. He who thinks that he is on our side when he steps out armed into the street has been deluded.

We must state that such actions conform not to the path of the revolution, but to the path of counterrevolution. We must state that the decision of the revolutionary democracy cannot be dictated by bayonets. And we must call on everyone who is loyal to the cause of the revolution to defend the plenary organ of democracy and the cause of the revolution.

DAN. At a time like this, my comrades are speaking of the harmful split in the Central Committee. But the whole horror of the situation lies not in the decision we adopted here, but in the fact that for some comrades there exist no central organs of the revolutionary democracy. We are meeting at a time when the Tauride Palace is surrounded by armed masses of people. . . .

At the very time when the revolutionary army is shedding blood at the front and is asking for our help, the revolutionary people are separating one city from the whole country, from the revolutionary army. The whole revolutionary democracy has clearly expressed its will at the All-Russian Congress, but the revolutionary people of Petrograd are making an armed attempt to foist their will on the democracy. It is our duty to say that their action benefits the counterrevolution—it categorically contradicts the will of the revolutionary democracy of the whole country. . . .

SOROKIN. It is with deep satisfaction that I heard comrades Tseretelli and Dan. We are passing through a time when the voices in authority must be heard openly and forcefully, and nobody, no threats, including death threats, can stop us from saying that what is now occurring is, essentially, a counterrevolution.

. . .

Around 3:00 A.M. a delegate of the 1st Machine-Gun Regiment came to the meeting and delivered the following speech:

"What is happening today," said the delegate, "is being done in the name of the revolution, in the name of the whole revolutionary International. Yesterday representatives from the front arrived at the Regiment and demanded machine guns from us—because otherwise they would be shot. We didn't give them the machine guns. (*General shouts of indignation:* "Shame, shame.") We didn't give them the machine guns, not because we didn't want to, but because we knew that there were machine guns in Tula. We hope that you will not put us in disgrace and that those who have been with us up to now will be with us in the future.

COMRADE SAAK'IAN. . . . Trotsky and Lenin think that the people want to transfer the power to the Soviets, but the masses, carrying the placard "All power to the Soviets" essentially want bread, which, however, will not appear automatically on the streets; the masses want the war to be terminated, come what may; the 40-year-old servicemen want to be allowed to go home.[3]

Even at the time of the Congress I said that we certainly were not panic-stricken at the thought of power, of the possibility of taking it in our own hands. But we cannot come into power only because the Lenins and Trotskys desire this.

Bayonets and machine guns must belong to the people and not to individual army units, for in this event the history of praetorianism in Rome will repeat itself [*here*].

They want to force us to go against the will of the revolutionary democracy which has elected us, but we cannot be coerced into this by machine guns.

TROTSKY voices a protest on behalf of several members of the Central Committee against the resolution of the meeting: on the necessity of submitting to the decisions of the majority or not participating in the meeting.

CHERNOV. I propose, comrades, that a certificate of authorization be required of all those who speak on behalf of military units. The fact of the matter is that a "representative" of the 1st Machine-Gun Regiment delivered a speech here, but the comrade machine-gunners present declare that they do not know this "representative," that there is no such person whatsoever in the regiment.

A comrade machine-gunner speaks and declares that there never was such a person in his regiment as the "representative" who spoke. We asked this machine-gunner for his documents, but he declared that he had no document, that it seems he gave the document to Ensign Semashko. But you all know about Semashko—he is a well-known deserter.

REPRESENTATIVE OF THE PUTILOV PLANT speaks. The whole Putilov Plant is at the Tauride Palace. The putilovites say that they will not disperse until the ten capitalist ministers are arrested and the Soviet takes the power into its hands.

. . .

ABRAMOVICH. We are witnesses to a plot. I do not approve of it. It does not have the same meaning now for the initiators as it may have had earlier. Even so,

[3] See Doc. 1147.

a decision on the transfer of power was begging the question: the social base from which the revolution drew its support has narrowed down to the base from which the Soviets draw their support. The question would anyway have been decided in terms of a transfer of power, and suddenly—a plot. I have no doubt that should the power be transfered to the Soviets, the Bolsheviks would demand that the power be transferred to the Central Committee of the Russian Social Democratic Workers' Party.

The peasantry has passed its resolutions, it has expressed its will. The peasants expressed their thoughts and the way in which they would want to resolve the land question, but they are being told of immediate seizures. Let them go out and say directly: this is our work. It must be established once and for all whether or not they want to submit to the will of the democracy or whether they will continue playing hide-and-seek as previously, provoking surreptitiously the [events] which we are now witnessing. If, however, they do want to answer all our questions openly, we must ask their electors whether they were instructed to follow the tactics we are now observing.

People come out with irresponsible slogans, but they don't undertake constructive revolutionary work, and they also do not let us carry it out.

Let the power be transferred to the Soviets tomorrow, but then, without taking anything into consideration, they will demand the socialization of the means of production.

We have been sent by a peasantry of 130 million, but delegates from small groups are coming to us here and want to foist their will on us. I propose that we ignore their armed strength and calmly answer what we think.

. . .

[Excerpts from] the Joint Meeting of the Central Executive Committee of the Soviets of Workers' and Soldiers' Deputies and the Executive Committee of the Peasants' Deputies: July 4.

. . .

ZINOVIEV: Comrades, the crisis was created, on the one hand, by the bourgeoisie's refusal to participate in the Government, and on the other hand, by the way in which Petrograd workers and soldiers reacted to this.

The departure of the Kadets is far from being a case of doctrinairism. It is naïve to think that they rejected the portfolios on account of the Ukrainian question. They acted with calculation. They acted in accordance with their class interests. They left the Government at a time when the country found itself in a critical and threatening position. It was at this point that they relieved themselves of responsibility. To think that the movement of the past few days is the work of agitators is a prejudice. This is a spontaneous movement, evoked by the extremely difficult economic position.

Our party did everything to lend an organized character to the spontaneous movement of the workers, and at the present moment our party is publishing an appeal to the Petrograd workers and soldiers to go out into the streets and to stop the demonstrations. (*Exclamations*: "After mountains of corpses.")

The Congress, having expressed itself in favor of a coalition government, never gave its word that it would under no circumstances take the power into its hands.

Now the situation has changed; now conditions have arisen under which the question of power must be decided over again. And it must be decided over again in terms of what we have been proposing.

In place of the former position with the bourgeoisie, you have substituted an agreement with individual members of the bourgeoisie; for, I ask, who is standing behind the Octobrist Godnev? Who is standing behind other bourgeois members of the Government?

Such a situation has arisen that there remains only one way out—to take all the power into your hands. If you will do this, you will save the revolution. You will enjoy the confidence and support of the whole democracy. You will save the revolution. (*Applause from the galleries.*)

.   .   .

TSERETELLI: Comrades! The fate of the revolution has never been in such danger as now, and never have we had such responsibility in our decisions as at the present moment. The question now being decided is: do we possess sufficient authority and strength to avert the civil war which is on the verge of developing? If we fail—the revolution will perish.

I will now analyze the essence of the question of power as well as [the reasons] why this question cannot be decided now. It has been pointed out here that with the resignation of the K.D.'s the bloc with the bourgeoisie has been broken.

But this is not so. When the problem of the coalition government was being decided, it was formulated in a way that depicted this as a bloc, not with the Constitutional Democrats, but with all those forces of the country that were ready to follow the path of fufilling the national tasks put forth by the revolution. Then it was also pointed out that we would break with them only at such a time as one or another stratum of the bourgeoisie turned out in practice to be a hindrance in carrying out the legislation which followed from the national platform of the democracy. It is not with parties that we form blocs. We form blocs with all those who stand on one and the same platform with us. This constitutes the essence of a coalition ministry.

From this point of view, which is shared by the majority of the democracy, the resignation of the Kadets does not signify that the bloc has been broken.

When our opponents propose that we break with the bourgeois elements and take all power into our hands, they forget to add that they are also demanding that we change our entire policy. If we, the Soviet majority, should take all the power into our hands, then wouldn't all of you, from Martov to Lenin, demand actions from us which, in our opinion, would lead to a separatist war and wouldn't you direct against us your slogan of "To an armistice, not to an offensive"? But, then, we will not adopt this policy. If, after seizing power, we did not allow you to dictate your policy to us, then wouldn't you start to say the same [things] about us as you are now saying in *Pravda*: "They are worse than the bourgeoisie. They are pretending to be socialists and are deceiving the workers even more"?

Comrades! Don't forget that there is a difference between the attitudes expressed in Petrograd and the attitudes in the provinces and on the front. There the Petrograd events are regarded as attempts to foist by force the will of the minority on the whole Russian democracy. (*Exclamations:* "Right!") I was in the provinces and on the front, and I am stating that the authority of the Provisional Government in the country is great, much greater than it is thought here.

.   .   .

1154. APPEAL OF VTsIK AND THE ALL-RUSSIAN EXECUTIVE COMMITTEE OF PEASANTS' SOVIETS TO THE WORKERS AND SOLDIERS OF PETROGRAD
[*Izvestiia*, No. 108, July 4, 1917, p. 1.]

COMRADE SOLDIERS AND WORKERS:

Contrary to the clearly expressed will of *all* socialist parties, without exception, certain obscure persons are calling on you to go out armed into the streets. It is in this way that you are asked to protest against the disbandment of regiments which have discredited themselves at the front by criminally violating their duty to the revolution.

We, authorized representatives of the revolutionary democracy of all Russia, issue this statement to you:

The disbandment of regiments at the front was carried out at the insistance of army and frontal organizations and in compliance with the order from our Minister of War, Comrade A. F. Kerensky, who was selected by us.

An action taken in defense of the disbanded regiments is an action against our brothers who are shedding their blood at the front.

We remind comrade soldiers that no military unit has the right to go out armed without a call for such action by the Commander [of the Military District], who acts in complete accord with us.

Anyone who violates this resolution during the troubled days that Russia is going through will be denounced by us as traitors and enemies of the revolution.

All available measures at our disposal will be adopted for implementing the present resolution.

> BUREAU OF THE ALL-RUSSIAN CENTRAL EXECUTIVE COMMITTEE
> OF SOVIETS OF WORKERS' AND SOLDIERS' DEPUTIES
> BUREAU OF THE ALL-RUSSIAN EXECUTIVE COMMITTEE OF
> PEASANTS' SOVIETS

1155. *Izvestiia* ON THE DANGER TO THE REVOLUTION
[No. 108, July 4, 1917, p. 2.]

Only two months have passed since the memorable April Days, and Petrograd, the heart and brain of revolutionary Russia, is once again experiencing alarming, tragic days.

The revolutionary democracy succeeded in creating a single all-Russian plenipotentiary organ—the Central Executive Committee—after enormous and intensive work by the best revolutionary forces of the country; at the same time, at the Congress of Soviets, representatives of all the organized elements of the democracy in a concerted effort worked out a consistent and all-round program for consolidating the gains of the revolution. Furthermore, a really strong revolutionary army was successfully created—through the heroic efforts of all the organs of the revolution, from the Provisional Government to the regimental and volost committees. This army, for the first time since the revolution and only two and a half months before the convocation of the Constituent Assembly, can alone bring final victory to the cause of the revolution. It was at this moment that persons and parties appeared which once again placed the revolutionary cause in the most dangerous and critical position.

On one and the same day two attacks were made against the revolutionary power, on the plenary organs of the revolutionary democracy, on their clearly expressed will.

One attempt came from the right, the other from the left.

Kadet representatives in the Government, defending the interests of the more imperialistic section of the bourgeoisie, which has been taking a more and more definitely counterrevolutionary position with every day, announced their resignation from the Government, and thereby initiated the *crisis in power*, at the very moment when there can be no question that the only surety for the salvation of the revolutionary cause lies in a single, strong revolutionary power.

.　.　.

The Ukrainian question is a detail; the Kadets left the Government even without the Ukrainian question, for they oppose further gains of the revolution; they oppose its expansion, for they do not want to assist the revolutionary cause, they do not want to take part in either its failures or its successes.

And inasmuch as the departure of the Kadets has conclusively revealed the line of our imperialistic bourgeoisie, the Kadets themselves have decisively and irrevocably cast themselves into the camp of the enemies of the revolution.

The revolution does not fear an open break with the Kadets and with imperialists of all shades.

. . . But it is not the Kadets alone who are attempting to smash the revolutionary power and place the fate of the country at stake.

At the very moment when a conspiracy against the Provisional Government and against the whole democracy was being prepared in the Central Committee of the Kadets, a significant section of the Petrograd proletariat and Petrograd soldiery was also preparing an attack on the revolutionary democracy. *It was preparing to commit violence on the will of all revolutionary Russia*, embodied in the Central Executive Committee of the Soviets of Soldiers' and Workers' Deputies.

Under the influence of completely irresponsible agitation by the Bolsheviks, who exploited for their own ends the natural dissatisfaction and discontent of the proletarian and soldiers' masses, evoked by the serious economic crisis, a part of the Petrograd proletariat and army went out armed into the streets.

What did the blinded comrade soldiers and workers want to attain yesterday?

Their banners spoke of the transfer of all power to the Soviets, of the termination of war.

But were they not themselves demonstrating, first of all, against the will of the Soviets of all Russia; was it not they who were shattering the authority and strength of the Soviets; was it not they who were shattering the strength of revolutionary Russia, thereby delaying the end of the war?

The workers and soldiers who went out into the streets yesterday wanted to foist their will on all revolutionary Russia by means of armed strength.

What will happen if this or a comparable attempt is crowned with success? . . .

This day will be the day of the downfall of the revolution. For the revolution can only develop victoriously when by its side and at its head stand organs which are fulfilling the will of the majority of the democracy.

.　.　.

In this awesome hour, when the destinies of Russia and, perhaps, of the whole world, are being decided—for the whole beginning struggle of world democracies against imperialism depends upon the outcome of the Russian revolution—we call upon the workers and soldiers of Petrograd to save the revolution, to save it not by reckless demonstrations which have already caused bloodshed of fraternal workers and soldiers, but by conscious, revolutionary discipline, by the subjection of their own will to the will of the majority.

The revolution is in danger!

1156. *Delo Naroda* ON THE BOLSHEVIK CALL FOR A DEMONSTRATION

[No. 92, July 5, 1917, p. 1. Reference is to the Proclamation of July 4. See Doc. 1157.]

At the very moment when armed detachments pass one after another in front of the gates to the Tauride Palace, pushing the doors in an attempt to enter the hall of conferences and demanding that the Central Committee of the All-Russian Soviets take power in its hands, at the moment when armed groups of machine-gunners ride around, shooting right and left; at a time when blood has already been shed—at this very moment the Bolsheviks decide that their time has come; that the time has come to act—and oh, of course, lawfully and peacefully!

They find this time most propitious to call a "peaceful" and "organized" demonstration!

Our loud reply in the face of the entire country is that this is insanity, stupidity, or simply *hypocrisy* and mockery of us.

At such moments of alarm, fraught with civil war and bloodshed, the Soviets of Workers' and Soldiers' Deputies have always had one simple and unequivocal slogan: No demonstrations of any kind!

The Bolsheviks choose precisely this moment to shout to their kind: "Into the streets!"

The more people there are in the streets, the more accidental innocent victims there will be at every step, victims of the skirmishes which inevitably arise when automobiles with machine guns and trucks full of soldiers armed with rifles dash as if crazed throughout the city. [The soldiers] do not say where the "counter-revolution" is concealed, the struggle against which is their shield, and aiming now at "main" streets, now at store windows and large houses, they hope that the "bullet will seek out the guilty one."

And the hands of those who signed yesterday's appeal, in the name of a whole series of Bolshevik organizations, will already be stained in the blood of these innocent victims. Oh, what irony!—to a "peaceful and organized" demonstration!

1157. THE BOLSHEVIK PROCLAMATIONS OF THE NIGHTS OF JULY 4 AND 5

[*Collected Works of V. I. Lenin: Toward the Seizure of Power*, XXI, Bk. II, 299–300. Word of the Government's possession of evidence linking the Bolsheviks to the Germans began to circulate the night of the 4th. When it became known that some of the documentation had been released to the press, the Government, early in the morning of the 5th, authorized the arrest of the leading Bolshevik suspects before they could flee. These accusations had a pronounced sobering effect upon the demonstrating workers and soldiers, and especially upon the hesitating and uncommitted regiments in the capital, which then came to the support of the Government. This aspect of the July uprising is covered in the next section.]

A

Fellow Workers and Soldiers of Petrograd!

Since the counterrevolutionary bourgeoisie has already come out openly against the revolution, the All-Russian Soviet of Workers', Soldiers' and Peasants' Deputies must take all power into its own hands.

This is the will of the revolutionary population of Petrograd, which has the right to bring this will by means of a *peaceful* and *organised* demonstration to the attention of the Executive Committee of the All-Russian Soviet of Workers', Soldiers' and Peasants' Deputies now in session.

Long live the will of the revolutionary workers and revolutionary soldiers!

Long live the power of the Soviets!

The coalition government has collapsed: it fell to pieces because it was unable to carry out the tasks for which it was created. The revolution is faced with most tremendous and difficult problems. A new power is needed which, united with the revolutionary proletariat, revolutionary army and revolutionary peasants, will decisively take up the task of consolidating and extending the victories already gained by the people. This power can be only the power of the Soviets of Workers', Soldiers' and Peasants' Deputies.

Yesterday the revolutionary garrison and the workers of Petrograd demonstrated and proclaimed this slogan: All power to the Soviets! We call upon this movement that arose in the regiments and factories to become a peaceful, organised expression of the will of all the workers, soldiers and peasants of Petrograd.

> CENTRAL COMMITTEE, RUSSIAN SOCIAL-DEMOCRATIC LABOUR PARTY
> PETROGRAD COMMITTEE, R.S.-D.L.P.
> INTERBOROUGH COMMITTEE, R.S.-D.L.P.
> MILITARY ORGANISATION OF THE CENTRAL COMMITTEE, R.S.-D.L.P.
> COMMISSION OF THE WORKERS' SECTION OF THE SOVIET OF WORKERS'
> AND SOLDIERS' DEPUTIES

B

COMRADES! On Monday you came out on the streets. On Tuesday you decided to continue the demonstration. We called you to a peaceful demonstration yesterday. The object of this demonstration was to show to all the toiling and exploited masses the strength of our slogans, their weight, their significance and their necessity for the liberation of the peoples from war, hunger and ruin.

The object of the demonstration was achieved. The slogans of the vanguard of the working class and of the army were imposingly and worthily proclaimed. The scattered firing of the counterrevolutionaries on the demonstrators could not disturb the general character of the demonstration.

Comrades! For the present political crisis, our aim has been accomplished. We have therefore decided to end the demonstration. Let each and every one peacefully and in an organised manner bring the strike and the demonstration to a close.

Let us await the further development of the crisis. Let us continue to prepare our forces. Life is with us, the course of events shows the correctness of our slogans.

CENTRAL COMMITTEE, R.S.-D.L.P.
PETROGRAD COMMITTEE, R.S.-D.L.P.
INTERBOROUGH COMMITTEE, R.S.-D.L.P.
MILITARY ORGANISATION OF THE CENTRAL COMMITTEE, R.S.-D.L.P.
COMMISSION OF THE WORKERS' SECTION OF THE SOVIET OF WORKERS'
AND SOLDIERS' DEPUTIES

1158. B. O. BOGDANOV ON THE BOLSHEVIK ROLE IN THE UPRISING
[I. Tobolin, "Iiul'skie dni v Petrograde," *KA*, XXIV (1927), 68–70.]

On October 5, 1917, the examining magistrate of the Grodno District Court for the more important cases of the district interrogated in Petrograd as a witness, in accordance with article 443 of the Code of Criminal Procedure, the person mentioned hereunder, and he testified:

Bogdanov, Boris Osipovich—supplementarily.

On the question which was put supplementarily with regard to the events of July 3–5, he replied as follows:

. . .

The role of the Bolsheviks in the demonstrations of July 3–5 was beyond doubt negative. They gave an ideological [meaning], so to speak, to a movement which had all the external signs of a suspect movement, because, judging by its beginning, it was not provoked by any political party of the democracy. It could be imagined that the mutiny of the machine-gunners was provoked and organized by enemy agents; one could believe that it was caused by the intrigues of the counterrevolutionaries who had camouflaged and concealed themselves in the guise of friends of the people; only in the best of cases could the movement of the machine-gunners be ascribed to mutiny or the flaring up of primitive, irresponsible-minded men. The Bolsheviks intervened in this movement. They gave it slogans and blessed the movement itself. They helped to attract to it the sympathies of the working masses. Later on they undertook to organize it. When it was formed, this movement went under the slogan: "All power to the Soviets"; it was a movement directed against the Provisional Government, and in the first place against the Central Executive Committee, which was supporting the Provisional Government. I will say even more directly: the movement was against the Central Executive Committee in order to inflict a blow on the Provisional Government indirectly. This probably explains why the whole action took place around the Tauride [Palace] and not around the Mariinskii Palace. Second, politically the question boiled down to forcing the Central Executive Committee of the Workers' and Soldiers' Deputies to recognize the necessity of taking the power into its own hands. In this latter case, the first aim, that of overthrowing the Provisional Government, would also have been solved immediately.

The most serious pressure was organized against the Central Executive Committee. During the events the Soviet of Workers', Soldiers', and Peasants' Deputies was in session continuously. At that time also the Workers' Section of the

Petrograd Workers' and Soldiers' Deputies was in session. At that session many of the leaders of the Central Executive Committee, occupied in organizing the cessation of the disturbances taking place, were absent. In the Workers' Section the Bolsheviks put the question of transferring power into the hands of the people, and a special committee was elected, the purpose of which I do not see clearly even now. Whether this was a committee to prepare the organization of a movement which had flared up spontaneously, whether it was created for the purpose of exerting pressure on the Central Executive Committee of the Soviets of Workers' and Soldiers' Deputies, or, finally, whether the Workers' Section of the Executive Committee was organized for the event of power being transferred into the hands of the Soviet of Workers' and Soldiers' Deputies [I do not know], but it is certain that the decision of the Workers' Section in the excited atmosphere of the days of July 3 and 4 was intended to give definite political significance to the rebellion of the machine-gunners. In the days of July 3, 4, and 5 yet another means of pressure on the Central Executive Committee of the Soviets of Workers' and Soldiers' Deputies was organized, so to speak, from the "inside." Probably the Bolsheviks had ordered all of its organization to send delegations from factories, plants, and barracks demanding the transfer of power into the hands of the Soviets and authorization to admit these delegates to the sessions of the Central Executive Committee with a decisive vote. The delegations, with mandates usually written on the farms of factory [or] plant committees, usually Bolshevik, in uniform, monotonous, and almost literally the same wording, assembled at the Tauride Palace and demanded admittance to the sessions of the Central Executive Committee of the Soviets of Workers' and Soldiers' Deputies. This took place while the Tauride Palace was surrounded by crowds of armed people.

What was the nature of the movement of July 3–5? I have difficulty in answering in a definite manner. I still do not know whether it was an armed rebellion or an armed demonstration. The external signs would seem to indicate that it was an armed rebellion. To us who were in the Tauride Palace at that time it seemed almost completely obvious. The situation then was such that at any moment armed mobs could break in, wreck the Tauride Palace, arrest and shoot us down if we refused to take the power into our hands. There were many external reasons for such views. On the other hand, there are reasons to doubt that this movement was actually an armed rebellion. And the most striking of these is that the armed crowds could have overthrown us on at least one or two of these days, could have overthrown the Provisional Government during these days, but they didn't do either, in spite of their strong resolutions and all their strong words, and even some isolated actions like the arrest of Chernow and the shooting. Therefore, I am inclined to characterize the movement of July 3–5 as an armed demonstration, which had for its purpose to force the Central Executive Committee of the Soviets of Workers' and Soldiers' Deputies to take power into its own hands under the direct pressure of physically strong masses and thereby at last to compel the Provisional Government to withdraw.

In spite of all the danger of the situation, we refused to take power into our hands before the threat of bayonets, and on the 5th, toward night, we had at our disposal "for the Central Executive Committee of the Soviets of Workers' and Soldiers' Deputies" and "the Provisional Government" almost the whole garrison, which on July 3, 4, and 5 had demonstrated under the slogan: "All power to the Soviets."

1159. Resolution of the Regimental and Company Committees of the 1st Infantry Reserve Regiment on July 5

[I. Tobolin, "Iiul'skie dni v Petrograde," *KA*, XIII (1927), 49–50. See Doc. 1149, B.]

1) Regarding the demonstrations carried out by the Regiment, the following resolution proposed by Comrade Ust'vol'skii was approved:

"The regimental and company committees of the 1st Infantry Reserve Regiment at a joint session on July 5, 1917, have decided:

1. The demonstration of the Regiment on July 4 was a peaceful demonstration. The clash that took place was due to a sad misunderstanding whose clarification is entrusted to a Special Commission of Inquiry.

2. Being satisfied with the solution of the current question, that is, with the resolution of the joint session of the Executive Committees of the Soldiers' and Workers' and Peasants' Deputies, the Regiment places itself at their entire disposal until the convening of the All-Russian Congress.

3. While continuing to hold in principle its former point of view, that the cabinet crisis may be solved only by transferring all the power into the hands of the Soviets of Workers', Soldiers', and Peasants' Deputies, the Regiment declares that it considers the will of the revolutionary people which will be expressed in the forthcoming Congress as obligatory for itself and that it will implicitly obey the decisions of the latter.

4. The present decision is to be brought to the knowledge of the Executive Committee of the Soviet of Workers' and Soldiers' Deputies.

· · · ·

After the aforementioned resolution was approved by the members of the committees, Ensign Sakharov, Gavill, and Ivan Osipov demonstratively left the hall of the meeting as a protest against the nonapproval of their resolution, which had gathered fewer votes, and did not return to the meeting until its end.

Acting Secretary Makarov

1160. Government Action to Restore Order in Petrograd
[*Zhurnaly*, No. 124, July 6, 1917.]

Resolved:

v) To delegate the Minister of Labor, Skobelev, and the Temporary Acting Minister of the Navy, Lebedev, together with the representatives of the All-Russian Central Executive Committees of the Soviets of Workers' and Peasants' Deputies, Gots and Avksent'ev, to concentrate in their hands all actions of military and civilian authorities in restoring and maintaining revolutionary order within the bounds of the Petrograd Military District.

1161. Government Decree on Arbitrary Acts
[*VVP*, No. 98, July 7, 1917.]

The Provisional Government declares that:

All arbitrary actions, arrests, and searches carried on by individual persons, civilian or military, as well as by groups of persons, are intolerable and violate the revolutionary order. As such they will be suppressed most vigorously by the Government and the offenders prosecuted with all the severity of the law.

July 6, 1917

1162. PENALTIES FOR PUBLIC INCITEMENT TO CRIMINAL ACTS
[*Sob., Uzak.*, I, 2, No. 1508. See Doc. 1128.]

LAW OF THE PROVISIONAL GOVERNMENT

The Provisional Government has decreed:

1. Anyone guilty of public incitement to murder, brigandage, robbery, pogroms, and other heinous crimes, as well as to violence against any part of the population, is to be punished by detention in a house of correction for not more than three years, or by detention in a fortress for a period of not more than three years.

2. Anyone guilty of public incitement to disobedience to lawful orders of the authorities is to be punished by detention in a fortress for a period of not more than three years, or by detention in prison.

3. Anyone guilty of inciting officers, soldiers, and other military ranks during wartime to disobey the laws in effect under the new democratic system in the army and the orders of the military authorities consistent with them is to be punished as for state treason.

4. The present law to be put into effect by telegraph before publication by the Senate.

PRINCE L'VOV, Minister-President
SKARIATIN, Acting Minister of Justice
July 6, 1917

1163. ORDER TO THE COMPOSITE DETACHMENTS OF THE FIELD FORCES
[*Izvestiia*, No. 111, July 7, 1917, p. 1. The Composite Force was sent from the front by Kerensky to aid in the restoration of order. It included armored cars, infantry, artillery, and cavalry.]

Petrograd, July 6, 1917. No. 1

In accordance with the instructions of the Provisional Government in agreement with the Central Executive Committee of the All-Russian Congress of Soviets of Soldiers' and Workers' Deputies and the Executive Committee of the Soviets of Peasants' Deputies, I have been appointed commander of the composite detachments of the field forces.

Citizen Soldiers!

The supreme organ of the revolutionary democratic power calls on you to support and consolidate the triumph of freedom and the revolution.

It is our duty to strengthen and defend the cause of the revolution against malignant encroachments from any source.

We who have come from the battle front have the duty to save the capital of revolutionary Russia from the irresponsible groups which are attempting to foist their will by force of arms on the majority of the revolutionary democracy, covering up for their own cowardice and unwillingness to go to the battle front by extremist slogans, and which are resorting to violence, sowing discord in our ranks, and causing innocent blood to flow on the streets of Petrograd.

The field forces are honestly performing their duty in the fields of action and cannot permit themselves to be stabbed in the back at a time when they are performing their revolutionary duty on the front. . . .

. . . .

We will take action against those who are violating the will of the revolutionary people and the decrees of the revolutionary government, who are leading Russia back, whether consciously or unconsciously, to the previous reign of violence and arbitrary rule, and [we] will execute the orders and instructions of the central organs of the revolutionary democracy and the Provisional Government, coordinating our actions with the units of the Petrograd garrison which have remained loyal to the cause of the revolution.

We know each other, and I am sure that with the strength you have gained through revolutionary discipline, which is based on a conscientious attitude toward one's duty to the people, you will carry out honestly and forcefully the responsible and honorable task which we have been called upon to perform by our elected organs of the revolutionary power.

> COMMANDER OF THE COMPOSITE DETACHMENT
> MEMBER OF THE CENTRAL EXECUTIVE COMMITTEE
> OF THE ALL-RUSSIAN CONGRESS OF WORKERS'
> AND SOLDIERS' DEPUTIES
> Lieutenant Mazurenko

1164. THE DISBANDMENT OF MILITARY UNITS WHICH PARTICIPATED IN THE UPRISING

[*VVP*, No. 99, July 8, 1917, p. 1. Among the first to be disbanded was the 1st Machine-Gun Regiment.]

The Provisional Government resolved:

To disband the military units which participated in the armed rebellion on July 3, 4, and 5 of 1917 in the city of Petrograd and its outskirts, and to distribute their personnel at the discretion of the War and Navy Minister.

> PRINCE L'VOV, Minister-President
> A. KERENSKY, Minister of War and Navy

1165. ORDER TO THE ARMY AND NAVY CONCERNING THE MUTINOUS ACTIVITIES OF UNITS AT KRONSTADT AND IN THE BALTIC FLEET DURING THE UPRISING

[*Izvestiia*, No. 112, July 8, 1917, p. 1.]

From the beginning of the revolution, there were persons in Kronstadt and in some ships of the Baltic Fleet who, influenced by the activities of German agents and provocateurs, called for actions threatening the revolution and the security of our native land. At the time when our valiant army, sacrificing itself heroically, entered into bloody combat with the enemy, at a time when the navy, loyal to the democracy, was tirelessly and selflessly fulfilling the heavy task of combat imposed on it, [those in] Kronstadt and in certain ships, headed by *Respublika and Petro-*

pavlovsk, stabbed their comrades in the back by their actions, by adopting resolutions against the offensive, by calling for resistance to the revolutionary power embodied in the Provisional Government which was established by the democracy, and by attempting to exert pressure on the will of the elective organs of the democracy as personified by the All-Russian Congresses of the Soviets of Workers', Peasants', and Soldiers' Deputies.

During the offensive itself, disturbances started in Petrograd, threatening the revolution and exposing our army to the blows of the enemy. When ships were summoned in accordance with an order of the Provisional Government in agreement with the Executive Committees of the Soviets of Workers', Soldiers', and Peasants' Deputies, in order to bring quick and decisive influence to bear on the Kronstadters who were participating in these treasonable disturbances in Petrograd, the enemies of the people and the revolution, acting through the Central Committee of the Baltic Fleet, brought sedition into the ranks of the ships' companies by falsely interpreting these measures. These traitors prevented the dispatch of ships, loyal to the revolution, to Petrograd, prevented the adoption of measures for the most rapid termination of disorders organized by the enemy, and incited companies to arbitrary actions—the replacement of Commissar General Onipko, the resolution on the arrest of the assistant to the Minister of War, Captain Dudarov, and the presentation of a series of demands to the Executive Committees of the All-Russian Congresses of the Soviets of Workers', Soldiers', and Peasants' Deputies.

The treasonable and traitorous activity of a number of persons forced the Provisional Government to issue instructions for the immediate arrest of their leaders. Among these the Provisional Government resolved to arrest the delegation from the Baltic Fleet, which arrived in Petrograd, and to investigate its activities. In view of the above, I hereby order:

1. That the [present] Central Committee of the Baltic Fleet immediately be dissolved and that new elections be held.

2. The announcement to all companies and ships of the Baltic Fleet that I call upon them to exclude at once from their midst all suspicious persons calling for insubordination to the Provisional Government and agitating against the offensive, and to bring them to Petrograd for trial and investigation.

3. The commands at Kronstadt and the crews of the battleships *Petropavlovsk*, *Respublika*, and *Slava*, whose names are stigmatized by counterrevolutionary acts and resolutions, to arrest the instigators . . . [unclear in text] within 24 hours and send them to Petrograd for trial and investigation and, also, to bring assertions of the complete submission to the Provisional Government. I announce to the commands at Kronstadt and these ships that if my present order is not executed, they will be declared traitors to their native land and the revolution, and the most resolute measures will be taken against them.

Comrades! Our native land is on the brink of ruin as a result of treachery and treason. Her freedom and the gains of the revolution are threatened with a mortal danger. The German armies have already assumed the offensive on our front. Any hour one may expect decisive actions from the enemy fleet, which is capable of taking advantage of the temporary disorganization. Resolute and firm measures are required for eradicating [this disorganization]. The army had adopted such measures, and the navy must follow in step. In the name of our native land, the revolution and freedom, in the name of the welfare of the working masses, I call on you to rally around the Provisional Government and the all-Russian organs of democracy and to repel bravely the heavy blows of the external enemy, protecting the rear against the treacherous blows of traitors.

This order is to be announced immediately in all commands and ships of the Navy.

A. F. KERENSKY, Minister of War and Navy

[July 7, 1917]

1166. REPLIES TO KERENSKY'S ORDER OF JULY 7 TO THE BALTIC FLEET
[*Rech'*, No. 163, July 14, 1917, p. 4.]

The Chairman of the Assembly and of the Ship's Committee of the battleship of the line *Petropavlovsk* sent to the General Staff of the Navy a resolution of the Assembly answering the order to the army and fleet issued on July 7 of the current year.

The crew of the battleship of the line *Petropavlovsk*, having discussed the political situation which has been created in connection with the events of July 3 and 4 in Petrograd, on July 12 adopted the following resolution: 1) The crew expresses its complete confidence in the Provisional Government, invested with the plenitude of power by the Central All-Russian Executive Committees of the Soviets of Workers', Soldiers', and Peasants' Deputies, and recognizes that it is obligatory to fulfill all the orders of the Provisional Government which rely on this plenipotentiary organ of the Russian democracy. 2) The crew requests the appointment of an investigative committee in order to detect all those guilty of creating the shameful events of July 3 and 4, and is ready to render every assistance to such a committee. 3) The crew, bearing in mind that its resolution against the offensive had been adopted at the moment when the question of the offensive already had an immediate practical significance, expresses its deep regret with regard to the adoption of this resolution. At the same time the crew declares that it never hesitated in fulfilling every order of the naval authorities in respect to the offensive [operations]—as is proved by its behavior throughout the war. At the present time the crew will fulfill its revolutionary and military duty, and, at any moment, at the order of the revolutionary Provisional Government, will move against the enemy. 4) The crew asks the Central All-Russian Executive Committees of the Soviets of Workers', Soldiers', and Peasants' Deputies to take all necessary measures in order that the accusation of participating in the counterrevolutionary actions should be cleared and that it should be published for everybody's knowledge.

IVANOV, Chairman of the Battle Committee
KARKLIN, Secretary

The crew of the battleship of the line *Respublika* joins the present resolution.

KORNEV, Chairman
TRUKHATOV, Secretary

The crew of the battleship of the line *Slava* at its meeting of July 12 has unanimously joined the present resolution.

RULOV, Chairman of the Assembly
and of the Ship's Committee
SOROKIN, Secretary

.   .   .

Having read in the newspapers a notice according to which a group of sailors of the cruiser *Aurora* has sent to Minister Kerensky a letter full of cynical abuses and the demand containing threats that he should leave his post, the crew of the cruiser has immediately met and has decided: "The special committee should establish a committee which would find out whether the letter which shames the name of the vessel has actually been received. In case the notice were to prove correct, the special committee should undertake a very strict investigation in order to find out those guilty of such an odious provocation and to prosecute them. The crew of the cruiser *Aurora* declares that it is indignant over the odious letter sent by unknown people to Minister Kerensky, a letter that throws a shadow on the whole crew, and in the most categorical manner protests against this miserable cowardice of provocateurs who hide themselves behind the back of the whole crew; it will take all necessary measures in order to discover their names."

By the authority of the crew of the cruiser *Aurora*: Ensign Zladogorskii; Kurkov and Maslovskii, sailors.

G. Agababov, appointed by the Temporary Committee of the State Duma to the vessel *Aurora*, joined this resolution.

1167. *Rech'* ON THE RESULTS OF THE UPRISING
[No. 157, July 7, 1917, p. 1.]

The capital is rapidly quieting down much more quickly than could be expected at the beginning of the revolt. . . . For the time being it is possible to speak only of external calm, . . . but the external calm is striking . . . The impression is so vivid that a person feels he has been transferred to another city and finds himself among other people. . . .

· · ·

Let us speak bluntly: bolshevism is hopelessly compromised; the absurdity of its revolt, which assumed all the features of disgusting hoodlumism, seemed simply incomprehensible until the shameful accusation of being a hireling of the Germans was flung at Lenin. . . . At that moment there occurred an exceptionally sharp change of feelings, and bolshevism died, so to speak, a sudden death.

· · ·

Petrograd has quieted down much more quickly than could be expected. Bolshevism proved to be a bluff . . . But the danger to the revolution from those who tolerate bolshevism is much more serious, and if, at the last moment, they do not change their minds, the revolution will be threatened by a far more serious crisis.

1168. *Rabochaia Gazeta* ON THE DANGERS STEMMING FROM THE BOLSHEVIK ATTEMPT
[No. 100, July 7, 1917, p. 1.]

What we long ago predicted has happened.

Bolshevik tactics—we asserted—lead to the isolation of the revolutionary proletariat. They open wide the doors to the very counterrevolution against which the Bolsheviks are allegedly fighting.

If the senseless attempt of the Bolsheviks had succeeded, if, profiting by the spontaneous dissatisfaction and the obscure discontent of the workers' and soldiers' masses, they had succeeded in overthrowing the Provisional Government by force of arms and in thrusting power upon the Soviets of Workers' and Soldiers' Deputies at bayonet point, the cause of the revolution would have been lost. The government forced upon the country would have been quickly overthrown. The dictatorship of superrevolutionaries would have been replaced by the reign of counterrevolution.

Fortunately the revolution proved to be stronger. The organs of revolutionary democracy succeeded in liquidating the armed insurrection of soldiers and sailors drawn into the adventure. Before the revolutionary government was compelled to resort to force, the mad attempt of the Bolsheviks and anarchists collapsed of itself and deteriorated into plunder, violence, murder.

The [attempted] overthrow of the revolutionary government failed. *Only because* of this, counterrevolution—and this can be said with certainty—will not rush in the footsteps of the Bolsheviks into the gap which by their tactics they pierced in the stronghold of the revolutionary democracy.

But by their efforts the Bolsheviks nonetheless *opened the doors slightly to counterrevolution.* With many the sobering process threatens to lead toward a proclivity for the right. Failure calls forth disappointment; disappointment calls forth hatred and anger against the "bad shepherds," against the leaders who brought them to defeat.

Among the broad masses panic takes the form of open hostility toward the revolution. The narrow-minded revenge the fear they experienced, the days of alarm, the violence to their conscience and will.

This turn in mood is fraught with dangers. The wave of anarchical-Blanquism has receded; in its turn the muddy counterrevolutionary wave grows and widens. From the stone cast by the Bolsheviks into the turbulent sea of Philistinism radiate wide pogromist and anti-Semitic waves.

Revolutionary organizations and all enlightened workers and soldiers must give a most vigorous rebuff to the pogrom agitation, no matter whence it comes or at whom it is directed. All efforts must be exerted to establish a revolutionary order, so needed now, when we face such tremendous problems as the struggle against economic breakdown, the struggle for universal peace, preparation for election in the Constituent Assembly.

1169. *Izvestiia* ON THE "ACHIEVEMENTS" OF THE UPRISING
[No. 110, July 6, 1917, pp. 1–2.]

The central organ of the Bolshevik organization, *Pravda*, finally gave its reaction to the bloody events of July 3 and 4.

The July 5 issue of *Pravda* carried an appeal signed by the Central Committee, the Petrograd Committee, and the Military Organization of the Bolsheviks. Calling for an end to the demonstration and for resumption of work, the Bolsheviks say in this appeal . . . [that] the demonstration of July 3 and 4 achieved its aim.[4]

What then did the demonstrators of July 3 and 4 and their acknowledged official leaders—the Bolsheviks—achieve?

---

[4] Doc. 1157, B.

They achieved the death of 400 workers, soldiers, sailors, women, and children . . .

They achieved the destruction and looting of private flats and shops . . .

They succeeded in weakening our front . . .

They attempted to seize the counterintelligence department where all the information on German espionage is kept—which attempts, fortunately, were not crowned with success.

They achieved the insulting by a frenzied crowd of a proved fighter of the revolution, the recognized leader of the Socialist Revolutionary Party, V. M. Chernov, by its brazen attempt to arrest him.

They achieved dissension, a mutual animosity between individual parts of the democracy . . .

Such, so far, are the results of the demonstration of July 3 and 4. And if these constituted the aims of the demonstration, then the Bolsheviks are a thousand times right when they say that the aims of the demonstration have been achieved.

But if the demonstration had other aims, if it was based on the desire to hasten the conclusion of peace, to give bread to the people and to crush the inception of a counterrevolution, then does anyone really have the nerve to think that the days of July 3 and 4 will bring bread, peace, and freedom to the people?

The days of July 3 and 4 dealt a terrible blow to the revolution, while the counterrevolutionary cause was given powerful support.

. . .

The honor and glory of saving [the cause of] the revolution will now and forever belong to the majority of the revolutionary democracy and its plenary organs, the Soviets of Workers', Soldiers', and Peasants' Deputies.

THE CHARGES AGAINST THE BOLSHEVIKS[5]

1170. The Published Charges Against the Bolsheviks

[*Zhivoe Slovo*, No. 51, July 5, 1917, as translated in the *Collected Works of V. I. Lenin: Toward the Seizure of Power*, XXI, Bk. I, 280–81. This communique was released on the authorization of Minister of Justice Pereverzev on the basis of the information at the disposal of his department. Tereshchenko and Nekrosov, who had been carrying on

---

[5] A summary of the evidence on Bolshevik-German relations may be found in David Shub, *Lenin*, pp. 211–16. See also A. F. Kerensky, *The Crucifixion of Liberty*, Chap. XVI, as well as Colonel B. V. Nikitine, *The Fatal Years*, Chap. XI, in which the head of military counterintelligence at that time quotes and discusses the documents which were in the hands of the Provisional Government. Refutations of the accusations can be found in M. N. Pokrovskii, *Oktiabr'skaia revoliutsiia*, pp. 115–36, and Leon Trotsky, *History of the Russian Revolution*, II, Chap. IV. A recent collection of translated documents from the German Foreign Ministry Archives, edited by Z. A. B. Zeman, *Germany and the Revolution in Russia, 1915–1918*, which should certainly be consulted, adds new information on German support of the Bolsheviks, though many details remain, and perhaps will continue to remain, unclear. Because of the availability of this volume and for considerations of space, only one excerpt from it has been included (Doc. 1180).

a separate and secret investigation of the matter, were, together with Kerensky, indignant at the premature disclosure of the charges before more complete evidence could be obtained and arrests of the accused carried out. See Kerensky, *The Crucifixion of Liberty*, pp. 322–24, and Doc. 1174.]

The following letter, signed in their own handwriting, was submitted by G. Alexinsky and the former inmate of the Schlüsselburg prison, V. Pankratov, members of the Second State Duma, to the Committee of Journalists attached to the Provisional Government:

"We, the undersigned, Gregory Alexeyevich Alexinsky, former member of the Second State Duma representing the workers of the city of Petrograd, and Vasily Semyonovich Pankratov, member of the Socialist-Revolutionary Party, who spent fourteen years in the Schlüsselburg prison at hard labour, believe it to be our revolutionary duty to publish extracts from documents just received by us, from which the Russian citizens will see how and from what direction are endangered Russian liberty, the revolutionary army and the Russian people who won this liberty with their blood. We demand an immediate investigation. G. Alexinsky, V. Pankratov; July 17, 1917; Petrograd."

In a letter dated May 16, 1917, under the number 3719, the Chief of Staff of the Supreme Command sent the Minister of War the record of the examination, April 28, of Ensign Yermolenko of the 16th Siberian infantry regiment. From his statements to the chief of the Investigating Division of the General Staff the following is established: on May 8 of this year he was dispatched to us behind the lines of the Sixth Army, to agitate for the speediest conclusion of a separate peace with Germany. This commission was accepted by Yermolenko at the insistence of the comrades. Officers of the German General Staff, Schidtzki and Lübers, had told him that propaganda of a similar kind was being carried on in Russia by the chairman of the Ukrainian Section of the Union for the Liberation of the Ukraine, A. Skoropis-Yoltukhovsky, and Lenin. Lenin was commissioned to use every means in his power to undermine the confidence of the Russian people in the Provisional Government. Money for the propaganda is being received through a certain Svedson, employed in Stockholm at the German embassy. Money and instructions were forwarded through trusted persons.

In accordance with the information just received, these trusted persons in Stockholm were: the Bolshevik Jacob Fürstenberg, better known under the name of "Hanecki" [Ganetskii], and Parvus (Dr. Helfand); in Petrograd: the Bolshevik attorney, M. U. Kozlovsky, a woman relative of Hanecki—Sumenson, engaged in speculation together with Hanecki, and others. Kozlovsky is the chief receiver of German money, which is transferred from Berlin through the "Disconto-Gesellschaft" to the Stockholm "Via Bank," and thence to the Siberian Bank in Petrograd, where his account at present has a balance of over 2,000,000 rubles. The military censorship has unearthed an uninterrupted exchange of telegrams of a political and financial nature between the German agents and Bolshevik leaders (Stockholm-Petrograd).

The letter was accompanied by the following note by G. Alexinsky and V. Pankratov: "Owing to technical considerations the original documents will be published by us later as a supplement."

1171. The Bolshevik Denial of the Charges that Lenin Received German Money

[*Zapiski Instituta Lenina*, II, Part 4, 155–56. Government forces raided and closed the office of *Pravda* on the morning of July 5. The Appeal below was published in *Listok Pravdy*, a two-page paper which appeared on July 6 in place of *Pravda*. Lenin's disclaimers and articles on the charges, published in various places, including *Listok Pravdy*, may be found in the *Collected Works of V. I. Lenin: Toward the Seizure of Power*, XXI, Bk. I, 17 ff.

Although a number of Bolsheviks were arrested by the Government after the disclosure of the charges against them, Lenin and Zinoviev went into hiding, first in the suburbs of Petrograd, then over the border in Finland. According to V. D. Bronch-Bruevich, in his *Na boevykh postakh fevral'skoi i oktiabr'skoi revoliutsii*, pp. 83–85, N. S. Karinskii, an assistant to Minister of Justice Pereverzev, and the prosecutor in charge of the subsequent preparation of the case against the Bolsheviks (see Doc. 1176), called him on the evening of July 4 to tell him of the impending disclosures in order that he might warn Lenin.]

TO THE POPULATION OF PETROGRAD!

TO THE WORKERS! TO THE SOLDIERS!

TO ALL HONEST CITIZENS!

THE SLANDER MUST BE EXPOSED!

SLANDERERS TO BE PROSECUTED!

An unheard-of accusation is made against *Comrade Lenin* that he apparently received or is receiving money from German sources for his propaganda. The newspapers have already publicized this monstrous slander. Underground leaflets with reference to the former deputy Aleksinskii are already being printed. Calls are already heard to kill the Bolsheviks. And lists with people marked for destruction circulate among the soldiers who are being deceived.

The aim is clear. Counterrevolution wants to behead the revolution in the simplest way—by sowing discord among the masses and by baiting them against the most popular leaders, honored warriors of the revolution.

We declare that everything that is reported about money and other connections of Comrade Lenin with the ruling circles of Germany is a lie and a slander.

The instigator of the matter, Aleksinskii, is a notorious slanderer who has accused a number of persons of bribery by the Germans. For his dishonest acts he has already been condemned by the Union of Russian, English, Italian, and Neutral Journalists in France. For his malicious slander he has been expelled from all the democratic organizations of Paris and was not admitted to the Petrograd Soviet of Workers' and Soldiers' Deputies.

We demand that the Provisional Government and the Central Executive Committee of the Soviets of Workers' and Soldiers' Deputies make an immediate and open investigation of all the circumstances of the foul conspiracy by the pogromists and hired slanderers against the honor and life of the leaders of the working class.

Complete light should be shed on this matter. And all the people will be convinced as a result of this investigation that there is not one single blemish on the revolutionary honor of Comrade Lenin.

Slanderers and disseminators of slander to be prosecuted! Pogromists and liars to the pillory!

Central Committee of RSDWP

1172. Statement from the Central Executive Committee of the Soviet

[Izvestiia, No. 110, July 6, 1917, p. 6.]

In connection with the news which has circulated around town and has already seeped into the press concerning the charges leveled against N. Lenin and other politicians to the effect that they have been receiving money from an obscure German source, the Executive Committee wishes to inform the public that at the request of representatives of the Bolshevik faction it has appointed a committee to investigate this matter. In view of this, the Central Committee requests that [the public] refrain from spreading derogatory condemnations or expressing its attitudes on this matter until the Committee completes its work, and [it] considers any kind of [demonstrative] actions on this subject to be inadmissible.

1173. Pereverzev's Comments on the Charges

[Novoe Vremia, No. 14820, July 7, 1917, p. 2.]

. . . In his interview with a reporter of *Vechernee Vremia*, P. N. Pereverzev stated: *"Personally, I have been convinced for a long time that Lenin has been working for German money.* I am just as deeply convinced—and I have expressed it openly—that I consider him incapable of taking the money for himself personally. I still hold this conviction, but Lenin is an almost mad fanatic who has never been and is not now interested in knowing from what sources he receives offers of funds for the struggle on behalf of his ideals. The persons around him might, and did, use this circumstance. The information that I had led to a firm conviction on that point. When we received information that soldiers and Kronstadt sailors had decided to arrest the whole Executive Committee, without considering the incalculable danger that was threatening Russia and the course of the revolution, I did not deem it possible not to open the eyes of the troops to the activities of the men who had started the sedition and were leading them against the highest organs of the democratic government which had been elected by the very same soldiers and workers. I communicated to the troops the information in my hands, and I communicated to them a great deal more than was published in the press. My communication created a very strong impression. I consider that the revelation of the data I had played a considerable part in the change of mood in the direction of the restoration of order."

· · ·

1174. Views of Tereshchenko, Nekrasov, and Kerensky on the Charges Against the Bolsheviks and on the Resignation of Pereverzev

[Novoe Vremia, No. 14821, July 8, 1917, p. 2.]

Minister of Foreign Affairs M. I. Tereshchenko made an official declaration through our reporter concerning the revelations that have appeared in the press about German agents and about the resignation from the Provisional Government of the Minister of Justice, P. N. Pereverzev. The entire interview with the Minister was conducted in the presence of N. V. Nekrasov. An interesting announcement was also made by A. F. Kerensky, who was in the Ministry of Foreign Affairs, where a conference of the Provisional Goverment was taking place.

"The resignation of P. N. Pereverzev," the Minister of Foreign Affairs said, "had been predetermined some time ago, in view of his exhibition of lack of energy during the liquidation of anarchistic raids, and in particular the capture of the Durnovo villa. Governmental weakness contributes neither to the interest nor to the dignity of the State.

"Information has reached the newspapers that N. V. Nekrasov and I argued against the arrests connected with the revelations of the activity of Lenin and his comrades, and also against the publication of the document—which has been printed since—regarding the relations of the Bolsheviks and the German agents. In reality, we found out only *post factum* about the fact that the documents had been handed over to the newspaper, so that it is absolutely inadmissible to ascribe to us any involvement in this affair. The members of the Provisional Government were informed only at 12:30 A.M., July 5, concerning the intention to make public certain data about the criminal activities of German agents.

"I must tell you frankly," the Minister said with agitation, "that we were literally horrified at the thought of publication of the document, and first of all we asked the basic question: Have the necessary arrests been made yet? This was answered in the negative.

"As is known, Prince L'vov requested, in the name of the Government, that the editors of newspapers postpone the publication of the document received by them. The request of the President of the Council of Ministers was quite natural, in view of the fact that the premature publication of certain data which we have at our disposal might give the culprits an opportunity to flee justice. It must not be forgotten that P. N. Pereverzev himself spoke against printing in the newspapers the part of the document relating to Mrs. Sumenson, precisely because of the fear that she might use that warning and slip out of Russia. Thus, that part of the document was made public without the knowledge of the Minister of Justice.

"Despite the lateness of the hour, we deemed it necessary immediately to undertake the necessary arrests, of which the proper authorities were at once notified. At first the difficulties of making the arrests because of the Bolshevik propaganda were pointed out to us. Nevertheless, the detention of persons mentioned in the document did take place, and it is only just to note that N. V. Nekrasov and I vehemently insisted on that. The order was given at half past five in the morning.

"We shared completely the point of view of the Minister of Justice concerning the necessity of using the information which we had at our disposal, but only on condition that the publication of the secret information in the press would not interfere with the Government's efforts to pursue the investigation to the end. Despite the desirability of creating a decisive change of mood among certain strata of the population, we agreed that the publication of the documents would be possible only after all the culprits were in our hands. The consequences of the premature publication have already manifested themselves. The arrival of two prominent and extremely dangerous German agents had been expected in Petrograd. They would, of course, have been arrested, and very great significance was attached to their detention in view of the fact that they are among the central figures of German espionage. Now, of course, it is useless to count on their arrival and on the complete unmasking of their activity. We have also received information that certain agents, who were to be detained later in connection with the unraveling of the case, have already disappeared. Competent persons who are well acquainted with the circumstances were just as horrified as we were when they read in the press the now well-known information on Lenin, Kozlovskii, and others. Many of them had even thought that this was a new German plot.

"I must add," the Minister said, "that A. F. Kerensky shared our opinion fully."

Just at that moment, the War Minister arrived and made the following declaration:

"I wired concerning the necessity of publishing the data on the activity of German agents, but not prematurely, on condition that the press carry weighty charges and that the accused could not escape."

"But, in reality," M. I. Tereshchenko resumed, and he was supported by N. V. Nekrasov, "the published information represents only an insignificant part of the whole case. This part, however, spoiled everything. We had contemplated the possibility of publishing in full the information we had at our disposal, but haste might affect the outcome of the case disastrously. Secrecy is still necessary, but I find it possible to communicate to you one of the numerous facts that shed light on the relations between the Bolsheviks and German agents. On June 16, i.e., two days before the Sunday demonstration in Petrograd, the editors of *Pravda* sent, over the signature of Bronislav Veselovskii, a telegram addressed to Ganetskii (Fürstenberg) containing the detailed information about all the slogans that the Bolsheviks were planning to use in the demonstration. Among other things, the telegram also mentioned the well-known slogan: 'Neither separate peace with Wilhelm, nor secret treaties with the Allies.' On June 20, the newspaper of the German Crown Prince, *Lokal Anzeiger*, printed, from its correspondent in Copenhagen, an identical telegram, which repeated verbatim the text of the editors of *Pravda*, with the exception of the phrase 'neither separate peace with Wilhelm.' And yet we were able to establish authentically that only one telegram regarding the slogans of the Bolsheviks was sent abroad with the Veselovskii signature."

When asked about the methods of investigating the activity of German agents, M. I. Tereshchenko and N. V. Nekrasov answered that the investigation was being pursued by all the forces of governmental power, independent of the Party investigation of the affair.

1175. Lenin on "The Question of the Bolshevik Leaders Appearing Before the Courts"[6]

[*Collected Works of V. I. Lenin: Toward the Seizure of Power*, XXI, Bk. I, 34.]

Judging by private conversations, there are two opinions on this question.

Comrades yielding to the "Soviet atmosphere" are often inclined towards appearing before the courts.

Those who are closer to the working masses apparently incline towards not appearing.

In principle, the question reduces itself to an estimation of what are commonly called constitutional illusions.

If one thinks that a *just* government and *just* courts are possible in Russia,

---

[6] An explanatory note in the *Collected Works of V. I. Lenin: Toward the Seizure of Power*, XXI, Bk. I, 284, reads: "There was vacillation among a part of the members of the C.C. on the question of whether Lenin and G. Zinoviev should appear in court. V. Nogin regarded it as necessary that the leaders of the party give themselves up and appear in court for the

that the convocation of the Constituent Assembly is probable, then he may arrive at the conclusion that it is necessary to appear.

But such an opinion is thoroughly erroneous. The latest events, especially after July 17, have shown in the most flagrant fashion that the convocation of the Constituent Assembly is improbable (without a new revolution), that no just government or just court exists, or can exist (at present) in Russia.

The court is an organ of power. The liberals sometimes forget this. It is a sin for a Marxist to forget it.

Where, then, is the power? Who constitutes the power?

There is no government. It changes daily. It is inactive.

The power that is active is the military dictatorship. Under such conditions it is ridiculous even to speak of "the courts." It is not a question of "courts," but of *an episode in the civil war*. This is what those in favour of appearing before the courts unfortunately do not want to understand.

Pereverzev and Alexinsky as initiators of the "case"—is it not ridiculous to speak of a court in such a case? Is it not naïve to think that, under such conditions, any court can examine, investigate, establish anything?

Power is in the hands of a military dictatorship. Without a new revolution this power can only become stronger for a while, first of all for the duration of the war.

"I have done nothing unlawful. The courts are just. The courts will examine the case. The trial will be public. The people will understand. I shall appear."

This reasoning is childishly naïve. Not a trial but a campaign of persecution against the internationalists, this is what the *authorities need*. To seize them and hold onto them is what Messrs. Kerensky and Co. need. Thus it was (in England and France), thus it will be (in Russia).

Let the internationalists work underground as far as it is in their power, but let them not commit the folly of voluntarily appearing before the courts!

1176. Report of the Public Prosecutor on the Investigation of the Charges Against the Bolsheviks

[*Rech'*, No 170, July 22, 1917, p. 5.]

The Prosecutor [N. S. Karinskii] of the Petrograd Court of Appeals issued to the representatives of the press some data established by witnesses and documents which led to the prosecution of the following persons in accordance with articles 51, 100, and 108 of the Criminal Code (on treason and organized armed rebellion): Ul'ianov (Lenin), Apfelbaum (Zinoviev), Kolontai, Helfand (Par-

purpose of an open struggle with the slanderous and lying accusations. J. Stalin and S. Orjonikidze decidedly objected to this, fearing a lynching party of the counter-revolutionary military cadets or a secret murder in jail. After a consultation with Lenin and Zinoviev, Nogin and Orjonikidze, at the insistence of Lenin, set out for the C.E.C. to clear up the situation, and, in the case of voluntary appearance, to secure a guarantee of safety. At the negotiations with the members of the C.E.C., Anismov (Menshevik worker) explained that it was impossible to secure such a guarantee, as the actual power after the July days had passed into the hands of the counter-revolutionary militarists. Anisimov's statement finally overcame the hesitation of the individual members of the C.C., and the question of the appearance in court was decided in the negative. At the Sixth Conference of the R.S.-D.L.P., the question of appearance in court was again submitted for consideration, and the Conference decisively came out against it, in view of the absence of a guarantee of the personal safety of the accused. . . ."

vus), Fürstenberg (Ganetskii), Kozlovskii, Sumenson, Ensigns Semashko and Sakharov, Midshipmen Ilin (Raskol'nikov), and Roshal'.

The Street Revolt

On the evening of July 3, racing automobiles and armored trucks with armed soldiers and workers appeared on the streets of Petrograd. They stopped private automobiles, ordered out at gun point the drivers and passengers, took the cars over, installed machine guns in them, and joined the other previously armored motors.

Shortly afterwards, confused shooting and machine-gun firing ensued, resulting in casualties among peaceful citizens who happened to be on the street.

Ensign Semashko

On the same evening the 1st Machine-Gun Regiment joined the rebellion. The leader was Ensign Semashko. He was ordered to the front in April (1917) with the machine-gun company, but he arbitrarily refused to follow this order and continued to appear in the Regiment, where he staged general meetings without the knowledge of the regimental committee. He formed a "collective" of Bolsheviks, which prevented all those who were not in accord with them from speaking at the meetings. This "collective" was in contact with the Military Organization of the Central Committee of the Social Democratic Party, ensconced in the home of Kshesinskaia[7] on Bol'shaia Dvorianskaia Street.

Around 10:00 o'clock in the evening the regiment drew up in formation; fully armed and accompanied by trucks and automobiles with machine guns, they marched in the direction of the house of Kshesinskaia. They were greeted from the balcony by several people who called for armed rebellion.

The regiment then proceeded toward the Tauride Palace, where Zinoviev and Trotsky greeted them with speeches. In hailing the armed rebellion the latter stated that victory was on their side already, inasmuch as the Workers' Section of the Soviet of Workers' and Soldiers' Deputies agreed to having all power concentrated in the Soviet of Workers' and Soldiers' Deputies.

All this took place around 2:00 o'clock in the morning, whereupon the army units returned to the barracks.

Later in the day, on July 4, Ensign Semashko appeared in the regiment, accompanied by sailors and workers, and began to incite the soldiers to take up arms and machine guns and demand the overthrow of the Government.

Midshipman Raskol'nikov

On July 3, Midshipman Ilin, who called himself Raskol'nikov, arrived in Kronstadt from Petrograd, accompanied by several delegates from the machine-gun regiment. He spoke at a meeting in Yakornaia Square calling for an armed rebellion in Petrograd in order to depose the Provisional Government and transfer all power to the Soviet of Workers' and Soldiers' Deputies. Raskol'nikov stated that the Workers' Section of the Soviet of W.S.D. had already approved this slogan and that the majority of the Petrograd garrison would make the same demands.

The same evening the Executive Committee of the Soviet of Workers' and

---

[7] A well-known dancer whose home the Bolsheviks took over for their headquarters.

Soldiers' Deputies of Kronstadt met under the chairmanship of Raskol'nikov and passed a resolution for all military units to meet at six o'clock in the morning in the Yakornaia Square with arms in hand and then to proceed in a well-organized fashion to Petrograd and, jointly with the troops of the Petrograd garrison, to stage an armed demonstration under the slogan "All power to the Soviet of Soldiers' and Workers' Deputies."

This resolution, over the signature of Raskol'nikov, as president of the committee, and in the name of the chief of all naval units of the city of Kronstadt, was transmitted by telephonograms to all the land and sea units of the city.

At the siren signal, the soldiers, sailors, and workers, armed with rifles, began to gather on the morning of July 4 in Yakornaia Square. There, from the platform, speeches were made by Raskol'nikov and Roshal' calling for an armed rebellion. There, too, cartridges were distributed among those who assembled. Raskol'nikov and Roshal' were the leaders and the number of participants was approximatly 5,000 men.

Arriving at about 11:00 o'clock at the Nikolaevskii Bridge (in Petrograd), they drew up in formation and, under the leadership of the same persons, moved toward the house of Kshesinskaia. There soon appeared on the balcony first Lunacharskii and then Lenin. They hailed the Kronstadt men as the "flower and pride of the revolution" and called upon them to march on the Tauride Palace to demand the deposition of the capitalist ministers and the transfer of all power to the Soviet of Workers' and Soldiers' Deputies. Lenin said, in the event the demand was not granted, to await instructions from the Central Committee.

The Shooting

On the way to the Tauride Palace, on Liteinyi Prospekt, they opened fire, which lasted for about an hour and resulted in many casualties.

On approaching the Tauride Palace these units attempted to arrest some of the ministers who were participating at the time in a session in the Tauride Palace of the Committee of the Soviet of Workers' and Soldiers' Deputies.

The Directives of the Military Organization

The Military Organization at the Central Committee of the Social Democratic Party issued a written order to send a cruiser from Kronstadt.

It was established that many of the sailors did not sympathize with the armed rebellion but were forced to take part in it at the threat of being shot.

The 1st Infantry [Reserve] Regiment

The coming out of the 1st Infantry Reserve Regiment took place on July 4 at the initiative of Ensign Sakharov.

On July 3 several soldiers from this Regiment, together with workers, came to the president of the regimental committee and stated that the entire Petrograd garrison resolved to march with arms and that the 1st Infantry Reserve Regiment must join this resolution. The president of the regimental committee replied that he could not take their word and must ask that an official resolution be brought to him. Nevertheless, part of the Regiment, armed, left the barracks at 10:00 o'clock in the evening and proceeded toward the Tauride Palace. A delegation from the Regiment entered the Tauride Palace and, in the name of the entire Regiment, made the request of "All power to the Soviet of Workers' and Soldiers' Deputies" and "Down with the ten capitalist ministers!"

Having done this, the Regiment returned to the barracks. But the same night Sakharov called a meeting and forced a promise from the soldiers of the Regiment to make another armed march on July 4. Sakharov stated at the meeting that he assumed responsibility for the armed march and for the possible shedding of blood.

Persuasions of the Commander of the Regiment and of the regimental committee not to do this had no effect, and almost the entire Regiment took armed action on July 4.

On arriving at the Tauride Palace and presenting their demands, the regiment agreed to return home, but in spite of the order by the Commander of the Regiment, Sakharov persuaded the soldiers to proceed to the Nevskii Prospekt, where, as he put it, the Regiment must "show its strength to the bourgois."

On the Liteinyi, after a shot was heard from an unidentified direction, the Regiment opened fire. As a result there were many dead and wounded.

Appeals to Armed Action

Definite data exist to the effect that the armed action on the part of military units on July 3–5 was far from a unanimous expression of their sentiment. Rather, it was artificially aroused by the incitement of individual leaders who, by means of demagogic and at times also provocative methods, set up intensive propaganda on the need to overthrow the government. These individuals advocated the disobedience of military units to commanding officers and refusal to go to the front to fight the enemy.

Investigation revealed that armed action was preceded by systematic meetings in military units where speeches were made urging the troops to revolt.

Thus, on July 2, the 1st Machine-Gun Regiment held a meeting and concert at the Narodnyi Dom where Lunacharskii, Trotsky, and others spoke. They all appealed for the overthrow of the Provisional Government, disobedience of military authorities, and refusal [to participate] in the offensive at the front. They pointed out that the offensive just concluded was the result of the deceiving actions of War Minister Kerensky and the officers and was the result of the arrival of the American capitalists [Root Mission?].

Trotsky's appeal, which tried to convince them of the necessity of armed action against the Government, aroused particular excitement. His speech was interrupted by cries: "Death to Kerensky," "Down with war," "Down with the capitalist ministers," "We don't need the offensive," "All power to the Soviet of Workers' and Soldiers' Deputies."

During the month of April, May, and June, Kolontai and Ensign Semashko attended the meetings of the Machine-Gun Regiment and spoke there. They urged the soldiers not to send companies to the front, not to obey the decisions of the regiment committees to send soldiers to the front, to overthrow the Provisional Government and thus achieve the transfer of all power to the Soviet of W. and S. D.

The Participation of the Central Committee of the Social Democratic Party in the Organization of the Revolt

It is established further that the revolt took place and continued according to the instructions of the Central Committee of the Social Democratic Party.

All leading instructions emanated from the house of Kshesinskaia, called by witnesses the "headquarters of Lenin." The Central Committee of the Social Democratic Party was also lodged there.

Forms of a military organization attached to the Central Committee of the Social Democratic Party were discovered in the house of Kshesinskaia. These were the very forms used for written instructions on armed action distributed in the army units.

It was on such a form that the Petrograd Military Automobile Shop received, during the night of July 4–5, a proposal to prepare armored cars for combat-readiness and to put them at the disposal of the Military Organization. The order to send a cruiser from Kronstadt was written on the same form.

Moreover, the following were also found there: 1) Notes on the distribution of military units and "armed workers" according to regions; on the distribution among various persons of responsibilities on "armed workers" according to regions; on the distribution among various persons of responsibilities on taking charge of armed forces, on reconnaissance, and outside watch; on contacts with units; on the Peter and Paul Fortress, on the military units comprising the Vyborg and Petrograd sections and Marsov field, and on establishing contacts with various regiments. 2) A resolution worked out at the session of the all-city conference of the Social Democratic Party and delegates from factories and military units on July 3, at 11:00 in the evening. The resolution recommended: "The immediate demonstration of workers and soldiers on the street in order to show their will." This resolution was signed by the Central Committee of the Social Democratic Party and the Military Organization of the S.D. Party. 3) A telegram from Stockholm, dated April 20, addressed to Ul'ianov (Lenin) and signed by Ganetskii (Fürstenberg): "Steinberg will try to get a subsidy for our organization. I must request his action be controlled, because social tact is completely lacking." 4) Literature of the "Union of the Russian People" and a large number of postal cards, published by *"Pauk"* [spider] and illustrating a ritual murder in Hungary in 1882.

The relation between the armed insurrection and the activity of the Central Committee of the S.D. Party, which maintained a military organization, is established, in addition to documentary data, by the fact that the armed units which participated in the insurrection, both from the Petrograd garrison and from Kronstadt, proceeded to the house of Kshesinskaia, where they received instructions from Ulianov (Lenin) and other persons. Suggestions to the military units about battle-readiness of armored cars and machine guns also emanated from there, and, finally, it was there that the armored trucks and automobiles gathered.

Aid to the Enemy and Espionage

The intensive propaganda campaign for an insurrection, which was waged among the troops and the civilian population over several months and which resulted in the insurrection of July 3–5, was staged for the purpose of aiding the enemy in its hostile actions against Russia.[8]

In this connection data have been obtained by the investigation indicating that a large espionage organization working for Germany exists in Russia. But in the interests of the investigation only the following data are released thus far:

A number of witnesses questioned in the case attested that while residing in the German part of Switzerland, Lenin was in contact with Parvus (he also being Helfand), who had the definite reputation of being a German agent; that Lenin frequented the camps for the Ukrainian prisoners, where he carried on propaganda for the separation of the Ukraine from Russia.

[8] See also Volume II, Doc. 851.

Evidence Pointing to Lenin as a German Agent

The data of the preliminary investigation point directly to Lenin as a German agent and indicate that, after entering into an agreement with Germany on action designed to aid Germany in her war with Russia, he arrived in Petrograd. Here, with financial assistance from Germany, he began to act to achieve this aim.

Relations with Germany

Relations with Germany were carried on through Stockholm. In April of this year an attempt was made from Stockholm to publish outside of Petrograd a newspaper for the purpose of waging a campaign against England and France.

Large sums of money appeared among the German agents in Copenhagen and Stockholm in the early days of the revolution, and an extensive recruiting of agents for Russia was launched among our deserters and emigrants. Sums of money (800 thousand rubles, 250 thousand rubles, and other sums) were remitted to Russia from Stockholm through one bank which received orders from Germany.

It was also revealed that Lenin and Zinoviev, while living in Austria near Krakov, were arrested in October 1914 by the Austrian authorities as Russian subjects, but were soon released with the right of free departure for Switzerland, where they started publication of the journal *Sotsial-Demokrat,* which advocated the idea of the necessity of Russia's defeat in the present war.

An important role in freeing Zinoviev and Lenin was played by Ganetskii, who, according to his own words, told one of the witnesses to "break off" the examination of Lenin and Zinoviev by the Austrian authorities. It was subsequently revealed that Lenin and Zinoviev were released from Austrian arrest by personal order of Count Stürgkh, the Austrian Prime Minister.

The investigation established that Yakov (diminutive "Kuba") Ganetskii-Fürstenberg, while residing in Copenhagen during the war, was closely connected in financial matters with Parvus, agent of the German government.

Moreover, the activity of Parvus as a German and Austrian agent was directed toward the defeat of Russia and its separation from the Ukraine.

The investigation established that Kozlovskii traveled from Copenhagen, where he represented himself as legal adviser to the prominent capitalist Helfand. Helfand (Parvus) proposed the financing of a steamship company in Russia. During the negotiations in this connection it was revealed that Parvus had at his disposal a large amount of capital, but was completely ignorant of the business which he proposed to finance.

On making inquiries the representatives of the steamship company learned that Helfand had over a million rubles in a bank in Copenhagen.

When it became clear to the representatives of the steamship company that the business activity of Helfand (Parvus) was merely a cover-up for his work for Germany, they ended all negotiations with him.

Simultaneously with this it was revealed that Helfand-Parvus, together with Fürstenberg and Kozlovskii, made trips from Copenhagen to Berlin and back.

Helfand-Parvus, Lenin, and Others

From the numerous telegrams in the hands of the legal authorities it is established that a constant and extensive correspondence was carried on between Sumenson, Ul'ianov (Lenin), Kolontai, and Kozlovskii residing in Petrograd, on the one hand, and Fürstenberg (Ganetskii) and Helfand (Parvus), on the other. Although this correspondence refers to commercial deals, shipment of all sorts of goods, and money transactions, it offers sufficient reasons to conclude that this correspondence was a cover-up for relations of an espionage character.

According to data in this matter, it is clear that some Russian banks received large sums, paid to various people, from Scandinavian banks. And it is interesting that within half a year Sumenson withdrew from her personal account 750,000 rubles deposited to her credit by various persons and that the current balance on her account is 180,000 rubles.

The Forthcoming Investigation

In investigating the present case the inquest authorities are guided by the materials secured only through inquest, and this material gives entirely sufficient reason to brand the action as criminal as well as to uncover many of the persons who participated in it. The forthcoming numerous cross-examinations of witnesses, examination of material evidence found, detailed investigation of money transactions—all this complex work of the future should yield abundant material uncovering the criminal espionage organization and its participants.

In reviewing all of the indicated questions, the inquest authorities were concerned, not with the political platforms of the persons involved, but only in uncovering criminal activity and finding sufficient grounds for prosecuting the accused.

Conclusion

On the basis of the data outlined, as well as of data that cannot as yet be made public, Vladimir Ul'ianov (Lenin), Ovsei-Gersh Arenov Apfelbaum (Zinoviev), Alexandra Mikhailovna Kolontai, Mecheslav Ulievich Kozlovskii, Ev'genia Mavrikievna Sumenson, Helfand (Parvus), Yakov Fürstenberg (Kuba Ganetskii), Midshipman Ilin (Raskol'nikov), and Ensigns Semashko, Sakharov, and Roshal' are accused of having entered—in 1917, while Russian citizens, by a preliminary agreement between themselves and other persons, and for the purpose of aiding the enemy countries at war with Russia—with said countries into an agreement to assist in the disorganization of the Russian army and the rear in order to weaken the fighting strength of the army. For this purpose and with the money received from said states, they organized propaganda among the civilian population and in the army, appealing to them to refuse immediately to continue military actions against the enemy; also, toward the same end, to organize in Petrograd, from July 3 to 5, 1917, an armed insurrection against the existing order in the state supreme authority. This was accompanied by murders and violence and attempts to arrest some members of the Government. As a consequence of this, some military units refused to carry out orders of their commanding personnel and arbitrarily abandoned their positions, thus aiding in the success of the enemy's armies.

1177. *Vlast' Naroda* ON THE REPORT
[No. 73, July 22, 1917, p. 2.]

Criminal prosecution is instituted against the culprits of the Petrograd revolt. The Prosecutor of the Petrograd Court of Appeals, in announcing the data secured through preliminary investigation which served as the basis for the accusation of Lenin and company of armed revolt and state treason, states:

"In reviewing all the indicated questions, the inquest authorities were not concerned with the political platform of the persons involved and were only interested in uncovering criminal activity and finding sufficient grounds for prosecuting the accused."

The case of the Bolsheviks is treated correctly, as it should be dealt with in a democracy.

Events similar to the Petrograd revolt are a crime first of all against the democracy organized into a state. All these crimes must be investigated. The guilty ones are revealed through these investigations. The country will see who it was that covered the police uniform with a red banner and who it was that betrayed the Russian proletariat while guilty of state treason. This inquiry at the same time absolves those accused by rumors, be it perhaps the hundred-mouthed goddess, but false nevertheless. The inquiry will separate the innocent from the guilty and, among the latter, will separate those who had evil designs and intentions from those who were careless in their actions.

How and by whom should these inquiries be conducted? There can be no two answers to this question. All criminal acts against the state must be investigated and the guilty ones tried by the organs of state law and penalized by penalties established by the state. In view of the exceptional gravity of the acts, a special commission may be organized in the legal order to assist the departments of the Office of Prosecution and the organs of inquiry. The authority for making the decision and the force of the authority must belong to the prosecuting organs of the state and to them alone.

The slogan has been devised, which at the present time apparently enjoys general recognition and support, that *all power* belongs to the *Provisional Government*—now the government for the salvation of the revolution and, moreover, the government destined to save the country and the entire state. If all power belongs to it, it should also concentrate in its hands all *legal power*. We consequently think it entirely impossible to concentrate the inquiry of criminal events in the hands of any organizations other than the legal organs of the state.

1178. Excerpts from Lenin's Reply to the Report

[*Rabochy i Soldat*, Nos. 3, 4, July 26, 27, 1917, as translated in the *Collected Works of V. I. Lenin: The Seizure of Power*, XXI, Bk. I, 51–61.]

I

On August 4, the papers printed the communication issued by the "Public Prosecutor of the Petrograd Supreme Court" about the inquiry into the events of July 16–18,[9] and about the summoning before the Court of a group of Bolsheviks, myself included, charged with treason and the organisation of armed uprising.

The government was forced to make public this communication because this heinous case has become too scandalous and appeared to all intelligent persons as an obvious forgery, perpetrated with the aid of the slandered Alexinsky, in fulfilment of the persistent desires and demands of the counter-revolutionary Cadet Party.

But by the publication of this communication, the government of Tsereteli and Co. disgraced itself the more, for now the grossness of the forgery, particularly, stares one in the face.

I left Petrograd on Thursday, July 12, on account of illness, and I only re-

[9] All dates in this document are New Style.

turned on Tuesday morning, July 17. But of course I assume full and unequivocal responsibility for all steps and measures taken by the Central Committee of our party, as well as by our party as a whole. I call attention to my absence to account for my lack of information concerning some details and for my alluding mainly to documents which have appeared in the press.

* * *

Incidentally, I, personally, owing to illness, delivered only one speech on July 17, from the balcony of Kshesinskaya's house. The Prosecutor mentions it, attempts to give its contents, but not only does he not mention any witnesses, he even suppresses the testimony of witnesses which was published in the press. I am far from having a complete set of the newspapers, but I have seen two references in the press: first, in the Bolshevik paper, *Proletarskoye Dyelo* (Cronstadt), and second, in the official Menshevik paper, *Rabochaya Gazeta* [*Workers' Gazette*]. Why not verify the contents of my speech by these documents and by public appeals to the population?

The entire speech consisted of the following: first, an apology for confining myself to only a few words on account of illness; second, a greeting to the revolutionary Cronstadtians in the name of the Petrograd workers; third, an expression of confidence that our slogan "All Power to the Soviets" must, and will, conquer, despite all the zigzags of the path of history; fourth, an appeal for "firmness, steadfastness and vigilance."

* * *

We, as representatives of the party of the revolutionary proletariat, maintain that our party always has been and always will be with the oppressed masses, when the masses express their thousand-times-justified and legitimate indignation against the high cost of living, against the lethargy and treachery of the "Socialist" Ministers, against the imperialist war and its prolongation. Our party did its imperative duty by going together with the justly indignant masses on July 17, and by trying to give their movement, their demonstrations, as much of a peaceful and organized character as possible. For on July 17 a peaceful passing of power to the Soviets was still possible, a peaceful development of the Russian Revolution was still realisable.

How stupid the Prosecutor's fairy tale about the "organization of an armed uprising" is, may be seen from the following. No one denies that among the armed soldiers and sailors who on July 17 crowded the streets of Petrograd the vast majority were on the side of our party. Our party had every opportunity to commence the unseating and arrest of hundreds of officials, to occupy dozens of government and official buildings and institutions, etc.

Nothing of this sort was done. Only people who have become so confused that they repeat all kinds of fairy tales disseminated by counter-revolutionary Cadets can remain blind to the ridiculous absurdity of the assertion that on July 16 and 17 the "organisation of an armed uprising" took place.

* * *

II

The accusation of espionage and of relations with Germany, another Beilis case, deserves but cursory notice. Here the "investigation," after a particularly crude perversion of the facts, simply parrots the slanders of the notorious calumniator Alexinsky.

It is untrue that in 1914 Zinoviev and I were arrested by the Austrian authorities. I alone was arrested.

It is untrue that I was arrested as a Russian subject. I was arrested on suspicion of spying. The local gendarme mistook the diagrams of agrarian statistics in my notebook for "plans"! Clearly, the Austrian gendarme was right on a level with Alexinsky and the *Yedinstvo* group. It seems, however, that I have broken the record in my pursuit after internationalism, for I have been persecuted by *both* the warring coalitions as a spy—in Austria by the gendarme, and in Russia by Alexinsky, the Cadets and Co.

It is not true that Hanecki played a part in my release from the Austrian prison. A part was played by Victor Adler, who put the Austrian authorities to shame. A part was played by the Poles, who were ashamed that such a despicable arrest of a Russian revolutionist could take place in their country.

It is a contemptible lie that I had relations with Parvus, that I visited military camps, etc. Nothing of the kind happened, or could ever happen. Upon the appearance of the very first numbers of Parvus's magazine, the *Kolokol* ["Bell"], our paper, the *Sotsial-Demokrat*, branded Parvus as a renegade and a German Plekhanov. Parvus is just as much of a social-chauvinist on the side of Germany as Plekhanov is on the side of Russia. As revolutionary internationalists we had and could have nothing in common with any German, Russian, or Ukrainian (Union for the Liberation of the Ukraine) social-chauvinist.

Steinberg is a member of the emigrant committee in Stockholm. The first time I met him was in Stockholm. About May 3, or a bit later, Steinberg came to Petrograd and, if I remember correctly, tried to obtain a subsidy for the emigrants' society. The Prosecutor could have verified it quite easily, if he had wanted to verify it.

The Prosecutor plays up the fact that Parvus is connected with Hanecki, and that Hanecki is connected with Lenin. But this is simply the trick of a swindler, for every ones knowns that Hanecki had financial dealings with Parvus, while I and Hanecki had not.

Hanecki, as a tradesman, worked for Parvus; they conducted business together. There are a great many emigrants who have admitted in the press that they have worked in establishments and undertakings belonging to Parvus.

The Prosecutor brings out the point that commercial correspondence might serve as a screen for relations of an espionage nature. It would be interesting to know how many Cadets, Mensheviks and S.-R.'s could be accused, according to this wonderful prescription, for commercial correspondence.

But if the Prosecutor is in possession of a series of telegrams from Hanecki to Sumenson (these telegrams have been published); if the Prosecutor knows in which bank, when, and how much money Sumenson had (and the Prosecutor has published a few figures of this nature), then why should he not summon two or three office and business employees to take part in the investigation? In two days they would put at his disposal a complete abstract of all the commercial and bank records.

Hardly anything reveals the nature of this "Beilis case"[10] so well as the fragmentary figures cited by the Prosecutor: "Within half a year Sumenson drew 750,000 rubles; she has 180,000 rubles left on her account." If you do publish

---

[10] A notorious trial, shortly before the war, used to incite anti-Semitism and marked by grave infractions of judicial procedure.

figures, why not publish them in full? Exactly when, exactly from whom did Sumenson receive money "within half a year," and to whom did she pay it out? Exactly when, and exactly what consignments of goods were received?

What is easier than to gather such complete data? In two or three days this could and should have been done. This would have uncovered the whole cycle of commercial dealings between Hanecki and Sumenson. It would have left no room for obscure innuendoes for the Prosecutor to manipulate!

Alexinsky's vilest and meanest slanders, paraphrased to sound like a "state" document by the officials of the Cabinet of Tsereteli and Co.—this is how low the S.-R.'s and Mensheviks have fallen!

III

Of course, it would be extremely naïve to regard the "judicial cases" instituted by the Cabinet of Tsereteli, Kerensky and Co. against the Bolsheviks as actual judicial cases. It would be absolutely unpardonable constitutional illusion.

The S.-R.'s and Mensheviks, having entered into a coalition with the counter-revolutionary Cadets on May 19 and having adopted a policy of offensive warfare, *i.e.*, the renewal and continuation of the imperialist war, inevitably found themselves captives of the Cadets.

As captives, they were forced to participate in the filthiest Cadet deals, in their basest and most slanderous plots.

The "case" of Chernov is rapidly beginning to enlighten even the most backward, that is, it proves the correctness of our views. Besides Chernov, the *Ryech* is beginning to denounce Tsereteli as a "hyprocrite" and a "Zimmerwaldist."

Now the blind shall see, and stones shall speak.

The counter-revolution is closing its ranks. The Cadets are at the bottom. The staff, the military leaders, and Kerenesky are in their grip; the Black Hundred press is at their service. Such are the allies of the bourgeois counter-revolution.

The despicable slandering of poltical opponents will help the proletariat sooner to understand where the counter-revolution is, and to sweep it away in the name of freedom, peace, bread for the hungry, land for the peasants.

N. LENIN

1179. RESOLUTION OF AUGUST 18 OF THE PETROGRAD SOVIET

[*Izvestiia*, No. 148, August 19, 1917, p. 4. Some of the Bolsheviks were released for lack of evidence. Soon after their arrest. Others, including Trotsky, who was arrested only on July 23, were released on bail after the Kornilov Affair, while still others remained in prison until the Bolshevik revolution. Lenin, of course, remained in hiding with a warrant for his arrest in force until his seizure of power. The preparation of the case against the Bolsheviks continued in a somewhat desultory fashion to the fall of the Provisional Government.]

"The Petrograd Soviet of Workers' and Soldiers' Deputies, having discussed the question of the arrests and persecutions of representatives of extremist trends in socialist parties, including members of the Soviet, vigorously protests against the illegal arrests and the excesses which have taken place, and insists, first, on the immediate release of all arrested persons who have not, to date, been presented with any charges; second, on setting an immediate date for a trial by jury for all the accused; and third, on indicting all persons guilty of unlawful deprivation of freedom."

Comrade Lunacharskii submitted a fourth part to this resolution, which read:
"4) The establishment of a public committee of inquiry with the participation of members of the Soviet of Workers' and Soldiers' Deputies."
The meeting adopted this point.

1180. EXCERPT OF A TELEGRAM FROM THE GERMAN STATE SECRETARY (KÜHLMANN) TO THE FOREIGN MINISTRY LIAISON OFFICER AT GENERAL HEADQUARTERS CONFIRMING GERMAN FINANCIAL SUPPORT OF THE BOLSHEVIKS

[Zeman, *Germany and the Russian Revolution*, pp. 94–95.]

Berlin, 3 December 1917

The disruption of the Entente and the subsequent creation of political combinations agreeable to us constitute the most important war aim of our diplomacy. Russia appeared to be the weakest link in the enemy's chain. The task therefore was gradually to loosen it and, when possible, to remove it. This was the purpose of the subversive activity we caused to be carried out in Russia behind the front —in the first place promotion of separatist tendencies and support of the Bolsheviki. It was not until the Bolsheviki had received from us a steady flow of funds through various channels and under varying labels that they were in a position to be able to build up their main organ, *Pravda*, to conduct energetic propaganda and appreciably to extend the originally narrow basis of their party. The Bolsheviki have now come into power; how long they will retain power cannot yet be foreseen. They need peace in order to strengthen their own position; on the other hand it is entirely in our interest that we should exploit the period while they are in power, which may be a short one, in order to attain firstly an armistice and then, if possible, peace. The conclusion of a separate peace would mean the achievement of the desired war aim, namely, a breach between Russia and her Allies. The amount of tension necessarily caused by such a breach would determine the degree of Russia's dependence on Germany and her future relations with us. Once cast out and cast off by her former Allies, abandoned financially, Russia will be forced to seek our support. . . .

. . .

1181. *Rabochaia Gazeta* ON THE NEW BOLSHEVIK PROGRAM AFTER THE JULY DAYS

[No. 129, August 10, 1917, p. 1.]

Since the arrival of Lenin from abroad, the Bolsheviks who are led by him got hold of two formulas, in the name of which they opened a struggle. One was the goal: the dictatorship of the proletariat and of the poorest proletarian and semi-proletarian strata of the peasantry. This formula was making its way diffidently, shyly, and self-consciously, evidently in order not to alienate prematurely that majority of the peasants which the Bolsheviks had at first planned to use for support.

The other formula—the one that was preparing the way for the Bolshevik goal —on the other hand, resounded with strength and assurance, and was being advanced as a slogan calling directly to the masses.

That formula was: all power to the Soviets [of Workers' and Soldiers' Deputies].

Of course, for the Leninites it was only a temporary, transitional stage. This was, as it is clarified now in the brochure of N.L. [Nikolai Lenin], an experiment of peaceful development. By peaceful means, by means of winning power within the Soviets, they hoped to come to the proletarian dictatorship.

But the Soviets did not cooperate with the Bolsheviks. They did not dare to take power in their own hands. And that peaceful way of development, which the Leninites had planned for their experiment, began to provoke evident impatience among them.

As a result, the clang of arms sounded on the "peaceful" road.

The masses of workers and soldiers, carried away by Leninist propaganda, rose with weapons in their hands in order to force the Soviets to do things they did not want to do.

This move was defeated. It only resulted in senseless bloodshed in the streets of Petrograd. And the masses of soldiers running away from the enemy at the front threw a beam of light on the danger which Leninism presented to the revolution, to the consolidation of its gains, to the protection of it against external and internal dangers.

Between the Soviets and Leninism an abyss opened up which was not there before.

Such is the logic of events. And this logic has now been assessed by Leninites.

The Leninites have lost the hope of arriving at their dictatorship by "peaceful means," i.e., by means of peacefully endorsing the developing anarchy. So they are abandoning the peaceful means. They are throwing away their slogan "All power to the Soviets." Of this, the brochure "On Slogans" by N.L., speaks definitely.[11]

"This struggle, the struggle for the passing of power to the Soviets in due time, is finished. The peaceful course of development has been rendered impossible. The non-peaceful, the most painful road has begun."

"Non-peaceful, most painful"—these are euphemisms for "bloody."

In other words, N.L. calls for a second revolution, a proletarian revolution, the revolution which must give power not to the majority of the population but to its insignificant minority.

The attempts at such a revolution will bring about not the triumph of the proletariat but the defeat of both the proletariat and the revolution. And the most decisive rebuff must be given to the propaganda for such a revolution.

[This must be done] not by violence and not by measures of repression; particularly, since N.L. himself does not call for the immediate revolution, right away, but suggests waiting for "the new upsurge of the revolution."

We must respond to the campaign that the Leninites have started on behalf of the second revolution by means of creative work; we must answer it by means of work directed toward saving the country from external danger, by saving industry, transportation, and finances from a crash; and by putting into effect the urgent measures on behalf of workers and peasants.

On the basis of this work, our propaganda addressed to the workers—concerning the madness and destructiveness of the road to which the Leninites call them—will sound convincing.

[11] *Collected Works of V. I. Lenin: Toward the Seizure of Power*, XXI, Bk. I, 43–50.

CHAPTER 25

The Political Crisis

THE END OF THE FIRST COALITION

1182. THE KADETS EXPLAIN THE RESIGNATION OF THEIR MEMBERS IN THE GOVERNMENT

[*Rech'*, No. 155, July 5, 1917, p. 2. The resignations were submitted on July 2.]

The Central Committee of the Party of the People's Freedom, having been obliged to recall its representative from the Provisional Government, considers it to be its duty to explain to the country why this act was unavoidable at this trying moment for the country.

From the very first days of the revolution, the Party of the People's Freedom was of the opinion that the only way to save the freedom won and to drive off the external enemy was to form a united national government, resting upon the population as a whole. Therefore, in the beginning of May, the Party responded to the Government's call for the formation of a so-called coalition cabinet, hoping that it would mean the establishment of a government inspired by the desire to find a middle course for all the trends existing in the country and to carry out the national will. Unfortunately, it did not work out that way. The fundamental idea of a coalition, an all-national agreement, was not realized in its true form, and that explains why the coalition was incapable of giving the country a united and strong government. In a large number of questions, both foreign and domestic, which touched the principles of unity and power of the Government, the members of the Party of the People's Freedom were left in a minority. The latest and especially striking event of this kind was the acceptance by the Government, in its definite form and excluding the possibility of introducing any alteration, of an agreement concluded with the Ukrainian Rada by three members of the Provisional Government, who went to Kiev in order to carry on preliminary negotiations. This decision was taken notwithstanding the warnings given by our comrades as to its possible consequences.[1]

In regard to the Ukrainian question, the Central Committee recognizes the necessity of preparing a plan for the regional autonomy of the Ukraine for submission to the Constituent Assembly, and the Committee has even started work on this measure. But the Central Committee is of the opinion that [1] the immediate formation of a local government, responsible to a public organization of the same local character, which will have to function with an indefinite authority and an undefined territory, and [2] the Government's welcoming, in advance, of a plan of regional autonomy, whose contents remain unknown to it, constitute an inadmissible and highly dangerous precedent, predetermining, contrary to the oath taken by the members of the Government, the will of the Constituent Assembly and the future organization of the Russian state. The Central Committee of the Party takes the stand that its followers in the Government, who are deprived of the

[1] See Volume I, Doc. 354.

possibility of exerting any influence as to the substance of the act and of harmonizing it with the fundamental demands of public law, should not bear a responsibility for this measure and for its possible consequences.

The Party of the People's Freedom holds that a united and strong Government can be created either by increasing the homogeneity of its membership or by organizing it in such a way as to compel its members to act on matters of fundamental national interest, not through the preponderance of majority over minority, but through mutual agreements, tending toward the fulfillment of all-national problems.

The Party would like to believe that the Government about to be formed will stand back of the offensive which has just commenced at the front and will strive to re-establish normal life in the interior. The Party will support wholeheartedly the new Provisional Government in its efforts for the good of Russia and in its fight against the external foes.

The heroic deeds of our army, which is making final, determined efforts to hasten peace by a mighty offensive, should call forth the unconditional and steady support of all citizens regardless of party lines. Today, as heretofore, the Party of the People's Freedom urges all the people to stand together and fulfill their patriotic duty for the sake of Russia's welfare, for the sake of her regeneration and reconstruction on foundations of popular government and social justice.

THE CENTRAL COMMITTEE OF THE PARTY OF THE PEOPLE'S FREEDOM

1183. *Den'* ON THE KADET WITHDRAWAL

[No. 102, July 6, 1917, p. 1. For Lenin's comment, see the *Collected Works of V. I. Lenin: Toward the Seizure of Power*, XXI, Bk. I, 15–16.]

The Provisional Government has emerged with the honors out of the tempest of the last days. It has coped simultaneously with two blows, from the Kadets and from the Bolsheviks. Both expected to overthrow it, but only raised its prestige among the popular masses.

The Kadets have withdrawn from the Provisional Government because of their dissent over the Ukrainian question. But it is precisely on this question that the Government has won an important political victory, having reached an agreement with the Rada.

The Universal of the Rada is a document that should silence all those who wished to overthrow the Government over precisely that issue. From this quarter the danger to the revolution is over.

The Government has lost a more or less important group of militant Kadets, but has won the sympathies of the many millions of Ukrainians, personified in their organized representatives.

And if the Kadets boycott the Provisional Government because of the Ukraine, then the Ukraine will undoubtedly boycott the Kadets even more than before. Let them enjoy the fruits of their nearsighted policy.

But also the Bolsheviks have strengthened the Government. They have strengthened it by covering themselves with shame before the whole country and by justifying the resolute attitude which the Government took toward them. Henceforth it will be able to act much more decisively in its struggle against the Bolshevik and anarchic excesses, and this will strengthen its power and authority all over the country.

Fate, or more exactly the Kadets, chose that the Government be confronted by the senseless rebellion precisely at the time when a cruel blow was inflicted upon it by the partisans of Miliukov. And the fact that under this unfavorable trend of circumstances it could nevertheless honorably cope with the problems that fell to its lot bears witness to its strength and solidity.

All these symptoms are comforting. We cannot know what the near future will bring us. Ahead of us may yet lie many ordeals, but, as the revolutionary Government has coped in these tumultuous days with the menace [confronting both] itself and Russia, the hope that it will cope also with future complications does not appear groundless.

The revolutionary power strengthens and there is reason to believe that it will bring the country to the Constituent Assembly, which will lead us out of the critical stage into the stage of organized development.

The Government grows stronger—such is the comforting conclusion to be drawn from these grievous days.

1184. The Acceptance of the Resignation of the Kadet Ministers and the Submittal of the Resignation of Prince L'vov
[*Zhurnaly*, No. 125, July 7, 1917.]

Heard:

1. The presentation of the Minister-President of the statements submitted [to him by the following ministers] to relinquish their titles as members of the Provisional Government and to release them of their posts: Minister of Education, A. A. Manuilov; Minister of Welfare, Prince D. I. Shakhovskoi; Minister of Transport, N. V. Nekrasov; Minister of Finance, A. I. Shingarev; Minister of Justice, P. N. Pereverzev; and Acting Minister of Trade and Industry, V. A. Stepanov.

Resolved:

I. To release as of July 3, 1917, [the above mentioned] of [their] titles of members of the Provisional Government and of their posts . . .

II. To recognize that the Provisional Government preserves all plenary power in its present membership.

III. Immediately upon restoring order in Petrograd and assuring the population of safety, to begin the solution of the question of enlarging the membership of the Provisional Government.

IV. To entrust the deputy ministers . . . with temporary charge of the administration of the ministries: of Education, Welfare, Transport, Finance, Justice, and Trade and Industry.

Heard:

2. The statement of the Minister-President, Prince G. E. L'vov, to relinquish the duties of Minister-President and Minister of the Interior and to entrust his duties as Minister of the Interior temporarily to Assistant Minister D. M. Shchepkin.

Resolved:

To take under consideration.

1185. THE DECLARATION OF THE PROVISIONAL GOVERNMENT
[*VVP*, No. 100, p. 1.]

Citizens! A fateful hour has struck. The armies of the German Emperor have broken the front of the Russian national revolutionary army. This terrible operation was facilitated for them by the criminal levity and blind fanaticism of some and the treachery of others. Both threatened the very foundations of the new Free Russia. At this fateful moment when, taking advantage of the general confusion, the hidden forces of counterrevolution can raise their heads, the re-organized Provisional Government clearly realizes the responsibility which weighs so heavily on its shoulders. But the Government possesses full and firm confidence in the strength of the great Russian people. The Provisional Government has confidence in the rapid recuperation of the political life of the country now that the contagious sickness which shook the national organism has declared itself and burned itself out in an acute crisis. The Provisional Government firmly believes that that crisis will lead to recovery and not to death.

Strong in that belief, the Provisional Government is ready to act, and will act with all the energy and resolution that the present exceptional circumstances demand.

The Provisional Government regards as its first and major problem the application of all its strength to the struggle against the foreign foe, and to the defense of the new state order against every anarchical and counterrevolutionary attempt, without hesitating to take the most rigorous measures in its power. At the same time, it will again make it clear by its foreign policy that the revolutionary army can only go forward to the fight with the firm conviction that not a drop of the blood of a Russian soldier will be shed for foreign ends, and will again confirm the sentiments of democratic right which it has openly proclaimed to the whole world in its pacific pronouncement. With this end in view the Provisional Government, in keeping with the principles of foreign policy proclaimed in the Government's Declaration of May 6 [*sic*], intends to propose to the Allies to gather at a conference of the Allies during August in order to determine the general course of the Allies' foreign policy and to coordinate their actions in carrying out the principles proclaimed by the Russian revolution. Russia will be represented in this conference by members of the diplomatic corps as well as by representatives of the Russian democracy.

Pursuing the work of state organization in other areas also on the principles promulgated by the Declaration of May 6 [*sic*], the Provisional Government deems it necessary to carry out immediately a number of measures which will realize the indicated principles.

The Provisional Government will take all steps in order that elections to the Constituent Assembly take place on the appointed date (September 17) and that the preliminary measures be completed in advance in order to guarantee the correctness and freedom of elections. In the field of internal policy, the Provisional Government's principal problem is the introduction at the earliest possible moment of municipal and zemstvo self-government on the basis of universal, direct, equal, and secret suffrage widely distributed. Attributing at the same time particular significance to the creation locally of organs of authority vested with the confidence of the entire population, the Provisional Government will immediately bring into the organization of local authority representatives of public organizations in order to form collegiate organs of regional administration, combining a number of guberniyas.

In its desire for a consistent introduction of principles of civil equality into the life of the country, the Provisional Government will establish in the near future laws on abolishing estates [*soslovie*] as well as final liquidation of civil ranks and orders, except those granted for battle distinctions.

In order to cope energetically with the economic disorder and to take further measures for the protection of labor, the Economic Council and the Central Economic Committee, appointed by the Provisional Government, will begin their work immediately. Their tasks will consist of working out a general plan for the organization of the national economy and of labor, the working out of draft laws, and general measures to regulate economic life and the control of industry, as well as carrying them out in a planned and coordinated fashion. In the domain of labor policy, bills will be shortly prepared and put into effect regarding the freedom of trade unions, and regarding labor exchanges and arbitration courts. Bills are also being drafted relative to the eight-hour day, the protection of labor, and the introduction of all kinds of workers' insurance.

With regard to the agricultural question, the Provisional Government is convinced, as before, that, in view of the vital requirements of our national economy and the repeatedly expressed desires of the peasants, as well as the programs formulated by all the democratic parties in the country, future agricultural reforms must be based upon the principle of transferring the land to the toilers. On this basis a scheme of agricultural reform is being drawn up which will be submitted to the Constituent Assembly.

The measures which the Provisional Government will take in the immediate future are:

1) Complete doing away with the old agrarian policy which ruined and disorganized the agricultural communities;

2) Measures safeguarding the complete freedom of the Constituent Assembly as to the distribution of the country's land reserve;

3) Improvement of land relations in the interests of state defense and supplying the country with food by means of expanding and consolidating the network of land committees organized by the state, with well-defined legal authority in the area of deciding the current questions of agricultural-economic policy, except the basic question of the right to land ownership, which is within the authority of the Constituent Assembly; and

4) The elimination, by means of such legal regulation of land relations, of that grave danger with which the state and the future agrarian reform is threatened, such as land seizures and similar arbitrary local methods of solving the land needs which contradict the principle of the general national plan of the future land reform.

In announcing its proposed aims the Provisional Government thinks it has the right to count in its grave and responsible work upon the wholehearted and enthusiastic support of all the vital forces of the country. It demands of all of them sacrifice and readiness to give everything—all their strength, possessions, their very life—for the great cause of saving the country that has ceased to be the stern stepmother to the people inhabiting it, and it strives to unite all of them on the principles of complete liberty and equality.

July 8

1186. STATEMENT BY PRINCE L'VOV CONCERNING HIS RESIGNATION

[*Russkiia Vedomosti*, No. 155, July 9, 1917, p. 4.]

In today's [July 8] session of the Provisional Government, G. E. L'vov read his statement of July 7, which formalized his resignation from the Provisional Government, as follows.

After the suppression of the armed revolt in Petrograd, under the influence of the representatives of the extreme socialist movement, the Provisional Government passed a resolution to put into effect immediately the program of the government's further activity proposed by the socialist ministers. This program is acceptable to me only in those parts that are a repetition and development of the basic principles declared by the Provisional Government in the declarations it formerly published. But it is *unacceptable to me in its entirety* in view of the obvious deviation from the nonparty principles in the direction of the realization of purely party socialist aims, particularly in those parts of it that were formerly submitted to the Provisional Government for decision and against which I have already not infrequently expressed myself. Among those is the immediate declaration of a republican form of government in the Russian State. This is an obvious usurpation of the supreme rights of the Constituent Assembly, which is the only actual spokesman of the people's will. Such infringement upon the rights of the Constituent Assembly is the implementation of the proposed agrarian program. By consenting to this I would violate the obligation which I assumed in line with my duty pledged to the people. Further, there follows the dissolution of the State Duma and State Council and some secondary points of the same program of lesser importance, but bearing, nevertheless, the character of sacrificing national and moral values to the masses in the name of demagogy and as a play to the galleries.[2]

While an adherent of the transfer of land into the hands of the toiling peasantry, I nevertheless find that the land laws submitted by the Minister of Agriculture for confirmation by the Provisional Government are unacceptable to me, not only in their content, but because of the politics which they actually contain. The declaration of the Provisional Government of May 6 [*sic*] established the organization of land use in the interests of the national economy and the toiling population. But in my opinion, by deviating from it the Ministry of Agriculture passes laws which undermine the people's respect for the law. Not only do they fail to combat illegal seizures, not only do they fail to normalize and guide land relations into proper channels, but they seem to justify the ruinous arbitrary seizures which are taking place all over Russia. They also legalize the seizures which have already taken place; and as a matter of fact, they try to confront the Constituent Assembly with an accomplished fact. I see in them the fulfillment of a party program and not measures for the welfare of the entire country. I anticipate that in their final development they will betray the people's expectations and will result in the inability to realize the state land reform. I regard the land program which the Minister of Agriculture is conducting as ruinous for Russia, for it will leave her ravaged and undermined, both morally and economically. And I fear that it will create within Russia that which the Provisional Government vigorously combated in recent days in Petrograd.

[2] For a discussion of why the statements concerning the establishment of a republic and the abolition of the Duma and State Council did not appear in the Declaration, see Oliver H. Radkey, *The Agrarian Foes of Bolshevism*, pp. 286–93.

I am not touching upon those numerous differences of opinion between myself and the majority of the Provisional Government in the interpretation of the essence of the questions of state life and those conditions under which the Provisional Government must work. I cannot but point out the approval on July 4 of the resolution of the Executive Committees of the Soviets of Workers', Soldiers', and Peasants' Deputies, with the participation of the socialist ministers, on the obligation of the entire Provisional Government to be guided in its activity by the decisions of the All-Russian Congress of these deputies. These differences of opinion have increased, particularly in recent days. Not infrequently they made me question whether it was possible for me to remain at the head of the Provisional Government. But to the last days I always thought it my duty, because of the country's grave condition, to find a conciliatory course in the interest of preserving unity within the Provisional Government.

Now, in view of the profound differences of opinion on problems that confront the Government, my duty to the country tells me that I have no right to participate in carrying out the programs approved by the Provisional Government.

I resign from the cabinet of the Provisional Government and lay down my duties of Minister-President and Minister of the Interior.

1187. PRINCE L'VOV ON KERENSKY AS HIS SUCCESSOR AS MINISTER-PRESIDENT

[*Russkoe Slovo*, No. 157, July 12, 1917, p. 3.]

Today your correspondent received from G. E. L'vov information on the circumstances preceding his resignation and the causes that led to it.

Incidentally Prince L'vov touched upon the appointment of his successor, A. F. Kerensky:

"I laid down the heavy burden, convinced that I am fulfilling my duty to the motherland, and I deliberately proposed the candidacy of Kerensky to succeed me, for I am deeply convinced that it is precisely he who is necessary at this, perhaps the most dangerous, moment of the revolution, in the post of Minister-President.

"The extreme socialist tendencies," continued Prince L'vov, "expressed in so-called bolshevism, suffered complete collapse. The Russian people and the Russian army were convinced that German agents and traitors were in the majority in the above-mentioned movement. The sound Russian organism withstood this poisonous current. Bolshevism is buried, and this psychological break testifies to the fact that conscience, truth, and loyalty to the state are still alive and strong among the people.

"At such a time a strong government is needed. And to bring it about, a combination of elements of authority is needed such as are embodied in the person of Kerensky. In the army he is a recognized leader, in the country he is a symbol of the revolution. Actually he possesses real power, and among the socialists he is perhaps the only man of action. His devoted service to the country gives him the right and gives Russia the hope of realizing the power which the country awaits so eagerly. And most important, having assumed the leadership of the military power, he must have the greatest freedom of action in order to form a new government, in order to rally everybody into one whole, in order to create that high spirit in the country which alone can save the motherland."

1188. THE DEBATE AND RESOLUTION OF VTsIK AND THE EXECUTIVE
COMMITTEE OF THE SOVIETS OF PEASANTS' DEPUTIES
[*Izvestiia*, No. 114, July 11, 1917, pp. 3–4, 6.]

On July 9 the first, terrible news of the events at the front reached Petrograd.

The Central Committee of the Soviets of Workers' and Soldiers' Deputies and the Executive Committee of the Soviets of Peasants' Deputies were immediately called to a special meeting.

The meeting opened at 8:30 P.M.

Comrade Tseretelli gave a report.

Tseretelli's Speech

Comrades. The Provisional Government has been reorganized. It is composed of nine members. As you know, comrades, the Government must be composed of ten members, and it was decided that the principle of parity will be preserved in this connection; the [principle of] equal representation of the Soviets and non-socialist elements will be preserved.

You have read the declaration of the Provisional Government—this is not a new covenant; it points to a series of concrete measures which fulfill the declaration issued on May 6 by the coalition government.

This platform is not only a platform of a socialist movement; it is the platform of a covenant which is upheld by all the vital forces of the country. As this program is gradually being put into practice, some groups which supported it in the beginning are now withdrawing their support.

You have read Prince L'vov's letter; you know what prompted him to leave the Provisional Government. On my part, I must tell you that the letter presents the whole matter in a false light. I assume that you yourselves have discerned the incorrect account he has given of all the ramifications of the reorganization of the Provisional Government. Prince L'vov, the representative of moderate liberalism who joined the revolution, has resigned. The point of disagreement between him and the Provisional Government was the agrarian legislation of the Provisional Government.

This problem has acquired in his imagination the aspect of a monstrous plot.

No, this is not our policy, the policy of encouraging seizures, which he attributes to us. This is not the policy of the Ministry of Agriculture. We know that [land] seizures and anarchy can destroy the land reform, and that is why we are fighting them.

But the Constituent Assembly will be free to distribute and transfer the land to the people—and a series of measures which we submitted in order to guarantee this freedom to the Constituent Assembly frightened Prince L'vov.

.   .   .

The foreign and domestic situation of the country is critical. You know about the breakthrough on the front; and now it is a question of life and death for us to prevent the growth of the success which the enemy has achieved.

I will read you, comrades, a communiqué from a commander of one of the armies, and you will see what confusion reigns there and how imperative it is that the army hear of the decision that you will support the fight.

The communiqué was received by direct wire. The Minister of Labor, Comrade Skobelev, left for the front immediately upon its receipt. (The communiqué of the army commander and Kerensky's telegram on the demoralization in the army, which was brought on by the Petrograd revolt and which led to the enemy's success, were read aloud.) Comrades, we in the Provisional Government have discussed this question with representatives of the Ministry of War and have resolved to make a nation-wide announcement of the difficult situation in the army, concealing nothing.

This is not the time to hide one's wounds. Let the democracy know the situation and take a vigorous stand in defense of the revolution in order to raise the morale of the army.

Comrades, we are in the process of making forceful preparations to offset the breakthrough, but in order to come to the assistance of the army, it is necessary to exert all the strength of the country. Representatives of organizations from all parts of Russia must be sent to the front in order to encourage the army and turn it against the enemy. Commissars must be dispatched to the front, so that the country, the rear and the front, can thus be united in one powerful entity. This is the opinion of the Government and the Ministry of War, which know the situation and can appraise our strength and which know that with the concentrated efforts of all the forces of the democracy Russia will be saved. We must appeal for this and work for the cause of the revolution. The Government must be in a position to feel that it is united with all the people. This position is that of a strong Government which will be able to call to order all those who are ruining the cause of the revolution in any way, be it by anarchic or treasonable attempts to organize an uprising in the rear or by attempts of the counterrevolutionary forces, equally disastrous to the country, to take advantage of this confusion for achieving their own ends.

Only a single revolutionary, popular power which leans on the support of the democracy can save the country from disintegration and bring it to the ultimate victory of the revolution. I am saying that our revolution and the country are in danger. Everything depends on whether the democracy, rallying together with all the vital forces of the country, will be able to establish a power that will unify the whole country. The whole future course of our revolution depends on the creation of such a power, commanding the confidence and support of all the people and endowed with unlimited powers for saving the country. (*Prolonged applause.*)

Dan's Speech

Comrades! I am speaking on behalf of the Menshevik faction. The 3rd of July will remain a memorable day. This day marked an assault at the very heart of the revolution—[at] the Soviets of Workers' and Soldiers' Deputies.

It stands to reason that, had there not been such disorganization in the country as a result of the war, the demagoguery could not have enjoyed such success.

But this does not diminish the damage inflicted on the revolution on that day; it does not diminish the responsibility of that party which precipitated the revolt by its demagogic treatment of all the issues.

Fortunately, we succeeded in suppressing this movement in Petrograd, but it must be stated that this blow brought the country to the brink of ruin.

We are facing another great danger.

Our front has been broken and it still remains to be seen just what we will be able to do in this direction.

The danger lies in the fact that the counterrevolution is collecting all its forces—and it is clear to anyone who keeps his eyes open that a military dictatorship is imminent.

In order to avoid this possibility, in order to knock the weapons out of the hands of the counterrevolutionaries, our government must be given the most comprehensive powers while we retain for ourselves the right to exercise a restraining influence on it.

If we are unable to take the power into our hands at the present moment—if we are unable to take the initiative in liquidating the revolt—then others will do so who will at the same time crush the revolution itself.

The counterrevolution must be wiped out at its very inception. For this reason we are proposing to proclaim our government—the government *salut publique*—a government of dictatorship.

We must give it the most comprehensive, unlimited powers, in order to preserve and save the cause of the revolution.

Today, in this hall, a historical question is being decided. Today we must decide the future course of our revolution.

It is only through a strong government which will work together with the whole revolutionary democracy that the revolution can be saved from the blow which was just inflicted upon it.

Lunacharskii's Speech

Comrades, we, Social Democrats, Internationalists, realize the terrible dangers which surround the country and the revolution. It is imperative that we unify all the socialist forces. Our disunity has assumed the aspects of a sharp conflict. This is not the time for argument. . . . Comrades, if you take a man from the front, you will discover that it requires a tremendous exertion of all forces, an enormous struggle in order to . . . [achieve this unity of all the socialist forces].[3] And you will not achieve this by appeals to fight anarchy. You must at all costs arrive at an agreement between yourselves and the Bolsheviks in order to fight against the counterrevolution. We, Internationalists, and, I think, the Bolsheviks, consider that if it is impossible to reach this agreement at the present time, we are willing to make concessions—we extend you our hand for a union of forces despite the accumulated grievances and our mutual distrust. In this menacing hour we have extended our hand in the name of saving the revolution. The one point which may not be acceptable to you is the point regarding the demands of the avant-garde, but we know that in order to govern a state, it is necessary to have a ministry, it is necessary to have a power; so I think that even on this question there is no gulf between us. We are only speaking of accepting this power from the Soviets in order to satisfy the demands of the democracy, in order that revolutionary Russia can tell the soldier and worker what she is going to give them. No one can state with certainty that the situation has been saved, but a unification is imperative and the demands of the democracy must be satisfied. It does not seem to me that a situation could now arise which could break up this socialist bloc. The Bolsheviks are saying: we want to work together with you in order to save the country. Many listen to us and you will lose the sympathy of the socialist elements if you reject our proposal. I think that even strictly

---

[3] Error in text.

political considerations must force you to weigh this situation and accept our proposal. Otherwise, the gods are depriving you of reason and you are doomed to ruin.

Avksent'ev's Speech

I am speaking here on behalf of the Socialist Revolutionary faction of the Executive Committee of the All-Russian Soviet of Peasants' Deputies and the Central Executive Committee of the Soviets of Workers' and Soldiers' Deputies.

Comrade Dan has already read the resolution which has our wholehearted support.

Comrade Lunacharskii said that the gods are probably depriving us of our reason.

And where has the reason of Comrade Lunacharskii and his friends been during the past three months? We have been continuously saying, continuously warning Comrade Lunacharskii's friends that if they persist in conducting their type of propaganda and agitation we would come to a tragic denouement.

On that recent day when the masses ran riot in front of the Tauride Palace, we here, from this rostrum, heard the very same words which they were uttering on the streets of Petrograd, at the palace walls.

Only now do they speak of an agreement. But now it is no longer a question of an agreement, but of everyone subordinating himself to the directive, to the decision which will be adopted at the present meeting. (*Storm of applause.*) There is only one thing—unconditional submission to the will of the revolutionary democracy. (*Storm of applause.*)

Everyone who is not with us now is an enemy.

Now is not the time for words but for deeds, actions which may, perhaps, be tragic, but which were made incumbent on us by the Russian revolution. Even if we fall, we will fall with honor, defending the cause of the great revolution. (*Applause.*)

Comrade Lunacharskii said that soldiers and workers will be asking you what gains the revolution brought them. But we are raising another question, a more tragic one, namely, what will they *lose* if the revolution is defeated?

If the people lose their revolutionary position, they will lose everything that the revolution has given them.

We are appealing to the people for sacrifices, for the need to put everything at stake.

It was stated here: We speak bluntly and explicitly about the necessity of fighting against all manifestations of anarchy because we are afraid of losing the popularity of the man in the street.

But it is not a question of popularity. This is not what we fear. We are faced with an enormous responsibility. This responsibility can give rise to an inner determination to stop at nothing, to take every step that might save the great Russian revolution.

Such is the significance we are attributing to the present moment and to the resolution proposed to us. (*Prolonged applause.*)

We are saying that if you have understood the danger of a counterrevolution, we welcome this. But do not squelch your friends; let us work together. Then a counterrevolution will no longer frighten us.

.   .   .

At 2:10 [A.M.] the roll-call vote ended and the chairman announced the results: the resolution was adopted unanimously, by 252 votes, with 47 abstaining.

Resolution

Recognizing that the situation on the front and within the country threatens military devastation, the downfall of the revolution, and the triumph of counter-revolutionary forces, the joint meeting of the All-Russian Central Executive Committee of Soviets of Workers' and Soldiers' Deputies and the Executive Committee of Soviets of Peasants' Deputies resolved that:

1. The country and the revolution are in danger;

2. The Provisional Government is declared the Government to Save the Revolution;

3. The Government shall be vested with unlimited powers for restoring organization and discipline in the army by a resolute struggle with all manifestations of counterrevolution and anarchy, and for carrying out the same program of constructive legislation as was outlined in the Declaration;

4. The socialist ministers are to report on all their activities to the Joint Meeting of the Executive Committees no less than twice a week.

1189. AN APPEAL TO ALL THE POPULATION

[*Izvestiia*, No. 114, July 11, 1917, p. 1. Similar appeals to the workers and peasants calling for unity, sacrifice, and support for the Government to Save the Revolution, were published in the same issue.]

CITIZENS!

The all-Russian central organ of Workers', Soldiers', and Peasants' Soviets is turning to you with an appeal.

The menacing hour has struck. The front of revolutionary Russia has been broken through. Our republican troops are retreating in disorder and flight. New regions of our native land are threatened with enemy occupation.

The menacing hour has struck. Blinded madmen, with arms in hand, are attacking the power of the revolutionary Government in the capital, and the will of the whole revolutionary democracy. Deterioration and anarchy are beginning to reign in Russia. The dark forces have come back to life. They got wind of the prey. They are getting ready to turn you once again into oppressed slaves, to torture once again our native land which has suffered so much. They are seeking to subvert the organs of revolutionary democracy and the revolutionary Provisional Government; they are pitting the dark masses against Jews and are calling for arbitrary arrests, violence, lynchings, and pogroms.

Coming out under the guise of saviors of the revolution, they are putting you off your guard. They are promising you order. Actually, they are dreaming of a military dictatorship, and will bring you the restoration of that disgraceful order all the horrors of which must still be in your memory, citizens.

.   .   .

Heroic remedies are needed.

He who values Russian freedom, who has not forgotten the horrors and disgraces of autocracy, who does not want to surrender his country to the enemy power must, in practice, serve for the defense of his native land against internal and external attacks.

The Central Executive Committees have resolved to invest the revolutionary Government with extraordinary powers.

Let the Government crush with an iron hand all anarchical outbursts and all attempts to destroy the gains of the revolution. Let it establish order and discipline in the army. And let it carry out all those measures which are necessary to the revolution and which have already been drafted in its declarations.

Every one of us must assist in every possible way. There must be no disobedient or apathetic people in this menacing hour.

The front is in need of reinforcements, the home front needs workers, the state is in need of enormous financial resources.

Anyone who shuns the performance of his duty, who takes advantage of the difficulties of the revolution in order to work for the restoration of autocracy, is a traitor to the revolution, a betrayer of his native land.

We are appealing to you: fulfill your duty; rally around the dumas and zemstvos which you elected, around the organs of the revolutionary democracy; support the Provisional Government; give all your forces and all your resources to it.

The revolution and our native land are in danger. Then let every one turn out to be worthy of the name of citizen in this menacing hour.

We are appealing to you, citizens: stand guard over the revolution.

CENTRAL EXECUTIVE COMMITTEE OF THE SOVIET OF WORKERS' AND SOLDIERS' DEPUTIES
EXECUTIVE COMMITTEE OF THE SOVIETS OF PEASANTS' DEPUTIES

1190. *Rech'* ON THE WITHDRAWAL OF THE KADET MINISTERS AND PRINCE L'VOV

[No. 158, July 8, 1917, p. 1.]

During the day the cabinet crisis has deepened. Now not only the Kadet ministers but the President of the cabinet, Prince L'vov himself, deems it impossible to bear the collective responsibility for the future policies of the Government. Again, the complications were raised by the "bourgeois" ministers—and not, moreover, by those ministers who are more to the right, not by Messrs. Vl. L'vov and Godnev, who will probably retain their positions even when the power passes to the Bolsheviks. . . .

. . .

The coalition is nonexistent when one of its elements wants to command over the rest and dictate to it its decisions. In effect, the coalition was also nonexistent during the last period of the participation of the Kadets in the cabinet. Their presence served only to preserve the *fiction* of the existence of a coalition. That is why they left it . . .

The coalition cannot exist when the socialist parties, represented in the Soviets, pretend to be the only masters of Russia's destinies. . . . The secret of the "coalition" has finally been exposed after the walk-out of the Kadets . . .

Thereby, for the first time, the line of demarcation between the past and the future of the Russian revolution is clearly outlined. In the past the revolution was—or wanted to be, or, finally, wanted to seem—unanimous. In the future it will actually be, as once expressed by A. F. Kerensky, a socialist revolution. The whole of nonsocialist Russia shall be flung aside and shall soon be declared "counterrevolutionary."

Do the leaders of the Soviets and of the Executive Committees realize the extent of the risks they shoulder? Obviously they do, and the best proof is that, while retaining the power, they still seek to appear to be cooperating with the "bourgeoisie." . . .

. . .

. . . The inner contradictions of two tendencies are visible within the Soviets and within the Provisional Government itself. One calls to the front, approves the offensive, attempts at last to suppress the malicious Bolshevik propaganda. The other declares internal war, officially proclaims the sharpening of class struggle, while designating as "ideological opponents" the real enemies of revolution and freedom. One tendency is expressed in the policy of Kerensky. The other is expressed in the policy of the Soviets' majority. . . .

1191. *Delo Naroda* ON THE RESIGNATION OF PRINCE L'VOV
[No. 96, July 9, 1917, p. 1.]

The surviving members of the first Provisional Government are dwindling. Following the Octobrist Guchkov, the Progressist Konovalov, the Kadets' Miliukov, Shingarev, and Manuilov, the head of the Provisional Government of the first two governments—the nonpartisan, Prince G. E. L'vov—has also left.

The Minister-President and Minister of the Interior, Prince L'vov, accompanied his withdrawal from the Government and resignation from the heavy responsibility, especially during these latter days, with a letter addressed to the "Provisional Government."

The reason for his withdrawal is not personal, nor is it due to differences of views and outlook, but rather to a "profound difference of opinion" on a question, basic to the Russian revolution, the *land question.* And this deep *social* difference of opinion prevented the continuance of the symbiosis which survived the blood-and-iron tests of two months.

Prince L'vov emphasized quite frankly that, while in principle he is an "adherent of the transfer of land into the hands of the toiling peasantry," he finds nevertheless that "the land laws" submitted by the Minister of Agriculture for approval to the Provisional Government are unacceptable not only in content but in substance as well because of the entire policy contained in them.

In the opinion of Prince L'vov, the Ministry of Agriculture "passes laws which undermine the people's respect for the law." These laws, in the assertion of the Prince, "not only do not combat illegal seizures, not only fail to normalize and guide land relations, but they seem to justify the ruinous arbitrary seizures which take place all over Russia. They also legalize the seizures which have already taken place, and, as a matter of fact, they try to confront the Constituent Assembly with an accomplished fact."

The Prince was right when, of all the questions which caused a "deep difference of opinion" among the members of the coalition Government, he chose the most important, the most basic one which determines the course and outcome of the Russian revolution. But the Prince was profoundly wrong in the evaluation of those draft land laws which were worked out by the Ministry of Agriculture. He is wrong also when in the ban on all land, speculative, and "simply" trade transactions he sees a "justification" and approval of "arbitrary seizures of land." He is also wrong when he sees in the legal regulation of the "seizures which have already taken place" an attempt to confront the Constituent Assembly with an accomplished fact.

· · ·

The laws worked out in the Ministry of V. M. Chernov do not "undermine the people's respect for the law," but on the contrary, they proceed from it and strive to strengthen the people's awareness of law with regard to land. In order to prevent wholesale pillaging of the land fund, in order to preserve the people's resources to the day of judgment, when the question of land will be decided in the Constituent Assembly, the Ministry, guided by the S.R.'s, worked out appropriate draft laws.

The measures outlined by these laws may, from some points of view, seem unprofitable, solving the "transfer of land into the hands of the toiling peasantry" —which Prince L'vov defends also—in a way that does not seem desirable or just to him or to some others, namely, Lenin, P. P. Maslov, and N. N. Chernenkov. One might think that the proposed measures are not "for the welfare of the entire country," but we cannot see in the proposed laws "the realization of a party program," "an obvious deviation . . . in the direction . . . of purely party socialist bases."

It suffices to spend a short time in the conferences of the Soviets of Peasants' Deputies, to breathe the *muzhik* air of land committees, to be convinced how artificial and how unjust is the accusation that the land laws are proposed for party or even socialist interests.

· · ·

Prince L'vov was one of those accidental guests of the revolution. He has left it now. There is one less unintentional participant in the revolution. No doubt the ranks of the revolution will decrease more than once. Revolutionaries will come and go, but the revolution, the process of the revolution, will endure until the questions proposed, not by individual parties but by the entire course of Russian history, are solved.

1192. *Delo Naroda*'s Attack on the "Bolshevism" of the Kadets
[No. 98, July 12, 1917, p. 1.]

It is now quite clear that bolshevism is not localized in one party. "Bolshevism" is a sort of psycho-political ailment of our times.

There are various forms of bolshevism. There is, for example, "national bolshevism." It has almost triumphed in the Ukraine, where in an obviously predatory manner its representatives attempted to assess and levy taxes, to separate the Ukraine from Russia, to call their own constituent assembly prior to the convening of the All-Russian Constituent Assembly, etc., etc. . . .

There is *industrial* bolshevism of the dark strata of the proletariat, supported by the anarcho-Maximalist and Lenin-Communist elements. Its ideal is an immediate seizure of all factories and mills, arrest of capitalists, etc. There is *international* bolshevism, ready to sacrifice the future of the Russian revolution, disrupting the army at the front, in the hope that such a "heroic self-declaration" will break through the thickest crust of the peoples of other countries, to spread the revolutionary contagion over all of Europe and thus compensate for the great losses suffered by the fate of the people's cause in our motherland. . . .

What is the psychological trait common to all these "bolshevisms"? It is that all these people, as if hypnotized by one distant illuminated point that beckons them, break their way through with blinkers on their eyes which prevent them from seeing anything on the sides.

.   .   .

. . . There is "bolshevism to the right"—the Kadet and the commercial-industrial [groups]. It is not as bold as the international or Lenin-Communist. . . .

The "Bolshevik" character of the method of action of the Kadets in this connection is striking. Assuming that their tactics were completely successful and that none of the "minister-capitalists," as the notorious demagogic formula called them, would agree to join the Provisional Government of the new alignment, we would then have a purely socialist "Soviet" ministry and thus we would get, as a result, a "recall" and "boycott," organized by the Kadets, something the Leninists failed to achieve by means of an armed coup d'état. In other words, defeated on the frontal attack, the Leninists won, thanks to the rear attack of their unexpected allies to the right, the Kadets. As you can see, *les extrêmes se touchent.* . . .

This "attraction of the extremes" is of course no accident. From their point of view the Kadets are right. They think that the victory of the Bolsheviks' political line would be the forerunner of their own victory. They are convinced that this is the best road to counterrevolution. . . . And there is no gamble they would not resort to in order to achieve this aim. In reality they are the same Bolsheviks in a different disguise. They are the same stubborn men, the same doctrinaires, embittered by past political failures, just as vindictive and ready for the most blazing demagogy. And they are just as indiscriminate in their search for allies. Just as, in the case of the Bolsheviks, every ideology down to semi-anarchism poured in from the left and joined their side; so, in the case of the Kadets, the ill-assorted remnants of the old parties poured in from the right, and they were joined by elements bordering on pogrom instigators. Bravo, "recallers"; bravo, "Bolsheviks" of the Constitutional Democratic Party.

1193. *Volia Naroda* ON THE GOVERNMENT TO SAVE THE REVOLUTION
[No. 62, July 11, 1917, p. 1.]

We wrote in the last issue of *Volia Naroda* that in order to save the revolution and the country circumstances of the moment insistently call for the establishment of a stable revolutionary authority. We wrote that this demand is no prosaic longing for firm authority and no desire for a dictatorship, but an urgent problem, dictated by the "to be or not to be" of the revolution: "To be or not to be" a state?

.   .   .

The revolutionary country must answer this question. It must answer it clearly and firmly. It has answered through its plenary organs, in the Soviets of Peasants', Workers', and Soldiers' Deputies. It said loudly and imperatively:

"To live, to live, at all costs." And having said it, it made all the necessary deductions from this answer.

The first and basic deduction is *the establishment of authority with unlimited plenary power.* Without and outside such authority there is no salvation. We need a flexible, resolute, plenary organ of authority whose decrees are compulsory and unquestioned. The plenary organs of democracy understood this. And having understood it, they proclaimed: "The revolution and the country are in danger. It is necessary to form a government to save the revolution. Unlimited plenary power must belong to the Provisional Government. Twice a week it must give an account to the Soviets."

Such is the substance of the resolution passed by the Committees.

We hail this decision. It is unavoidable. It is the best of all possible ways out.

As a matter of fact, four basic ways were possible out of the situation that had been created. The first was seizure of power by the Soviets. But that would have meant narrowing the foundation of the revolutionary forces, for the bourgeois classes would in this case have split off from the revolutionary forces.

A split of this kind now would be ruinous. The Soviets could not take power into their hands because now, when speed and decisiveness of action are necessary, the Soviets, because of their great numbers, are unable to exhibit these qualities.

The second way out was to proclaim a genuine dictatorship. But it was unacceptable in its pure form.

The third way out was to leave the *status quo ante.* But everybody realized what fruits are born from the indecision and absence of authority that existed up to this time. Things could not continue in this way. It would have been tantamount to ruin. What then remained to be done?

The fourth solution remained, which the Committees adopted. A government was formed with unlimited plenary power. A dictatorship was established.

If it does not exist, it is only because the government in the name of the socialist ministers must still be responsible to the Committees.

From now on the Committees cannot interfere in the actions of the Provisional Government, but they reserve the right to express their lack of trust in their ministers. This does not mean that after expressing their distrust in the ministers the latter are juridically compelled to resign. No. The resolution excludes such juridical obligation. But there remains a moral responsibility. To the socialist ministers this responsibility is tantamount to juridical responsibility.

Such is the state of affairs.

We are no admirers of dictatorships. We are not even admirers of an authority with unlimited plenary power. But when the house is on fire, when danger is obvious, when further indecision is perilous, there is not time to argue about tastes. Then the unavoidable must be accepted. And we accept it. We accept it and hail it as the least of all evils, as the only chance of salvation from ruin.

But it would be naïve to suppose that, having formed and recognized such authority, the citizens could sit with their hands folded. Without active support from the citizens any authority is powerless. Without active participation by the people any authority is a fiction. It is time to stop the game of fiction. It is time to understand that now no authority, be it the most dictatorial of all dictatorships, is able to do anything unless all citizens merge into one whole, unless everyone surrenders all of his resources, all of his efforts, even life itself in the cause of saving the revolution. It is time to put an end to the passivity of some, the fruitless verbosity of others, and the clearly detrimental destructive work of still others.

We need action, united, quick, planned. The country and the revolution are dying. They must be saved!

THE RECONSTRUCTION OF THE GOVERNMENT[4]

1194. THE TEMPORARY COMMITTEE OF THE STATE DUMA ON THE ORGANIZATION OF THE NEW GOVERNMENT

[*Rech'*, No. 162, July 13, 1917, p. 3.]

The Temporary Committee of the State Duma, having discussed during its sessions of July 11 and 12 the question of its attitude toward the new reorganization of the Provisional Government's membership, has approved the following resolution:

In the fatal days of danger to the very existence of Russia a strong government enjoying general confidence and free of any party entanglements should stand at her head striving toward one common goal—that of saving the homeland from the external foe and from internal disintegration.

A government appointed by a group of individual political parties, which has accepted within its membership persons picked at random and not representing the opinion of many influential circles of the population, cannot achieve this goal.

The Temporary Committee has already expressed its opinion that only an honest and direct agreement between the organs having authority to represent the public can grant to the Government the recognition of the whole nation. Now the Committee is compelled to acknowledge that the method applied for the constitution of the new government, without consulting the Committee as the organ which represents the source of the two first revolutionary governments, cannot guarantee a sound realization of the idea of coalition and undermines the confidence of the population, which is necessary for the government.

If the Government has not abandoned the thought of uniting all the vital forces of the country, it should not, under the guise of a coalition, subordinate representation of the country to its socialist minority. It is the more inadmissible and fatal, as the country cannot fail to be conscious that precisely the activity of some socialist parties is the cause of the disintegration of the army, of the conscious destruction of civic peace, and of the weakening of the labor discipline of the people; that is, the cause of the elimination of those basic conditions without which it is impossible to continue the war or to restore internal order.

The Temporary Committee visualizes the solution of the painful trials and mortal dangers threatening the homeland with destruction, not in the deepening of party problems, but in the unity of all political trends and all strata of society in coordinated and energetic work for the salvation of the homeland.

Therefore, while giving credit to the energy and patriotism of the new Minister-President, A. F. Kerensky, and calling upon all the citizens to obey the Gov-

---

[4] At its meeting of July 13, the members of the Provisional Government authorized Kerensky to begin the reconstruction of the government and, in order to facilitate his work, placed their posts at his disposal.

ernment as the only authority [existing] in Russia, the Temporary Committee cannot keep silent in these times of menace for Russia and is compelled to declare that it declines all responsibility for the consequences which could result from the aforementioned defects in the composition of the new government and in the method of its appointment.

1195. The Resolution of the Petrograd Union of Trade and Industry
[*Rech'*, No. 164, July 15, 1917, p. 1.]

The force of the Russian revolution lay in the fact that [it reflected] all of the nation.

The revolution was weakened from the moment that one group after another, one class after another, began to turn from it.

Now the revolution is indubitably in danger because it has been transformed into a cause of class, into a cause of doctrinaire party circles.

The trade and industrial class which, with criminal thoughtlessness, was referred to as the enemy of the people, but which nevertheless is completely imbued with active love for our suffering homeland and for the ideal of liberty, loudly proclaims that the salvation of the revolution—more than that, the salvation of Russia—lies in the return of the revolution to its all-national [basis], in the subordination of party slogans and ideals to one single idea—that of saving our homeland and the liberty which has been achieved.

The times demand one single, strong, and firm authority!

If for that purpose a coalition government is necessary, then every element of the coalition should exert all its energies and make every concession in order to create a really all-national government with a program acceptable to all of the people.

The Petrograd Trade and Industrial Union asserts that these conditions were not respected when the Government to Save the Revolution was created and that therefore the strength of this government has not been secured.

One part of the coalition did not concede enough of its narrowly partisan goals and slogans; the other part, formed by means of personal selection from candidates having no real support in broad and influential circles of the population, is organically powerless. More than that, no serious attempts have ever been made to attract within the government the representatives of the most powerful organizations of the country.

Therefore, while taking the obligation of giving support to the Provisional Government as the only authority existing in the country, the Petrograd Trade and Industrial Union must openly state its grave doubts as to the correctness of the course that has been chosen for the purpose of saving the revolution.

1196. Letter from the Kadets to Kerensky
[*Rech'*, No. 166, July 18, 1917, p. 2, as translated in Golder, pp. 472–73.]

Dear Sir, Aleksandr Fedorovich:

You were pleased to invite us to join the Provisional Government. We realize that at this difficult moment no one has a right to refuse to share in the labor of the Government, provided conditions are such that results can be attained. After having considered your proposition, we are now ready to indicate the basis on which we can accept your offer.

We recognize that the question of the moment is to form an all-national ministry that has the confidence of all the people and sets for itself the task of saving the country from foreign destruction and internal disintegration. We can join the ministry only on condition that all members of it are independent, and that the cabinet is composed of men who have full confidence in one another and work on a basis of mutual understanding for the good of the country. With this in mind, we consider the following [fundamentals] necessary:

1. That all members of the Government, regardless of their party affiliations, are responsible to their conscience, and that their actions and presence in the cabinet are no reason for interference in the direction of State affairs by any kind of committees and organizations.

2. In matters of internal policy, the Government is to limit itself to guarding the conquests of the revolution and not to undertake measures that might lead to civil strife. Therefore, the carrying out of all basic social reforms and the determination of all questions relating to the form of government are to be left absolutely to the Constituent Assembly.

3. In matters of war and peace, the Government is to be guided by the principles of complete union with the Allies.

4. Steps are to be taken to develop a mighty army by restoring strict military discipline and putting a definite stop to interference by soldier committees in questions of war tactics and strategy.

5. As a fundamental in internal administration, an end is to be made to the many authorities; order reestablished in the country; a vigorous fight waged on anarchistic, anti-governmental and counter-revolutionary elements; and a stable local administration organized as soon as possible, so that the new, regularly selected local organs of government can begin to function.

6. State courts are to be brought back to a position that will enable them to carry on their procedure in a proper manner. Prosecuting attorneys and judges are not to be interfered with by politicians or other outside influences.

7. Elections for the Constituent Assembly are to be conducted in a manner to enable the people to express the true national will. Elections are to be under the supervision of the legally selected organs of local government or institutions formed by them. They are to guarantee the freedom of electioneering campaigns.

N. ASTROV
N. KISHKIN
V. NABOKOV

July 15, 1917

1197. THE KADETS' OBJECTION TO CHERNOV IN THE GOVERNMENT
[*Rech'*, No. 165, July 16, 1917, p. 1.]

.   .   .

Last Friday A. F. Kerensky . . . offered three members of the [Kadet] Party, V. D. Nabokov, N. M. Kishkin, and N. I. Astrov, [membership in the Government]. The reason for this personal approach was the desire to form a government really independent of any external influence. As this point of view corresponded exactly to the oft-repeated declarations of the Kadets that the country should have only one government and that no other organization should compete with it, imposing on it its own will, the Central Committee of the Party acknowledged that A. F. Kerensky's method of approach fully corresponded with the intentions of the Party. . . . With all the restraint [shown] by the Party, with all its willingness not to create further difficulties, . . . the Central Committee nevertheless deems it necessary to eliminate M. V. Chernov from the Government. Having met opposition from A. F. Kerensky, the Party declined to raise this issue in the form of an ultimatum. But three of its candidates (F. F. Kokoshkin, N. I. Astrov, and V. D. Nabokov) consider their entry [into the Government] impossible unless this condition is accepted. The same position has been taken by Tret'iakov, the representative of the Moscow industrialists.

. . .

1198. The Resolution of the Representatives of Trade and Industry
on the Entrance of S. N. Tret'iakov into the Government:
The Statement of the All-Russian Union
of Trade and Industry

[*Russkiia Vedomosti*, No. 163, July 19, 1917, p. 6.]

Resolution

In conclusion, the conference unanimously authorized S. N. Tret'iakov to accept the post of Minister of Trade and Industry offered to him, provided the political situation does not change, and unanimously passed the following resolution:

"Having heard the report of the President of the Moscow Stock Exchange Committee, S. N. Tret'iakov, and after studying his statement to the Minister-President, A. F. Kerensky, on behalf of the commercial and industrial class on the question of conditions under which representatives from the commercial and industrial class could become members of the Provisional Government, the joint session of the elected representatives from the Moscow Stock Exchange and merchant organizations, with the participation of representatives from the Moscow special exchanges and other commercial and industrial organizations, resolved unanimously to approve S. N. Tret'iakov's statement to the Minister-President and to rule that entry into the Provisional Government by anyone from the commercial-industrial group as official representatives of the commercial-industrial class is possible only with the approval, by the newly formed coalition cabinet of ministers, of the conditions outlined in S. N. Tret'iakov's statement."

[July 18]

The Council of the All-Russian Union of Trade and Industry

Yesterday [July 18] at the sitting of the Council of the All-Russian Union of Trade and Industry, after a discussion of the question of the political situation, the following statement to the Provisional Government was approved:

"During one of the most trying and responsible moments in Russian history," reads the statement, "the Provisional Government, where socialist representatives predominate, appeals to the representatives of the liberal bourgeois groups in

Russian society with an offer to join its ranks in order to form a coalition ministry which they call the Government to Save the Revolution, but which they should have called the government for the preservation of the dying motherland. Representatives of the commercial-industrial class think it their duty to join the ministry on conditions already outlined. We do not evade our duty to the motherland. But we are impelled to say a word of truth about the present situation in Russia, lest our entry into the government is overrated. We have no illusions. And we do not think that a genuine government of national salvation can be formed unless a radical break is made with the system under which the revolution has developed during these past months. The policy of the government destined to save Russia cannot have a class or party character. It must be a national and people's policy only. Prompted by a sense of national survival, the Russian people overthrew the old regime and brought about a national revolution. But the disillusionment came much too soon. They are now asked to change the national revolution into a social revolution . . . In bringing about the social revolution, advantage was taken of the people's ignorance. They cast to the masses demagogic slogans in whose actual realization no one believed. And they poisoned the people's souls with hatred and anger. They ended the war at the front and began it inside the country. As a matter of fact, power was soon transferred from the Provisional Government to the Soviets of Workers' and Soldiers' Deputies—a casual gathering of people, for the most part still ignorant, with no name, unenlightened and irresponsible as a result of past oppression, and unprepared to participate in state and social construction. The leaders of the socialist parties, who subsequently became members of the Provisional Government, themselves felt all the weight and danger of the dictatorship of the masses when they came face to face with the street demonstrations of the Bolsheviks, who took them in tow also. The spontaneous development of the revolution, unguided by a firm authority, brought Russia to complete anarchy and decay. The national unity of great Russia disintegrated . . . There is even less law and order in the country than there was under the old regime. And the Government does nothing in the primordial force of the revolution to guard the liberty and rights of the citizens. The Government, during the past months, has permitted the poisoning of the Russian people and the Russian army and the disruption of all discipline, thereby following the Soviets of Workers' and Soldiers' Deputies, who must bear the responsibility for the disgrace and humiliation of Russia and the Russian army. Only by a radical break by the Government with the dictatorship of the Soviets, which lead to disintegration; only by the restoration of the masses to health and the awakening in them of a national, state consciousness; only by revealing the true soul of the Russian people, which has lived, built, created, and spoken over the centuries, can Russia be saved. Unless this takes place, Russia will perish, and no shifting of new ministers will help. All the sound, responsible, and creative forces of the Russian people and society must save Russia at any cost—Russia, and not the revolution. The future of Russia cannot be abandoned to the power of the dictatorship of parties and the dictatorship of classes—its lot today. If a dictatorial power is needed to save the motherland, such a power can only be a genuinely national power which is above parties and above classes, born of national enthusiasm. Russia and Russian freedom and not the revolution are in danger. This danger stems from the false direction of the revolution and its internal disintegration. Free Russia must be saved from the disintegration of the revolution."

1199. KERENSKY'S REPLY TO THE KADETS: THE KADETS' REFUSAL TO PARTICIPATE IN THE GOVERNMENT

[*Rech'*, No. 169, July 21, 1917, p. 2, and No. 170, July 22, p. 4.]

Letter from A. F. Kerensky to V. D. Nabokov, N. M. Kishkin, and N. I. Astrov

Having received your letter of July 15, I affirm that the Provisional Government is vested with plenary power and is not responsible to any public organization or party, but to the country alone, [guided by] its own conscience and understanding. [Therefore,] I believe that the statement contained in your letter does not hinder your entering the Provisional Government, whose work shall be invariably guided by the principles contained in its declarations of March 2, May 6 [*sic*], and July 8, its main task being, at the present moment, that of saving the country and [our] freedom.

Therefore, I reiterate my proposal to you to join the Provisional Government and, through common effort and on the basis described, to do everything possible to lead the country along the road of freedom and light, after mobilizing its energy and efforts, and after [restoring] order.

A. KERENSKY

Letter from V. Nabokov, P. Novgorodtsev, and N. Astrov

DEAR ALEKSANDR FEDOROVICH:

Recognizing the importance, under the exceptionally difficult conditions of the present moment, of uniting within the Government all the living forces of the country, we have deemed it our duty to respond to your invitation to join the Provisional Government. We informed you in our letter of July 15, signed by N. M. Kishkin and two of the undersigned, of those basic principles without realization of which the salvation of our country seems to us impossible and our participation in the Government morally inadmissible and politically useless.

During the negotiations which have since taken place, you expressed your agreement with our statements, and afterwards your readiness to confirm this in writing. Unfortunately, in the course of further negotiations, and before we had the opportunity to conclude the discussions about our participation in the Government, essential differences in principle were revealed between us on the basic question of the relationship between the program approved by you and the previous program and work of the Proivsional Government.

You have found it necessary to emphasize in the draft you sent us of your written answer to our letter of July 15 that the Government which you are now renovating remains entirely based on the Provisional Government declarations of March 2, May 6 [*sic*], and July 8; consequently our participation in the Government could not alter its activity. On our part, we believed that your proposal itself was proof of your desire to put before the Provisional Government new tasks, to be achieved on a new basis.

Having shown our readiness to make concessions on questions concerning the membership of the Provisional Government, we are unable to renounce the declarations of principle which we have made. Their significance is completely undermined by the inclusion in the text of the letter of the point in question, while the declaration of July 8, which was issued after the representatives of the Party of the People's Freedom had withdrawn from the Government, is in many ways unacceptable to us.

In view of the foregoing, we are compelled to state that our participation in the Government is deprived of any political significance by your stand that the basis of the former activity of the Government, in so far as it is expressed in the aforementioned declarations, cannot be subject to any alteration; moreover, this stand is equivalent to your abandoning any further endeavor to come to an agreement with us on a really national program.

V. NABOKOV, P. NOVGORODTSEV, N. ASTROV

July 20, 1917

Letter from N. M. Kishkin to A. F. Kerensky

N. M. Kishkin sent to Minister-President A. F. Kerensky the following telegram:

DEAR ALEKSANDR FEDOROVICH:

Having learned the contents of your letter to us and the reply of my comrades, I deeply regret being forced to agree that, under these circumstances, it is impossible for us to participate in the Provisional Government. We asked to enter the Provisional Government in order to bring the country, by common efforts, along the road of freedom and light, after mobilizing the country for intense labors and [after restoring] order. But this could be achieved by joint action only if every one of us understood in the same way, first, what the road of freedom and light is, and second, what the methods [for reaching it] are. That was the reason for addressing to you our letter of July 15 in which we expressed our ideas on the subject in detail. It would seem that there could be but two answers: the Provisional Government, either sharing completely the point of view expressed by us, would ask us to enter the cabinet, or, not sharing it, would cease further negotiations. You have given us a third answer, namely, that the statements contained in our letter should not hinder our joining the membership of the Government, whose activity will be directed by the principles laid down in the three declarations. At a time when the country is swiftly moving toward disaster, a Government that wishes to be a truly national Government and not a partisan or class one should reveal everything about the country, while you, as Minister-President, wishing to save the country, should not refer solely to old Government declarations, from which, under the pressure of terrible events, you have lately, and quite rightly, already withdrawn yourself. For the authority of the new coalition government, it was necessary that the country should be informed of the points on which the agreement was reached between the members who remained in the Government and those who joined it now. It was our wish to bring about this clarification, and [for this purpose] we submitted the seven points. [However,] you have not desired this clarification, and this has rendered impossible the formation of a really national Government.

With my respects,

NIKOLAI KISHKIN

1200. THE PRIVATE CONFERENCES OF THE MEMBERS OF THE STATE DUMA

[*Rech'*, No. 167, July 19, 1917, p. 3–4; *Izvestiia*, No. 122, July 20, 1917, p. 3.]

A

A private session of the members of the State Duma under the chairmanship of M. V. Rodzianko was held in the library of the State Duma on July 18.

. . .

The President then read the address of the Temporary Committee of the State Duma.

[The address is given in section B of this document, pp. 1414–15.]

M. V. Rodzianko asked the members of the State Duma whether they were willing to join and to approve the address worked out by the Temporary Committee.

Statement by I. F. Godnev

"The address states," said I. V. Godnev, "that the army was not safeguarded by the Government and that the local organs of administration were deprived of governmental leadership. I consider that it is correct there was no authority within the army. But there is no reason to blame the Government for it, because the question arises whether the Government had anything at its disposal for putting into effect its instructions directed toward the restoration of order."

Rodzianko noted that the words in question were an excerpt from an official report of General Kornilov from the front.

Continuing his speech, I. V. Godnev also protested against the words "local administrative organs deprived of governmental leadership." Administrative directives were given. A number of telegraphic instructions regarding land seizures have been sent. But they were not carried out.

The question was raised: "And the actions of Chernov?"

I. V. Godnev retorted that he spoke of the actions of the Provisional Government and not of those of individuals.

. . .

The Speech of A. M. Maslennikov

. . .

"Everything contained in this address is felt by the population itself," said A. M. Maslennikov. "There is no doubt that we have now already reached the moment when the state is dying. The question now is not one of eloquent proclamations; we must find a way to save Russia. The country is perishing; there is no army; industry is disorganized. At this time, when intensive work is required, the population is idle and thinks only of how better to profit, whom to plunder. (*Cries:* "Correct!")

"How did it happen that our valorous army, which in 1915, without weapons or ammunition, courageously defended the homeland with their bodies and their fists, turned into a multitude of cowards betraying their homeland?

"It is time to say, gentlemen, why we have reached this shame, this humiliation. Those dreamers and lunatics, who imagine that they are the creators of world politics, are guilty of it. The petty career-seeking [individuals], who wish, thanks to the revolution, to drive in cars and live in palaces, are guilty of it. The traitors like Lenin and Company, who have sold Russia to the Germans, are guilty of it, and we are guilty of it."

"The Government first of all," remarked V. M. Purishkevich.

"When on February 27," continued the speaker, "the mutinous Volynskii Regiment and crowds of workers arrived here, the leaders of the revolution, Kerensky, Skobelev, Chkheidze, came and implored the State Duma to head the rebellion, thereby guaranteeing a revolution and not a mutiny of soldiers, which could be easily suppressed. The State Duma headed this movement. Thanks to the Duma the revolution really took place, but in this great tragic moment of our history, a group of mad fanatics, of shady individuals and betrayers, calling themselves the Executive Committee of the Soviet of Workers' and Soldiers' Deputies, stuck to the revolution."

"I would ask you not to use such strong expressions," remarked the President.

. . .

"Only the State Duma can save Russia. I recommend that this address be approved; that the President be asked to call all the members of the State Duma, not for a private, underground session, but for a real session of the State Duma; a demand that the whole government in its entirety come here and report on the conditions of the country; and that the State Duma indicate to the Government how and by whom the Government should be reinforced or replaced.

"I will be told that the army is in their hands and that physically they can prevent such a session and dissolve us. Perhaps you are right. But let them dissolve us by force; we have not the right to take such dangers into consideration. We do not have the right to conceal ourselves any longer. We must come out from the underground; the State Duma is a trench which defends the honor, the dignity, and the existence of Russia, and in this trench we must either win or die. (*Applause.*)"

The Speech of V. M. Purishkevich

The floor was taken by V. M. Purishkevich, who agreed completely with the words of A. M. Maslennikov.

"Minister-President Kerensky, who is correctly called the minister of the civil war, could not find, after the horrors experienced by the Russian army, better words to address himself to the army and to the people than by shouting: 'Save the revolution!' They still continue to shout about the revolution at a time when Russia is at the brink of ruin, and, as a matter of fact, more because of the internal than because of the external foe. I am a thoroughly convinced monarchist and I will not alter my convictions. But I am ready to serve any intelligent Social Democrat in power and hide my sympathies, if I could believe that this would lead Russia to safety.

"Certainly the faith that we will save our tormented fatherland and will win should not be forsaken. But to this end we must not proceed along the way of Herostratus, which is followed by the present Russian Government, headed by Minister-President Kerensky. Kerensky is as crystal-pure a man as Tseretelli. They are crystal-pure people but they are removed from the daily life of their own land and do not know it. First of all, it is necessary that the Government show combativeness and that the party of "the frightened intelligentsia" cease to exist.

"In the first place, the State Duma should take the road of recovery. It is necessary to chastise in order to avoid a massacre in a St. Bartholomew's night which threatens the Russian intelligentsia in the future. It is necessary to prevent popular lynchings, which will be the first consequence of an absence of government and of legal order. It is necessary to chastise not only those who run away from the front, but also those who corrupt that front.

"We know that over there many soldiers have been executed, but have those guilty of disintegration at the rear been punished? Where is the author of Order No. 1? He is a senator, this man who has made impossible the work of the army and has brought numerous Kronstadt officers and numerous valorous officers of all branches of service at the front to their graves. In the Surazhskii Regiment he was beaten up, and they say that as he ran away from there he shouted: 'They should be punished by death, these traitors; it is the only way to cope with them!' But it was too late.

"When, in former times, the representatives of the 'Union of the Russian People' invited one part of the population against another, it was said that they should be prosecuted. And now, when Minister of Agriculture Chernov permits himself to provoke the peasants against the nobles and *pomeshchiki* . . . ? The Government cannot tolerate parallel to itself the authority of the Soviet of Workers' and Soldiers' Deputies. If it wants to preserve its prestige, it should order and show them their place." Then Purishkevich read the names of the members of the Executive Committee, revealed their pseudonyms, and continued.

"Tell me: is there here even one single peasant? Here we have people who clothe themselves in soldiers' uniforms and workers' blouses, but who have nothing in common with soldiers or peasants or workers. . . . It is necessary that the Government be a government; it is necessary to put in its place and to dissolve the Soviet of Workers' and Soldiers' Deputies before it is done by the people themselves. . . .

. . .

"I will say now: Long live the State Duma, the only organ that is capable of saving Russia, and let all those dark forces which sit on the neck of the Provisional Government, of which the Provisional Government is afraid, be destroyed. These forces are headed by people who have nothing in common either with the soldiers or with the workers.

"The moment the State Duma speaks loudly, names the criminals, states that nowhere in the world is there a country which is ruled by a Soviet of Workers' and Soldiers' and Peasants' Deputies; by pseudo-soldiers', pseudo-peasants', and pseudo-workers' deputies; when it puts them in their place—at that moment, gentlemen, we will be able to say that we are statesmen; we will take the road to recovery, and along this road we will lead Russia toward victory both over the external foe and over the internal foe, who undoubtedly is more dangerous than the external one, because he threatens us not only with defeat but with complete annihilation forever. (*Applause.*) "

Speech of F. I. Rodichev

"In a difficult moment," said Rodichev, "the duty of everyone for whom the destinies of the fatherland are dear is not to yield to panic.

"The address which is proposed to us suffers from this defect.

"We are told that we need authority; yes, we need it, but it is not through words that authority will become strong. If we, having gathered here, issue an order it will not be obeyed. For you cannot take the power, you have no means of taking it; therefore we must abandon this course. We are told here that all the trouble is the result of the fact that people advancing their careers, and so forth, have appeared on the surface of the revolution. I believe . . . that the power of individuals is not so great; I consider, for instance, that Order No. 1 is a great calamity, but I am sure that the people who issued it did not know what they did. (*Voices:* "This is a great question.") And the Provisional Government, which accepted the demand not to withdraw the Petrograd garrison—did it realize that this promise destroyed the energies of, and that this act was ruining, the Petrograd garrison? I know that the members of the Provisional Government did not want to corrupt the Petrograd garrison, but events turned out to be stronger than they; and I, personally, do not blame them."

F. I. Rodichev protested against the personal accusations made by Purishkevich against Senator Sokolov—it was not the moment for personal attacks.

"We are told that everything would have been [all right] but for the self-appointed organizations. We are asked: who has elected the Soviet? I do not know. But I know that at the present time there are in the cities, or soon will be, a real elected democracy and I am astonished that the Soviets of Workers' Deputies continue to hold power in the cities where representatives have been elected by universal suffrage. But if we insult them and the Government, if we address unfriendly demands to them, then what are we doing at a time when our army is miserable, when it loses its strength and its honor—must we at such a time strengthen disorganization and enmity inside of Russia? Where is that unity which alone can create unanimity within the army?

"It is true that the Government ignores us, but we ourselves have not demanded any accounting. At the present time, when the Government seeks new bases on which it can reconstruct itself, our business is to indicate to it these bases.

. . .

"These are the demands which are indicated in the letter [of July 15][5] of my party comrades Kishkin, Astrov, and Nabokov, and I think that this national demand is a demand of the entire Russian land. (*Voices:* "Correct.")

"Confirm this declaration by your vote; abstain from exclamations of panic, which would reach the country; show it to the road of safety and organization. At this time, when the courage of the Russian people has apparently faltered, remain at your post and say to them: the honor of Russia and hope in the Russian army are not yet lost. (*Applause.*)"

. . .

The Speech of P. N. Miliukov

. . .

"I welcome the declaration presented by the Temporary Committee of the State Duma because I find expressed in it all the fundamental ideas which the Party of the People's Freedom has made the basis of its activity within the Provisional

[5] Doc. 1196.

Government; we [maintained] them when we were there and we were compelled to withdraw because they were not followed; now our party advances them as a condition for its participation. We are blamed for not wishing to abandon our party prejudices. I am very glad that the declaration of the Temporary Committee of the State Duma stresses that our demands addressed to the Government contain nothing partisan, and here it was correctly stated that the declaration addressed to the Government represents that minimum of all-Russian demands the fulfill-ment of which can alone give to this Government a really all-national, and not only partisan support. Then what are our demands? [Miliukov reiterates the points in the letter of July 15.]

. . .

"We believe that in questions of foreign policy the Provisional Government should not carry on any longer the principles of Zimmerwald. We express our-selves with great restraint: in the questions of war and peace, the principle of complete unity with the Allies will be respected. In their time, Tseretelli and Kerensky called themselves Zimmerwaldians; I hope that now they do not call themselves thus. But, within the membership of the Government there is a definite defeatist, a participant of the Zimmerwald Conference—Chernov.

. . .

"I must admit that, astounded by the great events of our days, by our reverses at the front and the mutiny of the Bolsheviks in Petrograd, the members of the Government understood that they must change their course sharply. The death penalty has been re-established. Perhaps other measures will be taken, but we consider it absolutely essential that the Minister-President either yield his post or in any case take as his assistants authoritative military leaders and that these authoritative military leaders really act with all the independence and personal authority required."

. . .

Then P. N. Miliukov dwelt in great detail on the reasons for which the party demanded a postponement of the elections to the Constituent Assembly and on the necessity of guarantees essential for the expression of the genuine will of the people. He finished his speech with the following words: "Having presented everything that we consider advances the only right way toward salvation, I ask my comrades whether they would consider it right if, under any conditions, even if the Government were to remain with the old programs of May 8 and June 6 [*sic*], the Party of the People's Freedom were to place its members in the role of buffers, a role that we have not wanted to play up to now; do they consider that the Party of the People's Freedom should nevertheless enter the Government? (*Voices:* "No, no.")

"Do you consider that it would represent the classes it does represent, that liberal bourgeoisie? . . . (*Exclamations:* "We don't think so; our duty is to withdraw.")

"We believe not. We believe that our duty is to withdraw from this Government in order to show all of Russia with whom she has to deal, in order not to cover with the authority and the name of our party deeds which lead to the ruin of Russia. We consider that we are obliged to show reality to the country, a hard, unseemly, and gloomy reality, which can be altered only after everyone becomes aware of it. We consider that in the days we are going through it is impossible to conceal anything, and we consider that by accepting the proposal that has been addressed to us, under any conditions and not under the conditions that we have advanced— and, I am glad to say, together with the Temporary Committee of the State Duma —we would be merely deceiving and creating the illusion that now everything was all well again in the Government. (*Tremendous applause.*)"

. . .

The Second Speech of P. N. Miliukov

The rostrum was occupied for a second time by P. N. Miliukov.

". . . I participated very closely in the compilation of the document by which we protested on behalf of the Temporary Committee against the appointment of ministers without the opinion of the State Duma being asked. We stressed that it would be completely incorrect if the next cabinet were to ignore the existence of one of the sources of power which had created the two first cabinets. It is impossible to ignore the fact that if the State Duma began to function in its former form it would find itself in difficult relations with the Provisional Government, which undoubtedly both legislates and even exercises in practice, sometimes incautiously, the rights of a constituent power. Nevertheless it is clear that the destruction of the Tsar's authority has made a large breach in the old Fundamental Laws and has displaced certain parts of the state apparatus. (*Maslennikov from his seat:* "But not the State Duma.") Consequently, it is rather difficult to refer to the Fundamental Laws. Because you are mistaken in thinking that Mikhail Aleksandrovich transferred his power to the Temporary Committee; he actually transferred his power, or the plenitude of this power, as he said, to the Provisional Government. (*A voice:* "Chosen by the State Duma and by the Temporary Committee.") And it is beyond doubt that the juridical situation is far from being as clear as you imagine it to be. It is also beyond doubt that the State Duma could appear on the scene as an institution preserving all the significance and dignity which befit it, not in a conflict with the Provisional Government, but in some other manner. While the Provisional Government exists, while it is strong and enjoys general recognition and the support of the whole nation (*Maslennikov:* "Very weak support"), I think that the State Duma was right to preserve itself, so to speak, as a reserve in the background: quite consciously it simply did not want to complicate the situation by stepping into the forefront.

"For our common task was to support the Provisional Government, and we constantly insisted that the Provisional Government should be the sole authority which would not recognize any other authorities; thus we ourselves did not want to hinder it. But I must say that I envisage the moment when the State Duma could itself play a role as an institution, as well as through its Temporary Committee; that would be not only if the authority of the Provisional Government was denied national recognition—which, in my opinion, it has already lost—but if it would lose all authority. (*Maslennikov from his seat:* "But it has lost it.")

"I must say that now the Provisional Government has not lost all its authority. First of all, at the head of the Provisional Government stands a man to whom all of Russia is most certainly indebted. Of course, one person cannot do everything. But Kerensky did more than could have been expected from him and, although he did not save Russia from defeat, he nevertheless saved her from shame and dishonor, from loss of dignity. It is beyond doubt that such a man also brings the stamp of authority to the Government at the head of which he stands. I would not say that the situation is lasting—on the contrary, the incompleteness of Kerensky's success is demonstrated day by day; the weakness of his personal efforts becomes obvious. But in any case I think that now the Government still enjoys some remnants of authority; it is being recognized mainly thanks to the fact that Kerensky is at its head.

"I do not think this is the time for us to recognize that the Government has absolutely no authority. Such a sad time may come, even perhaps quite soon; let us not try to be prophets. (*Maslennikov from his seat:* "Then it will be too late.") I think that then the State Duma will play its role. But I would not like it to enter the scene in a manner leading to conflict before the real conditions for such a conflict are apparent."

. . .

Further, P. N. Miliukov spoke of the negotiations, already known from the papers, of the members of the Party of the People's Freedom with A. F. Kerensky, regarding their entry into the cabinet, and, in conclusion, he dwelt on the attitude of the party toward Chernov.

"We considered," said he, "that if we join [the cabinet] we would do so in full membership. But what restrains us is the following: three of the five [ministers] expressed the understandable feeling that it was difficult for them to work with Minister Chernov, and perhaps many of you, sharing this sentiment, will understand its origin. Nevertheless I must say that I entertain certain doubts. Perhaps it is necessary to perpetrate a degree of moral violence and say to our comrades: Go, in spite of the feeling that has arisen in your soul; go, because sometimes it is necessary to sacrifice oneself. Therefore, in particular, it is necessary to find out how you envisage this question; even in the event of agreeing to the program and to the membership in the cabinet, should we nonetheless present an ultimatum regarding the withdrawal of Chernov? I personally have certain hesitations on the subject."

. . .

Declaration of M. V. Rodzianko

"The list of speakers is exhausted," declared M. V. Rodzianko. "In concluding our session I must say a few words on the essence of the document under discussion. F. I. Rodichev considers that it contains elements which could spread panic in the country, but having looked once more at this document and recalling the debates which we had in the Temporary Committee, I find absolutely no foundation for any kind of panic. . . .

". . . This document, which has been written calmly and objectively, can arouse no kind of panic among the population, because not only are all of the phenomena mentioned therein known to the population, but both the rural and the city populations, and the country in general, suffer from all of them.

. . .

"Therefore, as this document apparently corresponds to the feelings of all the members of the State Duma, permit me to consider it approved."

"Please, please."

. . .

"As for the question of convening the State Duma," continued M. V. Rodzianko, "I think that we should not today or in general present the question in a blunt or definite manner. For a long time I belonged to those of you who share the point of view of the member of the State Duma Maslennikov regarding the convening of the State Duma, but I agree with the member of the State Duma Miliukov that the psychological moment when the Duma as such could be convened has not yet come. I would take the liberty only of expressing one wish: I consider that our private sessions would be much more powerful and important if they were attended not by 50–60 persons but by 360 . . ."

The floor was given to A. M. Maslennikov, who declared:

"I respect our President to such a degree and I value so much his lofty and selfless activity at the present time that I accept his proposal in its entirety. As for myself, I would propose to convene a private session of the State Duma, attended by many [members], summoning them by telegram. Furthermore, I am delegated by the elected members of the State Council to announce to our President their request that, in the event of a private conference being convened, they be given the possibility of attending it."

M. V. Rodzianko entirely agreed with the proposal of A. M. Maslennikov.

"I will send telegrams and letters, but the representatives of the different parties should in this instance assist their President, whom the members of the Duma do not listen to. I ask you for your support."

Recalling that the deputies had decided to admit to the private conference members of all the four State Dumas, M. V. Rodzianko declared that he did not see any reason to prohibit the elected members of the State Council from attending these conferences.

P. N. Miliukov recalled that for the next private conference of the members of the State Duma there is an important theme—the question of the Moscow Conference.

"Perhaps," said P. N. Miliukov, "this question should be discussed together, because I know that the Government after some hesitation is nevertheless inclined toward calling the Moscow Conference for July 26. Whether we will be there I do not know, but in any case we should discuss the question together."

The session was closed. The next session was set for July 19 at 3:00 P.M.

B

The Address of the Temporary Committee of the State Duma

An army of ignorant men deprived of sense, whom the Government does not safeguard against systematic corruption and disintegration, who have lost the feeling of human dignity, is fleeing. On the fields, which cannot even be called battlefields, reign complete horror, dishonor, and shame, such as the Russian army has not known from the very beginning of its existence. Such are the reports from the front.

What has happened to the army is a reflection of what is going on in all of Russia. This compels the Temporary Committee of the State Duma to raise its voice resolutely in a moment of general calamity.

There is one underlying cause of this—the seizure by irresponsible organizations of the rights of the Government and the creation by them of dual power in the center and of anarchy in the provinces.

The elemental movement of the dark popular masses, confused by the instigations of demogogues and unchecked by duly organized procedure of administration or justice, threatens the economic life of the country with complete catastrophe.

At its full height the threat of national bankruptcy stands before us: the ruin of the zemstvos and of the towns; the destruction of industry, trade, and agriculture; complete disorganization of the railroads; and the menace of famine and cold for the city populations.

A catastrophe in the rear would result in the ruin of the army, and the ruin of the army would be the ruin of Russia.

There is only one course—that of a firm and strong government which would sternly demand of everyone and everybody the fulfillment of their duty.

The Government must not follow the directions of party organizations or separate classes, but, strong by itself, it should pursue in its unanimity only one goal—that of safeguarding our great homeland from the mortal danger of disintegration.

The revolution has wiped out all local authority. The new representatives of the government in the guberniya and uezd centers are completely dependent on local party class organizations, which imperiously dictate their own will. The judicial authorities are inactive. Local areas are dominated by committees and soviets of various denominations and of various often self-appointed origins, which constantly change their membership. They are not aware either of their rights or of their obligations. Deprived of governmental leadership and not being restrained by anyone, they consider that they possess the plenitude of national authority.

The very first task of the Government, and the most urgent one, is the organization of a new system of administration of justice, without which none of the reforms outlined by the Government can be carried out.

All the force of the governmental authority should be directed exclusively to the restoration of the fighting capacities of our army, for supplying it with food and with what is necessary in order to fight the enemy, for the organization of the economic life of the country, for the food supplies of the population, for the good condition of the means of transportation.

Until the Constituent Assembly is convened, no legislative acts introducing a basic change in the national or social structure—which would bring still greater confusion into the legal concepts of the population—are admissible.

The fatal [influence] of party politics in the realm of national construction has been clearly demonstrated. Within the country it threatens a catastrophe to economic life, while in the war it threatens the shame of defeat.

The rights acquired by the will of the people should be safeguarded by a firm government, which would rest on the recognition of the whole nation.

Otherwise, instead of a popular authority, another authority will arise, which will be merciless toward the liberaties achieved by the Russian revolution.

> M. Rodzianko, President of the Temporary Committee,
> President of the State Duma

. . .

C

On July 19, the members of the Fourth Duma resumed their private conference in the Tauride Palace. Up to 60 delegates attended. Of the government representatives, Baryshnikov was present.

Concerning the Political Situation

The meeting opened with a statement delivered out of order by A. A. Bublikov . . .

He said:

"I was unable to attend the private conference yesterday, and it was only from newspapers that I learned of what was said here. At the same time I learned of the general characteristics of yesterday's speeches from the account given in the official organ of the Soviet of Workers' and Soldiers' Deputies. *Izvestiia* . . . found it possible to equate yesterday's speeches with the aspirations of the counterrevolutionaries and it also included heavy industry—the bourgeoisie—in this [category]. I believe that I am the only person of those present here who has the right to claim that he reflects the view of the upper bourgeoisie. Although I have not been officially authorized by the bourgeoisie, I nevertheless think that it would officially confirm [my statements], and I consider it my duty to declare that the upper bourgeoisie in no way pursues the same policy as the counterrevolution, and that, like the whole country, it, too, yearns for the earliest onset of an era of law and order. But I believe that this must not be achieved at the price of betraying the revolution; the way to achieve this is not by increasing the tension in our relations through heedless speeches—which are absolutely astounding and, I would say, an inadmissible characteristic of the leading organs of the democracy—but, rather, through self-restraint, calmness, mutual concessions, and mutual respect.

"These are the statements that I consider necessary to make on my own behalf, and to declare categorically that I am in absolute disagreement with this type of characterization."

Protest by Trudovik Sukhanov

Trudovik Sukhanov took the floor with the following out-of-order statement:

"I arrived toward the end of the meeting yesterday and therefore did not hear the speeches that were made here. I became familiar with these speeches only today. And I consider it my duty to request that it be placed on record that I was not present at the time these speeches were made. I deeply regret, I am deeply grieved that a few dozen members of the State Duma who gathered together at the private meeting yesterday departed from that high, patriotic stand which they were able to adopt on February 27."

. . .

V. M. Purishkevich firmly protested against the uproar raised in the Soviet of Soldiers' and Workers' Deputies on account of the speeches [delivered] by members of the State Duma and against the attempts to squelch them. He expressed confidence that silent Russia, the Russia that has not yet emerged, this Russia will support the speeches of the members of the State Duma and will recognize these members as being worthy representatives of the people.

1201. The Resignation of Chernov

[*Izvestiia*, No. 123, July 21, 1917, p. 5. For Chernov's account of the charges against him and his subsequent actions, see his *The Great Russian Revolution*, pp. 245–47; for a detailed analysis of the episode, see Radkey, *The Agrarian Foes of Bolshevism*, pp. 293–313.]

In view of the too-oft-repeated slanderous attacks on him, V. M. Chernov considered it necessary to address the following letter to Minister-President A. F. Kerensky:

To MINISTER-PRESIDENT A. F. KERENSKY:

Having been subjected for too long a period to embittered attack by my political opponents, who have shown no scruples recently about circulating all manner of slanderous rumors about me or using the vilest and no less slanderous police-gendarme sources, I consider it necessary for me to have full freedom of action at the present time in order to defend my political honor and to prosecute libelers who are private persons. Therefore, I ask you to accept my resignation.

VICTOR CHERNOV, Minister of Agriculture
July 20, 1917

Having heard the above letter of V. M. Chernov, the Provisional Government expressed its complete confidence that he will in a very short time be in a position to refute all the attempts to cast aspersions on his name; it also recognized the complete legitimacy of V. M. Chernov's desire to have full freedom of action in defending himself and that this would not be possible unless he were relieved of his duties as a member of the Provisional Government.

At the same time, the Provisional Government resolved that the post of Minister of Agriculture would not be filled by anyone at the present time and that the Ministry would be headed by Acting Minister P. A. Vikhliaev.

1202. THE RESIGNATION OF KERENSKY
[*Rech'*, No. 170, July 22, 1917, p. 3.]

Charged by the Provisional Government to broaden the Ministry, A. F. Kerensky has had to wage in the past days a struggle on two fronts, or, to be more exact, he was under the influence of two opposing currents: one coming from the side of the representatives of the Party of the People's Freedom and the other from the side of the Soviet of Workers' and Soldiers' Deputies.

As a result, A. F. Kerensky found it impossible to remain in his post of Minister-President and on July 21 submitted the following letter to Deputy Minister-President N. V. Nekrasov:

"In view of my inability, all my efforts in this direction notwithstanding, to broaden the membership of the Provisional Government in such a way that it would answer the demands of the exceptionally historic moment which the country is experiencing, I can no longer bear the responsibility before the State [and remain] true to my conscience and understanding. I therefore request the Provisional Government to release me from all posts that I now hold. A. F. KERENSKY."

After handing over this letter, A. F. Kerensky departed from Petrograd.

Representatives from the press contacted one of the prominent members of the Provisional Government about this letter, with the request for an appropriate explanation, particularly in the light of the prevailing rumors that one of the immediate causes for A. F. Kerensky's resignation was the demand he received on July 21 from the Executive Committee of the Soviet of Workers' and Soldiers' Deputies for immediate reinstatement of V. M. Chernov in the membership of the Provisional Government.

The reply was that the immediate reason for Kerensky's resignation was only the circumstance that he found himself between the irreconcilable demands of two sides.

As for the alleged demand about the immediate reinstatement of V. M. Chernov in the Government, it is true that a sincere wish had been expressed about the necessity to institute at the earliest possible moment an investigation of the incident about V. M. Chernov in order to exonerate him immediately, and those who demanded the investigation were completely certain of the need for urgency.

A. F. Kerensky's letter to the Provisional Government was immediately followed by the resignation from their posts of several more members of the Provisional Government.

The Deputy Minister-President, N. V. Nekrasov, then made the following announcement:

"Following A. F. Kerensky's resignation, by right I should resign because the two-week period for which I agreed to accept the appointment expires tonight. It was on the night of July 6–7 that I was urgently summoned, immediately following my resignation simultaneously from the Party of the People's Freedom and from the Provisional Government, to the headquarters of the Petrograd Military District, where the post I am occupying now was offered to me. The invitation was extended to me then, in view of the breakthrough on the Southwestern Front and the subsequent arrest that night of the Bolsheviks, upon which I had been insisting all the time. Nevertheless I cannot take advantage now of this right, because we should then not have that Provisional Government to which A. F. Kerensky appeals in his letter."

After this, M. I. Tereshchenko, Minister of Foreign Affairs, who was the first to announce his resignation, and then the other members of the Provisional Government who intended to resign from their posts announced that they were withdrawing their intention [to resign] for the time being.

At the same time, it was decided not to accept A. F. Kerensky's resignation, but to call immediately a conference of representatives from five of the most important political parties (People's Freedom, Radical-Democratic, Trudovik National-Socialist, Social Democratic, and Socialist Revolutionary); also representatives of three revolutionary organizations of Russia: the Temporary Committee of the State Duma, the Executive Committee of the Soviets of Workers' and Soldiers' Deputies, and the Executive Committee of the Soviets of Peasants' Deputies.

This resolution was adopted almost immediately following the reading of the letter of A. F. Kerensky to the Provisional Government at 6:00 o'clock in the evening. At 6:30 that evening the members of the Provisional Government were already extending invitations to various organizations to attend the conference set for 9:00 o'clock in the evening. N. V. Nekrasov called on P. N. Miliukov, representing the Kadets-Democrats, and I. N. Yefremov called on the Radical-Democratic Party, etc.

All parties were invited in the name of their central committees. Moreover, each one of them had the right to delegate an unlimited number of representatives in order that they could accept the decisions legally. The State Duma and the Executive Committees of the Soviet of Workers', Soldiers', and Peasants' Deputies were invited in the names of their representatives, M. V. Rodzianko, N. C. Chkheidze, and N. D. Avksent'ev.

In the opinion of the Provisional Government, which was the initiator of the extraordinary conference, the conference should be, so to speak, a "Council of Peoples," and in this respect could perhaps replace the Moscow Conference. It should analyze the political forces of the country and their interrelation, and should determine what decision in the final analysis would guarantee the success of the organization of the Provisional Government. The extraordinary conference should not of course pass any definite unequivocal decisions. Instead it should mainly clarify the situation in encountering extreme views.

Incidentally, in answer to the question whether the rumors that found their way into the press that N. V. Nekrasov and M. I. Tereshchenko allegedly insisted on the resignation of V. M. Chernov, the former explained that it was not quite true:

"Rumors about Chernov were never any secret to us," said N. V. Nekrasov, "but two days ago when these rumors were circulated with particular insistence, M. I. Tereshchenko and I did raise the question point-blank about the advisability of retaining V. M. Chernov in the membership of the Provisional Government until the circumstances are clarified."

"And how, in your opinion, should this clarification proceed?"

"At first it was supposed that the investigation should be conducted in the usual manner, but now that one of the newspapers has printed the substance of the accusation in full, the simple solution for V. M. Chernov is to hold this paper responsible for slander," said N. V. Nekrasov.

. . .

M. I. Tereshchenko, Minister of Foreign Affairs, withdrew his resignation, and, on July 21, continued to conduct the affairs of his office and receive Allied diplomats. M. I. Tereshchenko had a long talk with the French Ambassador, Mr. Noulens.

Mr. M. I. Tereshchenko's withdrawal of his resignation was effected, so it is reported, by the circumstance that V. M. Chernov resigned from the membership of the Provisional Government. M. I. Tereshchenko, according to the report, did not deem it possible to remain in the membership of the Government together with the Minister of Agriculture, V. M. Chernov, until the complete exoneration of the latter.

1203. THE CONFERENCE OF THE NIGHT OF JULY 21 IN THE WINTER PALACE

[*Izvestiia*, No. 124, July 22, 1917, pp. 3–4, and No. 125, July 23, 1917, p. 2; *Rech'*, No. 170, July 22, 1917, p. 4, and No. 171, July 23, 1917, p. 4.]

The joint session of the Provisional Government and the Central Committees of the parties began at 10:30 [P.M.] under the chairmanship of N. V. Nekrasov.

N. V. Nekrasov read the letter from Minister-President A. F. Kerensky. Then N. V. Nekrasov pointed out that the question facing the Government was that of finding a way out of the present situation. Three alternatives presented themselves: the Provisional Government could transfer its power to the original source from which it received this power; it could transfer all its plenary powers to one person who would form a cabinet; it could turn to the major political and social organizations in the country and hear their opinions. The Provisional Government decided on the latter. . . .

. . .

I. V. Godnev's Speech

I. V. Godnev pointed out that the one thing that must be done at the present time is to cast aside all party and group [affiliations] and to do everything necessary in the interest of Russia, and not in the interest of individual parties whose ambitions and desires assume such uncompromising forms. The only thing that is necessary is to endow the Provisional Government with power independent of all parties and for it to lead the country with a firm hand along the path of organization which will bring it to the Constituent Assembly.

M. I. Tereshchenko's Speech

"Today the country is in mortal danger. I do not want to blame any groups for this. This is a result of the revolution, and it [in turn] is a result of the old regime. I am afraid that the time which separates us from the past is short, but we must, at all costs, create a strong, vigorous, democratic Russia. There can be no return to the past. It spells inevitable ruin to our native land. Times of personal rule have been swept away along with the old regime. Now this is no longer possible, and government must be concentrated in the hands of institutions.

"I must state that during these months of the revolution, various groups wanted to take advantage of the situation that has developed. Unparalleled excessive demands have brought an inordinate strain on all the financial resources of the state and it now finds itself on the verge of bankruptcy.

"I will say a few words about Order No. 1. It is the greatest crime. Perhaps it was provoked by the conditions of the times, but it should have been openly recognized as a mistake.

"The offensive which was made possible by the incredible efforts of A. F. Kerensky has saved the honor of our country. The officers perished dauntlessly; they went in for practical suicide. Together with them perished the heroes of the army and regimental committees.

"I am in a better position than anyone else to know the state of morale in the country at that time. It was hopelessly excruciating. For months I had to convince [foreigners] that Russia would not betray [them], that the truce at the front which came about at the wish of the Germans had not penetrated the heart of the Russian man. The offensive restored the honor and dignity of Russia.

"I do not want to belittle the significance of the Soviets of Workers', Soldiers', and Peasants' Deputies, but the national problem, in its full scope, cannot be satisfactorily resolved in such a one-sided manner. The Government must rely on the support of all the strata of the population. Otherwise it will not succeed in evoking the enthusiasm which alone can save Russia.

"It is impossible to go on living in this way; we must all unite, unite with the army, with the population."

. . .

P. N. Miliukov's Speech

P. N. Miliukov first of all made common cause with the speeches of Tereshchenko and Godnev and emphasized that the Kadets are insisting on independent power, not only in the center but throughout the whole country.

Examining Tereshchenko's views further, the speaker emphasized that the Soviets are still speaking of peace.

"On the other hand, I. G. Tseretelli continues to speak about saving the revolution and the country, but the salvation of the country remains in the background while the salvation of the revolution is pushed to the fore.

"One could have subscribed to the political program of Tseretelli, but when one knows that a Zimmerwaldist is speaking, then the expressions assume a different meaning.

"Turning to the field of domestic policy, I must admit that here the situation is even more difficult. There are measures which really must be carried out before the convocation of the Constituent Assembly. But it all depends on the scope of these measures. If one speaks about better utilization of economic forces and about raising the economic productivity of the country, then, of course, there will be no argument. But do the measures which the committees are carrying out on a local level contribute to productivity?"

The speaker read excerpts from an article, sent to him today, which tells of the destruction of model farms, of the destruction of pedigreed cattle, and of the excesses that destroy the wealth [of the country] that cannot be restored in the near future.

"Everything that is going on at the local level," continued the speaker, "is to a certain extent a result of the permissiveness of the Government and, in part, has become legalized by it."

Regarding the way in which the new Government is to be formed, the speaker believed that A. F. Kerensky, who commands all the necessary authority and possesses all the qualities for this task, should be asked immediately to form a cabinet consisting of those persons whom he sees fit to invite. It might be said that A. F. Kerensky has already tried to do this, but his endeavor failed. Now, however, he will feel that he has been authorized to do this. In the past he ran up against the Kadets at one end and the "Soviets" at the other. Now, however, he will have an opportunity to choose his side.

. . .

A. V. Peshekhonov's Speech

A. V. Peshekhonov expressed surprise that the Provisional Government is accused by some people of introducing some sort of party program. Everything that the Government did, all of the measures it initiated, were called for by the acute needs of the country. In fact, these measures were short of meeting fully the actual needs, so loudly proclaimed on all sides. And while the former Minister-President, Prince G. E. L'vov, looked askance at V. M. Chernov for his agrarian measures, the latter looked with an unfavorable eye at the Prince for his orders in the Department of the Interior. Therefore, to talk about introducing any definite program is futile. But now a common ground could unquestionably be found. All that is needed is that the individual parties fully understand those points in common, which undoubtedly they have and which at the present moment could serve as a common platform.

The Speech of M. I. Tereshchenko

M. I. Tereshchenko said that he took the floor again in order to emphasize, with pain in his heart, that he fails absolutely to feel in all the preceding speeches any awareness of the exceptional character of this moment, which is unprecedented in Russian history. Again he begs that we forget individuals and think only of the harmony that can save Russia.

[A recess was announced at this point. The conference reconvened at 1:00 A.M.]

.   .   .

Lieber's Speech

In behalf of the Organizational Committee of the Russian Social Democratic Workers' Party (of Mensheviks), Lieber elucidated the terms on which the Social Democratic Party would be prepared to support the Government.

"Essentially, these terms are that the Government should lean upon the working masses of the population [by acting] through the revolutionary-democratic institutions.

"The Government must be creative and must aim to satisfy the interests of the democracy in so far as these interests do not conflict with the interests of the state.

"It must conduct a vigorous struggle for peace, because the struggle for peace is a potent weapon of national defense, while national defense, in its turn, is a potent weapon in the struggle for peace.

"We need the dictatorship of the Government to save the Revolution, but [it must be] a creative dictatorship, and not a dictatorship of repressions.

"And if the new government does not lean upon the masses, if the time comes that the Soviets cease to exist, then the country will find itself at the mercy of anarchy."

.   .   .

N. D. Avksent'ev's Speech

Avksent'ev spoke with great pathos and, greatly carried away, pounded the table with his fists.

"I do not wish to talk, I will not talk about the sins of the past, for it is necessary to talk about the problems of the moment. We must rescue our motherland at any cost from the deadly danger with which she is threatened and provide the people with the gains of the revolution. But how are we to do this? It is necessary that we have a general burst [of enthusiasm], combined effort, tremendous exertion, and all the sacrifices that will be asked of us. Only in this way will we achieve a union of strength. To our great misfortune, the moment we pass from words to action, party discords begin which should have no place here. Do not forget that we deal with a revolutionary element. The only salvation at the present moment is to rally round the Provisional Government, which is not composed of socialists alone. It pursues no political program, but executes the essential needs of the people. If you do nothing until the Constituent Assembly, you will turn the popular masses against yourselves and plunge the country into anarchy. Do not forget that at this grave moment we are experiencing, we must think of saving Russia and not about slogans of party programs. We, socialists, are ready to work with this government, headed by Kerensky, and we call upon you to join in this work. But if you do not do so at the present fateful moment and bring the country to ruin, all the weight of the dreadful consequences will fall upon you and not upon us."

.   .   .

N. V. Nekrasov's Speech

N. V. Nekrasov began his speech by pointing out that the country faces a catastrophe: "We cannot delay a moment. We must act. And at this very moment the Provisional Government remains without a head. All work has stopped.

"General Kornilov, for example, awaits an answer from the Provisional Government to the demands he makes before assuming the post of Supreme Commander. But we cannot give this answer now, because who will sign the consent of the Provisional Government to General Kornilov's conditions?

"Quick and responsible decisions on various questions related to national administration must be made almost every minute. At one moment we must debate the Finnish question, at another, settle a conflict with the Ukrainians, at still another, put down a revolt. And all this at a time when it is revealed that our finances are almost exhausted and havoc reigns in all spheres of national life.

"To waste so much strength on talks and negotiations at such a frightening time is criminal. Why has A. F. Kerensky left? He left because he was exhausted from the painful realization that he bears a tremendous responsibility for the future of Russia, that he must decide the most important national questions, that he must give answers both at the front and in the rear, and at the same time engage in fruitless negotiations about filling the cabinet and averting a complete breakdown of power. Do you realize the dreadful situation of the country, which may plunge into anarchy tomorrow, for there will be no authority?

"I am withdrawing from the Government. My political career will come to an end. This enables me, finally, to tell you, comrades from the Soviet of Workers' and Soldiers' Deputies, the whole truth. For you, too, are responsible for what takes place now. Have you not held the socialist ministers in constant fear of possible expression of lack of confidence? Have you not forced the socialist ministers to come to you twice a week and report on every one of their smallest steps? When calling on you, the ministers were afraid they would slip on some detail, as on an orange peel. Could this contribute to the peace of mind in the work of the Provisional Government, that peace of mind so necessary at the present responsible time in which we are living? The withdrawal of one minister who slipped inevitably created a government crisis. And you did nothing to make our work easier.

"Take, then, this power into your own hands and bear the responsibility for the fate of Russia. But if you lack the resoluteness to do so, leave the power to the coalition government, and then do not interfere in its work.

"There can be no half-decisions tonight. Either you trust A. F. Kerensky implicitly and those he will call to share the power, or you do not trust them. Then form a purely socialist cabinet and we will yield the power to you."

Statement by P. N. Miliukov

Following the speech of N. V. Nekrasov, P. N. Miliukov spoke as follows:

"In the name of the Party of the People's Freedom I state that we support completely the formulation [of the question] presented by N. V. Nekrasov. And we address the Soviet of Workers' and Soldiers' Deputies with the question: is it prepared to take the power into its own hands or [is it willing] to show confidence, without reservations and reports, in the government which will be formed by A. F. Kerensky?"

. . .

I. G. Tseretelli's Speech

I. G. Tseretelli stated that he was speaking both as a member of the Provisional Government and as member of the Executive Committee of the Soviet of Workers' and Soldiers' Deputies, and he nourished the hope that he would express the point of view of both organs. I. G. Tseretelli sees no irreconcilable discrepancy in what disturbs P. N. Miliukov in the responsibility of socialist ministers to give an account to the Soviet. In view of the peculiar position of the Soviet, its sessions are public, and their purpose is not interference in the actions of the Government, but merely the informing of those strata of the democracy that listen keenly to the voice of their organ. The demand of the K.-D.'s seems to I. G. Tseretelli illogical. Inasmuch as the Soviet has the right to vote in delegating ministers, how could we deprive them of further connection with their delegates.

In addressing the Kadets, I. G. Tseretelli said further:

"You demand that the Soviet have full confidence in you. Have this confidence then in us also. Put a stop to the boycott and to the attacks that are launched against the Government. I appeal to you, P. N. Miliukov. I demand that your party not undermine the power if you cannot form this power from your own party. I demand of you that you do not boycott that power which is in existence already, that you do not paralyze it, do not undermine the population's trust in it. And since you, Pavel Nikolaevich, have no hope of giving the country another government tomorrow, you must abandon the tactics of boycott."

The speaker asked P. N. Miliukov to state definitely that he was against the program minimum which the Provisional Government advanced in its declarations. If the Kadets categorically state that this program—the cry of the people's masses—is unacceptable to them, this will truly assure us of the people's confidence in us. And we shall take the power then. The speaker demanded a clear answer, whether or not the Party of the People's Freedom would support the power of the Soviet of Workers' and Soldiers' Deputies, and whether it accepted the program established by the declaration of July 8.

"The demands that you make upon the Soviets are demands that they destroy themselves, and with them also the revolution; whereupon you will undertake the salvation of Russia. Personally I entertain the same feelings toward the Kadets as they do toward the Soviets, but I never would appeal to them with a demand for self-destruction. I repeat, if you are unable to create a strong power, which you seek, do not paralyze the action of the existing power; do not throw the country into a civil war at the moment when it is already at the edge of a precipice."

.   .   .

F. Dan's Speech

F. Dan, member of the Executive Committee of the Soviet of Workers' and Soldiers' Deputies, said that he was amazed at the demands on self-limitations made upon democracy. In no sphere, in no stratum of society, he said, was such capacity for self-limitation and the submergence of particular interests to those of the State revealed as in the Soviets. Having all the opportunity to take power into their hands, the Soviet did not do so; it did not do so even under the threat of bullets. N. V. Nekrasov pointed out here the burden of power: "I can state, however, that when the moment arrives this burden will not stop us."

Referring to the words of Miliukov about the relations between the Party of the

People's Freedom and its representatives in the State Duma, Dan asked whether Miliukov thought it was possible to establish a revolutionary Russia under such relations. Should the relation between the masses and the Government be lost even for a day, he said, would not the power, too, collapse immediately. The connection between the masses and its representatives also exists in the privileged strata, but here it is not as intimate and not as firm as in socialist organizations.

The speaker concluded by repeating the words of Tseretelli, that the entire policy of the Party of the People's Freedom is reduced to a campaign against the Government and that only isolated brave personalities like Nekrasov, Tereshchenko, and others opposed this tactic.

. . .

Statement by Chkheidze

N. S. Chkheidze stated that to vent eloquence in speeches and pour out useless words at the present time was a crime. N. S. Chkheidze protested against the remark made by P. N. Miliukov that the Soviets of Workers' and Soldiers' Deputies must abandon the political arena if they are unable to administer the affairs of the State. "We work openly," said N. S. Chkheidze, "and history will appreciate our work in due time. And you, Pavel Nikolaevich, respond straightforwardly to the questions we put to you. Perhaps this is the last chance and we will not meet together again." [N. S. Chkheidze then addressed three questions to P. N. Miliukov: What was his attitude on the foreign policy program of the Russian democracy? What was his attitude on the agrarian question, and what was his attitude on social legislation?]

P. N. Miliukov's Speech

P. N. Miliukov replied that the Soviets are a class organization and do not embrace all of the people. Therefore a socialist ministry would not meet with popular support. In this respect P. N. Miliukov fully agreed with I. G. Tseretelli. But, not wishing to "take over the power" openly, the socialist ministers camouflage their power by having alleged representatives of the "bourgeoisie" aid them in carrying out their program. Therefore, by denying the Bolsheviks their demand to put "all power" into the hands of the Soviets, they achieve the same thing indirectly and destroy completely the basic condition of honest coalition—subordination to general national aims.

"If you are unable to form authority with your own strength, if you cannot take it into your own hands, I ask you then, would you oppose the authority which A. F. Kerensky creates? Up to this time you have put obstacles in his way by constantly controlling him.

"The answer to the question, what program we propose, is contained in the letter by three of our candidates for the posts of ministers, published on July 15.

"So far as my views on questions of foreign policy are concerned, they of course remain the same. However, I think that now is no time to discuss them. We must first create a mighty Russia and then talk about realizing the national aims and fulfilling our obligation to the Allies.

"Finally, the question of what is and what is not acceptable in the agrarian reform can be decided in drawing up the declaration of the future government."

. . .

Statement by M. M. Vinaver

M. M. Vinaver thinks that the general situation is sufficiently clear and the danger hanging over Russia is obvious. Two questions should be clarified now: Are the socialist parties and the Soviets of Workers' and Soldiers' Deputies willing to give A. F. Kerensky complete freedom to form a cabinet, and are they willing to free the future socialist members of the government from the control of party and other organizations?

The statement by M. M. Vinaver aroused considerable excitement among the representatives of the Soviet of Workers' and Soldiers' Deputies. Although the list of speakers had been completed, Gots threw a question at M. M. Vinaver in a raised voice. [He asked] whether the Kadets would be included in the government if they were requested to approve the declaration of July 8.

To this, Vinaver replied that the Kadets regard the declaration of July 8 as unacceptable to them, but that if Kerensky forms the government of members who accept this declaration, the party will support him.

"And will this support be complete?" pursued the questioning of the representatives of the Soviet.

"The support will be complete and absolute—much more complete than was the Soviet's support of the Government in its first composition. We shall not institute a control, we shall not assume executive power and shall demand absolute subordination of all to the authority which Kerensky formulates."

Following this, the representatives of the Soviet asked for a recess.

After the recess N. V. Nekrasov announced that there would be no balloting, but that only statements would be made.

Resolutions

Toward 6:00 o'clock in the morning the Malachite Hall was once more filled with members of the extraordinary meeting, and the leaders of all parties present announced their resolutions.

The resolution of the Social Democrats, read by Dan, stated the following: "The Organizational Committee of the Russian Social Democratic Workers' Party declares that it fully empowers Comrade A. F. Kerensky with the formation of the cabinet and with the bringing in of representatives of all parties willing to work on the basis of the program worked out by the Provisional Government on July 8 under the Presidency of A. F. Kerensky."

To this resolution Dan added orally that the socialist ministers from the party who enter the Provisional Government must be responsible to the organs that delegated them to the Government.

In the name of the Socialist Revolutionaries, Gots stated: "The Central Committee of the Socialist Revolutionaries states that it fully empowers Kerensky with the formation of a coalition cabinet, with the inclusion of representatives of all parties prepared to work on the basis of the program proclaimed by the Government under the Presidency of Kerensky on July 8."

M. M. Vinaver in the name of the Party of the People's Freedom read the following resolution: "The Party of the People's Freedom believes that A. F. Kerensky should be empowered with the formation of the Provisional Government on an all-national basis, composed of members not responsible to any organizations or committees."

In the name of the Trudovik Popular Socialist Party, V. A. Peshekhonov stated that the party thinks the only way out of the situation is to entrust A. F. Kerensky with the formation of the cabinet, without limiting him by any conditions.

The resolution passed by the Radical-Democratic Party read: "Recognizing the program of the Provisional Government of July 8 as acceptable, although it admits of various interpretations, the Radical-Democratic Party deems it indispensable to give A. F. Kerensky complete freedom both in the selection of people in order to create a firm government, and in questions of clear definition of the program of further action by the government created by him."

After the announcement of the resolutions, N. V. Nekrasov declared the conference ended. About 6:00 o'clock in the morning participants of the conference began to leave. Some of them went to the Tauride Palace to attend the conference of the Soviet of Workers' and Soldiers' Deputies.

1204. Kerensky Withdraws His Resignation
[*Rech'*, No. 171, July 23, 1917, p. 4.]

"The apparent inability on my part to create by means of the mutual agreement of the various political parties, both socialist and nonsocialist, a strong revolutionary government, indispensable in the crucial hour in which we are living, forced me to tender my resignation.

"The Conference of July 21 of representatives of the principal socialist, democratic, and liberal parties after extensive deliberation led to the decision that the parties represented there resolved to entrust me with the reorganization of the Government.

"Finding it impossible under the present circumstances, when the country is in danger of destruction from outside and a breakdown from within, to decline the serious duty now imposed on me, I regard it as an unfailing command of the country to form in the shortest time, and in spite of all possible obstacles, a strong revolutionary government.

"In realizing this task, I shall be guided by my unshakable conviction that the salvation of the motherland and the republic calls for the abandonment of party controversies and the consecrated work of all Russian citizens under the circumstances and forms imperiously dictated by severe necessity to wage war, to maintain the fighting morale of the army, and to restore the economic power of the State.

"Having been in the Provisional Government from the first hour of the transfer of all power into the hands of the people, I deem it necessary to proceed in reorganizing the Government on those principles which it has successively elaborated and which were expressed in its declarations.

"At the same time, as head of the Government, I find it unavoidable to introduce changes in the order and distribution of the Government's work. And I do not think I have the right to stop short of fulfilling to the full extent the tasks confronting the Provisional Government, in spite of the fact that these changes will increase my responsibility in the affairs of the Provisional Government."

A. Kerensky

July 22, 1917

On July 22, at approximately 4:00 o'clock in the afternoon, members of the Provisional Government arrived at the Winter Palace. At approximately 5:00 o'clock a meeting of the Provisional Government took place. Present at the conference was A. F. Kerensky, Minister-President, who had tendered his resignation, but had been recalled by an urgent telegram to Finland where he had gone the day before.

Members of the Provisional Government gave A. F. Kerensky an account of the debates and the results of the night conference at the Winter Palace.

As a result, A. F. Kerensky agreed to withdraw his resignation and immediately exchanged opinions on the formation of a new cabinet.

. . .

During the evening of July 22 A. F. Kerensky carried on negotiations with some prominent political leaders, it being reported that A. F. Kerensky had an audience with P. A. Kropotkin and G. V. Plekhanov.

. . .

To the representatives of the press A. F. Kerensky announced:
"The declaration of July 8 I signed myself and I do not intend to repudiate it."

. . .

In view of the diverse rumors and reports on the resignation of the Minister of Foreign Affairs, M. I. Tereshchenko, which occurred on July 19, we are informed by authoritative sources that his resignation was provoked by the same general reasons that forced Minister-President Kerensky to resign prior to that.

On the insistence of the Provisional Government M. I. Tereshchenko withdrew his resignation immediately in order not to interrupt the work of his department.

. . .

Late at night it became known that the S.R. Central Committee resolved to request the Provisional Government to investigate within a period of three days the accusation against V. M. Chernov, emphasizing that in the event they are unconfirmed V. M. Chernov must be reinstated in the membership of the Provisional Government.

1205. RESOLUTION OF THE TEMPORARY COMMITTEE OF THE STATE DUMA
[*Rech'*, No. 171, July 23, 1917, p. 4.]

On the evening of July 22, an extraordinary session of the Temporary Committee of the Duma took place under the chairmanship of M. V. Rodzianko.

M. V. Rodzianko opened the session by giving a detailed report on the results of the extraordinary meeting which took place the night of July 21 in the Winter Palace.

After a prolonged exchange of opinions on the report of M. V. Rodzianko, the Temporary Committee adopted the following resolution:

"Having acquainted ourselves with the debates during the sessions held at the

Winter Palace on the night of July 21 and July 22, and having heard the statement of the President of the State Duma, who participated in the session, the Temporary Committee of the State Duma thinks there should be no further delay in the formation of a strong government. There is no time to be lost. Everybody must rally round one aim: that of rescuing the motherland. In the face of this patriotic mission all party and class differences and interests must be abandoned at this grave moment.

"While maintaining the positions [stated in] previous resolutions, the Temporary Committee of the Duma deems it necessary to entrust A. F. Kerensky with the formation of a cabinet by the invitation of persons united by the great mission of rescuing Russia at any cost."

1206. THE RESOLUTION OF THE SOVIET EXECUTIVE COMMITTEES
[*Izvestiia*, No. 126, July 25, 1917, p. 5.]

Resolution

1) Recognizing the necessity of forming a strong, revolutionary, democratic Government in the interest of defending the country and the revolution, the Central Executive Committee of the Soviets of Workers' and Soldiers' Deputies and the Executive Committee of the Soviets of Peasants' Deputies call upon the democracy to give its most vigorous support to the Government in its measures aimed at defending the country and consolidating the gains of the revolution on the basis of the July 8 program.

2) Approving the socialist comrades' entry into the Provisional Government, the Central Executive Committees shall retain the right of recalling their members from the Provisional Government in the event that the Government deviates from the democratic aims outlined above.

3) The Central Executive Committees express their firm belief that only by relying on the organs of the revolutionary democracy within the country and on the front will the Provisional Government be able to adopt a course [leading] to the salvation of the country and the revolution.

4) The Central Executive Committees call upon all the Soviets of Workers', Soldiers', and Peasants' Deputies and all army and navy organizations to stand steadfastly on guard over the country and the revolution, rallying broad masses of the democracy around themselves, and announce that they, for their part, will offer the most energetic resistance to any encroachments on the rights of these organizations and their freedom to function.

1207. *Novoe Vremia* ON THE NEW GOVERNMENT

[No. 14835, July 25, 1917, p. 4. The membership of the Government was as follows: A. F. Kerensky, Minister-President and Minister of War and Navy (the Assistant Ministers of War and Navy were B. V. Savinkov and V. I. Lebedev); N. V. Nebrasov, Deputy Minister-President and Minister of Finance; M. I. Tereshchenko, Minister of Foreign Affairs; M. I. Skobelev, Minister of Labor; A. V. Peshekhonov, Minister of Food; V. M. Chernov, Minister of Agriculture; S. F. Ol'denburg, Minister of Education; A. S. Zarudnyi, Minister of Justice; I. N. Yefremov, Minister of Welfare; P. P. Yurenev, Minister of Transport; S. N. Prokopovich, Minister of Trade and Industry;

A. M. Nikitin, Minister of Post and Telegraph; F. F. Kokoshkin, State Controller; A. V. Kartashev, Ober-Procurator of the Holy Synod; N. D. Avksent'ev, Minister of the Interior.]

The list of ministers invited by A. F. Kerensky to save the revolution has been made public.

There are no indications that they will be equal to such heroic action.

The inclusion in the new government of Minister Chernov, who regards international socialism and not Russia as his fatherland, colors the entire list. By what process of thinking they have arrived at the conviction that a minister whose interests are in international socialism, which are practically the interests of the German Empire, is fit to save the motherland at a moment when it is precisely Germany who threatens her hardly anyone will understand.

No national government was formed. What was created was a repetition of the government which preceded it.

This predetermines the future of the new government. May it not carry along with it all of Russia.

1208. *Russkiia Vedomosti* ON THE NEW GOVERNMENT
[No. 170, July 27, 1917, p. 1.]

The Minister-President's appeal to the population rings with new notes, long awaited by the country. The appeal talks of freedom, welded national unity, and the restoration of Russia's honor, degraded by treason, faintheartedness and despicable cowardice. It speaks of iron authority and the selfless impulse of the people themselves, who will forge a formidable and creative national power.

Words about motherland, about national power, about national unity—could we talk about these only two months ago when our motherland was replaced by Zimmerwald, national power by anarchical ruin, and national unity by appeals to class hatred? The July days and the disgrace at the front forced many to wake up from the nightmare which threatened to choke the young Russian freedom, forced us to make the first step to replace the factual dictatorship of only one class by a national union of all the vital forces of the revolution for the cause of saving the perishing motherland.

It is the final stake. Now for the last time the question is being decided: are we or are we not to succeed in resurrecting the national power of our country by creating an iron government? We know that this attempt has many shortcomings, obvious to everyone and undoubtedly not unknown to A. F. Kerensky himself. The coalition government was not launched on the basis of a clear and lawful agreement of all the vital forces of Russia. Its formation demanded very effective, forceful methods, such as the temporary resignation of A. F. Kerensky. In the composition of the government we see no representatives of the genuine bourgeoisie—representatives of the commercial-industrial class. Still vague is the relation between the government and those public and party organizations to which individual members of the government belong. The Party of the People's Freedom only permitted its members to join; it did not delegate them. The Party of the S.R.'s put as an ultimatum the question of including the Minister of Agriculture, V. M. Chernov, in the government. The ministers who are at the same time members of the Soviets of Workers' and Peasants' Deputies formulate in a new way their relations to the Soviets: they are not responsible to them, but merely inform them.

Therefore it is still too early to say what concrete form the mutual relations between the coalition government and the organizations they lean upon will take.

It is impossible as yet to determine whether, once having definitely and sharply broken with old traditions, the government can be that iron power which moves toward the creation of the national power of our motherland.

But in any event the Rubicon has been passed. The chaotic period of state and national breakdown is over. The new government calls upon the citizens to rally around the great sacrificial deed to create a great free Russia. This call must be heard.

1209. *Volia Naroda* ON THE NEW GOVERNMENT
[No. 75, July 26, 1917, p. 1.]

The government crisis has been resolved. After prolonged negotiations, accompanied by well-known incidents and interparty wranglings, Comrade A. F. Kerensky suceeded in forming a revitalized ministry. We now have a government which conforms in its character, composition, and program to the unusually exceptional conditions experienced by the country at present. It is a nonpartisan government, with no one political group predominating. Rather, it is an all-Russian, national government that takes upon itself the general national problems which merge with the interests of the revolution. It was not without difficulty that this agreement was achieved between organizations and parties now comprising the basis of revolutionary authority. Down to the last minute each one of them exhibited little inclination to compromise, firmly holding to its irreconcilable position. Even at the famous historic conference in the Winter Palace it seemed impossible to find a unifying formula for the organs of revolutionary democracy and the liberal bourgeoisie. The awareness of a terrible and deadly danger which gathers over Russia, threatening equally all classes, all strata of the population, no matter what their interests and ideals; the realization that in this tragic fatal hour of history only the union of all vital forces of the country affords a chance for salvation, finally triumphed over class irreconcilability and factional pride, and both sides compromised. The Kadet Party consented to join the ranks of the Government, which based its activity on the declaration of July 8. The Soviets consented to curtail their demands for the responsibility of the Soviet ministers to them. They merely reserved the right to recall their members delegated to the Government, should the latter deviate from its program; the right enjoyed everywhere by political parties and taken advantage of on July 3 by the Kadets, so strictly adhering to the principles of traditional statecraft.

. . . The present situation calls for great sacrifices by all parties and organizations. In the name of general interests the Soviets sacrificed and imposed a limit upon themselves. The parties of the liberal bourgeoisie sacrificed and adopted the program which they repudiated, promising support to the Government. This total self-limitation should not be short-lived, the result of a quickly extinguished flame. It must endure until all dangers surrounding Russia are finally eliminated. The slightest violation of those conditions upon which the agreement had been reached between the Russia of the workers and of the privileged classes, the slightest deviation from the conciliatory position which both sides took by surrendering to the pressure of objective necessity, will be a blow to the Government, will weaken its strength, and thus will in this menacing hour strike a blow at the country and the revolution. . . . But in order to create such an atmosphere of total self-limitation and sacrifice, in order that the country may rise to this moral height and prove itself truly worthy of freedom, it must be challenged by a clear and definite idea, concentrating within itself all the demands of the moment and at the same time being broad enough and all-inclusive; this will kindle in all hearts the fire of self-sacrifice, which burns up all egotisms, class, group, and individual. This idea, dictated by the entire course of events and the situation in the country, is the idea of revolutionary *defense*.

1210. *Rabochaia Gazeta* ON THE NEW GOVERNMENT
[No. 116, July 26, 1917, p. 1.]

The new Provisional Government is finally formed.

The country has been following the government crisis with the greatest tension and can now draw a sigh of relief. For every day, every hour of anarchy is fraught with the gravest danger to the revolution, because it is precisely the absence of government that paves the way to counterrevolution.

A. F. Kerensky succeeded in forming a coalition ministry with the support of outstanding and responsible parties. Remaining outside the coalition are only the irresponsible groups of the Bolsheviks in the "left" wing and both covert and avowed counterrevolutionaries in the right wing.

The new Government unquestionably bears a democratic character, both in its structure, predominantly composed of representatives of revolutionary democracy, and in its program, akin to the declaration of July 8.

But the Party of the People's Freedom, comprising a large number from the propertied classes, also gave the government, according to the reports in *Rech'*, "its best men, best theoreticians and statesmen, and best practical leaders and specialists."

Thus the coalition Government formally consolidated all the vital forces of the land ready to unite in order to save the country from military devastation.

The Provisional Government enjoys unlimited dictatorial power. It is guaranteed the support of all parties who sent their representatives. It is assured of the support of the plenipotentiary organs of revolutionary democracy—the Soviets of Workers', Soldiers', and Peasants' Deputies.

Under such conditions the new Government can launch its responsible work boldly, counting on all-national recognition and the support of the overwhelming majority of the population.

Problems of the greatest difficulty and complexity confront the new Government. No revolutionary government in the past has ever faced such difficulties. . . .

.   .   .

Revolutionary democracy will fulfill its duty to the end. To the government of revolutionary defense and the vigorous democratic reform of the country, to the government of merciless warfare against counterrevolution, a most active support is pledged. *This* support of the coalition will steadfastly withstand the pressure from hostile forces.

Will *another* support of the coalition, from the bourgeoisie, prove to be as unyielding and firm? Is the organized bourgeoisie ready now, after the K.D.'s have joined the government, to support the Provisional Government in its attempts to save the motherland and the revolution and bring the country to the Constituent Assembly? Will it, following its political leaders, understand that a coalition is a necessity; that no salvation for the country is possible without coalition; that neither the revolutionary democracy without propertied classes nor the propertied classes without the revolutionary democracy are able to take power into their hands and save the country from ruin?

The future will answer this question.

The Government has just been formed. But already, before it has begun work, a campaign against it is launched by the opposition. Forces which remained outside the coalition have been attempting from the outset to undermine the confidence in the new Government. They are suspicious of it and openly oppose it.

. . .

The situation is clear. The right and the "left" wings will wage an underground and an open campaign to undermine the revolutionary Government. The right and "left" wings of irresponsible groups, or people either avowedly dangerous to the revolution or blinded by group doctrinairism, will throw sticks into the wheels of the new Government.

But large groups of people and, above all, the working class will realize the seriousness of the moment. They will be infected with that holy concern for the future of the country and the revolution of which Tseretelli, who withdrew from the Government, spoke, and through their work will strengthen the organs of revolution, shattered by the blows of anarchy and counterrevolution.

Democracy will rally closely around its revolutionary organs and with all its might help the Provisional Government in the solution of the problems it faces in the matter of defense of the country and the strengthening of the conquests of the revolution.

1211. *Delo Naroda* ON THE NEW GOVERNMENT
[No. 110, July 26, 1917, p. 1.]

The crisis of power lasted precisely three weeks. The crisis passed through a number of phases, each subsequently complicating the situation still further and more hopelessly, so it seemed. The withdrawal of the K.D.'s from the power; the adventure of July 3–5; the breakthrough of the front, and as a result the so-far uninterrupted retreat of our army; the resignation of Prince L'vov from power; the slanderous campaign against Comrade Chernov and his resignation from the Government; and finally the resignation of Comrade Kerensky—all these events, building up like a rolling snowball, formed in their total a mountain of obstacles which finally stopped the state mechanism. It would seem there was no way out of the deadlock: if you went to the right, you would destroy the revolution; if you went to the left, you would destroy the country; if you remained in the same place, you would destroy both the country and the revolution. . . . Neither the revolutionary democracy nor, far less, the ruling classes by themselves, with their own strength, could solve those problems raised by the objective course of events, which called for a general national high spirit, enthusiasm, and sacrifices, not from any one party or class, but from all of the people.

Both socialist and nonsocialist parties realized but too well, and frankly admitted, that coalition was the only expedient way out of the situation—a *union* of forces, each in itself individually incapable of guarding the country and the revolution, and service to which was recognized as a twofold task of our time.

People of various parties and opposite classes were equally aware of the fact that Hannibal was at the gates; that together we must strike the enemy of the country and the revolution; that the time has not come yet for the parting of the ways of classes and parties welded by history and a common fate. Nevertheless, in spite of all attempts to "combine" them, coalition did not succeed, stumbling each time against insurmountable obstacles on one or the other side.

By his political genius, wisdom, and tact, A. F. Kerensky finally succeeded in arriving at a mean balance of forces, reconciling both sides by mutual compromise. The new Government was formed on the basis of the declaration of the former Government of July 8. Comprising the new Government were representatives of all those five parties whose leading organs were invited to attend the historic conference in the Winter Palace on July 21.

Thus the coalition was effected, the combination of forces for the time being took place, a "civic reconciliation" in the name of saving the country and the revolution was temporarily declared.

. . .

Some people think that it was impossible to form a national government and that what was shaped was merely a "repetition" of the former government, of that coalition which did not live up to its expectation and collapsed on July 2 with such a crash.

Perhaps it is so. But if the new coalition is merely a "repetition" of the former unsuccessful experiment, the Petrograd events of July 3–5 are responsible for it. Revolutionary democracy paid for the revolt not only with the blood of its sons, but also by the fact that it stopped the movement and development of the revolution. . . .

. . .

Resolutely and with no delay, forward—let this be the course from which the new Government will not deviate! Let the Government consistently realize the obligations it assumed by the declaration of July 8. Let it gain confidence in its strength and trust the mind of the Russian people, and then, once a national government, it will have the strength to satisfy both the interests of the people and the needs of the revolution and defense!

The new Government will have the more chance of becoming a national government the more pronouncedly national its policy becomes. Because only people who actually see and realize that "The law—it is I" will be able to give the authority the support which any pressure will be powerless to overcome, [pressure] either to the right in the name of "sound" reaction, or to the left in the name of seditious freedom.

1212. *Izvestiia* ON THE NEW GOVERNMENT
[No. 126, July 25, 1917, pp. 1–2.]

The most important, fundamental task of the new Government is the defense of the country against military devastation. The wounds inflicted by the breakthroughs that have riddled our front must be healed at all costs. Otherwise the situation spells downfall to Russia, downfall to the revolution. The country, torn into shreds and worn out with suffering, will fall prey to predatory imperialists; the Russian people will not see liberty, the Russian peasant will not see land; disintegration, corruption, and deterioration will be the lot of the once-great country of Russia.

This must not happen. The Russian democracy will not permit it. Soldiers, workers, peasants—everyone as one man must put his strength, his courage, his energy and resolution into the cause of saving the country, at the head of which stands the new Government.

But it must be remembered that a successful national defense is possible only on the basis of an equally stubborn defense of the revolution. Those who demand in the name of the salvation of the country that revolutionary reforms be discontinued and that revolutionary democratic organizations be weakened or destroyed are hypocrites and liars.

It is precisely now that there must be an exertion of all creative powers, so necessary to carry out urgent measures in the realms of agrarian, socioeconomic, and financial policies. A delay in the passage of such measures will undermine the entire economic life of the country and will cause loss of faith and a fall of morale in the population. . . .

Furthermore: there must be iron discipline, there must be revolutionary order, and there must be the greatest self-restraint on the part of each and every person. But he who does not see that he is dealing with people who have already breathed the bracing air of freedom is blind. Only a madman can cherish a dream that a discipline and an order based on the strong-arm methods of the tsarist regime might be introduced in revolutionary Russia.

. . .

A government for the defense of the country must also be a government for the defense of the revolution. In saving the country by employing every revolutionary means, it must also save the revolution with the assistance of all the vital forces of the country. A ruthless struggle against the counterrevolution which avidly awaits moments of national disasters is essential to the interests of national defense.

In the eyes of the democracy, the new Government, which was formed on the basis of a definite political program and which has incorporated representatives of all the vital forces of the country, is precisely the kind of government of revolutionary defense that is needed at the present time. And for this reason the Government will be guaranteed the support of the democracy in this work.

1213. *Novaia Zhizn'* ON THE NEW GOVERNMENT

[No. 83, July 25, 1917, p. 1. For Lenin's comments, see the *Collected Works of V. I. Lenin: Toward the Seizure of Power*, XXI, Bk. I, 76–79.]

By the time these lines reach the reader, the cabinet will no doubt finally be formed. At the present moment the fate of some of the candidates is not entirely clarified. But on the whole, the physiognomy of the new Government—"the Government to Save the Revolution"—is apparently pretty clearly defined. . . .

As heretofore, the cart of the Russian revolution will be drawn by the swan, the crawfish, and the pike, the only difference being that the swan has his wings badly clipped and his spine injured, whereas the pike and the crawfish, well fed by carrion during the past three weeks, are full of unusual high spirits and strength.[6] It is easy to foresee where the cart will roll. The new ministry will no longer represent a picture of complete paralysis of authority. It has a chance to move from dead center, but of course not forward, but backward. . . .

The socialist ministers and the democratic ministers are destined, it seems, to play the role of that cover-up without which the reaction cannot as yet get along, and then be thrown overboard from political life at the moment the leaders of the Kadet and all other "national" parties no longer need the screen of a protective revolutionary coloring. If the representatives of the Russian revolutionary democracy lacked the knowledge, strength, and courage to create a government capable of moving the revolution forward, they at least should have had sufficient courage to admit their helplessness openly and remove themselves from power altogether, exposing the game of the reactionary circles to all the people and not giving even one popular name among the Russian democracy to the reactionary ministry.

ATTEMPTS TO STRENGTHEN GOVERNMENTAL POWER AND RESTORE REVOLUTIONARY ORDER

1214. GOVERNMENTAL AUTHORITY TO SHUT DOWN SEDITIOUS AND INFLAMMATORY PUBLICATIONS

[*Zhurnaly*, No. 129, July 12, 1917.]

. . .

Resolved:

To publish the following law:

With reference to the change of and supplement to the Provisional Government's law of April 27, 1917 (*Sob. Uzak.*, No. 597),[7] resolved:

To grant permission to the Minister of War and Acting Minister of the Interior to shut down, as a temporary measure, current publications which advocate disobedience of orders by military authorities and nonfulfillment of military duty and which contain appeals to violence and civil war, holding the chief editors at the same time responsible before the law.

1215. MEASURES FOR MAINTAINING ORDER IN PETROGRAD

[*Izvestiia*, No. 116, July 13, 1917, p. 1.]

The Provisional Government has adopted [the following] resolute measures in order to prevent a recurrence of the July 3–5 events which dangerously imperiled the fate of the Russian revolution:

1) The Ministry of Justice is instructed to conduct the most thorough inquiry into the events of July 3–5.

---

[6] The reference is to a fable of Krylov's.
[7] Volume I, Doc. 207.

2) All persons who are directly or indirectly responsible for these events shall be arrested by the investigating authorities and brought to trial.

3) All processions and street assemblies in Petrograd shall be prohibited pending a new directive.

4) Appeals for violence and attempted revolts, regardless of their origin, shall be suppressed by every means, including the use of armed force.

5) Unauthorized searches and arrests shall be prohibited under threat of severe punishment for those [persons] who, by interfering with due process of law, undermine the prestige of the Government and disrupt its activities, which are directed at restoring revolutionary order.

In suppressing anarchy: It is not the purpose of the Provisional Government to give irresponsible groups an opportunity to sow new discord in the country under the guise of a struggle against anarchy and thus pave the way for a counter-revolution.

I am calling on all officials within the jurisdiction of my department—the Commissar of the Provisional Government in charge of the former Prefecture of Petrograd and all officers of the Petrograd militia—to adopt all appropriate measures for the effective fulfillment of the demands made by the Provisional Government.

All those who fail to carry out the demands of the Provisional Government shall be subject to arrest and prosecution by legal authorities.

TSERETELLI, Acting Minister of the Interior

1216. TELEGRAM OF THE MINISTER OF THE INTERIOR TO LOCAL COMMITTEES AND ORGANS OF SELF-GOVERNMENT

[*VVP*, No. 107, July 18, 1917, p. 2. No. II in this series of three communications is printed in Volume II as Doc. 488.]

I

To Committees of Public Organizations, Soviets of Workers', Soldiers', and Peasants' Deputies, and Organs of Municipal and Zemstvo Self-Government:

On taking over the administration of the Ministry of the Interior, I am giving to the commissars under my jurisdiction a number of guiding instructions for their activity in circulars dated July 17.

The grave days experienced by Russia impose upon the Provisional Government the responsibility to direct all the plenary power with which it is invested to rescue the revolution and defend the country from military ruin. Restoration of revolutionary order and creative democratic work—such is the course of Russia's salvation.

The Government cannot tolerate any further demonstrations of anarchy such as the treacherous blow dealt the revolution during the days of July 3–5. It cannot allow either appeals to civil war or acts of violence and arbitrary actions which threaten the very existence of the country. It cannot permit any attempts to cause disintegration in the army, to shake its order and discipline, and thus prepare the ground for military defeats.

Nevertheless the Provisional Government is well aware of the danger with which the country is threatened by the counterrevolution which is rearing its head in an attempt to take advantage of the internal discord and of misfortunes at the front in order to turn the country back, to deprive the people of the fruits of their revolutionary struggle, and to restore the system under which, in the interests of a few, the most basic interests of the country and the wide popular masses were betrayed and sold.

Rigorous suppression of both anarchical and counterrevolutionary undertakings constitutes one of the most important tasks of the Government.

Realizing that the strengthening of the revolution is the only course to save the country, the Government deems it urgently necessary to create an invincible support for the revolution in the devotion to it of the broad popular masses. At the same time, while rigorously combating all expressions of anarchy and counter-revolution, the Government sets itself the aim of the most expedient introduction of the program of external and internal policy as outlined in the declaration of the Government on July 8.

In order to carry out all these exceptionally important tasks, a strong and stable revolutionary authority is necessary in the center and locally, vested with extraordinary powers in the name of the defense of the country and the salvation of the revolution.

But such power will lead to the desired end in the suppression of anarchy and counterrevolution, as well as in the restoration of the fighting efficiency of the army and in the field of positive revolutionary creative work, only if the state authority and its local representatives act in the closest unity with all the public revolutionary organizations of the country imbued with all of its vital strength.

Therefore I address myself to all the democratically re-elected organs of city and zemstvo self-government, to all the committees of public organizations, to the Soviets of Workers', Peasants', and Soldiers' Deputies, with an appeal to render energetic and active support to government commissars in the execution of the tasks imposed upon them, bearing in mind that the commissars of the Provisional Government are the representatives and executors of the will of the plenary central government of revolutionary Russia.

Anticipating in the nearest future the introduction of organs of oblast administration and the selecting of representatives of revolutionary-democratic organizations in the work of this administration, and attributing primary importance to the personal qualifications of the commissars, I request all of the named institutions and organizations to submit to me as soon as possible their suggestions on the desirable forms of organization of the regional and guberniya administrations, as well as on new candidates for approval, acceptable to all named organizations, in the event of unfitness of some of the commissars for the tasks imposed upon them.

All such considerations and suggestions will receive the most careful attention on my part.

Only in intimate relation with organized popular forces can the work of internal organization of Russia, the defense of the country, and the salvation of the revolution be realized.

Ir. TSERETELLI, Acting Minister of the Interior

July 17, 1917

1217. TELEGRAM OF THE MINISTER OF THE INTERIOR TO GOVERNMENT
COMMISSARS

[*VVP*, No. 107, July 18, 1917, p. 2. No. II in this series of three communications is
printed in Volume II as Doc. 488.]

III

To Guberniya, Oblast, and Municipal Commissars

The treacherous blow of anarchy aroused discord in the land. In the hope of
wrenching from the revolution her gains, counterrevolution reared its head. The
breakdown and anarchy in the rear spread to the front. In the name of the salvation of the country the Provisional Government is vested with full powers and
will not stop short of any measures in order to avert the impending danger to the
country. You, in your places, are called upon to represent the revolutionary
authority of the Provisional Government. Your duty to the revolution enjoins
you at the present grave moment to carry out unflinchingly and resolutely all the
orders of the Government and to assist with all your strength in cementing the
authority of the revolutionary power. In fulfilling the will of the plenipotentiary
revolutionary government, you have the right—you are required—to demand
unqualified obedience to each and all of the orders of the Provisional Government
and its representatives. In its activity the Government responds to the will of
organized popular forces. You, too, must appeal for support and organize all local
public and revolutionary democratic organizations while standing on the firm
ground of the program declared by the Provisional Government in its declaration
of July 8. Wide use should be made of the experience and creative initiative of
these organizations in the matter of organizing local, public, and economic life.
Guarding the interests of revolutionary Russia, you are obliged to suppress with
all energy all attempts to provoke anarchy and discord. No arbitrary seizures of
property or land, no acts of violence, no appeals to civil war and violation of military duty are to be tolerated. But you must remember that counterrevolution is
attempting to utilize for its own purposes the struggle of the revolutionary government with the anarchical uprisings among various elements of the democratic
population. The counterrevolutionary elements attempt to provoke the representatives of the Government to a struggle with the entire organized democracy or to
take repressions arbitrarily into their own hands, in order to demolish with their
help all democratic organizations and to violate the legal interests and rights of
workers, peasants, and soldiers. Counterrevolution hopes thereby to shatter the
faith in revolution among the wide masses of the population, to interfere with the
realization of the positive program of reforms proclaimed by the Provisional
Government, and to return Russia to the rule, condemned by the people, which
brought the country to the brink of ruin. As representatives of the Government,
whose aim is defense of the country and the salvation of the revolution, you must
assume the duty, along with a vigorous struggle against anarchy, to avert just as
resolutely all counterrevolutionary designs. Acting in union with organized
popular forces, you must fulfill the tasks imposed upon you through the people
who are sincerely devoted to the cause of freedom. In defending the revolutionary
order and the freedom gained, you must take all measures toward the realization
of the Government's decision to convene the Constituent Assembly by September 30. To this end you should have direct supervision over uninterrupted preparation for elections to organs of local self-government. The revolution is in

danger. The country is passing through a severe trial. The salvation of revolutionary Russia calls for the exceptional exertion of all the vital forces, for the devotion of everyone to the interests of the people, and for selfless fulfillment of one's duty. All citizens and all representatives of the revolutionary government must be imbued with this thought. Notify immediately and widely all the population about the expressed will of the Provisional Government.

Ir. TSERETELLI, Acting Minister of the Interior

1218. GOVERNMENTAL AUTHORITY TO CLOSE ALL MEETINGS AND ASSEMBLIES

[*Sob. Uzak.*, I, 2, No. 1246. On July 26, military censorship was established over postal and telegraphic services, exempting only governmental and diplomatic communications. *Ibid.*, I, 2, No. 1229.]

LAW OF THE PROVISIONAL GOVERNMENT

For the duration of the war, the Minister of the Interior and the Minister of War are granted the right to prohibit and close all meetings and assemblies which may constitute a danger to the war effort or to the security of the state; this law to be put into effect before its promulgation by the Ruling Senate.

A. KERENSKY, Minister-President
ZARUDNYI, Minister of Justice
July 28, 1917

1219. GOVERNMENTAL AUTHORITY FOR ADMINISTRATIVE ARREST AND DEPORTATION
[*Sob. Uzak.*, I, 2, No. 1131.]

LAW OF THE PROVISIONAL GOVERNMENT

The grim experience of recent times has led the Government to the grievous necessity, in order to safeguard the fatherland and the revolution, of resorting to the emergency measures now proclaimed, so that an end may be put to the activity of those persons who wish to take advantage of the freedom bestowed by the revolution on all citizens only in order to inflict irreparable damage on the cause of the revolution and the very existence of the Russian State.

Under the present conditions of war and revolution in the country, the Government would not be fulfilling its duty to the homeland if it assumed that the responsibility incumbent upon it for protecting the independence and integrity of the State and the inviolability of the achievements of the revolution consisted only of taking judicial action against persons who have already committed criminal acts.

It is the duty of the Government to cut short the maturing of criminal designs before they can be put into practice, for in time of war even a brief disturbance of the tranquillity of the State harbors great dangers.

Therefore the Government, defending the civil and political rights of all and protecting the right to existence and open activity of all political tendencies, will nip in the bud the aforesaid activity of individuals endangering the State, for which purpose it grants the Minister of War and the Minister of the Interior emergency powers in the present time of emergency.

At the same time the Government has consciously refrained from conferring these powers on any other organ of state authority, thereby ensuring that the measures now proclaimed will be applied only for the good of the State, the observance of which is now more than ever the duty of the Government.

Accordingly, the Provisional Government has decreed:

I. To authorize the Minister of War and the Minister of the Interior, by mutual agreement:

1) To order the detention under arrest of persons whose activity constitutes a particular threat to the defense and internal security of the State, and to the freedom achieved by the revolution;

2) To enjoin the persons mentioned in para. 1) to leave the confines of the Russian State within a period specifically fixed for this purpose, with the proviso that in the event of their failure to do so or their willful return, they be detained under arrest by the procedure outlined in para. 1) of the present law.

II. The Minister of War and the Minister of the Interior are authorized to establish rules for the procedure to be followed in taking the measures mentioned in section I.

A. KERENSKY, Minister-President
ZARUDNYI, Minister of Justice
August 2, 1917

1220. AMENDMENTS TO THE PENAL CODE
[*Sob. Uzak.*, I, 2, No. 1132.]

LAW OF THE PROVISIONAL GOVERNMENT

The Provisional Government has decreed:

Articles 100 and 101 of the Penal Code (Code of Laws, Vol. XV, ed. 1909) to read as follows:

100. A person guilty of an act of violence designed to change the existing state structure in Russia or to sever from Russia any of its parts, or to remove organs of the Supreme Power in the State, or to deprive them of the possibility of exercising such power, is subject to the following penalty: an indefinite or fixed term at hard labor.

Both the commission of the present heinous crime and an attempt [to do so] are deemed to constitute the above act of violence.

101. Anyone guilty of preparations for the heinous crime provided for in Article 100 is subject to the following penalty: imprisonment in a house of correction or imprisonment in a fortress.

If the culprit had explosives or a store of arms in his possession for this purpose, he is subject to the following penalty: hard labor for a term of not more than eight years.

A. KERENSKY, Minister-President
ZARUDNYI, Minister of Justice
August 4, 1917

1221. *Russkiia Vedomosti* Questions the Necessity of the New Measures

[No. 176, August 3, 1917, p. 1. The reference to the Minister of Justice rather than the Minister of War and to administrative banishment rather than deportation abroad in connection with the law of August 2 (Doc. 1219) was probably the result of a mistake in transmission by telephone or telegraph from Petrograd to Moscow that evening, when the law was approved and communicated to the press bureau attached to the Government.]

A resolution has just been published by the Provisional Government granting the right to the Minister of the Interior, with the consent of the Minister of Justice, to put under guard and banish to regions especially designated for the purpose persons "whose activity is particularly endangering the freedom gained by the revolution and the state order now established."

The new resolution is directly related to a series of measures previously adopted by the Provisional Government as a result of the July events—restoration of the death penalty at the front, granting the right to the War Minister to close organs of the press instigating military mutiny and disobedience to military authorities at the front, granting the Ministers of the Interior and War the right to forbid and close all meetings and congresses which may represent a military danger and a danger to the safety of the country. Added to these now is the restoration of one of the most hated recollections of the old regime—administrative arrest and banishment. Of the basic human rights and the rights of the citizen fought for by every revolution—which as a matter of fact are the most valuable of its conquests—of these rights, after five months, we have preserved very little. And now we defend freedom, gained by the revolution, by means which, though temporary, suppress that very same freedom.

. . .

But are all these measures so necessary? Could not the Government really get along without the extraordinary powers, without revoking the basic guarantees of inviolability of person in order to defend the gains of the revolution? We doubt [that they are necessary] . . . To be sure, our chief misfortune in the period we have just experienced, the main cause of the total chaos and disintegration, was our weakness of power and helplessness. But this weakness was due to the fact not that the Government lacked sufficiently wide plenary powers, but that these powers remained untried. The Government did not sufficiently combat the various outbursts of anarchy, accompanied by the crudest violence toward the individual and by direct violations of law, although it had at its disposal the plenary power. Why this was the case, we shall not discuss, but at any rate, the fact remains a fact. . . . The Government must be firm and strong, but it attains this strength only by unrelenting observance of the law, application of it without any partiality and without any weaknesses, and not by resort to special plenipotentiary powers and administrative consideration. This testimony of internal weakness cannot make the Government strong, as the Statute on Enforced and Extraordinary Security now reintroduced in parts did not make the Tsar's government strong.

We should also consider the possible future. The present composition of the Provisional Government presents certain guarantees against misusing the new measure, against applying it simply to people displeasing to the Ministers of the

Interior and of Justice, or to those who disagree with them in their political views. But what will happen if the present Provisional Government should disappear from the scene without waiting for the Constituent Assembly and be replaced by a government supported exclusively by the Soviets of Workers' and Soldiers' Deputies or, vice versa, by a government headed by some enterprising general? Then surely the new measure would find the widest and most varied application. But then it will be too late to oppose it. Deviations from great principles of justice never go unpunished.

1222. The Debates and the Resolution of the All-Russian Central Executive Committee of the Soviets of Workers' and Soldiers' Deputies

[*Izvestiia*, No. 136, August 5, 1917, pp. 4–5; No. 137, August 6, 1917, pp. 3–5. For Lenin's comment on this meeting, see the *Collected Works of V. I. Lenin: Toward the Seizure of Power*, XXI, Bk. 1, 98–103.]

The Speech by Minister of the Interior N. D. Avksent'ev

Met with general applause, the new Minister of the Interior, N. D. Avksent'ev, said:

"I entered the Provisional Government not long ago; I don't have the backlog of experience that the Minister-President has, nor the long history of trials that many of the members of the Provisional Government have. When you find yourself in the central government you can clearly see the whole menacing danger, not in a counterrevolution or in anarchy, but in the general disorganization, in the general disorder in supplies, in transport, and in the whole common cause, which requires the greatest sacrifices, exceptional efforts, and exceptional measures.

". . . I can speak only in general terms about the policy of the Minister of the Interior. We are now holding a conference of commissars and civic leaders. In my speech at this conference I indicated what we must do. We must consolidate the revolutionary power so that all the orders of the central government will be executed at the local level. I declared that only by leaning on the democracy will this power be able to acquire the force of influence and compulsion, which, alas, is a necessity.

". . . The democracy must either assume the full responsibility for state organization or declare openly: 'I refuse [to participate in] the organization of the State; let someone else do it . . .'

". . . The central government does not know what is happening in the outlying districts, and in the localities they don't know what is happening in the central government. I will say more: the guberniya commissars do not know what the uezd commissars are doing, and vice versa. Every uezd pursues its own policy, works for itself, and thinks that this expresses the highest idea of democracy. We must strive for [conditions where] all the separate organs of state authority would be united under one plan.

"Our third problem is to create a civil machinery for the protection of citizens; since it must not draw upon military forces that are needed elsewhere, the Ministry of the Interior has set for itself the urgent task of organizing a militia. Citizens must know that the revolutionary power knows how to defend their interests.

"The Minister of the Interior and the Minister of War have been granted the right to close down organs of the press that create alarm in the country. . . . On these grounds I closed down the *Narodnaia Gazeta* today and instigated legal proceedings against its editors. (*Applause.*) I will act in the same way in regard to anarchy and counterrevolution. The law on administrative arrests and deportations, confirmed on August 2, will be promulgated in a few days. And I have already taken advantage of this law to arrest Yuskevich-Krassovskii. (*Applause.*) Do you have confidence in me when I act in this way in the struggle against the enemies of both the right and the left? (*Voices from the audience are heard:* "We have, we have.") Will you have confidence in me and in us no matter what measures we adopt? I ask you to feel the full anxiety, the anxiety and the tragedy of the situation. Remember that you must have only one duty—to save the revolution at all costs. (*Storm of applause.*)"

After a break, Comrade Tseretelli delivered a long speech in which he proved the necessity of supporting the Government. . . .

At the end of his speech Tseretelli, speaking on behalf of the Mensheviks and Socialist Revolutionaries, proposed that the meeting adopt the following resolution:

Resolution

At a time when the revolutionary country has endured hard blows both from within and on the front, and when the revolutionary democracy is exerting every effort to cope with internal disorder and to organize the resistance against the onslaught of external foes, a considerable segment of the bourgeoisie, unwilling to bear the sacrifices demanded by the revolution, have joined forces with counterrevolutionary elements and are taking advantage of the difficulties of the country by launching an open onslaught on the empowered organs of the revolutionary democracy and by undermining the Provisional Government which the revolution established. At the same time all the open and hidden supporters of imperialism are trying to exploit the misfortune on the front in order to return the foreign policy of Russia to the aims and methods that have been unanimously condemned by the popular masses, to restore [this policy] just when the revolutionary democratic policy has begun to produce real results in the Western European countries.

Under these conditions, having recognized the necessity for a strong revolutionary power, the democracy is obligated to give its energetic support to all endeavors of this Government that are directed at saving the country from military devastation and saving the revolution from the menacing danger.

At the same time the democracy has the duty of warning the Government against such mistakes which, in an atmosphere of disorganization and sedition created by recent events, may weaken the forces of the revolution and facilitate the criminal work of the counterrevolutionary elements.

Such a mistake is the manner in which individual government agents have carried out the prosecution of persons arrested for the affair of July 3–5, which gave the counterrevolutionary elements the opportunity to exploit for their own ends the struggle against anarchy that the revolutionary power is conducting in the name of the salvation of the country and the revolution.

The obscure game of the counterrevolutionary circles and the gutter press [consists of] throwing unfounded accusations of espionage and bribery in order to create an unhealthy atmosphere of slander, insinuation, and suspicion, and to betray the interests of the country for the sake of their fight against the revolution and the destruction of organs of the revolutionary democracy.

In exactly the same way, the counterrevolutionary [forces] will utilize for their own interests any indulgence of the criminal activities of the old regime or its police and security agents, any indecision in discharging unsuitable personnel from positions of authority, any vacillation in the cause of protecting the rights of democratic organizations, particularly those of army organizations, and any ambiguity in the realm of foreign policy.

Welcoming the explicit and clear declaration of the Provisional Government, which has put an end to misunderstandings that have arisen in connection with the foreign policy of the revolutionary government, and likewise the statements of the Minister-President, Comrade Kerensky, and the Minister of the Interior, Comrade Avksent'ev, concerning the general direction of the Government's policy, delivered at the Central Executive Committee meeting of August 4, the Central Executive Committee expresses its firm belief that the Provisional Government, without relaxing the resolute struggle against anarchy, will just as resolutely suppress the slightest manifestations of a counterrevolution and, relying on the support of the democracy and its organizations, will be able to consolidate the gains of the revolution and organize the defense of the country, carrying out the program of July 3.

Organizing all the forces of the nation for fulfilling the heavy and responsible tasks that confront the country at the present time, the Provisional Government will achieve the goal it has set for itself only by relying on the creative power of the revolutionary democracy and by decisively repulsing the counterrevolution which strives to destroy the revolutionary-democratic organizations in the rear and on the front in order to undermine the revolutionary power and inflict a mortal blow to the revolution.

The Central Executive Committee calls upon all workers, peasants, and soldiers to rally even more closely around their organizations in order to throw all their strength into assisting in the realization of the democratic policy of saving the country and the revolution.

Kamenev's Speech

The meeting welcomes the next speaker, Kamenev, with a storm of prolonged applause.

"I do not attribute this applause to myself," says the speaker. "I interpret this applause to mean that you want to express your censure of that campaign of slander against us which is now under way and which is inadmissible in any revolutionary country.

"As I see it, our policy has not changed during the entire period of my absence. This is evident from the resolution submitted by Tseretelli. You have no right to adopt such ambiguous resolutions which have nothing to say.

"We must state explicitly that every experiment in joining forces with the bourgeoisie constitutes the first step toward the downfall of the revolution.

"The Soviets wash their hands of the situation and keep themselves aloof, when the organized workers and soldiers sincerely request them to take the power into their hands. The revolution can only assume an international [scope] by rupturing its ties with the bourgeoisie."

. . .

Martov's Speech

Comrade Martov speaks on behalf of the Menshevik-Internationalists and sharply criticizes the activities of the Provisional Government.

"Comrade Tseretelli criticized the activities of the Provisional Government far too mildly in his speech," began Comrade Martov. "He touched on questions of domestic policy and foreign policy, as well as the question of war. But the discrepancy between his depiction and reality, as we observe it, is far too great. The situation is far worse than the picture drawn for us by Comrade Tseretelli. Let us just take the Ministry of War, where Kerensky and Savinkov show absolutely no objection to the attempts of counterrevolutionary forces to do away with army organizations. This presents the greatest danger to the cause of the revolution. When a struggle is conducted under the flag of the Provisional Government, which is endowed with our confidence, against the democratic organizations on the front, the popular masses cease to understand where the sphere of revolutionary power ends and where the work of the counterrevolution begins. . . .

"It is not our aim to discredit the Government, or, even more, to strive for its downfall. In controlling the actions of the Government, we must exert strong pressure on the Government, in order to counteract the pressure on the Government that is coming from the other side, from the side of the bourgeoisie and the counterrevolutionary elements.

"In speaking of foreign policy, Comrade Tseretelli left certain things unsaid. He forgot that the Minister of Foreign Affairs, Tereshchenko, announced at the conference in the Winter Palace that no one in Russia is now thinking about peace. Doesn't this contradict our program of July 8?

"At the present time the transfer of power into the sole hands of the democracy is impossible without a civil war. The moment is much too unpropitious. But this does not mean that we must refrain from exercising vigilance over the Government and must close our eyes on all its mistakes. We must tell the Government that we will not let it go beyond a certain point. . . .

.   .   .

"I have no intention of calling people out into the streets; I have no intention of insisting on the necessity of any kind of demonstration in order to force the Government to follow our policy; but in our resolution we must tell the Government that, apart from the vital forces of the Kadets and the military which are leading the Government, there exist still other forces, the forces of the revolutionary democracy, on which the Provisional Government should primarily lean. . . ."

.   .   .

Bogdanov's Speech

.   .   .

". . . There were many defects in the activities of the new Government. Let us only take the dismal events of July 3–5. We considered that the actions of individual persons and organizations that took part in organizing the street demonstrations of July 3–5 were criminal, and we believed that the most drastic measures should be taken for suppressing such demonstrations. Every action of the Government aimed at protecting the interests of the revolution against such demonstrations will continue to have our support, as has been the case up until the present time. But here something else has occurred which compels us to adopt a cautious attitude toward present events. The Counterintelligence [Service] became involved in this affair and confused all the issues. The street revolt and its organization were intermixed with German espionage. I assert that arrests are necessary and they are necessary to the extent dictated by the interests of the revolution."

"Within limits!" [cries] are heard from the benches of the Bolsheviks.

"Yes, within limits," continued Comrade Bogdanov. "And I am firmly convinced that, were Lenin and Kamenev in power, the majority of those present at this meeting would not be here, but at another place.

"The arrests were necessary, but the picture that is created by the manner in which these arrests were carried out gives rise to anxiety in the revolutionary democratic milieu. Alongside of arrests of Bolsheviks and the heavy penalties inflicted on them, Government representatives were freeing undisputable criminals, not only against the revolution, but against the new Russia as a whole. . . .

"The disbandment of regiments which participated in the events of July 3–5 was carried out extremely unsuccessfully. Whole regiments, which [claimed] only isolated cases of individual participation in these events, suffered alongside of the culprits.

"A gross error was also committed in the disarmament of workers. . . . There were cases of raids on organizations which were devoid of any guilt. This must be noted and acknowledged.

"The foreign policy of the Government remains the same. It rests on the platform of July 8. I consider it necessary to tell the Government about its defects, and I am sure that the democracy will regain its composure, [that it will] straighten out the activities of the Government and, unquestionably, benefit the democratic cause. Strict criticism and uninterrupted creative work are necessary if the democracy is to regain its force [in the country]."

. . .

Dan's Speech

. . .

"At a time when the wounds from the July 3–5 revolt have not yet healed, when the strength of the Soviets has considerably diminished after the revolt, we are again being requested to take the power into our hands. And if the proposal of the Bolsheviks were accepted by us, it would mean that we were consciously opening the way to a military counterrevolution. The Provisional Government is the product of the real correlation of forces and conditions in the country. The Government organization is not perfect, it makes mistakes, but the Soviets, as organs of action, cannot restrict themselves solely to criticism. A litigation is in process between the counterrevolutionary forces and the forces of the revolutionary democracy.

"Considering the conditions under which the Provisional Government has to work—when, on the one hand, it has to defend the country and, on the other hand, adopt drastic measures for increasing the combat potential of the army and take heroic steps in the struggle against economic disorganization—it is easy to criticize the Government, especially when the revolutionary who criticizes speaks in the role of an agitator and gives vent to his feelings.

"I have to say that we are disturbed most of all by errors which the Provisional Government commits in the rear and the front of our armies. . . .

". . . Having enumerated a number of errors committed by Government representatives, we would like to see a Government policy that is more revolutionary, more direct [in its course], and leaning primarily on democratic organizations.

"The Government itself realizes very well that the real strength and its support lie in the democratic organizations. . . . A Government that is strong by virtue of the support it receives from revolutionary organizations will act as a bulwark forestalling the expansion of the counterrevolutionary forces. However, if we were to destroy the established Coalition Government, we would achieve but one thing—we would remove the obstacles that are delaying the triumph of the dark counterrevolution. In criticizing and straightening out [the policy] of the Provisional Government, it is our duty at the present moment to support the Government in every way, for if we were to overthrow it, we would kill the last obstacle in the way of the counterrevolution. (*Applause.*)"

Riazanov's Speech

Comrade Riazanov followed, speaking on behalf of the Bolsheviks.

. . .

Comrade Riazanov gave a very sharp criticism of the activities of the Ministry of Justice and the Counterintelligence [Service] in connection with the arrest of Bolsheviks. He declared that Comrades Lenin and Zinoviev will appear in court and will give their explanations, in order to nail down the slanderers, but they do not want to go to prison now for the satisfaction of the Counterintelligence, which in no way differs from the Okhranka of the old regime.

. . .

"I would like to ask you," said Riazanov, "why the head of the Government has not once visited you in the Tauride Palace and has come here now for the first time. His visit reminds me of that of Nicholas II to the State Duma, while your speeches on the subject of this visit remind me of the speeches [delivered] by the Kadets on this subject in the State Duma, six months before the revolution."

The whole audience was in an uproar.

Presiding Comrade Gots called Riazanov to order and declared:

"I cannot allow any comparisons of this nature, and if you will in the future permit yourself to speak in this manner, I will deprive you of your right to speak."

. . .

Tseretelli's Second Speech

At the end of the meeting, Comrade Tseretelli delivered a long concluding speech.

"When I was listening," he said, "to the speakers who were hurling invective at the Provisional Government and the Central Committee, I thought that many could envy the vantage point of their position. It is always attractive on the surface to be in opposition to the Government. Attacks against the Government always give the impression of determination and courage. And grounds for such attacks are always available, because there is no government that makes no mistakes; especially now, in Russia, when both the war and the internal disorganization are undermining the power. Any power, by virtue of the fact that it stands at the head of the state, would reflect all the difficulties weighing upon the country, and personify the desperate position of the country. This is why the struggle for power in Russia has now assumed such unprecedented forms. [Everyone] is trying to throw [the reins of government] into the lap of the opposing side, calculating on the fact that when this opposing side finds itself incapable of coping with its task, the transfer of power to the other side will then be guaranteed as a change to something new. I repeat—it is very easy to attack the power at the present time.

. . .

"We must point out the mistakes of the Government, and point out ways of adjusting these mistakes, but we must also make note of the merits of the Government. One of the principal merits of the Government is its decisive action in defending democratic principles in foreign policy. Thanks to this policy, the struggle against the onslaught of foreign and domestic imperialistic forces has been made easier for the democracy.

"The events of July 3–5 inflicted an immense blow on the whole Russian revolution; they inflicted a blow on our international policy. We see the repercussions of this blow, not only at home but abroad.

"Irresponsible elements were operating in the ranks of the democracy. Accusations were flung at me here to the effect that I have sanctioned and have assumed responsibility for the charge of German espionage leveled at the Bolsheviks. This is not so. The very next day after the arrests, I gave a verbal reply to the Bolsheviks' inquiry in the Central Committee, and I said: 'I do not suspect the Bolshevik leaders, charged with instigating the revolt of July 3–5, of connections with the German Staff, but I consider that the instigation of the revolt was in itself a crime and a betrayal of the cause of the revolution.'

. . .

"Kamenev has rebuked us here for lack of courage. I will ask why it is that Kamenev and his friends lacked the courage, if they considered that the demonstrations of July 3–5 were beneficial to the revolution, why it is that they did not have sufficient courage to display their solidarity with this demonstration and announce openly: yes, we are acting for the good of the revolution and are prepared to assume the full responsibility for our actions. That is how Russian revolutionaries usually act, and have acted in the past. (*Storm of applause.*) If, however, they consider, or have considered, such demonstrations to be a betrayal of the revolution, then why is it that they did not and do not find sufficient courage within themselves to say openly: Anyone who rises against the majority of the revolutionary democracy, anyone who marches with arms in hand against the empowered organs of the revolutionary democracy, is an enemy of the revolution.

. . .

"I now turn to Comrade Riazanov and to those who are conducting a campaign against the Soviets, in defense of the Bolsheviks. Do you know that the only reason your proud speeches are pronounced here and are heard all over Russia is because the Soviets of Workers' and Soldiers' Deputies are still in existence? If you succeed in undermining the authority of the Soviets, then where will the revolution find its support? The Bolsheviks will not defend the revolution, Comrade Riazanov, and they will not create the support [necessary] for saving exhausted revolutionary Russia.

. . .

"I understand the psychological basis of the criticism of Comrade Martov, who does not take the altered correlation of forces into account. There is no question but that our Soviets have to consolidate the positions they held in the past. . . .

"Only with a sober revolutionary policy that takes the real correlation of forces into account can we succeed in strengthening the Soviets. If we were to start pushing the Soviet ahead, on the basis of its present strength, and knowing that it would be hard to expect victory, we would be taking an irresponsible and criminal step similiar to the one taken on July 3–5. It is time to realize that the Soviet alone cannot save the country. It is its duty, therefore, to unite the broad, popular masses and guide them on to the course of saving the country and the revolution. I am firmly convinced that this Government of ours will never enter into combat with the Soviets, because before that ever happens there would be a crisis as a result of the resignation of our comrades [from the Government]. We must display civic courage not only in criticizing this Government, but also in saying that we support this Government which has no miraculous remedies for the sudden recovery of the ravaged country. We must have the courage to tell the masses the truth about the position of the country and the revolution, and not keep throwing irresponsible slogans at the masses as in the past. We believe that the Provisional Government will unite all the forces for the salvation of the country on the basis of the platform of July 8, and only in the event that the present coalition government finds itself incapable of carrying out this general democratic policy will the democracy be compelled to seek another government. (*Applause.*)"

After Tseretelli's speech, the resolution submitted by Comrade Tseretelli on behalf of the Menshevik and Socialist Revolutionary faction, published by us in the preceding issue, was adopted by the majority of the meeting, with the Bolsheviks and the Internationalists opposing.

. . .

CHAPTER 26

The Moscow Conference

THE CALL

1223. CALL FOR THE MOSCOW CONFERENCE

[*Gos. Sov.*, pp. 330–31. The decision to call a conference was taken on July 12. *VVP*, No. 103, July 13, 1917, p. 2.]

(To the municipal dumas, zemstvo boards, universities and academic institutions, cooperative and trade union organizations, Soviets of Workers', Soldiers', and Peasants' Deputies, army soviets of the front, etc.)

In view of the exceptional current events, the Provisional Government, for the purpose of addressing all the organized forces of the country, has resolved to convoke the State Conference in Moscow from August 12 to August 14. [The following] are invited to participate in this Conference: representatives of political, public, democratic, nationalities, commercial, industrial, and cooperative organizations, leaders of organs of the democracy, highest representatives of the army [and] academic institutions, and members of the four State Dumas. Special invitations will be sent to the Supreme Commander and the former Minister-President, Prince L'vov. It is planned to hold the Conference in the Nicholai Palace in the Kremlin. The State Conference shall be opened by an address from the Minister-President, who will acquaint the members of the Conference with the situation of the country and the program of the new government. Speeches will follow by representatives of individual ministries, devoted to elucidations on individual branches of . . . state administration and the national economy. The organization of the State Conference has been assigned to the Minister of Post and Telegraph, conjointly with the Minister of Trade and Industry and the Minister of Transport. Over a thousand participants are anticipated.

1224. INSTRUCTIONS OF THE CENTRAL EXECUTIVE COMMITTEE OF THE SOVIETS OF WORKERS' AND SOLDIERS' DEPUTIES TO THE DELEGATION OF THE CENTRAL EXECUTIVE COMMITTEE AT THE MOSCOW CONFERENCE AND THE RESOLUTION ON THE CONFERENCE, AUGUST 10

[*Izvestiia*, No. 141, August 11, 1917, p. 4.]

Instructions

1. At the Moscow Conference members of the Central Executive Committee take part as delegates of the Central Executive Committee.

2. Member delegates of the Central Executive Committee have no right to speak either in their own name or in the name of any faction without the permission of the Presidium of the Central Executive Committee.

3. Member delegates of the Central Executive Committee cannot sign the declarations of this or that group at the Moscow Conference without the permission of the Presidium of the Central Executive Committee.

4. Only those groups and individuals may be delegates of the Central Executive Committee of Workers' and Soldiers' Deputies who accept the three points just indicated.

5. Individuals and groups belonging to the Central Executive Committee who violate its regulations will immediately be deprived of their mandates.

6. The delegation of the Central Executive Committee of Workers' and Soldiers' Deputies cannot make a single responsible statement without a previous preliminary deliberation by the delegation as a whole.

7. The delegation of the Central Executive Committee at the Moscow Conference has all the rights of the Central Executive Committee of Workers' and Soldiers' Deputies.

8. In order to attend to current matters of exceptional importance needing immediate attention, the Central Executive Committee authorizes a committee of five to act in its name.

9. A general meeting of the Central Executive Committee at Petrograd, during the Moscow Conference, can take place only under point 8.

Resolution

Standing at the head of the revolutionary democracy, the All-Russian Central Executive Committee of the Soviets of Workers' and Soldiers' Deputies has accepted the invitation of the Government and will participate in the Moscow Conference in order to defend, before the whole country, the path to the salvation of our exhausted native land as outlined by the revolutionary democracy.

The Central Executive Committee will point out that the only way to save the country and the revolution is by [achieving] the solidarity of all the vital forces of Russia around a strong revolutionary government which vigorously defends the country and fights for its salvation on the basis of the national platform in the sphere of domestic as well as international policy, proclaimed on July 8.

The toiling democracy is prepared to bear the heaviest sacrifices in this direction, but it will expect the same from all the other classes.

Any attempt to use the Conference for the purpose of inflicting a blow on the revolutionary democracy will be regarded by the All-Russian Central Executive Committee as a grave betrayal of the popular cause, and it will take every step to [gain] the solidarity of all the democratic participants at the Conference for [administering] the most decisive rebuff to the enemies of the people and the revolution.

The resolution was adopted.

1225. APPEAL OF THE CENTRAL COMMITTEE OF THE BOLSKEVIK PARTY
[*Gos. Sov.* pp. 333–34.]

The development of the counterrevolution is entering a new phase. From destruction and demolition it passes to the consolidation of the positions occupied; from excesses and outrages to "legal channels" of constitutional construction.

The revolution can and must be defeated, say the counterrevolutionaries. But this is not enough. They must also receive approval for this. Moreover, it must be so arranged that the approval will be given by "the people" themselves, by the "nation," and not only in Petrograd or on the front but in all of Russia. Then the victory will be secure. Then the conquests obtained can serve as grounds for new, future conquests of the counterrevolution.

But how is this to be arranged?

One could speed up the convocation of the Constituent Assembly, the only representatives of the whole Russian people, and request its approval for a policy of war and ruin, raids and arrests, massacres and executions.

But the bourgeoisie would not agree to this. It knows that at the Constituent Assembly, where the peasants will constitute the majority, it will obtain neither recognition nor approval of the counterrevolutionary policy.

But where is "the way out"?

"The way out" lies in substituting the "Moscow Conference" for the Constituent Assembly.

To call together a conference of merchants and industrialists, *pomeshchiki* and bankers, members of the tsarist Duma and domesticated Mensheviks and S.R.'s, in order to obtain, after proclaiming this conference a "national assembly," its approval of the policy of imperialism and counterrevolution and shift the burdens of war onto the shoulders of workers and peasants—this is "the way out" for the counterrevolutionaries.

The counterrevolution needs its own parliament, its own center; and it will create it.

The counterrevolution needs the confidence of "public opinion," and it will create it. This is the whole point.

In this respect the counterrevolution is following the same course as the revolution. It is learning from the revolution.

The revolution has its own parliament, its own effective center, and it felt that it was organized.

Now the counterrevolution is trying to create this right in the heart of Russia, in Moscow, through the hands of—the irony of fate—S.R.'s and Mensheviks.

And this at a time when the parliament of the revolution has been brought down to the position of a simple appendage of the bourgeois-imperialistic counterrevolution, when a deadly war has been declared on the Soviets and the committees of workers, peasants, and soldiers.

It is not difficult to understand that under these conditions the Conference which convenes in Moscow today will inevitably turn into an organ for the conspiracy of the counterrevolution against workers who are threatened with lockouts and unemployment, against peasants to whom land "is not given," against soldiers who are being deprived of the freedom obtained in the days of the revolution; a conspiracy covered up by the "socialistic phrases" of S.R.'s and Mensheviks who support this conference.

Therefore, the task of the leading workers is:

1. To tear the mask of national representation off the Conference, exposing its counterrevolutionary, antinational essence to light.

2. To expose the Mensheviks and the S.R.'s who are covering up this conference with the flag of "the salvation of the revolution" and leading the people into delusion.

3. To organize mass meetings of protest against this counterrevolutionary machination of "the saviors" . . . of the profits of the *pomeshchiki* and capitalists.

Comrades! Organize meetings and carry resolutions of protest against the "Moscow Conference."

Join the putilovites and organize collections today for the benefit of the hunted and persecuted party press as a sign of protest against the "conference."

Do not give way to provocation and do not stage any street demonstrations today.

1226. *Rech'* ON THE CONFERENCE
[No. 188, August 12, 1917, p. 1.]

.   .   .

It is already obvious that the Moscow State Conference will not consolidate the shaky position [of the Provisional Government], but will only [serve] to stress the inner contradictions of the irreconcilability of the two tendencies, the inevitability of the final choice, which was already manifest at the Winter Palace conference. On the one hand, the all-national Kadet program of July 15, which the Kadets later adopted during their congress, and which was further developed in the resolution of its Moscow Conference of August 10; on the other hand, a stubborn insistence on the program of July 8, an insistence that has grown stronger since the Party of the People's Freedom . . . has declared this program unacceptable. . . . Thus, as could be foreseen, the Moscow Conference, instead of strengthening the Government, will lead to a new crisis.

.   .   .

However, it may also be that such a consequence is not absolutely unavoidable, that even after the exposure of inner contradictions, the Government shall continue to exist, hesitating between the two opposite tendencies, which are splitting it.

. . . As the Government promises "to sell at a high price" its errors, then there remains nothing else but to follow it along this costly road, taking comfort [in the thought] that further errors would have cost the country still more.

Therefore, it is necessary to choose. If the Moscow Conference makes this choice, it will fulfill its historic role.

1227. *Rabochaia Gazeta* ON THE CONFERENCE
[No. 125, August 5, 1917, p. 2.]

And so, the Moscow Conference will take place. Apparently, the Provisional Government has firmly decided to gather in Moscow representatives of all organized public opinion, to unfold before them, without any concealment, the picture of the tragic situation of the country, and to pose the question of the support for the Government in saving the country and preserving the revolution.

Amid the revolutionary democracy, isolated voices are already speaking about a boycott of the Moscow Conference by democratic organizations. Indeed, why should democracy sit at the same table with the Philistines? Wouldn't it be better to demonstrate before the whole country—by refraining from participation in the Conference—that the bourgeoisie is isolated, that the propertied classes have no place among the living forces of the country, that the bourgeoisie, in its entirety, *has already passed* into the camp of counterrevolution?

If the revolutionary democracy should adopt this position of boycott, of undermining the Moscow Conference, it would commit a very grave political error.

It is not proved that all strata of the bourgeoisie have already passed to the side of counterrevolution. There is reason to believe in the possibility of agreement, at the Moscow Conference—in the name of the salvation of the country and the preservation of the revolution—with certain elements of the organized bourgeoisie which are still traveling a common road with revolutionary democracy.

But, suppose even that a considerable part of the bourgeoisie comes to the Conference with a rock in its pocket. Suppose it comes with a secret aim of struggling against the [Workers' and Soldiers'] Soviets and against the Provisional Government, which is being supported by them. Do we have, even in that case, reason to avoid a "face-to-face meeting" with the organized bourgeoisie?

On no account!

Revolutionary democracy is not afraid to find itself under the cross fire of attacks and accusations. It is not afraid of criticism.

Why, it is only because of its organized efforts that Russia has been saved from disintegration and ruin. Admittedly, there have been mistakes and blunders in the activity of the revolutionary organs of power, but the only person who does not make mistakes is the one who does not do anything!

Revolutionary democracy has no reason to fear that it will stand convicted in the eyes of the people and the whole world. . . .

1228. *Izvestiia* ON THE CONFERENCE
[No. 133, August 2, 1917, pp. 1–2.]

The Provisional Government has decided to call a conference of representatives of public organizations to convene in Moscow on August 12. A total of up to 2,000 participants is anticipated.

The very fact that such a conference is being called shows how critical is the position in which the country finds itself. The Government is forced to turn to all the vital forces of the country in order to explain the state of affairs to them and to call upon them for sacrifices without which the salvation of the State is inconceivable.

. . .

Everyone knows that the root of all the evils that have descended upon Russia lies in the World War, which for three years has been sucking all the lifeblood out of the country, which has for centuries been sucked by the vampires of autocracy. The earliest possible achievement of universal peace based on the principles already formulated by the Provisional Government of revolutionary Russia, has been, and continues to be, the only way leading to the real salvation of the country and the salvation of the revolution.

But until the international situation offers the possibility of achieving this desired international peace, the war must continue to be waged, and the 200 million population of Russia must be given the opportunity to live.

. . .

If patriotism, the salvation of the country, and the salvation of the revolution are not empty words, then let all the classes of Russian society show at the Moscow Conference what they are prepared to do and the kind of sacrifices they are willing to bring to the altar of revolutionary Russia.

. . .

The point is this: we know of dozens and hundreds of resolutions by political and trade union workers' organizations on restricting the struggle for wage increases; by peasants' congresses on repudiating seizures of land; by soldiers' meetings on the willingness to sacrifice their lives. But where can one find a single resolution by capitalists on restricting profits, or by industrialists on regulating production in the interests of the many millions of the poverty-stricken masses, or by landowners on the state control of rent, or by the propertied [classes] on increasing the taxation of income and capital?

We know of no such resolutions. Instead, we hear the same stereotyped, hypocritical words about the salvation of the country; we hear the barely suppressed sighs about the good old times when the worker, the peasant, and the soldier could be kept "in check" with the fist. And only in one respect does their unrestrained generosity manifest itself—in devising newer and newer repressions.

The Moscow Conference must show whether there still exists the moral fortitude among the propertied classes of Russia to enable them to forego their selfish mercenary interests at this time of national calamities and rush to the assistance of the country.

And then let all of Russia see. Let her see and judge.

1229. The Atmosphere in Moscow at the Opening of the Conference
[*Izvestiia*, No. 143, August 13, 1917, p. 2.]

The Moscow State Conference opened under somewhat unusual conditions: the trams are not running; coffee shops and restaurants are closed. At yesterday's meeting of the Soviet of Workers' and Soldiers' Deputies it was resolved to call upon the Moscow proletariat not to strike. However, the attitude of the proletariat toward the Moscow Conference turned out to be so negative that a meeting of the Bureau of the Central Trade Union, attended by representatives of all the district sections, was held late at night. And the meeting, which represented the 400 thousand Moscow proletariat, resolved almost unanimously to call a strike. The Union of Employees in Trade and Industry and the Printers' Union were the only ones who did not support this resolution. The newspapers will be out tomorrow in Moscow.

Enormous crowds, estimated at over 10,000 people, [began to gather] early in the morning at the Bolshoi Theater, where the State Conference is in session. The entire district adjoining the Bolshoi Theater was blocked off by a triple cordon of soldiers and cadets. Order was maintained by the regular and mounted militia. There was no disorder. No demonstrations occurred, since all the organizations, including the Bolsheviks, were making forceful appeals to the workers not to stage any demonstrations.

The crowd met the arriving delegates with considerable reserve. Only a negligible number of people expressed approval; for the most part, however, the attitude of the crowd was hostile; whistles were even heard. The scene reminded one of the historic days of the convocation of the First State Duma in Petrograd.

At 3:00 P.M. the conference hall was filled to capacity. The only empty seats were those reserved for the representatives of the Soviets of Workers' and Soldiers' Deputies. Their appearance at the Conference was somewhat delayed; they arrived when Minister-President Kerensky had already begun his speech.

The presidents of all the State Dumas—Rodzianko, Guchkov, Golovin, Khomiakov—were among the delegates attending [the Conference]. Only the late Muromtsev was missing. Veterans of the revolution—Kropotkin, Breshko-Breshkovskaia, Lopatin, and others—were present. Here, too, was the high command, headed by Alekseev and Brusilov. Here, too, were the captains of industry and banking. One gains the general impression that the representatives of the so-called "bourgeois" world overshadow the democratic elements. Morning coats, frock coats, and starched shirts dominated over blouses, but there was no way to determine the exact composition of the Conference. A particularly inscrutable element is the so-called "intelligentsia," representing the local and municipal self-governments.

THE PROCEEDINGS[1]

1230. KERENSKY'S OPENING ADDRESS
[*Gos. Sov.*, pp. 1–16.]

By the authority of the Provisional Government I declare the State Conference, called by the supreme power of the State of Russia, open under my presidency as head of the Provisional Government.

On behalf of the Provisional Government I greet the citizens of the State of Russia who have gathered here. I welcome especially our brother warriors who, under the leadership of their superiors, are now defending with great courage and wholehearted heroism the frontiers of the Russian State (*applause*).

. . . The Provisional Government called you to come here, sons of the motherland, in order to tell you frankly and directly the real truth of what awaits you and what our great, but weary and long-suffering motherland is experiencing now. We called you here to proclaim this truth in the very heart of the Russian State, in the city of Moscow. We called you in order that in the future no one should be able to say that he did not know and use this pretext to justify his actions that might lead to further disintegration and the ruin of the free Russian State (*applause*).

Frequently, as the hour of this great Conference approached, many were disturbed and others thought that this hour could be utilized against the tranquility of the State and against the safety of the motherland and the revolution. The Provisional Government was and continues to be guided by its great faith in the understanding and conscience of the Russian people. While changing in its membership, the Government remained true to its basic aims from the moment of the overthrow of the old despotic government. And it regards itself as the sole repository of the sovereign rights of the Russian people until the Constituent Assembly convenes (*tempestuous applause*).

May everyone know, and may those know who have once already attempted to raise their armed hand against the people's government, that these attempts will be stopped with iron and blood (*tempestuous, prolonged applause*). Therefore let those beware who already participated once in an unsuccessful attempt and who

---

[1] The Conference met in Moscow from August 12 to August 15. The selections that follow are from some of the more important and revealing speeches given by participants, who numbered about 2,400 and represented all social, economic, and political classes and organizations, excepting the Bolshevik, as well as the armed forces.

think that the time has come to overthrow with the help of bayonets the revolutionary government (*outcries*: "Bravo!" *and tempestuous applause*) . . .

We believe that we can freely and openly speak the truth. We have no fear that this truth will be heard only by our friends, it will also be heard by our enemies, and by those who destroy our troops and by those who here await the time when they can raise their heads and attack the free Russian people (*applause*). It makes no difference, because they often know the truth better through their agents than many Russian citizens (*outcries*: "Correct").

As before, this time we hide nothing from you. After the revolution we come for the first time as the Provisional Government to you, Russian citizens; we come to you with an open heart and with a profound sense of an intolerable, superhuman, infinite responsibility, which we bear and will continue to bear in spite of all the blows we suffer. Only by the taking of our life could the body of the great Russian democracy be torn and destroyed (*applause*. "Hurrah").

The situation is very grave. Our State experiences an hour of deadly danger . . .

. . .

. . . I have but one wish: that all of you here present, and each one individually, carry our words to the people, the parties, and the groups with which you are connected; that you carry them just as we in all our conscience tell you, without reinterpreting them, without putting into them a meaning they do not contain, without consciously and unconsciously distorting them in order to increase yet more the breakdown, disintegration, and ruin of our motherland. To see everything and to speak only of the joyous and pleasant things is impossible. One must tell everything, hoping that everyone will find sufficient strength within himself to detect in what has been said that grain of bitter truth which bears upon himself or his friends. Once more: our aim which we shall not abandon, our aim which we shall put forth all effort to carry out, this aim is the salvation of the State, the preservation of the honor and dignity of all the Russian people and the Russian State, and the struggle with everything which destroys this sole force and with those who interfere with the aims that the Provisional Government has set for itself.

I shall not speak about the detailed program. We shall not pause on what not infrequently has been said to the entire population in the Provisional Government's declarations (*applause*). For, if there was a period in the Russian revolution which was for the most part destructive, which destroyed the old foundations and created the new bases of the right to self-government for the entire people—now the time has arrived for organization, consolidation, and defense of the achieved rights of the Russian State as such. And as a government that respects its citizens but also respects itself, we have told you and shall continue to tell you frankly and openly what should be done, what we are doing and what we are aiming at . . .

To be sure, citizens, you must be interested in what we want, where we see the hidden and greatest danger, and [that for which] we appeal to the mind and conscience of our people. This of course is the army; this, of course, is that great hope and the only force which in the great union with the will of the people and the Provisional Government is the *ultima ratio*.

With the support of the democratic armed forces, of the revolutionary will and free expression of our people, we came into this world with our head raised high and we remained there, equal among equals, in the great battle and at the death feast of the peoples of Europe. But we came there with our own words and our own will. Beware lest these blows at the army, these blows at the will and authority of the sovereign authority of the Russian people make a breach in the very ideas for which we fight and open the gate to the enemies of the idea of freedom which you thought we defended poorly. We desire and we will see to it that no one dare relegate the Russian empire to second place in the chorus of world nations (*tempestuous applause*). We are asking no alms and we need no condescension. ("Bravo!" *Applause*). . . . I swear to you that whoever strikes the blow, whoever contributes toward our disgrace will face those who have no fear and do not run away from machine guns.

Following the unsuccessful proposals to us for a separate peace, we have just experienced an infamous attempt—an appeal to our allies through a neutral, most holy person with the same proposal for a separate peace.[2] However, the name of Russia did not appear among the addressees. (*Voices:* "Bravo!" *Applause*). Several months ago such attempts of the enemy aimed at us were rejected with indignation by the will of the people . . . Such attempts aimed in another direction were rejected with the same indignation and contempt by the governments friendly toward us. In the name of our great people I want to say one thing: we did not and could not expect any other answer. (*Tempestuous, prolonged applause of the conference addressed to the representatives of Russia's Allies, which becomes an ovation. All rise and continue to applaud while facing the box occupied by the representatives of the Allied powers.*) Misfortunes bring you closer. Of those who suffered great trials I must mention the Rumanian people, who suffered particularly; and I must say that if, as a result of common misfortunes and common errors, they (the Rumanian people) have to abandon their native land, they will find sufficient room and hospitality within the borders of our country.

We see signs of the weakening of our military front because of the breakthrough, also signs of the weakening of the international and national life of our free, revolutionary, and democratic Russia. The Provisional Government sees these symptoms which threaten us not alone in the insufficiently objective and neutral step of the papal throne; we see them also in the aspirations observed within the Russian State itself among some of the peoples who seemed to be indissolubly, vitally, and permanently bound with the free democracy by the common merciless fight for mutual freedom. We could have argued that languishing and dying in the chains of the tsarist autocracy, hateful to the Russian people, we did not spare our blood, we did not fear any sacrifices. For the good of all peoples inhabiting our country, we often forgot our own needs by exerting the will and the strength of a strong man (*applause*). And now, when the yoke of autocracy is overthrown, when the Russian free people—long-suffering, wounded, and disgraced—stretch their arms, when there are still some gangrenous parts, when as yet we have not settled with all the accursed heritage of the past, we can say: and where are you? Why do we fail to hear your voices casting your lot with us unconditionally, with no bargaining, in the fight for the common freedom with a great terrifying despotism? We do not hear them because of the suspicion and hatred toward the old regime.

---

[2] The Pope's peace offer. See Volume II, Doc. 1011.

The latter directed other blows at the non-Russian nationalities. To all the horror it added ridicule of what is most holy—the name of Jew or Ukrainian, Finn, Swede, or Armenian. This hatred, like a disease, is transferred to us, and they see in us the successors of the old oppression. But . . . hard as it is for us, the Russian democracy, for us, the Russian people, to bear this test of friendship which failed in time of misfortune, we will continue to keep our promise. We shall not retract what we gave and what will be given by the supreme master of the Russian land, the Constituent Assembly. The Provisional Government as the authority which has no unlimited right to deal with our forefathers' heritage and the future of our land will fulfill its duty to the entire state. And where the struggle goes beyond all bounds, where they try to take advantage of our difficulties by preventing the Russian people from expressing their free will, we say and we will say: Hands off! (*Applause.*) . . . It grieves me greatly to have to say that we might be confronted with a trial in the next few days: in our northern autonomous republic, Finland. In spite of her complete internal freedom and in spite of our professed good will, as testified by a special state act that gave or restored full power inside the country to the Grand Duchy of Finland—in spite of this, it is expected that an attempt will be made to take advantage of our difficulties and bring about by physical force the triumph of objectives and aims which are at this time impossible and which would spell ruin to the entire state. As head of the Provisional Government, as Minister of War, I will give appropriate instructions. This will not be tolerated . . . (*Boisterous applause. Shouts*: "Bravo.") And we hope that our decision will be supported by the full authority of all the people of the entire nation. (*Applause.*) We never went beyond the bounds of the constitution. We remain the protectors and guardians of both Russian and Finnish freedom. And the Finnish people will very soon be convinced that where there is no violence the Russian Government does not forget but gives yet more.

I do not wish to touch upon an intimate and fraternal strife. I have faith that the many millions of peasants, workers, and urban masses of brothers, bound by blood ties and common faith—the Ukrainians—in spite of many grievances and differences, perhaps due to misunderstanding, will never follow the course that would justify our saying: "And why, my brother, dost thou kiss me? And who gave thee thirty pieces of silver?" But these internal tensions, these moments when we experience a certain anxiety for the most immediate future, all these are signs of the same thing; they are signs of the decline in the eyes of others of our authority and the decline of their faith in the understanding, the might, and the will to live of our own people. (*Boisterous applause.*)

Our army is a force that we must keep pure, bright, and excellent. But this army is infected by a deadly cancer of the same heritage left to us from the past, the same faults in understanding, conscious bravery, and willingness to sacrifice that characterize all the Russian people. Before casting a stone at those who failed to pass the test, search your own souls. Did you pass the test? Did you always remain at your post? Did you merely use words about sacrifice or did you actually sacrifice? And did you see at the head of those who sacrificed voluntarily, as really was the case in the past, not only those who were poor, ignorant, and hungry, but those who were educated, rich, and wise? . . .

. . . And to you who have come here from the front I say, I, your Minister of War and your Supreme Commander, as a member of the Provisional Government I govern and I convey to you its will. There is no will and authority in the army higher than the will and authority of the Provisional Government. (*Tempestuous, prolonged applause. Cries*: "Bravo.") You may rest assured that we will protect you against demoralizing influences which creep into the army from the bottom and destroy at the bottom—it is the most terrifying thing—the shame which enables people who fear death to say that they do not want to fight for an idea. (*Tempestuous, prolonged applause. Cries*: "Bravo.") We fight them with all our strength. This anarchy from the left, this bolshevism, or whatever it is called, will find its enemy in our country, in the Russian democracy, which is imbued with the spirit of love for the State and with the idea of freedom. (*Applause.*) But I say once more: every attempt of bolshevism . . . any attempt to profit by the weakening of discipline, will be put to an end by me. (*Temptestuous, prolonged applause.*)

While still Minister of Justice I introduced in the Provisional Government the question of abolishing capital punishment. (*Applause. Cries*: "Bravo.") And as Minister of War it was also I who introduced in the Provisional Government partial restoration of capital punishment. (*Cries:* "Right!" *Boisterous applause, suddenly interrupted by the sharp and excited voice of the President.*) Who dares applaud when it is a question of capital punishment? Don't you know that at that moment, at that hour, a part of our human heart was killed? (*After the ensuing silence the Minister-President continues his speech.*)

But if it is necessary for the preservation of the State, if our words, warning of great trials, do not reach those who demoralize and pervert our army in the rear, we will pluck our heart out, but save the State. (*Tempestuous, prolonged applause.*) But let everyone know that this measure is a great temptation, that this measure is a great trial, and let no one dare submit absolute demands upon us on this point. We will not tolerate this. We merely state that if the elemental destruction, breakdown, faintheartedness and cowardice, treacherous murder, attack upon peaceful citizens, burning of inhabited and vacant dwellings, plunder—if all this continues, in spite of our warning, the Provisional Government will find sufficient strength and will use the means dictated at the time to fight these.

Moreover, citizens, no one will take away from us what was gained by the Russian people and the Russian army. You will recall that we gained our freedom only because, at the hour of deadly danger this winter, the armed and unarmed people clasped each other's hands in a union of life and death. Together we won, and we are all equal masters at the new free helm of the Russian State. The experience of these months showed that all that had been created casually, at times feverishly, at times insufficiently thought through, is now subject to revision and proper implementation as the rights as well as the duties of every man who serves in the Russian army. And, gentlemen, that for which many now blame the revolution was an expression of elemental forces and not the play of deliberately evil forces of the revolution. This may be seen from the fact that all that shocks and provokes indignation on the part of the present restorers of the army was carried out before me and in spite of me by their own hands. (*Voices*: "Right.") It was only the elemental force, it was only a process of the breakdown of the old ties and [the erection of a] casual hasty structure. This haste was necessary. Otherwise the whole tremendous body of material following the fall of the despotic military authority would have collapsed. It was held back from this inclination to fall apart. Now this rough draft will turn into a clean copy. Everything will be put in its place; everyone will know his rights and duties! And not only the duties to command but also the duties to execute the commands (*applause; voices*: "Right") ; not only the duties of those who give orders, but also the duties of those who receive them. Those who formerly were unlimited in giving commands as well as those who execute the commands should be aware of their rights. Commissars and committees and disciplinary courts will be preserved . . . (*applause, chiefly from seats occupied by military representatives*). But everything will be given those forms which the army needs now and which must be, not transitory phenomena, but an unchanging part of the army organism. We army people and those who have been in the army, we know where the limits of the possible end and where the impossible and the adventurous begin. And wherever those limits exist, the Provisional Government will say: not one step farther! The Provisional Government will be able to make its voice heard to such an extent that no one will have reason to think that the plenary power of the Provisional Government is a one-sided power which leaves an opening on the other side.

Permit me, citizens, not to dwell at length on these measures. I must merely testify to one thing, namely, that from the moment of my joining the Ministry of War, not one measure was passed that might have weakened the force of the army or the authority of the commanding personnel. (*Applause.*) At the very outset I initiated a systematic and planned revision, codification, and coordination of all the new institutions in the army which must become law. But more than anything else I regard it as necessary and important to say here that the entire army from bottom to top and from top to bottom, that the entire army, regardless of rank and position, must be a model of discipline and subordination of the junior to the senior, and of all to the supreme authority. (*Applause.*) As Minister of War, I take the liberty of telling you, citizens of the Russian land: the ills of the army were just as accidental and transitory as those of the entire Russian State. But under the stunning blows of great trials the will to live is born, the will to discipline, the will to fulfill one's duty. And in this will, in this reason and conscience lies the guarantee of resurrection and salvation of Russia and the Russian army. (*Prolonged applause.*)

My colleagues, members of the Provisional Government will present to you in greater detail those aspects of the life and economy of the Russian State which they have studied more carefully than I. I merely want to say that you will be confronted with a picture of great collapse, great processes of destruction, frequently with impoverishment. You will have a picture of the threat of famine which faces us. Therefore I think you will understand why we called you and why at this hour we talk with you chiefly not about what should be done, but how it should be done . . . And, I repeat, if we lack understanding and conscience, if—I repeat again—we are inundated by the wave of collapse and breakdown through personal interests and interparty disputes, we will tell our country about this, we shall call to her for help. But now we shall ourselves, using our unlimited power, move with iron and all the strength of the compulsory apparatus of the state power wherever there is violence and arbitrary action. (*Applause.*)

1231. Prokopovich's Speech
[*Gos. Sov.*, pp. 20–32.]

Citizens, the Provisional Government has instructed me to give you an account of the general features of the present state of the national economy and the general principles of economic policy to which the Provisional Government subscribes, which are being carried out by its organs. It stands to reason that, inasmuch as we are speaking of the present state of the national economy, the dominant factor which determines all and everything is the war. The war has diverted masses of workers from the national economy. The war is costing us a colossal price.

With your permission I will read you the basic figures: in the first year of the war, from July 1914 to July 1915, the war cost us 5.3 billion rubles; in the second year, 11.2 billion; and in the third year we have already spent 18.6 billion on the war. In order to evaluate the significance of these figures, we must juxtapose them with the amounts of the national income and the aggregate of all material values which our national economy produced during normal times before the war. In accordance with my instructions to the Economic Council, the national income of the country was computed for the year 1913, the last year before the war. The following results were obtained: our total national income in rubles for the pre-war period amounted to approximately 16 billion rubles in normal rubles. This is what we had at our disposal. Enormous demands were made on this national fund as a consequence of the war. There was no way in which we could have covered the 18.5 billion rubles which we expended in the third year from this fund of 16 billion rubles, had not, of course, the value of this ruble fallen sharply. In general, it must be estimated that during the third year of the war we spent up to 40–50 per cent of our national income on the war, [that is,] from 40 to 50 per cent of all the material goods which the country produces and by which it exists. There can be no doubt that we were inadequately prepared for waging such an enormous and expensive war.

Furthermore, there is still another factor which has an extremely adverse effect on our economic position, namely, the fact that from the very beginning, from the first year of the war, we were cut off from the world market. Our allies have the possibility of receiving these material goods, the manufactured goods and arms which they need: guns, bread, clothes, material for clothes; all these they can receive from the world market. Consequently, the burden on their domestic economy, on their national economy, is relatively insignificant, in comparison, of course, with ours: we are forced to obtain everything from our own country. According to the data which we have at our disposal, only approximately 16 per cent of the war expenditure is furnished by foreign imports, [whereas] 84 per cent is furnished by the domestic market. Under this state of affairs, when we are forced to give away almost 40–50 per cent of the national income to the war, it stands to reason that the first condition that had to arise within the country was a shortage of goods. . . .

Finally, as concerns industry, this state of affairs necessarily produced a disastrous drop in production; the average output per worker in the Donets Basin has now dropped 50 per cent. The extraction [of minerals] has fallen to approximately half. These are the conditions that inevitably arise as a result of such a diversion of material goods into the war, and this would have proved absolutely fatal had not the government intervened at this point [to exercise] its regulating authority.

Under such a state of affairs, absolute freedom of trade and absolute, unrestricted ownership rights over goods and the means of production would have necessarily led to impoverishment and extreme hardship for the popular masses. Therefore, the regulating intervention of the state—regulating in the sense of establishing fixed prices, in the sense of exercising a determining influence in the distribution of goods among the different classes of the population, and, finally, in the sense of a regulating intervention, in certain cases, in industry—is essential to the country. The Government has followed this course.

I am convinced that there is not a single person in this audience who would advocate absolute freedom of trade and unlimited rights of private ownership during a war which is as heavy to bear as the present one. . . .

At the present time, citizens, the Provisional Government has created a Central Economic Committee which will become the regulating center of our whole national-economic life. During the past few days the Economic Council has studied and approved the plan for its [projected] organization, and will submit it to the Provisional Government within the next few days.

. . .

. . . One can hope that in the not-too-distant future we will have at our disposal a public-administrative apparatus capable of satisfying completely the needs of both the army and the population. In the meantime, while we are on the subject of satisfying these needs, [I must say that] the situation is extremely grave. I must say this openly, citizens.

I will begin with the work of the Ministry of Food. I ask you to look carefully at the picture which this Ministry presents. The position of the country with respect to food supply is very difficult at the present time. Total procurements of grain and forage, assigned to the Ministry of Food, are approaching the level of 700–800 million poods* for this fourth year of the war.

Meanwhile, only 300 million poods were required for the first year, 500 million for the second year, and 600 million poods for the third year. You can see how the procurements are increasing, how the demand for grain is growing in the country. The amount of fat which must be procured for the army alone is 8.5 million poods; the amount of meat is 50 million poods. These demands on the national economy are staggering. Meanwhile, in many areas the population is not provided with that basic food product—bread. . . .

. . .

The Ministry's available grain reserves have recently fallen to a very low level (26 million poods for August 1), perhaps to a critical minimum. It was only toward the end of February that the grain reserves fell to such insignificant proportions (around 20 million poods for March 1, not including a similar amount which was stored at the docks awaiting the opening of navigation), i.e., at the time of the revolution. In addition, the extreme disorganization in transport . . . makes it difficult to use these reserves for eliminating cases of dire need.

In the beginning of July [the Ministry] succeeded in raising the level of grain reserves at the front to the norm of a month and a half [supply], i.e., to a relatively favorable condition. But the Tarnapol' breakthrough on the Southwestern Front, accompanied by the loss of its supplies and the disorganization in its rear, left the front in a very difficult position. Supplies were transferred from other fronts for its relief, in particular from the Western and Northern fronts, to which it is especially difficult to send grain. In addition, there was a noticeable drop in the middle of July in the quantity of grain shipped to the army. As a result, the food [supply] situation on the front took a sharp turn for the worse.

* The original initially read 700–800 million, which was corrected to 1,000–1,100 million; the newspaper accounts also give [the figures of] 700–800 million poods.

August is undoubtedly the most difficult month in the food [supply] campaign, which is being conducted on a nation-wide scale. During the harvesting season, which has far from ended in many places, the conveyance of grain to wharves and [railroad] stations naturally falls to a minimum. One can count on a slight improvement in the situation in the future. The rural population of the consumer guberniyas is now gathering the crops and will be supplied with its own grain for the coming months, while in the south, procurements for towns and for the army from the new harvest can be begun. In general, the grain resources of the country must be considered as being in a very precarious state, with quite a serious shortage of groats. There will be enough grain, and [some] left over. But it is extremely difficult to obtain this grain and distribute it. The parity in the interchange [of goods] has been disturbed and it is inconceivable to restore it under the present conditions: under no circumstances can the village receive equal value in exchange for its products. Even should the demands which are made in this respect by the village population be satisfied, they could not produce the necessary results.

These demands are as follows:

a) An increase in fixed prices. . . .

b) The establishment of fixed and equitable prices on manufactured goods, iron, and other industrial products necessary to the village. . . .

c) Enactment of labor conscription. (*Applause.*) . . .

The technical apparatus at the disposal of the food supply organization is very weak and in many places it cannot satisfy the most modest desires. This is explained by the fact that the people who were forced to take charge of food supply were often completely inexperienced in [this field], possessed no professional training, and, furthermore, were forced to carry on this work without having the proper technical equipment at their disposal. Thus, they are forced to work under highly unfavorable and extremely difficult conditions. Naturally, they commit blunders and mistakes and they often lose control of the situation. It must be said that the law did not prevent them from inviting the [cooperation of the] commercial apparatus in this work, and that no obstacles of this kind were set up by the Ministry. This [choice] was left entirely up to the local organs. In certain places they are using the commercial apparatus quite extensively. For example, in Ufa guberniya the grain sacking in 320 out of 376 [instances] is carried out by large-scale and average merchants who were recommended by a special public organization and are working under the control and supervision of local food and other committees. In Samara guberniya 40 per cent of the grain is sacked in this manner. In other places the commercial apparatus is used to a more moderate extent, preference being given to the cooperative and zemstvo apparatus and even to their own [apparatus] established specifically for this purpose. In many places, however, the commercial apparatus is not used at all. The principal reason for this is the extreme distrust and even outright hostile attitude toward the commercial class on the part of the local population. Even should they so desire, the food committee workers are incapable of overcoming this [attitude]. Cases of food supply boards and even committees being dissolved for their attempts, or even mere intentions, to avail themselves of the services of the merchants are not infrequent. The extremely negative attitude of the population toward the commercial class is explained, partly, by the attitudes they bring to the work of the grain monopoly, [i.e.,] their unwillingness or their inability to reconcile themselves to the role of commissioners and agents of the state acting under strict control and within a definite framework, and, chiefly, by the hatred which the merchants, personified by speculators and marauders, have inspired against themselves among the population, especially during the war. However, the Ministry has not lost hope that the technical apparatus, which is undergoing gradual improvement, will finally be perfected. The commercial class, by its loyal actions and organizational activities, perhaps may be able to overcome the hostile attitude of the population, and thus place its professional experience and its technical apparatus at the disposal of state institutions, renouncing its self-interested class pursuits—at least for the duration of the war—and offering no resistance to the most stringent control by organs of the democratic power. In addition, the rapidly expanding and increasingly better-organized network of cooperatives will become even more . . . adapted to carrying out its social and legal obligations in the field of food supply. And the food supply organs will develop their own apparatus. But most important of all, the experience and the professional practice which they are gradually acquiring will insure them against new mistakes and blunders.

Regulating control, similar to that exercised in providing the country with articles of prime necessity, is also needed in the realm of agriculture. A general land reform must be the concern of the Constituent Assembly. A draft of this reform is being worked out by the state committee on land, but a certain amount of regulating control over the utilization of private property is already necessary at the present time. Of course, any regulation of land relations before the convocation of the Constituent Assembly can be carried out only in the interest of the country as a whole and under the systematic guidance of the Provisional Government; no prejudgment of questions that lie in the province of the Constituent Assembly must be allowed, nor must the determination of land policy be left up to any local institutions or organizations. It is in precisely this light that both the Provisional Government and the Ministry of Agriculture regard their tasks in the realm of land policy. In this respect the work of the land committees provoked much criticism. I consider it necessary to establish one chronological date: the statute on land committees was approved on April 21 (the Ministry [headed by] Shingarev), and at that same time [it was announced] in a special proclamation that these committees were charged with the responsibility of "settling arguments and misunderstandings regarding land affairs." The task of the Provisional Government and the Ministry of Agriculture at the present time is to restrict the sphere of competence of local land committees, and to regulate and subordinate their activities to law. The contemplated direction of this regulation can be judged by the three bills submitted by the Ministry of Agriculture—on the preservation of forests and their exploitation, on regulating land relations, and on courts of conciliation.

I read a completely false report in the newspapers to the effect that the bill on the rules governing the preservation of forests and their exploitation has been rejected by the Provisional Government. Certain corrections had been inserted at a session of the Provisional Government, but there had been no rejection whatsoever of the bill submitted by the Ministry of Agriculture. This newspaper report does not conform to reality; it is not true. In order to judge the contemplated direction [to be taken] in regulating land relations, I will pause on this bill. Its substance consists of assigning the supervision over cutting the timber essential for satisfying the needs of the nation to a central organization on satisfying fuel needs, the so-called "Special Council on Fuel," or, abbreviated, "Osotop." The function of local land committees is to regulate the forest exploitation necessary for satisfying the needs of the local population.

Thus, we see that this bill attempts to satisfy equally the national needs of the country regarding the preservation of forest resources and their protection against sometimes unwitting and totally unnecessary plunder, as well as the national needs regarding fuel and construction material, and, at the same time, the needs of the local population. This, strictly speaking, is the substance of this bill. These basic principles of the bill met with the complete support of the Provisional Government. . . .

I will now turn to the third ministry, the Ministry of Trade and Industry. I emphasize "the Ministry of Industry," and not of industrialists. I think that the whole nation is interested in the development of industry; all the people [are interested], everyone—consumers as well as producers, industrialists as well as workers. (*Storm of applause.*) . . . Therefore, the basic tasks of the Ministry of Trade and Industry are indisputable for all political currents: 1) it is necessary to safeguard existing industry, 2) it is necessary to assist in the development of new branches, and 3) it is necessary to be concerned in the development of the most perfect forms within each individual branch of industry.

Three sets of questions now confront the Ministry of Trade and Industry as it sets out to accomplish these tasks. The most urgent and difficult . . . question is that of arresting the destruction of industry, which is occurring for a variety of reasons, and of applying every means to increase its productive capacity in most of the branches of the national economy. Next in importance is the preparation of a plan for the transition of industry to peacetime conditions in order that this transition will not be accompanied by the termination of business in those branches of industry which are now geared entirely to war production. The third question concerns the elaboration of a sound plan regarding those principles which, in the interests of the Russian national economy in general, and of industry in particular, must be insisted upon in concluding postwar trade agreements.

.   .   .

As basic measures, it is necessary to increase the procurement of fuel and raw materials of all kinds and to achieve maximum production on the railroads and in car and train construction, since the root of all these evils is the poor state of transport and the shortage of fuel and raw materials. Another important factor in the industrial chaos is the conflict in the sphere of industry and the decline in productive forces. The Ministry of Trade and Industry, in complete accord with the Ministry of Labor, considers that the following are basic measures which must be adopted in combating this evil: 1) the rights of the enterprise owners in the management of business must be guaranteed by an appropriate clarification of workers' rights, and the interests [of the enterprise owners] must be protected against manifestations of anarchy by appropriate Government measures;* 2) there must be state control over enterprises such as will assure the workers that no malicious measures are being undertaken against them by the employers (*applause*); 3) fixed prices must be established on most consumer goods, and

* In *Russkoe Slovo* there follows: *Stormy applause from the seats of the industrialists.*

fixed wages in the most important branches of labor (*applause*) ; 4) there must be a restriction on the size of profits of enterprise owners by means of a normal percentage [rate] (*applause from the left*), which would guarantee a working capital in industry and, at the same time, would insure the population against the excessive enrichment of industrial enterprise owners at its expense; 5) a general law on labor conscription, or a series of partial laws introducing a compulsory minimum number of working days per month and a minimum daily output, must be issued; 6) the Central Economic Committee must unify all the economic legislation on [furnishing] the country with supplies, and carry out a single nation-wide plan for supplying all branches of the national economy. Such, citizens, are the tasks of the Ministry of Trade and Industry. As I have already said, the Ministry of Trade and Industry is acting in complete accord with the Ministry of Labor on questions regulating labor.

Now I shall turn to a brief characterization of the basic principles which govern the activities of the Ministry of Labor. First of all, it considers all those coercive measures that had, unfortunately, taken place in many areas of Russia and in many industrial enterprises, such as the conveyance by wheelbarrows[3] or coercion over the administration, to be absolutely inadmissible manifestations of anarchy. (*Applause.*) Every measure must be taken to protect the management against persons guilty of such coercive measures, including the prosecution of such persons . . . for criminal liability. (*Applause from the right. Cries:* "Right!") The Ministry of Labor considers the interference of workers in the management of enterprises to be inadmissible. The right of hiring and firing employees and workers belongs wholly to the management, unless a special agreement on this score exists between the workers and the administration and providing this [agreement] conforms to law. Having an extremely negative attitude toward any worker's interference in the matter of management, the Ministry of Labor supports in every way the development of collective agreements on employment, the so-called agreements on wage scales, which alone, in the belief of the Ministry of Labor, can settle the labor question. As for the usual conflicts, which contain the features neither of coercion nor of interference in the rights of the management to manage the enterprises—all these conflicts, in the opinion of the Ministry of Labor, must be first of all subject to examination by [a court of] arbitration, and conflicts in enterprises which are considered vital to the national interest must be subject to compulsory examination by a court of arbitration. Proceeding from these basic principles, the Ministry of Labor worked out a whole series of bills, and several of these bills have already been approved by the Provisional Government and have received the force of law. Such, for example, are the law on the protection of woman and child labor, the change in the old law on workers' sickness and accident insurance, and, in addition, the law on courts of conciliation. At the present time the Ministry of Labor is drawing up bills on the freedom to strike, on labor markets, on labor agreements, on unemployment insurance, and on courts of arbitration.

. . . Collective agreements establish the rate of payment for piecework and make provisions for prohibiting the shortening of the working day below the

---

[3] Reference is to the practice of carrying unpopular owners and managers out of factories in wheelbarrows.

established norm of eight hours. This norm is computed from calculations based on one month; consequently, the Ministry is fighting against a decrease in the number of working days per month and a decrease in working hours per day. Furthermore, it stands for prohibiting any gatherings or meetings during working hours. (*Applause and cries:* "Right!") It is the deep conviction of the Ministry of Labor that all these measures may be systematically carried out only if state control over enterprises is exercised and profits are restricted. (*Applause.*)

I now turn to the work of the Ministry of Transport. In view of the great strain on the whole railroad mechanism during the entire course of the present war, in view of the sharp, recent fall in labor productivity, the decline in the authority of railroad managers and in the discipline of employees, and in view of the shortage of material and spare parts, the situation that has arisen in the railroads is extremely grave. Comparing the seven months of the present year to the same period of last year, 980,000 cars remain unloaded, 250,000 of which fall within the one month of July. This [figure] constitutes approximately 15 per cent of a normal commercial turnover on our railroads. . . .

. . . .

. . . We should abandon all illusions with regard to a possible increase in railroad transport in the near future; we cannot count on American rolling stock, since not more than 375 steam engines will be received before January; at the same time autumn is approaching and the percentage of damaged steam engines, progressively increasing since the [level of] 16.8 per cent in January of the current year, reached the unprecedented figure of 25 per cent on August 1 and shows a tendency for further growth, whereas last year this comprised a mere 18 per cent. Having 800 more steam engines at hand on August 1 than in the previous year, we have at the same time 1,427 fewer steam engines in operation than in the past year. The number of cars impossible to repair has almost doubled in comparison to last year. This enormous increase in the amount of damaged steam engines is explained, on the one hand, by the wear and tear on these engines during the course of the war—during these three years of monstrous work which fell to their lot—and, on the other hand, by insufficient work in railroad workshops, where repair and reconditioning of damaged steam engines is proceeding at an extremely slow rate at the present time. Previously, the work proceeded slowly owing to the absence of raw materials and metals. At the present time the steam-engine workshops are supplied with all the raw materials and metals designated in the requests submitted for July and August by the railroad management, and the chief difficulty now lies in the slow rate of work in these railroad workshops. Apart from [the measure] calling for the transfer of steam engines that require repair to the shipbuilding and locomotive construction plants, the Provisional Government has outlined a series of resolute measures for improving sanitary conditions and restoring normal working conditions on the railroads. These measures will be published and put into practice within the next few days. Nevertheless, one cannot close one's eyes to the fact that during the winter there will be major transport difficulties and it will be necessary to cut down the shipment of even priority and urgent items in every way.

Such, citizens, is the ugly, grave picture of our economic situation.

With every month the productive capacity of our country progressively declines.

Only sacrifices can save our native land, save the Russian State, save the revolution, save the cause of the revolution and our freedom. And the Provisional Government calls on you [to make] these sacrifices. The Government asks, it demands sacrifices from you. Let the capitalist renounce excess profits (*applause*), let the worker renounce excess rest (*applause*).

We know how the profits have changed during the years of the war. They have grown. The critical moment has now arrived. The profits must be renounced, the country must be saved.

We know how labor productivity has fallen. . . . In general, we are seeing an enormous decline in labor productivity. Of course, this decline can be attributed, to a certain extent—perhaps to a large extent—to the worn-out state of equipment, to the wear and tear on the machines, but, at the same time, this decline is partly attributed to the slackness of labor. And this must be taken into consideration. It is an indubitable truth, and we must state it flatly.

Citizens, our economic life cannot go on like this. A continued decline in productive forces threatens ruin to the whole state, the whole people, the army, to all of us, to the cause of the revolution. Citizen-capitalists, place your managerial talents and your capital at the disposal of the Provisional Government. Citizen-workers, give your labor to the state. Citizen-peasants, feed the army and the town and those who work in the defense of the country with your grain. The salvation of the country lies in your sacrifices. (*Applause. Commotion in the hall.*)

1232. Nekrasov's Speech

[*Gos. Sov.*, pp. 33–43.]

CHAIRMAN: The Deputy Minister-President and the Minister of Finance, Nekrasov.*

NEKRASOV: . . .

. . .

From the report of the preceding speaker—the Minister of Trade and Industry—you have already heard those figures that characterize the problems of the Minister of Finance at the present time. I will permit myself to remind you of them only once again so that this picture will be completely clear to you. The picture is simple and definite. Essentially, it adds up to only one figure: 15 billion rubles outstanding for the period through January 1, 1918. It seems to me that there is no point in giving you further details . . . This figure speaks for itself. Everything else that must be said on other subjects necessarily pales before this figure.

How did we get ourselves into this position?

Citizens, there is a very widespread opinion at present that the revolution was the factor which had a vitiating influence on Russia's finances. And I will say that there is a certain element of truth in this assertion. The objective language of figures tells us that even after taking into account the whole growth of

---

* According to the account in *Russkoe Slovo: The appearance of N. N. Nekrasov on the rostrum is met with weak applause; the right and part of the center are demonstratively silent.*

unfavorable circumstances which had accumulated up to the time of the revolution, and taking into account all those unfavorable circumstances which arose [later], producing what is called involution in mathematics—all those factors still do not explain that financial distress in which we find ourselves [today] unless we take into account the influence of the revolution and those special circumstances that it created.

Not a single period in the history of Russia, not a single tsarist government, has been marked by such extravagance; I will not touch on the motives behind this extravagance, but not one was as generous in its spending as the government of revolutionary Russia. Citizens, we must bear this truth in mind, because we now have to pay for all the sins of the past, and it would be a mistake, on the one hand, to lay the entire blame on the previous tsarist government and, on the other, to transmit the results of all this onto the shoulders of the future generations of our successors. These are the two basic considerations which guide the Provisional Government.

Now it is necessary not only to look for the mistakes and failings of the old regime, but, also, to look completely objectively and dispassionately at the activities of the revolutionary period. . . . If I am to speak in the language of figures, I would not know of another more eloquent table characterizing this role of the revolutionary period than the figures showing the issuance of bank notes for the entire period of the war.

. . .

In order that you may have a clear understanding of what we have to do, permit me once again to cite you a few figures which will illustrate the basis of our present national budget, and permit me to say, first of all, that this budget is highly aberrant in its construction, that it does not in the least reflect the picture of the real expenditure with which we are concerned. The blame for this rests with that 18th clause of the budget rules against which the State Dumas have led a long and futile fight. This clause [calls for] setting apart all the expenditure on the preparations for, and the conduct of, war in a special military fund, separate from the normal budget. As a result, we now have two budgets: one presenting a picture of a relatively illusory state of well-being, and the other harboring all the elements of the menacing danger in store for us. . . .

. . .

. . . Only when you turn to the military budget will you see the real picture. For the four-year period you see 49 billion rubles of expenditure and 35 billion rubles of revenue. Here lies the source of our staggering deficit. . . . The Provisional Government could not remain indifferent to what it had to face in making disbursements from the military fund. Here, more than anywhere else, it could not afford such disbursements. Here, more than anywhere else, we encountered criminal irresponsibility which reached the verge of complete permissiveness. . . . Disbursements from the military fund must be placed on a basis such as to permit the verification and control of these disbursements, not four months after they are made, but at the very moment that they are being contemplated. (*Applause; voices from the audience:* "Right!") And the Provisional Government accepted this basis. Representatives of the Ministry of Finance were introduced into all those institutions where it was necessary to work together with the State Control, in order to be present at the very time that funds were expended, at their place of origin, and in order to have the opportunity, without causing any detriment to the fighting capacity of the army, to stop those unnecessary expenses with which we have had to deal only too often. . . .

At the same time, citizens, we must say that in appealing for economy on the front, we cannot ignore [the need] for economy in the rear. . . .

. . .

At this Conference one can only state the truth, regardless of how bitter it may be. I must say that the new revolutionary order is proving to be much more costly to the state treasury than the old order. Citizens, this truth cannot be ignored. . . . According to preliminary estimates, the expenses of food supply committees on their organizations may reach 500 million rubles per year. (*Exclamations of amazement.*) According to the preliminary estimates of the Ministry of Finance, the expenses of land committees were calculated to be 140 million rubles a year. (*Exclamations of amazement.*) I don't have to tell you that the state treasury cannot endure such expenses and that there must be a limit to them. (*Storm of applause; cries:* "Right!") . . .

And I will say that there is still another factor which has an extremely strong influence on the state treasury. It is unnoticeable at first, and it, too, becomes evident and patent only afterwards: it is the increase in workers' wages. (*Cries:* "Right!") Let me tell you that in the Putilov plant alone, the demands that were presented for the period ending this year, the demands for credit from the state treasury, are reaching 90 million rubles. (*Commotion in the audience.*) . . .

At the very beginning of the revolution the demands for wage increases were easily satisfied, particularly in enterprises that worked for national defense and in certain private enterprises. It seemed as though this was, so to speak, a family matter, that the industrialists and the workers would regulate this problem among themselves. This was a profound error. All these demands ultimately find their way into a memorandum to the Minister of Finance. For even private industry cannot endure the expenses that it is forced to incur, and, in one form or another, it makes its appearance either at the desk of the Minister of Finance or at the State Bank with demands for emergency credit and with demands for unauthorized loans, to which the Ministry of Finance cannot accede. It is characteristic that the representatives of the workers' democracy are the first to come to the support of these demands.

. . .

. . . The other side of the coin, the question of our source of revenue, is far from being in such a satisfactory state as to enable us to regard it with equanimity. I still do not have any data on tax returns and public revenues covering any considerable length of time. But even that [information] which I do have at my disposal gives me grounds to say that in this regard we are running up against partisanship and inadequate understanding of the immediate problems of state.

Comparing the first three months [of this year] with [the same period] in 1916, the returns from the tax on state lands dropped 32 per cent; from the tax on urban real estate, 41 per cent; from the dwelling tax, 43 per cent; from the special wartime tax, 29 per cent; from business licenses, 19 per cent; from mortgage payments, 11 per cent; from inheritance taxes, 16 per cent; from insurance taxes, 27 per cent; from redemption payments, 65 per cent. . . . And only if increased pressure is exerted in assessing and collecting taxes will it be possible to reduce to a certain extent this difference in the yields from revenue.

Our sources of revenue are similarly strained to the extreme, and I will say that that aspect of them which is called direct taxation is under particular strain. According to the account given by the Chairman of the Commission on the problems of taxation, these direct taxes add up to the following: if two more of those measures which are already outlined by the Provisional Government are passed . . . —[namely,] the inheritance tax and the property tax—then after this, says the Chairman of the Commission, a financial reform will be carried out in Russia which, in all fairness, will take one of the first places, if not the first place directly, among all the financial reforms that were ever carried out in any country. After carrying out this truly grandiose reform we will be able to say confidently that everything that is possible to take will be taken from the propertied classes. But since this is still far from sufficient for the purpose of covering the financial needs of the state, it becomes absolutely inevitable that we resort to taxation on the broad strata of the population, i.e., to increased indirect taxation.

. . . .

. . . We consider it necessary not to refrain from incurring certain expenses at the present time which carry the promise of bringing us great gains at a future date. We will not shrink from [ordering] the immediate utilization of water power, because we know that this power will serve us in good stead during the fuel crisis which awaits us after the war. . . . The Provisional Government stands firmly on the definite line of preparing legislation which the future bearers of power will have to carry out. Here, too, we will be confronted with the principle about which the Minister of Trade and Industry has spoken: the necessity of preserving and encouraging private enterprise. We will probably be compelled to adopt the course of forming special commercial monopolies: on sugar, tea, matches. But I consider it my duty to state that this type of monopoly does not represent, in our minds, the introduction of new foundations for state socialism. We consider these to be strictly fiscal measures; we consider it necessary to enact them for enlarging and improving our sources of revenue, and we do not in any way see that these measures contain any systematic attempt to inhibit private enterprise. We know that after the war we will belong to a family of nations where this private enterprise has not been undermined, or abolished, and we will have to make allowances for it in competing as equals in the world market. . . .

The Ministry of Finance, in its turn, will consider it necessary to adopt at the same time all measures to ensure that our national credit potential can be used to its fullest extent. Those diverse and singular loans that are being projected by the Ministry of Finance in accord with the Provisional Government will give us the opportunity to appeal to the country for assistance, basing this appeal not only on a sense of duty to the country—which everyone should possess—but, also, on a definite concern for the economy. In this regard, I consider it my duty to state that financial adventures of any kind are completely alien to the intentions of the Provisional Government. . . . Troubled times breed all kinds of rumors, and among these is the supposition that the Provisional Government is prepared to confiscate private property to obtain revenue for the state. I consider it my duty to state that the Provisional Government has no such ventures in mind, that it stands firmly on the basis of a scientifically prepared financial policy, and that it will under no circumstances embark on risky experiments of this nature. (*Applause.*)

· · ·

I have already told you at the beginning, citizens, that finances reflected like a mirror all the unfavorable factors of the present, and I must state to you that, in this respect, the Ministry of Finance represents, in fact, an extremely sensitive index of all the changes. By examining the subscription list to the "Liberty Loan" which I have at my disposal, you can clearly, consistently, and accurately trace [the relation between] the changes in the subscription [rate] and the changes in the internal situation. It inevitably registers a drop during a governmental crisis or when changes or difficulties occur. And it shows an increase when these difficulties are overcome, and when the country develops confidence in the stability of the contemporary situation. . . . And, finally, this financial policy of ours is intimately connected with national defense; it is intimately connected with the confidence that exists, both within the country and outside of it, in the strength of the state. I will not speak to you of the problems of our foreign credit. I will only say one thing—that in this respect our internal might and our strength at the front are directly proportional to the means at the disposal of the Ministry of Finance. Today, the whole Provisional Government has turned to us, citizens, with these three basic requirements: order, sacrifices, and defense. . . . I ask you, together with the whole Provisional Government: are you, and those who sent you, prepared to accept these three basic conditions and put them into practice to the best of your ability? (*Prolonged applause.*)

· · ·

1233. KORNILOV'S SPEECH
[*Gos. Sov.*, pp. 60–66.]

KERENSKY: Yesterday the Provisional Government outlined before you the general position of the army and those measures that are being contemplated by the Provisional Government and that will be put into effect. In addition, the Provisional Government deemed it necessary to summon the Supreme Commander and to request him to give an account before the State Conference of the situation at the front and the condition of the army. (*Addressing L. G. Kornilov:*) The floor is yours, General.

(*The Supreme Commander ascends the rostrum and is met by a prolonged storm of applause from the whole audience, with the exception of the left section of the aisles. The whole audience, with the exception of representatives of the Soviets of Workers' and Soldiers' Deputies, rises from the seats and applauds the Supreme Commander, who has ascended the rostrum. Growing shouts of indignation are heard from different corners of the audience, addressed to those on the left who remain sitting . . . Shouts ring out: "Cads!" "Get up!" No one rises from the left benches, and a shout is heard from there: "Serfs!" The noise, which has been continuous, grows even louder. The Chairman tries to calm down the audience and, after achieving a certain degree of quiet, addresses [the following words to the audience].*)

I request the audience to maintain order and to hear out the first soldier of the Provisional Government with the respect due him and out of respect to the Provisional Government. (*Cries:* "Right!" *Applause.*)

KORNILOV: As Supreme Commander I greet the Provisional Government . . . and the whole State Conference on behalf of the field forces. I would have been happy to add that I greet you on behalf of all those armies standing out there, on the border, like a firm and impenetrable wall, defending the Russian territory and the dignity and honor of Russia. But it is with deep sorrow that I have to add and declare openly that I do not have confidence that the Russian army will staunchly perform its duty to the country.

My telegram of July 9 concerning the restoration of the death sentence for traitors and betrayers in the theater of war is well-known to everyone. The immediate object of this telegram, the incident that provoked this telegram, was the disgrace of the Ternopol' breakthrough. And this pogrom, which the Russian army had never known during its entire existence, is continuing to this day. The disgrace of the Ternopol' debacle is the inevitable and direct consequence of that unheard-of disorganization brought on our once glorious and victorious army by influences from without and by imprudent measures adopted for its reorganization. The measures that the Government adopted following my telegram contributed, undoubtedly, somewhat to the restoration of normal conditions in the army, but the destructive propaganda for disorganizing the army is still continuing, and I will furnish you with the facts. During this short period of time since the beginning of August, the men have become like animals and, losing all semblance of soldiers, have killed the following commanders: the Commander of the Riflemen Guards Regiment, Colonel Bykov (*voices:* "Let us honor his memory by rising"), and Captain Kolobov of the same regiment; the two brothers Abramovich, officers, were killed at the "Kalinichi" station; the Commanders of the 437th and 43rd Siberian regiments were severely beaten and wounded; Commander Dubnenskii of the Purgasov Regiment was raised on bayonets by his own soldiers. (*Cries:* "Were the guilty ones hanged?") But when the regiment, which refused to surrender the instigators and criminals, was surrounded by a composite detachment, and the commissar demanded that they surrender them under threat of opening fire immediately on the whole regiment, then a wail was raised and pleas for mercy [resounded]. (*Cries:* "Disgrace!") All the criminals were surrendered. They were tried by revolutionary court-martial and are awaiting their fate, which they cannot escape. (*Cries:* "Right!") After this the regiment promised to wash away the disgrace of their treason. Thus, before the face of the invincible revolutionary power, the crime was liquidated without shedding a single drop of blood, and the possible further growth of crime was intercepted. All these murders were committed by soldiers in a nightmarish atmosphere of irrational, hideous club law, of interminable ignorance and abominable hooliganism. A few days ago, when it became clear that the Germans were advancing on Riga, the 56th Siberian Riflemen Regiment, the regiment that received so much acclaim in previous battles, voluntarily abandoned its positions and ran, leaving its arms and munitions behind it . . . (*Cries:* "Disgrace!") And only under the pressure of arms, after I issued a telegraphic order to exterminate the regiment, did the regiment return. (*Cries:* "Right!" *Applause from the right.*) Thus——— (*The Chairman interrupts Kornilov with the following words.*)

KERENSKY: Excuse me, General. I request the audience to hear out those portions of the speech that tell about the great misfortune and the suffering that befell our land without such disrespectful interruptions.

KORNILOV: Thus, the army is conducting a ruthless struggle against anarchy, and anarchy will be crushed. But the danger of new debacles still hangs over the country. There still hangs the threat of new losses of territory and towns and the direct danger to the capital itself. The situation on the front is such that, as a consequence of the collapse of our army, we have lost all Galicia, we have lost all Bukhovina and all of the fruits of our victories of the past and present years. In certain areas the enemy has already crossed the borders and is threatening the most fertile provinces of our south. The enemy is trying to beat down the Rumanian army and exclude Rumania from among our Allies; the enemy is already knocking at the gates of Riga, and if the instability of our armies prevents us from holding our lines along the coast of the Gulf of Riga, then the road to Petrograd will be open. As a legacy from the old regime, free Russia received an army, the organization of which was, of course, marked by great defects. But nonetheless, this army had combat potential, it was staunch and ready for self-sacrifices. By a whole series of legislative measures passed after the revolution by people whose understanding and spirit were alien to the army, this army was converted into the most reckless mob, which values nothing but its own life. There were cases where individual regiments expressed the desire to conclude peace with the Germans and were ready to return the conquered provinces to the enemy and pay indemnities of 200 rubles per head. The army must be restored at all costs, for without such an army there can be no free Russia, there can be no salvation for the native land. In order to restore the army, the Provisional Government must immediately adopt the measures that I have proposed in a report. My report has been submitted, and this report bears the signatures, without any reservations, of Assistant Minister of War Savinkov and the Commissar of the Supreme Commander, Filonenko. (*Cries:* "Bravo!")

I will give you a brief account of the basic principles of my report. Historical inferences and combat experience show that there can be no army without discipline. Only an army welded by iron discipline, only an army that is led by the single, inflexible will of its leaders, only such an army is capable of achieving victory and is worthy of victory. Only such an army can endure all the trials of battle. Discipline must be affirmed in the daily, routine work of the army by vesting the superiors, the officers, and the noncommissioned officers with corresponding authority. They must be assured of having a real possibility for bringing order into the necessary internal work of forcing the soldiers to clean and feed the horses, clean up their quarters—which are incredibly dirty at the present time—and thus save the whole army from epidemics, and save the country from pestilence. I must remind those of you who have set your goal as the fight for peace that with the present state of the army, even if it were possible to conclude peace to the great disgrace of the country, peace could still not be achieved, since the accompanying demobilization could not be accomplished, for the undisciplined mob would destroy its own country in a torrent of disorders. (*Cries:* "Right!" *Applause.*)

The prestige of the officers must be enhanced. The officers who fought valiantly during the entire course of the war, the majority of whom had joined the revolution at the very start and remained loyal to its cause, must now be morally rewarded for all the humiliations and systematic mockery they have endured through no fault of theirs. (*Cries:* "Right!") The material position of the officers, their families, widows and orphans of fallen heroes, must be improved—and, by the way, it should be noted, by rights, that this is practically the only corporate body in Russia that still has not even broached the subject of its needs and has not demanded improvement of its material position. As for what this position is like, it can be illustrated by the recent case of that ensign who was picked up in the streets of Petrograd when he collapsed from emaciation as a result of hunger due to lack of funds.

I do not oppose committees. I worked with them as Commander of the 8th Army and as Commander in Chief of the Southwestern Front. But I demand that their activities be confined to the sphere of economic and internal life of the army within limitations which must be clearly specified by law, without any interference in military operations, in questions of combat, or in the selection of superiors. I recognize the commissariat to be a measure that is necessary at the present time. But the assurance of the validity of this measure lies with the personnel of the commissariat whose democracy-minded political outlook must exhibit tact, energy, and the absence of a fear of responsibility, responsibility which is often very heavy. There is no army without a rear. All the measures that are being carried out at the front will prove fruitless, and the blood which will inevitably flow with the restoration of order in the army will not be expiated by the welfare of the native land, if the disciplined, efficient army is left without the same kind of replenishments, without food supplies, without munitions and clothes. The measures that are adopted at the front must also be adopted in the rear. And the principal idea governing these measures must be that they should conform to the goal of saving the native land. Meanwhile, according to my information, according to the accurate information I have at my disposal, the condition of our railroads at the present time is such that by the month of November they will be incapable of transporting everything that is required by the army, and the army will be left without supplies. I will not go on to point out in detail the repercussions of such a situation.

On the Southeastern Front, which, owing to local conditions, should be the best-provided at the present time when the crops are being gathered in, the position is as follows; I will read you a telegram which I received from the Commander in Chief of the Southwestern Front: "There is a need for flour at the front; there is absolutely no flour in the stores at the base. Shipments from guberniya food supply committees are negligible. All the hardtack bakeries have closed down and are idle. Existing hardtack reserves are beginning to be rationed for use of the garrisons in the rear for the first time in the entire course of the war. But they will not last long. I consider it my duty to report on this distress as a case of emergency. For the last two weeks the military districts have resorted to exploiting the local resources of the district. As a temporary expedient for saving the present situation and for avoiding hunger riots, the Chief of Supplies of the Southwestern Front issued an order for the urgent organization of garrison commissions in Kiev, which, under the leadership of guberniya food supply committees, would immediately proceed to procure supplies in the rear of the district, resorting, if necessary, to commandeering. Intervention by the Government is nevertheless urgently required, because the front can no longer go on living in this way."

I will cite several figures which may give you an idea of the situation regarding the question of supplying the army with other requirements—in particular, with military supplies. At the present time the productive capacity of our defense works has fallen to such a degree that, speaking in round figures, the production of the chief requirements of the army, in comparison with the figures for the period of October 1916 to January 1917, shows a 60 per cent decrease in firearms and a 60 per cent decrease in ammunition. These are the only figures I will cite. Consequently, if this continues, our army will find itself in exactly the same position as at the beginning of spring, 1915, a situation which, as you well know yourselves, caused the withdrawal of our armies from Poland, Galicia, and the Carpathians.

I will emphasize one more figure. For the successful action of the army at the present time, it must have "eyes." What I call "eyes" are airplanes. Airplanes are also needed for artillery action. The position of our air force is such that we cannot replenish the losses in our airplanes by either our own plant production or foreign imports. Without the possibility of replenishing our losses, we are likewise incapable of replenishing pilot losses, because there is nothing in which to train them. At the present time the productive capacity of our aircraft construction plants has decreased almost 80 per cent. Thus, if the most resolute measures are not adopted, our air force, our valiant air force, which has contributed so much toward victory, will become extinct by spring. If resolute measures are adopted at the front for restoring normal conditions in the army and increasing its combat potential, then I believe that there should be no difference between the front and the rear in terms of the severity of these measures necessary to save the country. But in one respect the front, standing as it does directly in the face of danger, must be given preference. If fate has willed it that we be underfed, then let the rear be underfed, but not the front.

I will add one thing to what I considered it my duty to report to you—it is something that I had always believed in my heart and the presence of which I now observe: the country wants to live. Like a spell cast on us by the enemy, that atmosphere of suicide of a great and independent country, brought on by the irresponsible slogans thrown into the darkest, ignorant masses, is now dispelling. In order to effectively realize the popular will, it is imperative that the measures which I have just outlined be put into practice. I do not doubt for a minute that these measures will be passed without delay. But it is impossible to allow the resolution to carry out these measures each time to be achieved under the pressure of defeat or concessions of our native territories. While resolute measures for raising the discipline at the front followed as a result of the Ternopol' debacle and the losses of Galicia and Bukhovina, it cannot be tolerated that order in the rear should have to come as a consequence of our loss of Riga, or that order on the railroads should have to be restored at the price of our concessions of Moldavia and Bessarabia to the enemy.

I believe in the genius of the Russian people, I believe in the reason of the Russian people, and I believe in the salvation of the country. I believe in the bright future of our native land, and I believe that the fighting efficiency of our army and her former glory will be restored. But I declare that there is no time to lose, that not a single minute must be lost. Resolution is necessary and the firm, steadfast execution of the measures outlined. (*Applause.*)

1234. KALEDIN'S SPEECH
[*Gos. Sov.*, pp. 73–76.]

Having heard the report of the Provisional Government on the grave position of the Russian State, the Cossacks, personified by the representatives of all the twelve Cossack forces—the Don, Kuban, Terek, Orenburg, Yaitskii, Astrakhan',

Siberian, Amur, Transbaikal, Semirech, Enisei, and Ussur—standing on a national, statesmanlike point of view and noting with deep sorrow that private, class, and party interests have prevailed over the general interest in our national domestic policy, welcome the determination of the Provisional Government to free itself finally, in the realm of statecraft and national construction, from the pressure of party and class organization ("Bravo!"; *applause*), together with the other causes which have brought the country to the verge of ruin. (*Voice:* "True.")

The Cossacks, who have not known serfdom, who have been free and independent since time immemorial, who have enjoyed extensive self-government even in the past, and had always enjoyed equality and fraternity in their midst, did not become drunk with freedom. When they received it once again, when [the freedom] that was taken away by the tsarist government was returned to them, the Cossacks, strong by virtue of their sound sense, and imbued with healthy principles of statesmanship, accepted freedom calmly and with dignity, and converted it immediately into fact by creating a democratically elected government of their forces during the very first days of the revolution, combining freedom with order. It is with pride that the Cossacks announce that their regiments have known no deserters (*applause;* "Bravo!"), that they have preserved their strong formation, and in this strong and free formation they are defending and will continue to defend the long-suffering fatherland and freedom. (*Applause.*)

Serving the new regime in truth and in faith, having sealed with blood their devotion to the system, to the [cause] of saving the native land and the army, and dismissing with complete contempt all provocative slanders [leveled] against them—the charges of reaction and counterrevolution—the Cossacks declare that at a time of mortal danger to their native land, when many army units have forgotten about Russia and have covered themselves with disgrace, they will not deviate from their historic path of serving their native land with arms in hand, [both] on the battlefields and inside the country in the struggle against treason and betrayal. At this point the Cossacks wish to point out that this charge of counterrevolution was leveled at them just after the Cossack regiments [responded to] the appeal of the socialist ministers on July 3 and, saving the revolutionary government, came forth resolutely, as always, with arms in hand, to defend the State against anarchy and treason. (*Cries:* "Right!" *Applause from the right.*)

. . .

We have outlined the following principal measures for the salvation of the native land: 1) The army must be kept outside of politics (*applause from the right; cries:* "Bravo!"), and meetings and assemblies with their party struggles and disputes must be completely prohibited (*cries from the right:* "Right!"); 2) all Soviets and committees must be abolished (*noise from the left, applause from the right; cries:* "Right!"*) both in the army and in the rear (*cries from the right:* "Right!" "Bravo!"; *noise from the left*), with the exception of regimental, company, battery, and Cossack troop [committees] whose rights and duties must be limited strictly to the sphere of internal routine† (*applause from the right; cries:* "Right!" "Bravo!"); 3) the declaration of Soldiers' Rights must be revised (*ap-*

---

* According to *Russkoe Slovo: strong commotion on the left; cries:* "This is a counterrevolution"; *the Chairman rings the bell.*

† In *Russkoe Slovo* there follows: *Karaulov shouts from audience:* "Perfectly right!"

plause from the right; cries: "Right!"; *noise from the left)* and supplemented with a declaration of his duties (*cries:* "Bravo!" "True!"; *applause*) ; 4) discipline in the army must be raised and strengthened by the most resolute measures (*noise; cries from the right:* "Right!") ; 5) the rear and the front are an indivisible whole guaranteeing the fighting efficiency of the army, and all measures necessary for strengthening discipline at the front must likewise be implemented in the rear (*cries:* "Right!" "Bravo!") ; 6) the disciplinary rights of the commanding personnel must be restored (*cries from the right:* "Bravo!" "Right!"; *storm of applause, noise and whistles from the left)* ; the leaders of the army must be given full powers (*cries from the right:* "Right!"; *applause*).

In the menacing hour of grave ordeals at the front and complete internal collapse from the political and economic disorganization, the country can be saved from ultimate ruin only by a really strong government in the capable and experienced hands (*cries from the right:* "Bravo, bravo!") of persons who are not bound by narrow party or group programs (*cries from the right:* "Right!"; *applause*), who are free from the necessity of looking over their shoulders after every step they take to all kinds of committees and Soviets (*applause from the right; cries:* "Right!"), who are clearly aware of the fact that the source of the sovereign power of the state resides in the will of the whole people and not in individual parties and groups (*cries from the right:* "Bravo!"; *storm of applause*). There must be one single power for the central and local levels. The usurpation of state power by central and local committees and by the Soviets must be immediately and abruptly brought to an end.* (*Cries:* "Right!") Russia must be an indivisible whole. All separatist tendencies must be nipped in the bud. In the sphere of national economy, it is imperative to have the most thrifty administration, carried through consistently, strictly, and implacably in all spheres of national life. A law on labor conscription must be immediately drawn up and enacted; fixed wage scales and [restrictions on] employers' profits must be introduced without delay; the market values of agricultural and industrial products must be brought into correspondence without delay; the strictest and most efficacious measures must be adopted for protecting the productivity of agriculture, which is suffering immeasurably from the lawless acts of various committees and individual persons that are violating the fixed system of land utilization and land tenure relations.

1235. CHKHEIDZE'S SPEECH AND THE DECLARATION OF THE UNITED DEMOCRACY
[*Gos. Sov.*, pp. 77–86.]

([*Chkheidze was*] *met with a storm of prolonged applause from the left benches. His appearance on the rostrum was accompanied by cries of* "Long live the leader of the revolution!"; *applause.*) Citizens: In spite of the fact that it has just been proclaimed that democratic institutions must be immediately abolished— and the Central Executive Committee of the Soviets of Workers' and Soldiers' Deputies and the Executive Committee of the Soviets of Peasants' Deputies are

---

* In *Russkoe Slovo* there follows: *Storm of protest from the left. Cries are heard:* "Out with him!" "Counterrevolutionary!" *Storm of applause from the right.*

such organizations—I must begin my speech with a reference to these institutions. Thus, on behalf of the Central Executive Committee of the Soviets of Workers' and Soldiers' Deputies, the Executive Committee of United Public Organizations, the cooperative organizations, the chairmen of food supply committees, members of the State Conference, the representatives of front and army organizations and the soldiers' section of the Central Executive Committee of the Soviets of Workers' and Soldiers' Deputies, the Central Committee of the All-Russian Union of Disabled War Veterans, the Executive Committee of the Petrograd Union of Disabled War Veterans, the representatives of the All-Russian Union of Zemstvo Workers, the Central Union of Employees in Government Service or in public and private institutions, the All-Russian Railroad Constituent Congress, and the majority of representatives of municipal governments, I have the honor to make the following declaration:

"Russia is passing through days of grave, almost mortal, danger. The enemy forces are invading the interior of the country. The army is retreating. The finances of the country are undermined. The railroads are in a state of complete disorganization. Industry is being destroyed and is failing to satisfy the demands of either the army or the population. Starvation is imminent in the towns. And at the same time incidents of corruption in the army and anarchical outbreaks in the country indicate that the dissatisfaction of the popular masses, worn out with suffering by three years of war, threatens to assume a form that would endanger the very existence of the State. All the open and secret enemies of the revolution are avidly making use of every misfortune on the front, of every difficulty and disturbance within the country to buy their own personal welfare at the price of Russia's ruin and to turn back the great, revolutionary country to the conditions which drove her to the brink of ruin and which were unanimously condemned by the people.

"In this grave and difficult hour, the united organizations of the revolutionary democracy testify once more before all Russia to their unshakable determination not to stop at any effort of sacrifice to save the country and the revolution. From their very inception, these organizations set for themselves the goal of unifying all the vital forces of the country for the execution of those great tasks which the revolution has placed before Russia and for the struggle against that decomposition and decay with which the cadaveric poison of autocracy had infected every part of the national organism. Personified by its Soviets of Workers', Peasants', and Soldiers' Deputies, the revolutionary democracy did not strive for power, it sought no monopoly for itself. It was ready to support any power that was able to protect the interests of the country and the revolution. Amidst the chaos of destruction it strove to organize and discipline the popular masses for creative statesmanship, to channel the spontaneous movement of the giant nation which had cast off the age-old chains into systematic work on restoring the fighting efficiency of the army, which was rotting to its very foundations from the old regime, to organize the national economy, and, always, and in all things, to place the interests of the whole, the interests of the country and the revolution above the interests of individual classes or groups of the population.

"Considering the innumerable difficulties through which revolutionary Russia has to fight her way, the unbearable burdens from which the popular masses want to free themselves, the inexperience in organized activity due to centuries of slavery, and in the face of the resistance which the activities of the revolutionary democracy encountered from all the defenders of special privileges and selfish interest—not everything that should be done has yet been done, and not everything was done in the way it should have been done. If the incidents of corruption in the army and the anarchical outbursts still bespeak the pernicious legacy of the old regime and the menacing phantom of unvanquished anarchy, then still, surveying at a glance the past five months of the revolution, we can safely say that it is only thanks to the organizations of the revolutionary democracy that the creative spirit of the revolution has been preserved and the country saved from dissolution and the rule of anarchy. And only with the active participation of the revolutionary democracy is it possible to regenerate the army, reconstruct the country, and save Russia and the revolution. The democracy is inseparable from the revolutionary country.

"During these unparalleled ordeals that have descended upon Russia, it is only the self-reliance and awareness of the people that can save the country which has already breathed the invigorating air of freedom. Only a government that rests on the strength of many millions of people, concentrated in its innumerable organizations, is capable of extricating the country from the tragic situation and coping with the onslaught of its foreign and domestic enemies. Under these conditions, any attempts to destroy the democratic organizations, to undermine their significance, to dig a gulf between them and the Government, and to convert the Government into an instrument in the hands of the privileged and the propertied [classes], is not only treason to the cause of the revolution but a direct betrayal of our native land, which will perish on the very day that the conscious, disciplined, self-reliant, and organized masses of the laboring people cease to stand guard over her. In demanding of the Government that it carry out the program of July 8 with greater determination and consistency, the revolutionary democracy is defending not the exclusive interests of any one class or group, but the common interests of the country and the revolution.

"The program of July 8 is not a program [designed] exclusively for the democratic classes. It does not express the full range of their demands. This program is nothing more than a development of the program of May 6, which served as the basis for forming the coalition [government] and it contains only such points without which there could be no question of organizing for national defense, raising the level of the national economy, establishing the political structure of Russia, or safeguarding the gains of the revolution.

"In these days when the enemy invasion is jeopardizing the very existence of the revolutionary State, the democracy demands that all citizens and the Government exert every resource for organizing the defense of the country against military devastation. The Government must bear in mind that only by relying upon the active participation of democratic organizations in the rear and on the front will it be able to fulfill this enormous task.* It must impress this idea on the entire commanding staff and must thwart every attempt made under the pretext of organizing for defense to revert to those methods which corrupt the army and lead inevitably to defeat and to the betrayal of our native land. The Government must demand absolute subordination of the military authorities to itself, as the bearer of the supreme power of the State.

* In *Russkoe Slovo* there follows: *Loud applause. The left rises as one man and gives a stormy ovation to the delegation from the front.*

"The Government must bear in mind that a vigorous pursuance of a foreign policy in the spirit of repudiating all imperialistic aims and of striving for the earliest possible achievement of universal peace based on democratic principles will serve as a powerful instrument for raising the fighting efficiency of the army and [strengthening] national defense. A clear awareness that the attainment of this peace, so necessary for the regeneration of the country, constitutes the sole aim of the Government's policy will inspire the revolutionary army which is shedding its blood with courage, enthusiasm, and the willingness [to endure] great self-sacrifices.

"The Government must remember that the earliest possible organization of of the rear and the regulation of the economic life of the country are mandatory in the interest of [national] defense. At a time when the blood of the people is flowing in torrents, when the wealth of the nation is being dissipated, the democracy is prepared for any sacrifices to save the country and the revolution. And the privileged and propertied [classes], for whom the very calamities of war have, during the course of three years, served as sources of immeasurable enrichment, must also yield their interests to the higher interests of the country.

"Proceeding from all the above considerations, the united revolutionary democracy asserts that the vital interests of the country and the revolution urgently demand the strict implementation of the following measures:

"I. *In the field of purveyance and the matter of food supply.* 1) Considering that one of the most important problems is that of providing the army and the population with food supplies, and recognizing the necessity of having a single, uniform government policy on the matter of purveyance and food supply, we believe that the grain monopoly and fixed prices on agricultural products must remain unchanged despite the sacrifices that the peasantry is forced to bear on this account; a return to free enterprise, or even a fluctuation of prices on agricultural products would prove disastrous to the country under the present conditions and would lead to an inevitable collapse of the economy. 2) On the other hand, this method of providing the army and the population with food supplies makes it imperative to have a system of measures designed for supplying the rural population with industrial goods, in so far as this is possible under the present condition of industry. In addition, fixed prices must be established on all the basic industrial commodities, and wages must also be subject to regulation. Only these conditions will protect the peasants against the destructive effect of fixed grain prices, especially during a period of the devaluation of the ruble. 3) The successful implementation of the policy on food supply and on supplying the population with industrial products is inconceivable without the widest participation both in the procurement and in the distribution of agricultural and industrial products under the general supervision of state food supply organs. 4) In addition to enlisting the widest participation of cooperatives in the work on food supply and purveyance, the whole remaining apparatus of private commerce must be utilized whenever the possibility or necessity for this arises. The enlistment of private commerce under the exceptionally strict control of food supply organs prevents the development of speculation and is dictated by the interest of the State.

"II. *In the field of trade and industry.* 1) The problems of national defense and the organization of purveyance make it imperative that the most resolute measures be adopted for regulating transport service and raising the productive capacity of industry. 2) In order to increase industrial production, the first requirement is that the Government establish control over production and intervene actively in the management of enterprises to the point of organizing industry into state syndicates and trusts and introducing monopolies. 3) Only the large-scale participation of democratic organizations can assure that this control over production and regulation of industry will serve the true interests of the country and not the interests of individual groups. 4) The immediate achievement of such control over industry is the principal condition for increasing its productive capacity, which has declined on account of poor technical equipment, extreme impairment of the instruments of production, disorganization of transport services, the shortage of raw materials, the sudden drop in the nutrition standards of labor, and the change in personnel, which sometimes includes industrialists, as a result of a series of mobilizations. 5) In so far as the decline in productive capacity can be ascribed to the negligence of workers and to manifestations of irresponsibility among the working masses, the labor organizations will continue to struggle with still greater energy against these manifestations of irresponsibility, which contribute to the general disorganization and thereby endanger the cause of the revolution. 6) The Government must not delay the implementation of the program of urgent measures on labor protection, which would contribute to increased production. At the same time, a network of labor exchanges for keeping account of and distributing manpower, as well as networks of courts of conciliation, must be established. The right of workers to form unions and coalitions in all branches of labor must be preserved. Labor organizations, for their part, must actively strive to increase labor productivity for the sake of saving the country and the revolution. With this goal in mind, they must: (a) fix a minimum output [required] for every enterprise, depending on the technical facilities of the given enterprise; (b) see to it that the eight-hour working day is strictly observed, permitting overtime work when there are no unemployed workers in the given branch of industry or when the interests of national defense and the revolution so require; (c) offer every assistance in settling conflicts by means of arbitration, resorting to strikes only when all other means of settling the conflicts have been exhausted; in addition, must firmly condemn the use of violence on representatives of management and must seek to refer all conflicts arising between workers and the administrative-technical personnel to courts of conciliation; (d) must exert every effort to conclude collective wage agreements as the absolute condition for the normal work of enterprises. 7) The above-mentioned control over production and purveyance and the establishment of fixed prices must be accompanied by a regulation of the relation between labor and capital and between wages and the working day, and also, if the necessity arises, by the introduction of labor conscription, which must apply to all classes of the population and which should have as its only object the interest of the country and should under no circumstances assume the form of militarization of labor, which is capable of utterly destroying the national economy. 8) While exerting every effort in safeguarding the interest of national defense, the Government must at the same time adopt preliminary measures for the gradual and painless demobilization of the national economy and for alleviating the disaster of the inevitable and catastrophic unemployment. In particular, it must immediately draw up a program of public works for the purpose of reconstructing the economy destroyed by the war.

"III. *In the field of finances.* 1) In addition to the strict enforcement, without any eliminations or restrictions, of the last laws of the Provisional Government relating to the income tax and the war profits tax, reforms must also be enacted in the inheritance tax, the tax on incomes from interest-bearing securities or funds, and the tax on luxuries. 2) At the same time, in order to avert a financial catastrophe, it is absolutely necessary to pass an emergency measure in the immediate future, namely, a high extraordinary capital levy, which would act as the single most important source for covering the extraordinary expenditure of the State. 3) To the extent that loans and the taxation of the propertied classes prove insufficient for covering the extraordinary needs of the State, it will be necessary to increase the present taxes on articles of mass consumption and to establish new taxes. This must be accomplished chiefly in the form of financial monopolies inviting the large-scale participation of cooperatives and other public organizations in the distribution of the products of the monopoly. 4) In order to carry out successfully the reconstruction of the taxation system, it is necessary to reorganize all the tax collection agencies, revise all procedures of tax assessment, and adopt broad measures of control for preventing tax evasion and incorrect payment of taxes. 5) With respect to the loan, the Government must apply resolute measures for compulsory subscriptions. 6) As all these financial measures are carried out, the issuance of bank notes can be slowed down and reduced to a minimum by establishing fixed prices on all essential products, standardizing profits and wages in connection with the general regulation of the entire national economy, and by exercising strict economy in making disbursements from the State Treasury, eliminating all unnecessary expenses. 7) In order to increase the revenues of the State Treasury, it is necessary to pass a series of measures designed to draw funds into the State Bank. The State Bank itself must be reorganized. The best method of inducing the population at large to deposit its funds—which is extremely important at the present time—is with the assistance of credit-savings associations and other cooperative establishments and their associations. 8) Private credit establishments must be placed under strict control in order to prevent their policies from conflicting with the national interest. 9) The united democracy, for its part, considers it necessary to exert every effort in supporting the financial legislation of the Government relating to successful tax collection and subscription to the Liberty Loan.

"IV. *On the land question.* Prior to the revolution, land tenure was not governed by any specific legislation, but was determined by the interests of the propertied classes, which had the support of the tsarist government. Thus, with the downfall of the old regime, there were absolutely no legal provisions for the regulation of land-tenure relations. In many localities the legitimate aspiration of the laboring peasantry for satisfying its land needs has therefore assumed the sporadic forms of an ever-growing spontaneous movement. In some cases this movement adds complications to land-tenure relations and gives rise to conflicts, misunderstandings, and disputes over land; in other cases, it creates difficulties in organizing the supply of articles of prime necessity, and, finally, it creates obstructions in the way of a systematic resolution of the land question in the Constituent Assembly. Therefore, it is imperative to have a vigorous, consistent, and systematic regulation of land-tenure relations. During the present transitional period prior to the convocation of the Constituent Assembly, this regulation must be founded on the following basic principles: 1) It is necessary to repudiate all seizures of any other person's land (*applause*), whether by individual persons, or by groups of persons, or associations. 2) The direct adjustment of land-tenure relations must be assigned to local land committees. Without violating the existing forms of landownership, these committees must have jurisdiction over lands designated for agricultural purposes in order to assure their fullest utilization for the sake of saving the national economy from complete disorganization. 3) With this end in view, the central government must immediately issue laws and instructions which provide explicit definitions of the rights and duties of land committees (*applause*) and also their rules of procedure. Moreover, these laws and instructions must provide every protection of the interests of the agricultural population as regards landownership, as well as the interests of food supply and agricultural production as a whole. (*Prolonged applause.*)

"V. *On the organization of the army.* Considering that the salvation of the country and of the revolution at the present time depends upon the restoration of the strength of the army, the democracy insists on the implementation of the following measures: 1) The rights and duties of the commanding personnel, the commissars, and the army organizations must be clearly and explicitly delineated: (a) the commanding personnel must be accorded complete independence in the realm of [active] operations and campaign tactics, and a decisive influence in the realm of drilling and field training; (b) the commissars must act as bears of the united revolutionary policy of the Provisional Government, and as organs which stand guard over revolutionary law in the army; the activities of the commissars must be brought into close relation to army organizations; (c) the army committees must act as organs representing soldiers as a whole and as leaders of their social and political life; as such, the rights of the committees which follow organically from their actual role in army life must be confirmed by law. 2) Extraordinary measures of revolutionary reprisal that are introduced under exceptional circumstances must be implemented only in agreement with the commissariat and must under no circumstances apply to the healthy elements of the army; the prepossession with, or abuse of, coercive and repressive methods destroys the fighting spirit and the combat potential of the army. For this very reason the restoration of personal disciplinary authority to commanding personnel is inadmissible. In order to enhance the authority of the commanding personnel, all those persons who have clearly revealed themselves to be counterrevolutionaries must be removed from the high command and their posts filled by individuals who have distinguished themselves within the rank and file of officers, the majority of whom have staunchly and selflessly borne all the hardships of war along with the masses of soldiers. (*Storm of applause; the soldiers' section—left wing—rises to welcome the comrade officers, members of the frontal committees.*) 3) There must be increased work in the rear to provide for the needs of the soldiers. In this connection it must be asserted that it is the duty of the state and society to assist the disabled war veterans and their families in every way and to give more comprehensive support, within the limits of financial resources, to the families of all those who have been called into active service.

"VI. *In the realm of local self-government and administration.* 1) The earliest organization of local self-governments and administrations is necessary in the interest both of strengthening the revolutionary order and of carrying out systematically some of the measures of the Provisional Government. 2) The organs of local self-government, elected on the basis of universal suffrage, must fulfill the functions of local state administration and they should not be opposed by any other organs of local self-government. The representative of the central government, however, must be given the right to pass on the legality of the actions taken by the local self-government. 3) In this connection, it is necessary immediately to revise and bring into correspondence the municipal and rural statutes and the regulations on the militia, and to broaden the sphere of competence of local self-government in questions of public order and safety, finances, labor legislation, and so forth. 4) Commissars of the Provisional Government, selected locally and confirmed by the central government, shall act as the organs of administrative government only for the transitional period of the revolution. 5) As soon as the organs of local self-government are elected, the full powers of the executive committee of public organizations in the corresponding region shall cease to have force.

"VII. *On the nationality question.* All the vital, creative powers of all the peoples of Russia must and can be applied to the difficult and responsible work of national construction, which the salvation of the country and of the revolution imperatively demands of the democracy. These national efforts by peoples inhabiting Russia will serve as a powerful instrument in the creative work of the state. Awakened to a free, organized, national life, these broad, national masses will create reliable support for the revolutionary power. Recognizing that the resolution of national questions in their full scope lies within the jurisdiction of the Constituent Assembly, and considering it necessary to preserve the unity of revolutionary forces, the democracy declares itself opposed to any attempts to resolve national problems by way of a *fait accompli*, by creating separate entities out of individual parts of Russia. But at the same time, the democracy insists that the Government carry out immediately those parts of the democratic national program which satisfy the most vital needs of the peoples inhabiting Russia and which weld them together into an integral, powerful instrument of the revolutionary state organization. In particular, the democracy considers it necessary [to adopt the following measures]: 1) To issue a declaration of the Provisional Government which recognizes the right of all nationalities to full self-determination, to be realized by means of a covenant concluded at the all-national Constituent Assembly. 2) To issue a decree on the equality of rights in [the use of] language: to grant citizens of all nationalities, upon their achievement of civil and political rights, the right and opportunity to use their native language in schools, courts, organs of self-government, and in their relations with the central government, etc. 3) To form a Council of Nationalities in the Provisional Government, which would include representatives of all the nationalities of Russia, in order to prepare materials on nationality questions for the All-Russian Constituent Assembly and to work out methods of regulating national relations and polities, granting nations the opportunity to settle their own internal affairs."

Such are the aims, the earliest and complete realization of which is absolutely necessary in the interest of saving the country and the revolution. The democracy calls upon the Government and all the forces in society that value the cause of revolutionary Russia to realize these aims. Let the Government, which is vested with full powers and which enjoys the support of the democracy, find the strength and the vigor to pursue this course steadfastly and consistently. In this grave hour of trials, when all our strength must be concentrated on defending the country against military devastation, do not let the interests of Russia be sacrificed to the importunities of irresponsible or self-interested groups. In suppressing any manifestations of anarchy, let the revolutionary power ruthlessly intercept all the feeble intentions of counterrevolutionary conspirators who are exploiting the population of our native land for their own criminal ends. Let the popular masses see everything that is being done to save the country. Let them know that the Government will not tolerate the slightest encroachment on the revolutionary gains of the people. Such a government will have the determined support of the broad, popular masses. Such a government will have no reason to fear anarchical riots or counterrevolutionary plots. (*Applause.*) The people will react with confidence to the exceptional measures that such a government will find necessary to adopt in the interest of consolidating the revolutionary order, because in these measures they will see no manifestations of arbitrary rule, or political vengeance, or faint-hearted concessions to the pressures of any group, but only the necessity that is dictated by the vital interests of the country and the revolution. Such a government will be able to cope with the grave and responsible problems which confront it: [those of] national defense, the protection of revolutionary gains, and the urgent convocation of the Constituent Assembly that will consolidate the democratic republic in Russia which, in reality, has already been proclaimed by the people. (*Loud applause. The deputies of the left and part of the center give a stormy ovation to Comrade Chkheidze.*)

1236. MAKLAKOV'S SPEECH
[*Gos. Sov.*, pp. 116–17.]

. . .

There is only one program, one way to save the revolution—it is a program of the sensible governing of Russia, without utopias, sins, and needless mistakes. Be capable of applying it, show that you are in command of the situation, and then the revolution will be strengthened. And I want to tell the Government, which has already started the program and has taken the initial steps—let it follow this program to the very end. . . . The Government does not see that the people are not a party, the people are not those who vote for party lists. The Government does not want to see that parties, as such, may be wrong, even the most progressive, the most popular parties. . . . The political program of the present moment must be dictated not by the will of political parties, but by the will of history. Let the Government understand what Russia needs, what she really needs, and let it follow this policy boldly regardless of any resistance that it may encounter. And I will say more: the Government is mistaken if it thinks that on parting with political parties it will lose its real strength, for the Government will be backed not by an organized minority, not by a party, but by the deep, dark masses of people which are now, through lack of understanding, quietly casting their votes for party lists. These masses whose voice, it is said, is "the voice of God," these masses will instinctively understand who is destroying them and who is leading them to salvation. (*Loud applause from the right; cries:* "Right!") And it will surround those who are leading them to salvation with the love, the sympathy, and the loyalty against which the malignity of political parties will be powerless. (*Applause.*)

. . . Let the country believe that everyone in the Government loves his native land as much as he loves the revolution, that our native land is dear to the Government not only in terms of the dignity of the revolution, and not only because it has become free, but that our native land is dearer to it than anything else, no matter how ill-fated or even servile it may be. Let the Government not rely on the formal resolutions of political parties, but rely on and believe in those at the front who are now dying for their ungrateful native land. Let it listen to them, see the support it has in them, and let it find the courage to take daring steps and lead the country onward, for the Day of Judgment is approaching. . . . Russia, gentlemen, will not sell herself for the revolution. What Russia needs is to be saved, and not a revolution. Russia loves the revolution only because, in her opinion, the revolution will save her, and if she ever nourishes doubts about this, no force [on earth] will be of avail to you in holding on to the conquests of the revolution. And those who are trembling [in fear of losing] these seizures and conquests of the revolution will very soon see how mistaken they are in their policy. (*Storm of applause from the right.*)

KERENSKY. I request the gentleman members and participants of the Conference to refrain in the future from abusing their right of expressing their opinions with complete freedom and to the very end; I mean this only in one sense: I request the gentleman speakers to refrain from repeating what has already been said if that has caused undue disturbance in the audience. (*Applause. Noise. A shout from the left:* "O ho! Why?") This is because I am preserving order in the whole audience with equal measure. (*Addressing himself to the right.*) You are asking, Why. Because it is not your side that is disturbed: I envision the possibility of the opposite [case], and am therefore telling you beforehand that we must preserve order in the general interest of the State. (*Applause.*)

1237. TSERETELLI'S SPEECH

[*Gos. Sov.*, pp. 118–28.]

Citizens and comrades. I have the honor to speak on behalf of the All-Russian Central Committee of the Soviets of Workers' and Soldiers' Deputies, as well as on behalf of the All-Russian Central Committee of Peasants' Deputies. Always, in all its actions, the democracy combines its efforts to achieve a common goal, ignoring local, group, and personal interests. And in the present case we found it [necessary] in the interest of the cause to combine our speeches because our views do not differ, in essential aspects, with regard to that tragic problem, the solution of which will determine the fate of the country. The views of the organized peasantry, the organized working class, and the organized army are identical. I speak here before the All-Russian State Conference not in order to enter into a polemic with representatives of various groups of the population, regardless of how far removed they may be from the point of view held by the organizations which I represent. I consider that the fundamental task, the fundamental purpose of the present conference is that of establishing the one policy that would unite —not in words or in declarations of principles, but in practice—all the forces capable of fighting in the name of the salvation of the country. Combining their efforts and strengthening the revolutionary government, they must take up the cause of saving the country with greater energy and intensity than has been the case up to the present moment. For the hour has indeed struck when delays will spell disaster to our free native land and when all the strength that is left in the people must be thrown into the balance in order that people can vindicate their existence and their freedom.

If I touch on certain positions with which I decidedly disagree, it is not for the purpose of demonstrating once again the special point of view which I represent, but it is because I consider that a thoroughgoing examination of all the basic issues which divide some parts from that whole, called revolutionary Russia, can only serve to promote its unity as it exerts every effort in the cause of saving the country. Therefore, I must begin with a reference to one incorrect position that was maintained here by the preceding speaker. V. A. Maklakov said that the immediate task of the Government is to act independently of the social forces which have supported this Government up to the present time.

. . . I say that if the point is that this is the way to save Russia, then what prevents any one group, or any individual person who shares the views of Citizen Maklakov and accepts his way of saving [Russia], from making a nation-wide announcement to this effect and rallying the popular masses? (*Applause; cries:* "Right!") It is obvious that only the awareness and the endeavors of the organized masses can save Russia at the present time. . . . The common sense of the people, their instinct of self-preservation, and their keen perception prompted them [to believe] that there could be no salvation outside of organization, outside of this network which envelops all of Russia and unites the popular masses. If the Provisional Government, which personified the whole of revolutionary Russia and acted as its bearer of power, was established, then this was possible only because the source of its power resided in those organizations which, without perhaps having achieved the complete unification of the popular masses, had nevertheless received nation-wide recognition.

. . . Everybody knows that if the great Russian revolution had not occurred, we would have concluded a separate peace by now. (*Voice:* "Bravo!" *Applause.*) This is admitted by everyone, and everyone, even the right, speaks about the great revolution as having been accomplished in the name of saving the country; even those whose hearts lay close to tsarism—as, for example, Shul'gin, who just made a statement to this effect—even they are saying that they recoiled from tsarism because, by their own admission, tsarism was bringing, and had brought, the country to the brink of ruin, and it was only the revolution that saved the country from this ruin. (*Applause.*) *

. . . Citizens! General Kornilov, the Supreme Commander, has drawn a terrible picture for us here. Yes, it is through cruel blows that the democracy has to receive its baptism in state administration and in shaping its destiny. Yes, the democracy did not come fully prepared for this cause, and it is maturing and gaining strength in severe times, it is straining its every nerve. But still democratic Rusia is growing stronger. She has to pass through severe trials. The Supreme Commander made a very graphic and very forceful statement that struck at the heart of every person. . . . Yes, this is terrible, but still, if under these conditions, under these bloody blows, the people are closing their ranks, there is still hope left that both Riga and the lost parts of the territory will be recaptured. (*Applause.*)

But I will tell you that there is one price—and take careful note of this—there is one price at which one cannot buy order in the country: one cannot buy order

---

* In *Russkoe Slovo: Storm of applause from the left; cries from the right*: "Not true."

at the price of people's loss of faith in national strength, in the strength of the democracy. Were you to establish such order in the country, it would be the order not of a living, fighting state, but an order [that reigns in] a cemetery, or at a funeral held for the destinies of Russia. It would mean the loss of all Russia. (*Applause.*) . . .

. . . Tell [me], was it by force that the democracy was compelled to recognize the absolute power of the Government and transfer all [its] state functions to the coalition government, when this was nationally proclaimed in a time of grave ordeal by the revolutionary democracy? The democracy realized that the moment had arrived when, in order to save the country, the power must be centralized in the hands of the coalition government. The time had come when this became possible, because through the efforts of the democracy the relations between various groups had become more or less stabilized. And those who speak about the shortcomings of the previous government, about the interference of democratic collectives in the functions of the central executive authority, must not forget that no such strong, self-contained government, which can carry out, in practice, all the most important functions of the state, could have been established outside of this collective, outside of this organized democracy. . . .

. . . Here it is being asked: But why is this sentinel necessary at the present moment? This comes from the very same people who have the most to say about the impotence of the revolutionary government. These people are inviting us to abolish the democratic organizations; [they are saying] that there is no danger from any side threatening the gains of the revolution. But in this atmosphere in which Russia now lives, in this atmosphere of irresponsible fomentations and demonstrations when the truly critical period for the country has arrived, if the insane mind of some person, or group of persons, should conceive of the idea that the hour has struck when the cause of freedom can be subjected to a test and should try to establish order in the country at the price of destroying all the organizations that were born at the initiative of the people, and if these intentions were to become converted into fact—then who will there be to stand up staunchly in the defense of national freedom and the existence of the country? (*Applause.*) Who stood in the defense of the country when irresponsible demonstrations from the other side jeopardized her very existence? Who stood staunchly in the defense of the country against anarchy and in favor of re-establishing the revolutionary order? Cossacks and Kadets.* Yes, the Cossacks also participated in this cause, and this service to the cause of the revolution will not be forgotten by those who were then defending the revolution. But I will say to you that if at that moment the authoritative organization of the revolutionary democracy, whose voice is heeded by the masses of soldiers, workers, and peasants more than any other, if this organization faltered and reeled—tell [me], would the Cossacks have been able to preserve order in the country? (*Cries:* "Bravo!" *Applause.*) . . .

Now there remains only one course to adopt, which is the resolute course of democratic reforms, and the unification of all the revolutionary forces not in the name of satisfying one class or another, not in the name of selfish interests, but in

---

* In *Russkoe Slovo: Voices from the right*: "Cossacks and Kadets."

the name of the common interest, in the name of the whole country. And we are firmly convinced that a power which does not lean on the democracy, on its support and on its sympathy, cannot even pretend to have the nerve to undertake the salvation of the country. When words were heard here from the ranks of the organized democracy about making demands on the Government, there were many who ironically contrasted these statements with the statements made by the Minister-President concerning the impossibility of [making] demands, but I am firmly convinced that this was the result of a misunderstanding.

When the Minister-President spoke about the supreme power, of which he is the bearer, what the Minister-President had in mind, of course, was that the source of this power [resided] in the people, and not in himself. (*Applause.*) He, together with the other ministers, is the bearer of this supreme power, endowed with the confidence of the people; and all those who lean on the people, on the popular masses, and who express their will have the right to present demands to the bearer of power who exercises exceptionally wide powers but who likewise carries exceptionally great responsibilities. It is their duty not only to uphold and safeguard these rights, but, also, to make demands that the responsibilities be carried out. Only that government will be strong which is able, at a time like this, when an efficient machinery for expressing the will of the people has not yet been created, to sense the common will of the people from the statements of various strata [of society] and various democratic and nondemocratic organizations. . . .

The specific weight and importance of those who are strong by virtue of their property qualifications cannot be denied, especially at a time like this. The revolutionary power cannot fail to take this into account, and if there are forces among them which are able to support the common cause of saving the country without undermining the unity and the common efforts of the people, then both the Government and the organized democracy must do everything [in their power] to open the way for them to [participate in] the cause of saving the country. But if it would so happen that these propertied [*tsenzovye*] classes, relying on their weight and importance, confronted the popular government with the choice of leaning exclusively on the privileged elements in the cause of saving the country, brushing aside the aspirations and the forces of the vast majority of the people, or leaning on the organized democracy, then the choice of the popular government would be clear. By leaning on the organized, vast majority of the population, it would have the hope of saving the country through the efforts of these strata of society, and it would have the possibility of forcing everybody else to yield to the highest interests of the state. (*Applause from the left.*) . . . After the resounding applause here, following the Minister of Finance's statement that the coalition Goverment is thinking of revising the financial laws that have already been passed in order to lighten some of the burdens of the propertied [classes], I would like to see a representative of the propertied [classes] come up here and say that it is not about lightening the burden of taxes that the propertied class must think, that in this unprecedented time, when the impoverished, emaciated state is spending 32 billion [rubles] a year, at a time like this the propertied class must not stop at any sacrifice for the State. (*Loud and prolonged applause from the left.*)

. . . You have read our declarations. They fall into two parts: one, directed at taxing the propertied [classes], at the sacrifices which the state must accept from the propertied [classes], and the other, at what the working class on its part can give. And no sacrifice is regarded as a means of increasing the well-being of any one class. Everything must go to the consolidation of the whole.

You will say: but in practice, there have been cases and there continue to be cases of a different attitude by the working class. Yes, there have been cases and there continue to be [such] cases, and the organized democracy, the progressive constituent of all the laboring classes, is exerting every effort in the name of the country's salvation to decrease the incidence of such cases, to make them disappear. Where are the progressive strata of your classes, where in your rank and file is the struggle, in the name of the general national [interest, against those who have not themselves reached the level of understanding these]* interests? You are say-ing: the cream of the intelligentsia, the cream of the educated, is found in these classes. Yes, indeed, the cream of the intelligentsia, the cream of the educated. We would like to see a resolute struggle of the progressive strata of this class with the democracy, in the name of enlisting the sacrifices of all those other strata of your class, which are destroying the country. Only in this case will the coalition receive the name of a real coalition.

Many cries have rung out here, and there was applause first from one side, then from the other. I declare: Long live the honest, real, democratic coalition that stops at no sacrifice. I know that there will be applause here. But will it come from there? (*He makes a gesture to the right. Storm of applause. A voice:* "Long live the Soviet of Workers', Soldiers', and Peasants' Deputies!" *Storm of applause.*) Long live the democratic revolutionary coalition Goverment! (*Storm of applause, turning into an ovation for the Provisional Government.*)

1238. MILIUKOV'S SPEECH
[*Gos. Sov.*, pp. 128–34.]

([*Miliukov is*] *met with applause.*) I do not have sufficient time to trace all the odd meanderings in the speech [given] by the representative of the organs of the so-called "revolutionary democracy." He did not want to argue (*noise from the left*), but he argued all the time. He advanced a number of dubious assertions in which truth was mixed with error. It is true, as this speaker said, that the revolu-tion was accomplished in the name of saving the country. It is not true—or at any rate it has not been proved—that under different conditions we would have already had a separate peace by now. It is true that the revolution was started by the spontaneous outburst of the popular masses and not by a planned conspiracy. It is not true that the revolution owes its victory to the unorganized, elemental forces. It owes this victory to the State Duma (*laughter from the left, applause from the right*), which united the whole people, and not [just] to individual parties, and it gave sanction to the revolution. (*Voices:* "And Mikhail, Aleksei?" "Right." . . . *Noise from the left.*)

KERENSKY. I ask for the meeting to be quiet; otherwise I will double the time of the speaker.

MILIUKOV. It is true that the democratic organizations tried to organize the revolution; it is not true that will be able to save the revolution from the

---

* The words enclosed between the brackets were omitted in the original and were supple-mented according to the *Izvestiia Moskovskogo Soveta.*

disastrous consequences of their own mistakes. It is true that, while the machinery for properly expressing the will of the people has not yet been created, the Government's task is to discern this common will; it is not true that the common will of the people finds its sole expression in the hastily concocted party organizations. It is true that the Government must not lean exclusively on the propertied [*tsenzovye*] elements; it is not true that the nonpropertied elements are not at odds with the organs of the so-called revolutionary democracy. It is true that at the present time the unorganized masses have submitted to the party slogans that sound most promising; it is not true that the parties which advance these slogans have a monopoly on democracy, for Russia does not consist of socialists alone. (*Applause from the right.*)

. . .

It is true that the seeds of everything that is happening now were sown at the very beginning of the revolutionary period, in those first days and first months (March and April) when the Government was not yet a coalition cabinet. At that time, the Government was satisfied with moral support while it was preparing the country for the Constituent Assembly. And during these two months the parties, that were to gain in strength at a later date, organized the country for the immediate realization of their party aims.

Thus, on the one hand, we saw the theory and practice of nonresistance. "The Government does not act by means of coercion, but by the voluntary submission of its citizens"—such was the constant refrain of our speeches. And I heard the echo of [this refrain] in the Minister-President's speech. But on the other hand . . . a tactic was developing, the exact formula of which I heard even at that time, in those first days of the revolution, from a certain prominent socialist who said to me: "Everything now depends on whom the army will follow—you or us." We were not the ones who formulated the problem of the day in this light.

. . .

. . . I remember the long succession of delegations from the army, which was not yet demoralized at that time, passing before us in the Mariinskii Palace and inquiring anxiously of us, the first Provisional Government: "It is true that there is dual power in Petrograd; is it true that self-constituted organizations are interfering with you? Tell us, and we will free you from them." I remember also our embarrassed replies: "No, no, this has been exaggerated . . . There were attempts, true, but now everything is assuming stability and order."

However, the time came when this first government, too, could no longer ignore the consequences of this notorious support of "in so far as." After the days of April 20 and 21, the Government wrote its first address to the country, an address which, in its original form, was a strong indictment against the Soviets of Workers' and Soldiers' Deputies for bringing disorder and disintegration into the country, but which later, after a whole series of corrections, turned into a sociological treatise about how the old social relations had been destroyed, but new ones had not yet formed. This document concluded, over my personal objections, with an invitation to all the socialist parties of the Soviet to come and share the government power. I objected to this, believing that a mixed government would be not stronger but weaker than the government that emerged from the revolution. But, in general, my views at that time struck no responsive chord among my colleagues. For example, I considered then that the days of April 20 and 21 were, essentially, a victory for the Government (*voices from the left:* "O ho!"), which strengthened its power. Others found that it was a defeat, that it was proof of the necessity of sharing the power with the very people who came to us then and said: "Excuse us, but we are not ready yet."

Tseretelli just confirmed here that at that time they did not seek power . . . (*Tseretelli from the audience:* "We never sought power." *Voice from the left:* "Contrary to you.") Between these two views, the group that had the most influence in the Government from the beginning to the end of its existence chose the coalition. And the coalition was formed. Simultaneously with the change to a coalition cabinet occurred the first two capitulations of the Government to the utopianism of the socialist parties: the capitulation in the army, which was accompanied by the resignation of Guchkov, and the capitulation in foreign policy, which was accompanied by my own resignation.

. . . .

. . . The two months of government by this cabinet were marked by two other capitulations; it capitulated to the extreme utopian demands of the nationalities, demands which predetermined the future state organization of Russia. The first capitulation provoked the resignation of Minister Konovalov; the second, the resignation of the remaining members of the Party of the People's Freedom. I failed to mention the fifth capitulation—to the tendencies of the masses toward expropriation in the agrarian question, a capitulation which provoked the resignation of the first Minister-President, Prince L'vov.

. . . .

. . . Three spheres of life arouse particular concern in the country, these are the military, the internal administration, and social harmony. We all recognize the services of our Minister-President in raising the spirits of our forces. But the report of the Supreme Commander today has confirmed the inadequacy of the measures for bringing moral influence to bear. And we would wish that the demands made by specialists and experts who recognize the necessity for the immediate adoption of other measures, indicated by the Supreme Commander, would not serve as cause for suspicion, verbal threats, or even dismissals, but as subjects for serious and thoughtful discussion and immediate execution. (*Cries:* "Right!" *Applause.*)

We listened to the report of the Minister of the Interior. In this report we heard the frequent repetition of the words "statesmanship," "order," and "strong government." But we found out nothing about the system that must be based on these principles, and we have strong fears that the present executive body is making no provisions for the restoration of order and offers no guarantee of securtiy of person and property. With reference to the principal social problem—the land problem—we cannot, in general, speak about a government policy, because the question concerns the policy of the Minister of Agriculture, who remains inactive whenever he pleases, and who acts, also, when and how he pleases. It remains for us to see when and in what form our land policy becomes a government [policy]. But we cannot help but be concerned over its outcome for the selfsame reason, that a certain part of our Government is bound by party allegiance. I do not want to draw final conclusions today from all these remarks. The Minister-

President wanted to receive the support of the [Kadet] Party, and he received it. The Minister-President wanted to receive the support of the members of this Conference, the representatives of the Russian land, and probably, he will receive this too. The rest depends on the way the Government is able to make use of this support, which we are giving to it willingly and without arguments. (*Applause.*)

1239. Speech by the President of the Moscow Guberniya Zemstvo Board, A. E. Gruzinov

[*Gos. Sov.*, pp. 160–63.]

I am speaking at the request of the group of guberniya zemstvo representatives. This group includes members of both the democratized zemstvos and the zemstvos that have not been democratized, whose membership is drawn from the electorally qualified groups of society [*tsenzovye*]. But we, representatives of the latter type of zemstvos, representatives of the institution which for fifty years has stood guard over the organized public of Russia, the institution which performed its role during the revolution—we believe that our voice must now be heard, and we believe this because the persons who make up this group have remained at their places and have not been washed away by the wave of the revolution. . . . But we cannot fail to point out what is happening in the country now. The situation is extremely serious. We speak about unity here. But even here, in this hall, we see disunity, and the same disunity exists locally. We speak about teamwork, but in various localities a great number of educated workers in the zemstvos and in other institutions—in the railroads and factories, and everywhere else—are being discharged from work for the sole reason that they are ranked with the class that is called "bourgeois."

. . . One must look further. From the very beginning of the revolution, the revolutionary democracy organized large Soviets of Soldiers' and Workers' Deputies on a centralized basis. And these Soviets had significance. Then gradually, under the influence of the very same Soviets, partly by their own instigation and partly by instructions from the Provisional Government, an endless number of various committees and councils was organized throughout Russia and in the army. The functions of these committees and councils were not defined; their tasks overlapped each other and overlapped the tasks, responsibilities, and rights of the representatives of the Provisional Government. . . . As a result, there was complete diversification, complete disorganization locally, the absence of any authority, the absence of any security of person or property, and not even the possibility of upholding the rights which came with the revolution.

. . . . .

. . . The law enforcement authority is also paralyzed, because there are no organs that can assume these functions. We believe, therefore, that the court must begin to function in the immediate future, and that executive authority must be constituted.

. . . . .

Now we come to a very serious question, to the question of finances. . . . Tax payments are not coming in, there is nobody to collect them, expenses are growing precipitously, and I must note that everywhere, in all localities, in the zemstvos old and new, and in the committees, a new strange kind of attitude has appeared—that money is also something bourgeois, and, for this reason, money can be spent to one's heart's content. Never has there been such reckless spending as is occurring at the present time. (*Applause.*) . . . One must look at things from a realistic point of view, and here we are looking from the point of view of the land in which we live. So we, who can see, from here, everything about which I have spoken—we have to say that not only a general financial crash, but a financial crash at the bottom [level], can utterly destroy those cultural undertakings that have existed in our country thanks to the same zemstvo which has been working for fifty years in this direction.

. . .

1240. Speech of the Guberniya Zemstvo Representative,
S. S. Salazkin
[*Gos. Sov.*, pp. 165–66.]

Citizens and comrades: At the joint conference of representatives of guberniya zemstvos who gathered together for the purpose of formulating a common answer to the Provisional Government, it was discovered that no common answer could be given. There turned out to be two trends, and the guberniya zemstvo representatives split into two groups accordingly. You have just heard the representative of one of these groups, and I am appearing as the representative of the other group, which instructed me to speak on its behalf. (*Voices:* "Why didn't he say so?" "He must have forgotten.") I will take the liberty of enumerating the zemstvos on behalf of which I am appearing here; only I must point out beforehand that representatives of certain zemstvos split among themselves, and some of them joined the first group, others the second [group]. First I will enumerate the zemstvos that are in complete agreement on the declaration to be made by me, and then I will indicate those that are divided. [The following zemstvos] have given their full support: Riazan', Vitebsk, Saratov, Kostroma, Vologda, Vladimir, Nizhnii Novgorod, Simbirsk, Kazan', Orenburg, Kherson, Lifland, Tauride, Tver, Astrakhan', Ekaterinoslav, Estland, and Ufa. Then, out of the three representatives, one or two have supported it from the following zemstvos: Minsk, Penza, Khar'kov, Petrograd, Mogilev, Chernigov, Kaluga, Viatka, Kiev, Novgorod, Tambov, Samara, and Kursk. There are thirty-one zemstvos, and all the representatives from eighteen [zemstvos] support the declaration which I shall now make. (*Storm of applause.*)

As is well known, there still are no new democratic zemstvos at the present time. The zemstvos are democratized in part and not all to the same extent. This circumstance presents a certain amount of difficulty in delivering [this] address. This, perhaps, explains the fact that the zemstvos' representatives were unable to come to an agreement on a common platform. You must have heard the platform of the first group; as concerns our platform, it is completely answered by the declaration of the united democratic organizations, read yesterday by Comrade Chkheidze. (*Loud applause;* "Bravo!") Therefore, we declare that we subscribe to it in full and request that we be included in the list of those organizations on behalf of which the resolution was read. (*Applause.*) . . .

. . .

1241. CHKHENKELI'S SPEECH
[*Gos. Sov.*, pp. 178–79.]

. . .

Citizens of free Russia: I have been given the floor as the representative of the Georgian nationality, but I will say a few words as a member of the Special Transcaucasian Committee of the revolutionary Provisional Government, the committee that personifies the complete solidarity of all the nationalities in Transcaucasia, [their] unity of thoughts and ideas, [and their] unity in revolutionary work. Citizens, the nationalities of Transcaucasia—and I have the full right to testify to this before you—are united and solid not only among themselves, but . . . with both the Russian people and the other peoples inhabiting [this] great country. (*Applause.*) I am turning to the so-called *inorodtsy*, and I must state: there no longer are any *inorodtsy* in Russia. There is [only] one united people of Russia who have one united goal. (*Applause.*) I wish to express my deepest congratulations to the nationalities of Russia which have suffered terrible oppression under the old regime, congratulations on behalf of all the nationalities of Transcaucasia, on their emancipation from the yoke of tsarism, on their emancipation from the ignominy of persecution and oppression. If there were some people among the nationalities that were oppressed in Russia who, back under the old regime, were thinking or asking themselves the question: do we really have one fatherland? can Russia be considered as being one fatherland for all of us?—if a shadow of a doubt on this score crept into the minds of any one of them, then [let me say that] we never nourished such doubts, and even [in times of] misfortune we were saying that for us there was only one fatherland—Russia. (*Applause.*) And so, if such doubts existed in the minds of some during times of misfortune or oppression, it stands to reason that now, with a free regime, with a free Russia, in the period of the great revolution, we must have no such doubts; we have one united fatherland—Russia. (*Applause.*)

Turning once again to my subject, I must state that up until the present time the nationalities of Transcaucasia have not taken a single action in the direction of separatism, nor will they take such action in the future. (*Applause.*) These nationalities as a whole, even the privileged [*tsenzovye*] elements of our nationalities, will, I hope, wholly subscribe to the declaration read from here by Comrade Chkheidze. (*Applause.*) As concerns the Georgian nation, the overwhelming majority in this nation stands and has stood—not only today, but even under the old regime—on a line with the democracy of Russia. (*Applause.*) There is no need for us to advance any reasons; I am not in the habit of justifying myself, I am only in the habit of making accusations. And the Georgian nationality has its representatives here—Chkheidze and Tseretelli. (*Voices from the audience:* "Long live the leader of Georgian democracy, Tseretelli!" *Applause.* "Long live Chkheidze!")

1242. R. A. ABRAMOVICH'S SPEECH
[*Gos. Sov.*, pp. 183–84.]

On behalf of all the Jewish socialist parties, on behalf of the Jewish proletariat and all the Jewish revolutionary democracy, I make the following statement:

The Jewish proletariat and all the Jewish working people have always considered themselves to be a part of the whole workers' democracy of Russia. And it was together with [the Russian democracy], together with the proletariat, that they fought for the realization of the ideals of democracy and socialism. This struggle was not an easy one: we were the poorest, the most humiliated, the most oppressed nation in Russia. The cruelest, the most ruthless blows of tsarism and reaction rained on us: the tested weapon has always been the inflammation of national hostility and the gospel of hatred against the Jews. There is no accusation too infamous or too wild that has not been hurled at the Jewish people; there is no arbitrariness that has not been considered permissible with respect to the Jews. And there is no form of violence which has not been applied by the old regime. All these persecutions descended with particular force on the poorer classes, primarily on the Jewish working people who were thereby doomed to physical and moral degeneration. But the Jewish working class did not surrender to violence. It accepted the challenge and answered the atrocities of tsarism by a courageous revolutionary struggle within the ranks of the working class of all Russia. (*Applause.*) Without stooping under the weight of the blows that rained upon the proletariat, without fearing persecutions, repressions, pogroms, turning away from the cowards in contempt, the Jewish proletariat bravely chose the path of revolutionary struggle, impelled by its deep conviction that the [attainment of] freedom can only be understood in terms of the victory of the revolution in Russia. The pledge for this victory lies in the unification of all the democratic, revolutionary workers' elements in Russia. We were strengthened in this conviction, in this faith, by that unremitting sympathy to our needs and suffering, by that fraternal support which the Russian working class and the revolutionary peasantry have always extended to us. (*Applause.*)

Our path, the path of revolutionary struggle, was difficult. It was rich with sacrifices and the blood we shed. But the Jewish working class followed this path courageously and steadfastly, arm in arm with the laboring masses of Russia. Our hopes, our cherished dreams were justified—the revolution happened and brought the long-awaited freedom to Russia and all her peoples, and gave the Jewish people the opportunity to take their place, as equals, among all the nations of free Russia. The centuries-old tragedy of a vast people had come to an end; the disgrace of a great nation had been washed away. (*Storm of prolonged applause.*)

1243. SPEECH OF THE REPRESENTATIVE OF MOSLEM ORGANIZATIONS, A. TOPCHIBASHEV

[*Gos. Sov.*, pp. 185–88.]

Citizens: To my lot fell the high honor of appearing before the present All-Russian Conference on behalf of all the Moslems who are participating in the Conference and who represent the following democratic organizations: 1) the All-Russian Moslem Council, 2) the All-Russian Moslem Military Council (Shura), 3) the Committee of Moslem Public Organizations of Baku, which are performing the functions of the Transcaucasian Central Committee, 4) the Central Committee of United Caucasians of Northern Caucasus and Daghestan, 5) the Turkestan Krai Council, 6) the Crimean Oblast Committee, 7) the Kirghiz and Bashkir Oblast Councils.

. . .

No sooner had the sun of freedom appeared over Russia than the Moslem people, having thrown off the hated chains of despotism, took heart and, rejoicing in the hope for a better life, took their place in the ranks of the most fervent supporters of the new regime that is based on democratic principles. [They acted] not only as supporters but as defenders of the Provisional Government which personifies this system and decided to give every support to all the measures that the supreme power of the nation should undertake and to follow the road of freedom together with the revolutionary democracy. . . .

. . .

With regard to the national question, the Moslems find that it is necessary to achieve the unification of all the peoples and to establish contact between them, and they also declare that they will support all other nationalities in their [attempts] to realize their national and political ideals based on democratic principles, subject to final discussion at the Constituent Assembly. The Moslems declare that, standing firmly on the path they have chosen, they feel that they, too, have the strength and the will for order, sacrifice, and labor, so necessary for the consolidation and consummation of revolutionary gains. They are certain that the day is close when free, democratic Russia will realize the equality and fraternity of peoples, Moslems among them, and will show the world an example, unparalleled in the history of mankind, of respect to the rights of all peoples, inviting European nations to liberate all their subjected peoples, including the Moslem peoples in Europe, Asia, and Africa, on the basis of free self-determination. Then we will proclaim enthusiastically, in one voice: *ex oriente lux!*

1244. Speech of the Estonian Representative, Pipp
[*Gos. Sov.*, pp. 188–90.]

At a terrible hour in the life of the great State of Russia, the Provisional Government turned to all the peoples with an appeal to give an honest answer on all problems of national life. The revolutionary Provisional Government calls upon everyone and all the peoples of Russia for order, sacrifice, and unity in the name of the cause of defense. We, representatives of the Estonian people, consider it our civic duty to point out the basic conditions that are necessary for saving our native land, the freedom, and the cause of the revolution. We state that in questions of a general nature we stand for the complete realization of the measures outlined by the Russian democracy, and we will give every support to the revolutionary Provisional Government in this direction. But we consider it necessary to make a special note of one question of tremendous importance to the State— the nationality question.

First of all, we must point out that the statement made by the head of the Provisional Government harbors no kind words toward us. On the contrary, we, non-Russian peoples, are being reminded of the possible accounting and of the magnanimous forgiveness for the absence of friendship at a time of danger. We consider that this attitude toward us is profoundly unjust, for our desire to satisfy the most vital and urgent national demands is not a destructive or centrifugal phenomenon, but the only correct and sound principle of state construction. In resolving this question, we are not weakening the might of the Russian State, we are not ruining the revolution, but, rather, we are consolidating its gains. That is why the Estonian people—who have never striven for separatism, who have never betrayed the Russian democracy, who suffered through the horrors of punitive expeditions in the years of the first Russian revolution and the derision of the rights and person of peasants, workers, and their laboring intelligentsia—firmly convinced that their fate is inextricably bound with the interests of the whole democracy, consider it necessary to the best of their judgment and inexorable will, to proceed to the resolution of the nationality question. There can be no delays. No people can live by promises alone. The vagueness of the situation can only increase the spontaneous unrest among the people. The basic needs of the people must be given timely satisfaction. At the same time, preliminary work must be started for reorganizing the State on principles providing the highest guarantee of freedom and national self-determination in a democratic Russian republic based on the federal principle of a friendly family of Russian peoples, where autonomous regions—Estonia among them—would constitute equal members.

Before this ultimate goal becomes a reality at the Constituent Assembly, the Provisional Government, in order to achieve its immediate aims of order, sacrifice, and defense, must carry out the measures on the nationality question as outlined in the declaration made by the organs of the revolutionary democracy. . . .

1245. Speech by the Representative of the Navy, Commander Kallistov
[*Gos. Sov.*, pp. 206–8.]

I have too little time to relate the whole truth about the Navy, but I must begin with bitterness and sorrow in my heart, which you, perhaps, who are seamen may understand, [when I say] that in the speeches which we heard on August 12, not only was there nothing said about the position of the Navy, but even the word "navy" itself was not uttered a single time here in Moscow, before the whole country. It would be too painful for me to draw the logical inference from this. But how can this silence be understood? Does it mean that all is well with the Navy, [or] does it mean that something is wrong with the Navy? Since it cannot be assumed that in this threatening hour Russia would be indifferent to the Navy that has been called upon to defend her, then mentally raising over the Moscow State Conference our glorious St. Andrew's flag, which has been flying for three centuries over oceans and seas, I declare that the Russian Navy is still not abolished. I declare that no matter how seriously the Baltic Fleet may have been disorganized by Kronstadt, the German Navy has not as yet tried to measure its strength against it after the engagement at Riga; that the Black Sea Fleet has remained as it was, although it, too, is ailing, as the master of the Black—once "Russian"—Sea; and that the fleets of the Arctic and Pacific oceans and our other fleets are performing their duty to Russia.

I have come here from the deck of the destroyer *Pronzitel'nyi*, which is entrusted to me, and which has covered almost 85 thousand miles in the Black Sea and in campaigns during the war, or, in your terms, almost 150 thousand versts. Let these figures, at least, convince you that the Navy is working as well as it can.

But let my other words convince you also that naval service, in general, has now become immeasurably more difficult. We have come here to Moscow to be cured, and I will name you the chief ailments of the Navy.

The first ailment is the lowered status of officers who have been deprived of their rights and who feel themselves to be the least important persons in the State. Admiral Kolchak who is in America and whose very name could not help but disturb our revolutionary conscience, Admiral Kolchak whose services in the fight for freedom will be appreciated differently, perhaps, by the American democracy[4] (*bell of the Chairman*) than they were by us, this Admiral Kolchak said—and I will repeat it after him—that the sailors, our valiant comrades-in-arms, are not to be blamed for this ailment, but that the blame must fall on those who until recent days have consistently viewed the officers as an institution to be tolerated only as an annoying [but] necessary evil in the structure of a free state, as people whose only place is on the sidelines of the revolution. And these suppressors of the national spirit did not tell the sailors about the fifteen Decembrist naval officers who languished for decades in penal servitude in Siberia, or about Lieutenant Sukhanov who was executed, or about Lieutenant Schmidt who was shot, or about Lieutenant Nikitenko who was hanged . . .

The second ailment is the lowered capacity for work that is observed among a considerable number of sailors and port workers and, in part, among officers, as an inevitable reflection of the general state of disorganization in Russia, as a result of the excessively tense political life of the country.

The third ailment is the negative aftereffects of abolishing the corps of warrant officers and re-enlisted men—[a measure] carried out recently by way of an improvisation. This abolition deprived the Navy of thousands of expert technicians in all specialties, the majority of whom were servicing the most delicate, the most complex mechanisms. It cost the working people hundreds of millions of rubles. It threatens—and this, alas, is already making itself felt—to reduce the material working order of the Navy and, consequently, the combat potential of the Navy. If strengthening the central authority and raising the spirit of the whole country can serve as a remedy against the lowered capacity for work, then in order to cure the third ailment it is necessary to assure not the adoption of timid half-measures, but rather the earliest possible return into the Navy of all the valuable workers who have been thrown overboard.

One last word. When I was leaving for the State Conference, the sailors and officers of my destroyer requested that I place a candle at the ikon of the Iberian Mother of God, and I have fulfilled this request. We know that Moscow was once burned down from a candle. May God grant that the candle that was lit in Moscow by the Black Sea Fleet will flare up into a bright flame and that everything that is ruining Russia will be consumed in this flame.

1246. Speech by the Representative of the Front Organizations, Kuropatkin
[*Gos. Sov.*, pp. 224–26.]

I have been authorized to make the following statement on behalf of the entire group of delegates from the front representing all the field forces (*he reads the statement*):

---

[4] At the end of July, Admiral Kolchak was sent to the United States as head of a naval mission.

"Subscribing to the general declaration read here on behalf of the united democracy of the country, we consider it necessary to emphasize and expand on those of its points which concern the question of organizing and increasing the combat potential of the army. The army stands at the center of all the basic problems of the country's life. The salvation of the country and the revolution is dependent upon the restoration of the army's strength. The might of the army lies in a united, strong revolutionary power. Strong authority in the army arises only providing there is harmonious work among all the vital, creative forces of the army, and, therefore, everyone capable of understanding the danger threatening the country must unite for energetic, dedicated work in accordance with his strength, ability, and the task before him. The officers' corps alone will not be able to increase the combat potential of the army. Since the vast majority of the officers [came from] the former, prerevolutionary [army], they do not command the necessary confidence of the soldiers, even to this day. Only through close teamwork with soldiers' organs of independent action which grew out of the process of the revolution and which have organic ties with the masses is it conceivable and possible to restore the combat potential of the army and raise the revolutionary discipline to the proper heights. There must be a clear and explicit delineation of the rights and responsibilities of all the principal forces of authority in the army: the officers' corps, the army organizations, and the commissars. The officers' corps must be granted complete independence in the sphere of operations and combat, and decisive importance in the sphere of drill and field training. At the same time, the officers' corps must be completely excluded from political leadership in the army. The commissars must be the executors of the united revolutionary policy of the Provisional Government, which represents the will of the revolutionary majority in the country. The [sphere of] competence of this important and indispensable body in the period we are passing through must be broadened and strengthened. The activities of this body, which stands guard over lawfulness in the army, must be placed in close relation to the army organizations. The soldiers' organizations, being organs of soldiers' self-government, must receive complete legal sanction of their rights and responsibilities corresponding to their actual role in the life of the army. Only with such an interrelationship of the basic elements of authority in the army will there be results from the work intensively conducted by army organizations, strengthening the authority of the officers' corps while [providing] full guarantee of the personal and public rights of the soldiers.

"Taking into consideration the large [degree of] irresponsibility, the low level of civic consciousness, and the presence of outright criminal elements in the army, we recognize the necessity of [bringing] firm, revolutionary influence to bear and [using] constraint in the event of certain crimes [committed] in combat or in the routine work of the army. Extraordinary measures of revolutionary influence must be implemented with the consent of the commissars. But we protest most resolutely against the tendency that is observed in certain circles to apply repressive measures even to the healthy elements of the army—to build the strength of the army on repressions alone. The infatuation with, and, at times, the conscious abuse of, the system of constraints and repressions, [while] creating an imaginary submissiveness of the soldiers, brings about, in reality, a mass exodus from the revolution—even of the responsible elements in the army—embitters the masses, revives and increases the discord between the officers' corps and the soldiers, and destroys, instead of strengthening, the fighting spirit and the fighting strength of the army. Similarly, the restoration at the present time of independent disciplinary authority of commanding officers would serve to destroy, rather than to raise, the combat potential of the army. Under the conditions of the present state of awareness of the soldiers, the restoration of the disciplinary authority of commanding officers would be interpreted as a return to the old regime; it would not create any authority and would undermine the very foundation of the necessary and complex work of establishing a normal system of revolutionary courts in a democratic army.

"We insist on the necessity of energetically promoting to the highest posts of command all outstanding line officers, the majority of whom have staunchly endured, together with all the soldiers, all the burdens of campaign life throughout the entire course of the war. By removing all the incapable and obviously counterrevolutionary persons from the high command, a healthy state of the officers' corps would create normal conditions for the work of restoring and increasing the combat potential of the army.

"There must also be increased work at the center on satisfying the needs of the soldiers. In addition, it is the duty of the Government and society to pay greater attention to provisions for disabled veterans and their families, as well as increased aid, within financial possibilities, to families of those called up for military service, which measures, among others, will give the soldier a feeling of assurance that the country and the Government have not forgotten him. The frame of mind and the state of the army are intimately connected with the general policy of the country and the Government. The refusal of the propertied classes to boycott the Government, the willingness of all classes to make sacrifices, the consolidation of the creative revolutionary work in the country, the widely organized participation of all the democratic forces in national defense and in assistance to the army, and a strengthened policy of the international struggle for peace can create the conditions [necessary] for saving the army and restoring its fighting power."

1247. Speech of the Representative of the Navy Central Committee, Abramov

[*Gos. Sov.*, pp. 226–27.]

Comrades and citizens: Speaking on behalf of the Central Committee of the All-Russian Navy, which encompasses the whole Russian Navy, I have been instructed to state that the All-Russian Navy, being one of the detachments of the revolutionary democracy, fully supports the declaration that was read here by Comrade Chkheidze. (*Applause.*) Second, I was instructed to say a few words about our views on the question of the combat potential of the army and the navy. We declare that it is impossible to raise the combat potential of the army and the navy without [working through] the military, army, and navy organizations; that to abolish or undermine the authority of naval organizations at the present time would lead to the complete destruction of the combat potential of the navy. On the one hand, we fully support the preceding declaration of the army committees that the officers' corps must be accorded complete independence in technical and operational matters pertaining to combat. On the other hand, the Russian revolutionary navy, which is a component part of a united front and which has defended the Russian territory both before and during the revolution, has guarded and continues to stand on guard over the gains of the revolution, and the Provisional Government need have no hesitation in relying on the strength of the Russian Navy for the defense of the country and the revolution. (*Applause. Cries:* "Bravo!") In contrast to General Kaledin's declaration on behalf of the Cossacks, which contained the points demanding the immediate addition of the Soviets of Soldiers' and Workers' Deputies and the immediate abolition of the military organizations in the army, we declare that this may only be accomplished when the Russian Navy ceases to exist. In the points read by General Kaledin, it was declared that the Cossacks had no deserters in their midst. I can declare on behalf of the navy that the Russian Navy likewise does not know and has not known deserters in its midst, but it has not and does not advertise this, because it considers [loyalty to be] its duty. (*Cries:* "Not true, there were [deserters]! What about Kronstadt?")

I am reminded of Kronstadt. There were no deserters in Kronstadt; there was irresponsible agitation in Kronstadt which led to a partial disintegration of the navy. The same happened in the army. But neither in Kronstadt nor anywhere else were there any deserters. And so, comrades, in concluding my speech, I want to say on behalf of the All-Russian Navy that our thoughts conceiving the necessity of naval and army organizations are not the opinion of some one isolated, high-ranking organization. The seamen of the faraway Pacific squadrons and the river fleet of Amur think the same way about this, as do also the seamen of the North Sea and Pacific fleets, the Black Sea Fleet, and . . . the Baltic Fleet. Without increasing its combat potential and without the friendly teamwork between the officers' corps and these organizations, the Russian Navy cannot exist. (*Applause.*)

1248. Bublikov's Speech
[*Gos. Sov.,* pp. 267–69.]

Citizens: I come to this rostrum only to answer the question that was aimed directly at the commercial and industrial bourgeoisie, the question of sacrifices, the question put by the noble leader of the Russian democracy, Comrade Tseretelli. . . .

.   .   .   .

We have been accused here of desertion. But who has prevented us, from top to bottom, from working for the benefit of the native land? Were we ourselves the ones to leave the commercial organizations at the lower levels? Were we the ones who refused to participate there? We were ousted from the top and from the bottom. (*Applause.*) But it is not resentment which fills my words, but [a feeling of] deep sorrow that during a period which required the most intensive national construction, our native land was seized with the unfortunate idea that this could be accomplished quickly and easily, without the participation of one of the major forces in the country, a force which long ago demonstrated in one way or another its creative capacities. And now, when on the third day of our conference we heard the long-awaited words, when for the first time a fraternal hand was extended to us, this hand—I declare on behalf of the commercial and industrial class—will not remain suspended in the air. It will not remain suspended; even if it is the first time that it is extended, it will not remain suspended, even if you have made the great mistake of applauding the words saying that the commercial and industrial [class] is the enemy of the country. We wait and believe that these old vestiges, these themes borrowed from the West, where everything, perhaps, is built on conflict, where love has been forgotten—[that] these words will fall into disuse in Russia, and that in offering us a coalition you will enter it not only honestly, as you proposed, but also with the greatest respect for the other side. (*Applause.*) And then the commercial and industrial class will have the greatest happiness of standing with you, shoulder to shoulder, in the ranks of those working for the benefit of a new, happy Russia, a Russia which for many years it has yearned to see free, [a Russia] in the creation of which it has participated through its representatives, and from which it will now never withdraw. For it is only in this atmosphere of freedom that it will be able to fulfill the greatest task that confronts it: [that of] accomplishing the creative work for the benefit of Russia on the basis of which all Russia could become prosperous, the creative work which would give her the same opportunity as has the rich, strong, foreign industry to pay its beloved co-workers generously according to their deserts and not to force them into exhausting labor for a worthless price as formerly, when this industry itself had one foot in the grave. ("Bravo!" *Applause.*) And we are offering you all our knowledge and experience so as to avoid unnecessary upsets and to accomplish this creative work in the shortest possible time and with the maximum advantage not to us, but to our native land, dearly beloved by us all. (*Applause from the whole audience. Bublikov and Tseretelli shake hands. Stormy ovation.*)

1249. SPEECH OF THE REPRESENTATIVE OF THE CENTRAL COUNCIL OF TRADE UNIONS, V. P. GRINEVICH

[*Gos. Sov.*, pp. 273–78.]

Citizens and comrades: [I speak] on behalf of the workers' trade unions which have asked to be represented at the Moscow State Conference by the Presidium—in the persons of its Chairman and his two deputies—of the All-Russian Central Council of Trade Unions, elected at the All-Russian Conference of Trade Unions which was held in Petrograd in the month of June and was attended by 220 delegates representing 1,475,000 workers organized in trade unions. Citizens and comrades: before I begin to deliver my speech, I wish to state on behalf of the majority of the workers organized in trade unions that we wholeheartedly support the declaration read here yesterday by our Comrade Chkheidze. (*Applause on the left benches.*) And if, comrades and citizens, I was forced to word the first [statement of our] support, unfortunately, on behalf of only a majority, now on behalf of all the organized workers in trade unions, we [give our] support to the economic, financial, and labor program adopted by the All-Russian Congress of Soviets of Workers' and Soldiers' Deputies. (*Applause.*) And, comrades and citizens, even more energetically we give the powerful support of the organized trade union workers for the defense of those organizations, those Soviets and committees which were created in the process of the Russian revolution, thereby establishing a united, revolutionary front of the Russian democracy on the extreme left wing. (*Applause.*)

. . .

I will permit myself a short digression. It has been said here that the workers are responsible for the disruption of industry, that it is owing to their exorbitant demands that there is disorganization in transport, and so on and so forth. But, citizens and comrades, one must, after all, speak the truth. . . . The representative of the front committees who spoke here drew us a terrible picture of [what happens] when one has to face spontaneous [outbreaks] of the workers' masses. But you know that the whole criminal policy of the tsarist regime is responsible for the illiteracy and the lack of culture that prevail among the broad masses of workers, and it required the tremendous energies of the more mature, leading elements of the working class—in this respect the Soviets of Workers' Deputies gave us tremendous assistance and performed a tremendous service—in order that the spontaneous movement of the workers for the improvement of their until-then starvation existence, a movement that was often irresponsible, [marked by] all forms of violence, could be directed, step by step, into organized channels.

. . .

Comrades and citizens, I want to pause on the question of labor productivity. As you know, this is the question with which the whole bourgeois press is daily intimidating all of Russia; this is the question with which it wages war against the working class. . . . You can see that the organized actions of the working class do not pursue [the end of] wages alone. . . . In addition, I will tell you that whenever they speak about the decrease of labor productivity, it is worded in such a way as to imply that the decline in the production of Russian industry resulted entirely from the negligence of the workers and their unwillingness to work. But, citizens and comrades, aside from the noble words heard within these walls, it is necessary to exhibit their noble spirit outside of these walls, too; the noble spirit is needed in the actions that are taken, and let the representatives of the commercial and industrial capital truthfully indicate why Russian industry has declined so much. It is because there was no impetus for [industry], enriched by excess war profits, to improve its machines, its benches, to raise the productive capacity of the nation. Let them indicate truthfully that the productivity of labor has declined owing to the disorganization of food supply, owing to that terrible position in which the working class finds itself, owing to the abolition of the laws on restricting woman and child labor passed during the war with the support of the industrial class, owing to the influx into the working class of new elements of woman labor and the labor of adolescents who are untrained, unprepared, unqualified, [and] who cannot produce according to the former standards.

So, citizens and comrades, in discussing these questions it must be said—my time, unfortunately, is coming to an end and I did not have time to touch on other questions—that, yes, we will find a way out of this impasse, out of this political, military, and industrial-economic impasse, when we will all come to understand each other and when we will say that our new democratic regime, our new revolutionary Russia, must be built on the basis of a determined application of the principle of initiative in all spheres as well as of the most equitable distribution of the national income. (*Storm of applause.*)

1250. SPEECH OF TRADE UNION REPRESENTATIVE, D. B. RIAZANOV
[*Gos. Sov.*, pp. 278–81.]

Citizens and comrades: The speaker who preceded me told you that he is the representative of the majority of all the workers organized in trade unions. We won't argue here about [what constitutes] a majority or a minority—the fact is that I represent those workers, organized in trade unions, who are known by the name of Internationalists. (*Applause of the extreme leftists.*) Comrade Grinevich found it necessary to emphasize that the section of the workers whose opinion he considers he has the right to express wholly supports the political program of the Soviets of Workers', Soldiers', and Peasants' Deputies. But this does not mean that I, as the minority representative, do not support this program, [or] that the minority which, if you will, stands behind us is separating itself from the revolutionary democracy. It merely retains the humble honor of being the extreme left wing of this revolutionary democracy. (*Applause from the left.*) . . . Our disagreement [revolves] essentially around the question of how strong is that combination of power [represented by those who] addressed you at today's [session] of the State Conference. Our disagreement is essentially [around the question of] how strong and how sound are the hopes that are placed on (*a gesture to the right*) this sector. (*Laughter.*) And now I must say that I know Citizen Bublikov through our joint work in the Economic Council. I have already had the occasion there to point out his thorough knowledge of the field of transportation and his understanding of the failings of the old regime in this field. Even so, although I saw him shake hands with Comrade Tseretelli, although I listened to his well-wishings, his assurance that the commercial and industrial class and this sector are ready [to accept] this unity, I am compelled to say: I hear this wish [expressed] but I have no faith. I would not believe it even if Citizen Riabushinskii had kissed Comrade Chkheidze. (*Laughter.*) The history of the French Revolution has preserved for us the memory of Lamouré's kiss, the kiss that was exchanged between two sections of the National Assembly—not the working class and not the bourgeoisie, but the two sections of the bourgeoisie—and you know that never did this struggle flare up so fiercely as after that kiss. (*Laughter*). . . .

· · ·

1251. Speech by the Representative of Cooperative Organizations,
A. M. Berkenheim
[*Gos. Sov.*, pp. 297–301.]

Citizens: I am speaking here as the representative of 50 thousand cooperative organizations of Russia which include 20 million members, encompassing around half of the population of Russia through its economic organizations. . . .

The Russian cooperatives have made only one political appearance since the time of the Russian revolution. This was right after the February Days when we declared that we all needed but one thing: a democratic republic and the free expression of the will of the people at the Constituent Assembly. At that time we were invited to assist the Government in the field of food supply and the distribution of the products of prime necessity. And modestly, without a single word, withdrawing from the political arena, we of the cooperatives—the unskilled workers of Russian society—settled down to this work. We consider that now, in this grave and terrible hour, we, too, must express our views once again. We know no parties in our midst. Our organizations include everyone, and different elements of Russian society are working peacefully side by side, shoulder to shoulder, in our midst. On behalf of these nonparty cooperatives I declare that we give our full support to the declaration of the revolutionary democracy that was read here. (*Cries:* "Bravo!" *Applause from the left.*)

We more than anybody else know the tremendous public role which the Soviets played in the history of the Russian revolution and the role they now play in consolidating Russian society. We have all the more right to declare this because, by its present statement, extending its hand to the other strata of the Russian population, the revolutionary democracy—personified by the Soviets and other public organizations—has now demonstrated in practice its political maturity, its preparedness, and its ability to analyze the state of affairs and to give a serious, historically correct appraisal of it. We declare that in supporting the declaration of the revolutionary democracy we do not conceive of the government of Russia as being other than a united, integral Government that stands above party [considerations]. We assert that what Russia needs now more than anything else is a united, integral, and strong government power. We have the utmost confidence in this government which has been selected from the best of Russian people; we trust it and we commit ourselves to support it in every possible way. (*Storm of applause.*)

. . .

In the economic sphere, I must state that the cooperatives have never sought to strengthen their position by government legislation. The cooperatives are free. . . . We consider that the force of the cooperatives and their tremendous economic power are not being put to sufficient use by the revolutionary government. . . . And we believe that greater reliance ought to be placed in practice on the free creative work of the people, on their cooperative organizations. We think that a system of properly and consistently enforced state monopolies in conjunction with consistently and properly enforced regulation of the economy must now underlie all economic legislation. We consider, first of all, that the grain monopoly must remain intact. We consider that the fixed prices on grain must remain constant. . . .

It stands to reason that the proper regulation of industry must subsume the regulation of profits, the regulation of industrial life, and the regulation of labor, and must conclude, in the long run, with universal labor conscription.

Citizens and comrades, during the past days we have been hearing how two views come up against each other, as though there were [two] separate trends in one Russia: the labor and the bourgeoisie, the laboring democracy and the forces of the bourgeoisie. We consider—that is, we of the cooperatives consider —that in the face of this moment in the history of Russia there can be no place for the perpetual opposition of these concepts. . . .

We have heard long [speeches] here where much has been said to us about the downfall of Russia. Citizens, this is not true. Russia's downfall is out of the question—there can be no downfall of Russia; she will not fall. Do we actually know the meaning of real privation? Is it not true that in our privation with regard to food supplies we are approaching the [situation] which Germany has already experienced in two years of war? . . .

. . .

Comrades and citizens, I do not know whether Russia will ever have to experience a turning point in her history as dreadful and as decisive as the one through which we are now passing. It seems to us that this is what we must do in our role, the role of the practical cooperative organizations: we must say openly and definitely, for everyone to hear, that—recognizing the full significance, cor-

rectness, and integrity of the position of the revolutionary democracy, being completely at one with it in all our thoughts, with all our past and with all our future,
now, at this critical moment, on this terrible day of judgment—we, together with
the others, consider it our duty to call upon all Russian citizens to unite for a
common goal, to rally together as [closely] as possible in a common drive and
declare together with everybody else: "In unity there is strength." (*Applause.*)

1252. KERENSKY'S CONCLUDING ADDRESS

[*Gos. Sov.*, pp. 301–7.]

The State Conference is drawing to a close. In spite of all the difficulties and
doubts entertained by many persons before this Conference, the Provisional Government summoned it anyway, and has no regrets for having done so. The Provisional Government believed and believes that even if this Conference produces
no immediate, tangible, concrete results, its enormous significance would still rest
in the fact that the citizens of the State of Russia of all classes, parties, and nationalities assembled and openly expressed their thoughts to one another on what,
in their opinion, is necessary for the State at this moment of truly great danger.
. . . The Provisional Government received the opportunity to take, so to
speak, a snapshot of the political moods of the country. The whole range of
moods, shades, and aspirations was displayed before it. It is not only what was
said here that was displayed, but also what was felt and what was partly left
unsaid and what was being carried away to those obscure levels of socio-political
life for which the time has not yet come, perhaps, to express themselves aloud.

The Provisional Government does not, of course, interpret this Conference
as an expression of a feeling of general unity and general agreement. The life of
the State is such that it encompasses interests that are both compatible and incompatible, and, sometimes, those that are completely irreconcilable. This Conference has strengthened our conviction that the task of any Provisional Government, and, in general, of any Russian government at the present time, consists of
reconciling conscientiously, as well as conciliating, everything that is at all conceivable in the name of the one, in the name of the whole, State . . .

The Provisional Government came here with the words "The State requires
order, sacrifices, and labor." And you who had to answer, each for himself, said:
"We will sacrifice, we will give our labor, and we want order." Unfortunately,
this was often accompanied by a qualification: "We will do this if our neighbors
will do the same." This means that it is necessary for someone to begin. I am
deeply convinced that the ones who will begin will be those to whom a free country
is dearest of all, to whom dearest of all is the struggle which we are carrying on
for the future, and to whom most odious of all is this apparition of imminent
disgrace and humiliation. (*Applause from the whole audience.*) The Provisional
Government hears and knows about everything that is happening in the country.
The Provisional Government—as I said on Saturday—cannot conceive of and
cannot understand how it can be possible to govern against the will of the country,
or without fulfilling the will of this country in at least certain respects. But at
the same time, the Provisional Government, and every [person] who has been in
government, knows how difficult it is to find [the solution] that would truly conform to the real will of the country. Each one who comes speaks with authority,
each one sees only a part; but we, by virtue of our position, see the whole. If we
do not see it, then this is our fault, for we must see everything. (*Voices:* "Bravo!"

"Right!") And it often happens that as soon as a person leaves the government, he ceases to see the whole, and, seeing only a part, he can attack those who are in power that much more vigorously. (*Applause from the left.*)

Is it not clear to you, citizens, from what you have heard here, that it is so difficult, sometimes almost impossible, to reconcile the various points of view, the various interests, and to establish a common understanding of things? Did not the people here, striving alike only for the good of the State, speak of the very same things in completely different ways; and did not each one of you, after hearing an opposite analysis of a given problem or a point of view—did not each one of you understand that he had not quite seen everything [that there was] to the problem, but that he now sees more? (*Voice:* "Right.") It is precisely this that constitutes the unbearable difficulty for the Government, which honestly strives only for this common will and these common aims. Where are the criteria? Who can tell? And where are the scales? It is the human being with his weaknesses, with his ability to perceive only in his own limited way. If we are told here, "You have already sold yourselves out to the bourgeoisie, you have already sold the interests of the revolution and the people, you are practically serving to restore the old regime," then they who say [this] are not those who sit here and who understand the problems of the State, but those who are not represented here and with whom we coped successfully when it was necessary and crushed their revolt against the national power. But we are told at the same time that we are merely mirages and shadows, that, in reality, we are in the power of some—in your opinion (*pointing to the right side*)—dark forces. We are told that we are no longer free in our actions. Here I must also say that the Provisional Government is not dependent on any forces outside of the Provisional Government, with the exception of only one, single force—the force of the will of the people, which we seek. (*Applause.*) Such a Government will always encounter many critics in its course, but few supporters, because each one feels, every class and every party feels, that his desires have not been gratified to the fullest extent, and each one thinks that this is because the shadowy power, occupying a place that does not [rightfully] belong to it, does not dare to gratify all his desires. Perhaps you have seen that even this is not so, because in the arguments that have been presented here, you have sometimes heard a truth which you yourselves had not known before.

I will not summarize the opinions that have been voiced here. I must only state that everything that has been expressed here will be taken into consideration by the Provisional Government for guidance and coordination in the name of the interests of the country and her salvation. (*Loud applause.*) I must state likewise that whatever, in our belief, does not conform to the national interests will not be acted upon, regardless of the pressure exerted upon us, even if this pressure turns into physical coercion or threats—we will not do anything which, according to our conscience, does not conform to the common views. (*Storm of applause.*) We are told: how quickly the Provisional Government is leading the country to ruin. There was no end to the number of crimes and sins attributed to us! But these people forget that the Provisional Government has existed for a mere six months, while the empire existed for 300 years. They forget that many—and this I know—did not want to take the power away from the old government, reasoning very wisely and very well for themselves: "Why should we, in the last hours of the war, assume the responsibility for other people's sins?" The Provisional Government was not afraid of assuming this responsibility; it was not afraid during its first composition, and it is not afraid even now, because it knows that, apart from the judgment of contemporaries, there is still the judgment of history. (*Storm of applause.*)

They forget still another thing—they forget the war. They forget this terrible phantom which is destroying lives and plundering wealth, which is leading all the peoples to improvishment, and with which the old power, based on [strong] cultural traditions—which are no match for us—could hardly cope after the third year of the war. And this sin that is not ours—the war—we take upon ourselves. Not only do we not say: stop now, but we say: curse him who will tell us to stop the fight now. (*Storm of applause.*)

Yes, it is difficult for us, because we know the force of human ignorance, not only of the lowest classes of society, but of all Russian society; ignorance not in elementary matters, of course, but in questions of statesmanship, in questions of government. ("True," "Right!") And we know that perhaps we will succumb to these blows. . . . because [the responsibility for] everything that has happened in the past is laid upon the last [statesmen] who entered [the Government] with the sole aim of banishing this past forever beyond recall. (*Cries:* "Right!" *Applause.*) This policy of steering the middle course, this policy that is not even at the middle, this policy is the only genuine policy that considers the State. This path is thorny and difficult, and it is no wonder that the Provisional Government has been changing its composition. Many of the things for which we who sit here are now being blamed became converted into fact at a time when I alone represented the whole democracy in the first Provisional Government. (*Applause.*) What, then—is it that I possess or possessed such strength that I forced people to do what I wanted, instead of what they wanted? No, it is because that was the kind of life and those were the things that had to be done and there was no other way of going about it under the historical conditions of the times. Whoever comes to power will set out right away to do what has to be done for the country. And the Provisional Government, which is more democratic in its present composition, is adopting measures for bringing influence to bear and measures of physical coercion which the first Provisional Government would not have adopted. (*Cries:* "Right!") The things for which the first Provisional Government is now being reproached, I gave it credit for, because it is precisely the first Provisional Government which exhibited the self-restraint and, I might say, the wisdom of statesmanship when it refrained from adopting measures which, under the conditions of that period, would not have been understood by the populace, which would not have been understood by you who are now sitting here on the right, and which would have brought about the opposite results and would have made our future course more difficult and complicated instead of bringing us closer to it. (*Applause.*)

I will never forget the day, gentlemen, members of the State Conference, when we were sitting in the office of the Minister of War, Guchkov, and when we were informed that armed people were coming to remove us. We all replied, unanimously: "There are to be no steps taken for our protection." (*Loud applause from the whole audience.*) This was genuine faith in the strength of the reason and the wisdom of the people. It was only when this violence was used against the Government, which [itself] had never made use of violence and had not followed the policy of the old regime in any way, that we said: "Here reason, and perhaps conscience, too, has come to an end, and here we will fight." . . .

Today, permit me to say, not on behalf of the Provisional Government but on my own behalf, I feel that not everyone understands the necessity of a policy that does not have as its aim the use of physical force, which is demanded today. I feel that this experiment will be adopted by one side or another, but then only will you see that the power which appeared impotent was the only possible power under the present conditions. As soon as the Provisional Government or anyone else adopts the most iron-fisted, the most drastic measures in order to carry out some one task to the very end or to gratify somebody's particular interests and destroys what now exists, he will usher in a civil war and a great calamity in which all of us, perhaps, will perish. ("True!") That is why we must defend to the last hour that one and only policy which the Government can now pursue—that of reconciling everything that can be reconciled, of leading everyone toward one objective, sweeping aside and, if need be, chopping off only those [elements] which do not want to subordinate their desires to the common will, but, on the contrary, want to subordinate the common will, by force, to their own desires. (*Applause.*)

. . .

The Provisional Government considers that the most fundamental, the most important, the most vital questions at the present time are the question of the army and the questions of regenerating and strengthening the financial and economic life of the country. [On this latter point] we want to do everything that can be done in this direction. We are waiting for the assistance of the wisdom of the country. We are expecting that everything that has been said here will be carried out in practice, and that this symbolic hand-shake will bring the necessary practical results. On our part, we will do our utmost to contribute to this present *rapproache-ment* of interests, protecting at the same time the legitimate needs and requirements of every side. (*Applause.*) It may happen that both sides will say that they are dissatified, because each one of them will not have been satisfied to the fullest extent.

But the even more frightening and more vital question for the country is that of the army. And I, as Minister of War and Navy, and all of us, as members of the Provisional Government, grieve that in the opinions expressed here concerning the army certain statements were permitted which disturbed the [various] sides too greatly. . . . When the army is, really, the people in arms, when the army is open from all sides to all kinds of political influence, every careless word, every statement that is too sharp, is bound to react painfully on the nerves of all those who are at the front, and I am already receiving comments regarding these discussions and the statements that have been made here. The feelings of every member of the army—officer or soldier, irrespectively—are equally and endlessly valuable to me. My problem, the problem of the Minister of War, and the problem of the Provisional Government, is to know the right measure of things in this question in order to fight for and create conditions under which the fighting capacity of the army will not decrease and its strength will not collapse. I will take the liberty of assuring you once again that we refuse to [adopt] this or that measure only when we feel that it may yield the opposite results. And I think that to the army—to its diverse parts and elements—a somewhat greater truth was revealed about itself than it had known before, because yesterday and today the balance sheet of these five months, since the day of the revolution, was drawn up. I must retain my objectivity in this matter, gentlemen, members of the State Conference. And I must remind those of you who have spoken here about the necessity of a radical, abrupt change in the life of the army, which is not supported by the Supreme Command—these persons have either forgotten or do not even know the present-day reality. They have forgotten that the commissars and I did not come to the army and the navy of our own accord, but only because this was necessary then, as it is now, because the army and the navy are still unable to lead a regular life and perform their functions, because their fundamental elements still do not see eye to eye. . . .

Many commanders under the present conditions are resorting to forceful measures which are inadmissible, and both the Supreme Commander and I have to take urgent and drastic steps. Even here the individuals who are responsible for the army both at the front and in the rear must be allowed to do what is necessary without attracting or arousing the unhealthy curiosity which surrounds the army and those attempts at repression which are harmful to both our native land and the army. (*Applause from the left.*) In closing this Conference, gentlemen, members of the State Conference, the Provisional Government wishes to express once again its deep appreciation to each one of you for having come here, [for] each person who was invited has come here. You came to help us in the difficult and burdensome work, unbearable in its responsibility, which has fallen to our lot. Perhaps the hope which binds each one of us present here to this State Conference will not come to pass. Perhaps our State will not have sufficient strength to find the road to salvation as quickly as is necessary. But each of you, I hope, will always remember that in a grave and difficult hour the Russian citizens were able to come to an agreement and put aside all that is petty and insignificant, all that consciously or unconsciously increases animosity. Every person, according to his perception and awarenes, spoke only of the State, of the native land, of her ills, and appealed only for the common, united cause of saving what is so profoundly dear to us, that which is of immeasurable value to us, which has no name, because one speaks too often of the native land, forgetting the meaning of the word. . . .

I am often told that I have too much faith and that I dream too much. Now, members of the State Conference and citizens of the Russian land, I will not dream any more. I will try to have less faith—it often happens that the Government is blamed for having this boundless faith, the faith in man, in his soul, in his conscience and his reason. . . . If each one of you could glance for just a moment at everything that is happening in the country, if you could take a glance and see everything and understand, you would not be speaking in the way you do. Since it must be, so let it be. Let my heart turn to stone, let all the chords of my faith in man fade away, let all the flowers of my dreams for man wither and die. (*Cry from above:* "Don't let this happen!") These have been scorned and stamped upon today from this rostrum. Then I will stamp on them myself. They will cease to be. (*Cry from above:* "You cannot do this—your heart will not permit you this.") I will cast away the keys to this heart that loves the people and I will think only of the State. And let everyone know that everything you had wanted and which has not been, is possible. (*Cry:* "Long live the Provisional Government!") Perhaps all those forms of government for which you yearn, this yearning for a power that brings pressure to bear from above, [perhaps] it is a yearning for the autocracy which you abolished (*cry:* "May it be damned!"), [perhaps] it is the lack of understanding that the power of the government resides only in public opinion and in the will of the whole people. In every measure that is associated with brutality, the Government must exercise even greater caution than with respect to the life of one it holds dearest of all, because there is no more valuable a good and no greater a value than our native land and the people. (*Applause.*)

Tomorrow we will return to the heavy duty, work, and service to the State; tomorrow we will return to our routine conditions. Today, however, allow me to say to you on behalf of the Provisional Government that never will our native land perish; no one will ever deprive her of the freedom which was won by all the people.

(*Members of the Conference rise from their seats and give a fervent ovation to Kerensky, lasting several minutes. Cries:* "Long live the revolution!" "Long live the Russian republic!" "Hurrah!" "Long live Kerensky!")

I announce the State Conference closed, its work being completed. (*Cries:* "Long live the revolution!")

The Conference closed at 1:20 a.m.

REACTIONS

1253. *Novoe Vremia* on Kornilov's Speech
[No. 14853, August 13, 1917, p. 5.]

The most outstanding features of the second day's session of the State Conference in Moscow was the speech of General Kornilov.

He was the first to put a finger boldly in the wound. Russia is threatened with destruction because of the disgraceful condition in the army. Owing to the abolition of military discipline, the heretofore valiant army has degenerated in places into a mob of robbers. It surrenders at the first gunshot, it raids and violates the peaceful population, it concludes peace treaties with the enemy for a price of 200 rubles per head, it murders its leaders. The shield and sword of the State and the people have turned into the knife of a murderer and the axe of an executioner.

The source of this terrible transformation is the "ill-advised measures introduced in the army in order to reorganize it by people who do not know what the army is [*sic*]." The situation is further aggravated by the fact that at the helm of the ship of state are people who oppose the idea of defending the State.

In contrast to other government leaders, the Supreme Commander indicated quite definite measures without which the restoration of the army is impossible.

. . .

The demands of the first soldier of the revolutionary army are direct, straightforward, and useful. They preserve the army as a weapon of national defense, reserve in it a proper place for the influence of the democratic elements through committees, and, finally, introduce a strict revolutionary control over the commanding personnel through government commissars.

But in the eyes of the imported politicians and their local servants, this plan suffers from one major defect. It preserves the strength of the Russian army. It promises to convert the disordered hordes of armed people dangerous only to their compatriots into a mighty weapon of national defense. Therefore, even in the State Conference people were found who thought it propitious to show particular contempt for the first soldier of the revolutionary army. They were met with shouts of traitor and other deserving epithets.

These shouts embrarrassed and brought a few to reason. But this is merely an episode.

The important thing for Russia is: will the State Conference be able to insist on the implementation of the Supreme Commander's demands or not?

General Kornilov stated that his views are shared completely by the administrator of the Ministry of War, Savinkov, and by Commissar Filonenko, at Stavka.

The administrator of the Ministry, it seems, was removed from his post. He was removed for agreeing with the views of the Supreme Commander.[5]

And so, everything will remain as before?

That is the crucial question now.

Either the restoration of the Russian army along the lines indicated by General Kornilov—there are no other ways—or its final disintegration, with the unavoidable ruin of Russia and all of her freedoms.

All of Russia favors the former move. The latter is supported by the imported politicians who place their own fleeting power above all. Which of the tendencies will triumph will depend upon the head of the Provisional Government.

1254. *Russkiia Vedomosti* ON KORNILOV'S SPEECH
[No. 186, August 15, 1917, p. 3.]

The most arresting moment of the Moscow State Conference was the address of the Supreme Commander, General Kornilov. His was a guileless speech, devoid of all oratorical embellishments. It was an account of the illness of the army, but the effect it produced was great. In an even, restrained voice, in a tone in which one relates something that is painful and hard to talk about, General Kornilov painted a picture of the disintegration of the army. He told of the unmerciful beating of officers, of the desertion of whole regiments, of the onset of famine in the army, of the appalling drop in the production of guns and shells, and the even sharper reduction in the production of our plants of fighter and reconnaissance airplanes, etc., etc. Much of what Kornilov had to say was already known before. But when the entire picture of the breakdown of the army was revealed to the audience, and when this picture was painted by no other than the Supreme Commander of the same army, a truly sinister impression was gained. The words of General Kornilov took on a sinister shading; they expressed doubt that we will hold back the further pressure and the impending danger to the capital. We are well accustomed to the words "the fatherland is in danger." But General Kornilov's speech contained no fine words; it was saturated with the menacing truth in all of its stern reality, and because of this it was the more terrifying. When the General began to talk about the measures necessary to restore the army to health, even the thought of arguing against these measures seemed strange. Could there be any question of arguing; is there any need to prove the necessity to undertake immediately, stopping at nothing, all the measures that could protect the country from ruin?

General Kornilov did not deal at all with questions of the internal life of the state; he did not touch, even indirectly, upon any political or social themes, which arouse such discord among us. He was what he had to be—a strictly non-party

[5] See Volume II, Doc. 887.

leader of the army who grieves because of its needs and who thinks only of defending the country. This strictly non-party position of General Kornilov, together with the exceptional restraint of his speech, gave every reason to believe that precisely this speech would become the center of the national unity which was the purpose of convening the Moscow Conference. But this has not happened. To be sure, part of the Conference was deeply shaken by what it heard, but then the other part remained indifferent to the speech of the Supreme Commander. More-over, this part deemed it necessary to demonstrate its restrained attitude to the address of the leader of the Russian army. These refrained from any expressions of sympathy toward him and toward his recommendations. And this spoke for the failure of the whole Moscow Conference. Of course, all speakers talked about the necessity of union and solidarity. The recommendations introduced at the Conference testified to that. But unity of sentiment has not been achieved at the Conference. There was no outburst of feeling that could rally everyone around the common task of saving the motherland. Part of the Conference still was not kindled with sacred alarm about the salvation of the motherland from the external enemy; it remained deaf to the danger threatening the country. And if General Kornilov failed in his speech to awaken a sacrificing enthusiasm, a readiness for heroic deeds, if he failed to dissipate the concentrated atmosphere of party and class egotism, it is doubtful that any of the subsequent speakers at the Conference will succeed in doing so. The purposes of the Conference remain unachieved.

1255. *Rech'* ON THE SIGNIFICANCE OF THE CONFERENCE
[No. 192, August 17, 1917, p. 1.]

. . . By contributing to the destruction of the present, the Moscow Conference has undoubtely helped to shape the near future. Will this near future preserve the present membership of the Government? If it is to this end, the purposes of self-preservation, that the Government convened the Moscow Conference, then it has made a grave mistake. The Moscow Conference has shifted the line of demarcation between the representatives of the population into two camps, and has thereby opened the question of the present composition of the Government, because its membership has to a considerable degree passed from the now outmoded and completed stage of revolutionary utopianism to the stage of sober reality. For the mentality of the Minister-President himself, who reacted with nervous sensitivity to the rise of the new wave, the necessity of following this shift in revolutionary stages represented a singular [personal] tragedy, which he expressed in a gloomy readiness to destroy his own soul. These statements astounded the majority of the Conference by their spontaneousness and . . . intensity. They reflected the difficulty and tragic impossibility, as demonstrated by A. F. Kerensky at the Conference, for men irrevocably linked with the history of the Russian revolutionary movement to willingly and freely proceed into the promised land, which they attained in the wake of their pillar of fire, the land of liberated Russia. Another way of life, another training, other habits and actions are required for consolidating the conquests of the revolution, for creating a revolutionary legality by means of self-asserted Jacobinian organizations.

Utopianism does not always acquire the noble features reflected in the burning emotionalism of A. F. Kerensky or in that of an Avksent'ev. . . .

. . . Whether they wished to bring forth all these issues or not, the organizers of the Moscow Conference did so. Whatever course historical events take, as from the days of this Conference the Russian revolution is beginning a new chapter.

1256. *Den'* ON THE CONFERENCE
[No. 139, August 18, 1917, p. 1.]

One went to the Moscow Conference as to a battle. The revolutionary democracy expected an attack from bourgeois Russia; it prepared itself to repel it and even to start a counterattack.

Now, summing up, after the Conference, the combatants try to find out who has won.

One side exults that democracy has won; the other believes as firmly that democracy has retreated.

The Moscow Conference acquires great importance for the country, precisely because it has mixed up the cards and forced a sharply defined struggle on a completely different plane. No one has come as a victor from this battle, or, if you wish, everybody has suffered defeat. The Moscow Conference has consolidated all the separate groups into two large camps.

For the first time the democracy has met face to face a great social force in Russia, the existence of which she knew but which she could not fathom. The democracy felt that the words regarding bourgeois revolution began to take on flesh and blood in the form of a mighty force which wishes to live and act in the bourgeois way, a force with which it is necessary to reckon not in proportion to its number, but in accordance with its social significance.

But also bourgeois Russia has felt that the time of its undivided power has not yet arrived.

And the struggle for power which was ready to seethe did not break out, although a contest was going on.

By themselves, the formulas, which boiled down to the issue of who is capable of saving Russia, turned in another direction and were forced to give a reply to the question: what is capable of saving Russia?

The answer broke through with elementary force; an honest coalition of opposing and, at the same time, inseparable forces.

The fact that democracy was the first to pronounce this word represents its merit but not its victory.

By saying these words regarding an honest coalition, democracy has thereby condemned everything that up to now has hindered on its part an honest coalition.

Sentence was pronounced not only against the Bolsheviks, who were not allowed at the Conference, but against all programs, against whole tactics, in so far as they contain a spirit of domination over the other side and not a spirit of mutual agreement and of concessions.

Not only Leninism but in the same measure its opposite, Miliukovism, suffered a defeat. . . .

1257. *Delo Naroda* ON THE CONFERENCE
[No. 129, August 17, 1917, p. 1.]

The Moscow State Conference did not live up to the hopes placed in it or the apprehensions it suggested. And since our hopes were not shattered, but, on the contrary, that which we had feared did not come to pass, we must naturally evaluate the Moscow Conference with a plus sign rather than a minus.

In spite of its immediate tasks, the Moscow State Conference consolidated the ranks of the revolutionary democracy. It effected a unity of the revolutionary front which its enemies did not except and of which its friends could not be quite sure either. . . .

. . .

By its declaration the revolutionary democracy deprived its opponents of the ammunition they used against it. In developing the Government declaration of July 8 the democracy outlined a wide, concrete, and truly national program of salvation of the motherland and the revolution. What could the real and concealed enemies of the revolution say against the declared program? *No one* who sincerely wished the salvation of the country could *by one word* deny the importance of the measures proposed by the democracy. And the enemies of the revolution were compelled to capitulate in the face of the united democracy.

The hand tendered by Bublikov to Tseretelli symbolized the bourgeoisie's admission of its moral capitulation.

We do not overestimate the importance of the "moral capitulation." But even in the world of real things a moral victory, a victory of ideas, is not a hypothetical, but a real quantity. . . .

In this respect, without exaggerating the importance of the Moscow Conference one can rightly say that the Government also emerged from the Conference stronger than it had been before the Conference. Anyone who realizes how important it is for a revolutionary government to be strong in its creative work cannot but also view this consequence of the Moscow Conference as a positive achievement.

. . .

Some episodes which were not in tune with the general sentiment only set off the role of the leading actor on the stage of the Moscow Bol'shoi Theater—the Russian democracy.

No salvation either for the revolution or for Russia outside the democracy was the thesis publicly declared and triumphantly approved at the Moscow Conference.

1258. *Izvestiia* ON THE CONFERENCE
[No. 145, August 16, 1917, p. 1.]

What will be the outcome of the Moscow Conference? What direct results will it bring?

As we write these lines, only a conjectural answer to these questions is possible at the moment. But one result is already certain—it will be an impressive demonstration of all the inexhaustible forces that the revolution has at its disposal. Those who considered that the revolution was practically buried—all the counterrevolutionaries who were already hovering over the revolution like vultures over a corpse —all the "June 3rd" Kadets and Octobrists who were all set to give a sound kick to the dead lion—experienced deep disappointment during these [past] days of the Moscow Conference.

The revolution was wounded, but it did not die. Moreover, it possesses its own curative powers, which will place it back on its feet and enable it to progress. The malicious digressions aimed at all the organized forces of the revolution which have carried and continue to carry the revolution on their shoulders, the barely concealed dreams, here and there, about returning to "the good old times," the pathetic declamation on the theme of "national defense," and the cold phrases, devoid of content, about sacrifices, without a single concrete statement about any effective sacrifice—this is all that the enemies of the revolution had to offer to all Russia in a time of mortal danger to the native land, which they are taking upon themselves to save by their own methods.

The declaration of the united democracy presented a complete contrast. It gave a clear and concrete program of the legislation necessary for the efficient organization of [national] defense and the salvation of the country. The enemies of the revolution did not choose to fight on these grounds, but the declamatory phrases which continued even after the declaration was read sounded that much more pitiful and false. And that much more embarrassing was the silence in response to the democratic speakers' appeal for a united effort, on the basis of this practical and truly effective program, of all those for whom [the word] Russia was not an empty sound and the willingness to make sacrifices not an empty stipulation.

On the other hand, representatives of the real, living Russia—representatives of workers, peasants, the army and the navy, zemstvos, towns, cooperatives, teachers, various national groups—came forward one after another to testify to their solidarity with the organizations of the revolutionary democracy.

The democracy emerges with greater strength from the Moscow Conference. This fact will have to be considered by the government authorities and all the responsible groups which want, not only in words but in practice, to take part in the cause of saving our native land and of strengthening the democracy, which is based, not on the protection of their own special interests, but on the very fact that the whole country clearly feels that Russia can be saved only by adherence to a consistent democratic platform. The salvation of Russia and the consolidation of the revolution are inseparable from one another.

1259. "Half a Year of the Revolution"

[Editorial in *Izvestiia*, No. 155, August 27, 1917, p. 3.]

. . .

There are eyes that cannot see the forest for the trees. There are pessimists who predict general ruin as a result of every individual mistake or defect. But if one diverts one's attention from the confusions of every little day, if one has the courage to bear the unavoidable privations for the sake of the future and take a look at the past-half year without feelings of irritation over what each one of us has had to endure, then it must be said that in spite of all the wartime burdens, in spite of all the economic disorganization, in spite of all the chaos in domestic affairs and the whole instability of the present and all the dangers of the future, the revolution has accomplished an enormous amount of creative work and is forging ahead over all obstacles.

Civil liberties have been established, foundations for local self-government on a completely democratic basis have been laid, the sword of the democratic army is being forged in heavy battle, and the country is preparing to consummate the revolution by convoking the Constituent Assembly.

There has never yet been a revolution which proceeded so directly toward a set goal. This became possible in our country only because the democratic forces immediately stamped their seal on the whole revolution. The Constituent Assembly, convoked on the basis of universal and equal suffrage with a secret and direct ballot, is the basis of the revolutionary order. No one can raise the objection that this system of resolving all the problems of the state is unjust, or that it places the various elements of the population in positions of inequality. No, it is absolutely just, it is unimpeachably just, and every honest citizen can submit to this order, not as a formality, but in good faith. That is why complete democratization is the best guarantee for lasting internal peace. This social contract was concluded at the insistence of the democratic forces even under the first Provisional Government, and the new, free regime rests firmly on it.

Another guarantee for this regime is the organization of the democratic forces. The Provisional Government has already endured many crises. This is in the order of things, since the Government cannot have the indisputable sanction of the people under a temporary regime, and any composition of the Government or parts of the Government can cause the dissatisfaction of one or another segment of the population. But if to date these government crises have not developed beyond a cabinet crisis and have not ended in outright civil war, and if all the attempts of the lurking counterrevolution proved to be nothing more than the stratagems of provocateurs, then this is because on guard over the revolution and its social contract—which has not yet been fulfilled but is close to being fulfilled —stands a large, organized force: this force is the Soviets of Workers', Soldiers', and Peasants' Deputies. They are preserving the gains of the revolution until the day they place this treasure in the hands of the All-Russian Constituent Assembly.

Just as this time is approaching, a menacing cloud hangs over our country: heavy blows have descended on our revolutionary army. The army, disorganized in its technical machinery by the thieving tsarist regime, could not avoid being disorganized even further during the first weeks of the revolution in view of the contradictions between the officers' corps and the soldiers—contradictions which were driven to the extreme by the same old regime. The Soviets of Soldiers' Deputies tried their utmost to localize these conflicts, and it was only thanks to the Soviets that during the first two months of the revolution the army did not turn into a disorderly mob. They saved it from internal deterioration. And now, after six months of work, these same Soviets act as the source of moral strength for this army and as the principal factor in restoring its discipline, its awareness, and its readiness for action. The blows of the enemy are no longer destroying the army, but are "steeling" it, and we have faith that revolutionary Russia will be just as invincible as was revolutionary France.

The latter became an instrument in Napoleon's policy of conquest. We are insured against such a delusion by the same organization of the democratic forces. In exactly the same way as the realization of universal suffrage within the country is now beyond doubt, so also in foreign policy "peace without annexations or indemnities" will be converted into a fact by the victorious revolution.

The revolution has not yet ended. The greatest of dangers now threaten it. But it will find support in the courage of the revolutionary army and the inspiration of the revolutionary people, and it will achieve victory.

PART VIII
From Kornilov to October[1]

After weeks of preparation, the plot against the Government, organized at Stavka by General Kornilov and his military accomplices with the collaboration of certain conservative and liberal circles in the rear, was revealed on August 26.[2] But in the event, Kornilov's hopes for success proved illusory and his supporters impotent.

That evening, following the receipt of Kornilov's ultimatum, Kerensky reported to the Government on the imminent danger and was granted full power to suppress the counterrevolutionary attempt. He immediately issued orders halting the movement of Kornilov's vanguard under the command of General Krymov and interrupting railroad transport between Luga and Petrograd. Krymov's troops, as they became aware of their mission, defected, and other units were unable or refused to advance. Informed on the following morning of the night's events, the Central Committees of the Soviets of Workers', Soldiers', and Peasants' Deputies created a People's Committee for the Struggle Against Counterrevolution and organized a workers' militia as an auxiliary to support the Government's measures against the uprising.

Within four days the movement had collapsed. Meantime, the Government had offered the Supreme Command to General Alekseev, who declined it, but later agreed to serve as Chief of Staff, provided Kerensky assumed the superior post. This arrangement was accepted on August 30, after which Alekseev departed for Stavka, where he was able to carry out a peaceful arrest of Kornilov and his closest associates on September 1 with a minimum of disruption to the operations of the high command.

The revolt itself was a complete debacle. Its consequences, on the other hand, were far-reaching and ultimately fatal to the democratic regime in Russia. A wave of anarchy swept the armed forces and the country. In the army and in the Baltic Fleet numerous cases of open insubordination and lynchings were reported as soldiers and sailors, unsure where to put their trust, now suspected all officers, although the majority of them had, in fact, remained loyal to the regime. The efforts of Stavka, and of field commanders, together with army and front committees, to instill confidence in the officers and re-establish discipline met with tremendous difficulties and only limited success. In the rear, the incidence of agrarian disorders, workers' manifestations, arbitrary actions by committees, and outbursts by reserve military units rose alarmingly, forcing the Government with increasing frequency to use troops to maintain order. Attempts to restore normal life in the country were futile. Russia had returned to the rule of license that prevailed in the first weeks following the fall of the monarchy.

---

[1] In addition to the sources cited in the following part, valuable materials on this period are to be found in the volumes of *Velikaia oktiabr'skaia sotsialisticheskaia revoliutsiia* entitled *Revoliutsionnoe dvizhenie v rossii v avguste 1917 g.: Razgrom Kornilovskogo miatezha* and *Oktiabr'skoe vooruzhennoe vosstanie v Petrograd*, recently published in the Soviet Union.

[2] See also Volume II, Docs. 876–904.

Concurrently, the political situation rapidly deteriorated. Supporters of the military revolt, seconded and supplemented by the Bolsheviks, took the initiative in launching virulent charges against the Government and particularly the Minister-President, shattering the alliance of democratic forces. Confidence in the nation's leadership was shaken in both the liberal and socialist camps, while the conservative elements were completely alienated.[3] The Government recognized at once that the blow to political stability as well as internal order from a mutiny led by the Supreme Commander necessitated its reorganization. But negotiations were hampered from the beginning by irreconcilable disagreements over its membership. Meantime, on September 1, Russia was formally proclaimed a Republic, and it was announced that five ministers, Kerensky, Tereshchenko, Verkhovskii, Verderevskii, and Nikitin would constitute a directory within the Government to expedite decisions on the most urgent questions, pending the formation of a new ministry.

While Kerensky negotiated with parties and individuals, the socialists debated endlessly whether to approve participation in a cabinet with the Kadets, some of whom had been close to the Kornilov movement, or whether to demand an all-socialist government. To decide the question VTsIK called a Democratic Conference that opened on September 14. Its deliberations and resolutions were far from clarifying. It voted for coalition, then accepted amendments against the inclusion of the Kadets, a patent contradiction as there was no other liberal or moderate party of comparable strength and importance, and finally rejected the entire motion as amended. Disconcerted by their action, the members agreed to authorize a delegation to consult with the Government on a way out of the impasse.

As a result of these discussions, which were attended also by representatives from the Kadets, the socialist parties, and the Moscow industrialists, the third coalition came into being on September 25. Simultaneously, the organization of a Provisional Council of the Russian Republic was announced, composed of delegates of the same groups and parties, various social organizations, and the army, which was to act as a consultive body to the Government until the convocation of the Constituent Assembly. The Council convened on October 7. In the following weeks, it offered a tribune for the Government to report on its activities and aims and a forum for the debate of public issues. Yet, significantly, its first session was marred by an aggressive declaration by Trotsky on the refusal of his party to participate, followed by the withdrawal of the Bolshevik delegation.

Indeed, the Bolsheviks were the real and only gainers from the Kornilov affair. Lenin had understood its implications immediately, writing on August 30 to the Party's Central Committee from his place of hiding that the revolt had brought "an extremely unexpected . . . and downright unbelievably sharp turn in the course of events" and forwarding secret instructions for the new tactics to be followed.[4] In the shock of the Kornilov days and the fear of counterrevolution, the Soviet Executive Committees had accepted Bolshevik collaboration, and under

---

[3] The attitude of the conservatives was evidenced in the proceedings of the Second Congress of Public Leaders in Moscow. See Doc. 1391. P. N. Miliukov wrote in his *Istorii vtoroi russkoi revoliutsii*, I, vypusk 3, 179: "There existed in the press of various trends the almost unanimous conviction that the Bolsheviks either would not make up their minds to seize power as they had no hope of retaining it or if they did seize it would hold on to it for only a very short time. In moderate circles, it was considered that the latter experiment was highly advisable, in order 'to cure Russia of Bolshevism forever.' . . . Experience has shown that this light-minded self-assurance was a great mistake."

[4] *Collected Works of V. I. Lenin: Toward the Seizure of Power*, XXI, Bk. I, 127.

the guise of Soviet arming of the workers, the Bolshevik Red Guard revived. The splits and dissensions among the socialist parties soon also paved the way for Bolshevik control of the Petrograd, Moscow, and a majority of the provincial soviets, while accelerated Bolshevik agitation, propaganda, and disruptive tactics preyed upon the confusion and disillusionment of the masses to discredit the Provisional Government through a campaign of vilification and calumny.

Day after day, Bolshevik propaganda accused the Government of betraying freedom and all the revolutionary achievements of the people, of planning to postpone the Constituent Assembly indefinitely, and of intending to surrender Petrograd to the Germans. Meanwhile, Lenin and his close collaborators were convinced that the moment had come for armed action against the regime. In letter after letter to the Central Committee, he urged preparations for an uprising. Many of his associates demurred, voicing doubts of success. Finally, on October 10, returning to Petrograd in disguise, he appeared before the Central Committee and, after an all-night debate in which he hammered home his views, the Committee voted ten to two for an insurrection. The general staff was to be the Bolshevik-controlled Military Revolutionary Committee, headed by Leon Trotsky, the recently elected President of the Petrograd Soviet.

While Bolshevik preparations went forward and rumors of the impending action spread over the city, Trotsky blandly denied all knowledge of the coming event. But suspecting the real aims of Bolshevik activity among the troops in the capital and doubtful of the loyalty of some of the officers in the Petrograd Garrison, the Government ordered Stavka to dispatch some of the most disciplined regiments from the front.

On the morning of October 24, Kerensky unexpectedly appeared before the regular session of the Council of the Republic to demand prompt support for strong measures to quell the incipient revolt. The response of the overwhelming majority of the assembly left no doubt in Kerensky's mind upon his departure that a formal expression of solidarity with the Government would soon be forthcoming. Instead, the left leaders engaged in heated discussions over the policies of the Government and only late in the evening submitted the Council's answer in the form of a resolution urging the Government to issue a decree transferring the land to the land committees and to initiate immediately negotiations for a general peace, steps which they asserted would stop the uprising. Kerensky and the Government, appalled and indignant at the Council's action, rejected the document as worthless.

Directly following the departure of the delegation from the Council, representatives of the three Don Cossack regiments stationed in Petrograd appeared at the Winter Palace and, after a discussion with the Minister-President, declared their loyalty to the Government and their determination to defend it. Later, when the meeting of the Provisional Government recessed at about 2:00 A.M. on October 25, Kerensky and Deputy Minister-President Konovalov went to the District Military Headquarters to check on the accuracy of the reports from the Commander, which appeared unduly optimistic and at variance with the facts of the constantly worsening situation. His confused and unsatisfactory explanations convinced them of the necessity to attempt a reorganization of the command.

As the morning of October 25 advanced, the systematic seizure of strategic points throughout the city by detachments under orders from the Military Revolutionary Committee continued. The Cossack regiments upon which Kerensky had depended remained in their barracks as the result of a subsequent decision by the Council of Cossack Troops to remain neutral in the struggle between the Government and the Bolsheviks. The detachments summoned from the front failed to appear. In the light of these developments, the Minister-President, after consultation with Konovalov and Kishkin, left Petrograd around noon to locate the expected front units outside the capital and hasten their advance. Soon thereafter, the Provisional Government reconvened in the Winter Palace under the chairmanship of Konovalov and remained in session until its arrest late that night by the Bolsheviks after an assault upon the building. When word of this event reached Smol'nyi, the Second Congress of Soviets, which had just opened, proclaimed the end of the Provisional Government and the inauguration of the new Soviet order.

At about 10:00 P.M., the Minister-President and his aides finally reached Pskov, headquarters of the Commander in Chief of the Northern Front, General Cheremisov. Here they found that Cheremisov had, on his own initiative, countermanded the order for troop movements toward the capital, that the General was in close contact with the Military Revolutionary Committee in Pskov, and that he in fact believed that the army should remain aloof from the political struggle. Under these circumstances it was imperative that Kerensky leave Pskov as soon as possible. Accompanied by General Krasnov and a small advance guard of troops from the Third Cossack Cavalry Corps and some light artillery, Kerensky reached Gatchina early in the morning of October 27. En route he received word of the arrest of his colleagues in the Winter Palace and, after his arrival, of the formation in Petrograd during the night of October 25–26 of a Committee to Save the Fatherland and the Revolution, headed by N. D. Avksent'ev, President of the Council of the Republic. The Committee was composed of representatives from the Kadet, Socialist Revolutionary, and Menshevik parties, and from the Municipal Duma, the cooperatives, and some trade unions. In addition to its other activities in opposition to the Bolshevik uprising, the Committee was attempting to organize the loyal military units in the capital for armed resistance.

Kerensky and Krasnov were convinced that their best hope of success lay in a rapid march on Petrograd despite the continuing absence of reinforcements for their small expedition. After a brief consultation among the staff, it was decided to take Tsarskoe Selo on the following day and approach the suburbs of Petrograd on October 29. However, despite the welcome addition to their ranks of an armored train and some infantry, the Cossacks did not take Tsarskoe Selo until late in the evening and remained inactive during the 29th. That day in Petrograd the Bolsheviks suppressed the uprising of the military cadets called by the Committee to Save the Fatherland and the Revolution and timed to coincide with the arrival of Kerensky's forces. On October 30, Krasnov's troops engaged Bolshevik infantry and sailors at Pulkovo with indecisive results that forced a retreat to Gatchina. There, in the growing atmosphere of demoralization and disaffection, the last ordeal of the Provisional Government and its President took place.

The warning words of the first Russian Provisional Government's declaration of April 26, 1917, had proved prophetic: "Before Russia rises the terrible apparition of civil war and anarchy, carrying destruction to freedom. There is a somber and grievous course of peoples, a course well known in history, leading from freedom through civil war and anarchy to reaction and the return of despotism. This course must not be the course of the Russian people."[5]

---

[5] Doc. 1075.

CHAPTER 27

The Kornilov Affair

BACKGROUND AND PREPARATION

1260. THE RECOLLECTIONS OF A. I. PUTILOV

[A series of interviews with Putilov by N. Vakar in Paris, published in *Posledniia Novosti*, No. 5780, January 20, 1937, p. 2, and No. 5784, January 24, 1937, p. 5. It is noteworthy, in connection with Putilov's statements and those of Finisov which follow, that there is evidence that Admiral Kolchak was seriously considered, probably in early July, for the leading role in the movement to destroy the Bolsheviks by force and eliminate from the Government those who presumably tolerated them, after which he would assume the role of dictator. However, at the end of July, he left Petrograd under orders as the head of a naval mission to the United States. See Elena Varneck and H. H. Fisher, *The Testimony of Kolchak and Other Siberian Materials*, p. 228.]

I

A. I. Guchkov, in his memoirs published in *Posledniia Novosti*, and A. F. Kerensky, in his recent polemic with General A. I. Denikin and in a public lecture in . . . the Social Museum, touched upon a hitherto unknown aspect of General L. G. Kornilov's action and named two persons for the first time: A. I. Putilov and A. I. Vyshnegradskii.

"At this time (April 1917—N.P.V.)," wrote A. I. Guchkov, "a private committee, consisting of representatives of banks and insurance companies, was organized at the initiative of A. I. Putilov. I, too, joined this committee. In order to give an official justification for our existence, we called ourselves the Society for the Economic Rehabilitation of Russia. Actually, we set for ourselves the aim of establishing a large fund for supporting moderate bourgeois candidates to the Constituent Assembly and for combating the influence of socialists at the front. In the end, we decided to place the large funds that we collected at the disposal of General Kornilov for the purpose of organizing an armed struggle against the Soviets."[1]

"That is to say, not against the Soviets, but against the Provisional Government," added A. F. Kerensky. (*Novaia Rossiia*, No. 18.)

Referring to the well-known letter of General M. V. Alekseev to P. N. Miliukov (published in *Izvestiia* in December 1917) in which the former Chief of Staff of the Supreme Commander hinted at the connection between General Kornilov "and certain individuals,"[2] A. F. Kerensky publicly announced the names of these individuals at the November 13 meeting.

[These individuals], he said, "are Putilov and Vyshnegradskii, well known in all of Petersburg."

The former head of the Provisional Government added in this connection

---

[1] *Posledniia Novosti*, No. 5668, September 30, 1936, p. 2.
[2] See Doc. 1300.

that General Kornilov's orderly, Zavoiko, also belonged to the committee of Putilov and Vyshnegradskii.

Almost twenty years have passed since the Kornilov affair . . . there are no historical documents on the episode which A. I. Guchkov and A. F. Kerensky have now recalled. Most of the witnesses and the direct participants in it are beyond reach. General L. G. Kornilov was killed. It is rumored that V. S. Zavoiko is living in America under an alias. A. I. Guchkov and A. I. Vyshnegradskii have died.

But A. I. Putilov is alive and lives in Paris.

. . .

A. I. Putilov told us for the first time what, for 19 years, he did not consider proper to divulge to the public:

"What A. I. Guchkov says in his memoirs about our Society is, in general, correct," he remarked. "I myself do not remember exactly when it was formed. I think it was in April of 1917. At any rate, A. I. Guchkov was still the Minister of War at that time and had no connection with our initiative. But, on the other hand, the Provisional Government was already exhibiting such weakness that the danger from the left was becoming a certainty in our minds. After all, it was even beyond the powers of the Government to carry out the sentence of the Justice of the Peace (about the eviction of the Bolsheviks from the private residence of Kshesinskaia) . . . A struggle against the Bolsheviks should have been organized both on the front and in the rear. However, inasmuch as the Provisional Government intended to convoke the Constituent Assembly, we were also confronted with the task of seating our moderate bourgeois candidates in the Constituent Assembly. As is well known, one cannot conduct propaganda without money. Thus, those of us connected with banks, industries, and insurance companies began to exchange views on this subject. I do not remember who took the initiative. I will probably not be mistaken if I say that the first steps in this direction were taken by myself and A. I. Vyshnegradskii."

The Society for the Economic Rehabilitation of Russia

"The task before us was so obvious that all the banking, industrial, and insurance circles responded immediately to our initiative. There is no point in enumerating them. They began to raise funds. The committee consisted of N. N. Kutler, N. A. Belotsvetov, V. A. Kamenka, A. P. Meshcherskii, A. I. Vyshnegradskii, and myself. During the initial stage, we raised 4 million rubles, if my memory does not fail me. We raised it, but we did not know what to do with it.

"A. I. Guchkov was then Minister of War and was not *au courant* on the industrialists' ventures. As soon as he left the Government, the initiators asked him to head the Society and assume charge of its practical activities. A. I. Guchkov consented.

"During the entire summer A. I. Guchkov tried to set the propaganda going, he published proclamations, distributed leaflets, brochures, and all kinds of literature . . . I think that around 500,000 rubles was spent on this. We did not busy ourselves with preparations for the Constituent Assembly, of course, because there was a long time to go before the Constituent Assembly. We thought, I am sorry to say, that nothing would come of the propaganda. What could have come of it when we had to speak about 'war until a victorious end,' while the

Bolsheviks were proclaiming 'peace without annexations or indemnities' and were advancing so alluring a slogan to the uneducated masses as 'loot the looters'? But we did not interfere with A. I. Guchkov.

"In the meantime the Moscow State Conference convened."

In the Train with General L. G. Kornilov

"At the end of the Moscow Conference," A. I. Putilov continued, "General L. G. Kornilov sent his adjutant, I think it was Colonel Desimet'er, to request that A. I. Vyshnegradskii, A. P. Meshcherskii, and I visit him in his train. . . .

"Kornilov received us in the train and said:

" 'Gentlemen, you were present at the State Conference; you saw and heard what was going on there. I am not asking you about your political convictions. You are Russian people. The army is falling apart. Everything is going to rack and ruin. As long as the Bolsheviks are sitting in Smol'nyi, nothing can be done . . . I am not foisting my views on anyone. As soon as the opportunity presents itself, we will convoke the Constituent Assembly. Whatever its decisions . . . I will submit to them without question. It makes no difference to me whether there is a monarchy or a republic. I only need order and firm authority in the country and the army.'

"I do not remember his speech precisely but such, approximately, was its meaning. The General continued:

" 'In agreement with A. F. Kerensky, I am dispatching a corps to Petrograd to disperse the Bolsheviks. But it is not enough to disperse them; they must be arrested. In order that the Bolsheviks do not scatter from Smol'nyi, and in order to avoid street fighting, a movement must be organized within Petrograd to help General Krymov. This will require funds. Officers and cadets must be gathered together . . . Money is needed to accommodate and feed people before the action. Can you give the money?'

"To this A. I. Vyshnegradskii and I replied:

" 'There is money. We are not the only ones in charge of the money, but we are sure that our colleagues will agree to place all the collected funds at your disposal.'

"At that moment there was no doubt in our minds that General Kornilov was acting in agreement with A. F. Kerensky. We raised no further questions, either about the plan of action or about subsequent intentions. For us it sufficed that the Government and the Supreme Commander had finally decided to put an end to dual power in the country. We were ready to make any sacrifices in helping them to restore order."

But if General Kornilov was acting in agreement with the head of the Government, didn't it seem strange to you that he was turning to you for funds when he could undoubtedly have received these funds from the Government?

"No," A. I. Putilov rejoined, "this did not seem strange to us. One must remember the conditions under which all this was taking place. If General Kornilov were to have asked the Government for just one ruble for organizing an armed action in Petrograd, this would immediately have come to the attention of Smol'nyi . . . the whole operation would then have miscarried! The conditions were such that both the Government and the Supreme Commander had to act in secrecy."

Did General Kornilov say how much money would be necessary?

"No, there was no mention of the sum . . . In general, General Kornilov knew nothing about our funds until the discussion in the train. Had he known, he would probably have turned to the president of the Society, A. I. Guchkov, and not to us. Guchkov later learned of this discussion from us. General Kornilov had simply turned to us as representatives of the Russian industrial and financial world. He assumed that I, personally, A. I. Vyshnegradskii, and A. T. Meshcherskii would be able to raise the required sum. We informed him then and there that the money was already raised and could be turned over to him at any time.

" 'It will be difficult to communicate with each other on this matter,' the General then said. 'Here are four names for you: Colonels Sidorin, Desimet'er, Pronin, and—from Stavka.'

"He gave a fourth name, but I have forgotten it. But it is unimportant, because only the first two played a role in subsequent events.

" 'If one of the four comes to you,' the General concluded, 'you will know that he comes from me.' "

How large were the funds of your committee at that time?

"Having raised 4 million rubles at the start we temporarily stopped the collection of additional funds until such time as the first amount was spent. A. I. Guchkov spent around 500,000 during the summer on propaganda. It follows that around 3.5 million remained current on the Society's account in the Russian-Asiatic Bank, the Azov-Don [Bank], the International [Bank], the Siberian [Bank], and others . . . But I think that if General Kornilov were in need of it, we could have raised, by a new assessment, no less than 10 million rubles in short order."

A. I. Vyshnegradskii and A. I. Putilov left the General around midnight.

"In bidding us farewell," A. I. Putilov recalled, "the Supreme Commander said among other things: 'I see that you have done your part. But there might be a need for quite a lot of money. Couldn't you also induce the Muscovites . . .?'

"On the following day I went to see the President of the Moscow Stock Exchange Committee, S. N. Tret'iakov, and told him about the conversation with General Kornilov and the desire expressed by the Supreme Commander. To this S. N. Tret'iakov answered: 'I take no part in such adventures.' I left with nothing."

When the Moscow Conference ended, A. I. Putilov returned to Petrograd, while A. I. Vyshnegradskii remained in Moscow at the side of his ailing wife. He took no part in subsequent developments. A. I. Guchkov was touring the fronts.

"I was the one who had to bear the consequences . . . ," said A. I. Putilov.

II

Envoys from General L. G. Kornilov

A. I. Putilov asserted that after General Kornilov's meeting in the train with A. I. Putilov and A. I. Vyshnegradskii and right up to the contemplated action in Petrograd, there was no communication between the Society for the Economic Rehabilitation of Russia and Stavka. The organized industrialists and bankers of Petrograd were waiting for the time the Supreme Commander would need the money. Communications were re-established suddenly, two days before "the Kornilov revolt."

"Kornilov was to have started operations during the night of August 28–29," A. I. Putilov related. "This date, by the way, was unknown to us, as were, generally speaking, the plans of General Kornilov. It was our deepest conviction that he acted in agreement with A. F. Kerensky. August 29 fell on Monday [*sic*], and on Saturday Colonels Sidorin and Desimet'er came to see me, accompanied by Engineer X.

"The colonels presented General Kornilov's letter and demanded that 2 million rubles be issued right away. I opened the letter. General Kornilov mentioned only 800,000 rubles . . . the difference surprised me. The colonels explained that the necessity [for the 2 million] came up at the last minute when it was already too late to rewrite the letter. 'Excuse me,' I said, 'but the General knows perfectly well that there is no need to stand on . . . ceremony on this matter; without rewriting the letter, he could have crossed out the figure and entered a new one in his own handwriting!' Then the colonels declared that they had raised the amount themselves, because they became convinced upon their arrival in Petrograd that 800,000 would not be sufficient to provide food and accommodations for the officers . . . I did not argue, but I pointed out that I could not make the decision by myself and had to call a [meeting of] the Board. Why did not the General warn me earlier? The banks were going to close in 15 minutes! A second signature for the check was required. Where would I get it? 'For pity's sake!' said the colonels, 'do something. We can't wait any longer. The money is needed urgently, immediately. The action is all set for tomorrow night.' "

A. I. Putilov made an inquiry regarding the amount of money in the Society's account in the Russian-Asiatic Bank . . . 400,000 rubles . . . He decided to issue this money at his own risk and responsibility.

"Here, in addition," he said to the colonels, "is my personal check for 400,000 more. Thus, there are 800,000 rubles altogether, the exact sum that the General requested in the letter. Go downstairs and receive it. Thus I have fulfilled the General's request. As for the rest of the money, i.e., 1,200,000 rubles, I will find my colleagues this very day and call [a meeting of] the Board. We will discuss it. Come to the Bank for the answer at 5:00 o'clock tomorrow."

Colonels Sidorin and Desimet'er left. A. I. Putilov found V. A. Kamenka, N. N. Kutler, and N. A. Belotsvetov. A. I. Guchkov was out of town, but was expected to return by night. The Board decided to meet in his flat and wait.

"A. I. Guchkov arrived after midnight," A. I. Putilov related . . .

The Board members agreed with A. I. Putilov and wrote out checks . . . for 1,200,000 rubles.

"This is a large sum," A. I. Putilov said. "One cannot take receipts from the colonels. Give me two, or at least one, witness who will be present when it is handed over."

A. I. Guchkov burst out laughing:

"Aleksei Ivanovich wants to be insured. Well then, let us give him a specialist on insurance, N. A. Belotsvetov!"

So it was decided that on the following day, Sunday, August 28, A. I. Putilov and N. A. Belotsvetov would give an additional sum of 1,200,000 rubles to General Kornilov's envoys, without trying to obtain more specific information as to whether or not the envoys were acting with the knowledge of the Supreme Commander.

Malyi Yaroslavets

As was agreed, on Sunday, at 5:00 P.M., N. A. Belotsvetov and A. I. Putilov were sitting in the Russian-Asiatic Bank waiting for the envoys.

"We waited one hour, two hours—no colonels! . . . We waited until 8:00 o'clock, no one came . . .

"We took the checks with us and went [to Malyi Yaroslavets]. We entered and saw in the antechamber an engineer's coat on the hanger. 'Where is this gentleman sitting?' we asked. 'In Room No. 5.' 'Give him our visiting cards.' We handed our visiting cards to the waiter and followed him. Our engineer emerged from the [private] room, half drunk. 'Hello,' he said, 'how did you find me here?' 'Your cook told us.' 'What a fool! I have been hiding out for three days and she tattled . . . But then, that's all right! Come in . . . here we all are among our own people!' "

It was evidently unpleasant for A. I. Putilov to recall this episode. . . .

"N. A. and I crossed the threshold of the room and were thunderstruck," A. I. Putilov related reluctantly. "The room was enormous, a veritable hall. There was a banquet going on, and around 40 officers were sitting at a table. There were countless bottles. We were welcomed and asked: 'Would you like to have something?' Colonel Sidorin was presiding. Everyone was in uniform; some were in field dress. Only Colonel N. was dressed in civilian clothes. Why in civilian clothes? After all, the action was to start in several hours! Was the Colonel from Stavka so well known in person to the officers and cadets that they would recognize him in a jacket and coat? How was he going to lead the action? Why are they here? . . . Why did they not come at the appointed time for the money? . . . Noise, shouting half-drunk speeches. We sat and listened in horror. The company became tipsy and loudly discussed the action. They told where the units were stationed, who would go where, how everything would be! . . . We interrupted, we pleaded with them to keep quiet: 'You have gone out of your minds! Here the waiters are spies, the walls are like cardboard . . . In five minutes they will know everything in Smol'nyi!' They would keep quiet for a while, drink, and begin over again . . . N. A. and I were simply in despair. We did not know what to do.

"And then around 10:00 P.M. Ruma, a commissar of the Vyborg unit, ran into the office. 'Gentlemen!' he shouted. 'Kerensky has declared Kornilov a traitor! One thousand six hundred persons have been named for arrest! I saw half of the list; the names of those present here are not on it. But I did not see the second half!' . . . The colonels were confused and frightened. The first reaction was panic. They wanted to disperse. But they soon calmed down and ordered more champagne. N. A. Belotsvetov leaned over to me and said in my ear: 'I don't know how you feel, Aleksei Ivanovich, but I will not give the checks. By night their legs won't carry them. The money will be lost anyway.' We rose from the table and made our way to the exit. Someone started running after us shouting: 'But the checks? The checks?' Belotsvetov answered: 'Tomorrow.' . . . I don't remember how we got out of the room and found ourselves on the Morskaia. We stood on the street for a while. Belotsvetov said: 'Everything has failed!' . . . 'Of course it has failed. Can one go about it in this way? . . .' "

. . . He shrugged his shoulders hopelessly and ended his account:

"What happened further, I don't know. I heard that his subordinates could not find Colonel Sidorin that night and that later both colonels disappeared.[3] We gave the whole thing up as lost. The money remained in the banks . . . it was later lost, together with the banks themselves. On the following morning, I left Petrograd fearing arrest. I went through Luga to A. A. Bogdanov's estate, 22 versts away on the Novgorod highway."

A. I. Putilov passed the fronts of both opponents. Soldiers and officers were holding meetings in Luga (not a single platoon was ready for combat), but farther along the Novgorod highway stood units of the 3rd Cavalry Corps in exemplary form. "Ah," he thought, driving past them, "if they were to fire but a single shot at Luga, everyone there would scatter like rabbits." . . .

"No," he shook his head with contrition, "it was badly organized. Kornilov did not know how to select his collaborators . . ."

I was trying to find out whether in the opinion of A. I. Putilov there existed a "Kornilov plot" against the Government.

Twenty years is a sufficiently long period for a witness to acquire historical perspective in place of personal predilections. Was it actually the case that Kornilov's blow was aimed not only against Smol'nyi but against the Provisional Government too?

"Until the very end we did not doubt [the existence of] an agreement between Kerensky and Kornilov. Kornilov acted against Smol'nyi. Only against Smol'nyi. The demonstration in Petrograd was necessary as an aid to Krymov's corps . . . Actually, I do not know the extent to which Kornilov arrived at terms with Kerensky. It is possible that they understood some things differently. But, I repeat, I was not under the impression that Kornilov was conspiring against the Government. Even now, I do not clearly understand what compelled Kerensky to declare Kornilov a traitor and thus ruin everything for good."

. . .

"Permit me now to express my personal views on this subject. There is no doubt in my mind that Kornilov had Kerensky's consent to send the corps to Petrograd. . . . Kerensky hurled an open charge at Vyshnegradskii and myself (why not at the whole Board of the Society?) that we were counterrevolutionaries and were raising funds for an armed struggle, not against the Soviets, but against the Provisional Government. This, of course, is untrue. From what I have said, it can be seen that we took no steps against the Provisional Government. When we placed the money at the disposal of the Supreme Commander, we in no way separated him, in our thoughts, from the Government. And if some friction developed subsequently between him and the head of the Provisional Government, which led to a catastrophe, we had nothing to do with it. We placed the collected funds at the disposal of the Supreme Commander for the fight against the Soviets. Kerensky says: 'That is to say, against the Provisional Government.' . . . A

---

[3] In a letter to the editor, published in *Posledniia Novosti* (No. 5817, February 26, 1937, p. 3), Colonel, then General, Sidorin took exception to much of Putilov's account, including his presence in the industrialist's office on Saturday (which he correctly points out fell on August 26, not 27) with a letter from General Kornilov, the receipt of 400,000 rubles, the claim that any action was planned for August 27 or 28, the meeting planned for Sunday afternoon to receive the additional 1,200,000 rubles, the lack of organization among the Petrograd officers, and the boisterous scene at the Malyi Yaroslavets. See also Doc. 1261.

strange identification! It is especially strange after he himself was forced to escape from the Soviets under the protection of Cossacks brought from the front by General Krymov. Kerensky evidently wanted to make Vyshnegradskii and myself scapegoats for his own sins . . . I think that an accurate description of this unfortunate affair was given by the late V. V. Savinkov when he was summoned before the investigator appointed by Kerensky. When the investigator asked for his testimony in the case of Kornilov's treason, Savinkov replied: 'Permit me, first of all, to correct the description of the crime: it is not a question of General Kornilov's treason, but of Minister Kerensky's fright' . . . Such, in my opinion, was in fact the case."

At the request of A. I. Putilov, I wrote down his exact words, and then asked him . . . about Mr. Zavoiko.

"V. S. Zavoiko was never a member of our committee," he retorted, "nor could he have been, because he did not represent any industrial circles. Everyone knew him, of course. But since we are speaking about our committee and the funds, he played no role whatsoever in the events. Contact with Kornilov was established, not through Zavoiko, but through those colonels I have named. You now know how this contact originated and what finally came of it . . . It is possible that Mr. Zavoiko played a political role in Stavka, and was an adviser of Kornilov. This confirms my opinion that Kornilov did not know how to select people. Before the discussion in the train, we had no connections whatsoever with Kornilov. And the only connection after the discussion was the visit of the colonels who came for money."

The fate of the 4 million [rubles] collected by the Society for the Economic Rehabilitation of Russia is now known, thanks to the testimony of A. I. Putilov: 500,000 rubles were spent by A. I. Guchkov on antisocialist propaganda during the summer of 1917; 800,000 rubles were given to General Kornilov's envoys, Colonels Sidorin and Desimet'er, for organizing the action of August 28 in Petrograd, while 2,700,000 rubles, together with other deposits in the Russian-Asiatic Bank, the Azov-Don Bank, the International Bank, the Siberian Bank, etc., were lost in the process of nationalization by the Soviets.

1261. The Recollections of Finisov, Shidlovskii, and Miliukov

a. P. N. Finisov

[Interviews given to N. Vakar for *Posledniia Novosti*, No. 5818, February 27, 1937, p. 4; No. 5825, March 6, 1937, p. 3.]

I

The Republican Center

In May of 1917, there gathered in the home of F. A. Lipskii, member of the board of the Siberian Bank, in addition to the host, General L. G. Kornilov, K. V. Nikolaevskii, P. N. Finisov, former member of the Duma F. Alad'in, and Colonel Shuvaev. The Republican Center was founded at this meeting.

K. V. Nikolaevskii (Popular Socialist) was elected president and treasurer, and the three vice-presidents elected were A. A. Bogdanovskii (P.S.), L. L. Ruma (S.R.), and P. N. Finisov (no party affiliation). The purpose of the organization? To throttle the spontaneous revolutionary movement.

At that time Kornilov already felt that things would end badly. Down to the July revolt we engaged in propaganda only, acting within a legal framework and adhering approximately to the platform of the Kadet Party. The idea of establishing a strong power came later.

P. N. Finisov preserved many documents and notes. By referring to them he establishes the following details:

Chief attention was directed toward organizing a military section. At the beginning it was headed by Colonel of the General Staff Romanevskii; later, during a brief period, by Admiral A. V. Kolchak, and finally (from July 1917) by Colonel of the General Staff L. P. Desimet'er.

The section included representatives from the Military League (General I. I. Fedorov), the Army and Fleet Officers' Union (Colonel Novosil'tsev and Colonel Pronin), the Union of Cossack Troops (Colonel A. I. Dutov), the Union of St. George Cavaliers, the Union of Military Duty (Colonel Vinberg), the Union of Invalids, the Union of Escaped War Prisoners, the League of Personal Example, and many other organizations.

The military section included aides Baranovskii and Tumanov of the Minister of War (Kerensky); also Colonels Bagratuni, Geiman, Shuvaev, and Klerzhe (head of military censorship who had direct contact with Stavka). Nonmilitary espionage was led by L. L. Ruma, and the military, by Colonel Bantysh and Al'kimovich, who subsequently betrayed the Republican Center to the Bolsheviks . . . All propaganda was handled by A. A. Bogdanovskii, who had at his disposal a spacious apartment on Nadezhdinskii Street. Under his direction leaflets about the Bolsheviks were prepared and distributed everywhere (Leaflet No. 11, for instance, was distributed to all of Moscow during the State Conference).

The organization's headquarters was a huge private residence on the Nevskii, No. 104, which housed the offices of the Bessarabian Railway, Crimean Railway, Sviatogorsk Cement Company, and "Maiak" Lumber Company. Messrs. Lipskii, Nikolaevskii, and Finisov were directors or presidents of the latter.

Beginning with August 12, adds P. N. Finisov, after receiving word from both of our intelligence groups that meetings of the military section in the above building were beginning to attract attention, we held our meetings in private dining rooms of various large restaurants, changing the place each time. . . . All registration cards were burned by A. A. Bogdanovskii after information reached us of the betrayal by Captain Al'kimovich.

. . . .

Financing

In May, after the organization of the Republican Center in the home of F. A. Lipskii, a meeting was called in the Siberian Bank. Participating in the meeting were E. K. Grubbe (President of the Siberian Bank), N. A. Ass (Director, now residing in Paris), V. V. Andreev (passed away in Finland), V. V. Tarnovskii (former Director and later Director of Gosbank under the Bolsheviks), N. Kh. Denisov, F. A. Lipskii, K. V. Nikolaevskii, and P. N. Finisov.

It was decided that financial support was needed in the work against the growing influence of the Soviet of Workers' and Soldiers' Deputies, and a sum of 100,000 rubles was assigned for it. (I think that subsequently, in June, K. V. Nikolaevskii received an additional sum of 50,000 rubles.) This money was used for the initial propaganda. In so far as I can recall, only a negligible sum was allocated to the military section—for trips, postage, etc.

According to P. N. Finisov, down to the middle of July, the Republican Center heard nothing about the activity of A. I. Putilov, A. I. Guchkov, A. I. Vyshnegradskii, and others. Nor had it heard of the Society for the Economic Rehabilitation of Russia, created by them.

None of us saw what A. I. Guchkov printed and distributed with the 500,000 rubles about which Putilov speaks. There were no posters, no appeals, no publications of any kind . . . At no time was A. I. Guchkov a member of the Republican Center. He had no relations with us and couldn't have had, because his name was extremely unpopular in our organization, which worked intimately with the officers' corps.

The first contact of the Republican Center with the Society for the Economic Rehabilitation of Russia took place after the July revolt.

At that time F. A. Lipskii received a letter or a telegram from N. Kh. Denisov in Gurzuf, with a request to send a responsible representative from the Republican Center to the Crimea on an urgent matter, so reports Finisov. Neither Lipskii nor Nikolaevskii could leave Petersburg. I was asked to go. I arrived in Gurzuf. In N. Kh. Denisov's office I met A. I. Putilov. Putilov requested me to give a detailed account of the Republican Center. After listening to me with approval, he said: "Tell Lipskii and Nikolaevskii that I organized the Society for the Economic Rehabilitation of Russia, which will gladly support you. When I return to Petersburg at the end of July, we will discuss this further." I remained in Gurzuf two days and departed.

The recipient and distributor of all funds in the Republican Center was Nikolaevskii. Nobody interfered with his work. Just what he agreed upon with A. I. Putilov on the latter's return to Petersburg P. N. Finisov does not know. Prior to his departure from the capital for Odessa on August 2 or 3, Nikolaevskii left a note, stating the amount of money to be issued to the account of the Society for the Economic Rehabilitation of Russia, to various military organizations, and to intelligence organs.

By this time word came from Stavka, first by wireless and later personally from Colonel Sidorin and Colonel Pronin, that the second demonstration by the Bolsheviks was to take place on September 2–3. Complete readiness was demanded of us. It appeared that 500,000 rubles were needed to seize armed units and radio stations in Tsarskoe Selo, transport the armed detachment of Captain Orlov, dump stone-loaded barges in the canal to prevent the approach of warships from Kronstadt (this was assigned to Lieutenant Fomin, subsequently Navy Minister under Admiral Kolchak), replace guards with reliable units, etc.

The Trip of F. A. Lipskii and P. N. Finisov to Stavka

The Military Section of the Republican Center elaborated a detailed plan of seizing all strategic points in Petersburg until the approach to the capital of the troops sent by Stavka in agreement with the Provisional Government. According to P. N. Finisov, "everything was ready by August 20."

Whose order then did the organization await?

Nobody's, says P. N. Finisov. We were to seize Petersburg in response to the Bolsheviks' action.

To bring about an armed coup d'état?

No, our aims were more modest. We had to take Smol'nyi and await the arrival of the troops from Stavka.

And the Provisional Government?

We did not intend to touch it. Clothed with dictatorial power, Kornilov was to change its membership in part, but that is another question. If Colonel V. Vinberg writes that allegedly members of the Provisional Government were to be arrested, it is completely untrue. Vinberg did not belong to the leading center, did not know our plan, and wrote his book "by hearsay." When in Kiev in 1918 as head of the Sixth Brigade, he extended to me his personal apology for the inaccuracies in his book and promised to write a second part where everything would be corrected. He died before he could do so.

When "everything was ready" in Petersburg, Stavka sent a message, on August 21, for "responsible persons" from the Republican Center to appear for a report.

Nikolaevskii was out of town. Colonels Sidorin and Desimet'er were unable to leave the military organization, continued P. N. Finisov's account. They asked Lipskii and me to come to Stavka. On the evening of the same date, at the country estate of Lipskii (Sablino, Nikolaevskii R.R.), a meeting took place, with Colonel R. R. Raupakh participating. Final plans were worked out on the composition of the government (Kerensky was to remain in the post of Minister of Justice), on agrarian reforms, on the siege of Petersburg, etc. With all this data we departed for Stavka to Gen. Kornilov.

In his reminiscences (*Arkhiv Russkoi Revoliutsii*, V) Gen. A. S. Lukomskii writes: ". . . the two communications engineers who were requested to come arrived" . . . One of the engineers was P. N. Finisov, the other, F. A. Lipskii (the latter, incidentally, was not an engineer, but a Candidate in mathematical sciences).

At 12:00 midnight, Prince Trubetskoi ushered us into the study of the late Tsar, where the following had already assembled: General L. G. Kornilov, Gen. A. M. Krymov, Gen. I. P. Romanovskii, Gen. A. S. Lukomskii, and four or five military men (one general and the rest colonels). Kornilov told us that Savinkov was just in to see him, and that everything was coordinated with him. However, he said, the government was against appointing General Krymov and against including the "Savage" Division in the corps that was being sent to Petersburg.[4] V. N. L'vov also arrived from Petersburg with some instruction, the nature of which, however, was not known because General Kornilov had not talked with him yet . . . After this we made a detailed report, indicating also the new list of ministers. Kornilov immediately made some changes in the list (he removed, for instance, the name of P. P. Yurenev, Minister of Transport, replacing him with E. P. Shuberskii). We pointed out the extreme bitterness among the officers and suggested that Kerensky be called to Stavka in order to save his life, since an accidental assassination might result in real catastrophe . . . *Kornilov approved the entire plan. And in doing so the Supreme Commander added that he would discuss with Kerensky the final membership of the Government.*

Thus—was there, or was there not, a plot against the Provisional Government?

For goodness' sake! replied P. N. Finisov in indignation, what sort of con-

---

[4] The Native Division, organized by the Grand Duke Mikhail Aleksandrovich from members of Moslem Caucasian tribes. It was noted for its bravery and savagery.

spiracy was it if half of the old membership, and among them the most extreme left, was to be retained in the government? Kerensky and Skobelev? Only such ministers as Nekrasov, Chernov, and Tereshchenko were to be thrown out. If Kerensky looks upon it as a plot against him, in that sense it was a plot. We naturally did not think it possible to retain Kerensky, who was a prisoner of the Soviet of Workers' and Soldiers' Deputies, at the head of the Government. . . . It was precisely in this form that our plan was accepted by General Kornilov.

II

The plan for armed action by the officers' organization in Petersburg was approved and confirmed by General Kornilov on the night before August 24 at Stavka.

The conspirators' aim was to raid Smol'nyi, seize power in Petersburg, and give General Kornilov the opportunity, [with the support of] troops, to change the composition of the Provisional Government (A. F. Kerensky, incidentally, was to remain as Minister of Justice).

The overthrow was to have occurred "in answer to the Bolshevik demonstration." By this time, however, reports were received that the Bolshevik demonstration, set for September 2–3, was postponed and, possibly, was not going to be staged at all.

. . .

"On August 25 we returned from Stavka. This is what happened: we arrived with Lipskii and said to Putilov: 'Aleksei Ivanovich, we need 500,000 rubles desperately.' A. Putilov replied: 'Our checks, gentlemen, are signed by three persons. On hand I have only a check for 270,000 rubles. You can have it, but as for the rest of the money, you have to wait for Belotsvetov and Vyshnegradskii. But if it is a matter of urgency, then you, Fedor Aleksandrovich (Lipskii), give 200,000 yourself, under my word of honor. . . . Send for the money tomorrow. Shall the money be prepared in small bills for you?' After this, we left. On the next day we (Colonel Sidorin, Colonel Desimet'er, and I) received from the Russian-Asiatic Bank 270,000 rubles (and not 300,000 as General Sidorin writes). Then we wrote out two checks from our own funds: Lipskii, for 75,000 rubles, and I, for 125,000 rubles. The money was divided among all the organizations and receipts were given."

P. N. Finisov did not have any letter from General Kornilov to A. I. Putilov and there was no mention whatsoever of the figure of 800,000 rubles. Furthermore, there was no mention of the 2 million rubles, according to Finisov.

"The letter came later," recalled P. N. Finisov. "When the catastrophe had already occurred . . . , i.e., on Monday, August 28, Colonels Sidorin and Pronin went to A. I. Putilov and asked again for money. But when he read Kornilov's letter (here the question concerned 800,000 rubles), A. I. Putilov replied: 'We do not give money for funerals.' "

"And what of the scene in Malyi Yaroslavets, described by A. I. Putilov?"

"[This is] also untrue. In the first place, this did not happen on Sunday the 27th, because on Sunday evening we were all sitting in the six private rooms of Villa Rodé, when Colonel Klerzhe arrived at 1:00 A.M. and informed us that Kerensky had proclaimed Kornilov a traitor, which fact was reputed to him by direct wire from Stavka. [The scene in Malyi Yaroslavets] occurred then on Saturday, i.e., on the day before . . . In the second place, it was not an 'enormous' room which we occupied in the Malyi Yaroslavets, but one which barely accommodated twelve persons. Present there were Colonel Sidorin, Colonel Desimet'er, Ataman Dutov, Staff Captain Al'kimovich, Lieutenant Colonel Bantysh, Chief of Military Communications, General Ivanov, L. L. Ruma, and Lieutenant Berezovskii. F. A. Lipskii and Colonel Geiman arrived later. If Desimet'er and Berezovskii wore civilian clothes, this was because the action was intended not for that night but for a week hence . . . Only Dutov, I think, was slightly intoxicated; the rest were seriously discussing business. We knew nothing about the checks for 1,200,000 rubles. The arrival of Putilov and Belotsvetov, in general, amazed us."

"Then why did they come?"

"We could not understand ourselves. This explains my surprise at meeting A. I. Putilov. He came with Belotsvetov to ask us . . . not to divulge—in the event of failure—the source of financial aid from O.E.V.R. They stayed with us for about twenty minutes and left. All of us asked ourselves later, what did this mean? Was it that they had actually become frightened because they had issued us 270,000 rubles on the day before? I do not know whether or not they had given money to K. V. Nikolaevskii in the past.

"The remainder of the sum which General Sidorin mentions in his letter (what remained of the 470,000 rubles) was returned by P. N. Finisov and Colonel Sidorin to Nikolaevskii. It was this money (around 160,000 rubles) that later served to finance the publication *Obshchee Delo* under the editorship of V. L. Burtsev . . ."

Conference in Malyi Yaroslavets

The confusion in dates, fully understandable in view of the remoteness of these events, occurred not only with A. I. Putilov but also with General V. I. Sidorin. In reconstructing details of the past on the basis of the records he preserved, P. N. Finisov indicated that the meeting at Malyi Yaroslavets, mentioned in General Sidorin's letter, took place not on the evening of the 27th (on that day the organization met in individual rooms at the Villa Rodé) but on Monday, August 28, at 2:00 P.M., i.e., when the conflict between Kerensky and General Kornilov had already broken out.

"Persons in charge of individual sections of the military organization," P. N. Finisov related, "were summoned to this extraordinary meeting to decide whether to advance immediately or not. Practically speaking, the action could have taken place on that same day. But all communications with General Krymov were broken off (as a result of Minister Nekrasov's orders). Without communications with the Cossack regiments and without new instructions from Stavka, we hesitated to assume responsibility for operations in Petersburg. . . .

"It was decided at once to send Colonel L. P. Desimet'er and myself . . . to General Krymov, [and] K. V. Nikolaevskii to Stavka, and not to undertake anything until reports were received from us."

"How is one to understand the enigmatic words of General V. I. Sidorin that on the day following the conversation with General M. A. Alekseev, 'We were forced to reject any action,' bowing to . . . 'circumstances of exceptional importance'?"

P. N. Finisov hesitated. Then he decided not to conceal anything about events that have gone down in history and gave the following frank account:

"This is what happened. As I have already said, several days before this, it became known to us as a fact that the Bolsheviks had postponed their demonstration indefinitely. We considered it impossible to carry out our plan without these grounds. . . . At the last meeting in Malyi Yaroslavets we therefore decided to resort to an extreme measure. General Krymov's regiments continued to move toward Petersburg. It would have been a crime not to have taken advantage of this. If there were no grounds, they had to be created. A special organization was instructed at this conference to provoke a 'Bolshevik' demonstration, i.e., to ransack the haymarket, the shops; in other words, to incite a street riot. In response to this, the operations of the officers' organizations and General Krymov's Cossack regiments were to have begun on the same day. This assignment was given to General V. I. Sidorin. Right then and there he was given 100,000 rubles for this purpose (of this amount, General Sidorin spent only 26,000 rubles for preparing a 'Bolshevik riot,' and the remaining 74,000 he later returned to us) . . . The time for the artificial riot was to have been set by us, i.e., by Colonel Desimet'er and me, after we met with General A. M. Krymov and sent a coded order to Petersburg."

The Search for General A. M. Krymov

At 4:00 P.M., on Monday, August 28, P. N. Finisov and Colonel Desimet'er left Petersburg to find General Krymov and restore communications with him as soon as possible.

"After searching endlessly, we found him, on Tuesday at 5:00 A.M., in the village of Zaozer'e, 20 versts from Luga . . . The Chief of Staff, General Khreshchatitskii, met us, and finding us physically exhausted and weak, he sent us at once to bed; two hours later, he woke us up and led us to Krymov's office, which was located in the cowshed. We gave our report. General Krymov confirmed that, without a Bolshevik demonstration in the capital, his indoctrinated Cossacks would not march against Petersburg . . . A meeting of Cossacks was called on the spot, and Krymov, Desimet'er, and I gave speeches. At 8:00 A.M. a motorcyclist was dispatched with a coded message to General Sidorin, via Gatchina, containing the order: "Act at once according to instructions."

After bidding farewell to General Krymov, the envoys started on their way back to Petersburg convinced that they would arrive there in the midst of a revolt. Halfway between Gatchina and Luga they met . . . Colonel Samarin, who was on his way to General Krymov to deliver an order from Kerensky that he come to Petersburg.

"We took gasoline for our car from Colonel Samarin, shook hands, and parted," P. N. Finisov continued his account. "Krymov departed for Petersburg convinced that the 'Bolshevik' demonstration would take place and instructed General Khreshchatitskii to start moving the Cossack regiments when he received the prearranged signal . . ."

Conditions in Petersburg amazed him, because he found them to be contrary to all his expectations. They also amazed the envoys who arrived in the night and went to . . . the flat of Colonel Goncharov, a member of the organization, and assistant to the Commander in Chief of the Air Force.

The Failure of the "Action"

"With amazement we learned from Colonel Goncharov that everything was quiet in town, that there was no demonstration. We tried to call up General Sidorin, . . . but we could not locate him anywhere. At 3:00 A.M. Captain Kravchenko arrived and informed us that General Sidorin had a discussion with General Alekseev, who objected to the action . . . It is difficult to convey to you how profoundly shaken we were!"

"Did General Sidorin receive your message in time?"

"The message was received toward evening, but by this time the plan had already been abandoned. Alas! Thanks to Sidorin himself . . . On that very morning, while we were staying with Krymov, he told the whole plan to General Alekseev. Alekseev vigorously objected to 'the provocation' and declared: 'If you agree to such a measure, I will shoot myself! And before I die, I will leave a note explaining my reasons.' Sidorin submitted, canceled the orders, and returned the remaining, unspent money to the Republican Center. . . ."

When P. N. Finisov recalled this, his expression changed; he could barely control his emotions, and, in a voice filled with tears, he said:

"It is Sidorin's fault that the coup d'état did not occur!"

Perhaps General V. I. Sidorin will some day give a detailed account of his discussions with General M. V. Alekseev, to which there is a vague reference in his letter. But we can hardly be wrong in assuming that the whole plan of the Petersburg organization seemed too unsound to General Alekseev, whereas "the provocation" seemed too dangerous, since it would undoubtedly have been exposed in a matter of days and would then have provoked a new outburst of —this time genuine—indignation.[5]

That Which Remains Unclear

General Kornilov was not informed in time of the plan "for an artificial Bolshevik riot" in Petersburg. This idea belongs entirely to the Petersburg organization, which came to this decision at the last moment . . .

"Then why did Kornilov still send the Native Division to Petersburg, contrary to the agreement with Kerensky?"

P. N. Finisov assured us that the Native Division, which formed a part of the 3rd Cavalry Corps, was sent not to Petersburg but to positions on the Northern Front.

"A tragic misunderstanding occurred! Only four Cossack regiments were advancing with Krymov."

"But why, contrary to the agreement with Kerensky, did Kornilov retain Krymov as head of the corps?"

To this P. N. Finisov had no reply . . . He did not know and became lost in guesswork, since he knew of such an agreement with Kerensky from the lips of Kornilov himself.

"Did not the news that the Bolshevik demonstration was called off compel you to change the plan before the events of August 27?"

---

[5] Another, and revealing, account of General Alekseev's attitude during those days is given by V. A. Maklakov in his Preface to *La chute du régime tsariste*, pp. 84–86. See also Docs. 1299 and 1300.

"Yes," P. N. Finisov admitted. "By this time it was decided, in agreement with Stavka, to proceed irrespective of the actions of the Bolsheviks. The date still hinged on the arrival of officers from the Southwestern Front; however, it was not to be later than September 2–3. By this date, too, Krymov's Cossacks were to be concentrated at Petersburg . . . Incidentally, P. N. Miliukov also knew about this plan. He probably knew about it from Kornilov himself, who spoke with him during the Moscow Conference. Later on, P. B. Struve, F. A. Rodichev, and Prince Pavel D. Dolgorukov paid him a visit to propose that he establish contact with the Republican Center. As far as I know, this visit occurred in Petersburg around August 23. Not only did P. N. Miliukov refuse to participate personally, but he declared that he would not even report this to the Central Committee of the Kadet Party."[6]

P. N. Finisov regretted this deeply, believing that the Kadets' support "would have been very valuable at that time and might have changed the entire course of events."

"Did the military organization plan to assassinate the head of the Government? After all, Colonel Klerzhe, who was named by A. F. Kerensky, belonged to the central group of leaders of the Republican Center."

P. N. Finisov spread his hands in amazement and said excitedly:

"When I read this, I could not believe my eyes . . . Colonel Klerzhe? A military writer, the gentlest soul! It is absolutely incredible. Oh God! Why, he couldn't even have slaughtered a chicken! . . . No, this is sheer nonsense. Whoever reported this to the Winter Palace evidently wanted to cause a little alarm or, simply, to harass [the Government] a bit . . .

"And what of the naval cadets?"

"Yes, we had a cell among the naval cadets. I will say more: we even had a cell among the cadets on guard duty at Kerensky's office . . . but as for attempts [at assassination]!? I swear to you that such a thought never even crossed anyone's mind."

b. S. I. Shidlovskii
[Vospominaniia, Part II, p. 141.]

About this time [Moscow State Conference] a group of young officers from Stavka expressed a wish to have a strictly confidential talk with some of the more prominent members of the State Duma. A small secret meeting was arranged [in Moscow], during which the officers stated that they were delegated by Kornilov to bring to the attention of the Duma the fact that everything was in readiness at the front and in Stavka to depose Kerensky. All that was needed was the consent of the State Duma in order that the plot be carried out in its name and, so to speak, under its sponsorship.

The reaction of the members of the State Duma to this offer was most cautious. They questioned the officers at great length in order to determine precisely what had been organized and how. In the end they concluded unanimously that the plot could not be treated seriously. They consequently declined to even talk on the subject with Kornilov. The only member of the Duma who went to meet Kornilov in his train was Miliukov, who had a conversation with him, the content of which is unknown to me.

[6] See footnote 7.

c. P. N. MILIUKOV

[*Istoriia vtoroi russkoi revoliutsii*, I, vypusk 2, 173–74.]

. . . Now, as Kornilov told me personally during our meeting in Moscow, August 13, he did not want to miss this opportunity, and the moment for an open conflict with Kerensky's government was formulated in his mind quite definitely, even to a previously set date of August 27.

Did it mean that Kornilov was consciously preparing a "plot" against the government? Strange as it may seem, this thought was not associated in Kornilov's mind with his intentions. He was quite sincere when, subsequently in his testimony—that is, in the official document—confusing "conspiracy" with "counterrevolution" under a monarchy, he solemnly declared: "I am not and have not been involved in any plots." In all of my conversations with various representatives of different political parties, I declared that I did not belong to any political party and do not intend to belong, but that I always have supported and will continue to support those that have only one aim—to save the country from ruin and to deliver the army from collapse. I always declared and always will maintain the position that the future of Russia and the question of the type of government can only be decided by the Constituent Assembly, which alone can express the ruling will of the Russian people. I always declared that I shall never support any political combination that aims to restore the house of Romanov, because I consider that this dynasty in its last representatives played a fatal role in the life of the country." Without regarding himself as a "counterrevolutionary" in the sense in which in those days it was understood, Kornilov consequently did not regard himself as a "conspirator." To be sure, he wanted to replace the government. However, in the first place, this did not predetermine the question of the *form* of change: it could take place in a peaceful way with the consent of the government, including even Kerensky himself . . . In this sense the date of August 27 to his mind was not some fatal deadline. What had to take place on August 27 could occur just as well on August 10 or July 8. The important thing for Kornilov was to manifest his will. It was up to others to give this will a correct judicial expression. That was not his affair.[7]

1262. THE RECOLLECTIONS OF F. VINBERG

[Excerpts from Vinberg's diary, written while a prisoner of the Bolsheviks in the Trubetskoi Bastion of the Peter and Paul Fortress, published in Kiev in 1918 under the title *V plenu u obez'ian; zapiski kontr-revoliutsionera*, pp. 15–16, 98–107. See also Miliukov, *Istoriia vtoroi russkoi revoliutsii*, I, vypusk 2, 87–89, 164–65, 171.]

· · ·

December 14 [1917]. This [past] summer I met him [Purishkevich] in Petrograd. He was agitated, indignant, and certainly suffered dreadfully, like myself and all those who still loved our ill-starred, unbearably tormented motherland. It goes without saying that we talked and consulted about what might be done to

[7] Miliukov later reconfirmed this conversation with Kornilov during the Moscow Conference. Miliukov stated that he warned Kornilov that a fight with Kerensky then would be "untimely." The visit of Struve and others was denied by Miliukov. *Posledniia Novosti*, No. 5825, March 6, 1937, p. 2.

save Russia from the rule of doctrinaires and theorizers detached from reality, from those political impotents headed by the incapable, weak, and cowardly Kerensky.

Soon after that the absurd and ill-fated Kornilov venture started, undertaken by naïve people inexperienced in the reverses and snares of revolutionary life; by people who became toys in the hands of mean provocateurs and adventurers. In a somewhat subordinate and ill-informed but rather deeply implicated capacity, I also took part in that unfortunate affair . . .

. . .

January 27 [1918]. . . . Precisely in May . . . our officers' Union of Military Duty was formed, of which, I think, I am still listed as the President . . . The purpose of the Union was to contribute by all the means within our power to the regeneration of the past gallant spirit of the Russian army, its ancient fighting traditions and its basic way of life . . . Of course, the membership dues which we collected were far from sufficient to equip ourselves with an office-apartment and other material necessities for the Union's existence; a large political organization which was active at the time and known under the name of the Republican Center, headed by a president, a certain Nikolaevskii, came to our help . . . I was troubled by the name Republican, which conflicted absolutely with my political ideals, views, and hopes. . . . [Nikolaevskii] explained to me that this name was nothing but a *nom de guerre*: people of the most varied tendencies, but united in a spirit of patriotism and a desire that our country should continue the war until victory in unity with the Allies, could join them under this banner; all this required a dictatorship . . . After such an explanation, we, the presidium of the Union, deemed it possible . . . to act and to work together with the Center and to avail ourselves of their financial help, which amounted, as far as I remember, to 6,000 rubles for the initial installation and organization of the Union of Military Duty . . . As a result of the serious obstacles raised by the general political situation of the country . . . our official slogans, which remained unused, and the whole of our program became a mere "surface movement." Under the banner of these official slogans gathered, joined, and rallied a certain group of officers, who were linked together by common convictions and the feelings they experienced in those dreadful days of our ill-fated country's distress—this was our "underwater movement."

During all of last summer the intensive, wise, and energetic activity of the Republican Center proved to be an important political force, which attracted the majority of the outstanding and most popular people. The Military Section of the Republican Center was at first under the direction of Colonel of the General Staff D., a very intelligent and talented man, who was definitely inclined toward counterrevolution. [When he left for the Far East, he] turned [the management of] affairs over to a colonel, also of the General Staff, a certain Desimet'er, who was much inferior to his predecessor and who, in my opinion, did a great deal of harm to the development and strengthening of the tasks laid in the basis of the organization. . . . [At first it was intended to carry out a "cautious" policy, as the Republican Center had a great deal of money and did not begrudge its use to organize all the large cities under its guidance. But by the end of July the attitude changed under the influence of reverses on the front, "the fall of Kerensky's built-up prestige," and the expectation "of a new move by the Bolsheviks."] The sum total of these circumstances weighed with Nikolaevskii, with his assistant Finisov, and, especially, with the powerful, but anonymous, leaders of the Center. It was decided to pass to action in close solidarity and agreement with General Kornilov, who was destined for the role of dictator. It was agreed that upon his arrival at the head of the special corps assigned for the capital General Krymov would take power in Petrograd into his hands. Before the appearance of Krymov, Colonel of the General Staff Sidorin came to Petrograd as the representative of Kornilov at the "R.C."; with the full cooperation of Desimet'er, he was to direct the activities of the officers in Petrograd in coordination with the operations of Kornilov's troops approaching the capital.

January 28 . . . The main difficulty in the whole reckless venture—its deplorable failure permits me to call it thus—was that so many mean and mercenary characters were attached to it, not to speak of the dishonest, double-faced, ambiguous, and cowardly role played by Kerensky. But even in spite of these unfavorable circumstances, the undertaking could have been carried out successfully if the right moment had not been missed, if so much precious time had not been lost . . . As I played no role in the organization as a whole, I was not informed of all the details; I deeply regretted it later, for had I been better informed in the beginning, I would not have felt so deep a disappointment after playing a stupid role under the direction of all kinds of rogues and scoundrels; nor would I have suffered so much morally after my hopes were shattered had I not believed in the firm conviction of our leaders in the imminence of success . . . When the moment for beginning the action was approaching, a week or ten days previous, I made the acquaintance of Colonel Vasilii Vasil'evich Geiman, of the Native Division's Chechen Cavalry Regiment, who held, in a sense, the position of chief of staff with Colonel Desimet'er, and later with Sidorin. It so happened that Geiman became something of an intermediary between me and the two colonels, whom I personally saw only once or twice . . . I usually saw Geiman daily at fixed hours or, at least, I communicated with him by phone; in this way, I was kept in touch with the general situation of our cause. Geiman always announced joyful news regarding the successes, which, allegedly, accompanied all our preparations for the decisive day. As it turned out later, the stories of Geiman proved, if not pure invention, at least greatly exaggerated . . . *The decisive* day was to occur when Krymov's corps or its vanguard, consisting of the Native Division, would approach the suburbs of Petrograd. At that time, the officer conspirators assembled in Petrograd, and, divided in advance into groups, were to carry out the task assigned each group: seizure of armed cars, arrest of the Provisional Government, arrest and execution of the most prominent and influential members of the Soviet of W. and S.D., and so on. By the arrival of Krymov's troops, the main forces of the revolution would already be crushed, annihilated, and rendered harmless, so that Krymov's only task would be the restoration of order in the capital.

Desimet'er and Sidorin informed me through Geiman that they intended to have me at the head of the officers' reserve, which would probably be stationed somewhere in the vicinity of the Hotel Astoria and would operate according to circumstances, depending on the orders I would receive. It was assumed that I would have under my command around 100 officers and, perhaps, a certain number of enlisted men. To help our cause, a good friend of mine, commander of a large military unit stationed at Krasnoe Selo, promised to put at my disposal about

30 officers and 100 soldiers, absolutely reliable and trustworthy . . . I decided to temporarily place all this command, on its arrival in Petrograd, in the houses of my wife and acquaintances, so that their appearance would be as little noticed as possible . . . When I told Geiman that I had this reinforcement, he was very pleased and promised to advise me as to exactly when I might summon the command. Next day, he advised me in a definite way that our action would take place early next morning, at dawn, but that he would give me further more detailed instructions that same evening, around 10:00 o'clock. . . . All night I waited for them in vain. By the next day it was clear that our whole undertaking had failed. Next day it came out that Geiman with his more or less inseparable a.d.c. . . . spent the night at the Villa Rodé, where a large gathering of these "conspirators" was celebrating, while I impatiently awaited those famous "instructions" which he had promised.

. . .

January 29. Reminiscing now about all that was experienced at that time, it is easier to make a more or less correct appraisal of the whole undertaking, which, had it succeeded, would have given Russia great hope and the chance of recovering and halting in time on the path of dishonor into which she has sunk, but the failure of which hastened the disintegration and caused countless new victims among the martyrized officers. Great are the crimes of Kerensky, but this crime, when for the sake of his own selfish interests and ambition he sacrificed his country and contributed to the triumph of the Bolsheviks, surpasses in its foulness all the others. In spite of the clumsiness with which the conspiracy was handled, in spite of many unfavorable circumstances which played a fateful role, until the last moment the conspiracy might still have been successful but for the cowardice and the dishonesty of its Petrograd leaders.

. . .

1263. General Lukomskii's Account

[*Memoirs of the Russian Revolution* by *General Loukomsky*, trans. by Mrs. Vitali, pp. 94–113. Although this source is readily available in English, the account is so central to the Kornilov affair that excerpts have nevertheless been included. Dates are New Style, but in some instances Old Style dates have been added for clarity. Another important military account is that of General A. I. Denikin, *Ocherki russkoi smuty*, II, and its English abridgment and translation, *The Russian Turmoil*, especially Chaps. XXX, XXI, and XXXII.]

On August 19th–20th, if I remember rightly, General Romanoffsky transmitted to me General Korniloff's order to concentrate the 3rd Cavalry Corps, with the Native Cavalry Division, in the area of Nevel–New Sokolniki–Velikie Luki.

These units formed the reserve of the Roumanian Front. A few days before I had had a conversation with General Korniloff, and we had discussed the necessity of moving a considerable group of cavalry from the Roumanian to the Northern Front, in order to strengthen the latter.

"But why must they be moved to the area of Nevel–New Sokolniki–Velikie Luki?" I asked General Romanoffsky.

"I could not tell you why. I am only transmitting General Korniloff's order exactly."

"When and how did you receive this order?"

"Yesterday, after eleven o'clock at night, General Korniloff called me and begged me to transmit this order to you."

All this seemed very strange. Why had this order been sent to me through the intermedium of the Quartermaster-General, Romanoffsky, instead of being given to me directly, and why had the above-mentioned area of concentration been fixed upon?

I went to Korniloff, informed him that General Romanoffsky had transmitted his order to me, and begged him to explain why he had chosen the above-mentioned area for the concentration of the cavalry.

General Korniloff replied that he wished to concentrate the cavalry on a point from where it would be easy to move it, in case of necessity, to the Northern or to the Western Front. The area in question was quite suitable for this purpose.

I said that we had no ground to fear for our Western Front, where there were sufficient reserves at hand, and that it would be far better to concentrate the cavalry in the neighbourhood of Pskov.

Korniloff, however, kept to his decision.

"Very well," I said, "I shall take the necessary dispositions; but I have an impression, Lavr Georgievitch, that you are keeping something from me. The area you have chosen would have been perfect if there was any question of throwing the cavalry upon Petrograd or Moscow, but I do not consider it to be the right one if it is only necessary to strengthen the Northern Front. If I am not mistaken, and you are, indeed, keeping something back, I must beg you either to let me go to the Front, or else to inform me of all your plans and intentions. A Chief of Staff can only remain at his post if he enjoys the full confidence of his Chief."

After thinking for a moment, General Korniloff replied:

"You are right. There are certain considerations which I have not yet spoken to you about. I beg you to at once give the necessary orders for moving the cavalry, and urgently to call the Commander of the 3rd Cavalry Corps, General Krymoff, to the Stavka. I will tell you everything in detail on my return from Petrograd."

General Korniloff left for Petrograd in the evening of August 22nd.

. . .

On the morning of August 24th General Korniloff returned to the Stavka.

He told me with indignation that his journey to Petrograd had been fruitless. Kerensky was leading him by the nose, and evidently did not wish to carry out his requests. These had been very superficially examined at the sittings of the Provisional Government; Savinkoff had been entrusted to work out a definite project for restoring discipline in the Army, and to present it, with General Korniloff's consent, to the Provisional Government for ratification. "They only want to gain time, as you see," said General Korniloff. "Mr. Kerensky evidently does not wish me to be present at the State Conference in Moscow, but I shall certainly go there, and will insist on my requests being accepted and fulfilled at last," added he.

. . .

After this General Korniloff went back to the conversation I had had with him before his journey to Petrograd.

"As you well know," said he, "all the reports of our Intelligence Department tend to prove that a new manifestation of the Bolsheviks will take place in Petrograd at the beginning of next month, about September 10th–11th. It is indispensable for Germany to sign a separate peace with Russia, and throw the armies that are on our front against the French and the English.

"The German Bolshevik agents, local ones as well as those who have been sent to us in leaded railway carriages by the Germans, will do all in their power to produce a *coup d'état*, and take over the supreme authority in the land.

"I feel sure, when I think of the events of May 3rd and June 16th–17th, that the molluscs who form the Provisional Government will be swept away; and if they remain in power by some miracle, the leaders of the Bolsheviks and the Council [Soviet] of Workmen and Soldiers' Deputies will be left unpunished owing to Mr. Tchernoff and Co.

"It is time to put an end to all this. It is time to hang the German agents and spies, with Lenin at their head, to dispel the Council of Workmen and Soldiers' Deputies and scatter them far and wide, so that they should never be able to come together again!

"You are right. My chief object in moving the Cavalry Corps is to have it at hand in the vicinity of Petrograd, at the end of August, and, if this manifestation of the Bolsheviks takes place, to deal with the traitors of Russia as they deserve to be dealt with.

"I intend to place General Krymoff at the head of this operation. I know that in case of necessity he will not hesitate to hang all the members of the Council of Workmen and Soldiers' Deputies.

"As to the Provisional Government, I have no intention of going against them; I hope to come to an agreement with them at the last moment. But now is not the moment to speak of it to anyone, for Mr. Kerensky, and especially Mr. Tchernoff, will not consent to my plan, and all will be spoilt.

"If I do not come to an agreement with Kerensky and Savinkoff, I may have to deal the blow to the Bolsheviks without their consent. But afterwards they will be the first to thank me for this, and it will be possible to form a strong Government in Russia, independent of all kind of traitors.

"I have no personal ambition. I only wish to save Russia, and will gladly submit to a strong Provisional Government, purified of all undesirable elements.

"Will you go with me to the end, and do you believe me when I say that I want nothing for myself?"

Knowing General Korniloff to be absolutely honest and devoted to his country, I replied that I believed what he said, that I shared his views, and would go with him to the end.

Such was the beginning, the base, and the substance of the "conspiracy" of which the Provisional Government accused us later on.

.   .   .

"I did not speak to you before of all this," said General Korniloff, "because I thought that you wished to command an army. Now I beg of you to remain with me as Chief of Staff. . . . You have too much on your hands as Chief of Staff. Trust to me; I shall look after everything myself, and all shall be done as it ought to be. My Orderly Officer, Zavoiko, and my Adjutant, Colonel Galitzine, are enlightened as to my plans."

I unfortunately acquiesced to all he said, and did not take any part in working out the details of the operation. It appeared later on that General Korniloff, for want of time, did not direct the preparations in person, and those who were called upon to execute the scheme, not excepting General Krymoff, treated the whole affair much too lightly, this being one of the reasons why the operations ultimately failed.

General Krymoff arrived at the Stavka on August 25th [August 12 O.S.], but General Korniloff had not time to talk things over with him before leaving for Krymoff to accompany him to Moscow in order to discuss the matter on the way.

. . .

After having delivered his speech, General Korniloff immediately left for Mohilev.

During his sojourn in Moscow he had several times met with the Ataman of the Don, Kaledin; with the President of the State Douma, Rodzianko; and the representatives of different public organizations and political parties. His intercourse with them had given him the impression that all his requests would be supported, and had fortified his belief in the justice of his decisions.

After his return to Mohilev, General Korniloff waited impatiently for the final solution of the questions he had raised at the Conference, and before Kerensky and Savinoff wired to say that they were working out a plan of the necessary measures for restoring discipline in the Army; that Savinkoff would arrive in a few days at Mohilev in order to discuss them finally with Korniloff and come to an agreement with him, after which these measures would immediately be ratified by the Provisional Government.

Meanwhile, information from Petrograd confirmed the rumours of an intended rising of the Bolsheviks, which was to take place at the beginning of the next month.

Some time before this a secret society had been formed in Petrograd, which had for its object the organization of detachments for self-defence in case of a rising of the Bolsheviks. Colonel Lebedeff, of the General Staff, who was in touch with the heads of this organization, asked General Korniloff to enter into immediate intercourse with them, and to invite them to Mohilev.

General Korniloff consented, and two engineers, belonging to the organization in question, arrived at Mohilev.

They informed General Korniloff that they had about two thousand men at their disposal, perfectly well armed, but were short of officers. They did not risk enrolling them from among the officers of the Petrograd garrison for fear they should be indiscreet and betray the organization. They begged General Korniloff to send about one hundred officers to Petrograd at the end of August, and vowed that they would play an important role in case of a rising of the Bolsheviks.

General Korniloff consented to this, saying that he would send officers from the Front, under the pretext of giving them leave of absence. The necessary dispositions would be taken by the "Officers' Union."*

* An "Officers' Union" had been formed in June, with the object of helping the officers to keep in touch with each other, and strengthen them in their efforts for putting an end to the disorganization in the Army. The central organ of administration of the "Officers' Union" was at the Stavka, and local sections of this Union existed at all the Headquarters of different units of the Army: divisions, corps, armies, etc.

It was agreed among them that everything must be ready by September 8th [August 26 O.S.], and that, in case of a rising of the Bolsheviks, at the approach of General Krymoff on Petrograd, this organization should step forward, occupy the Smolny Institute (Headquarters of the Council of Workmen and Soldiers' Deputies), and try to arrest the Bolshevik leaders.

After the Conference in Moscow, Korniloff unfortunately spoke to many people who came to the Stavka of his intention to deal a decisive blow to the Bolsheviks, and to the Council of Workmen and Soldiers' Deputies. This intention had, in fact, ceased to be a secret, and part, if not all, of his plan had got to be known in Petrograd. I am deeply persuaded that these rumours, which had evidently reached the Council of Workmen and Soldiers' Deputies, made them postpone the proposed rising of the Bolsheviks, and insist on putting Korniloff out of the way.

Kerensky, on the other hand, who looked upon Korniloff as a dangerous rival, was only too glad to seize this opportunity for provoking what he called "a revolt" on the part of the Supreme Commander-in-Chief, and then getting rid of him.

On September 6th [August 24 O.S.] the new Chief of the War Office [Assistant Minister of War], Savinkoff, at last arrived at the Stavka.

I took him into General Korniloff's study. After shaking hands with the Supreme Commander-in-Chief, Mr. Savinkoff said that he was charged with a special mission for him from the Provisional Government, which he wished to impart to him alone.

I left them and went to my own rooms. In about an hour's time General Korniloff sent for me, and said that Savinkoff had brought with him the project of the measures which the Government intended to take for restoring discipline in the Army. He added that all his requests were seemingly accepted, begged me to examine the materials brought by Savinkoff, and make my report on the subject before dinner. After dinner he would come to a definite agreement with Savinkoff in my presence. In the evening, at nine, he would receive, at the latter's request, Kerensky's Director of Office, Colonel Baranoffsky, and would discuss with him the necessary measures for preventing the expected rising of the Bolsheviks to take place.

General Korniloff then said that Savinkoff was accompanied by the Chief of the Intelligence Department of the War Office, and begged for permission to make some arrests at the Stavka, if it should prove necessary to do so.

"It seems," added Korniloff, ["]that Mr. Savinkoff's arrival is not only due to his desire to come to an agreement with me. He evidently wishes to make an inquiry concerning the activity of the members of the Stavka."

I replied that they were welcome to make any inquiry they liked, but that I would admit of no arrests without my permission.

I set about to examine the materials brought by Savinkoff, and very soon saw that the circle of jurisdiction left by this project to the "Commissaries" and "Committees" was far too wide; that the "Commissaries," especially, retained the right of interfering with the orders of the Commanding Staff, if these orders did not concern strictly operative dispositions. (General Korniloff, on the other hand, had lately decided to insist on the entire suppression of "Commissaries" and "Committees.")

I reported all this to the Supreme Commander-in-Chief.

After dinner, Savinkoff and I went to Korniloff's study. Savinkoff insisted on the necessity of maintaining the institution of "Commissaries" and "Committees" in the Army, but consented to limit the circle of their activity and to define it more exactly. General Korniloff insisted on the entire suppression of the afore-said institution.

In the end it was decided to inform the Provisional Government of the desire of the Supreme Commander-in-Chief and, if the former did not consent to suppress the "Commissaries" and "Committees" entirely, considerably to curtail their rights. There was no difference of opinion as to the rest.

When all the materials brought by Savinkoff had been duly examined, the Chief of the War Office told Korniloff that it was necessary to agree on the means of paralysing the influence of the Council of Workmen and Soldiers' Deputies, who would, of course, protest categorically against the adoption of the measures proposed by General Korniloff. He said that, notwithstanding this protest, the Provisional Government would ratify the project, which had now been worked out in complete accordance with the Supreme Commander-in-Chief, but that a rising of the Bolsheviks would immediately follow. This must be mercilessly crushed, and the Council itself must be suppressed if it supported the Bolsheviks. The garrison of Petrograd, he said, was not sufficiently to be relied upon, and it was indispensable to bring trustworthy cavalry units to Petrograd, and the city must be placed under martial law at their approach. Savinkoff assured Korniloff that all he said was in strict accordance with the views of the President of the Provisional Government, Mr. Kerensky, and that he, Savinkoff, had brought with him the latter's Director of Office, Colonel Baranoffsky, in order to exactly define the frontiers of the area which must be placed under martial law. He begged General Korniloff to wire to Petrograd when the corps sent by him under General Krymoff's command would be approaching Petrograd, which would then immedi-ately be placed under martial law with all its environs.

"This is indispensable," added Savinkoff, "as it will give you the possibility of applying the most energetic measures for crushing the Bolsheviks. I hope, Lavr Georgievitch, that the General you have chosen to command this corps will deal mercilessly with them, and with the Council of Workmen and Soldiers' Deputies, should the latter support them."*

General Korniloff replied that Savinkoff need not worry; that all measures should be taken by him to do prompt justice on the Bolsheviks, and on the Council of Workmen and Soldiers' Deputies, in case of a rising of the former.

It was already nine in the evening, and General Korniloff invited the Quarter-master-General, Romanoffsky, and Kerensky's Director of Office, Colonel Baran-offsky, to his study.

Savinkoff once more repeated in their presence that, after the ratification by the Government of the measures which had definitely been worked out with General Korniloff, a rising of the Bolsheviks would inevitably follow; that General Korniloff, *in strict agreement with the Provisional Government,* was sending a Cavalry Corps to Petrograd with the object of crushing this revolt, and that it was now indispensable to determine the area which it would be necessary to place under martial law at the approach of this corps to the capital.

---

* My memory may fail me, and I may not render Savinkoff's declaration textually, word for word, but the essence and meaning of this declaration is absolutely exact.

The area in question was fixed upon conjointly with Colonel Baranoffsky, who took a copy of the map on which it had been outlined.

On taking leave of Korniloff, Savinkoff expressed his belief that all would go well, adding, quite unexpectedly: "But do not appoint General Krymoff Commander of this Corps."

On the morning of September 7th [August 25 O.S.], when I came to make my daily report to General Korniloff, he told me the following:

In the evening of September 6th [August 24 O.S.], Mr. Lvoff (formerly Procurator of the Holy Synod) had arrived at Mohilev, and demanded to see the Supreme Commander-in-Chief at once. The latter, being occupied, could not receive him, and he presented himself to General Korniloff on the following morning.

Mr. Lvoff informed Korniloff that he had come as delegate of the Minister-President, Kerensky, in order to learn the point of view of the Supreme Commander-in-Chief on the best and most expedient way of creating a strong authority.

The Minister-President, it appeared, considered the three following courses as possible:

1. Kerensky himself as Dictator, at the head of a new Government.

2. A Government of three or four members (one of which must be the Supreme Commander-in-Chief, General Korniloff) invested with unlimited powers.

3. General Korniloff as Dictator and Supreme Commander-in-Chief, at the head of a new Government.

Mr. Lvoff inquired whether General Korniloff considered it desirable—in the latter case—for Kerensky and Savinkoff to form part of the new Government.

General Korniloff voted for the latter of these three variants, saying that Kerensky and Savinkoff must be members of the new Government, and charged Mr. Lvoff to inform them that he invited them both urgently to the Stavka, as he feared for their personal safety in case of a rising in the capital, and it would, moreover, be necessary to discuss a whole series of questions which would, naturally, arise in connection with the expected events.

I inquired whether Mr. Lvoff had brought any written proof of his mission.

"No," replied Korniloff, "he had no letter with him. The questions he put were written down in his notebook, and he entered my answers in the same. Mr. Lvoff is an irreproachably honest man and a gentleman, and I had no reason to distrust him."

"I know him for a perfect gentleman," said I, "but I also know that he has the reputation of a blunderer, and is quite capable of making a mess of things. The very fact of Kerensky's charging a third person with this mission seems suspicious to me. I am afraid he is hatching some plot against you. All this is very, very strange. Why did not Savinkoff say anything about it? Why is Lvoff entrusted with this mission at the very moment of Savinkoff's arrival at the Stavka? God grant I may be mistaken, but I do not like the look of it all, and I profoundly distrust Kerensky."

Korniloff said that I was too suspicious, that Lvoff had left Petrograd after Savinkoff, which explains why the latter knew nothing about the subject of this mission. He believed that Kerensky was sincere in this case, as the question of Dictatorship had been discussed by him before.

The following telegram was sent to Savinkoff on September 8th [August 26 O.S.], as had been agreed:

"The Corps will be concentrated in the vicinity of Petrograd towards the evening of August 28/Sept. 10. Petrograd must be placed under martial law on Aug. 29/Sept. 11. No. 6394. KORNILOFF."

On September 8th [August 26 O.S.], Kerensky called General Korniloff to the direct cable and begged him to confirm whether "he had actually charged Mr. Lvoff to inform him, Kerensky, of his plans and purposes."

General Korniloff replied: "Yes, I have charged Mr. Lvoff to inform you of my plans and purposes."

Kerensky then inquired whether General Korniloff still considered it urgent for him and Savinkoff to come to the Stavka.

Korniloff replied affirmatively, after which Kerensky said: "It is too late to start to-day, Saturday, but we shall leave for the Stavka on Sunday."

General Korniloff said that he would expect them on Monday, September 10th.

I must note here what General Korniloff himself owned later on—that the latter acted most thoughtlessly in this case, for, in speaking by direct cable with Kerensky, he omitted to ask him *what* it was that Lvoff had said to him.

.   .   .

Meanwhile, Korniloff was sure that everything was going on well, and that he was acting in full accordance with the Provisional Government. When I entered his study, late on the evening of September 8th [August 26 O.S.], to report on something, I found him poring over the project of a new list of Ministers.

"I am elaborating the project of a new Cabinet," said he. "I want to have it ready for the arrival of Kerensky and Savinkoff, and to come to a full agreement with them. I will be glad, however, if I am freed from the necessity of being Dictator. It will be best, after all, to form a strong Government of three or four members, in which I must, of course, take part, as Supreme Commander-in-Chief of the Army."

On that same evening, Korniloff sent a telegram to Moscow, to the President of the State Douma, Rodzianko, begging him, and other public leaders, to come to the Stavka on the morning of September 10th. When the subsequent events took place, however, neither Rodzianko nor any other of the public leaders who had so warmly supported Korniloff at the State Conference in Moscow put in an appearance at the Stavka.

At seven of the morning, on September 9th [August 27 O.S.], General Roman-offsky, Quartermaster-General at the Stavka, brought me a telegram addressed both to General Korniloff and me.

This telegram informed us that General Korniloff was dismissed from his post and ordered to start at once for Petrograd. I was invited to temporarily take over the duties of Supreme Commander-in-Chief.

The telegram was simply signed "Kerensky," and did not bear any number. I took it to General Korniloff.

This was a terrible blow to him. All hope of saving the Army and saving Russia was now lost. It was clear that Kerensky was bent on setting Korniloff aside, and on going further towards conciliating the Council of Workmen and Soldiers' Deputies; it was clear that the Bolsheviks would get the uppermost, and that all that remained yet of the Army and the mechanism of the State, would irretrievably crumble away.

After reading the telegram, General Korniloff asked what I intended to do.

I replied that I considered it impossible to take over the duties of Supreme Commander-in-Chief, and would immediately draft an answer in that sense.

Korniloff then said to me:

"Yes, under the existing conditions, it is my duty to remain at my post to the end. I must have my own way, and force the Provisional Government to carry out my requests. Please wire at once to General Krymoff and tell him to hasten with the concentration of the troops near Petrograd."

.   .   .

On September 10th [August 28 O.S.] the post of Supreme Commander-in-Chief was offered to the Commander-in-Chief of the Northern Front, General Klembovsky, who was invited to remain at Pskov.

General Klembovsky took advantage of this to refuse the offer, saying that it was impossible to direct the movements of the Army from Pskov.

.   .   .

1264. RUMORS OF COUNTERREVOLUTIONARY ACTIVITY AT STAVKA AND ELSEWHERE

[*Rabochaia Gazeta*, No. 142, August 25, 1917, p. 1.]

The Provisional Government has finally directed its attention to the highly suspicious work carried on systematically by someone at Stavka.

Information published yesterday in our paper and in *Izvestiia* only confirms our worst suspicions. We read that: "A center of counterrevolution has built itself a strong nest at Stavka. Since the soldiery will not follow it, it has no hope of achieving any results by open and direct attacks upon the Provisional Government. Consequently, it tries to terrorize the Provisional Government by intimations of threatening events at the front. It thus hopes, if not to overthrow it, to force it, at any rate, to accept a number of measures aimed directly and indirectly at the revolutionary democracy and its organization."

News about the exposure of a counterrevolutionary monarchical conspiracy is gradually getting into the press. It is associated with the names of grand dukes. There is ever-increasing pogrom and anti-Jewish agitation, and pogroms have already begun as a result of difficulties in the food supply. Heading these disturbances occasionally are people in the uniforms of functionaries and even, as was the case in Moscow, of officers. Finally, there are the ever more insolent speeches by members of the former State Duma down to Purishkevich inclusive. All this, together with the mysterious organization at Stavka, is related, if not organizationally, then in "idea." All this is directed *against the revolution* and its victories, and, above all, against the Provisional revolutionary Government.

1265. STATEMENT OF SAVINKOV

[*Birzhevyia Vedomosti*, No. 16438, September 12, 1917, p. 1. See also *Rech'*, No. 215, September 13, 1917, p. 2.]

Undoubtedly a counterrevolutionary plot was being hatched at Stavka and in the country generally, but I am profoundly convinced that General Kornilov did not take part in the plot. I am no less convinced that his Chief of Staff, General

Lukomskii, and the other principal instigators, obstinately tried to influence General Kornilov. On the other hand, General Kornilov—I know this personally —was very dissatisfied with the policy of the Government. As he declared on several occasions, he considered its policy weak, bordering on the criminal.

Nevertheless, it would certainly have been possible to work conscientiously with General Kornilov for the good of the country. As far as I am concerned, I have always been of the opinion that liberty can only be assured by a powerful army, and that a German victory would put an end to liberty in Russia. I have always held the view that measures, even very severe measures, were necessary to re-establish discipline and to restore fighting efficiency to the army, but always provided that such measures had the support of the Provisional Government and the absolute consent of Kerensky and the authority of his name. . . .

. . .

At Stavka I found the Supreme Commander in a very excited state of mind, heaping reproaches on the Government and declaring that he had no more faith in it, the country was going to the dogs, that he could no longer work with Kerensky, etc. As soon as he had calmed down I informed him that his plans had been approved by Kerensky. At the same time I transmitted to him the request [of the Minister-President] for the dispatch to Petrograd of a cavalry corps to be placed at the disposal of the Provisional Government. I specified, however, that he should not send the so-called "Savage" Division, nor entrust the command of the troops sent to General Krymov. I had the most unfavorable information regarding the counterrevolutionary tendencies of General Krymov.

On learning that the measures urged by him had been approved, Kornilov altered his tone, agreed to all my requests, and stated that he now thought it would be possible to work with the Government. I left Stavka on August 24. General Kornilov, who saw me off, bade me convey to Kerensky the expression of his satisfaction and the assurance of his perfect loyalty to the Government. I carried away the impression that an agreement between General Kornilov and Kerensky had been practically accomplished. . . . Unfortunately, the situation changed radically between August 24 and 26.

While I was returning from Stavka to Petrograd, L'vov, the former Ober-Procurator of the Synod, was on his way from Petrograd to Stavka. Before leaving Petrograd he had solicited an interview on the general political situation with Kerensky, such as any politician might have. Arriving at Stavka on August 25, L'vov went to General Kornilov and informed him that he had been personally instructed by Kerensky to ask him to choose one of the three following alternatives, implying that it was impossible for Kerensky to continue to govern the state any longer:

1. Kerensky to resign and General Kornilov to become head of the Government and form a new cabinet, of which Kerensky agreed to be a member.

2. The whole Government to resign and hand over full power to General Kornilov, who would proclaim himself dictator until the Constituent Assembly met.

3. The Government to resign and a directorate to be formed, the principal members of which would be Kerensky, General Kornilov, myself, and some others.

After thinking it over, General Kornilov chose the third alternative. L'vov left Stavka the same day, and on the following day called on Kerensky at the Winter Palace and informed him that he had been instructed by General Kornilov to demand that the whole civil and military power be handed over to the Supreme

Commander, who would then form a new cabinet. In confirmation, L'vov handed Kerensky a historical document to this effect, written and signed by L'vov on behalf of the Supreme Commander. The document was in the nature of an ultimatum. Kerensky, stunned by this unexpected act, especially as I had assured him of the loyalty of General Kornilov, got into telephone communication with General Kornilov. Kerensky asked General Kornilov: "Do you subscribe to the words which L'vov has addressed to me on your behalf?" General Kornilov replied in the affirmative. Filonenko, to whom General Kornilov related his conversation with Kerensky, expressed his astonishment that the Supreme Commander should have thoughtlessly confirmed on the telephone a statement which had never even been read over to him. But it was too late. A fatal misunderstanding had already been created.

At once Kerensky relieved General Kornilov of his command, summoning him to Petrograd. General Kornilov replied (and here it is that the misunderstanding ends and the rebellion begins) that he did not consider himself relieved of his command, which he would continue to hold. He then ordered the arrest of the Commissar of the Provisional Government, Filonenko, and, at the same time, gave instructions to the "Savage" Division to march on Petrograd under the command of General Krymov.

At my own request I was authorized by Kerensky to converse with General Kornilov on the telephone. I spoke to him twice, trying to point out the inadmissibility of his act and its counterrevolutionary character. I explained that there had been a misunderstanding, and I urged him to agree to stop the march of his troops and come himself to Petrograd in order to clear up the incident, but General Kornilov answered that he no longer recognized the Government. . . .[8]

[Savinkov added, in conclusion, that although he considered General Kornilov's behavior unpardonable, he nevertheless persisted in the view that the ex-Supreme Commander had, down to the last moment, been no party to the plot of some of his generals.]

1266. A More Detailed Account of Savinkov's Conversations with Kornilov at Stavka

[Kerensky, *Prelude to Bolshevism*, pp. 212–15. This account was written down for Kerensky by Savinkov and was in Kerensky's possession when he wrote *Prelude* while in the underground in Russia following the fall of the Provisional Government. It was lost, along with all of his other papers and books, left behind when he fled Paris in advance of the German occupation in 1940.]

. . . . .

. . . [A] few extracts from Savinkov's conversations with Kornilov, as written down by Savinkov himself:—

"Lavr Georgievitch," Savinkov said to Kornilov on August 23rd, "I should like to speak with you in private." (At these words, Lukomsky and Filonenko got up and left the room.) "The matter is this: the telegrams lately received by the Ministry and signed by various persons belonging to the Headquarters Staff,

---

[8] See Kerensky, *Prelude to Bolshevism*, pp. 142–43, for a further account of this conversation.

I must tell you frankly, inspire me with alarm. These telegrams frequently treat of questions of a political character, and that in an inadmissible tone. I have stated to you already that I am convinced that you will loyally support the Provisional Government, and will not go against it. But I cannot say the same about your Staff."

Kornilov.—"I must tell you that I do not *trust any longer* Kerensky and the Provisional Government. The latter has not the strength to stand on the ground of firm authority which alone can save the country. As for Kerensky, he is not only weak and vacillating, but even *insincere.* He insulted me undeservedly [at the Moscow Conference]. Moreover, he carried on conversations behind my back with Tcheremissov, and wanted to appoint him Supreme Commander-in-Chief." [Nothing of the kind ever happened.—A. K.]

Savinkov.—"It seems to me that in questions of State there is no room for personal grievances. As for Kerensky, I can't share your opinion about him. I know Kerensky."

Kornilov.—"The composition of the Government ought to be altered."

Savinkov.—"As far as I know, Kerensky is of the same opinion."

Kornilov.—"It is necessary that Kerensky should not meddle with affairs."

Savinkov.—"This is impossible at present, even if it were necessary."

Kornilov.—"It is necessary that Alexeiev, Plekhanov and Argunov should be in the Government."

Savinkov.—"It is necessary rather that the Soviet Socialists should be replaced by non-Soviet Socialists. Is that what you mean?"

Kornilov.—"Yes; the Soviets have proved their impracticability and their inability to defend the country."

Savinkov.—"All that is a matter for the future. You are dissatisfied with the Government; talk it over with Kerensky. At any rate, you must admit that without Kerensky at its head no Government is conceivable."

Kornilov.—"I shall not enter the Government. You are right, of course, that without Kerensky at its head no Government is conceivable. But Kerensky is vacillating; he hesitates; he promises and does not fulfil his promises."

Savinkov.—"This is not correct. Allow me to inform you that during the six days that elapsed since the Moscow Conference, at which Kerensky declared that he was adopting methods of firm authority, the Ministry of War did much, namely . . ."

This conversation took place on the 23rd of August. Here are some extracts from a conversation on the following day:—

Kornilov.—"Very well, I shall not appoint Krimov."

Savinkov.—"Alexander Feodorovitch [Kerensky] would like you to appoint General D."

Kornilov.—"Alexander Feodorovitch has the right of objecting to an appointment, but he cannot instruct me whom to appoint."

Savinkov.—"Alexander Feodorovitch does not instruct you, he only requests."

Kornilov.—"I shall appoint D. Chief of the Staff."

Savinkov.—"And what about the Native Division?"

Kornilov.—"I shall replace it by the regular cavalry."

Savinkov.—"Many thanks. Alexander Feodorovitch also charged me to request you to detach for his disposal Colonel Pronin [Assistant President of the Main Committee of the Officers' League]."

Kornilov.—"Pronin! What for? I understand. It is a concealed arrest! I shall not let Pronin go. Give me proofs, and I will arrest Pronin myself."

Savinkov.—"Very well. I shall report it in that way to Alexander Feodorovitch."

Kornilov.—"Certainly."

.   .   .

Savinkov.—"Will you allow me, Lavr Georgievitch, to come back to yesterday's conversation? What is your attitude towards the Provisional Government?"

Kornilov.—"*Tell Alexander Feodorovitch that I shall support him in every way,* for the welfare of the Fatherland requires it."

Savinkov.—"Lavr Georgievitch! I am happy to hear these words. I never doubted you. I shall tell Alexander Feodorovitch what you have just said."

.   .   .

1267. FROM THE MEMOIRS OF V. N. L'VOV

[Published in *Posledniia Novosti*, No. 186, November 30, 1920, p. 2; No. 190, December 4, 1920, p. 2; No. 192, December 7, 1920, p. 2; and No. 194, December 9, 1920, p. 2.]

II

Right after the State Conference, an acquaintance of mine from Petrograd, named Dobrynskii, came to see me in my room. He wore the military uniform of the Red Cross and the Cross of St. George. He served earlier in the Ministry of Agriculture and was an official for special assignments while A. V. Krivoshein was Minister . . . After the revolution he settled in Vladikavkaz, where he established relations with the Caucasian mountain peoples. He commands great authority there and can bring out up to 40,000 Caucasians at the first signal given by him and direct them wherever he wishes. In view of his importance among the Caucasians, he was now summoned by telegram from Stavka to some kind of secret conference to be held on August 17 at Stavka. Before going there, he dropped in to ask my advice. Dobrynskii was a Board member of the Union of the Cavaliers of St. George. "But what advice do you want me to give you when I don't know what is the matter and what is going to be discussed at the secret conference?" Dobrynskii replied that in all probability the conference would discuss the question of Kornilov's dictatorship. I quickly retorted that I, personally, considered a dictatorship by Kornilov inconceivable. Kornilov does not have the backing of the soldiers. On the other hand, I know Kerensky and I know that he is by no means on the side of the Soviet. On the contrary, Kerensky is hesitating. However, if a course were indicated to him, he might pursue it. And therefore I suggest that Kornilov and Kerensky do not quarrel—God forbid —but make common cause. Let Kornilov be the chief of all the armed forces on the front and in the rear, and let Kerensky be the President of the Provisional Government. As for the Provisional Government, it must be formed on the basis of a national cabinet, as is the case in all the countries allied to us. War is not a time for party strife. All the parties that worked together during the revolution must be represented in the Government. In view of the disorders in Russia, special attention must be directed to the Ministry of the Interior. It would be desirable to grant special powers to the Minister of the Interior and place troops at his disposal for establishing order within the country. "That is my plan."

Dobrynskii asked me whether I would agree to be the Minister of the Interior.

Without attributing particular importance to this proposal, but simply giving my opinion, I answered that only provided a sufficient number of disciplined troops be placed at the disposal of the Minister of the Interior. Dobrynskii agreed with my plan and promised to relay it to the secret conference at Stavka. He left.

. . .

On August 20, Dobrynskii came to see me again in my [hotel] room, and jubilantly announced that my plan was accepted at the secret conference. True, they had thought of deciding in favor of a military dictatorship, but he delivered a speech . . . in defense of my plan, and the conference finally approved it. Then he added that late at night he was taken to the office of the Supreme Commander, and Kornilov told him confidentially that he had decided to be a military dictator, but that nobody must know about this. When he bade him farewell, Kornilov said: "Remember that you did not see me, and I did not see you." . . .

. . .

On the following day, August 21, Dobrynskii entered my hotel room and said that Alad'in, a former member of the First State Duma and the leader of the Trudoviks, wanted to make my acquaintance. I gave my consent. Alad'in entered [dressed] in a lieutenant's uniform of the British service. After greeting me, he began to complain about Kerensky, that the latter didn't want to see him, whereas Alad'in wanted to tell him the whole truth face to face. "What can he do to me? Not let me out of the office? That's all!" added Alad'in. A few minutes later Alad'in told me that he had received from Stavka a letter from Zavoiko.

"Who is Zavoiko?" I asked. "He is Kornilov's orderly," answered Alad'in. "The letter contains a very important mission. I sat two whole hours at Prince L'vov's, wanting to speak with him alone, but there were so many people there that I could not catch a convenient moment."

"Could you tell me what the mission is about?" I asked.

"Here is the place in the letter that refers to the mission," Alad'in said to me, showing me a piece of paper on which literally the following [words] were written: "At lunch the General, who was sitting opposite me, said: 'It wouldn't be a bad idea to warn the K.D., so that they could all resign from the Provisional Government by August 27 in order to put the Provisional Government in a difficult position and avoid troubles for themselves.'"

"Who is this General?" I asked.

"It's Lukomskii."

"And where did the lunch take place?" I continued.

"At the Supreme Commander's."

"What weight has this letter from a common orderly?"

"The point is," Dobrynskii explained to me, "that Kornilov never writes letters himself."

I gasped and understood the full meaning of the warning in Zavoiko's letter.

"The warning is of such great importance," I said, "that I could take a trip to Petrograd and give this piece of paper to the Central Committee of the Kadets." Alad'in agreed.

Then I told Alad'in about my plan and asked him what he thought of my going to Kerensky and persuading him to reorganize the Government in order to calm Stavka down.

Alad'in agreed that it would be very good if I could get Kerensky to agree to negotiations. "Perhaps you will succeed in preventing whatever it is that is being prepared for August 27."

"What is it that is being prepared?" I asked.

Alad'in answered definitely that he did not know.

When he left, I again asked Dobrynskii whether I should visit Kerensky to start negotiations with him on the basis of my plan. Dobrynskii fervently supported the necessity of my seeing Kerensky, saying that the secret conference at Stavka had authorized him to ask me this.

I asked my brother to come to my place, told him everything, and asked for his advice. He supported the necessity of my seeing Kerensky. "If they want an agreement with Kerensky in Stavka, then whom do they have to turn to if not to you, who have been on good terms with Kerensky?"

"How is it that they want an agreement when it seems that everything has already been decided there!" I exclaimed. However, I still decided to go in the hope that I might succeed in averting some [drastic action].

III

By evening I was on the train to Petrograd. As I sat in my compartment, I got into a conversation with a general who was sharing the compartment. The conversation became more and more involved—I learned from him that he was going to Petrograd to attend a military conference which was to formulate the demands that the conference intended to make to the Government.

"But what is expected on August 27?" I asked.

"I don't know," the General answered. "I only know that I was ordered by this date to bring up to Petrograd all the former police and *gendarmerie* of which I am the head. In any case, an ultimatum will be presented to the Government; if it does not accept the ultimatum, events will follow."

As soon as I arrived in Petrograd, early on the morning of August 22, I telephoned Miliukov. It turned out that he was out of town. I telephoned Nabokov, found him home, made an appointment to see him at his flat right away, and drove there the same morning. I entered the study, greeted him, and asked him to close all the doors so that no one could overhear us, because I had to tell him something very confidential. He closed all the doors, sat down, and listened.

I took out my piece of paper and said to him: "I was authorized by Stavka to give you the following to read. Read it!" And I handed him the paper.

Nabokov read it and then asked: "What does it mean?"

I answered him: "I know just as little as you do. My mission is fulfilled; it is limited to this paper. Now, do you want to know my opinion?"

"If you please."

"In my opinion, preparations for a coup d'état are being made in Stavka. I am making every effort to prevent them from taking this course. In my opinion, it is necessary for Kornilov to reach an agreement with Kerensky."

"With Kerensky?" exclaimed Nabokov. "But can't you understand that Kerensky is the symbol of the revolution? With the downfall of Kerensky, the revolution will be finished!"

"That's your opinion," I answered, "but I do not think so. If you honestly extend a hand of agreement to Kerensky, you will see that he will accept it."

"But you have seen for yourself at the State Conference that only Bublikov shook the hand extended by Tseretelli."

"With no agreement—it is civil war," I said.

"But what is going to happen on August 27?" Nabokov continued his questioning.

"I think," I said, "that an ultimatum will be presented and if it is not accepted something will follow."

I left Nabokov, amazed at his political blindness.[9] At 2:00 P.M. I was in the Winter Palace. I had to wait quite a long time for Kerensky. He was conferring about something with Savinkov, who was about to go to Stavka.

. . . Savinkov finally left . . .

"Just think, Aleksandr Fedorovich, the Government is hanging in mid-air. On the one hand, the Soviet is against you. On the other hand, the elements which you have pushed away from yourself are now against you."

"All of you out there are organizing plots," Kerensky interposed.

"I am not organizing any plots. The Soviet is organizing the plots."

. . .

". . . You must choose: either we or they."

"And who are you? The Union of Cavaliers of the Cross of St. George?" Kerensky smiled sarcastically. "But what sort of strength is that?"

"You are mistaken if that's what you think. There is, first, the Constitutional Democratic Party."

"I agree, this is a force," Kerensky interrupted me.

"Second," I continued, "there is the commercial and industrial class; third, there are the Cossacks; fourth, the regimental units; and, finally, the Union of Officers, and many others."

"What is it that you want me to do?"

"Break with the Soviet."

"You want me to be a traitor?"

"No, I do not want you to be a traitor, but I want you to think of Russia, and not the revolution. I am not against the Soviet. I have already told you that it only needs to be circumscribed by law. But I am against your listening exclusively to its voice, forgetting the existence of the rest of Russia, and especially when the Soviet is turning Bolshevik."

"Then what is it that you want me to do?"

"Offer your hand to those whom you have pushed away from yourself. Reorganize the Government so that it can satisfy a large element of all of Russian society and the people. Include some representatives to the right of the Kadets. On the other hand, let there be socialists in the Government, but not confined exclusively to representatives of the Soviet."

"But still one cannot do without representatives of the Soviet," Kerensky said.

"I do not argue; let it be so. But reach an agreement with those who hate you. A crucial moment has arrived. I know what I am saying. For the good of the country, I beseech you!"

Kerensky was moved.

"All right," he said. "I agree, and even if my resignation is required, I agree to resign, but understand that I cannot simply leave power; I must turn it over to other hands."

---

[9] V. Nabokov gave essentially the same account of this conversation in his "Vremennoe Pravitel'stvo," *ARR*, I (1921), 43–44.

"Then authorize me," I said, "to enter into negotiations, on your behalf, with all the elements I consider necessary."

"You have my authorization," said Kerensky; "only I ask you to hold everything secret." And he shook my hand firmly.

"I will inform you of the results obtained," I said.

"Where are you going?" Kerensky asked.

"I am going to the place I came from," I said, smiling. I left. Kerensky saw me off and waved to me for a long time as he stood outside of his study. I departed.[10]

Kerensky was won over. Now what would the opposing side say?

On the following day (August 23) I was back in Moscow.

I informed Alad'in at once that Kerensky was favorably disposed to an agreement. Alad'in answered with a sigh of relief: "Thank God, now we will avoid bloodshed."

"The basis of the agreement is as follows," I said; "the establishment of a national cabinet; if necessary, the resignation of Kerensky, keeping the negotiations secret; I was personally authorized to conduct negotiations on behalf of Kerensky."

Alad'in wrote all this down in his notebook. Dobrynskii was similarly pleased when he learned that Kerensky was amenable to an agreement. I called my brother . . . and told him that Kerensky authorized me to negotiate on forming a cabinet and that he was amenable to an agreement. My brother answered me that he had already talked with several persons, among them, incidentally, V. Maklakov. "It is difficult for us to go along with Kerensky," my brother said, "but we will still go along."

"And what of Maklakov?" I asked.

"Maklakov also will go along."

"And so the agreement is beginning to take shape," I said. Then I went downstairs to Alad'in's hotel room. It was noon. No sooner did we start to talk—there were three of us in the room: Alad'in, Dobrynskii, and I—than an orderly from Stavka, in field dress, appeared in the doorway and handed a package to Alad'in. Alad'in opened the package, read the contents, and turned pale. "I can't understand what happened in Stavka!" he exclaimed. "Read it." And he gave the package to Dobrynskii. Dobrynskii read it and raised his hands in dismay. "What is it?" I asked anxiously. "May I know? Since I have entered into negotiations, I think there is no reason to conceal it from me."

"Of course," said Alad'in. "The package contains a telegram from the Supreme Commander addressed to Kaledin, Ataman of the Don Cossacks, in which Kaledin is ordered to begin advancing against Moscow."

I read the telegram and cried out: "But this is madness!" Alad'in shrugged.

"Can't we detain the telegram and not send it?"

"This is impossible," said Alad'in.

"We are military men. If we receive an order from the Supreme Commander, it is our duty to carry out the order—that is, to send the telegram immediately."

"This is terrible," I said.

"This is still not a campaign against Moscow, but only the assembling of all Cossack units," Dobrynskii consoled me.

---

10 For Kerensky's account of this meeting, see his *Prelude to Bolshevism*, pp. 127–30.

IV

On the same day Dobrynskii and I left for Stavka. A Polish delegate entered our compartment who warned Dobrynskii that the Polish legion in Kiev was ready to advance at the first signal.

On the following day, August 24, we arrived in Mogilev . . .

.   .   .

. . . It was 10:00 o'clock in the evening when I entered Kornilov's office. I greeted him and said:

"I come from Kerensky."

Kornilov's eyes sparkled with an evil glint.

"I have a proposal to make to you," I continued. "It is wrongly believed that Kerensky is anxious to stay in power. He is ready to resign if he is in your way. But the power must be legally transferred from hand to hand. The power cannot be abandoned, but neither can it be seized. Kerensky has agreed to reorganize the Government so as to draw all elements of society into it. This is my proposal —an agreement with Kerensky."

Kornilov calmed down and replied:

"I have nothing against Kerensky. When he wanted to resign at the Moscow State Conference, I advised him against it. Then he asked me whether I would support him, and I promised him my support. But, then, Kerensky does not fight against the Bolsheviks. Days go by and he does nothing in this respect. This is wrong. If a Bolshevik uprising occurs in Petrograd, there will be an incredible mess. I was commander of the Petrograd forces and I know the mood of those men. Some of the regiments will support the Bolsheviks, others will be against it. In this mess the Provisional Government will perish. This must not happen. Some action must be taken to prevent this. I know Kerensky, and I know that one can reach an understanding with him. But Kerensky is hated and I cannot vouch for his life. Today Savinkov came here to complain to me about the Soviet. What can I do when I cannot get the Government to place under my command all the troops at the front and in the rear? Regimental committees interfere with military orders. However, I cannot complain about them as far as the economic [side of the question] is concerned: in this respect they are useful. But come at 10:00 o'clock tomorrow morning for the final answer."

I left, fully satisfied that Kornilov was in favor of an agreement.

.   .   .

At 10:00 A.M. on the following day (August 25) I was going up the stairs of the Governor's house where Kornilov was located, when an elderly enlistee met me on the top flight. He was a tall, stout man; his hair was dark with streaks of gray. He introduced himself: "Zavoiko." Zavoiko apologized on behalf of the Supreme Commander for asking me to wait. . . .

.   .   .

While Zavoiko was expounding to me his views on the *Zemskii Sobor*, the door of the office opened.

I entered Kornilov's office and sat down by his side at the desk. Kornilov started speaking to me in a firm and assured manner. The hesitating tone of yesterday was no longer evident.

"Tell Kerensky," Kornilov said to me, "that Riga fell because the draft bills I submitted to the Provisional Government have still not been approved. The fall of Riga arouses the indignation of the whole army. There can be no further delay. Regimental committees must have no right to interfere with military orders; Petrograd must be included in the sphere of military operations and placed under martial law; all units of the front and the rear must be subordinated to the Supreme Commander. From counterintelligence reports submitted to me, the Bolsheviks are planning to stage an uprising in Petrograd between August 28 and September 2. The aim of this uprising is to overthrow the Provisional Government, proclaim the power of the Soviet, conclude peace with Germany, and give up the Baltic Fleet to Germany . . . In view of such a formidable threat to Russia, I can see no other way out than to transfer the power of the Provisional Government to . . . the Supreme Commander."

I interrupted Kornilov.

"The transfer of military power alone, or civil as well?" I asked.

"Both military and civil," Kornilov explained.

"Allow me to write all this down so as to remember it."

"Please," said Kornilov, and offered me a pencil and paper.

"Perhaps it would be better simply to combine the office of Supreme Commander with the office of President of the Council of Ministers," I interposed.

Kornilov was embarrassed.

"Possibly your scheme is also acceptable," said Kornilov.

"Of course, all this is before the Constituent Assembly," Kornilov remarked.

"Furthermore," he continued, "warn Kerensky and Savinkov that I cannot vouch for their lives . . . , and, therefore, let them come to Stavka where I will personally be responsible for their safety."

I was moved by these words . . . and said to Kornilov:

"You are an honorable man."

Kornilov continued:

"It is not my concern who will be the Supreme Commander as long as the Provisional Government transfers the power to him."

I said to Kornilov:

"If it's a question of a military dictatorship, then who is to be the dictator, if not you?"

Kornilov nodded and continued:

"At any rate, if the Romanovs rise to the throne, it will only be over my dead body. As soon as the power is transferred, I will form my cabinet.

"I no longer trust Kerensky, he is not doing anything."

"And do you trust Savinkov?" I asked.

"No. I do not trust Savinkov either. I don't know whom he wants to stab in the back. It could be Kerensky, it could be me," Kornilov replied.

"If you have such an opinion of Savinkov, why didn't you arrest him yesterday while he was here?"

Kornilov was silent.

"However," Kornilov continued, "I could offer Savinkov the portfolio of Minister of War, and Kerensky—the portfolio of Minister of Justice."

At this point, to my complete surprise, Zavoiko . . . entered the office unannounced, interrupted the Supreme Commander, and said in a tone that teachers use toward pupils:

"No, no, not Minister of Justice, but Vice-President of the Council of Ministers."

I looked in amazement first at Kornilov, then at the orderly. Kornilov appeared disconcerted.

"Then is it your wish that I relay all this to Kerensky?" I asked Kornilov.

Zavoiko answered:

"Of course, of course, legal succession of power is important."

"In this case," I turned to Kornilov, "would you reserve a seat for me on the train since no tickets are being sold?"

Zavoiko said that he would personally accompany me to the station and arrange everything.

I bade farewell to Kornilov and left the office.

Zavoiko invited me for lunch at his place; he was located in the same building. I entered his place and found Dobrynskii and another gentleman whom I had not met . . . Zavoiko introduced us:

"Professor Yakovlev."[11]

Then Zavoiko sat at the desk, took out a piece of paper on which something was written, and began reading aloud. It was Kornilov's manifesto to the army in which Kornilov, calling himself a son of a Cossack, was taking Supreme Power in the name of saving the native land. Then . . . Zavoiko pulled out another paper from the desk and started reading. That was Kornilov's proclamation to the soldiers. It promised 8 dessiatines of land to every soldier when he returned home. This turned out to be the agrarian program drawn up by Professor Yakovlev who was sitting before me.

"Where are you going to find so many dessiatines for every soldier?" I asked.

Yakovlev explained that he had everything calculated precisely.

After reading the manifesto and the proclamation, Zavoiko slipped me a copy of each. I put them automatically into my pocket without knowing why he gave them to me. Then, taking a piece of paper with a casual air, Zavoiko said:

"And so, the Vice-President of the Council of Ministers will be Kerensky."

He wrote this down on the piece of paper.

V

"And so the Vice-President of the Council of Ministers will be Kerensky?"

"And who will be the Minister of the Interior?" asked Zavoiko and fixed his eyes upon me.

"Maybe you will take it?" Dobrynskii asked me.

I hastily refused. Zavoiko quickly wrote down: "Filonenko." He put his own name down for Minister of Finance and wrote in his own hand: "Zavoiko."

"Ober-Procurator of the Most Holy Synod," I said hastily: "Kartashev," and so forth.

Having completed the note, Zavoiko thrust it at me. I asked him what I was to do with it.

"You will see later!" said Zavoiko.

I hid the note in my pocket, but, unable to restrain myself, turned to Zavoiko and said:

"You are forming a cabinet. I see here that everything is ready for the coup

[11] See Miliukov, *Istoriia vtoroi russkoi revoliutsii,* I vypusk 2, 195–96.

d'état, and that you have decided on this without having sought the advice of civic leaders, or political parties, or any public organizations. This is impossible. One must immediately invite the prominent civic leaders to come here and discuss the situation with them."

Zavoiko stood up from the armchair by the desk and offered me a pen and paper.

"You can write to whomever you wish in the name of the Supreme Commander."

I sat down and wrote the following note:

"Kornilov requests the civic leaders, whom you deem it necessary to invite, to come at once to the Stavka."

"You will give this note to my brother," I said, addressing Dobrynskii. "Leave for Moscow immediately."

Then, addressing myself to Zavoiko, I smiled disdainfully, and added:

"I am glad that at least there is no one of the Black Hundred in your cabinet."

"I am not of the Black Hundred," Zavoiko answered. "I have a liberal past."

I bade him farewell and left with Dobrynskii for my own quarters.

.   .   .

Zavoiko came for me in an automobile and the three of us—Zavoiko, Dobrynskii, and I—sped to the station. At the station Zavoiko arranged a seat for me and we started walking up the platform while we waited for the train.

.   .   .

"So Savinkov came here," Zavoiko said to me, "to complain about the Soviet and ask us to save them from the Soviet. They are evidently losing their heads in Petrograd."

Reaching a quiet spot with no one around, I said to Zavoiko:

"If everything is decided among you, I do not understand the purpose of my going to Kerensky."

"It is important to arrange a legal succession of power!" Zavoiko answered me.

"But I don't understand why you placed Kerensky in your cabinet when you hate him?"

"How is it that you don't understand? After all, he is a well-known symbol for the soldiers. He must be retained."

"But is the cabinet you have planned really fit to govern Russia?"

"The socialists created this anarchy; then let them bear the consequences for it. This cabinet is [intended] only for three months. Later on, there will be another cabinet, a real one."

"Kornilov is guaranteeing Kerensky's life," I said.

"Ah, how can the Supreme Commander guarantee life to Kerensky!" exclaimed Zavoiko.

"He did say so, however."

"He may have said a lot of things! How can Kornilov vouch for every step Kerensky takes? So he leaves the house and is killed."

"But who would kill him?"

"Even the selfsame Savinkov—how should I know who!"

"But this is terrible!"

"There is nothing terrible. His death is necessary as an outlet for the pent-up feelings of the officers."

"Then why does Kornilov call him to Stavka?"

"Kornilov wants to save him, but he won't be able to. Don't forget," Zavoiko continued, "it is important to present three points to the Provisional Government: first, immediate transfer by the Provisional Government of all military and civil authority . . . to the Supreme Commander; second, immediate resignation of all the members of the Provisional Government, and third, announcement of martial law in Petrograd. And so, don't forget the three points," Zavoiko repeated over and over again to me.

Then, looking at me fixedly in the eyes, Zavoiko pronounced with deep significance:

"Bring Kerensky!"

Having pronounced these words, Zavoiko . . . disappeared and drove away without giving me time to come to my senses and ask him:

"What for?"

However, to bring Kerensky to Stavka after what Zavoiko expounded to me with such cynicism would mean to bring Kerensky to certain death. What did Zavoiko take me for!

A hangman?

Zavoiko formulated the Supreme Commander's demands to the Provisional Government clearly and explicitly, without leaving the slightest doubt of their meaning.

I was bringing an ultimatum. I knew, besides, that these demands would be bolstered by bayonets. Where are these bayonets? I did not know, but I felt them. Involuntarily, I recalled the General's words in the train about presenting an ultimatum to the Provisional Government. That meant that I was bringing this ultimatum!

. . .

But in addition to the ultimatum, I was bringing to Kerensky information of prime national importance about the Bolsheviks' schemes and their contemplated uprising between August 28 and September 2. I had to believe the words of the Supreme Commander. I spoke with the Supreme Commander on behalf of the President of the Provisional Government. There cannot be a shadow of untruth, I thought, in the words of the Supreme Commander. I was bringing a request from the Supreme Commander to the President of the Provisional Government, as a mediator between them.

I was bringing a warning to Kerensky that his life was in danger. Kerensky did not believe in bloodshed. If during the revolution the blood of the Ministers in the Tauride Palace was spared—this was only thanks to Kerensky; if no tsarist blood was shed in Tsarskoe Selo, it was only thanks to Kerensky. It was my duty to repay him with the same, i.e., to save his life and, at the same time, remain strictly within the boundaries of the mission assigned to me by Kornilov.

Why did not Kornilov accept an agreement with Kerensky? Only yesterday he spoke in a different tone, but today he was so vigorously opposed to it. This question was explained at a later date. When I met Zavoiko . . . in the Central Guardhouse in Petrograd I asked him about this, and he replied with self-satis-faction:

"Because on the evening of the 24th, when you were speaking with Kornilov, I was not present at Stavka."

As I was reflecting, Dobrynskii ran up to me and said to me in indignation:

"What kind of cabinet did they draw up there? The officers will not stand it for a second after the coup d'état! I was offered the post of Governor-General of Vladikavkaz. I refused. Now Tereshchenko is due to arrive here by train, and Zavoiko tells me that he will be killed, that he can't even vouch that he has not already been killed on the way. In the compartment."

"Wait for the train," I told Dobrynskii, "and warn Tereshchenko immediately to bypass Mogilev. Let him go wherever he wishes, even if it's to Kiev. And I am going to Petrograd."[12]

The train approached. I left.

Early next morning, on August 26, I was in Petrograd. I called Kerensky at once by telephone to ask when I could see him. Kerensky's aide answered me that Aleksandr Fedorovich was waiting for me.

I went to Kerensky immediately.

1268. KERENSKY'S ACCOUNT OF HIS SECOND MEETING WITH L'VOV AND HIS CONVERSATION OVER THE HUGHES APPARATUS WITH KORNILOV

[Kerensky, *Prelude to Bolshevism*, pp. 131–38.]

. . .

The second time he came, I met him with the following words: "You have come again to talk about the inclusion of new elements in the Provisional Govern-ment." (I am not certain about the actual words, but such was the meaning.) He answered: "No, I have come to discuss a totally different subject; the situation has completely changed." This time he made no mention whatsoever of the necessity to include new elements in the Provisional Government or of extending its range of support. He told me bluntly that he had come to warn me that my position was extremely precarious, that I was *doomed*; in the very near future there would be a Bolshevik rising, when the Government would re-ceive no support; that no one would guarantee my life, etc. When he saw that all this made no impression upon me and that I took it in a jocular way: "It can't be helped, such is fate," and so on, he abruptly broke off the conversation. Then, apparently much excited, he added: "I must make you a formal offer." "From whom?" "From Kornilov." When I listened to all this nonsense, it seemed to me that either he was insane or something very serious had happened. . . .

. . .

General Kornilov declared to me (Kerensky) through him (Lvov) that no assistance whatever would be given to the Provisional Government in its struggle with the Bolsheviks, and that in particular Kornilov would not answer for my

---

[12] I. A. Dobrynskii published an account of his role in the affair from August 20 to 26, which was published in the September 1 issue of *Vol'nyi Den'* in Novocherkassk and reprinted in *Rech'*, No. 211, September 8, 1917, p. 4. It corresponds in most instances with that of L'vov.

life anywhere but at Headquarters; that the continuance of the Provisional Government in power could no longer be permitted; that General Kornilov invited me to urge the Provisional Government to transfer its powers that very day to the Generalissimo, and, pending the formation by him of its new Cabinet, to hand over the direction of current affairs to the Assistant Ministers and to proclaim martial law throughout Russia. As to myself and Savinkov, we were urged to go away that night to Headquarters, where Ministerial portfolios awaited us —for Savinkov the position of War Minister, for me that of Minister of Justice.

To this V. N. Lvov added that this last condition—that is to say, our going to Headquarters and the rest—was put to me privately, and was not to be disclosed at the session of the Provisional Government.

This communication was an absolute surprise to me, and especially the fact that it came from the lips of V. N. Lvov, because his name had never before been mentioned in any of the reports or statements concerning the plot which I had in my possession.

At first I burst out laughing. "Don't joke, V. N.," I said.

"There is no time to joke; the situation is very serious," Lvov answered; and with extreme excitement and evident sincerity, he began to urge me to save my life. For that there was "only one way, to yield to Kornilov's demands." He was beside himself.

I walked hastily up and down my large room, trying to understand, to feel, what was the real meaning of all this—Lvov's coming, and the rest of it. I remembered what he had said at his first visit about "real force," and compared it with the feeling that existed against me at Headquarters, and with all the reports about the ripening conspiracy which was without a doubt connected with Headquarters; and as soon as I had got over my first surprise, or rather shock, I decided to test Lvov once more, to verify his statement and then to act. And to act instantly and resolutely. My mind was at work. I did not hesitate for an instant in my acting. I rather felt than understood all the extraordinary seriousness of the situation, if . . . if only Lvov's words were even remotely in accord with reality!

Calming myself a little, I deliberately pretended that I had no longer any doubt or hesitation, and that personally I had decided to agree.

I began to explain to Lvov that I could not convey such a communication to the Provisional Government without proofs. He reassured me, saying that every word he had uttered was true. At last I asked him to put into writing all Kornilov's points. The readiness, the assurance, the quickness with which Lvov agreed and wrote down Kornilov's proposals gave me full confidence that Lvov was not only fully informed, but that he had no doubt as to the realization of the plan.

Here is the text of the note Lvov wrote:—

General Kornilov proposes—

(1) That martial law shall be proclaimed in Petrograd.

(2) That all military and civil authority shall be placed in the hands of the Generalissmo.

(3) That all Ministers, not excluding the Premier, shall resign, and that the temporary executive power shall be transferred to the Assistant Ministers till the formation of a Cabinet by the Generalissimo.

V. Lvov

Petrograd, *August 26,* 1917.

As soon as he began to write, my last doubt disappeared. . . .

In those instants while Lvov was writing, my brain worked intensely. It was necessary to prove at once the formal connection between Lvov and Kornilov so clearly that the Provisional Government would be able to take resolute measures that very evening. It was essential to make Lvov commit himself, by making him repeat in the presence of a third person all his conversation with me. I felt I must act thus, and in no other way. . . . Meantime, Lvov finished writing, and giving me the document, said, "That is very good; now everything will end peacefully. People *there* think it very important that the powers of the Provisional Government should be transferred legally. Well, and as for you," he concluded, "will you go to Staff Headquarters?"

I do not know why, but this question stabbed me, put me on my guard, and almost involuntarily I replied, "Certainly not. Do you really think that I can be Minister of Justice under Kornilov?"

Here something strange happened.

Lvov sprang up; his face brightened as he exclaimed: "You are right! You are right! Don't go there. A trap is set for you; he will arrest you. Go away— somewhere far away; but get out of Petrograd you must. They hate you." Lvov said this excitedly.

We then "decided" that Kornilov should learn by telegraph of my resignation, and that I should not go to Staff Headquarters.

"And what will happen, V. N.," I said, "if you are mistaken, or if they have played a practical joke on you? What position will you be in then? You know, what you have written is very serious."

Lvov began energetically to prove that it was not a mistake, that it could not be a joke, that it was indeed a very serious matter, and that "General Kornilov would never take back his words."

At that moment the idea came into my head that I would get direct confirmation from Kornilov himself on the direct telegraphic line. Lvov jumped at the suggestion, and we arranged that we should meet at eight o'clock at the house of the War Minister to speak together to Kornilov on the direct telegraph.

Lvov had come to me a few minutes after five o'clock, and he left, as far as I remember, after seven. Nearly an hour was left before we were to meet at the War Minister's house. As he went out, at the door of my room Lvov met Virubov, who was coming to me. After I had acquainted him with what had happened, and asked him to stay with me, I sent my aide-de-camp to arrange for a direct line, and to summon to me at my Palace at nine o'clock in the evening the Chief Assistant of the Military Staff, Balavinsky, and the Assistant to the Commander of the Military District, Captain Kosmin.

At eight o'clock in the evening I went with Virubov to the telegraph. Everything was ready. Kornilov was waiting at the other end of the line. Lvov was not yet there. We tried to ring him up at his house, but there was no reply. Kornilov waited at the telegraph for twenty to twenty-five minutes. I decided to speak alone, as the character of the conversation made it indifferent whether only one or both of us were there; the subject had been agreed upon beforehand. I must confess that apparently both Virubov and I were still hoping that General Kornilov would ask in utter bewilderment: "What is there for me to corroborate? Which Lvov?" But the hope was not realized. Here is the full conversation as recorded by the Hughes tape machine.

The conversation by the Hughes tape machine of the Prime Minister (Kerensky) with the Commander-in-Chief (General Kornilov). Italics and figures are partly mine.

(1) "Good day, General. V. N. Lvov and Kerensky at the apparatus. We beg you to confirm the statement that *Kerensky is to act according to the communication made to him by V.N.*"

"Good day, Alexander Feodorovitch; good day, V. N. Confirming again the description I gave V.N. of the present situation of the country and the army as it appears to me, I declare again that the events of the past days and of those that I can see coming *imperatively demand a definite decision in the shortest possible time.*"

(2) "I, V.N., ask you *whether it is necessary to act on that definite decision* which you asked me to communicate privately to Kerensky, as he is hesitating to give his full confidence without your personal confirmation."

"Yes, I confirm that I asked you to convey to Alexander Feodorovitch my urgent demand that he should come to Mohilev."

(3) "I, Alexander Feodorovitch, *understand* your answer as *confirmation* of the words conveyed to me by V.N. *To do that* today and start from here is impossible. I hope to start tomorrow. Is it necessary for Savinkov to go?"

"I beg urgently that Boris Victorovitch shall come with you. Everything I said to V.N. refers *in equal degree* to Savinkov. I beg you earnestly not to put off your departure later than tomorrow. *Believe me, only my recognition of the responsibility of the moment urges me to persist in my request.*"

(4) Shall we come *only* in case of an outbreak, of which there are rumours, or in any case?"

"In any case."

"Good day. Soon we shall see each other."

"Good day."[13]

· · · ·

1269. Soviet and Other Worker Organs Deny Rumors of a Demonstration on August 27

[Izvestiia, No. 154, August 26, 1917, p. 5.]

Rumors have spread in the city that demonstrations are being prepared. It is said that a demonstration of the workers in the streets is being set for August 27. In the yellow counterrevolutionary press they write that a slaughter is being organized for August 27. Individuals dressed in soldier uniforms appear at the plants and call upon the workers to make armed demonstrations.

We, the representatives of the workers' and soldiers' organizations, declare as follows:

These rumors are being spread by *provocateurs* and the enemies of the revolution. They wish to bring the masses of soldiers and workers into the streets and to sink the revolution in a sea of blood.

We declare that not one single worker organization, not one single political

---

[13] L'vov arrived after this exchange. In the meantime he had been with Miliukov. See Miliukov, *Istoriia vtoroi russkoi revoliutsii*, I, vypusk 2, 210.

party of the working class or of the democracy calls for such actions or for any kind of demonstrations or processions.

The proletarians in the garrison of Petrograd will not submit to these provocations and will know how to respond to the call of counterrevolution with dignity.

Citizens, do not submit to panic!

Comrade soldiers and workers, be calm and self-restrained!

The worker and soldier organizations stand guard over the revolutionary cause.

> The Executive Committee of the Petrograd Soviet of Workers' and Soldiers' Deputies.
> The Petrograd Council of Trade Unions.
> The Central Council of the Factory Committees.

THE REVOLT

1270. RADIO-TELEGRAM FROM KERENSKY TO ALL THE COUNTRY, No. 4163
[*VVP*, No. 142, August 29, 1917, p. 1.]

I hereby announce:

On August 26 General Kornilov sent to me member of the State Duma Vladimir L'vov with a demand for the surrender by the Provisional Government of all civil and military power, so that he may form, at his personal discretion, a *new government* to administer the country. The authenticity of Deputy L'vov's authorization to make such a proposal to me was subsequently confirmed by General Kornilov in his conversation with me by direct wire. Perceiving in the presentation of such demands, addressed to the Provisional Government in my person, a desire of certain circles of Russian society to take advantage of the grave condition of the State for the purpose of establishing in the country a regime opposed to the conquests of the revolution, the Provisional Government has found it indispensable:

To authorize me, for the salvation of our motherland, of liberty, and of our republican order, to take prompt and resolute measures for the purpose of uprooting any attempt to encroach upon the Supreme Power in the State and upon the rights which the citizens have achieved by the revolution.

I am taking all necessary measures to protect the liberty and order of the country, and the population will be informed in due time with regard to such measures.

At the same time I order herewith:

1. General Kornilov to surrender the post of Supreme Commander to General Klembovskii, the Commander in Chief of the Northern Front, which bars the way to Petrograd; and General Klembovskii to assume temporarily the post of Supreme Commander, while remaining at Pskov.

2. The city and uezd of Petrograd under martial law, extending to it the regulations for regions declared under martial law. . . .

I call upon all the citizens to preserve complete tranquillity and to maintain order, which is so indispensable for the salvation of the country. I call upon all the ranks of the army and navy to carry on with calmness and self-sacrifice their duty of defending the country against the external enemy.[14]

A. F. KERENSKY, Minister-President, Minister of War and Navy
August 27, 1917

1271. KORNILOV'S RESPONSE TO KERENSKY'S RADIO-TELEGRAM
[E. I. Martynov, *Kornilov*, pp. 110–11.]

The Minister-President's telegram No. 4163 in its entire first part is a lie throughout: it was not I who sent the Member of the State Duma, Vladimir L'vov, to the Provisional Government, but he came to me as the envoy of the Minister-President. Aleksei Alad'in, Member of the State Duma, is a witness to this. A *great provocation* has thus taken place which jeopardizes the fate of the motherland.

People of Russia! Our great motherland is dying. The hour of her death is near. Forced to speak openly, I, General Kornilov, declare that under the pressure of the Bolshevik majority of the Soviets, the Provisional Government acts in complete harmony with the plans of the German general staff, and simultaneously with the forthcoming landing of the enemy forces on the Riga shores, it is killing the army and undermines the very foundation of the country.

The heavy sense of the inevitable ruin of the country commands me in these ominous moments to call upon all Russian people to come to the aid of the dying motherland. All in whose breasts a Russian heart is beating, who believe in God, in Church, pray to the Lord for the greatest miracle, the saving of our native land!

I, General Kornilov, son of a Cossack peasant, declare to all and sundry that I want nothing for myself, except the preservation of a Great Russia, and I vow to bring the people by means of victory over the enemy to the Constituent Assembly, where they will themselves decide their fate and choose their new form of government. But it is quite impossible for me to betray Russia into the hands of her ancient enemy, the German race, and to turn the Russian people into German slaves. I prefer to die on the battlefield of honor rather than see the disgrace and infamy of the Russian land.

Russian people, the life of your motherland is in your hands! August 27 1917. GENERAL KORNILOV.

1272. TELEGRAM TO THE MINISTER OF FOREIGN AFFAIRS FROM THE REPRESENTATIVE OF THE MINISTRY AT STAVKA
[*Sbornik sekretnykh dokumentov*, No. 1, pp. 23–24. See also Kerensky, *Prelude to Bolshevism*, pp. 184–85.]

. . .

Stavka. August 28, 1917, No. 262 (over direct wire).

A sober appraisal of the situation forces us to admit that the entire com-

---

[14] At about the same time Kerensky and Minister of the Interior Avksent'ev dispatched a telegram to guberniya and oblast commissars informing them of Kornilov's action and ordering them to inform the population of the events transpiring, to preserve order, and to combat any local counterrevolutionary actions. *VVP*, No. 142 (Supplement), August 29, 1917, p. 1.

manding personnel, the overwhelming majority of the officers, and the best combat units of the army will follow Kornilov. In the rear the entire Cossack host, the majority of the military schools, and the best combat units will go over to Kornilov's side. Added to the physical strength is the superiority of the military organization over the weakness of the government organs, moral support of all nonsocialist elements of the population, a growing discontent among the lower classes with the existing order. The majority of the popular and urban masses have grown indifferent to the existing order and will submit to any cracking of the whip. Undoubtedly, the overwhelming number of the March socialists will not hesitate to go over on their side. On the other hand, recent events at the front and in the rear, and particularly in Kazan',[15] revealed most manifestly the complete bankruptcy of the present order and the inevitability of impending catastrophe, unless an immediate change takes place. This consideration is apparently decisive for General Kornilov, who is aware of the fact that only resolute action can rescue Russia from the brink of the abyss toward which it is headed. It is idle talk to say that Kornilov prepares the triumph of Wilhelm at the moment when all that is left for the German armies is merely to cross our wide spaces.

It is up to the men now in power either to face the inevitable change, and thus make it painless as well as preserve the genuine guarantees of the people's freedom, or by their resistance to accept responsibility for countless new calamities. I am convinced that only the immediate arrival here of the Minister-President, the Assistant Minister of War, as well as yourself, in order to establish jointly with the Supreme Commander a foundation for a strong power, can avert the grave danger of civil war.

[PRINCE G. N. TRUBETSKOI]

1273. P. P. YURENEV'S ACCOUNT OF EVENTS WITHIN THE PROVISIONAL GOVERNMENT

[*Russkiia Vedomosti*, No. 200, September 1, 1917, pp. 4–5. See also F. F. Kokoshkin's account in *ibid*. In connection with this and the documents following, Kerensky's *Prelude to Bolshevism*, especially Chap. III, should be consulted.]

. . .

During the night of August [26-]27, A. F. Kerensky, unexpectedly for us, made his astounding declaration and requested to be given freedom of action. . . .

Kornilov stated he made his declaration on the advice of B. V. Savinkov and of V. N. L'vov. B. V. Savinkov objected that he had no relation whatsoever to the declaration of Kornilov and that he would immediately talk with Kornilov on the subject. In his negotiations with Kornilov, B. V. Savinkov implored him to abandon the action undertaken. To this Kornilov replied that he would think and would give his answer at 4:00 P.M.

At that time V. A. Maklakov and B. V. Savinkov went to the telegraph, which was connected by direct wire with Stavka. Their conversation lasted until

---

[15] Reference is to an explosion and fire in a munitions and supply dump at Kazan' in the middle of August which was widely blamed on German agents. See *Izvestiia*, No. 147, August 18, 1917, p. 3.

7:00 P.M. Then all the Ministers assembled and Kerensky informed them of the results of the negotiations.

Kornilov was ordered to resign his office of Supreme Commander and Kornilov refused to obey this order.

On Sunday a private meeting was held regarding the increase of the . . . price of bread. At that moment the situation was the following: All the Ministers withdrew and with this V. M. Chernov and F. F. Kokoshkin left definitely. A. F. Kerensky acted as a dictator, conferring with us in so far as he found it necessary. . . . [On Monday, August 28] General M. V. Alekseev arrived and had a talk with A. F. Kerensky. A. F. Kerensky offered to M. V. Alekseev the post of Supreme Commander, but the latter refused to accept this appointment. At 2:00 P.M. Alekseev was at the Headquarters of B. V. Savinkov[16] and at 3:00 P.M. he went with P. N. Miliukov to see Kerensky. . . . The question of the Supreme Commander was decided on . . . [August 30]. The question of M. V. Alekseev's appointment was also decided . . . [then].

At 3:00 P.M. all the ministers came to a meeting at which A. F. Kerensky declared that he invested himself with the office of Supreme Commander and appointed M. V. Alekseev Chief of Staff. Furthermore, Kerensky declared that L. G. Kornilov's attempt was not succeeding. Then the question turned to the necessity of reconstructing the governmental organs of authority.

All of us former members of the Provisional Government agreed that the whole power should belong to A. F. Kerensky and that a new collegiate organ should be created immediately, while for the time being the one in existence should be used. A. F. Kerensky was authorized to turn back the resignations of those who in his opinion should participate in the cabinet. This met with unanimous approval. . . .

As for the K.D.'s, they definitely declared that they never boycotted anybody and that they gave to A. F. Kerensky complete liberty of action and selection. He could select whom he wished.

As for the membership of the future cabinet, we declared that it would be necessary to have among the members of the cabinet a general or an admiral; as you know, this was done. In the new cabinet all the members are to be equal; there should be no kind of concealed directory.

. . .

Concerning my own opinion regarding the attempt perpetrated by General L. G. Kornilov, I would say that it was a terrible blow against the reconstruction of the country's forces. Little by little we were moving forward toward strengthening the Government, and what Kornilov has perpetrated drastically upsets our common task.

. . . Having resigned on the night of August 27, I gave A. F. Kerensky the opportunity immediately to carry out his dictatorial rights in the Ministry which I had administered until that time.

As a matter of fact, from August 27 I did not take any part in the administra-

[16] Savinkov was appointed Governor General of Petrograd by Kerensky on August 27, and, in accordance with his rights under the institution of martial law, prohibited public assemblies and enforced a strict censorship of the press. *VVP*, No. 142 (Supplement), August 29, 1917, pp. 1, 2; *ibid.*, August 31, 1917, p. 1.

tion, having transmitted the Ministry to my senior deputy, asking him to execute the direct orders of A. F. Kerensky.

As far as I know, all these orders have been executed without fail.

1274. INTERVIEW WITH NEKRASOV
[*Rech'*, No. 203, August 30, 1917, p. 2.]

The Deputy Minister-President, N. V. Nekrasov, in an interview with the representatives of the press on August 29 at 3:00 P.M., made the following declarations:

The general political situation should be considered favorable. Almost all the commanders in chief of the fronts are staying on the side of the Provisional Government and are obeying all its orders. Especially outstanding in this regard is the behavior of the Commander in Chief of the Caucasian Front, General Przheval'skii, and of the Commander in Chief of the Rumanian Front, General Shcherbachev. They have both declared that they are entirely on the side of the Provisional Government and are ready to support it.[17]

From the Commander in Chief of the Western Front, General Baluev, there are no direct declarations. However, judging by all his tactics and according to what has been communicated in the telegram from Commissar Zhdanov, all necessary measures are being taken on the Western Front, and the whole Western Front is in complete subordination to the Provisional Government.

The situation on the Northern Front is as follows:

The Commander in Chief of the Northern Front, General Klembovskii, has from the very beginning taken an undetermined position. Referring to the extreme military tensions on the front, he declared that he considered it difficult for him to accept the post of Supreme Commander which had been offered to him. To the question why he has let the echelons of General Kornilov pass through Pskov on their way to Petrograd, General Klembovskii replied that these echelons were not subordinate to him. At the present moment Pskov is surrounded by troops loyal to the Provisional Government. All the administration of Pskov and of the station of Pskov is in the hands of the Commissar of the Provisional Government. General Klembovskii was asked either to definitely and resolutely stand on the side of the Provisional Government or be removed.[18]

The Provisional Government has reason to believe that the troops which formed the detachment of General Kornilov were deceived. They were told that they would go to Petrograd at the invitation of the Provisional Government in order to liberate the capital from the Bolsheviks. Already today a delegation from one of the Cossack regiments has come to the Provisional Government declaring that the regiment, having learned the truth, was ready to stand on the side of the Provisional Government.

The Provisional Government has taken all necessary measures in order to

---

[17] See *Izvestiia*, No. 157, August 30, 1917, p. 5, for the texts of the telegrams from Przheval'skii and Shcherbachev. General A. I. Denikin, Commander in Chief of the Southwestern Front, supported General Kornilov and was arrested and held for trial along with Kornilov. For his account, see his *The Russian Turmoil*, Chap. XXXII.

[18] Klembovskii's equivocal replies to the questions addressed to him by Commissar Stankevich, on the authority of the Provisional Government, are reported in *Izvestiia*, No. 157, August 30, 1917, p. 6. He was relieved of command. *Ibid.*

protect Petrograd. But we hope that the matter will not culminate in bloodshed and we are taking all necessary measures in order that the troops that formed General Kornilov's detachment be informed of the actual state of affairs.

As you are aware, General Kornilov has referred to the fact that V. N. L'vov pretended to be the representative of the Provisional Government. V. N. L'vov himself categorically denies this. But even if one accepts as correct the version of General Kornilov, there is in any case not the slightest doubt that the whole action of General Kornilov was very thoroughly prepared beforehand. We were informed that a number of generals, having received orders to arrive at a certain place, did not go there and are now among the ranks of those who have mutinied. Incidentally, General Krymov, who is at the present moment in Luga, is among their number.

According to information received by the Provisional Government, discord has already begun within the ranks of General Krymov's detachment.

According to the information of the Provisional Government, the principal role in the organization of the rebellion was played by General Lukomskii.

Answering a question with regard to the reconstruction of the Provisional Government, N. V. Nekrasov declared:

All the information with regard to a governmental crisis is based on a misunderstanding. The Provisional Government continues to exist. Temporarily it has invested A. F. Kerensky with extraordinary powers but the ministers remain at their posts. Only P. P. Yurenev and F. F. Kokoshkin have made known their refusal to participate in the Provisional Government, while V. M. Chernov has considered that owing to general political considerations his presence in the Provisional Government would be inexpedient. There were no declarations of withdrawal from S. F. Ol'denburg and A. V. Kartashev; whether they are carrying out their duties as ministers I do not know.

In the event that at a certain moment Kerensky requires a harmonious group of people formally associated with him, he has been granted absolute freedom of action to organize such a group.

Now the whole issue is centered in the persons of Kerensky who defends the revolution and of Kornilov who defends reaction. And now it can be said quite definitely that all the country is with A. F. Kerensky. The shower of telegrams which is being received by the Provisional Government bears witness to this.

This mass of telegrams is all the more significant as the other side has taken measures in order that telegrams of an opposite nature should be received, and General Lukomskii has even asked one of the outstanding public men whether he had accomplished what he had promised to do. It must be openly acknowledged that the Provisional Government was completely unprepared for what has happened and that the betrayal of Kornilov was completely unexpected by it. The Provisional Government was meeting the plans of Kornilov half way with an open heart. And I can only recall with much bitterness how I, in a conversation with newspapermen, defended General Kornilov.[19] What happened at Stavka before the overt action of General Kornilov we do not know, and the communication from Lukomskii that party leaders were summoned to Stavka was quite unexpected for us. What party leaders were summoned to Stavka we do not know, but we know

---

[19] See *Daily Review of the Foreign Press*, Ser. 4, No. 29, September 4, 1917 (N.S.), p. 268.

that the leaders of the K.D. Party, the last party to the right, which the Provisional Government can take into consideration, have not been at Stavka and could not be there. A communication from Filonenko reported that if Kerensky and Savinkov were to arrive at Stavka they should not be surprised at seeing there persons of high social prominence. Who these persons of high social prominence are I do not as yet know.

The Party of the People's Freedom, as a statesmanlike party, could not, owing to its very essence, take any part in the plot of General Kornilov. For this would have meant a complete repudiation of its very essence! And there can be no question of the participation in this affair of P. N. Miliukov.

The Provisional Government, N. V. Nekrasov concluded, is taking every measure to avoid civil war. We are not the attacking but the defending side. We know that in the other camp irresoluteness reigns, and of course our behavior will take into account what the opposite side may undertake.

1275. ANOTHER STATEMENT BY NEKRASOV
[*Rech'*, No. 215, September 13, 1917, pp. 2–3.]

I remember very clearly the evening of August 26–27, N. V. Nekrasov related, when A. F. Kerensky called me from a meeting of the Provisional Government and showed me a document signed by V. N. L'vov, containing General Kornilov's ultimatum, and a record [by Hughes apparatus] of the conversation with General Kornilov, and asked me whether I was prepared to support him till the end. I distinctly remember his words . . . at that point: "I will not give them the revolution."

Of course, he received my agreement and from this moment on we started . . . making preparations for repelling Kornilov's attack. A. F. Kerensky and I were convinced from the very beginning that we were dealing with a very serious step which was carefully considered by General Kornilov.

As often happens, news of General Kornilov's ultimatum led to commentaries on a wide range of preceding events, which, taken separately, did not seem either threatening or symptomatic at the time.

Kornilov's entrance into Moscow, preparation of the guards in Moscow—evidently in the event of a proclamation of General Kornilov's dictatorship—all the activities of the Officers' Union in Stavka, General Kornilov's telegram to the railroadmen, support of their ultimatum[20]—all this in connection with General Kornilov's ultimatum made it clear that the forthcoming struggle was going to be a serious one.

Therefore, A. F. Kerensky immediately took all steps for repelling . . . Kornilov's forces. The order for halting the movement of echelons of Kornilov's troops by rail, signed by A. F. Kerensky, was transmitted by me to P. P. Yurenev, who had submitted his resignation the day before but had remained, together with other ministers, to attend to official duties: P. P. Yurenev announced that he had resigned from his post as head of the Ministry. I then called Liverovskii and Kizhenevskii and gave them A. F. Kerensky's order to stop Kornilov's echelons at once. I remember how two hours later Liverovskii informed me by telephone that the echelons were breaking through by force and that they could only be

[20] Volume II, Doc. 660.

stopped by similar use of force. In order to accomplish this, it was necessary to disassemble the rails and arrange an artificial wreck. I informed A. F. Kerensky of this at once and, without any hesitation, he issued an order to apply these heroic means.

These brief reports alone are entirely sufficient, I think, to see how preposterous are the . . . [illegible] that A. F. Kerensky was in collusion with General Kornilov. In this connection I must add that all these orders were issued by A. F. Kerensky before 4:00 P.M. on August 27, prior to the conversation of B. V. Savinkov with General Kornilov by the [Hughes] apparatus . . .

. . .

B. V. Savinkov absolutely correctly pointed out that the mounted corps was called out to replace the units removed from Petrograd when the instability of the Riga front became generally apparent and when the danger arose that Petrograd might become the arena of bloody events similar to those that occurred in Tarnopol', Kalush, and other places. Besides, there were grounds for fearing a repetition of the events of July 3–5 in connection with the events on the front. It was necessary to have disciplined troops near Petrograd in order to repel, in agreement with democratic organizations, any attempts at anarchistic demonstrations. It stands to reason that the cavalry, as B. V. Savinkov also indicated, was called out to Petrograd, not for the overthrow of the Soviet, but for the suppression of a Bolshevik plot which was then anticipated. The only untrue statement is one that is ascribed to B. V. Savinkov (I do not know whether he made it), that the troops were called out in the event that martial law was declared in Petrograd.

. . .

. . . The conversation by direct wire with General Kornilov was conducted on behalf of V. N. L'vov. General Kornilov was sent a Hughes telegram, signed by V. N. L'vov, which stated roughly the following: "A. F. doubts whether I can be absolutely trusted." The following answer was received from General Kornilov: "Yes, absolutely." By giving this answer, General Kornilov accepted the full responsibility for the contents of the ultimatum presented by V. N. L'vov.

The idea was not considered of transmitting to General Kornilov the full text of the ultimatum signed by V. N. L'vov. There are things that cannot be trusted even to the Hughes apparatus. After all, General Kornilov's ultimatum might have somehow become distributed in thousands of copies.

But one cannot draw the conclusion from all this that there was a misunderstanding in this case, and that V. N. L'vov incorrectly relayed what General Kornilov had asked him to communicate. No, there was no misunderstanding here. V. N. L'vov's role must be considered salutary for the revolution. . . . He revealed the plot prematurely and thus made it possible to liquidate it. In revolutionary circles they used to say in such cases: "But this is provocation; how can one reveal the cards before the proper time?"

Before General Kornilov's revolt, the Provisional Government made a supreme effort to coordinate the activities of the General and the high command subordinated to him. But, as it turned out, these efforts became paralyzed just when it seemed to us that coordination between the high command and the Provisional Government was being achieved.

In Stavka, responsible persons were working side by side with completely irresponsible people. But . . . there were also responsible persons who were . . . negotiating with the Supreme Commander on behalf of the Provisional Government, but without having been authorized by the Government to do so. I can allow that both B. V. Savinkov and M. M. Filonenko could have negotiated with General Kornilov on the reorganization of power, counting on the subsequent approval of their actions by the Provisional Government. But I assert that if B. V. Savinkov and M. M. Filonenko actually conducted such negotiations on the reorganization of power, then, at any rate, they did so without any authorization from the Provisional Government.

"Do you consider it possible that B. V. Savinkov participated in the plot, as is assumed by some newspapers [such as] *Novaia Zhizn'* and *Delo Naroda?*"

This is out of the question. I am so certain that B. V. Savinkov had no part in the plot that if [someone] were . . . to demonstrate the contrary to me, I would say with complete confidence: "I'll vouch for it with my life that this did not happen."

It is absurd to speak about the Kadets' participation in the plot. The Kadets and the plot may be said to be mutually exclusive. Whoever knows the Kadets' attitude toward any type of conspiratorial activities, it cannot help but be obvious to him that the Kadets did not and could not have taken any part in General Kornilov's plot, by virtue of their essential nature, their whole psychology, and their whole attitude toward conspiracy.

"Did M. M. Filonenko report to A. F. Kerensky, back on July 31, the existence of a plot in Stavka?"

I think that A. F. Kerensky will give you an answer to this himself. I can only say one thing—that A. F. Kerensky always paid such careful attention to any reports on possible counterrevolutionary actions that I cannot conceive how he could have missed a report on the existence of a counterrevolutionary plot in Stavka.[21]

.   .   .

1276. ORDER TO THE FORCES OF PETROGRAD
[*VVP*, No. 142 (Supplement), August 29, 1917, p. 1.]

Rising against the authority of the Provisional Government, the former Supreme Commander, General Kornilov, who has been proclaiming his patriotism and loyalty to the people in all his telegrams, has now revealed his treachery in practice.

He took the regiments from the front, weakening its resistance against the ruthless enemy—the German.

And he sent all these forces against Petrograd.

He speaks of saving the native land, yet he is consciously creating a fratricidal war.

He says that he stands for freedom, yet he sends the Native Division against Petrograd.

---

21 In *Rech'* of the same date, p. 2, Savinkov claimed that Filonenko had made such a report on July 31, but that it "was not received sympathetically." "It was pointed out to him," Savinkov continued, "that he did not know how to maintain good relations at Stavka—in particular with the Chief of Staff, General Lukomskii—and that if he did not succeed in establishing good relations he would lose his post. M. M. Filonenko was forced to be guided by these instructions . . . [and] I, too . . . right up to August 20."

Comrades! The hour has arrived when your loyalty to freedom and the revolution is on trial. Conscious of the sacrednes of your duty to the fatherland, be staunch and valiant in meeting your former army comrades who have been deceived by General Kornilov.

Let them see before them truly revolutionary regiments which have resolutely decided to defend the Government of the Revolution.

And before it is too late let them understand and become ashamed of the cause for which they have been criminally sent. If, however, they will not understand, I, your Minister, am certain that you will fearlessly perform your soldier's duty to the end.

KERENSKY, Minister-President [and Minister] of War and Navy

1277. IN THE BALTIC FLEET

[Extracts from the diary of Captain I. I. Rengarten, published in *Posledniia Novosti*, No. 5813, February 22, 1937, p. 3.]

. . . Kerensky has issued a declaration pronouncing Kornilov a traitor. Heaps of telegrams. Klembovskii has been appointed Supreme Commander. Troops are marching toward Petrograd; they have been ordered to halt. Martial law has been announced in Petrograd. Savinkov has been appointed Military Governor. The army and the navy have been called upon to remain calm. What is this? Is it really a civil war? . . . The Prince (Cherkasskii) came in to see me; he is alarmed; he says that Kornilov has taken an open stand against Kerensky, that he is sending out appeals. Each one is now confronted with the question—whose side to take? I read the appeal and I did not like it. Kerensky's declaration seemed more upright. I told Cherkasskii right then and there that I shall remain loyal to the Government, and that that is how I see my duty. The Prince agreed. We went to the commander. It turned out that he was of the same opinion. As a result, we are urgently sending out Kerensky's proclamation and orders from the naval commander [*komflot*] with an appeal for obedience to the Government. All our Hughes apparatuses, telegraph and telephone stations are working at full speed; everyone is on his feet. Fedia Kovkont (assistant to the flag captain of the operations section) is definitely against Kornilov; he considers Kornilov's actions baneful, thrusting us into the arms of anarchy. We reread the appeal. Who, then, is right? But what is going on? We now have a Directory, a dictator-usurper, and two Supreme Commanders. The orders themselves are contradictory. From Stavka it was ordered that officers be placed on duty at all the telegraph stations and prohibit the dispatch of telegrams hostile to Kornilov. . . .

Bloody excesses occurred in Helsingfors. On August 30, when the Kornilov movement could already be considered a failure, the company committee of the dreadnought *Petropavlovsk* called a general meeting of the company for taking the above-mentioned signed statements [*raspiski*] from the officers. As always in such cases, a thunderous resolution was adopted demanding the death sentence for Kornilov and all his adherents, and the transfer of power to the Soviets. The officers were asked to sign it, but they refused, stating that they would publish their own. A short while later, after holding a meeting in the wardroom, the officers did, in fact, adopt the following resolution: "Disapproving of General Kornilov's action as an action provoking civil war, we refuse to submit to his orders and will execute only the orders of the Government, acting in agreement with the All-Russian Central Executive Committee of the Soviet of Workers' and Soldiers' and Peasants' Deputies." Everyone in the wardroom, it seemed, agreed with this resolution. However, it did not satisfy the committee, which insisted that the officers subscribe to the resolution adopted at the general meeting, in which a death sentence for Kornilov was mentioned. Agonizing debates went on for one and a half hours. In the end, having rejected the resolution of the command, the officers agreed to add [the following words] to their [own resolution]: ". . . and the orders of the Central Executive Committee in agreement with the local revolutionary organizations." It stands to reason that there was no room for private consultations among officers during these one-and-a-half-hour debates, which proceeded in a tense atmosphere; each one acted independently. And then it was suddenly discovered that not all the officers were in agreement with the first resolution worked out in the wardroom. Midshipmen Kandyba and Kondrat'ev held to a separate opinion of their own, which they read right there: "We, the undersigned, pledge to submit unquestioningly to all combat orders of commanding officers appointed by the Provisional Government, in so far as these orders are directed against the foreign foe. Not wishing to shed Russian blood, we refuse actively to intervene in internal strife, and, protesting against the accusations made against us of [harboring] reactionary views, we request that we be given the opportunity to demonstrate our devotion to the native land on the positions at Tserel' in direct contact with the enemy." Lieutenant Tizenko, who had just returned from leave and came to the meeting straight from the railroad station, supported the two midshipmen on this separate opinion, as did also Midshipmen Mikhailov, who was keeping watch at the time that the resolution was drawn up. At first, the sailors seemed to react calmly to this action of the four officers, but in the evening agitation started. The fourth company suddenly announced that it did not want to have in its ranks Lieutenant Tizenko and Midshipmen Kandyba and Kondrat'ev, who were obvious "Kornilovites," and it demanded the appointment of other officers. At the same time, the ship's committee prohibited all four of them from going ashore.

During the night, the agitation increased even more. Ominous rumors about a lynching being prepared started to spread around the ship. Here and there, suspicious-looking little groups of sailors gathered together, whispering about something, and all night long shadows darted by the cabin where the above-mentioned officers slept, looking in and listening in.

In the morning Diuchkov, a sailor and electrician, representing the ship's committee, went to see the ship's commander, Captain D. D. Tyrtov, and announced that in view of the threat of lynching, he felt that it would be better to arrest all the four officers and send them ashore [placing them] under the supervision of "Tsentrobalt."[22] The chairman of the committee did not conceal the fact that there were individuals in the company who demanded that these officers—"Kornilovites"—be given "the third degree." And, in fact, after breakfast the lieutenant and the three midshipmen were called for questioning into one of the crew's quarters in the ship's bow . . .[23]

[22] Central Committee of the Baltic Fleet.

[23] The four officers were shot on the evening of August 31 by the crew, prompting strong reprimands and orders to cease such outrages from the Minister of the Navy, Admiral Vederevskii, and from Kerensky. *Rech'*, No. 207, September 3, 1917, p. 4; and *Russkiia Vedomosti*, No. 203, September 5, 1917, p. 4.

1278. ORDER OF THE COMMANDER OF THE BLACK SEA FLEET

[*Rech'*, No. 207, September 3, 1917, p. 4.]

The Black Sea Fleet has been, and remains, loyal to the Provisional Government—the only sovereign power of Russia. I am enjoining flag officers and commanders of the Black Sea Fleet and the commanders of army units under my command to adopt every possible measure for preserving complete calm in the units.

I consider any demonstrations and manifestations at this serious moment to be harmful to the fatherland. I am reminding all flag officers, commanders, commanders of individual units, officers, and companies that the enemy might take advantage of our confusion to deal its blows on the army and navy, and, therefore, it is the duty of each one of us to do everything in our power to maintain on a high level the fighting strength of the Black Sea Fleet and the fortresses during the highly tragic days of the present time.

This order shall be read in all units before a gathering of officers and companies.

REAR ADMIRAL NEMITS

1279. AN EXPLANATION OF KORNILOV'S INACTIVITY AT STAVKA

[Miliukov, *Istoriia vtoroi russkoi revoliutsii*, I, vypusk 2, 262–63.]

. . . Subsequently, the French correspondent Claude Anet [*La Revolution Russe, par Claude Anet*, II, 154] put a direct question to Kornilov: "How could it have happened that after breaking with Kerensky you did not march on Petrograd yourself? After all, had you been at the head of the troops, you would have entered the Winter Palace without a shot." According to Anet, General Kornilov's answer was as follows: "Minor reasons lead to major consequences. If I were the conspirator that Kerensky depicted me as being, if I had formed the plot to overthrow the Government, I would naturally have adopted the appropriate measures. At the appointed time I would have been at the head of my troops, and, like you, I have no doubts that I would have entered Petrograd almost without a battle. But, in reality, I did not organize [any] plot and made no preparations. Therefore, on receiving Kerensky's incomprehensible telegram, I lost 24 hours. As you know, I assumed that either the telegraph [agency] made a mistake or there was an uprising in Petrograd and the Bolsheviks had seized the telegraph [agency]. I was waiting for either a confirmation or a denial. Thus, I lost a day and a night: I permitted Kerensky and Nekrasov to steal a march on me . . . the railroad men had received orders: I could not get a train that would take me to the environs of the capital. *I would have been given a train at Mogilev, but I would have been arrested in Vitebsk.* I could have taken an automobile: but it was 600 versts to Petrograd along bad roads. Whatever the case, on Monday, in spite of all the difficulties, I could still have started action; I could have made up for the time lost and corrected the mistakes that were made. But I was ill, I had severe ague, and *I did not have my customary energy.*"

Behind the "minor reasons" there apparently was some one "major" [reason] which showed up equally in everything else. It was not in vain that General Krasnov noticed a general feeling of uncertainty at Stavka. "They warmly wished me success, but they themselves were worried; they were even afraid of Mogilev. I wanted to walk to the station. They did not let me." In the event of a failure, the awareness of the risk "of imprisonment, court-martial, death sentence" was not alien even to General Krasnov himself. In addition, he knew the soldiers and he knew that the reputation of General Kornilov, who was responsible for reverting the army "from liberties" to the death penalty, was already undermined among them.[24]

. . .

The question was actually decided not so much by troop movements, or by the strategic and tactical successes of either the Government's or Kornilov's detachments, as by the mood of the troops. The question was decided—here, as well as on the front—not by the leaders of regiments, but by the soldiers . . .

1280. ATAMAN KALEDIN AND THE DON COSSACKS

[The first item is from *Russkoe Slovo*, No. 197, August 29, 1917, p. 3; the second from *Russkiia Vedomosti*, No. 199, August 31, 1917, p. 2; and the third from *Delo Naroda*, No. 145, September 3, 1917, p. 3. See also Docs. 1263 and 1267. The evidence that Kornilov had received assurances of support from Kaledin is very strong. Before he could act, however, the movement was suppressed. He then publicly denied his complicity from the safety of the Don Cossack Territory.]

A.

The Provisional Government has received a telegraphic statement from General Kaledin in which he points out the necessity of abandoning all further hesitation and agreeing to the demand of General Kornilov, with whom he declares himself in full solidarity.

General Kaledin warns the Government that if it refuses to come to an agreement with General Kornilov, he, *with the help of the Cossacks which are under his orders, will take measures in order to cut Moscow and Petrograd off from the south of Russia.*[25]

B. Message from General Verkhovskii, Commandant of the Moscow Military District, to Ataman Kaledin

The Cossack echelons, having left the front, are proceeding to the Don region at the moment when the enemy is breaking through our front and attempting to push on to Petrograd. I do not know how to interpret this act. If it means that the Cossacks are declaring war on Russia, I warn you that the fratricidal war begun by General Kornilov has been blamed and condemned by the whole army and all Russia. That is why I shall consider the appearance of the Cossack troops, without my authorization, in the district of Moscow as a revolt against the Provisional Government. I shall order the immediate destruction of all those in revolt. You know that I possess sufficient forces to do so. I look forward impatiently for your reply to dissipate my doubts.

C.

The Provisional Government received a telegram from General Kaledin in

---

[24] For General P. N. Krasnov's account of the situation at Stavka and among the army commanders on the side of Kornilov, see his "Na vnutrennum fronte," *ARR*, I (1921), 113–25.

[25] Later, Kerensky denied having received any such ultimatum from Kaledin. *Izvestiia*, No. 200, October 18, 1917, p. 6.

which he categorically denies organizing the Cossack revolt that has been ascribed to him. In his telegram, General Kaledin expresses his willingness to submit to the orders of the Provisional Government and requests that the charge against him of [organizing] the revolt be withdrawn.

1281. THE RESIGNATION OF FILONENKO AS COMMISSAR AT STAVKA AND OF SAVINKOV AS ASSISTANT MINISTER OF WAR AND GOVERNOR GENERAL OF PETROGRAD

[*Volia Naroda*, No. 145, October 15, 1917, p. 1. This description of the meeting between Kerensky, Lebedev, Filonenko, Colonel Bagratuni, and Savinkov on the morning of August 29 was written by Lebedev in reply to a published statement by Savinkov in *Russkoe Slovo*, No. 231, October 10, 1917, p. 3, which claimed that Kerensky had found nothing untoward in Filonenko's dealings with Kornilov. Filonenko resigned immediately, and Savinkov was replaced by General Verkhovskii (as Minister of War) and by P. Pal'chinskii (as Governor General of Petrograd) on August 30.]

.   .   .

A. F. Kerensky addressed us thus: "I have called you together, gentlemen, for the following reason: V. T. Lebedev told me that in his report to B. V. Savinkov, M. M. Filonenko had used the following phrase: 'But I kept on defending our scheme: Kornilov and Kerensky as the two pillars of the dictatorship.' Do you confirm it, Colonel Bagratuni?"

"Yes, I confirm it," replied Colonel Bagratuni.

"And you, M. M. Filonenko?"

"Yes, I made that remark."

M. Filonenko then related that, after the arrival of V. N. L'vov, he had discussed with Kornilov a plan of dictatorship in the form of a "Council of Defense," composed of the following persons: General Kornilov, A. F. Kerensky, Savinkov, and himself. He had been discussing that plan in order to counteract the possibility of a sole dictatorship by Kornilov, which would otherwise become inevitable. The Minister-President was quite astounded at this confession.

"How could you, the Supreme Commissar of the Provisional Government, carry on such a conversation with Kornilov! Who authorized you to do so? General Kornilov might now indeed say that he had been led indirectly into error."

Filonenko endeavored to prove that he had put this plan forward as a counterpoise to the schemes of the conspirators; that there was no time to be lost, and last, that this conversation had been carried on in the spirit of private relations and personal friendship.

"For General Kornilov you were the Supreme Commissar, and this conversation of yours was a conversation between the Supreme Commissar and the Supreme Commander. You appeared to General Kornilov as the representative of the Provisional Government, which, however, had never authorized you to make any such declarations."

When Savinkov and Filonenko pointed out that an essentially similar plan of a Council of Defense had been advanced by the Provisional Government, A. F. Kerensky replied:

"Never, never! A question was raised and passed as to the formation of a 'Council of Defense' from within the Provisional Government itself, for concentrating in its hands the defense of the whole country, following the example of England. But it never occurred to anyone that General Kornilov, a subordinate of the Provisional Government, could ever enter such a Council. You, however, who are a Commissar of the Provisional Government, discussed with General Kornilov, without the Government's knowledge, plans for a directory into which there would enter three individuals who are not members of the Provisional Government—yourself, B. V. Savinkov, and General Kornilov—and one person who is a member of the Government, namely myself, who knew nothing about it!' "

As a result of the conversation, A. F. Kerensky said that he looked upon M. M. Filonenko's action as tactless, to say the least, and that he considered it impossible for the latter to continue any political work.

I, for my own part, declared that I considered M. M. Filonenko's behavior at Stavka to be criminal.

Filonenko consented to submit to A. F. Kerensky's decision and to retire from any participation in the political life of the country, whereupon Savinkov protested, defending the correctness of Filonenko's conduct and explaining away Filonenko's confession in such a manner that A. F. Kerensky corrected him several times by saying:

"All three of us—myself, V. T. Lebedev, and Colonel Bagratuni—have heard what M. M. Filonenko has said. He said something different."

As Savinkov went on insisting on the correctness of Filonenko's actions and expressing solidarity with him, the Minister-President offered to refer the whole business to the Provisional Government, which proposal, however, Filonenko declined, declaring that he preferred to submit to A. F. Kerensky's decision.

.   .   .

1282. Kerensky's Account of the Role and Suicide of Krymov
[Kerensky, *Prelude to Bolshevism*, pp. 114–16.]

Chairman.—We have a lacuna concerning General Krimov, as we had not examined him; therefore, the Commission begs you to state whether you have had any explanations with him.

Kerensky.—I have a vivid recollection of the whole scene, and I can describe it to you.

Chairman.—What information had you as to the movements of his corps before he put in an appearance?

Kerensky.—You see, we dispatched an officer, who had formerly served with him, to meet him at Luga and explain the situation. We did this after our telegrams ordering him to stay his march remained unacknowledged. This mission succeeded. General Krimov arrived here accompanied by this officer (General Samarin). When General Krimov was announced, I went to meet him, invited him to my study, and then we had a talk. As far as I can remember, General Iakubovitch, Assistant Minister of War, was also present. General Krimov began by saying that they had no special aims in marching here; that they had been sent at the disposal of the Provisional Government; that they had received orders to aid the Provisional Government; that no one dreamed of acting against the Government; that, as soon as the misunderstanding had been cleared, he had given orders to halt. Then he added that he was in possession of a written order to that effect. At first he would not produce the order, and I had no reason to doubt that he had been deceived by it. He apparently hesitated to deliver it, but did so at last. The order was absolutely clear and precise.

Chairman.—You were good enough to give it to me.

Kerensky.—You know it. . . . It is very cleverly written. I read the order. I knew Krimov and always greatly respected him, as a man of decidedly very moderate views, but highly honest and decent. I rose and slowly approached him. He also rose. He saw that I was greatly impressed by the order. He approached this table; I came up quite close to him and said, in a low voice: "Yes, General, I see. You are undoubtedly a *very* clever man. Thank you." Krimov saw that the part he played was perfectly clear to me.

.   .   .

After this, General Krimov told me that he had been at the Stavka, where they had drafted the disposition and the statute for proclaiming a *state of siege* at Petrograd; he added that, according to this plan, Petrograd was to be divided into military sections. I am sure he found the situation unbearable, because he, Krimov, had swerved from the truth; first of all, he did not openly confess his own part in the affair, and secondly, clause 4 of the order begins with the words: "From communications of the Stavka and information received by me, I learn that riots are taking place in Petrograd . . ." etc. I asked him what were his grounds for making this declaration in his own name about riots. He was driven to refer to some "officer," travelling he did not know whence or whither. In short, he could not explain it. Then we parted, i.e. I dismissed him, refusing to shake hands with him.

[It appears that in about an hour or two after Krimov left my study he committed suicide. It should not be thought that I ceased to respect him when I refused to shake hands with him. Not at all. The whole of Krimov's behaviour during his interview with me, his calm resolve—after momentary hesitation—to hand over to me immediately the convincing document (the order to his corps), his noble silence as regards General Kornilov's telegrams of August 27th–29th, his manly confession of his belief in a dictatorship, all give him an undeniable right to the highest esteem of his political enemies. All these facts clearly illustrate the honest, courageous, vigorous nature of the man. But I, as the most official person in the most official surroundings, as Premier and War Minister— I could not and had no right to treat this general guilty of a crime against the State in any other way. . . .]

1283. GENERAL SAMARIN'S ACCOUNT OF THE ROLE AND SUICIDE OF KRYMOV

[As related by General A. I. Denikin in *Posledniia Novosti*, No. 5713, November 14, 1936, p. 3.]

.   .   .

. . . Samarin was a man who was close to Krymov, who enjoyed, as I know from the words of Krymov himself, his complete confidence; and both under Guchkov and on Kerensky's staff he served *at the insistence* of Krymov. Therefore, having used bitter words in respect to General Samarin in my *Ocherki*, I deem it my duty here to also reveal, in the interest of truth, the explanations that General Samarin has given me during these past days.

"On August 28," writes General Samarin, "a mutual friend, Lieutenant Colonel Danil'chuk, came to see me in Petrograd on behalf of General Krymov . . .

From him I learned in detail of General Krymov's intentions and of the state of his divisions. Not a word was said with regard to destroying the Provisional Government; an order was being obeyed. On the 29th, Danil'chuk compiled a telegram to General Krymov regarding the sentiments in Petrograd; he coded it, and it was sent to Luga. On the same day, keeping silent regarding Danil'chuk, I said to General Baranovskii, chief of the cabinet of the Minister of War:

" 'Transmit to Kerensky that I know General Krymov well and am certain that if he had wished to hang the Minister-President he would not be staying at Luga, but would be sitting in the Winter Palace or would already have gone to meet his forefathers. Let them be calm and not commit stupidities (there was a project of inviting the sailors from the *Aurora* for the defense of the government).'

"To the objections of Baranovskii, I told him:

" 'If you wish, I will go to see General Krymov and will speak with him personally about the situation.'

"In an hour or an hour and a half Baranovskii came to me and told me *exactly* the following:

" 'Thank God, the fright (Baranovskii expressed himself much more roughly —A. D.) has passed and Kerensky asks you to go today to see General Krymov.'

"In about 40 minutes an old master sergeant who served in the cabinet of the Minister of War reported:

" 'If General Krymov comes here, he will be arrested.'

"I immediately summoned Baranovskii and said:

" 'If Kerensky intends to catch General Krymov in a mousetrap, then I will not go. Give me guarantees.'

"The guarantees were given. I categorically declare that not only did I not receive an order for the arrest of General Krymov, but I did not even receive the usual order 'to go'—such was the fright. How could Mr. Kerensky give an order 'for any eventuality' when he gave his word of honor that General Krymov not only would not be arrested but would be able, if he wished, to return to his Cossacks.

"In approximately an hour I was called by telephone by General M. V. Alekseev, who told me the following:

" 'Go immediately to see General Krymov; learn what he wishes. And if there is nothing exceptional, let him come here himself to speak with me and then everything will be clarified to everybody's benefit.'

"I left at dawn on the 30th with Lieutenant Colonel Danil'chuk and First Lieutenant Danilevich. Danil'chuk reported to General Krymov on the events in Petrograd; as to me, having met the General three-quarters of an hour later (I waited for horses in Luga), I told him some small details, enumerated the important generals who had betrayed General Kornilov, and transmitted the demand of General Alekseev and the word of honor of the Provisional Government. In my presence nothing had been said about Stavka.

"The General gathered his senior commanders and it was decided that he and the chief of his staff, General Diterichs, would go to Petrograd and that 25 officers and noncommissioned officers would also proceed there.

"We arrived in Petrograd at 1:00 A.M. on the 31st and stopped in my private apartment. The General went to the Tsarskoe Selo Station, summoned by General Alekseev. He returned at 3:00 o'clock and we went to sleep, having received an order to report to the Winter Palace at 10:00 A.M.

"In Kerensky's study (the former study of Emperor Alexander III) a tumultuous scene took place behind closed doors; present were only Generals Krymov, Diterichs, Yakubovich, and Baranovskii, and Kerensky (I. S. Shablovskii mentions also General Tumanov—A. D.). Shouts and loud voices were heard through the double doors. Also the procurator of the army and of the navy (Shablovskii), who was late, arrived there.

"In a quarter of an hour Generals Krymov, Diterichs, and Yakubovich left the cabinet, all of them very excited. I took Aleksandr Mikhailovich by the hand and asked him about the conversation. He answered:

" 'I am being prosecuted. Today I must report to the Admiralty to be interrogated by the procurator. For the time being I am under arrest.'

"Baranovskii, Yakubovich, and I demanded (through Baranovskii) that Kerensky immediately give a document certifying the complete liberty of Generals Krymov and Diterichs. In about 20 minutes the document was in my hands.

"Krymov was not arrested, but he was detained. Shablovskii relates this episode as follows:

" 'As soon as I closed the door behind me, Kerensky addressed himself to me with the words: "Mr. President of the Commission, this is General Krymov's order. Take a good look!" It was the order concerning the projected division of Petrograd into sectors, and the appointment of military commandants. I read the order slowly, and putting it into my pocket I said that the commission would examine it. After that Kerensky addressed himself to General Krymov and said: "General! You are at the disposal of the present extraordinary commission of inquiry." We left the cabinet. In the next room I presented myself to the Generals (Krymov and Diterichs) and said to General Krymov the following: "Your Excellency, you are free and can dispose of your time. But as I am leaving today for Stavka, I kindly ask you to come to see me at 5:00 P.M. in order to give your testimony." ' "

I continue to cite Samarin:

"At about 1:00 P.M. Aleksandr Mikhailovich and I entered the house on Zakhr'inskaia [Street] where the cabinet of the Minister of War was located and where I worked with my assistant, Captain Zhurvskii—a most intimate friend of the Krymov family. They kissed each other and left for the apartment of Zhurvskii, which was located in the same house. I started my reception. Not an hour had passed when Zhurvskii came in tears and told me that Aleksandr Mikhailovich had shot himself."

. . .

The president of the "extraordinary commission," Shablovskii, cites the last words of Krymov:

"The last card for saving the homeland has been beaten—living is not worth while any longer" . . .

. . .

A. DENIKIN

1284. APPEAL FROM THE ALL-RUSSIAN SOVIET EXECUTIVE COMMITTEES
[*Izvestiia*, No. 156, August 29, 1917, p. 4.]

General Kornilov has instigated a revolt against the revolution and the Provisional Government. He wants to restore the old regime and deprive the people of land and freedom. He is ready to open the front and betray the fatherland for the sake of his criminal goal.

Comrade Soldiers and Comrade Officers

The revolution and the fatherland call upon you to perform your duty. Let everyone stand up, as one man, in defense of land and freedom. Not a single order of General Kornilov must be obeyed. Submit only to the orders of the Provisional Government, which is acting in full agreement with the Central Executive Committees of the Soviets of Workers', Soldiers', and Peasants' Deputies; rally around them in a united family.

Now, when the external foe is threatening Petrograd, the army must be united, solid, and strong. Now every officer and every soldier is especially valuable in defending the country against the external foe.

Only an insignificant little group of traitors is taking part in the revolt against the revolution. There must be no [cases of] lynching of officers or soldiers. The Provisional Government and the Central Committees are doing everything in their power to discover all the participants in the plot and inflict upon them the punishment they deserve.

Comrade Soldiers and Comrade Officers

Act concertedly. In so doing you will save the fatherland from the external foe. In so doing you will save the land and the freedom; you will save the republic and the democratic organizations of the army. In so doing you will save yourselves and avert unnecessary casualties.

For the sake of all this, the Central Committee of the Soviets of Workers', Soldiers', and Peasants' Deputies calls upon all officers and soldiers to stand united in defense of the fatherland, the revolution, and the Provisional Government against the encroachments of the traitors on the people.

> THE CENTRAL EXECUTIVE COMMITTEE OF THE
> ALL-RUSSIAN SOVIET OF WORKERS' AND
> SOVIETS' DEPUTIES
> THE EXECUTIVE COMMITTEE OF THE ALL-RUSSIAN
> SOVIET OF PEASANTS' DEPUTIES

1285. THE ARMING OF THE WORKERS

[*Izvestiia*, No. 156, August 29, 1917, p. 6. In the face of the Kornilov threat, which appeared to be as much against the Soviets in general as against the Bolsheviks in particular, the Central Executive Committee of Workers' and Soldiers' Deputies agreed on August 27 to cooperate with the Bolsheviks in the formation of a Committee for the People's Struggle Against Counterrevolution. The Committee agreed to the organization of armed workers, which turned out to be, in fact, a rejuvenation of the Bolshevik-controlled Red Guard, largely suppressed since July. Evidences of the unexpected advantage gained by the Bolsheviks are to be found in the next document and throughout the remaining chapters of these volumes. See especially Lenin's letter to the Central Committee of the Party, dated August 30, printed in Chap. 29. For the proclamation on the revolt, issued by the Central Committee, see the *Collected Works of V. I. Lenin; Toward the Seizure of Power*, XXI, Bk. II, 318–19.]

After discussing the question of the necessity of countering the armed forces of the counterrevolution with the mobilized forces of workers, the Committee for the People's Struggle Against Counterrevolution resolved to recognize as desirable the arming of individual groups of workers for protecting workers' quarters, factories, and mills under the closest supervision of the district Soviets and under the control of the Committees. If the necessity arises, these groups will merge with the army units and be placed completely under the command of the army.

1286. Negotiations for the Release of Certain Individuals Arrested in Connection with the July Days
[*Izvestiia*, No. 158, August 31, 1917, p. 3.]

The Committee for the People's Struggle Against Counterrevolution, set up under the All-Russian Central Executive Committee of the Soviet of Workers' and Soldiers' Deputies, informs all comrade workers that it has taken all the relevant steps for the release within the next few days of all those persons arrested in connection with the events of July 3–5 who have not been proved guilty of acts of a criminal nature, espionage, etc. In its appeals to the authorities on this subject, the Committee insisted, naturally, not on terminating the investigations, but only on terminating the arrest of the largest possible number of persons who have been brought under investigation, and changing the measures of suppression that have been adopted against them. The current negotiations with the authorities on this subject give the Committee grounds to hope that auspicious results will be obtained within the next few days. While the Committee fully understands the heightened interest in this question, manifested by the broad masses of workers, it considers it necessary at the same time to point out that any arbitrary demonstrations on these grounds can only provoke panic and, by contributing to sedition, create the most dangerous complications. Remember, comrades, that Kornilovism has not yet been entirely liquidated and that now, more than ever before, it is necessary to have the strictest observance of revolutionary discipline.

1287. The Attitude of the Allies
[*Rech'*, No. 204, August 31, 1917, p. 3. The good offices of the ambassadors were refused with an expression of appreciation for the offer. For Sir George Buchanan's foreknowledge of the attempted coup d'état, which he did not transmit to the Provisional Government, and for his account of his and other Allied ambassadors' relations with the Government during the revolt, see his *My Mission to Russia and Other Diplomatic Memories*, II, 172–85. Somewhat later, it was alleged by certain newspapers that the British armored car unit in Russia, which Sir George had been asked on August 23 to place at the disposal of the Kornilov forces (*ibid.*, p. 175), had in fact participated in the revolt. Sir George protested the accusation, and finally, in the interests of Allied unity, the Government issued an official denial on September 19. A. Popov, "Inostrannye diplomaty o revoliutsii 1917 g.," *KA*, XXIV (1927), 160–61; and *Rech'*, No. 220, September 19, 1917, p. 5. Regarding the unexpressed but evident sympathy of the British Government for the Kornilov attempt, see C. Nabokoff, *The Ordeal of a Diplomat*, pp. 164–65. For the documents on the collective *démarche* of the Allied ambassadors in Petrograd on September 26, see Chap. 28.]

On August 30 the representatives of the Allied countries handed M. I. Tereshchenko, Minister of Foreign Affairs, the following communication:
"Some newspapers, mentioning the representatives of the Allied powers in

connection with the events now taking place, are ascribing to them attempts either to support or directly to suppress the actions of General Kornilov.

"It hardly seems necessary to refute such a communication, which is so utterly in contradiction with the attitude of the Allies toward Russian internal affairs.

"The representatives of all the Entente powers limited themselves, as dictated by their feelings of sympathy toward the great Allied democracy, to an offer of their friendly services for the purpose of avoiding bloodshed and civil war.

"In order to avoid any misunderstanding, attached herewith is the text of the declaration which Sir George Buchanan, acting as dean of the diplomatic corps, handed M. I. Tereshchenko on August 28: 'The representatives of the Allied powers, at a conference held under the chairmanship of Sir George Buchanan to discuss the situation which has arisen in connection with the conflict between the Provisional Government and General Kornilov, considered themselves duty-bound to remain at their posts in order to give, in case of need, protection to their compatriots. At the same time, they consider that, for the purpose of a successful continuation of the war, the maintenance of the unity of all the forces of Russia is of the utmost importance.

" 'In view of this they unanimously declare that from humanitarian motives and in their desire to prevent irretrievable steps they offer their good services solely for the purpose of promoting the interests of Russia and the Allied cause.' "

1288. EDITORIAL IN *Russkiia Vedomosti*
[No. 197, August 29, 1917, p. 3.]

The uprising of General Kornilov against the Provisional Government moved into the background all other issues of the day, even such important events as the fall of Riga and the offensive of the Germans on the road to Petrograd. And this is quite natural because we are now face to face with the greatest misfortune that could be imagined, with civil war into which a considerable part of the army is drawn.

There can be no two views on the action of General Kornilov. Regardless of the motives that prompted this step, the attempt on the part of the Supreme Commander to overthrow the Provisional Government and seize power by armed force is an entirely intolerable method of deciding national questions. The history of Western Europe knows of many examples of armed pronunciamentos undertaken in the name of popular welfare and freedom, but it knows of no pronunciamento from which freedom and welfare really profited. Even the restoration of the army to health, the reintroduction of military order, in the name of which General Kornilov spoke before, cannot serve as justification for the decision made by him. Because, by arousing the army against the Provisional Government, he thereby undermines even more the military discipline and the duty of obedience, which are, as it is, greatly shaken. You cannot restore order by means of even temporary, complete elimination of it. We sharply condemned at one time the armed insurrection of the Bolsheviks in Petrograd on July 3–5. And our attitude with regard to the step by General Kornilov is just as definite. Regardless of the motives of either side, resolving national questions in this manner is intolerable, particularly at the time of fierce war, when every internal quarrel can be utilized by the enemy and may lead to irreparable suffering at the front.

But while maintaining this negative attitude toward the attempt of General

Kornilov, we cannot close our eyes to the other side of the matter—to the presence of certain general conditions which create to some degree a favorable soil for military upheavals. From the very first days of its existence the Russian revolution committed a fateful error. It was unable to ignore the army. On the contary, it exerted all its efforts to win the army, granting her active participation and, in some instances, a chief role in deciding state questions. The army throughout is saturated with politics. The army committees are very often converted into purely political organizations with the same fractional divisions into S.R.'s, Mensheviks, Bolsheviks, etc., that we encounter in the Soviets of Workers' Deputies, in municipal Dumas, and elsewhere. Troops decide questions of war and peace, of the forms of state organizations, of land, and of the eight-hour workday, etc., and in general live a not less but perhaps more intensive political life than the peaceful civilian population. But mainly, the troops little by little learn to make *their* decisions on small matters, without considering the wishes of other public groups. Up to this time this concerned small things, but these small things cleared the way for the efforts at major decisions on basic state questions by force. And unless we return the army to what it should be, make it neutral again, standing outside of politics, we shall not rid ourselves of the threat of military revolt.

Another very significant circumstance is that Kornilov is not alone and that he undoubtedly has at his disposal numerous adherents among high-ranking commanders and among the officers. . . . This is no conspiracy, but something essentially even more dangerous than a conspiracy. It is an expression of a widespread and spontaneous dissatisfaction with the existing state of affairs in the army. The army is ill, gravely ill, and resolute measures are needed to restore her former fighting power. . . .

Eliminating politics from the army and restoring normal discipline are, however, problems of the future, although they brook no delay. And now we must think first of all about the methods of liquidating the grave crisis. Recent reports confirm the fact that very little hope is left for solving the crisis in a peaceful way without shedding blood. But while even the vaguest hope remains in this direction, while even one small chance remains for a peaceful solution, this chance must be exploited. . . .

1289. Editorial in *Rech'*
[No. 202, August 29, 1917, p. 1.]

Never before has Russia faced such a terrible situation as that which threatens her now—today. The papers report that from the south and from the north regiments are moving toward Petrograd—Russian regiments of General Kornilov. Defensive measures are hastily being taken against them, and the regiments of the Provisional Government, also Russian, are preparing for action. This takes place while the front is threatened with a new breakthrough by the enemy, after which the danger for the vital centers of the country may immeasurably increase. In the meantime, both sides quite sincerely assert that their only consideration is the welfare and the salvation of the country.

What is the matter? What colossal misunderstanding is dividing the two sides—if it is only a misunderstanding? Why cannot both sides join hands, before the split becomes too deep, in order to put an immediate end to the conflict which is tearing the country in two?

Alas, here in free Russia we are witnessing the repetition of a sight which is all too familiar to us from our knowledge of the old regime. Even those demands that are recognized as justifiable are not being given satisfaction because to satisfy them would mean the loss of governmental "prestige." Concessions are finally made, but . . . they are made too late. Or, even worse, instead of conceding to the demands of life, the Government takes a haughty pose, and behaves according to the principle that it is better to perish than to concede, forgetting that the struggle takes place on the living body of the nation and that Russia is suffering along with the Government. Little by little the defense of the country is being transformed into the self-defense of the Government, which gradually loses its contact with reality and begins to be obsessed with the phantoms of its own imagination. This Government ceases to see what everyone sees, is the last to learn what everybody knows, and scatters its fire upon imaginary opponents, without seeing the growing danger surrounding it.

The day before yesterday reconciliation was easy; yesterday it was still possible. For a whole day the members of the Party of the People's Freedom made every effort to re-establish the possibility of relations between the antagonists and to find the means by which the civil war already in progress could be stopped. These endeavors encountered the same punctilious argumentation. How could the legal Government possibly begin negotiations with rebels? How could concessions be made without loss of prestige for the Government? And should not the Government employ toward today's opponents the same treatment it employed toward the Bolsheviks?

In reply to this it can be argued, first, that the treatment of the Bolsheviks has always been much too lenient and that the Government has never dared to declare them criminals or rebels; second, that it is impossible to take a purely formal stand and ignore the fact that there is a difference between the partisans of Lenin and those of Kornilov: it is the difference between anarchy and national order.

.   .   .

1290. Editorial in *Den'*
[No. 148, August 28, 1917, p. 1.]

A serious attempt against Russian liberty has been perpetrated.

General Kornilov has chosen a moment of deathly danger for his homeland to set the fire of a civil war, to raise one part of the army against another, and to deflect all of it from the task of defending Russia against Wilhelm's bayonets and cannons.

In this dreadful hour of our history, Kornilov has directed his attention, not over there, where the crushing might of the enemy armies is moving on us, but here, where at the head of the Provisional Government the leader of Russia, A. F. Kerensky, stands guarding Russian freedom.

The hand that intended to inflict the last blow on Russian liberty has been stayed. The regiments, faithful to their homeland, will do everything to save exhausted Russia. But the danger is still great. The fate of Russia hangs by a hair. And in this terrible hour we appeal to you, citizens:

Calm and self-control!

Let us rally, all of us, around the Supreme Power; let us follow its orders implicitly. Now there cannot be either cowards or fainthearted or unconcerned. We must all guard the revolution, and everyone who runs away in fear or who indifferently steps aside will be a traitor.

Russia has never been in such danger as during these days. The external and internal foes are bringing death, shame, and slavery. Let us meet these enemies as citizens, and not as slaves.

1291. EDITORIAL IN *Volia Naroda*
[No. 104, August 29, 1917, p. 1.]

At the terrifying hour of grave trials in the life of the exhausted country, at the hour of the greatest outward danger threatening its very existence, a treacherous hand has risen armed with a fratricidal knife to strike a deadly blow.

General Kornilov, appointed to the highest military post by the confidence and trust of the Provisional Government, treacherously encroaches upon the very same national authority from whom he received the plenary powers of the supreme commander.

The dreams of all the dark forces of the past; the dreams of all those who from the very first days hated freedom; of all those who, because of class animosity and vindictiveness toward the revolution which gave the working people first place, united secretly and openly around the black banner of counterrevolution—[the dreams of all those forces] are being realized. "The general on a white horse" has become a reality. The troops of the rebel Kornilov are moving on Petrograd.

.   .   .

"Patriots" of the right camps, foaming at the mouth, demanded the restoration of discipline in the army . . . did everything to encourage Kornilov and his band to mutiny. They accused the leaders of revolutionary democracy—who guarded the freedom they won—of Germanophilism, whereas they themselves were helping the German Emperor. General Kornilov and all the social forces that support him at the present moment are the best accomplices of Wilhelm II and Hindenburg. . . . Kornilov's victory would mean an unavoidable separate peace—an unavoidable fall under the iron yoke of imperialist Germany. But the reactionary element is ready—it always has been ready for this—to sell the motherland and build its rule on her humiliation and disgrace.

The term "reaction" must be expanded now. The most diverse elements belong to its camp now: if not openly, at least as a matter of fact, many of those who hide behind a cloak of liberalism.

What is the role of the liberal bourgeoisie and its political leaders in the tragedy that is unfolding; what role did it play in its preparation?

The Kadet semiofficial organs, admitting the need for the union of all vital forces of the country in order to save the motherland, stubbornly and systematically sabotaged national unity. They demanded a strong government, savagely destroying the basis of coalition government and dooming it to insanity. They then argued to prove its weakness in order to show the need for a "sharp turn." They sent their representatives into the ranks of the Government only to create an opposition within and at the first sign of a crisis to withdraw; they have now withdrawn. They remained deaf to all calls to unity, unwilling to consider any compromises or sacrifices. . . .

The good Jesuits of *Rech'* regard the armed encroachment on the authority of the Provisional Government as a legal act that aims to establish a tie and succession of the cabinets, because Kornilov did plan to have A. F. Kerensky and B. V. Savinkov participate in the cabinet!

There can be no doubt here. In these grave hours democracy must count only upon its own strength. But its enemies are celebrating too soon. Democracy is not down yet. It will be able to defend the motherland and the revolution from all of their enemies, because by defending the revolution it also now defends the motherland.

But the danger that has been created also dictates appropriate measures for combating it. The pressure by the enemy must be counteracted with a united front. All internal disagreements must be forgotten, because we are now gambling with the preservation of Russian freedom. The entire revolutionary democracy of Russia, as one man, must rally around the Government which defends the motherland and the revolution. . . .

. . . History demands the greatest sacrifice of the Government and the revolution, in the name of the highest ideals of humanity, to suppress the feeling of pity and to crush with an iron hand those for whom violence is the usual basis of rule. They who were the first to draw the sword are responsible for this.

1292. EDITORIAL IN *Delo Naroda*
[No. 139, August 28, 1917, p. 1.]

Finally the enemies of the revolution begin to carry out their program openly, apparently carefully prepared and in detail.

. . .

And so the "preparation" begins. *Rech'*, the spiritual leader of the conspirators, launches a bitter campaign against the Provisional Government. Riga and the entire Riga region go over into the hands of the Germans. Stavka reports the treacherous desertion of soldiers. Panic spreads through the capital. Rumors are afloat about anticipated arson and explosions in factories manufacturing munitions and explosives. Rumors are spread about the "Bolsheviks" marching in the streets. Finally, a new government "crisis" is artificially created. When it appeared that the preparatory actions had created favorable ground, the military league publishes a proclamation—"support the leaders"—which calls for open action against the revolution.[26]

And now the "leaders" submit ultimatums to the Provisional Government. The demands are motivated by the helplessness of the Government and by the alleged action of the same Bolsheviks—danger of civil war—which automatically may open the front.

Simultaneously troops are marching on Petrograd . . .

As we see, complete unity of action has been established between the rear and the front of the counterrevolution.

. . .

No one should now have any doubt with whom we are dealing.

Betrayers of the people, traitors of the country—such are the true names of the counterrevolutionaries.

[26] *Novoe Vremia*, No. 14865, August 28, 1917, p. 1.

They are not ideological enemies of democracy, defending their views in the name of revolution as they understand their public aims.

We must consequently deal with them as with conspirators that have designs upon the very existence of the country. Vigorous and merciless measures against them—such must be the method of action on the part of the Government and the revolutionary democracy. The revolution was too lenient toward her enemies. Let her then turn her mercilessly severe face toward them.

1293. EDITORIAL IN *Rabochaia Gazeta*
[No. 145, August 28, 1917, p. 1.]

At last counterrevolution decided to strike at the revolution. For a long time it hid quietly; for a long time it stealthily spread discord and animosity; for a long time it awaited a propitious moment to strike at the very heart of the revolution.

Encouraged by the ambiguous conduct of the Kadets at the Moscow State Conference, it half-opened its hood. General Kornilov threatened the fall of Riga unless his demands were fulfilled; General Kaledin dared to proclaim publicly the reactionary aspirations of certain circles among the commanding personnel.

And when Riga surrendered, as if in fulfillment of the strangely accurate forecast of Kornilov—when the front was broken and a military storm hung over Petrograd, the mind and the heart of the revolution—*they* dared.

At the Moscow Conference Kornilov chose precisely the day of the semiannual anniversary of the revolution to overthrow the Provisional revolutionary Government, which is clothed with the confidence of the entire nation, and to proclaim his dictatorship. This miserable traitor took advantage of the greatest national misfortune—the surrender of Riga and the breakthrough of the front—the moment of the gravest danger to the motherland, with no concern for the state upheaval which may shake the country completely and break the ranks of the army, which can barely hold back the assault of the enemy.

1294. EDITORIAL IN *Izvestiia*
[No. 157, August 30, 1917, p. 2.]

What were General Kornilov and his supporters counting on when they openly raised the banner of revolt and counterrevolution?

They counted, in the first place, on the instability and weakness of the Government. They calculated that the Government would be inclined to negotiate with the counterrevolutionary rebels and would begin conceding revolutionary positions to them—and then the cause would have been won.

But they were fooled in their hopes. The Government remained firm and adopted a policy of a resolute struggle against the insurgent general who betrayed our native land. In vain did Messrs. Miliukov, Rodzianko, Alekseev, and their ilk try to incline the Government toward disastrous compromises which would have placed it completely in the hands of the counterrevolutionaries. At a crucial moment the Government understood its duty, and this card of the rebels and the traitors was topped.

But the conspirators had counted on one more thing: on the weakened strength of the revolutionary democracy as a consequence of internal strife and dissension.

But even here the calculations of General Kornilov and his open and secret friends were not justified. In the face of grave danger, the revolutionary wisdom prevailed in the democracy, and everyone, as one man, rallied around the Soviets. Hundreds of telegrams from the front and the rear, from army units and provincial soviets, bore witness to the readiness of the democracy to give every support to the Central Executive Committee and the Provisional Government in a resolute fight against the conspirators, who were not ashamed to open the front of revolutionary Russia to the hordes of German imperialism.

. . .

The strength of the revolutionary government and the solidarity of the revolutionary democracy—these are the two rocks against which the wave of the black counterrevolution will be dashed to pieces. Neither the Government nor the democracy must forget this.

SUPPRESSION AND INVESTIGATION

1295. PROCLAMATION OF THE GOVERNMENT
[*VVP*, No. 142 (Supplement), August 29, 1917, p. 1.]

*The Whole Country and the Army Are on the Side of the Revolution;
General Kornilov's Revolt Is Being Suppressed*

TO EVERYONE, EVERYONE, EVERYONE:

The attempted revolt by General Kornilov and the clique of adventurers gathered around him remain completely isolated from the rest of the active army and navy. With the exception of the Commander in Chief of the Southwestern Front, Denikin, the Commanders in Chief have remained loyal to the Provisional Government and have appealed for the same to all the forces under their commands.

Everywhere the Commanders in Chief are acting in complete accord with the revolutionary commissars of the Provisional Government and the committees of the front. General Denikin and all his staff have been detained at his headquarters. In the interest of defense, [Denikin] has been left in charge of operations but is kept under the strict control of the committee delegates. Erdeli, Commander of the Special Army,[27] and several members of his staff have also been arrested for insubordination.

The Baltic Fleet and its commanders have unanimously taken the side of the Provisional Government.

Only some small detachments, which, by means of deceit, General Kornilov has moved toward Petrograd, remained deluded, but the further advance of these echelons has been checked and the communications between them have been severed. Delegations from individual units of these forces have arrived in Petrograd with the request that they be furnished an order to arrest the commanders who have betrayed the Provisional Government.

The Provisional Government has adopted vigorous measures for the defense

[27] The Special Army was the name given to what would otherwise have been the 13th army because of the traditional superstitions associated with the number 13.

of Petrograd against any attempts to attack it, but there are grounds to hope that all bloodshed and civil war will be avoided.

Reports are coming in from all parts of the provinces regarding the complete loyalty of the troops and the population to the Provisional Government, along with declarations from various public organizations regarding their determination to support the revolutionary Government by every possible means. Complete unity of action must be preserved in order to save the native land. The Provisional Government enjoins absolute calm and unconditional submission to the Government and its loyal organs.

A. KERENSKY, Minister-President, Minister of War and Navy

1296. THE APPOINTMENT OF AN EXTRAORDINARY COMMISSION TO INVESTIGATE KORNILOV AND HIS ASSOCIATES
[Sob. Uzak., I, 2, No. 1387.]

LAW OF THE PROVISIONAL GOVERNMENT

The Provisional Government has decreed:

1. An extraordinary commission is appointed to investigate the case of the former Supreme Commander General Kornilov and his accomplices, who have engaged in open rebellion.

2. The aforesaid commission is empowered to bring criminal proceedings in military-revolutionary and other appropriate courts.

3. The same commission is granted the right to make arrests, searches, and seizures.

4. All officials and public institutions and organizations are required to carry out unquestioningly all orders of the aforesaid commission.

5. The Chief Naval Prosecutor, Shablovskii, is appointed Chairman of the commission, with the following members: the Military Examining Magistrate attached to the Extraordinary Commission of Inquiry, Colonel Raupakh; the Assistant Military Prosecutor of the Petrograd Military-Circuit Court, Colonel Ukraintsev; and the Examining Magistrate of the Petrograd Court for especially important cases, Kolokolov.

6. The Chairman of the commission is granted the right, if necessary, to request persons other than those named above to join the commission with the rights of members.[28]

A. KERENSKY, Minister-President, Minister of War and Navy
ZARUDNYI, Minister of Justice

August 29, 1917

1297. STATEMENT BY KROKHMAL' ON THE INVESTIGATION
[Novaia Zhizn', No. 143, October 3, 1917, p. 2.]

V. N. Krokhmal', member of the Committee on Inquiry in the case of Kornilov, informed our editor of the following:

Some part of the socialist press expresses the opinion that the Committee on Inquiry is allegedly limited in its authority and that its functions are narrowed

---

[28] Two additional members were added, elected by the Central Executive Committee of the Soviet: M. I. Lieber and V. N. Krokhmal'.

in certain directions. This is not true. The authority of the committee corresponds entirely to its tasks: to discover not only the intellectual and physical culprits of the Kornilov revolt, but also the broad social basis that supported it. With this aim the committee has already done a great deal and, incidentally, went to Mogilev twice, once to Moscow and Bykhov.[29] And at present the committee anticipates a trip to Novocherkassk. Many of those cross-examined are under arrest. The role of others is only being clarified. Incidentally, the committee devoted considerable attention to clarifying the role of Filonenko, Savinkov, and Zavoiko. The latter is under arrest as Kornilov's adjutant and author of his manifestoes.

The available materials are grouped in three categories, in accordance with which the following speculations are possible:

First: Kornilov is accused not only of the revolt, but also of a planned preparation for it by means of utilizing the resources and intellectual means placed at his disposal by the state authority.

Second: A certain group of people was preparing the overthrow of the Provisional Government and with these aims in view took advantage of the strained relations between the Government and Kornilov, using the latter as a tool for their aims.

Third: Using the support of certain groups sympathizing with him, Kornilov was responsible, along with them, for the revolt which was prepared by their mutual efforts.

The available material leads to the conclusion, however, that none of them aspired to the restoration of the monarchy.

So far as the role of Kerensky is concerned, the committee is not looking into this question at the present time.

1298. STATEMENT BY THE CHAIRMAN OF THE COMMISSION, SHABLOVSKII,
PROTESTING THE INACCURACY OF THE PUBLISHED
ACCOUNTS OF TESTIMONY

[*Russkiia Vedomosti*, No. 223, October 5, 1917, p. 2. Throughout the investigation, which was not completed when the Bolsheviks seized power, reports of testimony appeared in the papers (for an example, see the next document) which were usually incomplete and slanted to meet the political needs of the particular newspaper. No official publication has appeared of the materials of the Commission. Kerensky's *Prelude to Bolshevism* is, however, the annotated stenographic record of his evidence.]

I familiarized myself with the published material on the case of Kornilov only today. But I can say emphatically that the explanatory memorandum of Kornilov cannot serve as an undisputed basis to determine whether or not the conspiracy took place. In this case the General is the accused and this to a large degree predetermines the value of his testimony. As for the memoranda of Commissar Filonenko and General Alekseev, I would say that theirs are testimonies of more or less remote witnesses. They, too, cannot give a complete picture of the outbreak and development of the conspiracy, which up to this time is far from investigated. In particular the investigation commission is confronted with an extremely important problem, namely, to determine the role of V. N. L'vov, which up to this time remains very vague. The cross-examination of

---

[29] Where Kornilov and his associates placed under arrest were confined.

L'vov is fraught with certain difficulties. And his testimony should be treated with extreme caution. No deduction can be made so far in this respect.

Even if we admit, said Shablovskii further, that the published notes describe clearly and exhaustively the role of General Kornilov, they nevertheless bear only upon that period of time when General Kornilov had not as yet submitted the well-known ultimatum to the Provisional Government. From that time on, the conduct and motives of General Kornilov's actions are in no way explained in the materials published in the newspapers. Moreover, these materials in substance are not entirely accurate. I could correct not only some words and expressions but the whole testimonies of General Alekseev, which were recently published in the press.

For an all-round discussion, continued Shablovskii, of all the circumstances that preceded the famous ultimatum, the investigating commission cross-examined A. F. Kerensky, who himself wished to come and give the commission his competent explanations. It is possible that the Minister-President will be cross-examined again.

In general, concluded Shablovskii, all the noise aroused by the published memoranda only hampers the correct course of the investigation. As a matter of fact, while explaining nothing, the publishing of the data of the preliminary investigation leads to undesirable false rumors which disturb the public and prevent the investigating authorities from resolving calmly and objectively that sore question which received the historic name of "Kornilovshchina."

1299. REPORT ON GENERAL ALEKSEEV'S DEPOSITION TO THE COMMISSION

[Entitled "Was There a Mutiny?" *Novoe Vremia*, No. 14888, October 4, 1917, p. 3.]

After General Kornilov's resignation from the post of Supreme Commander, the post was offered to General M. V. Alekseev. The latter was requested to appear for this purpose by a special telegram sent to him en route to Smolensk. On the night of the 27th General Alekseev was in the Winter Palace and A. F. Kerensky offered him the supreme command of the army. General Alekseev asked if he might be given the documents in connection with the case in order that he might read them. He was given a number of telegrams.

These documents, says General Alekseev in his "memorandum," were incomplete. Several telegrams of importance were apparently missing. But even the material on hand gave full enough evidence to make the deductions: General Kornilov had previous negotiations with both the Minister-President and Savinkov. V. N. L'vov participated in these negotiations. It was impossible to find out at whose initiative he came to Mogilev. The ultimative request transmitted verbally by V. N. L'vov to A. F. Kerensky was not completely checked during the negotiations over the Hughes apparatus from the point of view of accuracy and correctness of content and explosition. The removal of General Kornilov from his post as Supreme Commander apparently came after General Kornilov's request was set forth by V. N. L'vov.

Feeling that the replacement of the Supreme Commander would have deplorable repercussions in the army, General Alekseev declined the offered post and expressed his conviction that the misunderstanding with General Kornilov should be clarified and ended in mutual understanding and thus spare the army from a shakeup by leaving General Kornilov in the post of Supreme Commander.

Representatives of the Union of the Cossack Troops also offered their services in settling the conflict. They offered to go to Mogilev and find ground for a mutual understanding between A. F. Kerensky and General Kornilov.

A. F. Kerensky replied that there could be no agreements with General Kornilov now.

The Minister of Foreign Affairs, M. I. Tereshchenko, declared that telegrams had been sent to all railway lines to the effect that General Kornilov had betrayed Russia and her government. Consequently none of his orders along the railway lines should be executed. The author of this telegram which prevented any opportunity to clarify the misunderstanding and come to an agreement was N. V. Nekrasov.

General Alekseev nevertheless did not abandon all hope of arriving at an understanding and made a second attempt in this direction on August 28. He suggested that several members of the Provisional Government and P. N. Miliukov be sent to Mogilev for personal negotiations with General Kornilov or that attempts be made to persuade him to come to an agreement by means of negotiations by the Hughes apparatus.

However, General Alekseev's second suggestion about coming to an understanding with General Kornilov was also emphatically declined by the Provisional Government, which thought it unnecessary to carry out any negotiations with Kornilov.

. . .

General Alekseev asked A. F. Kerensky to give him an opportunity to solve the matter in Mogilev calmly, without any jolts. Kerensky replied: yes, yes . . .

This was August 30. On the 31st, on starting out for Mogilov, General Alekseev learned by accident in Vitebsk that by order of A. F. Kerensky a detachment of Korotkov's regiment was mustered for action against Mogilev and for the arrest of Kornilov.

. . .

In Orsha General Alekseev found the Commissar of the Western Front, Zhdanov, and Colonel Korotkov with a detachment with three types of weapons. Colonel Korotkov told General Alekseev that, according to reliable information he had received, defensive works were erected around Mogilev and General Kornilov's forces consisted of artillery, 12 armored automobiles, four airplanes, and five thousand infantrymen.

General Alekseev emphatically forbade Colonel Korotkov to move on Mogilev and ordered the vanguard echelons of his detachment stopped at the station of Lotva, 15 versts from Mogilev. However Korotkov's regiment hesitated to carry out this order of the Chief of Staff of the Supreme Commander, since it had received an opposite order to move on Mogilev from the Supreme Commander himself.

On the night of September 1, Alekseev arrived Mogilev and talked with General Kornilov, who confirmed his promise to surrender. From General Kornilov General Alekseev went to the communication room in order to call A. F. Kerensky from Petrograd. But he received a telegram from Moscow from General Verkhovskii as follows:

"I leave today for Stavka with a large armed detachment in order to put an end to the mockery of common sense which has prevailed until now. Kornilov, Lukomskii, Pliushchevski-Pliushchik, Pronin, and Sakharov must be arrested immediately and prosecuted. This is the purpose of my trip, which I consider indispensable. On calling you over the [Hughes] apparatus, I trust I will hear from you that these arrests have already been made."

Over the [Hughes] apparatus from Petrograd A. F. Kerensky told General Alekseev: "During the last twenty-four hours I have received a great number of both oral and written communications to the effect that Stavka has at its disposal a large supply of weapons; that it is declared to be in a state of siege, and that over a 10-verst circumference outposts are erected, fortifications have been completed, and machine guns and arms distributed. Under the circumstances I do not deem it advisable to subject you and consequently the commission to the possible risk and suggested Korotkov move."

"Of all the information received by A. F. Kerensky," writes General Alekseev in his "memorandum," "only one thing corresponded to the facts—Mogilev and its environs over a radius of 10 versts were declared under state of siege. Everything else was an invention prompted by the fact that fear breeds terror."

Somebody's evil will pushed the troops toward Mogilev.

. . .

General Alekseev informed A. F. Kerensky that his safety and that of the investigating commission were guaranteed without the detachment of Colonel Korotkov. Colonel Korotkov would only create a slaughter if he moved on Mogilev. General Alekseev reported all this to A. F. Kerensky over the [Hughes] apparatus, but he was constantly interrupted by impatient exclamations. And subsequent events proved that General Alekseev was right when he insisted on stopping the detachment which was moving on Mogilev.

"I must testify," writes General Alekseev in his "memorandum," "that in accordance with his promise over the [Hughes] apparatus, General Kornilov surrendered his command of the armies without protest. He did not even express any protest against his arrest. So far as the garrison was concerned, his troops remained calm in their barracks, making no preparations to meet the approaching troops."

As seen from the telegram quoted below, reporting the conversation of V. V. Vyrubov and General Alekseev with the Assistant to the Minister of War, Colonel Baranovskii, promoted after the demotion of General Kornilov to Major-General, the delay in arresting General Kornilov aroused great agitation in Petrograd. And in order to quiet the "enraged revolutionary democracy," the immediate arrest of Kornilov and other "rebels" was demanded.

General Alekseev succeeded in crushing the entire notorious "rebellion" without shedding one drop of blood.

1300. LETTER FROM GENERAL ALEKSEEV TO MILIUKOV

[*Izvestiia*, No. 249, December 12, 1917, p. 2. See Doc. 1311.]

The following letter from General Alekseev to Miliukov has fallen into our hands:

September 12, 1917
Mogilev

Dear Pavel Nikolaevich:

I did not have an opportunity to see you before leaving Petrograd on August 31. Now, having surrendered my post, I cannot come to Petrograd and am forced to trouble you with this letter. Your assistance and that of other public men, of all those who can do anything, should be quiet, energetic, and far-reaching.

· · ·

Kornilov's undertaking was not that of a small group of adventurers. It relied on the sympathy and assistance of wide circles of our intelligentsia, which could not stand the torments of our motherland brought to [the brink of] ruin by the unhappy selection of her minister rulers.

No one would be able to demonstrate that the action was directed against the regime which existed on August 27–31. It was directed exclusively against individuals who in succession were joining the membership of the cabinet and quickly withdrawing from it, who could not constitute a solid and firm government, and who were leading the country toward her final ruin. The aim of the action was not to change the existing regime, but only to change individuals, to find such individuals as could save Russia.

Kornilov's action was no mystery for the members of the Government. The question was discussed with Savinkov, with Filonenko—and, through them, with Kerensky. Only a primitive revolutionary court-martial can conceal the participation of these individuals in the preliminary negotiations and in the preliminary agreement. Savinkov has already been forced to confess it in the press. Filonenko shall be exposed; in the future ministry he had pretensions to the post of Minister of Foreign Affairs, but next day he generously agreed to that of Minister of the Interior.

The participation of Kerensky is beyond question. I cannot explain why these persons retreated, why they repudiated their own words, when the action started.

The advance of the 3rd Cavalry Corps' division on Petrograd was made upon Kerensky's instructions, which had been transmitted by Savinkov. To what degree the agreement (which finds its explanation in the expected action of the Bolsheviks) had been worked out and established can be demonstrated to you by the following brief telegram:

"August 27. 2 hr. 30 min. To the Assistant Minister of War. The corps will concentrate in the outskirts of Petrograd toward the evening of August 28. I request you to declare Petrograd under martial law on August 29. 6394. GENERAL KORNILOV."

I think that it would be superfluous to explain the significance of this telegram. The members of the Government who participated in the action and who, for some reason, withdrew from it at the decisive moment had decided during the night of August 26–27, i.e., almost on the very hour when Kornilov was writing his telegram No. 6394, to remove him from the post of Supreme Commander. But then it was already impossible to stop the movement of the troops and to abandon the action, this [circumstance] was explained in General Lukomskii's telegram No. 6406 to Kerensky: "The arrival of Savinkov and L'vov, who on your behalf made a proposal in this sense to General Kornilov, has compelled General Kornilov to make a final decision, and, in accordance with your proposal, he gave final instructions, which now it is too late to cancel." The telegram is long; I am citing only one point, which is specially important in confirming my thought.

From this refusal of Kerensky, Savinkov, and Filonenko [to participate in] the action, which aimed at creating a government of a different composition, and from the fact of Kornilov's dismissal have come all the troubles of August 27–31. The action was collapsing; its visible participants were declared adventurers, traitors, and rebels. Its invisible participants either have remained masters of our destinies or have withdrawn from everything, leaving about 30 peoples to dishonor, trial, and execution.

As you are partly aware, some circles of our public not only knew everything, not only were ideological sympathizers, but even helped Kornilov as much as they could.

Kornilov did not seek power for himself personally. His aim was to create a solid, firm government of people on whom one could better rely in the matter of leading Russia toward her salvation. But, anyway, this is the wish and the aspiration of every honest man loving his country.

Why are only 30 general and officers, the majority of whom can be in no way responsible, to pay? Is it in order to gratify the all-powerful democracy and to save those participants who wish to conceal their participation?

It is time to start a press campaign in connection with this sad case. Russia cannot permit the crime which is being prepared for the very near future against her best and most valorous sons, [who are also] skillful generals.

Kornilov did not attempt to destroy the regime; he aspired to change, with the assistance of the members of the Government, the latter's composition, to gather active and energetic people.

It was neither treason nor rebellion. We are not confronted here by the crime provided for under article 110 of Code of Military Penalties. It could hardly even be brought under Article 100. Let it be brought with some stretch [of the law] under Article 100. This article does not provide for trial by revolutionary court-martial.

There cannot be such a trial. The trial should be the usual one, where the presence of a prosecutor, of a judge versed in law, and of counsels for the defense would guarantee the fairness of the investigation. Then the Messrs. Filonenkos would have a different kind of job from that of removing their hats before Kornilov's grave (*Russkoe Slovo*, September 10, No. 207, p. 3); then they would be compelled to sit beside General Kornilov.

Members of the Central Committee of the Officers' Union who did not participate at all in the action, and who addressed a proclamation to the officer members of the union only after General Kornilov's proclamation of August 27, are being prosecuted. Why are they being kept under guard? Why are they also under the threat of revolutionary court-martial?

General Denikin and others, who are at the mercy of Iordanskii and of the Southwestern Front's front committee are guilty (1) of expressing by telegram their solidarity with General Kornilov's ideas, (2) of distributing General Kornilov's proclamations. Let the jurists decide under which articles these generals could be accused; let them state aloud their authoritative opinion: (a) Can these eight people be tried separately from General Kornilov, and by iniquitous and hasty judgment? (b) Are the Commissar of the Southwestern Front and the Commander in Chief competent in the matter of prosecuting those secondary participants, while the main participants are being prosecuted by order of the Government?

. . .

I have yet another favor to ask you. I do not know the addresses of Mr. Vyshnegradskii, Mr. Putilov, and others. The families of those detained are being reduced to starvation. In order to save them, it is necessary to collect and to hand over to the Officers' Union Committee up to 300,000 rubles. I urgently request these men to come to their help. They cannot leave to their fate the families of those to whom they were linked by a common ideal and a common endeavor. I earnestly request you to take upon yourself this task, and to advise me of the results. We, officers, are more than interested in the matter.

It should be said that if the honest press does not immediately start an energetic investigation of the case, then in five to seven days our politicians will bring the case to the revolutionary court-martial, in order to hide the truth and conceal the true circumstances of this case. Then General Kornilov would be compelled to give before the court a broad picture of the whole preparation, of all his negotiations with individuals and groups, of their participation [in the action], so as to show to the Russian people with whom he was proceeding, what were the true purposes which he pursued, and how he, abandoned by everybody in a moment of hardship, had to appear with a small group of officers at a hasty trial, in order to meet this fate for his perishing homeland.

Here is the substance of my prayer to you.

Yours truly,

MIKH. ALEKSEEV

My address is: Smolensk, Verkhne-Piatnitskaia, Pastukhov's house.

1301. MEMBERS OF THE NATIVE DIVISION DENY KNOWINGLY PARTICIPATING IN THE REVOLT AND PLEDGE SUPPORT TO THE GOVERNMENT AND THE SOVIET

[*Izvestiia*, No. 160, September 2, 1917, p. 3. See also Kerensky's statement in *Rech'*, No. 207, September 3, 1917, p. 4, attesting to the loyalty of the troops of the 3rd Cavalry Corps.]

On September 1, several dozen officers, horsemen, and soldiers representing the Savage Division came to the Smol'nyi Institute. The delegation was received by members of the Executive Committee. In his welcoming speech, Comrade Tseretelli said that the revolutionary democracy had not for a minute doubted the loyalty of the Caucasians and their devotion to the revolution. At the same time, Comrade Tseretelli welcomed the delegation as countrymen from the distant freedom-loving Caucasus.

The representative of the Committee of the Caucasian Corps welcomed the central organ of the revolutionary democracy and read the following resolution:

"Having arrived in Petrograd to report on the situation of the corps to the Supreme Commander, the delegates of the Corps Committee of the Native Corps, which is composed of both natives and Russians, considered it their duty to come to the Central Soviet of Workers' and Soldiers' Deputies, whose voice is heeded not only in all of Russia but in the whole world. The freedom-loving Caucasians hope that the Soviet of Workers' and Soldiers' Deputies will be able to lead Russia out of the difficult position, defending our native land against the formidable enemy, which brings destruction to it and destruction of all the gains achieved by the revolution. We believe that you will do your utmost to create a really free country out of Russia, where even the smallest minorities, such as the mountain tribes of Caucasia, will be able to enjoy the blessings of this freedom.

"We declare that we are in complete solidarity with the political platform of the Soviet of Workers', Soldiers', and Peasants' Deputies.

"We thank you for your brotherly attention, which was expressed in your sending delegate Dobranitskii,[30] who so eloquently drew us a picture of the general political situation.

For this—thank you once again from the sons of the Caucasus.

"Long live the Soviet of Workers' and Soldiers' Deputies. Hurrah."

At the same time, the representative of the Committee of the Corps declared that the whole corps demands the strictest investigation of all the circumstances surrounding the revolt and the prosecution by a revolutionary court of all the conspirators who encroached upon the revolution.

. . .

1302. EDITORIAL IN *Rech'*
[Entitled "One Month After," No. 237, October 8, 1917, p. 2.]

As new documents disclosing facts relating to General Kornilov's undertaking appeared in the press, the ideas created about this tragic event through the communications and the actions of the Provisional Government, on the one hand, and those of the organs of the revolutionary democracy, on the other, must be considered destroyed at their very foundations. It is now impossible to deny that the simplified notion of rebellion and counterrevolution conveyed to the country by the first night telegram of the Provisional Government (according to a statement by General Alekseev, its author, as could be supposed, was N. V. Nekrasov) in no manner corresponds to the complexity of the circumstances which had preceded the action of General Kornilov. Already the first official communication sent by telegraph throughout the world on August 28 was in sharp contradiction with the negotiations regarding the cavalry corps and the reshuffle of the Government, and with all those circumstances which could not be unknown in the Winter Palace when V. N. L'vov was presenting his ill-fated ultimatum.

. . .

In the light of the documents published, it is already possible to appreciate objectively the attitude taken during the Kornilov days by the members of the Party of the People's Freedom and by *Rech'*, an attitude which provoked unheard-of attacks on the Kadets. These attacks constituted almost the whole of the revolutionary democracy's political platform and paralyzed attempts to form a coalition government. Only now has it been liquidated, although not completely, through the creation of the preparliament.

[30] Sent by the Soviet to Viritsa on the outskirts of Petrograd to explain to the Division the purpose of the expedition of Krimov and dissuade it from advancing.

What did the crimes of the K.D.'s and of *Rech'* consist of during the days of Kornilov? What was the basis of the assumption that the K.D.'s were participating in the counterrevolutionary action?

In the first official communication so thoughtlessly cast to the excited masses, General Kornilov was declared a counterrevolutionary, attempting to deprive the citizens of the rights gained by the revolution. This accusation was the point of departure of all the actions by both the Government and the revolutionary democracy. The fight against the counterrevolutionary "Kornilovshchina," sanctioned by the Government, proved to be healing water for a declining bolshevism. It increased its strength with the masses, brought it to victory within the Soviets, and pushed it to the first rank of political life. For the sake of defending the revolution against Kornilov, indulgences were handed to manifestly antigovernmental groups, which made wide use of them. . . . The struggle against the "Kornilovshchina" played the role of oil poured into the flame of bitterness and hatred against the officer corp. . . .

Such were the consequences of hastily proclaiming that General Kornilov was not only a rebel but also the leader of the counterrevolution.

Even prior to these horrors the members of the Party of the People's Freedom and *Rech'* had the courage to warn against undue haste in declaring the Supreme Commander of the Russian army a counterrevolutionary. . . .

The Kadets did insist upon a cautious evaluation of Kornilov's undertaking: they made of it a logical issue and submitted the supposition that the conspiracy was but a "fatal misunderstanding" which would do the country more harm than a real conspiracy. The members of the Party of the People's Freedom and General Alekseev made every effort to forestall the civil war by peaceful means, without coming to blows, and at the same time to not give to the anarchic group new materials for [promoting] chaos and the decomposition of the army. . . .

The efforts of the K.D.'s were not successful, and even then we considered ourselves entitled to say that the "haughty" attitude of the Government, which did not desire to negotiate with the rebels but had actually capitulated to the political organizations, would cost Russia too much.

. . .

How should the attitude of the K.D.'s be judged now, only a month later . . .

Not only the notes of Kornilov and Filonenko or the talks of Savinkov (these declarations may be suspected of onesidedness and partiality), but also the incontrovertible telegrams and the testimony of such authoritative witnesses as Prince Trubetskoi and General Alekseev have established beyond all doubt that at no moment did General Kornilov undertake or plot anything against the conquests of the revolution. . . .

And what about the existence of a supposed "misunderstanding" to be first of all dissolved and cleared up at all costs?

Now it is not a supposition, but a truth, which no one can dispute. For also after General Kornilov had been declared an enemy of the conquests of the revolution, the Supreme Commander was convinced that Kerensky and Savinkov were coming to Stavka for a definite agreement.

The documents clearly show that on August 28 General Kornilov was deeply convinced that he was acting in full agreement with the Government. As one reads the dramatic description of Prince Trubetskoi of how happy General

Kornilov was after his conversation of Saturday night by Hughes [apparatus], which took place after L'vov's ultimatum, that an agreement had been reached with the Government, one begins to believe in the historical fate which hangs over the country and creates the possibility of such "misunderstandings."

. . .

After one month, the attitude of the K.D.'s and of *Rech'* in the days of Kornilov requires neither justification nor explanation.

1303. EDITORIAL IN *Delo Naroda*
[No. 141, August 30, 1917, p. 1.]

For two days menacing bloody clouds hung over Russia. For two days hearts filled with anger and indignation were beating with anxiety over a possible treacherous assault upon the revolution.

For two days the revolutionary democracy gathered its strength in order to face the brazen enemy who dared to raise his criminal hand against the gains of the Russian people.

But at last a ray of light cut through the black clouds, the fluttering hearts can beat more calmly. The revolutionary democracy said: we are ready to accept the challenge of a battle we did not initiate.

But all this does not yet solve the burning and acute question of the Russian revolution, [the question raised] from the day of its blessed birth. The dissatisfaction with the tried combinations in the Government has not been put aside and cannot be put aside. Doubts continue to disturb the mind. The problem of a government capable of satisfying the creators and heroes of the revolution is again raised point-blank, and more acutely and earnestly than ever before. Not for a moment should we forget this. We must consider this wisely, with insight and due consideration for the immediate political consequences.

Without deciding ahead of time on the character and personnel of the Government, we think it our duty to state quite definitely and irrefutably only one thing: in order to save both our motherland and the revolution, to forestall audacious attempts similar to that of Kornilov, to consolidate the gains of the revolution and realize the social possibilities inherent in it, the Government must depend now upon the mighty revolutionary democracy, inexhaustible in its strength. It must place full confidence in the latter. This, it would seem, should become a political axiom of our days. And everyone who wishes no further shakeups, who truly wants to lead Russia to the Constituent Assembly and put it at last on the road of creative aspirations and genuinely constructive work, is obliged to learn this axiom well.

That is why it is with a feeling of sincere amazement that we read in the newspapers the information that Russia, weary and craving for some normal life, is to be presented with a "directory," composed of Kerensky-Nekrasov-Tereshchenko-Kishkin-Alekseev!

And why exactly a "directory"? On the basis of what pseudo-historic associations? Not really because the great French people some time ago had a "Directory"?

And if it is to be just this and nothing else, then what justifies its composition, planned by someone, perhaps by the press imagination of the newspaper reporters?

Or is the replacement of Avksent'ev, Chernov, and Skobelev by Kishkin and Alekseev that cure-all panacea with which they hope to heal the wounds of the Russian revolution and pacify the hearts of the revolutionary democracy?

No! Enough experiments! And particularly if they are more dangerous than the previous ones.

We are living in too grave and crucial times for such venturesome experiments.

1304. EDITORIAL IN *Rabochaia Gazeta*
[No. 148, August 31, 1917, p. 1.]

Kornilov's plot may be regarded as almost disposed of. The charred logs of the fire are still smoldering. But there is no longer any doubt that this time, at least, the insurrection against the revolution has been suppressed.

We must realize the causes that nourish counterrevolutionary moods and intrigues.

One such cause is the narrowing of the base—the foundation of the revolution. At first the revolution was nation-wide. However, one layer of the bourgeoisie after another gradually withdrew from it. The mood of the broad masses of the population also began to change. Our people have a short memory, and much too soon, under the influence of privations and poverty connected with the prolonged character of the war, the food crises, and the breakdown of economic life, disillusionment in the revolution began.

The base of revolution narrowed. This was expressed in the instability of the revolutionary government, in endless crises of authority, in the indecision, waverings, and instability of governmental policy. And crises of authority in their turn shatter the fragile foundations of the edifice of democratic Russia, just in the process of construction.

. . .

That is why invariably after each crisis of authority, after each such attempt to seize power, the eyes of the entire democracy turned to one bright spot—the Constituent Assembly—as an indisputable, sovereign organ of the people's will.

The convening of the Constituent Assembly should not be delayed a single day. This is clear. But what to do now? What to do in the remaining two months and more before elections, lest the convening of the Constituent Assembly again become an unfulfilled dream?

A more stable and durable foundation should be placed under the Government. But democracy itself must first be consolidated.

The events of July 3–5 disrupted the unified revolutionary front and brought confusion in the ranks of democracy. Following this the influence of the Soviets as organs unifying democracy unalterably declined—on the one hand, as the revolutionary mood in the country receded and, on the other, as one function after another was transferred from the Soviets to the organs of local self-government, professional unions, cooperatives, and organs of central authority. It seemed that the Soviets ceased to be the embodiment of democratic Russia. The democracy broke up into separate elements unrelated to each other, with mutual estrangement and misunderstanding growing among them.

This constituted the greatest danger to the revolution. That is why, while the Bolsheviks stubbornly led the way toward the dissolution of democracy, toward the political isolation of the proletariat in the country, we began a long time ago to sound the alarm and to call for the consolidation of all the heterogeneous elements of democracy.

The idea of convoking, prior to the Constituent Assembly, a permanent conference of all democratic organizations and organs of self-government is of tremendous political significance under present conditions. By consolidating democracy, such a conference will provide the revolutionary authority with a dependable support for a vigorous democratic policy and the suppression of counterrevolutionary intrigues. It will be able, to some extent at least, to weaken the waverings of authority and exert a stronger, or perhaps a determining influence upon its policy. Finally, such a permanent democratic conference, which no doubt will enjoy great prestige in the country and army, will help us avoid the repetition in our country of the Commune of Paris, the inevitable result of the political isolation of the proletariat.[31]

Following the suppression of the Kornilov conspiracy, the authority of the Central Executive Committee of the S. of W., S., and P.D. has noticeably increased. It proved to be a loyal guardian of the revolution. As during the first days of the revolution, the forces of democracy began to gather around it in military formation.

The Central Executive Committee should take advantage of this moment in order to consolidate the broken forces of Russian democracy, to reinforce, to use the words of Tseretelli, the unsteady scaffolding around the edifice of the Russian Republic which is being erected.

1305. *Izvestiia*'s CONCLUSIONS ON THE KORNILOV AFFAIR
[No. 158, August 31, 1917, p. 1.]

. . .

First of all, it is necessary to conduct the most rigorous and thorough legal investigations of the Kornilov plot, and exemplary punishment must be applied to all the instigators and conscious participators in it. The criminals from the supreme command who did not stop at [implementing] the most severe repressive measures—including the death penalty—against soldiers guilty of a breach of discipline must not count on any leniency for themselves.

. . .

. . . If there have been reports in the past that the whole picture of panic and desertion among our forces was to a large extent fabricated and exaggerated, then it is legitimate now to raise the question: Were not the very panic and desertion to a certain degree the result of the criminal orders of General Kornilov and his aides? Did these not enter their calculations in preparation for the treason planned long in advance? A rigorous and dispassionate inquest should furnish the answer to this question.

These conclusions refer to the liquidation of the past. In regard to the future, one must say to oneself: It is the duty of the Government to do everything possible to fill the highest offices with persons who instill confidence in the revolution, persons who have not been compromised either by participating in, or flirting with,

---

[31] See Chaps. 29 and 30 on the Democratic Conference and the Provisional Council of the Republic.

the revolt. And it must do everything possible to place the activities of these persons in conditions which exclude the possibility of [their] abusing the enormous authority given to them for the defense of the native land in the interests of dark, counterrevolutionary aims.

But what is true for the commanding staff holds true also for the Government itself. It must absorb representatives of all the vital forces of the country, but there must be no place in it for representatives of parties who have stigmatized themselves by their equivocal attitude toward the counterrevolutionary conspiracy. There is no place in the Government for members of the K.D. Party, after it had been paving the way politically for the success of the Kornilov plot and had come out in the role of Kornilov's defender and parliamentarian in the most dangerous moments for our native land and the revolution.

Only the Government which is clearly and consistently revolutionary in both its program and policy is capable of instilling the necessary confidence into the democratic masses. And recent events have demonstrated once again that only these masses are capable of safeguarding the gains of the revolution and defending the country against the external foe.

1306. *Novaia Zhizn'* on Kerensky's Role in the Revolt
[No. 139, September 28, 1917, p. 1.]

. . .

We are not familiar with the data at the disposal of Shablovskii's Committee on Inquiry. But judging from the fragmentary news that finds its way into the press and the speech delivered by the Minister-President at the Democratic Conference,[32] we must say that Kornilov's case does really contain much that is not clear. Could the inquiry, however, *under existing conditions*, overcome this lack of clarity? Could it illuminate the crime to the end in order to bring it honestly before the public court? We assert that, irrespective of the insight revealed by the representatives of the Central Executive Committee invited to participate in the commission, under the circumstances, this problem remains unsolved.

It may be regarded as well established that the testimonies of the chief accused, Kornilov and L'vov, and thus far the main witnesses, Savinkov and Filonenko, unavoidably lead to A. F. Kerensky himself. All threads of the case lead to the personality of the head of the Government. Of course the possibility is not excluded that the accomplices of the August crime falsely accuse the Minister-President and blame him for intolerable orders and actions. But we can be sure of it and make others believe it only after the case is investigated without any psychological obstacles.

. . .

The situation is complicated by the fact that Kerensky's speech contains admissions on some points which need further investigation. This speech delivered in such an injured and indignant tone could not contribute to the clarification of the actual state of the case. And the inquiry would lose little if the Minister-President had devoted his speech to the political questions on the agenda. Nevertheless A. F. Kerensky had but to touch upon the subject of the conspiracy in the briefest, most angry words when it became clear that he was perhaps the only

[32] See Doc. 1355.

member of the Government (not counting, of course, Savinkov) who was warned of it long before the explosion. It is established also that it was at his command that part of the fighting operation of the conspirators was undertaken. And the withdrawal of the troops from Petrograd? L'vov's trip? The unhampered activity of the Officers' Union at Stavka? Retaining General Lukomskii as Chief of Staff after the report of Filonenko? The appointment of Savinkov as defender of Petrograd against Kornilov? Finally, the disappearance of the entire Government on the fatal night of August 27, when the entire cabinet, as testified by Zarudnyi, absolutely without any cause melted like the snowmaiden?

This and a number of other more concrete questions the investigating authorities should have been under obligation to raise with all insistence were they not addressed directly to the head of the Government.

· · ·

Objection could be raised against us to the effect that there is no need to hurry with the Kornilov case in general. We can take our time. Perhaps . . . But at any rate it is either—or.

Either A. F. Kerensky remains at the head of the Government.

Or the case of Kornilov will be treated with clarity and dignity.

CHAPTER 28

Military and Civil Demoralization

THE ARMY AND NAVY

1307. ORDER TO THE ARMY AND THE FLEET
[*VVP*, No. 145, September 3, 1917, p. 3.]

As a result of General Kornilov's revolt, normal life in the army is completely disrupted.

For the restoration of order I command:

1. The cessation of all political struggle among the troops and the direction of all efforts upon our fighting strength, upon which alone the salvation of the country depends.

2. All troop organizations and commissars to function in a correct manner, free from political intolerance and suspicion and from any interference in the combat and operative work of the commanding personnel.

3. The restoration of unobstructed transport of military units in accordance with the assignments of the commanding personnel.

4. The cessation immediately of arrests of superiors, inasmuch as the right to such action belongs exclusively to investigative authorities, prosecutors, and the Extraordinary Investigating Commission, organized by me, which has already begun its work.

5. The cessation altogether of the replacement and dismissal of commanders from their posts, inasmuch as this right belongs only to the authorized organs of authority and is by no means within the competency of committee organizations.

6. The discontinuation immediately of the arbitrary formation of detachments under the pretext of combating counterrevolutionary action.

7. The immediate relinquishment of control of communication apparatus by troop organizations.

The army, which has expressed, in these trying troubled days, complete confidence in the Provisional Government and in me as Minister-President responsible for the future of the motherland, must understand that the preservation of the country lies in proper organization, in sustaining complete order and discipline, and in unity among all.

To these ends, invested with the confidence of the army, I appeal to all of you.

Let the conscience of each awaken and prompt each one to do his great duty for the motherland in this dark hour when her fate is being decided.

As the Supreme Commander, I demand of all the commanders, commissars, and troop organizations an unrelenting execution of the above order, and I warn you that evasion or refusal to execute my orders will be suppressed at the very outset with all the force of authority, and the guilty ones will receive severe punishments.

A. KERENSKY, Supreme Commander
ALEKSEEV, Chief of Staff, General of Infantry

1308. An Appeal for Order from the Central Executive Committee of the Soviets of Workers' and Soldiers' Deputies

[*Izvestiia*, No. 161, September 3, 1917, p. 1.]

Comrade Soldiers!

Your hearts are filled with wrath and fury, with grief and fear at the criminal betrayal of the traitor Kornilov and his accomplices.

With wrath and fury at the deceit by which the traitors almost involved you in a fratricidal civil war.

With grief and fear for the fate of the Russian revolution, for our whole country.

In the face of the enemy, the counterrevolutionary traitors led the forces of our native land against revolutionary Petrograd.

They marched in front of the echelons with the secret hope that they would succeed in stifling freedom with the hands of revolutionary soldiers.

Our hearts beat in unison with yours. But we now appeal to you for reason and will power. These words of authority are directed at you. We request, we urge, we order you.

Soldiers of the Russian revolution. Control your wrath. Let there be no reprisals or lynchings of officers. The vast majority of them are our comrades of the revolution. The counterrevolutionary enemy, mocking at you with malicious joy, will try to incite you against your friends, against our mutual comrades—the revolutionary officers. Innocent blood may flow in an unlawful, arbitrary reprisal, to the delight of the enemies of the revolution and to the advantage of the German General Staff. Your representatives are keeping a vigilant eye on developments to ensure that just punishment is administered to the traitors.

Each one of the traitors—from generals down to soldiers—will answer in court for the revolt against the power that was established by the revolution.

The revolution is punishing the traitors, but the interests of the revolution demand that the punishment of the guilty be by a public trial.

In the interest of the revolution, refrain from lynchings.

Use self-restraint, soldiers!

Put an end to lynchings!

Central Executive Committee of the Soviets of Workers' and Soldiers' Deputies

1309. Violence in Vyborg

[*Izvestiia*, No. 160, September 2, 1917, p. 5. See also Doc. 1277.]

The Temporary Military Committee [of the Soviet] received reports on the events in Vyborg. The picture of the lynching was terrible. At first three generals and a colonel, who were arrested earlier by the joint Executive Committee of the Soviet of Soldiers' and Workers' Deputies and the army committee of the 42nd Corps on charges of supporting Kornilov, were dragged out of the guardhouse by the crowd, thrown off the bridge, and killed in the water. This was immediately followed by lynchings in the regiments: commanders and some other officers were led out of the regiments and, after being beaten up, were thrown into the water and beaten [to death]; a total of approximately 15 officers were killed; the exact number is still not established, since some of the officers fled from the units. The killing continued until night. At the present time, there is no disruption of order in the town, but the mood of the soldiers arouses apprehension of a possible repetition of the excesses. Regular and mounted patrols [guard] the town. The use of force would undoubtedly provoke the gravest consequences, since the mere rumor of the possibility of calling out the Cossacks aroused extreme agitation among the soldiers. The local Soviet of Workers' and Soldiers' Deputies and representatives of the Central Executive Committee formed a Joint Court of Inquiry, which has already begun to function. Local workers, without distinction as to their party affiliations, attempted to prevent the excesses. With a view to establishing order and acquainting the soldiers with current events, meetings are being organized at which resolutions are adopted on the inadmissibility of lynchings and the [necessity of] combating them.

1310. "The Alarm Must Be Sounded"

[Editorial in *Rabochaia Gazeta*, No. 158, September 12, 1917, p. 1.]

It is hard to write about this . . . But it is impossible to be silent.

Things are not well in the garrisons stationed in Finland and particularly in the Baltic Fleet.

The blush of burning shame has not yet left our face for the executions without trial on *Petropavlovsk* and in Vyborg, which were a disgrace to the revolution. And again clouds are gathering, and again we live in unbearable anxiety for tomorrow.

As reported by the delegates of the C.I.C. who have returned from Finland, a tense atmosphere reigns in the Finnish garrisons and particularly on the ships of the Baltic Fleet. It threatens to explode any minute into a new tragedy before which the horrors of recent days will pale. An undercurrent of discontent continues among the sailors. They do not conceal their hostile feelings toward the officers. There are rumors of "Yeremeev night." There is something frightening in this peculiar translation into Russian of the Saint Bartholomew's Night, which tale—God only knows how—has penetrated the dark masses.

The alarm must be sounded. Hard by, hundreds of revolutionary officers live in fear of "Yeremeev night," of butchery by those who, together with them, are destined to engrave in blood their loyalty to the motherland and the revolution.

When the returned delegates were reporting to the Bureau of the C.I.C. the moral anguish of the officers, particularly during trials, a comrade sitting next to me quietly exclaimed: "But this is the way those condemned to die lived awaiting execution!"

Yes, condemned to death . . . doubly condemned to death! . . . Revolutionaries condemned to death awaited execution by their enemies, by the hangman of freedom. Officers condemned to death live from day to day under the oppressive expectation of execution without trial by their comrades, by the revolutionary soldiers and sailors.

Doubly condemned to death . . . Because with anguish the officers are forced to think also about the deadly combat with another, real enemy, who is preparing to take advantage of the discord in the fleet in order to penetrate into the revolutionary capital.

To lead his detachment into battle, perhaps to certain death, and to feel at the same time blind, vague, hostile distrust toward himself and to await sudden butchery—what emotions can compare with such anguish of officers, loyal to the cause of revolution?

These are the poisoned fruits of the Kornilov affair. The conspiracy of Kornilov is suppressed. But although suppressed, it continues its black deeds of disunion and destruction of the revolutionary forces.

The Kornilov affair revived once again in the soldiers and sailors an un-reasoning, dark, stupefying hatred and hostility toward the commanding per-sonnel. The Kornilov affair revived once again the painful heritage of the tsarist regime in the army, hostility and distrust toward officers—this undying echo of immemorial distrust toward the master renamed "bourgeois" now. All the in-justices of former years, dark fear of the return to the hateful past, a panicky fear of treason and counterrevolutionary intrigues from everywhere and par-ticularly from above—all this flared up after the Kornilov days with unprece-dented force. And all this is blown up, perhaps deliberately, by the dark propa-ganda of elements who strive to destroy the fighting efficiency of our fleet.

1311. MILITARY INTELLIGENCE REPORT FROM THE COMMANDER OF THE 6TH SIBERIAN CORPS AND OF THE 3RD SIBERIAN DIVISION

[Document 4, "Bylevskii Papers," ms. in the Hoover Institution on War, Revolution, and Peace. Extracts from a summary of information on army morale from September 20 to October 1, taken from the same source, are printed in James Bunyan and H. H. Fisher, *The Bolshevik Revolution, 1917–1918*, pp. 24–26. See also Doc. 1327.]

I. On the whole, the morale has worsened in almost all the divisions of the Corps, but especially in the 18th and the 3rd Siberian divisions, where there were cases of refusing and evading the carrying out of battle orders to attack, deriving from the battle task assigned to the Corps. The offensive operations undertaken for the purpose of improving an unfavorable situation, after the Corps had reached the Venden positions, were met with distrust by the soldiery, whose general opinion may be expressed by this sentence: "We gave away Riga without bloodshed, and now we are forced to move forward shedding blood." As a result of the shocks of the withdrawal, the psychological [condition] of the soldiers is unstable; every day this becomes especially obvious with the advent of darkness; the general nervous tension reaches the forward lines, and there were cases when, under the influence of this fear of darkness, companies and even larger units withdrew from the lines they had occupied during the day . . .

. . .

On the whole, propaganda on the part of some specific political parties is not noticeable; however, the internal events of the last days, showing that attempts against the Government are possible and giving rise to a deep fermentation among the soldiers, who suspect the commanding personnel of promoting counterrevolu-tion or of having counterrevolutionary leanings, have again brought into evidence trends of Bolshevik ideas and have created for them a favorable ground.

Only a definite consolidation of the Government's authority can put an end to this phenomenon.

Armed force was not used toward the 69th and 70th Siberian Rifle regiments

[which had refused to advance]. Taking into account their psychological instability, it was considered that for the time being the use of arms would be undesirable; personally I see [their behavior] not so much a manifestation of stark ill
will as the result of confusion in the minds of the soldiery, preventing them firmly
from deciding "whom are we finally to believe." All the subsequent events following closely one after the other, the withdrawal from Riga and the consequent loss
of faith in one's own military forces, the episode of General Kornilov and the
consequent loss of faith in the commanding personnel—all this represents psychological factors which are too complicated and too grave to pass without leaving
traces; they left their destructive influence on the already unstable and lately
undermined morale which has not been educated in the civic spirit of national
and soldierly duty.

II. In their conversations with the soldiers, the officer personnel, acting in the
interests of combat duty, always tried to raise in the eyes of the soldiers the prestige of General Kornilov as their Supreme Commander; now, when the Government has accused General Kornilov of treason and has started to pursue his partisans, even ordering them to be arrested as counterrevolutionaries, all the officers
who had spoken well of Kornilov have become in the eyes of the soldiers counterrevolutionaries who should be arrested. As a consequence of this circumstance,
the situation of the officer personnel has become very difficult; open hostility and
animosity are manifest on the part of the soldiers; the most insignificant event
may provoke unrest. Soldiers say among themselves that all the officers are followers of General Kornilov and partisans of the old regime, and that for this
reason they should be destroyed. Offenses and rudeness on the part of soldiers
toward the officers are an ordinary phenomenon, which I have often reported.
Under various pretexts the regimental courts do not function. The revolutionary
court functions slackly, apprehending reprisals against severe sanctions. There is
a complete lack of authority and no force that could compel the fulfillment of
service duty. Every attempt to establish order is foiled by the soldiers and their
organizations, for they fear losing the rights acquired from the revolution, which
they understand from the angle of personal comfort and lack of responsibility.
The situation is considered very serious. The possibility of an open rebellion
against the officers is not to be excluded, for the soldiery understand that by so
doing they would realize sooner their common desire of ending the war; because of
their intellectual backwardness, they do not think of consequences.

In the majority of cases the committees assist officers in matters of external
order and they adjust relations between officers and men; however, they are composed almost exclusively of soldiers and take the side of the soldiers on issues
that obviously harm the cause of the service; sometime this is done for fear of
vengeance, and sometimes because of the inability to understand and to penetrate
more deeply into the essence of the problem.

.   .   .

Propaganda by specific political parties has not been observed. There was and
continues to be agitation against General Kornilov and his followers on the part
of the Iskosol [Executive Committee of the 12th Army soldiers] acting through
its delegates and committees; this agitation inflames the passions of the crowds
and excites them against officers and high commanders.

The soldiers' committee has decided to prosecute the commander of the 9th

Regiment for an allegedly malevolent remark about the Provisional Government, while under the influence of drink.

In an unofficial decision, the officers of the 10th Regiment accuse the regimental commander of weakness and unfitness, and request his dismissal and his replacement by their own candidate.

The company commanders accuse the commander of the 11th Regiment of being offensively inattentive when evaluating their activity in combat and they condemn him for appointing Ensign Apzhel'skii as chief of N.C.O. cadres, allegedly because of former acquaintance.

The officers accuse the commander of the 12th Regiment of lack of preparedness and inability to direct the regiment during combat.

The officers consider that the commander of the first battery of the 3rd Siberian Artillery Brigade is unfit for the post he occupies and request his dismissal.

The soldiers have arrested Ensign Plinshchev of the divisional transport and Dr. Geller, allegedly for their attachment to General Kornilov; for the same reason Ensign Morozov has been dismissed from the artillery park battalion.

By its decision the regimental committee of the 9th Regiment has set the investigation by its delegate of the facts announced in my summary of August 24, which reported the flight of units of the 2nd and 43rd Siberian corps; in case the facts prove false, prosecution should be opened against me. (This information should be obtained from the Corps Headquarters.) . . .

1312. ORDER TO THE ARMY AND NAVY FROM THE PROVISIONAL GOVERNMENT
[*VVP*, No. 115, September 10, 1917, p. 1.]

To the Army and the Navy:

The Provisional Government of the Russian Republic[1] is convinced that in order to defend the Republic from all kinds of attempts against it, it should rely on an army and on a navy which are morally strong and battle-fit. The rebellion of Kornilov provoked again a burst of distrust on the part of the soldiers and sailors toward their commanding personnel, again undermining thereby the solidarity of the troops, which had started to become harmonious and which is the basis of their fighting capacity. The Provisional Government declares that the loyalty toward the Republic of the majority of the officer personnel is beyond doubt and that only a small part of the commanding personnel of the army proved that it was not worthy of the confidence which the Provisional Government had placed in it, and that therefore all those who preach a further deepening of distrust toward the commanding personnel as a whole are destroying our military might and act as criminals against the Republic by undermining that firm basis which alone can save Russia. In connection with the aforesaid, the Provisional Government declares:

1) The Provisional Government is providing for the replacement of all those commanders who, in its opinion, are incapable of leading the troops so as to repel the enemy through harmonious work tending to strengthen the republican regime in Russia.

2) The Provisional Government is providing for the replacement by new experienced officers, who are devoted to the Republic, of the whole command

[1] Russia was proclaimed a republic by Kerensky on September 1. See Doc. 1343.

personnel in Stavka, inasmuch as it was involved in the rebellion of General Kornilov.

3) The Provisional Government is removing from Stavka the troops that participated in the rebellion, replacing them with units that are absolutely loyal to the Republic.

4) The Provisional Government is prosecuting all those whose criminal intentions have become apparent during the rebellion.

5) The Provisional Government demands from the army and the navy an immediate return to normal military life on the basis of cooperation between the commanding personnel and the legally elected soldiers' and sailors' committees, providing that the commanders enjoy complete liberty [of action] in the realm of their operative activities and with regard to the drilling of the troops and of the fleets.

6) The Provisional Government demands the immediate transfer to the lawful authorities for purposes of investigation of all those arrested during the last crisis and the energetic investigation, with the participation of the representatives of the army and navy committees, of all cases, particularly abhorrent, assassination of persons who belonged to the commanding personnel.

7) Some individuals who without trial have executed their officers only on the basis of the suspicion [of involvement] in rebellious plans have been seized already and others will be seized and prosecuted. They have resurrected the old regime of arbitrariness and lawlessness for the overthrow of which the revolution took place.

The Provisional Government draws the attention of the army and the fleet to the fact that a lack of sufficient harmony from the top to the bottom, as a single whole, in the name of defending the fatherland, could render the army and navy unable to withstand a new attempt by some ambitious man to avail himself of a propitious moment and again make an attempt against the liberty of the Russian people.

A. KERENSKY, Minister-President and Supreme Commander
VERKHOVSKII, Minister of War
VERDEREVSKII, Minister of the Navy

September 9

1313. WAR MINISTER VERKHOVSKII'S REPORT TO THE CENTRAL COMMITTEE OF THE SOCIALIST REVOLUTIONARY PARTY

["Ts. K-t P.S.R. na rubezhe dvukh revoliutsii," unpublished ms. of Victor Chernov in the Hoover Institution on War, Revolution, and Peace. For excerpts from Verkhovskii's report to the Provisional Council of the Republic on October 10, see Bunyan and Fisher, pp. 35–37. For his report before the secret session of the Committees on Foreign Affairs and National Defense of the Council, which led to his resignation, see Chap. 30.]

On September 11 the Central Committee heard the information report of the Minister of War, General Verkhovskii. Not being a member of the PSR, General Verkhovskii wanted this report to testify to his high regard for the PSR and its role in establishing a new democratic-republican order and helping to strengthen the fighting efficiency of the army on the solid foundation of its democratization. General Verkhovskii gave a vivid picture of the disintegration of the army as a result of the Kornilov action, particularly in the light of the fact that on the heels of declaring Kornilov a rebel, the army received instructions from the government to continue to execute his operative orders. Nobody wanted to believe that an order in such contradiction to the preceding instruction could be true. In general, there was an increase of attacks on officers by soldiers, shootings, and throwing of grenades through the windows of officers' meetings, etc. Verkhovskii thought that the only way to keep the soldiers in the trenches would be for the government, simultaneously with its public demonstrative acts, to offer assurance that it had no intention of prolonging the war, but on the contrary was doing everything possible to bring about a democratic peace. Verkhovskii further proved that the army was too large; that it was impossible at the present time to equip and feed an army of this size; that compared with the number of actual fighting men the number of servicemen was too great, etc. All this called for a reduction of the army, while giving the army units a more militant character by radically purging the commanding personnel of all elements that aroused the complete distrust of the soldiers and by the introduction of a whole series of reforms generally. Verkhovskii did not ignore the presence in the Provisional Government of strong opposition to him and the fact that the Minister-President himself took such a vague position that Verkhovskii feared lest he be betrayed, together with his plan of reform, to this opposition. The latter, in particular, did not forgive Verkhovskii either his attempt to open military actions against the rebellious Stavka and Kornilov or his desire to establish friendly mutual work with the Soviets, including their left, Bolshevik wing when it remained within the bounds of certain moderation and loyalty.

The report had such a depressing effect in picturing the disintegration of the army that the question of "constructing a stable republican order" had to be postponed.

1314. The Resignation of Alekseev as Chief of Staff of the Supreme Commander
[*VVP*, No. 152, September 13, 1917, p. 2.]

In the awe-inspiring hour when, because of the open refusal of the former Supreme Commander, General Kornilov, to obey, the Russian army underwent great trials, General Alekseev selflessly accepted the functions of Chief of Staff of the Supreme Commander, and by his wise intervention he quickly and bloodlessly restored order and normal work in the most vital center of the army, in Stavka.

Now having accomplished this exceptionally important task, General Alekseev has asked me to relieve him of the functions of the Chief of Staff of the Supreme Commander. Yielding to this desire of General Alekseev, I requested the Provisional Government to relieve him of the functions of Chief of Staff of the Supreme Commander and to place him again at the disposal of the Provisional Government so that his experience in military matters and his knowledge may be used in future for the good of the homeland.[2]

A. KERENSKY, Supreme Commander

September 9, 1917

[2] Alekseev was replaced as Chief of Staff by Lieutenant General N. N. Dukhonin, *VVP*, No. 154, September 16, 1917, p. 4.

1315. GENERAL ALEKSEEV'S EXPLANATION OF HIS RESIGNATION
[*Rech'*, No. 215, September 13, 1917, p. 3.]

The . . . following interview with General Alekseev, [was] conducted by a correspondent of *Russkoe Slovo*, [and] received by telephone from Moscow:

Your correspondent was received by the former Chief of Staff of the Supreme Commander, General Alekseev. The General declared that his resignation was prompted by ethical considerations. In an emotional voice, he stated that he found neither the strength nor the will to remain at Stavka under the present conditions.

"The reasons for my resignation are threefold. First of all, the Kornilov affair. Even before the results of the investigation and the trial are known, General Kornilov is being treated as a rebel; I, however, think that this was a high-minded movement, deeply rooted in, and resting upon the broad masses of the population. It is said that it was a scheme of a small group of adventurers, but this is not true. Regardless of the outcome of the Kornilov affair, I can say that General Kornilov and those who have been arrested with him are not adventurers; these are people who sincerely love their country, who are passionately devoted to it. Kornilov saw that Russia was perishing from the weakness of the Government, or more precisely, from anarchy, and he demanded that there be a power so strong that it would arrest the disorganization in the army and the disintegration of the whole country. He never said: 'Give me the power,' but he said: 'Let anyone be in power as long as there is real power.' Everyone will agree with him that what we have is words, torrents of words, not power. We have people who wash their dirty linen, but there is no strong power. And what do they want to do with Kornilov? They want to create an artificial court atmosphere. His cause, as a cause that is popular and high-minded, requires a broad political interpretation, but they want to try him in a military-revolutionary court, which consists of three officers and three soldiers, individuals possessing no legal background and no broad social outlook.

"The primitive, military-revolutionary court will no doubt restrict itself to the framework of a revolt and will not view the case in any of its broader aspects. An injustice will be committed. Besides, they want to dismember the whole Kornilov case and to influence the trial of Kornilov by hurriedly convicting two subsidiary characters in the Kornilov drama. My conscience cannot accept all of this. I cannot view this calmly and I am resigning.

"The second reason is the corruption of our army. Practically speaking, in this hour of terrible danger, I can state with horror that we have no army (at these words the General's voice trembled and he shed a few tears), while the Germans are prepared, at any moment, to strike the last and most powerful blow against us. The position of the Germans is dismal. They are starving and they lack money; a separate peace is not coming off for them, and they want to make a last and desperate attempt to grip us in a vise. We are informed that they are massing their forces and are preparing to strike, probably on the Northern Front. We cannot counteract them. Our offensive near Riga,[3] [which entailed] a transfer of advanced units, is explained by the fact that the Germans have withdrawn their troops to Yakobshadt. The position of our army is irremediable.

"In Petrograd everyone is trying to give the army a discipline such as the

---

[3] In late August and early September, the Russian forces compelled the Germans to withdraw 12 to 15 versts in the Gulf of Riga area.

French, British, and German armies do not have—a new discipline based on the freedom of the individual. But all this, after all, is nothing but words and more words. They say that Kornilov wanted to introduce only the cane and the bullet as disciplinary measures. This is not true. He had a number of discerning measures which they want to implement even now. It is the situation of the army, which I am powerless to correct, that forces me to resign from the post.

"The third reason is the difficult position of the commanders. Our officers are martyrs. They are dying without a murmur, both from the bullets of the enemy and from torture [at the hands of] the soldiers. But it cannot continue like this. It is beyond my powers to do anything and I am resigning."[4]

1316. THE PROVISIONAL GOVERNMENT AND THE COSSACKS
[*Izvestiia*, No. 183, September 28, 1917, p. 2.]

Acting on the instructions of the Provisional Government, General Yudenich summoned Cossack representatives from the front and the rear to appear at a conference in the political department attached to the Ministry of War.

Representatives of the Council of the Union of Cossack Forces, [representatives] of the Cossack Section of the Soviet of Workers' and Soldiers' Deputies, and representatives of the forces attended the conference.

In his opening speech at the conference, General Yudenich declared that, in compliance with the instructions of the Provisional Government, he would like to establish, together with the Cossacks' representatives, the platform which could serve as a basis for reaching an agreement with the Cossacks, with the aim of clearing up as soon as possible all the misunderstandings that have recently occurred between the Cossacks and the organs of the Government. In this connection General Yudenich turned to the Cossack representatives with the concrete question: What are the Cossacks dissatisfied with and what do they want?

At the same time General Yudenich pointed out the necessity of clearing up as soon as possible the abnormal relations expressed in a whole series of undesirable events, such as the refusal of the Don Cossacks to dispatch their units to Khiva in compliance with an order of the Government or the unwillingness of the Don Cossack division to go to Finland in order to perform police and political duties.

The representatives of the Cossack administration on the Southwestern Front, Captain Gavrilov, gave a detailed answer to the questions raised by General Yudenich and made a note of the fact that in a difficult moment the Government always turns to the Cossacks for assistance. Once the crisis is over, however, the very same Cossacks are accused of counterrevolutionary activities and sedition. While it uses the services of the Cossacks, the Government at the same time ignores the voice of these same Cossacks.

· · ·

Continuing to elucidate the reasons for the misunderstandings between the Cossacks and the Government, Captain Gavrilov categorically emphasized the absolute inadmissibility of using the Cossacks alone for restoring order in the rear.

[4] See Doc. 1300.

"The Cossacks are either used as *gendarmes* or distributed by small units along railroads in the midst of 'an ocean of insurgent comrades,' where extreme hostility is manifested toward the Cossacks. Finally, the Cossacks are sent to put down insurgent regiments, which only provokes serious excesses."

General Yudenich pointed out that the Cossack forces are sent on dangerous missions evidently because they are considered to be reliable forces, to which Captain Gavrilov replied that this doesn't prevent the Government from accusing these reliable troops of sedition or chauvinism and, at the same time, from disregarding the elected organs of Cossack self-government.

The representative of the Orenburg forces, the Cossack elder [*voiskovoi starshina*] Protod'iakonov, gave a short résumé of the reasons for the dissatisfaction of the Cossacks: 1. The double-faced conduct of the Provisional Government with respect to the Cossacks. 2. The disregard of Cossack interests. 3. The infringement of the law manifested with respect to the Cossacks. 4. The assignment of police and political duties to the Cossacks.

Having pointed out these reasons, Protod'iakonov stressed the necessity of eliminating possible misunderstandings in the future when the following measures are carried out: 1. Respect for the organs of Cossack self-government. 2. Exemption of Cossacks from police and political duties. 3. Elimination of misunderstandings with the Don [region] as the father of all the Cossacks. 4. Independence of all the Cossack organizations. 5. A more considerate attitude toward the Council of the Union of Cossack Forces, which stands at the head of all the Cossacks. 6. A seeking of support by the Government, which the Cossacks think should be done, from all the segments of the population of the Russian republic, holding itself independent from any one class or group. 7. The increase of the number of seats designated for the Cossacks in the preparliament, if the Government sanctions this institution.

· · ·

Having heard the wishes of the Cossacks' representatives, General Yudenich promised to give a full report on this matter to the Provisional Government.

1317. COMMUNIQUÉ FROM THE SUPREME COMMANDER
[*VVP*, No. 158, September 21, 1917, p. 3.]

The July events on our Galician front followed by the breakthrough in August of our positions southeast of Riga in the region of Ikskuil'—the result of the reorganization of our army on new principles—and some events inside the country that undermined confidence in the stability of our armies arouse alarm and doubts in some quarters of the foreign press in our ability to fulfill further our obligations to the Allies. Such apprehensions of the Allied press which guard the interests of their countries are quite understandable. But they are apparently based on incomplete knowledge of the actual conditions, on a large scale, at the front. The deplorable incidents which took place in the combat life of our front and which could not be concealed by the free press, when summed up, overshadowed the tremendous work in the common cause of the Allies which our army fulfilled and continues to fulfill. More than six and a half months have elapsed since the day our revolution occurred, and our army as a whole continues to hold back the enemy forces on its front as before. Moreover, during this time these forces have not diminished, but on the contrary have increased. On June 18, when our armies took the offensive in Galicia, the number of the enemy's divisions on the Russian-Rumanian front was the same as it had been on February 27. By July 18, that is, in the very heat of fighting in eastern Galicia and Bukovina, the forces of the enemy increased along the entire front to nine and a half infantry divisions. At the present time, if we compare the enemy forces on our front with those at the beginning of the revolution, according to the data of September 12, the number of infantry divisions of the enemy is four more than on February 27. Moreover, the increase occurred chiefly in the German divisions, the number of which, compared with that of February 27, increased fifteen divisions, whereas the divisions of the Austrians and Turks diminished somewhat.[5] Irrespective of this, the artillery of the enemy during this period has also been increased to approximately 600 weapons of various caliber. The Caucasian front is not taken into consideration here. The armies there continue a successful battle with the Turkish armies in the mountains under particularly unfavorable climatic conditions, while compelled at the same time to defend themselves in the rear from the hostile and militant Kurdish tribes, who continually attack our transports.

. . .

Turning now to the present battle conditions, we must point out that the calm following the Riga breakthrough gives no cause to suppose that the enemy abandoned the thought of further actions on our front. As noted above, the number of German combat units has somewhat increased by autumn. And this reinforcement the Germans will probably attempt to put to use in one area or another. Not daring to make an open appearance in the North Sea, the German fleet is at the moment holding sway in the Baltic Sea. Therefore their attempts to make a landing are very likely. Although the fall season is not favorable for navigation on the Baltic Sea, there are days that are completely quiet, calm, and still, when even the smallest vessels can travel without difficulty in any direction. The object of the actions of the German fleet may be either the shore of the Gulf of Riga or the Finnish shore. In the event of the former, it would be to the advantage of the enemy to make a landing in the rear of our troops which occupy positions near Riga and to force them to retreat from the shore. This would enable the enemy to take a position on the Gulf of Riga, lay in supplies in its ports, and make it a base for its armies moving to the north and east of Riga. In the latter case the enemy might attempt to exploit the separatists' aspirations of some Finnish circles . . .

September 20.

1318. The *Démarche* of the British, French, and Italian Ambassadors on September 26

[*Sbornik sekretnykh dokumentov*, No. 43, pp. 108–10. The three secret telegrams were sent by Tereshchenko to the Russian diplomatic representatives in Rome, Paris, and London. One was also sent to Washington, requesting Bakhmet'ev to thank Lansing for the American Ambassador's abstention from the *démarche*. The Italian Government denied any intention of interfering in Russia's internal affairs and said it desired only to give the Provisional Government a weapon to use if it wished against elements of do-

[5] See Volume II, Doc. 808n.

mestic discontent. Balfour and Ribot as much as apologized for the incident, claiming that it had been poorly timed, but reflected only the desire of their governments to help Russia. The initiative would appear to have come from the French. *Ibid.*, pp. 107, 110–13. See also Sir George Buchanan, *My Mission to Russia and Other Diplomatic Memories*, II, 191–94, for a description of the meeting of the ambassadors with Kerensky.]

A.

The French, British, and Italian Ambassadors expressed the desire to be received together by the Minister-President; they made a statement to him in which they pointed out that the recent events give cause for misgivings regarding the force of resistance of Russia and regarding the possibility of her carrying on the war; as a result, public opinion in the Allied countries may demand that their governments render an account in respect of the material aid which they had granted to Russia. In order to make it possible for the Allied governments to appease public opinion and induce it once again to have confidence [in Russia], the Provisional Government should prove by deeds its determination to use every means for the purpose of re-establishing discipline and a genuine combat spirit in the army, and should likewise provide for a normal functioning of the government apparatus, both at the front and in the rear. In conclusion, the Allied governments expressed the hope that the Provisional Government would fulfill this task, which would guarantee it the full support of the Allies.

TERESHCHENKO

B.

In his reply to the three Ambassadors the Minister-President stated that the Provisional Government would take measures in order that their action should not be interpreted by public opinion in a sense that would be liable to provoke resentment against the Allies. He pointed out that the present difficult situation of Russia was largely due to the heritage of the old regime, whose government enjoyed in its time a support and a confidence from abroad that possibly did not correspond to its merits. He also drew [their] attention to the consequences caused by the hesitations of the Allies in the matter of supplying our army with ammunition; moreover, the results of such hesitations are being felt on the front two or three months later. As for the war, A. F. Kerensky pointed out that in Russia it always had been and still was visualized as an all-national cause and that, therefore, he deemed it superfluous to dwell on the sacrifices which have been borne by the Russian people. The imperialism of the Central Powers represented the greatest danger for Russia, and the fight against it should be carried on in close contact with the Allies. Russia, who has suffered from the war more than anyone else, could not conclude it without guaranteeing her own territorial immunity and independence, and would go on with the struggle whatever the international tension would be. As for the measures tending to the re-establishment of the army's fighting capacity, the Minister-President pointed out that the problem held the whole attention of the Government and that today's trip to Stavka of his Minister of War and of the Minister of Foreign Affairs was caused precisely by the necessity of working out a program to this effect. Concluding, A. F. Kerensky noted, in connection with the collective nature of the Ambassadors' move, that Russia was still a great power.

TERESHCHENKO

C.

The collective declaration of the three Ambassadors has made a painful impression on us, on account of both its substance and the manner in which it was done. Our Allies are well aware of the exceptional . . . [efforts][6] made by the Provisional Government to re-establish the fighting capacity of the army. Neither military reverses, nor internal unrest, nor, finally, the tremendous material difficulties were able to break the unswerving determination of the Provisional Government during the last six months to carry on to the end the fight against the common foe. Under these circumstances, we are at a loss to understand what kinds of motives have induced our Allies to make the aforesaid move and what tangible results they expect to obtain by it. Please communicate the contents of the present telegram to the Minister of Foreign Affairs. Transmit to him also my earnest request not to make public the move of the Allies without consulting us beforehand, so as to avoid dangerous feelings of resentment in our public opinion.

TERESHCHENKO

1319. ORDER OF THE COMMANDER IN CHIEF OF THE ARMIES OF THE NORTHERN FRONT AND THE FLEET OF THE BALTIC SEA CONCERNING RUMORS THAT POSITIONS WILL BE ABANDONED
[*VVP*, No. 171, October 7, 1917, p. 3.]

(October 1, 1917, No. 759)

Unfounded rumors are being spread in the region of the Northern Front. They allege that on a certain day part of our soldiers will leave the trenches and return home. I do not know whether those who engage in spreading these rumors are scoundrels and traitors or simply fools and gossipers. I am certain, however, that these rumors are an insult to our revolutionary army and a base slander upon the soldiers who selflessly defend the freedom and honor of Russia and who bear with resignation the heavy deprivations in the damp and cold trenches.

The privations of our troops after the recent battles and retreat from reinforced positions are infinite. There is a shortage of shoes, coats, warm underwear. Because of slush and poor roads, there is shortage of grain in places. But if the enemies of Russia and of the revolution think that hunger and cold can break the steadfastness of our army, let them not rejoice ahead of time. Measures have already been taken to improve the food and clothing supply of the troops. And, on the other hand, the soldier knows what awaits Russia in the event of defeat. No matter how great the privations of our army, no matter how strong the desire of the soldiers for peace, there shall be no traitors in the army. Our regiments will not betray their military and revolutionary duty. I declare for all to be known: All rumors about the forthcoming abandonment of positions by the soldiers is nonsense and slander. I demand the bringing to trial of all those persons who spread these rumors and thus insult the honor of the army. I request the soldiers' committees, people in authority, and combat officers to make a report on every instance discovered by them of spreading the above rumors and to turn over the guilty ones to the court authorities. I appeal to all to give a combined rebuff to the slanderers who trample under foot the banner of our revolutionary army.

GEN. CHEREMISOV
Commander in Chief of the Northern Front

[6] Error in text.

1320. "Are We Fighting or Are We Not?"
[Editorial in *Izvestiia*, No. 187, October 3, 1917, p. 1.]

On their return from the front, Comrades Kolerov and Malevskii reported at a closed session of the Central Executive Committee on the state of the active army. They pointed out many, very many, defects in all spheres of the situation. But shortcomings can be corrected, obstacles can be overcome. And as long as there is the desire and the energy—all this is not frightening. There was something in the report, however, before which the most dogged determination involuntarily falters. With a sincere feeling of indignation, Comrade Kolerov raised the question: Are we fighting or are we not?

.   .   .

 . . . They who have fought and who are really fighting have endured and are enduring the greatest privations without a murmur; they do not run from the burst of the first shrapnel. But those replacements that have been arriving from Petrograd, they do not want to dig trenches and they run at the first firing. With the replacements come people who are not disciplined, who are not inspired by their cause. The fighting soldiers scornfully call them *shkurniki* [self-seekers]. And so the army asks: Is it really so that everyone in the rear has become a self-seeker, and where are the comrades and the citizens? Where are the loyal comrades and the citizens who are conscious of their duty?

Or are we not fighting? But then tell us how to end the war! Must we simply abandon our guns and go home . . . ? Do we open the front, do we give up Dvinsk, Revel', Petrograd?

If we are not fighting, then know how to end the war. The German Government has stated sufficiently clearly that it wants peace at the expense of Russia, that it demands of us, if not indemnities, then at least vast annexations. He who does not want to fight under these conditions any longer, he who wants such a peace, let him have the courage to say so openly. But let him not hide behind the words that in general it is necessary to conclude peace. That peace is better than war, everyone understands. The army is not asking about this. The army has all the grounds to desire peace more ardently than the rear. But the responsible revolutionary army says: If there is no peace yet, if peace has not yet been concluded and we must remain in position, then we ask you: Why do you, sitting in the rear, forget about us and why do you not support us in our deadly struggle?

The army addresses this question to the rear, to the country, to the whole Russian Republic, and, above all, to the revolutionary democracy. Do not lay the blame on the bourgeoisie, because the army is not addressing itself to it, but to you—revolutionaries and democrats; because it is not the bourgeoisie, but you—Bolsheviks, Mensheviks, and Socialist Revolutionaries—who call the soldiers comrades.

Either [there is] the loyalty of a comrade until death, or the word "comrade" is a false one.

1321. Kerensky's Order in Anticipation of Imminent German Fleet and Landing Operations in the Gulf of Riga
[*Izvestiia*, No. 186, October 1, 1917, p. 4.]

On September 29 the Supreme Commander, A. F. Kerensky, sent the following telegram to the Commander in Chief of the Northern Front:

"Tell the Baltic Fleet that the terrible hour of trials has come to it. Russia awaits its valiant performance in saving [the country], and I, as Supreme Commander, demand dauntless and concerted efforts of the entire commanding staff and the sailors of the fleet.

"The hour has come when the Baltic Fleet has the opportunity of standing up for the honor of the country and for the great precepts of freedom and the revolution and to prove that it is worthy of them.

"It is time to collect one's senses, and one must stop playing, wittingly or unwittingly, into the hands of the enemy. The men of the Kronstadt Fortress have already reached the point where, at a critical hour, not all the [forces of] defense are on the job. Let everyone remember that the native land, which will live beyond this present day, will not forgive criminal thoughtlessness or intentional betrayal. Let the atrocious crime of the *Petropavlovsk* be expiated, and let the navy, under the command of its officers whose supreme love for their native land is known to all of Russia, repel the enemy with speed.

"KERENSKY"

1322. GERMAN CAPTURE OF THE GULF OF RIGA

[Editorial in *Izvestiia*, No. 190, October 6, 1917, p. 1. The German naval control of the Gulf and occupation of its islands took place between October 1 and 6.]

As of yesterday, the entire Gulf of Riga is in the hands of the Germans. . . .

. . .

We have endured another painful defeat. This time we can acknowledge this defeat without an overly great sense of shame; our navy fought bravely and without success against an enemy that was many times stronger.[7] One of our line-of-battle ships of the old model—*Slava*—was sunk, but our main naval forces remained intact and withdrew to defend the entrance to the Gulf of Finland.

. . .

The German Government is throwing its last forces into the fight, knowing that the war will not continue for long. It is hastening in the last moment to seize as much foreign territory as possible in order to force us to make bigger concessions during peace negotiations. [The German Government] thinks that this will save it from a revolution which is threatening it from within.

Not only do our own fate and the fate of our children depend upon our steadfastness in this last period of the war, but also the fate of the revolution both in our own country and everywhere else.

We speak often about the struggle for peace.

Now this moment has arrived, not in words alone, but in terms of a real struggle. We will carry out what we have said, what we have pledged under the banners in March—in the Tauride Palace and on the Mars field, on the graves of the victims of the revolution. We will carry this out courageously, unanimously, and unquestioningly, and then we will obtain the kind of peace for which we are striving.

Let the comrade sailors, soldiers, and officers go to battle in the name of peace

[7] The excellent performance of the navy and army in this action is attested to in all the official and press accounts.

and freedom, and let the civilians make all the necessary sacrifices . . . in the name of these comrades.

1323. SPEECH OF THE MINISTER OF THE NAVY, ADMIRAL VERDEREVSKII, BEFORE THE COUNCIL OF THE REPUBLIC, OCTOBER 10

[*VVP*, No. 174, October 10, 1917, p. 2. The speeches of the Minister of War and of General Alekseev are in Bunyan and Fisher, pp. 35–37.]

Like my colleague in the Ministry, the Minister of War, I will try to give you a brief but truthful account of the condition of the Navy, of what there is about the Navy that is precious and valuable for the country, of what forces us seamen, who are the flesh and blood of this Navy, to be so painfully concerned about it. I will take the liberty of passing over the statistics describing the material condition of the Navy, because, first, this might involve too much detail, and second, because I cannot bring myself to do this at an open session. . . . I will give a detailed report before the Commission on Defense, to be elected here, on the difficulties which will undoubtedly confront our combatant Navy in the near future. It has not come up against these difficulties to date, because during the period of 1916–17 . . . the Navy, for a variety of reasons, did not have the occasion to go into action. But as soon as the serious danger of prolonged skirmishes with the enemy appears on the horizon, the question of furnishing supplies to the Navy will assume a very grave aspect, and I have no doubt in my mind that, after hearing me, the Commission on Defense will find a way of avoiding the chief difficulties. In speaking of the Navy, I will take the liberty of not using too much of your time with a description of the operations of all the fleets, for the simple reason that the chief center [of operations] at the present time is, of course, in the Baltic. . . . From the very beginning of the war, the Baltic Fleet was confronted with an extremely responsible task—to defend the approaches to the capital against a formidable and, I would say, an immeasurably powerful foe. It performed this task with the greatest sense of duty and—I am proud to say— with great skill. . . .

. . . Permit me to turn now to the central and, indeed, the crucial question for the Navy—the question of its personnel. In contrast to the Army, the naval personnel is small, and it might seem that it should have been simple to establish during the past seven months the order that is necessary for the combat strength of the Navy. In reality, this is not so simple, and I will tell you why. First of all, I consider it my duty to state that orderly conditions in the Navy and teamwork among its personnel in achieving the one and only goal [of increasing] the fighting efficiency of the Navy are so highly necessary that if this is disputed for one reason or another . . . there will be no occasion to speak about any kind of fighting efficiency of the Navy. The rupture that occurred between the officers and sailors, just as it did between the officers and soldiers in the Army, is a much more tragic event in the Navy in terms of its consequences. One can disband a regiment and create another one in its place, but to disband the crew of a battleship which has learned its complicated mechanisms, which knows all the cells into which it is divided, which has been accustomed to handle all this mechanism under combat conditions and during operations, is not possible. There are no such cadres [to replace a crew]; they must be taught for years. Therefore, we must cherish what we have as the apple of our eye, and we must try to find ways and means of uniting the officers and sailors into one harmonious whole. In order to understand what has actually been happening in the Navy—very much has been said and written on this subject that, basically, is completely wrong—I will take the liberty of sketching the course that relations between officers and sailors have taken since the revolution. As you know, when the revolution occurred, the Navy was divided into two main groups: Revel' and Helsingfors. In Revel' there was not only no hostility toward officers during the revolution, but after the first few days—when the natural fear . . . of trusting officers disappeared in the face of the obvious fact that the officers fully deserved this trust, that they held the same views . . . as the vast majority of the crew—there came a period in Revel' which I felt I was correct in describing as a holiday period. Representative bodies of the crews were organized extremely rapidly into the Revel' Naval Committee and Ship Committees. Thanks to the activities of these elective committees and the close cooperation with them of officers and commanders, there was not a single case of excess in Revel'. Not only was there not a single case of excess in Revel', i.e., on the ships and in its institutions, but the fleet, in addition, protected the town against excesses, as much as this was within its power . . . As you know, matters took a completely different turn in Helsingsfors. I am not going to dwell on these distressing events; I am not going to speak about the reasons for them. I can say only one thing: that the basic reason for those horrors in Helsingfors was the habit of concealing the truth from the command—a habit to which we who have spent our entire military service under the old regime have become accustomed; this habit, this concealing [of the truth], was the fundamental cause of all the horrors. The various motifs that can be developed from this are another matter, but the cardinal fact remains the same. Thus, blood flowed between the commanding naval personnel . . . and the sailors in Helsingfors during the first days [of the revolution]. There was no real external reason for this bloodshed, and it brought discord between these two elements. There was no organic opposition of officers and sailors. The commissars who arrive [from Helsingfors] testify in all honesty that there are no counterrevolutionary aims or attempts on the part of naval officers, and if to this day there is still a gulf between [the officers and sailors], it is a gulf at the bottom of which lies the blood that was shed in vain. To bridge this gulf—and without this the fleet will undoubtedly perish— one cannot apply the usual methods. I maintain that the re-establishment of discipline is just as necessary in the Navy as it is in the Army, and, similarly, it cannot be established by means of threats and violence. The sense of responsibility for individual acts and crimes, although dulled in the command, is nevertheless alive, and if mutual relations between the commanding personnel and the sailors undergo a change, this sense of responsibility will revive. I am deeply convinced that those individuals who were monstrously cruel, who, in violation of all humanitarian [concepts] and [the dictates of] their conscience, caused innocent blood to flow, as was recently the case on the *Petropavlovsk*, will bear the punishment they deserve under the weight of censure from their own midst. . . . The Navy needs discipline even more, perhaps, than does the Army, because the men placed in the stokeholes, the men in the magazines—who do not know what is going on above them, who cannot participate directly in combat—these men can only fight when they are filled with great enthusiasm, and this enthusiasm can only come about when they develop equally great confidence in those who sit with them in the capacity of leaders. . . .

. . .

. . . During discussions yesterday with sailors' representatives, I pointed out that the American army is paying the utmost attention to the strictest adherence to form and punctiliousness in the giving of salutes and the mutual relations of servicemen. I also pointed out that there this discipline, this self-restraint, is undertaken voluntarily by all conscientious soldiers. And I do believe that this, actually, is the only way: one should reach an understanding with the masses on the basis of a common love for our native land, enjoining them voluntarily to assume all the burdens of military discipline, because this is dictated by the necessity of saving the country, which would otherwise be plunged into the greatest danger. Your opinion, gentlemen, members of the Council, and the public opinion in the country could be very instrumental in establishing this voluntary discipline. . . . On my part, I am adopting the following measures as soon as possible. There have been many delays, because until the present time the work of the commanding personnel and the sailors' organizations have been running up against the vagueness of the tasks before them. The first problem, therefore, is to channel the work of the committees and the organizations so as to produce the result which I have just mentioned. It stands to reason that individual cases of breach of discipline and order cannot be allowed to remain unpunished even under the conditions of voluntary discipline; otherwise there would be nothing voluntary. Therefore, it is planned to establish disciplinary courts in the Navy, just as in the Army, but, in view of the special conditions—the special conditions of the Navy —the officers, according to my bill—if it is accepted by you—will . . . be subordinated only to the personal authority of the commander. Otherwise, we will create ill feelings, because it is improper for a commander to be judged by his subordinates. By exerting my personal influence in Helsingfors, I hope that what I have stated about the central problem of relations in the Navy, about the necessity of raising the discipline, will be widely confirmed in the near future. And I am convinced that those remnants of, I would say, purely demagogic extremist methods which are still popular in some units will very soon give way to an honest, sensible, and conscientious attitude of the sailors toward their duty.

1324. SPEECH OF MARTOV IN REPLY TO THE SERVICE MINISTERS
[*Rech'*, No. 234, October 11, 1917, p. 4.]

L. Martov spoke on behalf of the Internationalists.

"We are told," he declared, "that the present state of the army is the result of the work of the revolutionary democracy. (*Voice from the right:* "Of course.") But when the revolution occurred, there already were full-fledged mass desertions and other phenomena [associated with] the loss of the stability and the organization of the army. I would like to remind General Alekseev that during his tenure as chief of our armed forces under our mutual friend, Nicholas Romanov, the Russian army experienced the practical application of the formula he is recommending here, which states that only the armies that represent a force in the rear and that are prepared to suppress a popular movement can emerge victorious. (*Noise from the right, applause from the left; cries from the right:* "Anarchy is not a popular movement.") . . . After all, it was no other than the members of the former Duma, Rodzianko and Miliukov, who, in the February Days, addressed speeches to the soldiers and officers who came to the State Duma against the will of their commanders and in defiance of their orders. This marked the beginning of the process which continued to develop with uncontrollable logic. In heated polemics, we were frequently reminded of Order No. 1, which is seen as the beginning of all our present troubles. But I will remind you that there was another order published before Order No. 1, signed by the Temporary Commandant of Petrograd—Baron Engel'hardt. This order prescribed that all armed officers must be disarmed, and that one must not stop short of execution in the event of resistance.[8] (*A cry from the left:* "They forgot!") Every politician should have understood in the February Days that there cannot be a political upheaval in the country that does not shatter the organization of the army as a whole; in place of the old organization, steeped in one principle, there should have been a quick reorganization, based completely on just the opposite principle. The revolutionary democracy's answer to this question was a concrete plan for reorganization. But since a part of society which participated, together with the democracy, in the overthrow of tsarism had, as of the second day of the revolution, placed its own private class interests above the general national interest, it aimed, first of all, to preserve the army at all costs as a weapon for the defense and protection of its own class interests. (*Cries from the right:* "Not true." *Applause from the left. Miliukov from the audience:* "You are remembering your Kienthal report.")

. . .

". . . The necessity of radical reforms has now been recognized even by the highest-ranking members of the War Department. The need for a firm policy has been recognized, but one is involuntarily filled with doubt that these reforms will be carried out and that the present Government is capable of carrying them out with enough consistency. We more than doubt this, because we cannot see how a government, based on a coalition with individuals who recognized and continue to recognize Kornilov's program, can consistently carry out democratic reforms in the army. And I am afraid that the trend in the direction of special concern over securing order in the rear might overshadow the clear, political principles which General Verkhovskii has advanced as the basis of his program! In order to make possible the work on democratizing the army, it is necessary to instill into the minds of the soldiers the assurance that they are driving back the enemy for the land which has been promised them by the revolution, that there will not be a single unnecessary day of the war. Either the Russian army will be a democratic, republican [army], or there will be no army at all, while any attempt to make a partial return to Kornilov's plan will serve to corrupt the army and undermine its combat potential."

. . .

1325. AN INCREASE IN THE ALLOWANCES OF MILITARY PERSONNEL
[*Sob. Uzak.,* I, 2, No. 2012.]

LAW OF THE PROVISIONAL GOVERNMENT

I. As of September 1, 1917, temporarily, pending revision and establishment

---

[8] Volume I, Doc. 37.

of new salary rates for all officers, physicians, military officials, and military chaplains of all units of troops, staffs, administrations, institutions, and organizations of the War Department, who receive maintenance (salary, food, and supplementary allowances) at the usual rates in all combat units, as well as in staffs, administrations, institutions, and organizations of the active army not in excess of 3,900 rubles per annum, and in other administrative offices, institutions, and organizations not in excess of 3,000 rubles per annum, there is established a grant of a special cost-of-living allowance, in addition to the maintenance received, amounting to 900 rubles per annum for bachelors and childless widowers, 1,000 rubles per year for married persons without children, and 1,200 rubles per annum for married persons and widowers with children.

. . .

IV. The allowances mentioned in sections I–III are paid monthly on the first for one month in advance; these allowances are not recoverable and are subject to no deductions.

. . .

A. KERENSKY, Minister-President
MAJOR GENERAL YAKUBOVICH, for the Minister of War

October 11, 1917

1326. THE INTRODUCTION OF STRICTER DISCIPLINARY MEASURES
[*Sob. Uzak.*, I, 2, No. 2054.]

LAW OF THE PROVISIONAL GOVERNMENT

With a view to maintaining military discipline and order among the troops on the proper level, the Provisional Government, in supplement to the existing regulations on disciplinary responsibility of military personnel, has decreed the establishment of the following:

I. In those military units and commands where disciplinary courts are prescribed, . . . if nothing is done to form such courts within a period of two weeks after the publication in the field of the present law, authority to impose disciplinary penalties shall be granted, pending the beginning of operations of the aforesaid court, individually to military commanders: the authority of the company court—to the battalion commander, or, if there is no commander in the unit or command corresponding to the battalion commander, to the company commander; the authority of the regimental court—to the regimental commander and his superior officers. The individual disciplinary authority of military commanders is exercised by them pending the beginning of operations of duly elected disciplinary courts.

II. If a disciplinary company or regimental court fails to announce its decision within 48 hours after a case of a disciplinary offense committed by a person subject to its jurisdiction has been brought to it, the aforesaid case is immediately withdrawn from the court and transferred for decision to the individual authority of the battalion commander (or, in the absence in the unit or command of an officer corresponding to the battalion commander, to the authority of the company commander), if the case was before a company court, or of the regimental commander if the case was before a regimental court.

III. Those individual military units and their subdivisions (companies, battalions, etc.) in which serious repeated or mass breaches of duty, order, and military discipline occur, in the form of refusal to obey the lawful authorities, failure to carry out battle orders, unwillingness to discharge duties, acts of violence or similar acts, are placed, in view of the overt and grave nature of the aforesaid breaches, on a special disciplinary footing by authority of the Commander of the Army (Chief Commander of the Military District) or the Commander in Chief of the armies of the Front, by agreement with the corresponding military commissars and appropriate army committees, or by authority of the Supreme Commander and War Minister. A unit or command placed on a disciplinary footing receives, in addition to its name, the term of "penal" unit and shall be deprived of the right to have elective military organizations, as a result of which all committees and disciplinary courts of this unit end their activity, and disciplinary authority is handed over to commanders on the basis indicated in paragraph 1 of the present Law.

Members of a penal unit or command, with the exception of those found by the appropriate authorities imposing the disciplinary penalty to be completely innocent of participation in the disorders that led to this penalty or drawn into them by violence and threats, are subject, regardless of criminal prosecution, to the following restrictions:

a) they may not be promoted to higher ranks or offices or nominated for decorations;

b) they may not be released on leave;

c) they receive salary and other forms of money allowance according to the rates that existed before March 1917; and

d) they receive the prisoner's food allowance . . .

The restrictions enumerated shall be withdrawn and the penal unit or command thus disciplined shall be restored to all service rights on condition of excellent conduct for not less than one month or outstanding and distinguished service in battle, by the same authority that placed the military unit on a disciplinary footing.

· · ·

A. KERENSKY, Minister-President
MAJOR GENERAL YAKUBOVICH, Assistant War Minister

October 20, 1917

1327. MILITARY INTELLIGENCE REPORT FROM STAVKA ON THE CONDITION OF THE ARMY FOR THE PERIOD OCTOBER 15–30, 1917

[Document 9, "Bylevskii Papers." See also Bunyan and Fisher, pp. 24–26 and Doc. 1311.]

The attached table [not printed] does not contain an exhaustive summary of the factual data, on the basis of which it would be possible to reach absolutely accurate conclusions regarding the real conditions of the entire active army and the degree of battle-fitness of its individual units; this is due to the fact that reports from Staffs usually note the more characteristic and vivid facts illustrating the manifestation of various negative phenomena observed in the army in connection with the events now experienced in the country and by the people.

· · ·

Also details of much interest pertaining to the positive phenomena occurring in the army and in the life of individual units are absent from these communications. This constitutes a lacuna on the manifestation in the army of a healthy spirit, which is capable of withstanding the effect of numerous disintegrating forces.

.   .   .

Furthermore, there is no doubt that reports on the morale of the army, which cannot be accurately determined until expressed in definite actions, bear the seal of a subjective estimate, for in the major part of the cases these reports are based on personal impressions.

.   .   .

There is no doubt that in a whole series of . . . violations the most important one is that of fraternization with the enemy; on the one hand, it represents the lowest point of the troops' demoralization, and, on the other, it undermines more than anything else the foundations of battle-fitness and discipline, provoking a whole series of excesses and complications.

The foregoing assertion is confirmed by facts: as the table shows, cases of fraternization are most frequently observed in the armies of the Western Front and in the Special Army, which are the least satisfactory armies also in other respects and are replete with excesses of every kind.

According to reports from the Staffs, cases of fraternization have lately become more and more frequent; in certain armies (3rd, Special, 10th) they have taken the character of a mass [action]. On the Western Front fraternization has considerably increased in connection with the last action of the Bolsheviks.

For the time being, individuals or small detachments make direct contacts with the enemy soldiers and negotiate with them, buying or bartering for bread, tobacco, and, especially, wine or alcohol. In every instance the enemy soldiers furnish our soldiers with Russian proclamations published by newspapers in Germany; they hold talks regarding the purposelessness of the war for Russia, who, allegedly, acts in the interests of England.

According to reports from the commanding personnel, the great majority of the soldiers do not take part in fraternization, but the personnel is very much in favor of fraternization and eliminates with great animosity everything that hinders it. This is demonstrated by the threats of infantrymen directed against the artillery for shooting at the fraternizers, by acts of violence against artillery observers for reporting from trenches to batteries acts of fraternization (152nd Regiment of the 5th Army, 690th and 3rd Turkestan Regiments of the Special Army).

The following incident occurred in the 196th Regiment (49th Division, 24th Corps, 4th Army): Fraternizing had been stopped by fire from artillery and the trenches. A delegation came to the commander of the battalion that had opened fire, demanding its cessation; the demand was rejected. During the night three bombs were thrown into the bunker of this commander; luckily they caused no damage.

The reports from all the Staffs note that the fight against fraternization by means of convincing or persuading on the part of the commanding personnel, the committees, or the commissar brings no result; thus far the only sure method has been to shoot at the fraternizers. There is no doubt that as fraternization develops, the use of arms will become more and more difficult, and thus this last means of counteracting this evil will gradually decrease.

Owing to lack of detailed data, it is impossible to establish the causes by virtue of which fraternizing takes the form of a mass [action] in some armies, while being less frequent or even absent in others.

In this connection serious attention should be paid to the report of the commander of the 1st Grenadier Corps (2nd Army), according to which those units of the corps which took part in combat action were emphatically opposed to fraternization and adopted an attitude of hostility and scorn toward those who fraternized. It is but natural that active operations against the enemy, when one is forced to look upon him as upon a real foe, exclude the possibility of fraternizing.

Perhaps precisely this fact should explain the almost complete absence of fraternizing on the Northern Front, where the memories of recent combats are still fresh in mind.

Unfortunately, the reports of the Staffs give little information with regard to the attitude of the rank and file of soldiery toward fraternization. On the other hand, the information given is most characteristic and shows that fraternization is carried on purposefully and with a definite aim: the soldiers of the 248th Infantry Regiment (38th Corps, 10th Army) declared that through fraternization they hoped to obtain an early peace, while at the meeting of the 38th Division's (5th Army) regimental, company and detachment committees a resolution was adopted to the effect that organized fraternizing was necessary because the Government was not conducting a resolute enough policy for the conclusion of an early peace.

As for the battle-fitness of the army, the testimonials from all the Staffs of all the fronts are increasingly pessimistic and gloomy.

At the present time, only the Cossack troops have preserved discipline and fighting capacity, in the full sense of these words; all the other troops can be distinguished only by a greater or lesser degree of disintegration.

In this connection it is interesting to note how battle-fitness has lowered in relation to the [various] branches of service: cavalry has preserved itself better, followed by special troops and artillery, while the infantry is in the worst condition.

According to reports from the commanding personnel, only a very small majority of infantry units carrying on their duty on the front line are satisfactory; according to the same sources, they fulfill their duties in a reluctant, slack, and weak-hearted way, with numerous violations of regulations and orders.

In the 7th, 11th, and Caucasian Armies service is maintained, although far from faultlessly, more evenly and satisfactorily than in other armies; moreover, the Caucasian Army, owing to the peculiarities of the front, finds itself in a somewhat different condition.

Owing to lack of data and information, it is impossible to establish why the aforementioned armies have been better preserved.

According to testimonials of the commanding personnel, reconnaissance, which at the present time is the only form of active combat operation, is carried out reluctantly and unsatisfactorily; in the majority of cases scouting is accomplished by volunteers, among whom there are many officers. . . .

. . .

Cases of disobedience to combat orders become ever more frequent. . . .

The majority of cases of disobedience to combat orders consist of refusals of individual units, including divisions, and of detachments to proceed to the lines for purposes of relief; cases of refusals to accomplish reconnaissance or guard duty are less frequent.

Almost all the cases recorded have many common traits; usually the pretexts given for disobeying combat orders are tiredness, poor food, defective clothing—especially defective shoes or warm clothes—reduced combat strength, and poor organization of the positions. Cases of discussion and criticism of combat orders are frequent . . .

With the exception of the 116th Division, which has been disbanded, it has proved possible to dispose of all the recorded cases of disobedience to combat orders, without recourse to arms . . .

In spite of this circumstance, each such excess always reflected very painfully on the relations between soldiers and officers, invariably aggravating and worsening them; which, in turn, led to a series of clashes and misunderstandings. This circumstance can be explained by the fact that the officers invariably opposed the wishes of the soldiery and remained true to their duty; sometimes, as it happened in the 24th Division (1st Army), they even occupied the lines alone, with their orderlies and a few volunteers.

In many cases the success of the committees in the matter of persuading units that intended to disobey was obtained at the cost of losing their authority with the soldiery, or even of provoking the hostility of the latter; for the soldiery had ceased to see in the committees the protectors of their interests.

. . .

Refusals of units to undergo training and to build works are gradually acquiring in the majority of the armies the character of a general [phenomenon] with which, apparently, it is becoming impossible to cope.

. . .

Without dwelling on the description of individual excesses, which usually manifest themselves in a most wild and coarse manner, it should be noted that, according to their nature, all the excesses recorded by the Staffs can be divided into three basic types: 1) those caused by the demands which, in the course of accomplishing their service duties, members of the commanding personnel or officers in general had made to soldiers in connection with their aforesaid service duties; 2) those caused by the indiscriminate suspicion that all the officers and high command personnel were counterrevolutionary and by the accusation that they prolonged the war intentionally; 3) those which were the result of the more or less organized demonstrations of the soldiery and of the lower committees against the privileges enjoyed by the officers: a salary larger than that of the soldiers, better food, the fact of being lodged in separate quarters or bunkers, and of having government-paid servants.

Lately the excesses of the latter type have increased considerably in almost all the armies. Units and committees approve resolutions and decisions according to which the officers should be given soldiers' rations, the allowances of the officers and their families should be reduced to those of the soldiers, commissaries should be forbidden to issue clothing to the officers, officers should be quartered with the soldiers, and so forth.

.   .   .

According to testimonials from all the Staffs, the attitude of the soldiery toward army organizations shows their insufficient understanding of them: because of their ignorance they are unable to follow or understand the meaning of the organizational and political activities of the higher committees. On the other hand, the lower committees which are in direct contact with the soldiery, owing to the lack of preparedness of their members for public work, exert little influence and often give in to the elemental feelings of the mob; they do not guide, but are guided in their decisions by the demands of the latter.

Therefore, the soldiery, while understanding their own interests as soldiers in a most elementary way, have accustomed themselves to consider the committees as organizations called to protect their interests.

In recent summaries the fall of the committees' authority is constantly underlined; this fact is explained by the resolute fight especially of the higher army organizations against the progressive disintegration of the army, in their endeavors to counteract, in harmony with the commanding personnel, the elemental manifestations of the soldiery to work against "the interests" of the latter.

Nevertheless, outrages against members of army organizations and statements expressing lack of confidence in committees are much less frequent than toward members of the commanding personnel or officers.

According to the reports of the commanding personnel, the attitude of the soldiery toward the war is extremely negative; aspiration for peace acquires an elemental scale, as amply confirmed by the enormous success of Bolshevik slogans and ideas at the front.

The aspiration for peace is so strong that, according to reports from the commanders of the 12th, 5th, and 11th Armies, our reverses on the Northern Front were met by some units with joy, as a circumstance that might hasten [the conclusion of] peace.

The theme of numerous [resolutions] expressing lack of confidence in the Provisional Government is that the latter is not resolute enough in its policy in the matter of peace. The last report from the Staff of the Western Front, dated October 30, gives this as the reason why many units have openly taken the side of the Bolsheviks so readily and rapidly.

According to the reports of the commanding personnel, peace at all costs has lately become the slogan of the soldiery.

.   .   .

The general mood of the soldiery, as mentioned in all the summaries of the Staffs and in all the reports of the commanding personnel, is subject to certain fluctuations; while being basically directed against the war, either it is rather calm and apathetic or it becomes more active, causing numerous excesses. If one examines data reflecting a somewhat longer period, one may observe that these fluctuations possess a certain regularity and are the result of certain causes which depend on the general political situation: passivity and an attitude of expectancy may be observed during periods of a certain equilibrium between the political forces; any attempt to strengthen either the rightist or the extreme left political tendencies is an immediate stimulus, causing greater activity, and a movement, invariably favoring parties of the extreme left, is at present under way in the army.

This phenomenon was clearly manifest during the Kornilov action and may be observed now as well.

. . .

The general conclusion of the commanding personnel may be summed up in the following statements: the army disintegrates; discipline is nonexistent; the commanding personnel is deprived not only of the prestige of authority but even of elementary consideration; the influence of the committees which endeavor to restrain the soldiery is weakening, while the influence of the committees which follow the latter is harmful; in addition to the foregoing, the army is in the imminent [danger of] famine.

Also the voices of some of the commissars join in this estimate of the situation. The following conclusions, arrived at by Zhdanov, Commissar of the Western Front, on October 22, are most characteristic in this regard: "The nervous tension of the army grows day by day; violations of discipline spread to further units. Bolshevik propaganda dominates and is successful.

"Slogans are simplified by the soldiery, which draws from them destructive conclusions, without any thought as to the repercussions which [the actions] perpetrated might have on the fate of the homeland and the revolution. There are threats to quit the front if peace is not concluded in the immediate future. Criminal elements cannot be prosecuted because investigation very seldom detects those guilty. Peace at all costs and under any conditions is the problem which agitates [the minds]. The high cost of consumers' goods and of tobacco products and the reduction of bread rations cause discontent.

"Confidence toward committees is on the decline; they are not obeyed; they are chased, beaten up.

"Intimidated committees lay down their powers without awaiting new elections. Hatred against officers grows in connection with the spreading conviction that they prolong the war. The morale of the troops at the front is getting worse. The morale of the committees, officers, and commanding personnel, who are crushed by the elemental scale of violations of discipline, is [in a state of] panic. There is nothing left but to give up. Disintegration has attained its limit."

LIEUTENANT COLONEL OF THE GENERAL STAFF,
CHIEF OF THE MILITARY POLITICAL SECTION,
Administration of the Deputy Chief of Staff of
the Supreme Commander

SECOND LIEUTENANT, for the Chief of the 1st Section

INTERNAL DISORDERS[9]

1328. THE RESIGNATION OF PESHEKHONOV AND THE INCREASE IN ECONOMIC DISORGANIZATION

[*Russkiia Vedomosti*, No. 203, September 5, 1917, p. 3.]

Sooner or later life shatters utopias and exposes all the banefulness of wrong

---

[9] Reference should also be made to the appropriate sections of the chapters on the agrarian problem, industry, labor, supply, local government, and nationalities.

steps. In the agitation of recent days in connection with the tragic events we are experiencing, the resignation of A. V. Peshekhonov from the post of Minister of Food passed unnoticed. Ministers come and go, and the resignation of A. V. Peshekhonov in this time of changing department heads might also indicate nothing in particular. However, there appears now in the *Narodnoe Slovo,* an organ of the Popular-Socialist Party, an extensive and very interesting statement by A. V. Peshekhonov on the reasons for his resignation from the ministerial post, which reveal that this resignation is related to the collapse of the entire economic system.

. . .

A harmonious economic plan was in existence, useful and intended only for the welfare of the country. It was built on the need for sacrifices on the part of all classes of the population. The state authority had to make "the most resolute and adamant demands": to workers for a cut in wages, to the owning classes for special taxation on unearned income and a considerable share of their property for the needs of the state, to peasants to force them to sell grain at established moderate prices, fixed by the state, to all classes for universal labor conscription. The realization of such a plan called for a high awareness on the part of the population and a stable organization of a strong government. It called also for a community of purposes and unity of goals for the general good. . . .

Precisely the opposite was done to create a community of interests and to make the general good the guiding principle. . . .

. . .

. . . "If," writes A. V. Peshekhonov, "we continue on this course, catastrophe is inevitable." The only way out is the creation of a stable government: "Sooner or later, we shall undoubtedly have to resort to 'a strong and stable government' to force the sale of grain, inasmuch as we do not have at our disposal economic incentives to prompt the villages to sell their produce. And psychological incentives for this are insufficient."

Thus bitter reality has shattered the dreams. The tendency toward voluntary sacrifices proved to be a utopian ideal, and the Government had no sufficient means to employ compulsory measures. We are faced with a collapse of the system and the impending danger of a catastrophe. . . .

1329. EDITORIAL IN *Volia Naroda* ON THE GROWING ANARCHY
[No. 123, September 20, 1917, p. 1.]

Against the background of merciless foreign war and defeats of the armies of the Republic, internally the country has entered upon a period of anarchy and, virtually, a period of civil war.

National class animosity has flared up everywhere—in the north and in the south, in the west and in the east, in Turkestan, near Moscow, in Finland, in the Urals, in Siberia, and in the Caucasus. From words people passed to action, and the singular devastation of Russian life is further complicated by strikes, revolts, upheavals, and outright robberies.

In a few more weeks, perhaps a few days, all of Russia will be swept by the fire of dissension, mutual discord, and the complete paralysis of all life.

An open revolt flares up in Tashkent, and the Government sends armies and bullets to suppress it.

A mutiny in Orel. Armies are sent there.

In Rostov the town hall is dynamited.

In Tambovsk guberniya there are agrarian pogroms; experimental fields are destroyed, also pedigreed cattle, etc.

In Novgorod-Voynsk uezd zemstvo storehouses are looted.

Grain reserve stores in Perm' guberniya are looted.

Gangs of robbers appear on the roads in Pskov guberniya.

In the Caucasus there is slaughter in a number of places.

Along the Volga, near Kamyshin, soldiers loot trains.

In Finland the army and the fleet disassociated themselves completely from the Provisional Government.

Russia is threatened by a railway employees' strike . . .

Unbridled, merciless anarchy is growing. Any cause is used.

Events of colossal importance take place throughout the country. The Russian state collapses. Whole regions secede . . .

How much further can one go . . .

Don't the leaders of democracy really understand, or are they unwilling to understand that further tolerance is impossible; that the policy of compromises and agreements with bolshevism has already disintegrated Russia and will eventually ruin the revolution, the country, and democracy itself?

In Tashkent the soldiers, egged on by bolshevism, stage a revolt which the Provisional Government is putting down with machine guns. Through its outrages bolshevism not only caused a revolt in Tashkent, but is encouraging the seceding of the entire oblast, because the local population in its turn takes up arms.

Here too the central organ of the Russian Social Democratic Workers' Party hails in its editorial the action of the Tashkent inhabitants, approves of them and promises them support:

"We are ready to support the Tashkent Soviet," write the Bolsheviks in *Rabochii Put'*—we shall fight in the same ranks with the revolutionary S.R.'s. We shall form a united front with them."

The Bolsheviks, Social Democrats, and Socialist Revolutionaries are with the Tashkents, and with the Finns, and with the Baltic, and with the Orlovtsy. They are for everything that causes anarchy, refuses to defend the country, or is against unity.

Their front is one, and the devastation of Russia moves at a gigantic rate.

And the other part of the democracy, the one that sits in session at the Aleksandrinskii Theater—is its front united, and what does it intend to do?

Does it seriously imagine that it is impossible to support the Provisional Government, to protest against the machine guns and troops sent into Turkestan, and to continue to seek compromises with the instigators of the Tashkent revolt?

Or perhaps it thinks that it is possible to condemn the conduct of the Finnish garrisons and seek an agreement with the Bolsheviks?

That it is possible to argue until exhaustion about the preparliament with those who sow discord and hostility throughout the Republic, who repudiate at bottom what it asserts, who will fashion a toy of the garrison from the preparliament as well as from the future government? . . .

No, these two currents are as incompatible as fire and water. And somebody must surrender.

1330. EDITORIAL IN *Russkiia Vedomosti* ON THE INCREASE IN DISORDER
[No. 214, September 20, 1917, p. 3.]

A great wave of disorders has spread throughout Russia. Kiev, Bakhmut, Orel', Tambov, Kozlov, Ufa, Tashkent, west and east, the center and the borderlands, by turns or simultaneously become the arena of pogroms and all sorts of disorders. In some places the disorders arise on the ground of food difficulties, in others it is spurred by the raid of a soldier mob on a wine store, in still others no one is able to answer the question why the disorders occurred. A city leads, it seems, a peaceful life. But suddenly a mob pours out into the street, begins to break up stores, to commit acts of violence on individuals, to subject representatives of the administration to lynching even if they are elected. The spontaneity and senselessness of the pogroms attract particular attention, and these peculiarities of the disorders more than anything else make the struggle against them difficult. To convince, to appeal to reason and conscience . . . , but it is precisely reason that is absent here, and conscience is sound asleep. To resort to measures of repression, to armed assistance . . . but it is precisely this armed force, represented by the soldiers of the local garrison, that plays the chief role in the pogroms. In the end, of course, the disorders are put down in one way or another, but only to cease in one city and break out immediately in another. Only two weeks ago the new War Minister spoke very reassuringly about the state of affairs in the Moscow Military District, and during these two weeks special military expeditions had to be mustered from Moscow to suppress soldiers' disorders in Orel', Tombov, and Kozlov.

The mob, in the worst sense of the word, more and more frequently pours out into the street and begins to feel itself master of the situation, acknowledging no authority but itself. . . .

.   .   .

Under the circumstances, there can, of course, be no question of the Democratic Conference leading to the formation of a strong government. Whether the Conference will favor coalition or be against it, whether the Provisional Government will approve the resolutions of the Conference, not only taking them under consideration but being guided by them, the Provisional Government will not become stronger than it has been as a result of it. And yet the weakness of the Government is felt most keenly by the Government itself, since before approving one or the other resolution, in both big and small matters, it is forced to pause and think; will the Government have strength to execute this decision. And very frequently we have to reply to such questions in the negative, because the Government is now deprived of the opportunity to insist on its decisions by forceful means. Only those who wish to, obey it, and to the extent they wish. Not only does the problem of forming a strong government remain a problem, but its solution as well is advanced into the depths of some vague and remote future.

And in the meantime events do not wait. Anarchy inside Russia is growing. The wave of senseless, spontaneous pogroms is spreading ever wider. And on our front new enemy units are appearing, transported even from France.

1331. Discussion in the Provisional Government on the Struggle Against Anarchy

[*Izvestiia*, No. 185, September 30, 1917, p. 5.]

. . .

Taking up the discussion of the struggle against anarchy, a number of telegrams from the provinces addressed to Kerensky were read. They contained urgent demands that the Government adopt immediate measures for putting down the disorders which have arisen on account of either the food question or the nationality question. The Jewish population in the former areas of the Jewish Pale, where all the commerce is concentrated in their hands and where clashes may be more frequent, is especially alarmed. Representatives of the Jewish community are very frightened by the sudden wave of anarchy, accompanied in certain places by murders. They do not restrict their petitions to telegrams and are sending their delegates to Petrograd to demand Government protection against street mobs. The Government has therefore found it necessary to draft measures which the local committees of safety could implement in the event of an outbreak of disorders. The general features of these measures involve the combined action of military and civil authorities. It has been found necessary to make extensive use of the right to introduce martial law. The Government realizes that the time has come when it is necessary to manifest firm authority and grant broad powers to the local organs of government for this purpose.

. . .

1332. The Report of the Prosecutor of the Saratov Court of Appeals to the Minister of Justice

[*Razlozhenie armii*, pp. 121–22.]

MR. MINISTER:

I deem it my duty to inform you that the city of Saratov, and the whole Saratov district in general, finds itself at the present time in a very painful situation; in all probability the situation will shortly become even worse.

The main evil against which there is no means to fight is the soldiers who at the present time are the irresponsible masters of the situation. Crimes, lynchings, arbitrary arrests and searches, all kind of requisitions—all this in the majority of cases is being carried out by soldiers alone or with their direct participation.

The guberniya authorities and public organizations are partly powerless to fight with them, partly they do not fight, evidently because they are afraid of losing their popularity in the eyes of the soldiery.

At the present time two calamities are threatening Saratov: the general searches of all the inhabitants and the resettlement in the city of the soldiers from the barracks situated beyond the city.

Having learned from the guberniya commissar that it has been decided to carry out within the new days a general search of the inhabitants of the city of Saratov, I deemed it my duty to intervene in a most emphatic way with reference to the existing laws, and I have declared that such a search would be illegal and would be prosecuted by the judicial authorities. The result of my intervention was that it has been decided to carry out the search only on the premises of trading firms and only in [the houses of] those [persons] with regard to whom there is information that they concealed goods and products for purposes of speculation. However, in spite of this, I am almost convinced that these searches will finally turn into pograms, because there we have neither forces nor means to prevent the soldiers from searching where they wish. All I could do was to arrange that in each commissariat the deputy prosecutors who will have to make the decisions concerning the lawfulness or unlawfulness of the requisitions will be on duty; however, I believe that this measure will prove to be insufficient.

On the other hand the guberniya commissar possesses neither authority nor power, and therefore, in his own words, he is not able to prevent the searches.

The matter stands similarly with regard to the resettlement of the soldiers in the city: the soldiers have declared that they would appear in the city and would occupy the apartments they liked. If they desire to do this, then I am convinced that no one will be able to prevent them.

I have informed the commander of the troops of this, but probably Saratov cannot expect any help from this side.

Matters are in no better shape in the uezd capitals and in the villages: the same demands . . . and the same complete absence of any kind of assistance to the judicial administration.

. . .

PROSECUTOR OF THE COURT OF APPEALS
September 29, 1917. No. 4617

1333. REQUEST FROM THE MINISTER OF THE INTERIOR TO THE CHIEF OF STAFF OF THE SUPREME COMMANDER FOR THE DISPATCH OF FORCES TO QUELL ANARCHICAL OUTBURSTS

[*Razlozhenie armii*, p. 137.]

I request that cavalry units be sent to the districts for the purpose of combating pogroms, confirming to the commanders of the troops the necessity of rendering assistance to the civilian authorities at their first demand by sending them detachments organized beforehand.

NIKITIN
October 1, 1917. No. 114 P. Petrograd.

Query: To the General Quartermaster

Please let me know whether you consider that such units can be spared. In any case, they should not be scattered but should be kept at the junctions of roads as mobile flying detachments.

LIEUTENANT GENERAL DUKHONIN
October 2, 1917.

1334. "THE WARFARE AGAINST POGROMS"

[Editorial in *Russkiia Vedomosti*, No. 224, October 1, 1917, p. 3.]

The wave of pogroms grows and expands to overflowing throughout Russia. Mountains of telegrams arrive daily bringing news about agrarian disorders, about city pogroms, about soldier mutinies. And only a small part of this news reaches the press. The columns of papers are unable to find space to print them in full. The Provisional Government is also snowed under with similar news. Moreover, this news in most cases is accompanied by remarks to the effect that the local administration is powerless to do anything to suppress the disorders and that it appeals for assistance from the central government. About two months ago everybody was horrified to learn of the soldiers' pogroms on the estate of Sheremetev near Mtsensk. Now such isolated reports no longer attract anyone's attention. They are drowned in a mass of similar facts. Khar'kov, Bendery, Tambov, Ostrog—all this merged into one dark picture of murders, pillages, arsons, and drunken debauches. Drunken, because almost everywhere the mob is particularly anxious to reach the liquor cellars, and on breaking into them everyone gets drunk until he loses consciousness.

The present disorders are completely devoid of any political coloring. The unbridled mob, with darkest animal instincts unleashed, loots and pillages everything that it finds at hand. It loots the *pomeshchik* estate, it loots a store, but it is just as willing to loot the zemstvo school. All objects in manorial homes arouses its hatred, but it treats treasures of culture with the same attitude of hatred and it destroys libraries and books with the same malicious joy. It strikes and kills the *pomeshchik* or shopkeeper suspected of speculation, but the same fate awaits Jews, just because they are Jews, and zemstvo employees and members of various committees elected by that same mob. These most senseless and cruel pogroms throw us far back into the depth of the age of barbarism, and shortly Russia will finally drown in this filthy wave. We must take the most resolute measures to combat the pograms. Words of admonition, appeals to reason and conscience are ineffectual here, because the brutal mob has neither reason nor conscience. It recognizes only force and submits to force only; all other means of coercion are in its eyes only testimony of the weakness of authority and consequently a guarantee to lawlessness. Sad and hard as it is to resort in a republican Russia to measures of severe, even merciless repression, this is truly a necessity, the bitter cup that cannot bypass us if we are earnestly concerned about the salvation of the State. From words, so numerous in recent times, we must finally pass on to action.

. . .

Now, when means of coercion are completely exhausted, an energetic suppression of disorders by armed force should be required of the military authorities. We must give them the necessary authority and render them proper support. And since many of the armed units, particularly those stationed in the rear, not only are incapable of combating pogroms but, on the contrary, play quite an active part in them and sometimes even a leading role, it is necessary to take steps to form special detachments for the warfare on disorders—detachments analogous to shock battalions at the front.

At any rate, we should be able to isolate from the multimillion-man Russian army a sufficient number of well-disciplined and loyal soldiers to form such detachments. These detachments need not be particularly numerous, because a violent mob, even if comprised of army soldiers, is, in the final analysis, infinitely cowardly, and a small but well-disciplined unit is sufficient to subdue it. We must make this mob aware of the return of authority; it should feel that the time of unpunished excesses has passed and that all encroachment on life and property of citizens and on the State order will be met with a proper rebuff.

Let the measures which will be employed by the military authorities be severe and even ruthless, but they must be such, because there are no other means to combat the growing anarchy and the wave of pogroms. An elementary civil order must be restored, no matter at what price. The simplest personal and property safety must be restored, for without this the State cannot exist.

1335. A Report of the Prosecutor of the Kursk District Court to the Prosecutor of the Khar'kov Court of Appeals

[*Razlozhenie armii*, pp. 122–24.]

On October 5 at about 1:00 P.M. arbitrary searches of some shops, stores, and also private apartments took place in the city of Kursk. These searches were carried out at the initiative of soldiers or persons dressed in soldiers' clothes. In the places where the searches took place, the gathering of a mob with obvious pogrom intentions could be noticed. These intentions were provoked by unknown persons who were not detained because the militia, owing to its lack of strength, could not show any real activity and because the militiamen just before that had presented to the chief of the militia a series of demands; among other things they had even declared that they would boycott him. This conflict is being examined by the municipal duma board and is not yet resolved.

In the evening of October 5 an arbitrary search was also carried out [in the house] of the member of the food board, Suprasskii, and the crowd pillaged the small reserves of flour and soap which he kept for personal use.

In connection with these circumstances, the commissar of the city of Kursk called a conference of the members of the public organizations and of the representatives of the municipal board (of new composition) and also of the military chiefs in order to take the necessary measures for the prevention of pogroms, and particularly the Jewish pogrom, which were being prepared.

At the conference it was disclosed that in the city of Kursk there is not sufficient military strength, nevertheless the majority of the members of the conference voted to request the commander of the troops of the Moscow Military District to declare the town of Kursk under martial law. However, the commander of the troops, who was driving through the town of Kursk, refused it.

It should be noted that a number of artillery ammunition dumps and a liquor storehouse are located in Kursk. This storehouse is guarded by a small sentry post of 11 men armed with revolvers and would represent in case of disorders a very great danger.

On the morning of October 6, on Kherson and Moscow Streets, crowds began to gather; in spite of small horse patrols of hussars who came from the village of Balakleia, the crowds did not disperse but increased considerably.

On Moscow Street the crowd went into the store of Voroshilin and started a search there; at the same time Second Lieutenant Palagin, chief of the militia, was compelled, at the demand of the soldiers present in the crowd, to arrest Voroshilin and his wife.

With great difficulty Palagin managed to save the Voroshilins from lynching at the hands of the crowd and to bring them into the building of the municipal militia. But later on, when the crowd of soldiers started to hinder the activity of the chief of the militia and the latter fired three shots into the air, the crowd rushed on the chief of the militia and began to beat him up. The cavalry hussar unit, which was on the spot, did not render assistance to the chief of the militia and Second Lieutenant Palagin was brought to the hospital with critical injuries. Simultaneously with the violence toward Second Lieutenant Palagin, the Voroshilins were the object of equal violence. They were severely beaten up by the mob, and in my presence, under escort of the hussars, they were also sent to the hospital.

The crowd created disorders on the premises of the militia, and at the same time money belonging to various persons was pillaged from the table of the chancellery.

I consider the situation in town extremely dangerous, pregnant with painful consequences, especially in view of the mood of the crowds, which are obviously hostile toward the Jewish population.

. . .

I would add that one of the instigators of the disorders was a man dressed in the uniform of a sailor.

N. Sysoev, Acting Prosecutor
of the Kursk District Court
October 6, 1917. No. 6318

1336. The Agrarian Movement and Anti-Jewish Agitation in Bessarabia

[*Russkiia Vedomosti*, No. 229, October 7, 1917, p. 2.]

SOROKI, Guberniya of Bessarabia. (*From our correspondent.*)

Widespread agrarian agitation is being waged in Soroki uezd, as well as in other parts of Bessarabia. One of the local agitators proposed resolutions, according to which every peasant deputy must, on return from the Congress, "personally choke to death one landlord." This same Arman declares that if they will give him two land surveyors he will solve within one week the entire agrarian question in the uezd once and for all! The agitation has created a strong agrarian movement. Lands are seized not only from the *pomeshchiki*, but from peasants as well. Resolutions are passed by the Moldavians on the eviction from the uezd of Malorussians, who bought lands from local *pomeshchiki*. Moreover, it is recommended that the Podolians return to Podolia to "their landlord" and that the long-occupied land for which the Podolians paid the bank for over one year be left for seizure by the Moldavians. As a result of all this, by the middle of September the sowing of the winter crop of wheat, the main cereal in Soroki uezd, was 40 per cent less than that of 1916. Even less [was done to prepare] the plowland.

Plunder and murder rage throughout the uezd. The authorities are powerless. The militia is unable to cope with the situation. The pogrom movement is mounting. Talk is heard of shifting all the blame to the Jews. The Soroki Municipal Duma cannot convene because the regional population refuses to put up with the fact that, of the 33 members of the Municipal Duma, 22 are Jews. Already, on one occasion, when a Jew was elected chairman, they dispersed the meeting and assaulted the members of the Duma. How rumors from the capital are interpreted by ignorant minds may be judged by the remark of one woman that things will get better now because "Kerensky having married the republic, soon a tsar will be born to them!"

1337. Circular of October 7 of the Minister of the Interior
[*Krest'ianskoe dvizhenie*, pp. 422–23.]

The ever-worsening internal situation of the country induces me to address myself to the [oblast, guberniya, and municipal] commissars with an appeal to rally all the sound elements of the population for the purpose of fighting the anarchy which is developing and which is irrepressibly driving the country to ruin. Without the active assistance of the population, the Government and its local organs are powerless to maintain order and prevent the violations which are perpetrated everywhere. In the meantime, in spite of the fact that the external enemy penetrates farther and farther into the depths of our territory and threatens further successes, in spite of the immediate danger for everyone from the wild disorders occurring in all places, the population does not [show signs of] the salutary ardour which love of the country, alarm for the country, and the instinct of self-preservation should have animated. The Government does everything in its power to prevent the growth of anarchy, but the results of its activity will be insignificant if organizations and individuals capable of realizing the seriousness of the country's situation but not their duty to rally and to work unceasingly for its salvation, remain passive. I suggest bringing this question up for discussion in all the public organizations and first of all in the organs of self-government formed on the basis of universal suffrage. Appeal to the population for their assistance in the measures taken to prevent and stop disorders; unite around you, without regard for party membership, all the local forces that have a statesman-like point of view. Relying in the first place on the organs of self-government and drawing them into the struggle against anarchy, consolidate your authority, which must have prestige among the population. If you consider that local conditions render it expedient, I suggest that you create and attach to yourselves a special committee for fighting anarchy, consisting of the representatives of the town and zemstvo self-government, of the commander of the local garrison, and the representative of the judicial authority. Take urgent measures for an adequate organization of the militia; reinforce its cadres by selected reliable men [drawn] from the servicemen now being discharged from the service or released for the purpose of reinforcing the militia, in accordance with the order issued to the commanders of the military districts by the Minister of War. Transmit this circular to the uezd commissars for execution. Communicate the results.

NIKITIN, Minister of the Interior

1338. Circular of the Central Administration of the Militia on the Violation of Religious Institutions
[*Krest'ianskoe dvizhenie*, p. 423.]

To Guberniya, Oblast, and Municipal Commissars:

The Minister of Confessions has announced that numerous reports have reached him and the Holy Synod concerning the armed attacks, ever more frequent of late, on monasteries and parish chruches, with the use, during the plunder, of the roughest kind of violence or even assassination; he notes that these facts cannot fail to create alarm and confusion among the faithful orthodox of the nation.

Therefore, the Minister of Confessions, having submitted to the Holy Synod a proposal regarding the necessity for the parish priests to appeal to the parishioners for the purpose of organizing the best possible protection of the churches and their property, at the same time has addressed a request to the Minister of the Interior that the latter should on his part take measures to safeguard the churches and especially the monasteries from the depredatory attacks and robberies [perpetrated against] them with ever-increasing frequency.

We inform you of the foregoing, and in view of the aforesaid communication from the Minister of Confessions, we consider it necessary to establish temporarily, until the present abnormal conditions come to an end, a vigilant guard of churches and monasteries and their property; militiamen should watch incessantly, especially at night, the goings on near the monasteries and the churches; they should make rounds and inspections as frequently as possible and ascertain each time the good condition of locks, doors, and windows; they should apply all their efforts, experience, and endeavor to effectively safeguard the temples and their property from plunder and destruction.

At the same time . . . make it obligatory for the rural communities to maintain guards for the protection of the local churches and monasteries and, in view of the exceptional circumstances occurring in the country, ask for assistance in this matter from the local public organizations.

> C. Sidamon-Eristov, for the Minister of the Interior
> S. Balavinskii, for the Chief of the Central Administration
> E. Simonovich, Witness

[October 7, 1917]

1339. Order of the Minister of War on Measures to Protect Public Safety and Property
[*Krest'ianskoe dvizhenie*, pp. 425–27.]

V[ery] urgent

To Guberniya, Municipal, and Oblast Commissars:

The Minister of War on October 11 issued Order No. 51, whose content is as follows:

"One of the tasks entrusted to the army at the present time is that of securing persons within the country from violence and of preserving real individual freedom.

"The militia now existing is not in a position to guarantee this foremost preoccupation of the State. The army has the duty to come to the assisance of the Government commissars and the town and zemstvo organizations with all its means and all its experience.

"The anarchy which grows in the country compels the urgent execution of this task, without the delay of even one day. The disorder in the rear, the pogroms, the setting fire to grain freight, the violence and atrocities threaten the front with famine and cold by rendering difficult the delivery of food and equipment. Personnel shortages in the cadres of the militia must be filled quickly. It is impossible to live in anarchy.

"The preliminary work in this direction is completed. In view of the urgent nature of the matter, as a first step I instruct the reserve units to fill the personnel shortages in the ranks of the militia; however, at the same time I intend to call on the active army immediately to secure order within the country. All the territory of the Republic is divided into reserve brigade sectors; the brigade regions are divided into regimental sectors. Every commissar or organ of self-government requiring reliable men for service in the militia shall call on the nearest brigade or regimental commander.

"I order:

"1) For the purpose of organizing the militia, the best officers from reserve regiments and reserve districts, preferably those who have seen combat duty and have received wounds, are to be placed at its disposal. Thus the Government can be sure that this important and at the moment especially responsible service will be entrusted to honest men, who have sacrificed their life for their homeland and who are used to military organization and discipline.

"I authorize the assignment for duty in the militia, at the request of town and zemstvo self-governments, of the best soldiers, preferably Cavaliers of St. George and those who have been wounded. Into the reliable hands of these defenders of the land, the citizens shall entrust what they cherish most—their liberty and their life.

"2) For the purpose of guarding the railways, the best officers and men, preferably Cavaliers of St. George who have been in battle and received wounds, are to be placed at the disposal of railway authorities (working in close contact with the All-Russian Railway Union. Their task is to organize the guarding of railway stations. I authorize the formation of similar detachments for guarding the wharves.

"3) For the purpose of organizing mounted guards, I authorize the district commanders to assign from cavalry units, at the request of Government commissars or the local self-governments, the best officers and men (with horses), preferably Cavaliers of St. George having been in combat action and having been wounded.

"4) The officers and men assigned for this service shall be immediately returned to the ranks of the army at the slightest evasion of duty or the slightest infringement of strict order or military discipline.

"It is the concern of the Minister of War to indicate the goal and furnish the necessary means. It is the concern of the local commanders to show the utmost initiative and render the utmost assistance in the task of organizing the militia.

"By common effort we must stop the growth of anarchy, which threatens to ruin our great homeland and the cherished hopes which the people link with the revolution.

"The goal is set, the means are furnished. I expect active creative work at the local level."

MAJOR GENERAL VERKHOVSKII, Minister of War

1340. TELEGRAM OF OCTOBER 21 FROM THE MINISTER OF THE INTERIOR ON MILITARY MEASURES TO HALT THE GROWTH OF ANARCHY
[*Krest'ianskoe dvizhenie*, p. 427.]

To Guberniya, Oblast, and Municipal Commissars:

The incessant growth of anarchy, which threatens the internal situation of the country, and the necessity to fight resolutely and swiftly all kinds of phenomena which violate public safety, compel the guberniya commissars, as the local representatives of the authority of the Provisional Government, to resort to the assistance of armed forces for the purpose of suppressing disorders.

Therefore, the Minister of War has instructed the commanders of the troops to place cavalry units from cavalry reserve regiments at the disposal of the guberniya commissars, following preliminary contact between the latter and the military districts.

While communicating the foregoing, the Minister of the Interior considers it necessary to point out that the utmost caution should be shown by the guberniya commissars in the exercise of the rights granted them; [to this end] they should take into account the local conditions, bearing in mind, however, that in order to localize and suppress the disorders it is essential to act firmly and resolutely and without the slightest delay.

While placing at the disposal of the guberniya commissars this extraordinary means necessitated by the difficult internal conditions of the Republic, the Ministry of the Interior expresses the certainty that in unity with the sound elements of the population and first of all with the organs of local self-government which express its will, the guberniya commissars shall not fail to make every effort to fight anarchy.

NIKITIN, Minister of the Interior

October 21, 1917

CHAPTER 29

The Dissolution of the Democratic Coalition

DISSENSION IN THE RANKS OF THE DEMOCRACY, THE
FORMATION OF THE COUNCIL OF FIVE, AND
THE PROCLAMATION OF A REPUBLIC

1341. Plenary Session of the Central Executive Committees of
the Workers', Soldiers', and Peasants' Deputies, August 30, 1917
[*Izvestiia*, No. 158, August 31, 1917, p. 5.]

Skobelev's Speech

Comrades, the counterrevolutionary revolt of General Kornilov has been put down. Stavka is surrendering without further resistance and the entire command of the front will be replaced in the very near future.

This success was achieved by the firm determination of the Government in fighting against the revolt. This government alone—in spite of that atmosphere of vacillation between political trends which even touched the confines of the Winter Palace—made it possible to carry out the technical measures in the struggle against the counterrevolution. Sometimes the initiative originated here, but it was always [carried out] in complete coordination with the Provisional Government.

.   .   .

The Provisional Government had to adjust its relations with the separate fronts, and, of course, the most pressing question confronting the Provisional Government was that of filling the posts that were occupied by the insurgent personnel, while the supreme command of the army was assumed by A. F. Kerensky.

But he cannot physically combine [the offices he holds]; there arose the question, therefore, of reorganizing the Provisional Government and transferring other persons.

In the course of reorganizing the Government, Colonel Verkhovskii, Commander of the Moscow Military District, was offered the post of Minister of War.

The post of the Minister of the Navy is held by Admiral Verderevskii. . . .

It stands to reason that the ideologically and politically mature awareness in the army of the necessity of defending our native land may be converted into a fact, but technically this can only be accomplished by a person with sufficient training, and under the present circumstances it became necessary for us to invite General Alekseev to [accept] the post of Chief of Staff.

.   .   .

There can be no place in the Provisional Government for persons belonging to parties that consider the Kornilov revolt to be an act of statesmanship. In this responsible moment in the fate of the Russian revolution, the members of the

Provisional Government must be above reproach, and we hope that we will succeed in preserving the idea of the coalition, drawing in elements of society who are able to march in step with the revolutionary democracy.

We hope that both the country and the Government will be able to emerge from this situation, perhaps undermined organically, but strengthened spiritually.

No single event could have had such an impact on the country as the revolt of General Kornilov.

And now the basic problem of the Provisional Government is, without doubt, the military resistance to the onslaught of the German forces. All [other] problems must be subordinated to this one basic problem. The question of the membership of the Provisional Government must likewise be subordinated to this problem.

It is necessary to re-establish the prestige of revolutionary Russia in the eyes of Europe, and then Russia may dare to entertain hopes in the realm of foreign policy.

Avksent'ev's Speech

Comrade Avksent'ev followed Comrade Skobelev on the rostrum.

At the beginning of his speech Comrade Avksent'ev informed the meeting that Stavka, preoccupied with the revolt, left all the fronts without any instructions for three days, so that the command was left completely uninformed as to the actions it should undertake against the enemy.

"If Hindenburg had wanted to take advantage of this," said Comrade Avkent'ev, "our whole army, which suddenly found itself without leaders, would have been doomed to inevitable destruction. (*Voices from the audience*: "Death to the traitors!")

"We resorted to the severe measures that we rejected in the first bright days of the revolution, among which, eventually, we restored the death penalty.

"If this was so persistently demanded for the lowly by Kornilov, in particular, and by those close to him, then it will be applied all the more vigorously against them.[1] (*Storm of applause.*)

.   .   .

"It is necessary, however, to defend our tormented country against her external enemies as well. In this respect the Provisional Government is completely unanimous. Now it will no longer contain persons who refused to disassociate themselves from certain bourgeois papers, who, in the grave days of treason, refused to stand openly with the Provisional Government for the same [objectives] and who were not ashamed to hurl the entire blame on the Provisional Government, instead of on Kornilov. It is clear that such persons cannot remain in the Provisional Government, which will not consider any compromises with the traitors." (*Applause.*)

.   .   .

Tseretelli's Speech

"Comrades! The revolutionary democracy must take into account the lesson to

---

[1] An editorial in *Delo Naroda*, No. 144, September 2, 1917, p. 1, strongly objected to the double standard applied to the death penalty—of objection to it when applied to the "lowly" and support for it when directed against the Kornilovites.

be derived from recent events in order to determine the correct course [to pursue] for strengthening the revolution, which is the hope of the country's salvation.

. . .

"There was only one hope that could have inspired Kornilov to commit his traitorous act—this was the hope for a split among the revolutionary democratic [forces]. But he was forced to become convinced that his hopes had not materialized; from the moment that the revolutionary democratic ranks closed instead of falling apart, the outcome of the conflict was determined. When he moved on Petrograd, he came up against a wall of united democratic [forces]; he encountered complete unity of action which arose from the united will of the whole revolutionary democracy.

"This experience must be welcomed and must be profited by for the defense of the revolution and our native land.

"The supporters of the counterrevolution revealed their true faces when they did not hesitate to leave the front unguarded in order to begin a civil war within the country. In this terrible hour the revolutionary democracy turned out to be the nucleus which united all the vital forces of the country. The conspiracy turned out to be isolated. And it is highly significant that not only the soldiers who came from the workers' midst but, also, the vast majority of the officers refused to follow Kornilov. The ideals of the revolutionary democracy, coinciding with the cause of the defense of the country and the revolution, triumphed over the force that was destroying the State. The organized democracy proved to be the nucleus personifying the unity of the country.

". . . If we now publicly eject one part of the coalition which has set itself in opposition to the interests of the whole country, it will be done painlessly for the country and in a way that will not confuse the ranks of the popular masses which support the coalition. It is my firm belief that this severance with the traitors of the revolution will not weaken us, because the revolutionary democracy has now closed its ranks more than ever before and has rallied all the forces of the country around it.

"This is the second experience that we must take into account. Closing our ranks in the struggle for saving the country and the revolution, we will unite all the real, vital forces of the country around a single revolutionary power.

"Now, more than ever before, it is necessary to create a body that will bring together all the democratic [forces]. We must now proceed to call a conference in which all the democratic organizations—of the army as well as the rear—will be represented.

. . .

"It is necessary to heal the wounds that were inflicted on the country and the army by Kornilov's treason. We must destroy the focal points around which the counterrevolutionary forces have become concentrated. We have spoken long ago about the dissolution of the State Duma. (*Applause. Voices from the audience*: "It is the first time we hear this from you.")

"I will tell you now why this is the first time you hear this from me. The Fourth Duma, if only for a brief moment, was stirred by the spirit of the revolution, and this brief moment, in the eyes of the broad masses, expiated all its sins.

"In the first days of the revolution, therefore, when the new, revolutionary authority was being established, the Petrograd Soviet of Workers' and Soldiers' Deputies did not even raise the question of abolishing the State Duma, in view of that one brief moment when it was baptized in the fire of the revolution. And up to the present time an attack against the State Duma could have been misunderstood by certain segments of the population which associated the State Duma with the memory of the first days of the revolution."

. . . Comrade Tseretelli concluded his speech by pointing out that the time has come when the State Duma, by its actions, has prepared the people to perceive correctly its present counterrevolutionary role, and it is the duty of the state power to take these lessons into account and strike out against this institution which has become the center of antinational forces.

1342. *Delo Naroda* ON THE GOVERNMENT CRISIS

[No. 143, September 1, 1917, p. 1. See Oliver H. Radkey, *The Agrarian Foes of Bolshevism*, pp. 394–402, 404.]

The prolonged crisis of the Goverment, which like a sinister shadow accompanied the Russian revolution during its entire existence, assumed a particular acuteness following the liquidation of the Kornilov conspiracy.

. . . It appeared that in a class state, based on oppression and exploitation of the toiling masses, the state authority as an organ of coercion is *actually* in the hands of the organizations of the proletariat and toiling peasantry. It appeared that the revolution set itself tremendous *social* tasks which inevitably led, in their realization, to the disappearance of large-scale agriculture and predatory-Asiatic means of exploitation of the proletariat.

This social character of the Russian revolution had to throw, and in reality did throw, agrarians and large industrial bourgeoisie into the camp of counterrevolution. We therefore cannot agree with the Menshevik view that the cause of the increased counterrevolution, which achieved forceful destruction of the gains of the revolution, is due to the agressive policy of the working class which was responsible for the isolation of the proletariat and which turned the bulk of the masses away from the revolutionary democracy. And proof of this is the bloodless liquidation of the Kornilov conspiracy, which manifestly revealed that the entire original body of the counterrevolutionary forces can be reduced to a handful of generals placed in power by the old regime and supported by the leaders of the landowners-gentry Fourth State Duma. Because even the most backward elements in the people's army whom Kornilov sent to revolutionary Petrograd immediately went over to the side of the revolution as soon as they learned that it was a case of an armed attack upon its gains.

Nor is this deduction contradicted by the exposed counterrevolutionary character of the Kadet Party, which obviously sympathized with General Kornilov's undertaking and politically prepared the ground for it by a definite campaign in the press; because the Party of the People's Freedom succeeded during the time of the revolution in becoming in the name of its central organs a genuine apologist for the banking and large-scale industrial bourgeoisie, accustomed by the tsar's regime to get tremendous profits not by work in the interest of the development of productive forces in the country but by means of the most brazen cheating of the consumer and by predatory exploitation of the proletariat.

But if such is the relation of the public forces in the country, if thus far *only* the toiling workers', soldiers', and peasants' masses are on the side of the revolution and against us, attacking with arms in hand the class of landowners and large capitalists, should not the Provisional *revolutionary* Government—that is, the Government which is based on the revolution—consist *only* of representatives of the toiling masses? After all, the Provisional Government cannot disregard the general law that any government is the reflection of a given relation of public forces. And are not all the crises of power we have experienced, all the instability of the government structure, explained by the fact that in violating this general law the authority was built on the coalition principle, on the understanding between the representatives of the toiling masses and the bourgeoisie, that is, on the obvious contradictory principle of reconciliation between *revolution* and *counterrevolution*?

Yes, revolution and counterrevolution, be the latter open or concealed, cannot be combined in building a single, strong, and energetic government authority. This is manifestly clear. Therefore we must say at the present time, when the counterrevolutionary nature of the Kadet Party has been exposed, that *no public leader, loyal to the revolution and furthermore to socialism, could or should participate with the Kadets in the exercise of governmental authority.* The Kadet Party has no place in the Provisional revolutionary Government. . . .

. . .

In spite of this, we express ourselves in favor of *coalition* government. We think that the Russian revolution did not eliminate the possibilities of capitalist development and that until a socialist revolution occurs in Western Europe, there can be no question of overthrowing the capitalist regime in Russia. . . .

The crash of Kadetism, which was an inevitable consequence of the crash of Kornilovism, signifies only the liquidation of that bourgeois world outlook which was formed as a result of the union of capital and large landowners with the tsar's regime. The interests of bourgeois society, and not the old bourgeois classes, are on the side of the revolution as long as it does not and cannot propose a program of a socialist revolution.

1343. THE PROCLAMATION OF A REPUBLIC

[*VVP*, No. 145, September 3, 1917, p. 1. The Senate refused to publish this act, deeming it in contradiction to the "constitution" of the Provisional Government, i.e., the agreement on principles arrived at between the Petrograd Soviet and the Temporary Committee of the State Duma on March 2, which forbade the predetermination of the form of government pending the convocation of the Constituent Assembly.]

General Kornilov's revolt has been suppressed, but the sedition brought by him into the ranks of the army and the country is great. And once again a great danger threatens the fate of our native land and her freedom.

Considering it necessary to put an end to the outward vagueness of the organization of the State and remembering the wholehearted and enthusiastic acceptance of the republican idea at the Moscow State Conference, the Provisional Government announces that the state system by which the State of Russia is governed is republican and proclaims the Russian Republic.

The urgent necessity of adopting immediate and decisive measures for restoring order in the shattered organization of the state has induced the Provisional Government to transfer its full powers of governing to five of its members, headed by the Minister-President.

The Provisional Government considers its principal task to be the restoration of state order and the fighting capacity of the army. Convinced that only through the concentrated efforts of all the vital forces of the country will it be possible to extricate our native land from the difficult position in which it finds itself, the Provisional Government will strive to expand its membership by inviting to its midst representatives of all those elements who place the permanent and common interests of our native land above the temporary and private interests of individual parties or classes.

The Provisional Government does not doubt it will accomplish this task in the very near future.

A. KERENSKY, Minister-President
ZARUDNYI, Minister of Justice
September 1, 1917

1344. *Rech'* ON THE PROCLAMATION
[No. 208, September 5, 1917, p. 1.]

. . .

. . . The word "republic" was used officially for the first time in the July declaration of A. F. Kerensky, when he was delegated with the authority to form the new cabinet; [then] it passed completely unnoticed. Now this republic is proclaimed by the Provisional Government, and the declaration of September 1 is completely silent with regard to the Constituent Assembly.

May we conclude from this that the decision of the future "sovereign master" [the Constituent Assembly] has been anticipated? Certainly not! And yet one must categorically recognize that the correct point of view is not that of the authors of the declaration of September 1, but the former point of view which was rejected by the declaration. By its actual significance . . . the declaration is not binding for the Constituent Assembly. But undoubtedly it will affect freedom of propaganda as well as the very attitude toward those currents which have not adhered to the republican idea. If these currents have up to now not been noticeable, it does not mean that they do not exist.

However, another remark is still more serious: . . . should one not beware that, in the light of the present regime, it is, on the contrary, the authority and the attractiveness of the "republican idea" that will suffer a considerable setback?

1345. *Volia Naroda* ON THE PROCLAMATION
[No. 110, September 5, 1917, p. 1.]

The recent Russian monarchy, later the legally vague "Russian power," has now become, not only actually but formally, a "Russian Republic."

The word that for decades had been forbidden has been pronounced. What not so long ago seemed distant and unrealizable has been realized.

A new act, foreign up to this time, will now be introduced in the Code of Laws.

The Provisional Government declared the Republic and thus separated the old order from the new.

We hail wholeheartedly this most important step of the Provisional Government headed by A. F. Kerensky.

Through its act it gave a legal definition to what already existed as a matter of fact. Through its act it summed up the achievements of the revolution. Through its act it made the return to the old impossible.

From the social and political point of view the declaration of Russia as a republic is of tremendous importance. Until now the word republic had not been used by the Provisional Government. And some possibility remained of the restoration of monarchy in one form or another.

Now all roads to the past have been cut off. No matter what evils may befall the Russian revolution in the future, this "little paper" cannot be destroyed. No reaction will make the Russian citizens forget it. Henceforth it will be the foundation stone and stronghold of the revolution that no shades of the past will be able to overcome.

Because of this, even though the act about the republic has added nothing and changed nothing in the actual state of affairs, its significance is tremendous. It is that frontier post beyond which no one can now venture on the road to the past.

1346. THE FORMATION OF THE COUNCIL OF FIVE

[*Osobyi Zhurnal*, No. 146, September 1, 1917.]

Heard:

The oral proposal of the Minister-President on entrusting the immediate direction of the affairs of the State, until the cabinet is definitely formed and in connection with the extraordinary circumstances of the moment, to a directory consisting of five persons.

Resolved:

To publish the following decision:

"Until the cabinet is definitely formed and in connection with the extraordinary circumstances of the present moment, the Provisional Government at its session of September 1 has entrusted the immediate direction of the affairs of state to the Minister-President, A. F. Kerensky; the Minister of Foreign Affairs, M. I. Tereshchenko; the Minister of War, Major General Verkhovskii; the Minister of the Navy, Admiral Verderevskii; and the Minister of Post and Telegraph, A. M. Nikitin.

.   .   .

1347. THE DIRECTORY

[*Rech'*, No. 207, September 3, 1917, p. 3.]

At 11:00 A.M. on September 2, the first session of the new Provisional Government, or, as it is customarily called, "The Council of Five," was held in A. F. Kerensky's office in the Winter Palace.

Only three members of the Directory were present at the session: A. F. Kerensky, M. I. Tereshchenko, and A. M. Nikitin.

It is believed in political circles that these three members of the "Council of Five" will virtually control all questions of internal and foreign policy, since the other two—General Verkhovskii, Minister of War, and Admiral Verderevskii, Minister of the Navy—will have to concentrate their attention on military matters.

It stands to reason that the greatest power will be concentrated in the hands of Minister-President A. F. Kerensky, of all the members of the Directory, especially since he is now at the same time the Supreme Commander.

The new . . . Provisional Government will have to settle the question of its functions in the very near future. In all probability, only the most important affairs of state will be concentrated in the hands of the "Council of Five." Business matters, in so far as they are not political in character, will be settled at conferences of department heads. It has been learned that I. I. Yefremov will preside over these conferences if he remains in charge of the Department of Welfare, in the capacity of [acting] head of the department.

From time to time conferences will be called by the Provisional Government, with the participation of all the [acting] heads of departments. Either A. F. Kerensky or M. I. Tereshchenko will preside over these joint conferences.

The [following] members of the former Provisional Government have not announced their final resignation: S. N. Prokopovich, Minister of Trade and Industry; I. I. Yefremov, Minister of Welfare; and A. V. Kartashev, Minister of Confessions. They have all been asked by A. F. Kerensky to remain in charge of their departments in the capacity of [acting] heads.

All the present heads of departments have also been asked to remain at their posts, including M. V. Bernatskii, head of the Ministry of Finance, and A. V. Liverovskii, head of the Ministry of Transport.

There are grounds to believe that the Directory will be temporary in character and that the question of the membership of the Provisional Government and its character (i.e., whether it will be a coalition) will be definitely established after the conference of representatives of democratic revolutionary organizations is held, which has been set for September 12 by the Central Executive Committee of the Soviet of Workers' and Soldiers' Deputies.

All organizations that adhered at the Moscow Conference to the declaration read by N. S. Chkheidze will participate in this Conference.

The final reorganization of the Provisional Government will depend upon the position adopted by this Democratic Conference.

In political circles it is considered probable that the Democratic Conference will pronounce itself a National Assembly, pending the convocation of the Constituent Assembly, and will declare in favor of establishing the Provisional Government's responsibility to it.

Incidentally, it is reported in government circles that the ministers were far from unanimous [in their views] during the discussions on the question of forming a Directory of five persons. Not only representatives of the Party of the People's Freedom, but socialist ministers, too, expressed their opposition to the Directory. However, in view of the hopelessness of the situation, it was decided to accept the idea of forming a Directory as a compromise.

One of the peculiarities of our Directory is the fact that not one of the persons composing it is a spokesman for the views of any one party. M. I. Tereshchenko does not represent any party. A. M. Nikitin, who belongs to the Social Democratic Party, is a rank-and-file member and has never had a position of leadership within the party. A. F. Kerensky far from agrees on everything with the present majority of the Socialist Revolutionary Party (there is even a rumor circulating that A. F. Kerensky has supposedly left the Socialist Revolutionary Party, but this rumor was not confirmed). Finally, the Ministers of War and the Navy, General Verkhovskii and Admiral Verderevskii, similarly do not represent any party.

The portfolios will be divided among the members of the new Provisional Government in the same way as before. Possibly, A. M. Nikitin, who until the present has held the post of Minister of Post and Telegraph, will be appointed Minister of the Interior.

* * *

On September 2, M. I. Skobelev visited the Ministry of Labor and attended to current business.

* * *

The fact that the position of the "Directory" is extremely difficult is not concealed in government circles. It is pointed out that up to the present time, the Provisional Government has been balancing between the "right" and the "left," resting on the support of first one, then the other [side]. In this lay its strength and this was the basis of its relative independence. Now the Provisional Government is forced to rest exclusively on the support of the left, and this makes it extremely dependent upon the Soviet of Workers' and Soldiers' Deputies, which, on its part, is moving closer and closer to the Bolsheviks.

1348. OFFICIAL CLARIFICATION OF THE FUNCTION OF THE COUNCIL OF FIVE
[*Izvestiia*, No. 163, September 6, 1917, p. 4.]

In view of the discussions in the press concerning the relationship and functions of the Council of Five and the Provisional Government, the following official clarification has been issued:

"The Provisional Government has singled out five members to discuss questions of a general political nature pertaining to the high command and national defense; these members constitute the Council of Five. The sittings of the Council of Five take place daily at 10:00 A.M. The regular sessions of the Provisional Government continue to be held during the day and are attended in full body, with participation by heads of individual ministries, during which [time] the members of the Council of Five report on the general course of events in the whole nation."

1349. THE RESIGNATION OF A. S. ZARUDNYI
[*Rech'*, No. 207, September 3, 1917, p. 3.]

On September 2, Minister of Justice A. S. Zarudnyi, who has handed in his resignation, was still working in his office.

In the morning, however, A. S. Zarudnyi announced to his closest co-workers that he had submitted his resignation to the Minister-President and that the Provisional Government had accepted it; he wanted to leave the Ministry at once.

Of the four Assistant Ministers, only A. A. Dem'ianov is now in Petrograd, and, with the resignation of A. S. Zarudnyi, he will assume the duties of acting head of the Ministry of Justice.

Yesterday A. S. Zarudnyi devoted almost the entire day to turning over the ministerial duties to A. A. Dem'ianov.

In the afternoon of September 2, A. S. Zarudnyi bade farewell to the employees of the Ministry of Justice.

In a brief speech, A. S. Zarudnyi said, among other things, that in the present difficult times ministers are merely guests in their ministries; they come for a short time, and then, regardless of the work in the Ministry, they must leave because of various influences and pressures.

"The real workers," A. S. Zarudnyi concluded, "are you; I was only your guest."

1350. THE REPRESENTATIVES OF TRADE AND INDUSTRY CONFER WITH KERENSKY ON A COALITION GOVERNMENT

[*Rech'*, No. 207, September 3, 1917, p. 3. Kishkin was also advised that, for the time being, it was impossible to form a coalition government. *Ibid.*]

On September 2, S. A. Smirnov and A. A. Buryshkin, representatives of commerce and industry who were summoned from Moscow by A. F. Kerensky for negotiations on forming a coalition cabinet, arrived in Petrograd at the same time as N. M. Kishkin.

A conference of representatives of commerce and industry was held in Moscow before the departure of S. A. Smirnov and A. A. Buryshkin.

Two points of view were outlined at the conference.

The minority found that A. F. Kerensky's proposal should be rejected, inasmuch as the Provisional Government did not consult the representatives of commerce and industry and was offering them two seats, not as a result of agreement but as a sort of handout.

It is said, incidentally, that P. P. Riabushinskii adhered to this point of view.

The majority of the participants in the conference did not agree with this, pointing out that, should the industrialists reject the proposal to enter the Provisional Government, they will continue to be reproached for sabotage.

In view of this, the majority of the participants declared in favor of S. A. Smirnov's and A. A. Buryshkin's trip to Petrograd. However, this trip turned out to be unnecessary, since the question of forming a coalition cabinet was dropped before the Moscow representatives arrived in Petrograd.

1351. THE PLENARY SESSION OF THE CENTRAL EXECUTIVE COMMITTEES OF THE SOVIETS OF WORKERS', SOLDIERS', AND PEASANTS' DEPUTIES, SEPTEMBER 1, 1917

[*Izvestiia*, No. 160, September 2, 1917, pp. 3–4; and No. 161, September 3, 1917, pp. 5–7.]

Skobelev's Speech

. . .

I know that the thought will not cross anyone's mind today that I am motivated by political speculation. Comrades, I am no longer a member of the Provisional Government, since I have most resolutely refused all the requests of A. F. Kerensky to withdraw my resignation.

It was said here that the principle of the coalition was not justified. I am of a different opinion. Regardless of the difficulty of the present situation, Russia has still remained a democracy. Regardless of the number of crises that the concept of the coalition had to endure, it has still succeeded in preserving Russia and her freedom to the present day. And this concept must not die.

Nevertheless I cannot remain in the Provisional Government if the revolutionary democracy is not wholly on its side.

I can only see the meaning of my stay in the Government in so far as I can express the will of the revolutionary democracy.

Now, comrades, I want to give you an account of my actions and experiences.

Three power combinations are possible: a coalition [government], a purely bourgeois [government], and a purely democratic [government]. A purely bourgeois [government] cannot be justified. There was a conflict of two forces in the Kornilov plot, one standing for autocracy and the other based on all the strata of the population. The latter won, and it could not have been otherwise. But one should not hurl sweeping accusations at the whole bourgeoisie, just as it was untrue, in its time, [to say] that the whole democracy had taken part in the street demonstrations of July 3–5. If certain bourgeois groups did, perhaps, take part in the Kornilov movement, probably the majority of them did not participate in it. Therefore, we have no right to exclude them completely from the Government.

A second concept of power consists of vesting it completely in the democracy. From the very first days of the revolution it was pointed out to us that only the slogan "All power to the Soviets" could save the country. During the past few days many of us have undergone a mental revolution, and the number of adherents to this slogan has increased.

But this revolution did not happen to me. I left the Provisional Government with the intention of carrying out my idea among you without my hands being tied. The graver the situation on the front lines and the domestic front, the more urgent it becomes to rally around ourselves all the vital forces for the defense of the country.

. . .

Don't forget, comrades, that Petrograd is not all of Russia, and that is why Petrograd must, first of all, inquire of all of Russia.

I have been on the front twice and I know that Petrograd does not enjoy the confidence of all.

The reason for this is the following: we are all overly possessed with the lust for power. Our eyes are on the Winter Palace and we strive too much to make our way into it. The provinces do not see it and they are therefore more sober.

. . .

Comrades, remember that the fate of democratic Russia is being decided. Think of Russia, comrades!

Bogdanov's Speech

Comrades: I am speaking on behalf of the Mensheviks, and I [wish to] inform you of the results we have reached from our thorough discussion of the circumstances in which we find ourselves.

. . .

I supported the coalition because this was the best way out of the impasse.

What Is the Solution?

Now the question adds up to whether we can form a coalition. Of course, we cannot have a coalition with the Kadets; the cruel facts have convinced us of this. We have never declined the responsibilities we assumed, but they have always slowed down our work. Now their cards are on the table and there can be no coalition with a party that provided the ideological inspiration for the Kornilov revolt.

We now face a government crisis and we may consider that the Kadets are completely excluded from it.

. . .

The Dictatorship of the Democracy

There are democratic parties, regardless of what they are called, which have a fundamental task before them, and in the process of the revolution we have approached the question of [vesting the] power in the democracy, but not in the socialists.

Some comrades raise the question of the possibility at the present moment of the dictatorship of the poorest class, i.e., the proletariat and the peasants. Those who speak of such a dictatorship of the proletariat are following the course of the Commune. Such a Commune may be possible in Petrograd and in other towns, but it cannot be accepted by the rest of Russia. It will be crushed by the vacillating elements which may join the bourgeois bloc, and, in this case, the time may come when we will be left no better off than at the start. The course of the dictatorship of the proletariat into which the workers are being pushed is a perilous course.

But there is another course—the dictatorship of the democracy, not of the Soviets of Workers' and Soldiers' Deputies, but of those democratic organizations whose cadres are working throughout the country, such as the cooperatives, the municipal dumas, and the new zemstvos.

This is the dictatorship of the democracy of which we speak and toward which we are moving. It means only one thing: all the democratic forces must be brought into play and all the organs for carrying out their decisions must be promoted.

The Immediate Tasks

Can the power be transferred to the Soviets without waiting for this? This cannot be done, because this would be a blow to the revolution. The whole country and the army are in a turmoil, not knowing in which direction to throw themselves. There can be no question of [vesting] the power in the Soviets at such a time. One must now recognize the following principle: it is necessary for the defense of the country and the revolution that the power be organized by the democracy itself. This is the first [point]. Then, it must immediately resolve that a congress of democratic organizations, municipal dumas, zemstvos, cooperatives, and so forth, be convoked in the nearest future, and this conference must decide the question of the organization of power.

What must we do in these days? The Kadets have left the Provisional Government and we do not regret this, but what remains of the Government must be preserved until the coming conference. We must rally around the remaining members of the Provisional Government, surround them with firm support and confidence, and tell our comrades, the socialist ministers, to remain at their revolutionary posts.

In its actions the Provisional Government must maintain contact with the Committee of the People's Struggle Against Counterrevolution at all times. It must select the persons it needs, guided in this selection by the instructions we give it, preventing at the same time all acts of provocation.

We must preserve strict discipline and this will constitute a pledge that we will bring the country to the democratic conference.

Riazanov's Speech

We have just heard two representatives of the Menshevik Party. Comrade Skobelev came to us only after everything had already happened. Is not everything that happened the consequence of the work of the party with which the coalition was formed—the Kadet Party? It has been said here that Petrograd is not all of Russia, but the provinces follow the events in Petrograd closely, and when the knot around the neck of the counterrevolution grows tighter here, we do not doubt that we will find support in the vast popular masses.

.   .   .

What we need . . . is a ministry that is responsible not to its own stupidity and unscrupulousness but to the united will of the people.

It is time to start thinking of the fact that the Soviets represent the majority in Russia; they must remember their strength. Let them pick a Provisional Government which would be responsible to them, which would bring the country to the earliest convocation of the Constituent Assembly. The Constituent Assembly alone is capable of concluding peace, carrying out the necessary reforms and bringing us closer to the socialist system, so that Russia may be the first to enter the united family of the revolutionary proletariat. (*Applause.*)

Chernov's Speech

Comrades! One has to make note of one fundamental difference in discussing the destinies of the coalition Government. It is the difference between the town and the village.

The symbolic gesture at the Moscow Conference of Bublikov extending his hand to Tseretelli cannot be applied to the village. The peasant representative could not extend his hand to the *pomeshchik* because large landownership is an element that is obviously not viable and is doomed to obliteration in the very near future. The bourgeoisie has also recognized this, and even Shidlovskii has admitted this in the Central Land Committee.

But the song of large industry is far from being sung. There can be no doubt of its viability. The interests of industrialists must be [viewed] separately from the interests of industry, to which the country cannot remain indifferent.

The commercial and industrial class now represents an economic, and not a political, group; thus, there remain the Kadets, who have taken up the struggle against the agrarian revolution.

.   .   .

The policy that provoked the conflict between the Party of the People's Freedom and the socialists, particularly the Socialist Revolutionaries, is the land policy. This policy was not of great importance to the commercial and industrial class and it could easily betray the large landowners; this betrayal would, in fact, be advantageous to it, since the enriched village would create a new consumer.

And no one will be surprised that yesterday the Socialist Revolutionary Party announced to Comrade Kerensky, who had outlined a cabinet which contained

Kadets, that such a list was unacceptable to the party and that the party will not give a single representative to the Government. (*Voice from the audience:* "And what about Kerensky?") It is not to me that you should address this question. The antagonism between Socialist Revolutionaries and the Kadets has reached a breaking point in the struggle against Kornilovism.

· · ·

Martov's Speech

Comrades, the cabinet crisis was resolved in a rather unexpected fashion. I am not familiar with the details, but the immediate demands which all the factions made of the head of the government were fulfilled: the Kadets have been removed, the democratic republic shall be proclaimed.

It was sufficient for those who until now were the ones to present us with ultimata to hear our ultimatum to them in order to produce immediate, tangible results.

· · ·

The closest ties and harmony must exist between the head of government and the revolutionary democracy. . . .

· · ·

I welcome the first attempt to form a democratic parliament. The first step has been taken; the rest will follow automatically. The revolutionary democracy will enter on this new course, without entertaining any doubts concerning its strength or its historical right to bring the struggle against its enemies to an end.

· · ·

Then let the revolutionary democracy carry out its policy to the very end in spite of even a hundred Kornilovs and Kaledins. (*Applause.*)

Kamenev's Speech

During the past few days we lived under the threat of the Kornilov conspiracy. Now, according to the statements of comrades Skobelev and Avksent'ev, the Central Executive Committee received a blow from the hand of Kerensky. It would be criminal to close one's eyes to this.

Two points unite all of us: the Government must be responsible to us and must look to the revolutionary democracy for support. Both of these demands were rejected.

· · ·

The composition of the Government that was announced to us is a government for Kerensky, while a government for Russia should be formed here, with or without Kerensky, depending upon our judgment.

Before taking action, Kerensky consulted Kishkin, but did he consult the majority of the proletariat which adopted the Bolsheviks' resolution of August 31?[2]

In view of the altered circumstances, I consider it necessary to enter the following supplement to the resolution which I submitted:

"Upholding the principles of the resolution on the government crisis, adopted by the Petrograd Soviet of Workers' and Soldiers' Deputies on August 31, and

---

[2] Passed by the Petrograd Soviet at a sparsely attended session and calling for immediate peace negotiations, workers' control, and confiscation of estates. See Doc. 1369.

finding that complete irresponsibility and personal dictatorship characterized the methods of forming [the Government] and of the new Provisional Government itself, the Central Executive Committee emphasizes that a genuine revolutionary government could be formed only on the basis indicated in the resolution."

This does not as yet mean that we plan to stage a demonstration against personal dictatorship. But if we were to restrain ourselves from doing so, we would not thereby be relieved of the responsibility of telling the people that Kerensky's government is a dictatorship.

You must issue a political statement to this effect, and if you will not do this, then fate will force you into it!

Tseretelli's Speech

We have just heard Kamenev's speech, which was based entirely on error. He said that we were confronted with the *fait accompli* of a government formed without our participation. Kamenev has probably forgotten that A. F. Kerensky turned to us on this score and that we adopted a decision which was published in the newspapers in which we granted Comrade Kerensky freedom of action in forming a cabinet for combating the counterrevolution. The steps taken by him conformed to this. He acted on the basis of our resolution.

Kerensky would have inflicted a blow on us only if, instead of forming a cabinet, he had confronted us with the fact of an absence of a Government and the necessity of forming one right now.

Such a state of affairs would have been a real blow to the comrade Bolsheviks, because they would have been forced to admit that they were not in a position of realizing a Soviet Government.

Now a government has been formed which has excluded the bourgeois elements that had compromised themselves in connection with the Kornilov plot. We are all in agreement on such a government. This will be a government for the defense of the country, and we will fully support its actions in suppressing the counterrevolution and its efforts in organizing the resistance to the external foe.

I suggest that you vote in favor of the resolution submitted by the Menshevik faction of the Social Democrats and the Socialist Revolutionaries. However, without changing its total aspect, we propose to make a few corrections in it, namely, to change the sense of its second article, in which the desire is expressed that the Kadets be excluded from the Government, since the Kadets have already been virtually excluded.[3]

Comrades, the idea of a coalition is, apparently, out of fashion. But I sometimes support old-fashioned ideas. In particular, I support the idea of a coalition.

. . .

The coalition principle always begins to collapse when democracy weakens. It is strong when democracy is strong.

. . .

On one [point], I think, we are all in agreement, namely, that everything possible must be done to unite, strengthen, and organize the democratic [forces]. It is with this objective [in mind] that we are calling a congress of all the democratic organizations.

[3] See Doc. 1355n.

I think that the democratic [forces] will be united at this congress. And if it turns out that there is not a single vital force in the country apart from ours, then we will take the power into our hands.

The course outlined in our resolution is just as acceptable to those who consider it necessary that full power be transferred to the democracy as it is to those who believe that, once the democracy gains in strength, it will attract all those who are now standing aloof and who, for the sake of the cause, must be placed in the service of the revolution and the salvation of the country.

———

After Tseretelli's speech, the resolutions of the Bolsheviks and the Menshevik-Internationalists were rejected, and the resolution submitted by the Menshevik faction of the Social Democrats and the Socialist Revolutionaries was accepted as the basis [for future action].

. . .

The resolution was put to a vote and was passed by an overwhelming majority.

Resolution of the Mensheviks and the Socialist Revolutionaries

The tragic situation created by the events at the front and by the civil war launched by the counterrevolution necessitates the establishment of a single revolutionary power capable of realizing the program of the revolutionary democracy and carrying on an active struggle against the counterrevolution and the external foe. Such a government, erected by the democracy and responsible to its organs, must be free of any compromises with the counterrevolutionary bourgeois elements. In view of this, the joint session of the Executive Committee of the Soviets of Workers' and Soldiers' Deputies and the Executive Committee of the Soviet of Peasants' Deputies has resolved:

1. A congress of all democratic organizations and democratic organs of local self-government must be convoked immediately for the purpose of deciding the question of forming a government capable of leading the country to the Constituent Assembly.

2. Until this congress [takes place], the Central Executive Committee requests that the Government preserve its present membership and, welcoming its first step —the proclamation of the democratic republic—relies on it for conducting a resolute struggle, in close unison with organs of the revolutionary democracy, against any counterrevolutionary conspiracies. The Central Executive Committee, on its part, calls upon the democracy to lend vigorous support to the Government in its work on organizing the defenses of the country and combating the counterrevolution, particularly by means of democratizing the army and decisively replacing the higher commanders.

3. For the purpose of preventing government agents from [taking] steps which may harm the cause or contribute needlessly to popular unrest, the All-Russian Central Committee considers it necessary that the Government, on adopting measures for maintaining order, act in close contact with the Committee of the People's Struggle Against Counterrevolution attached to the All-Russian Central Committee.

4. Under all circumstances, the Central Executive Committee emphatically charges the democratic elements of the population to resist provocation, to await

—giving full support—the decisions of the forthcoming democratic congress, to refrain from [taking] any spontaneous actions, and to counteract lynching with utmost determination.

1352. *Rech'* ON THE COUNCIL OF FIVE
[No. 207, September 3, 1917, p. 2.]

As is known, the reconstruction of the Government on the lines planned by A. F. Kerensky, and which had our complete approval, did not take place. M. V. Chernov's departure from the cabinet . . . produced an immediate change in the attitude of the Socialist Revolutionaries. Messrs. Gots and Zenzinov brought A. F. Kerensky an ultimatum—not to include Kadets in the cabinet, or else the Socialist Revolutionaries will quit it. For the second time since the reshuffling of the Government on July 25, A. F. Kerensky faced the dilemma of either insisting on his point of view and quitting the party, or bowing to the party's demands.

. . .

One should render full justice to A. F. Kerensky for not having as yet given in to the party moods. But it does not look as if he has taken a stand against them. He has simply stopped midway, at the point where he can rely upon the support of the organs of "the revolutionary democracy." The membership of the Government nucleus does not include the contested elements and it has decided to restrict itself to this membership for the next days. Thus has been formed a Provisional Government of five, or (more correctly) of three persons—Kerensky, Tereshchenko, and Nikitin—and the two military ministers, Verderevskii and Verkhovskii. The other ministers were left beyond the pale; at the same time that they were invited, they had to assume the rank of acting ministers, without voice in the most important matters of state. It was once again the same notorious "Directory," which previously had been condemned by the Soviets and rejected by them as a form of government. Thus, although the controversial question regarding the K.D.'s has been eliminated (or, more correctly, postponed) by the creation of the cabinet's political nucleus, this decision was nevertheless disapproved by the ministers linked with the Soviets, by Arksent'ev and Skobelev, who chose it as their motive for walking out of the Government. Officially (and, perhaps, in reality) the walkout was motivated by the desire to strengthen the Government's position within the Soviets.

And, in fact, the first session of the Executive Committee attended by the retired ministers ended with the rejection of the Bolshevik resolution, approved by the Petrograd Soviet, and the acceptance of the resolution of the Mensheviks and the S.R.'s. The Government in its present membership (of "five") obtained a provisional approval . . . At the same time the decision was taken that "the All-Russian Democratic Conference" will meet in Petrograd not later than September 12.

If this decision were to be put into effect, it would basically change the character of the Government. If the Government were to be created by a conference in which only those social groups that had "adhered to the Chkheidze declaration" during the Moscow Conference would participate, that would in reality be a seizure of power such as the Bolsheviks have been advocating up to now in vain.

The succession of power, which has existed until now, would be upset, and, in effect, we would be experiencing a new act of revolutionary creation of power.

However, for the time being, it is not a decision of the Government, but only a resolution of the Executive Committee. . . . These formulas [of the Executive Committee], produced by the needs of the moment, will hardly be entered in the future history of Russian public law; but they do satisfy current needs. It is another matter whether they will place the Government in a position of independence regarding the immediate intentions of the Bolsheviks and regarding the decisions of the conference of September 12, which, although "democratic," will nevertheless be a private conference. By preserving the most important, the succession of revolutionary power, [these formulas will] most certainly permit the Government to dispense with any new investiture. From this point of view it is impossible not to welcome the first act of the Government of "five," and one can hope that "in the very near future" it will raise its membership to normal, without making distinctions between ministers enjoying, and those not enjoying, the plenitude of rights. Thus not only would the succession of power be maintained, but the power itself would resume its original form—that which the revolutionary Government assumed after the events of February 27. We believe that such a restoration would be the best way of "bringing the country to the Constituent Assembly," and we will energetically support all the measures that the Government undertakes in this direction.

1353. APPEAL FROM MEMBERS OF THE SOCIAL DEMOCRATIC PARTY

[*Den'*, No. 157, September 7, 1917, p. 1.]

To the Comrades and to the Citizens!

The thesis which had been firmly established by the organs of the revolutionary democracy, that during the period of the revolution the Supreme Power of Russia should be built on the principles of a coalition between the democracy and the well-to-do classes, has been shattered.

The last attempt of the Government to create a coalition government was met by the resistance of the responsible organs of the democracy, and as a result, during very dangerous moments for the country, Russia is again deprived of [regular] authority with a "Council of Five" instead of a regularly organized government.

The solution of the problem regarding its organization has been postponed until the meeting of the Democratic Conference, set for September 16 [*sic*].

We, party workers, Menshevik-Defensists, address ourselves in this terrible moment to all our comrades and to all the citizens with a warning: the intention of some circles of the democracy to incite the Democratic Conference to abandon the thesis of the necessity of a coalition government, which was adopted by the democracy, threatens the country with terrible shocks. A homogeneously bourgeois government as well as a homogeneously socialistic government would be powerless in the matters of organizing the defense of the country or of safeguarding it against an economic disorder and would throw Russia into the abyss of a new civil war.

Neither side is strong enough to remove the other from the scales, and every attempt in this direction threatens us with a repetition of the days of July or August.

The Democratic Conference, if it were to decide to form a homogeneous socialist cabinet, would be a signal for an urgent mobilization of counterrevolutionary forces, which would be followed by the mass of the city and the rural petty bourgeoisie, which, in secret or openly, has manifested its sympathies toward the Kornilov adventure.

Even without that, the democracy is breaking away from the wide, nonsocialist strata of the population, while attempts to monopolize the creation of the Government would infuriate the dominating and middle classes not only against democracy but against the very foundations of our liberty.

Therefore we appeal to you: Unite; come as a solid mass to the Democratic Conference, in order to save Russia from the horrors of a civil war, in order to repel the anarchic and rebellious elements of democracy on the one side, and of reaction on the other, which are now raising their heads.

Outside of a coalition government, there is no salvation for a Russia torn by class hatred and class egotism. Let the Democratic Conference, leaving aside all attempts at a one-sided seizure of power, reaffirm by its authoritative decision a coalition government. [Signatures follow of 85 leading members of the Social Democratic Party (Menshevik).]

THE DEMOCRATIC CONFERENCE

1354. INVITATION TO THE CONFERENCE

[*Izvestiia*, No. 161, September 3, 1917, p. 4. The Conference did not convene until the 14th.]

The following telegraphic invitation to various democratic organizations was sent by the Central Executive Committee of the Soviets of Workers' and Soldiers' Deputies and the Executive Committee of the All-Russian Soviet of Peasants' Deputies:

"In these difficult days through which our native land is passing, when treason and betrayal carry the threat of military defeat and sedition within the country, revolutionary Russia must look to the democracy for her salvation.

"All the forces of the country must be assembled to organize for national defense, to assist in its internal organization, and to pronounce the final word on the conditions guaranteeing the existence of a strong, revolutionary authority capable of uniting all of revolutionary Russia for the purpose of repelling the foreign foe and crushing every attempt at [encroaching] on the freedom which has been won.

"In view of the above, the Central Executive Committee of the Soviets of Workers' and Soldiers' Deputies and the Executive Committee of the All-Russian Soviet of Peasants' Deputies have resolved to call a congress of all the democratic organizations in Russia, [to be held] in Petrograd on September 12, and invites you to send your representatives to it.[4]

> N. S. CHKHEIDZE, Chairman of the Central Executive Committee
> of the Soviets of Workers' and Soldiers' Deputies
> N. D. AVKSENT'EV, Chairman of the Executive Committee of the
> All-Russian Soviet of Peasants' Deputies

1355. THE OPENING OF THE CONFERENCE

[*Izvestiia*, No. 171, September 15, 1917, pp. 1–5; and No. 172, September 16, 1917, pp. 1, 2, 4.]

At 5:25 P.M. [on September 14], N. S. Chkheidze announced the opening of the All-Russian Conference.

Speech of N. S. Chkheidze

Comrades! . . . The extremely difficult moment through which revolutionary Russia is now passing has compelled the Central Executive Committee of the Soviets of Workers' and Soldiers' Deputies and the Executive Committee of Peasants' Deputies to invite you to this Conference.

. . .

Russia in Danger

The revolution has liberated the country from her age-old sworn enemy—tsarism. But to liquidate the legacy of this regime turned out to be a far more difficult matter than might have appeared at first sight.

Terrible Legacy and Tasks of the Revolution

The most terrible legacy we received is the war. It would seem that the principal task of the revolution with respect to the war is to rally all the creative forces of the nation for the purpose of resolutely defending the country, repelling the external foe, and liquidating the war on terms acceptable to revolutionary Russia and the revolutionary people.

Two Trends

Such should have been the task of the revolution with respect to the war. But it turned out to be different in practice. From the very beginning, ideologists of imperialist circles wanted to exploit the revolution for their own imperialistic desires, to include even Constantinople; and the tasks and aims which were foisted on the revolution were not only beyond its powers but were also completely alien to it.

On the other hand, it was prescribed that the Russian revolution be transformed immediately into a social revolution on a world scale so that, having leaped into the kingdom of freedom, it could immediately extinguish the fire of the capitalist war.

Six months of the revolution made it patently clear that the aspiration for [St.]

---

[4] On September 12, the Central Executive Committee of the Soviets of Workers' and Soldiers' Deputies voted for the coalition principle, but with an amendment, objected to by Tseretelli, that a coalition with the Kadets was inadmissible. *Izvestiia*, No. 169, September 13, 1917, p. 5.

Sophia was both counterrevolutionary and beyond the strength [of the country]. But the other aspect turned out to be no less fortunate: instead of a world socialist revolution it received fertile ground for counterrevolution, and instead of a leap into the kingdom of freedom it leaped into the kingdom of anarchy.

.   .   .

The Country Is Waiting for a Government

.   .   .

The country yearns for a government which would be responsible to all the elements that a government can lean upon as a firm base in carrying out the program it takes upon itself. But in order to [obtain] this, we ourselves must first of all come to an agreement on the platform and the program.

Common grounds for this exist, and these grounds are the platform which was announced at the Moscow Conference . . . (*General applause.*)

Speech of N. D. Avksent'ev

The floor went to N. D. Avksent'ev, Chairman of the Executive Committee of the Soviets of Peasants' Deputies.

Comrades: It is not for developing the political principles of the program that I am taking the floor . . . but in order to welcome those assembled here on behalf of the second organization which has taken the initiative in calling the Democratic Conference—on behalf of the Executive Committee of the All-Russian Soviet of Peasants' Deputies.

.   .   .

Urgent Tasks

After this heavy shock to the whole country, there arose the immediate task of leading our native land to the Constituent Assembly, the task of organizing the country along democratic principles. The democracy is confronted with great creative tasks, both in the realm of the struggle for the independence and safety of our native land and in the realm of organization for the sake of establishing a state system and a strong state power.

.   .   .

Hannibal's Oath of the Democracy

In resolving all the problems, the democracy must muster all its composure and statesmanship in order to act in the name of free Russia and [to consolidate] the gains of the revolution, which were obtained by the stupendous efforts of [many] generations and which the democracy has once and for all given a Hannibal's oath never to relinquish to anyone. (*General applause.*)

Speech of A. F. Kerensky

.   .   .

Greeting from the Provisional Government

The Provisional Government of the Russian Republic has instructed me to welcome the present meeting. . . . I cannot but welcome you also as the Supreme Commander of all the land and naval forces of the Russian Republic. The Provisional Government expects support from this meeting and desires to hear words of wisdom from the sons of the Russian land during this exceptionally difficult time for our country.

Just a month ago, at the State Conference, the Provisional Government openly announced its program, the tasks it had set for itself, and what it expected from the populace.

At the present meeting I will take the liberty of forgetting that I am the President of the Provisional Government and the Supreme Commander. I cannot speak to the conference of the democracy, whose will I carried out and with which I created the Russian revolution, until I can feel that there is no one here who would cast reproaches and slander against me personally of the kinds that have been heard in recent times . . . ("There is, there is," *a voice from the loge of the second tier was heard. But the noisy applause from almost the entire assembly hall drowned out this voice.*)

A. F. Kerensky and Kornilovism

Permit me to give you a brief account—ignoring individual cries—of what is called Kornilovism and of what has been opportunely and thoroughly exposed and abolished by me . . . ("By the Soviets and the democracy!" *the person from the same loge on the second tier shouted demonstratively, eliciting the protest and indignation of almost the whole audience.*)

Yes, by the democracy, because everything that I have done, I have done in the name of the democracy and on behalf of the democracy. (*Loud applause.*)

The Shadow of Napoleon

You recall the time, comrades and citizens, when the Russian offensive began. In a certain segment of the democracy they were saying at that time that I, Kerensky, was practically the pretender to the title of Napoleon.

I was then saying, comrades, that by undermining the authority of the revolutionary power, by destroying the solidarity and the strength of the troops organized on the basis of revolutionary discipline, . . . you are yourselves, by your own hand, preparing for the coming of a general on a white horse or a Napoleon.

In spite of all the measures that were adopted by the democracy and the Government for creating a revolutionary army through a regimen of confidence and persuasion, our work was subverted.

Kalushch and Ternopol'

And later the retreat from Galicia was not as terrible as were the unforgettable scenes of the pogroms in Kalushch, Ternopol', and other towns.

I will not recall these terrible scenes; they who created them will answer for them; but I must remind you that this was the great turning point when many began to doubt the strength of the revolutionary power, the revolutionary troops, and the ideas with which we went into the army to perform the great work of the new, revolutionary, military organization. From this point on, day in and day out, [we witnessed] the results of this blow endured by our native land, which was born for freedom on the fields of Galicia.

First Reports About the Plot

I find it necessary to declare categorically that information on the preparation for a possible military *coup* became known to me long before the events themselves. And from then on, I fought to forestall these events by every possible means. . . . ("The first general of Russia," *an ironic [voice] was heard from the loge of the second tier to the left.* "He let the cat out of the bag," *someone from the stalls picked up. Noisy protests followed these inadmissible outbursts, and Chairman N. S. Chkheidze was forced to announce that he would have to resort to unpleasant measures with respect to those who were disturbing the order.*)

"I Want to Tell the Country"

It makes no difference to me how those who obviously do not want to believe me react to my words. I want to tell the meeting as such, I want to tell the country, what really happened. This is not the first time—every time that attempts were made to overthrow the revolutionary order, either from the left or from the right, they were always preceded by indecent and sordid attacks on my person. This does not disturb me. The course that is dictated to me by the whole country and by the organized, statesmanlike democracy is, indeed, the path that will save the country from jeopardy, regardless of its source. (*Applause.*)

The Difficulty of the Struggle

You know, comrades and citizens, how difficult it is, in a new, free order, to struggle against those who, without restricting themselves to free assembly, press, and propaganda, are, in addition, forging an attack against the power and the country by means of a conspiracy. We do not have the means of combating them that the old regime had at its disposal. We despise these means. (*Cry:* "The Bolsheviks do not despise them!")

When the information relayed to me became reliable, I was compelled, in complete agreement with the democracy and the Provisional Government, to pass a law [granting] to the Minister of War the right to exile or imprison certain persons without bringing them to trial. I did this because we knew many things which, owing to the conditions of Russian life, we could not reveal.

. . .

A Matter of Systems

I must state flatly that this was a period of struggle between two systems, and at the Moscow Conference, on behalf of the Provisional Government, I said: "You can try to do away with the Provisional Government and try to attack the organization of the new country, but you can only do this over our dead bodies." (*Applause.*)

This commitment which I made at the Moscow Conference we have fulfilled, and we will fulfill it again if the danger of undermining the present system is great, from whichever side it may come. (*Applause.*)

Every misfortune on the front was used to present us with an ultimatum. . . .

Many at the Moscow Conference did not understand at whom the threat heard in the declarations of the Provisional Government was aimed, and it was felt that the Provisional Government knew something already.

Yes, we knew and we were prepared. We were on our guard, as ever-new demands kept coming in.

. . .

V. N. L'vov

The defeat at Riga and the retreat of the Russian troops strengthened the aspirations which nestled around Stavka. I will not name names. This will be revealed at the inquest, but I assert that even before V. N. L'vov came to me, a former civic leader approached one of the most prominent civic leaders in Moscow and demanded a meeting with me, declaring: "Let Kerensky bear in mind that henceforth there will be no changes in the Provisional Government without the consent of Stavka."

Kornilov and Petrograd

In view of the circumstance that the front was getting closer to the capital, it was necessary to make a change in the military conditions around Petrograd. At that time a demand was again made for the immediate transfer of all armed forces to the Supreme Commander, and it cost me a great deal of effort to keep Petrograd and its environs outside the jurisdiction of the Supreme Commander.

Mounted Corps

I also demanded that new forces be placed at the disposal of the Provisional Government for the purpose of protecting the Provisional Government against any attempted revolts.

I will not enter into polemics and refutations here, but I can only emphasize the fact that someone in the press took the liberty of stating that evidently Kornilov and Kerensky had jointly aspired for dictatorship.

Is not the present audience aware that when L'vov came to me he was arrested the very same evening, and that his last conversation with me took place in the presence of a witness who can confirm whether L'vov spoke to me as a returning envoy or whether he spoke with me as with a person who was flabbergasted at the unexpected demand?

There was no time for delay, because General Krymov, whom I had appointed to the Southwestern Front, was moving toward Petrograd in accordance with another order appointing him Commander of the Petrograd Army.

At this moment it was demanded that I leave immediately for Stavka for final negotiations.

"My Warning"

I cannot say very much here on this question. But I must firmly state that my warning which I issued in the months of June and July about the events I foresaw, pleading for avoidance of any line of conduct that could provoke such events, remained in vain.

When I was driving to Stavka and doing everything that was necessary to preserve the fighting capacity of the army, at that time——. But I won't speak about this. I only want to say that I can give but one reply to all the slanders and betrayals: not only had I given a warning, but I was on the post when I was needed.

The words I spoke have come true. Do not think that if I am being attacked by the Bolsheviks I do not [command] democratic forces, that I am hanging in the air. Bear in mind that if you only start something the roads will be blocked, the troops will not advance, and your dispatches will not go out. (*Applause from the left and the right.*)

Do not think that my person and attacks on my person interest me in this connection. That is not why I am saying this. I am saying this because I feel that this company is destroying the unity of the democracy and is giving rise to the greatest disasters.

I knew what they wanted because, before seeking out Kornilov, they were coming to me and were proposing that I take that course.

Meaning of the Events

The entire meaning of these events is that the Provisional Government, loyal to its oath, was struggling against any attempt, under any guise, to introduce a dictatorship into Russia. And now, just as in June, I must tell you: be on your guard; beware of the paths that might lead the democracy and the State Power astray from that one and only course that we have been pursuing until the present. . . . ("*And what have you done?" they asked, ironically, from the left. And once again, noisy protests against this cry were heard from all the benches, which quieted down only when N. S. Chkheidze declared unequivocally that he would see to it that all persons violating order would be "shown the door."*)

Comrades, citizens! The strength of the Russian State and the Russian democracy lies in the great wisdom which has illumined our course to the present. As Chairman Chkheidze has correctly stated, everything that provokes discord and internecine dissension is the means by which the old gods and the real counterrevolutionaries have been paving the way for their return. One cannot always prevent criminal work in time and with such success. If we deviate from our course, we might again come up against a movement that might take on such proportions that we would be unable to control it.

I have said what I think and what I know. . . .

Anarchy in the Country

In greeting this Conference, the Provisional Government has instructed me to state that, now as never before, it is necessary to strain every nerve and muster all the force of reason in the State. The Provisional Government is receiving telegrams from all corners about the ever-increasing anarchy which is sweeping over the country. Pogroms are beginning to occur, senseless plunder of other people's property by gangs of people who understand nothing and take nothing into consideration.

. . .

If the Government and the country do not hear the firm and resolute voice of this Conference, if the country does not hear that the real minds of the State have assembled here, placing the good of the people above everything else, then the revolution will collapse. Can it be that now, when every day we await with trepidation new telegrams about great losses and shocks, when we do not know with what strength or means we will be beating back with our bare hands this terrible campaign on the front—can it be that at this time we will not possess the awareness and the sense of responsibility to the great gains of freedom and the country which we serve? (*Noisy and prolonged applause.*)

. . .

The Only Path

As Supreme Commander, I must bear witness that, aside from insignificant exceptions, the army, from top to bottom, has shown itself to be loyal to the new fatherland, loyal in its service to it. (*Storm of applause.*)

All of us, leaders of the army, are in favor of organizing it along the principles of reason and harmonious work of all its elements.

The Death Penalty

("And what of the death penalty, Marat . . ." *was heard from the left. At first, Kerensky paused, then with a quiet, muffled voice, he continued:*)

Yes, at the beginning of the revolution the death penalty was abolished, but later, at the demand not only of the commanders but also the public organizations of the front, it was reintroduced. (*Shouts:* "Disgrace.")

The front curses and calls to shame those who, in spite of all the warnings, were perverting the ignorant people, [and creating situations] which reached the point of horrifying scenes where young children and nurses were raped by the dozen.

But I say to you, who shout from over there: When just a single death sentence will be signed by me, the Supreme Commander, then I will permit you to curse me.

One must work and fight only by truth. Truth saves, while lies and political gains will destroy those who toy with the country as well as the country itself. (*Applause.*)

When Kornilovism came, the army understood that it was precisely for the reason of its hesitation and the disappearance of military courage that these moods arose, that attacks against the free country were provoked. And everyone returning from the front testifies that the fighting power, the organization, and mutual trust have now increased.

But do not think that there is no one else in the army besides soldiers. There are valiant officers who are perishing and dying for Russia. (*Applause.*)

Let Him Be Cursed

Anyone who took advantage of these somber days to enter the army again with the intention of instilling hatred and dissension against the commanders, let him be cursed. (*A. F. Kerensky pronounced these words with great force, which gave rise to a stormy ovation.*)

. . .

The Provisional Government did not permit me to speak like this. I have to say that no matter what tomorrow and the future have in store for us, we will remain the same defenders of freedom, of our native land, and of the happiness of the people as we have been up to the present. (*Applause.* "To what native land?" *was heard from the left.* "Silence . . . Down with the friends of Wilhelm. Away with the Germanophiles . . ." "You are the grief of our native land," [*came an*] *answer from the upper loge. From all sides came noise and hissing in answer to this exclamation. It was with difficulty that Chairman N. S. Chkheidze succeeded in restoring order.*)

Heavy Cross

. . . When I come here, I forget the conventions of the position I occupy and I speak to you as a human being. But not everyone here understands a human being. I will speak to you now in the language of authority:

Anyone who dares to encroach upon the free republic, [anyone] who dares to plunge a knife into the back of the Russian army, will discover the might of the revolutionary Provisional Government, which governs by the faith and the confidence of the whole country. (*Noisy applause.*)

Long live the immortal revolution and the free Russian Republic. (*Everyone arose and applauded. "Long live the Supreme Commander," was heard from the ranks of the delegates from the front. Shouts of "Hurrah," a new ovation to A. F. Kerensky. "Long live the revolutionary army and the officers, who will all save us from ruin and disgrace," shouted A. F. Kerensky from the loge. And again applause, and again ovations, which continued long after Verkhovskii, the Minister of War, took his place on the rostrum.*)

Speech of V. M. Chernov

Comrades! The beginning of our meeting today reminded me of some of the scenes at the Moscow Conference. There, the mutually hostile demonstrations were understandable and the dividing line was indisputable—bourgeois Russia with her allies, including such famous names as General Kornilov, Kaledin, and others. (*Voice from the audience: "Do not touch Kaledin!" Noise and applause. N. S. Chkheidze announced that if the noise did not cease, the comrades who were disrupting the order of the meeting would be shown the door in order to restore silence. The noise subsided and V. M. Chernov continued his speech.*)

Bourgeois and Democratic Russia

Thus, comrades, the dividing line was clear to us: bourgeois and toiling, democratic Russia demonstrated on points of issue against each other, but here, comrades, before speaking about the necessity of one coalition or another, it is necessary to establish unity in our own midst, to create that great democratic coalition which alone can defend or not defend, accept or reject, such coalitions as it may find advantageous, but not such that would take advantage of it.

Two Foes

An enormous task lies before the democracy. It must fight against those centrifugal trends that are breaking up the cause of the revolution, in order to lead the country out of the impasse, out of the general, complete disorganization. We are confronted by two terrible foes. The first of these is a semicircle of fire which has enveloped us, which, like a pump, is draining all our resources, all our vital forces; and the second foe is the force of the general social, economic, and financial disorganization.

Democratic Coalition

If we create a coalition, a single, democratic, powerful [coalition], it will be an enormous force which will arouse the enthusiasm of the country, which will closely unite the broad democratic masses, and which will be able to pursue its foreign policy with an authoritative voice and place the domestic policy on a sound basis.

. . .

Its Results

The first coalition was an unavoidable experiment. The Russian people derived their lessons and conclusions from it.

The first coalition indicated the natural subsequent course. The reduced Provisional Government, formed on a parity basis, which was in existence for such a short time, was nevertheless a step forward.

A Step Backward

But after this step forward, a step backward was made. The democratic front was broken through. One fine day, the Tauride Palace was besieged by the Petrograd revolutionary proletariat and soldiers, and this was an immense blow to the democracy. The forces of the democracy weakened, and this was taken into account perfectly well by its political opponents. A shift to the right commenced. And this trend had to reach its logical conclusion. It was not difficult to foresee that it would result in a revolt and a conspiracy from the right.

An Interval of Sterility

The interval between the two seditions, the sedition that began from the left and the sedition that began from the right—this was an interval of sterility. . . .

Pressure on the Government

Just before the Kornilov revolt, under the pressure of higher commanders, a certain number of whom clearly saw the recovery of the country as their ultimate aim, this part of the commanders exerted pressure on the Government . . . in order to obtain from it the largest number of repressions, first on the front and later in the rear.

To our shame, people were found from the revolutionary milieu who undertook to be connecting links between Kornilov and the point on which pressure was to have been exerted.

Such was the situation. Before us is a whole series of accursed problems of Russian life which, by this one negative experiment, cannot be resolved.

Chronic Crisis

The central power of the Provisional Government is in a constant state of crisis. This instability, this changeability of the central power, is the source of discontent, of feverish agitation in the country; it makes the country feel nervous and interferes with the work.

How to Resolve the Question of Power?

Comrades, how is the question of power to be resolved? To date, we have proceeded from the principle of combining all that might be considered to be the vital forces of the country.

What does vital forces mean? Vital forces are those that stand for a new republican order.

We used to consider that a coalition of those determined forces decides the combination of the government, while the program of the government was, so to speak, a derivative from the fact of the coalition. And now, comrades, at this historical moment, I think that it is time to invert our reasoning, to place it on its seat [instead of] its head.

One must first proceed from the program and measure, by this program, the different forces which will be capable of carrying out this program with an open heart. Then create your program first of all, and, on its basis, become yourselves a single, great, toiling democratic coalition.

With Whom Is It Possible to Unite?

It is possible to fuse with those who are capable of subscribing to the program which was proclaimed at the Moscow Conference. But the following qualification must be made in this respect: *a coalition with the Party of the People's Freedom is no longer possible.* We have already had the experience of such a coalition. The central line of action of this party is calculated upon the collapse of the democracy.

You know the peril of this policy; you must say: no compromises, no coalitions with the central political headquarters of the party that brought its narrow party egotism to an entire popular slogan.

Summarizing all that has been said: you must find a program, follow it, join forces with those who can follow this program; if there are deserters, carry it out by yourselves. It will be the kind of work that will arouse general enthusiasm, [an enthusiasm] which can no longer be aroused by words which have been said over and over again.

Speech of Kamenev

Comrades! The Minister-President and the Supreme Commander has asked us to speak the truth here. It is true that this request was accompanied by threats. The threats we will ignore, but we consent to speak the truth.

Refusal of Confidence

Our first word of truth from the party, on behalf of which I have the honor to speak to you, will be that the six-month record of the different compositions of the Provisional Government compels us to refuse to give [a vote of] confidence to the policy which is now headed by Minister Kerensky. (*Voice from the audience*: "Impudent fellow." *Commotion and applause.*)

Comrades, I assume that we are living in a republic where, at this plenary session of representatives of the workers' democracy, the party of the proletariat has the right to say it does not have confidence in this or that government without its being construed as [an attempt to] overthrow the Russian State.

Kerensky's Mistake

Kerensky was mistaken in his belief that a policy of no confidence in him is a policy of no confidence in the Russian Republic. I believe that we must reject loud harangues as a means of settling the problem before us of [forming] a government. [This must be done] only on the basis of a realistic appraisal of that bitter experience of six months under a coalition government. And our lack of confidence is not based on lack of confidence in the person of A. F. Kerensky —not at all. It is based on the experiment that was made; it is based on taking stock of the class forces which have emerged during these six months.

. . .

Weigh the situation. If you want a coalition with the bourgeoisie, then form this honest coalition with the Kadets. But if the Kornilov revolt has taught you what the party of the proletariat has been saying from the very beginning of the revolution, then you must say that there is but one salvation for revolutionary Russia, that there is only one way of restoring the confidence of the army . . . only one way of restoring the confidence of the peasantry that they will receive the land, only one way of restoring the worker's belief that he is living in a republic—and this is the seizure of power by the very organizations of workers, peasants, and soldiers.

.   .   .

The Only Way Out

Can a new experiment with a coalition be made? My answer is in the negative. And this is why. If we accept the program adopted at the Moscow Conference, then where are the forces, the political groups that will agree to carry it out? The bourgeois elements have only one such political party—the Kadets. But it does not accept this program, as was revealed at the Moscow Conference. We cannot enter into a coalition with it on the basis of this platform, but if we reject the Party of the People's Freedom, then there are no other political groups with which we could enter into a coalition. (*Applause.*) There is no point in deluding ourselves. One cannot substitute Kishkin-Tereshchenko or Nekrasov for the large political party which is the only representative of the bourgeois elements in Russia. . . .

Thus, the only way out is [this]: the power must not be a coalition [government]; the power must pass into the hands of the democracy (*applause*), not to the Soviet of Workers' and Soldiers' Deputies, but into the hands of the democracy, which is quite fully represented here today. The government must be formed here. Here, too, a body must be nominated to which this government will be responsible (*applause*). Cognizant of the full weight of responsibility which may fall on our shoulders, and of the fear of responsibility which is apparent among us, I think that we must cast aside this dread of responsibility. Then take over this power. . . . (*He was applauded by a section of the audience.*)

Speech of I. G. Tseretelli

The Experience of the Past

Comrades, in discussing the question before us, reference was made here to past experience, and in particular to the experience of those representatives of the democracy who have already participated in the coalition government. Criticizing the work of the coalition government, they drew the conclusion that the time has come to change the basis of the policy and to recognize the necessity of forming an all-socialist government instead of a coalition. It seems to me that an evaluation of the past is indeed the only way in which we can determine our future tactics. If the idea of a coalition contributed nothing to the democracy . . . and ended only with the Kornilov conspiracy, if this was a result of the work of the coalition, then, of course, it must be discarded and the entire basis of our policy must be changed. But I think, comrades, that he who . . . proposes to form an all-socialist power is setting an impossible task before this power. If the coalition became bankrupt because it could not give much to the people, or because many of the principles toward which the democracy was striving were not realized, or because the interests of the workers, the interests of the whole population, were not sufficiently protected—if one is to approach the question from this point of view, then I fear that a strictly socialist government which we establish in its place, which must redouble its demand for immediate assistance from a population that is enduring heavy material privations and facing complete economic ruin—I fear that even a socialist government will be unable to withstand these demands. (*Voices:* "Bravo!" *Applause.*)

. . .

The Coalition Did the Work of the Democracy

We must state: If the all-socialist government about to be formed has to function under the same circumstances as the coalition government functioned, then many of your hopes, comrades, will be disappointed, and this program will not be realized. (*Voices:* "Right. This depends upon you.") . . .

. . .

. . . I will tell you this, comrades: the coalition government fought against great difficulties, against great obstacles, and still it succeeded in performing the work of the democracy under the difficult circumstances in which it found itself. (*Voice:* "What has it done?") I will tell you, comrades, what it has done, and this, above all, will go down in history as the great result of the coalition policy . . .

It was said here that General Kornilov's plot came as the result of the policy pursued by the coalition government. Comrades, the revolution fears these plots, which inflicted blows and caused it to collapse. But if the policy that brought about this plot led to the defeat of this very plot, making democracy master of the situation—as we now are, the day after Kornilov's plot—then evidently this policy has performed a great feat. It has consolidated democracy in its encounter with counterrevolutionary forces and has isolated the counterrevolution. (*Applause.*)

. . .

A Coalition Is Possible

I want to speak about my own point of view. It was one of the views that were developed in the Central Committee. The three others were presented here by other speakers. From my point of view, the objective position of the bourgeois elements makes it possible to propose a coalition on the basis of the democratic platform. In resolving this question, I do not think that it can be formulated in the manner [proposed] by V. M. Chernov. He said: "Yes, a coalition, but with the exclusion of such and such parties." I think, comrades, that the elements involved in the Kornilov affair who have taken an ambiguous stand toward it cannot of course be a part of this coalition. There can be no negotiations with them, and one of the conditions that the democracy must make is that this coalition government conduct an immediate, thorough investigation of the whole Kornilov affair and bring to a public trial the parties involved in the plot. This is so, of course; but can one say that the party as a whole is involved in this affair? Are there grounds for making this assertion? (*Voices:* "There are, of course.")

. . . But when you are told that you must establish the extent of the participation of individual persons or organizations and, on this basis, reject an entire political party which is heterogeneous in its elements, then it is my profound conviction that this is an incorrect political formulation of the question. (*Applause.*) . . .

. . .

. . . Is it correct, from the point of view of the development of the revolution, to take steps which alienate us from the forces that are still capable of serving the revolution, steps which jeopardize the implementation of the program upon which depends the salvation of the whole country? (*Applause.*) [5]

1356. THE SESSION OF SEPTEMBER 19: THE VOTE ON THE COALITION PRINCIPLE
[*Izvestiia*, No. 176, September 20, 1917, pp. 5–7.]

A conference of all factions was held yesterday morning, devoted to the discussion of the way in which the question of the organization of power should be formulated for putting it to a vote.

Following these conferences, an urgent meeting of the Presidium was held, devoted to the same question.

As a result, the Presidium decided to proceed with the balloting in the following way: the first question to be put to a vote would be the general question of a coalition. In the event that the majority adopted a decision in favor of a coalition, the second question to be put to a vote would be: Should there be a coalition with the participation of the Kadets or without their participation? If the Democratic Conference found it impossible to have the participation of the Kadets, a third question would be submitted to a vote, which would to a certain degree be an amendment to the decision on the second question, namely: Is the participation of reliable Kadets desirable?

In view of the fact that the meeting of the Presidium was protracted, the meeting set for 1:00 P.M. was very late in starting.

Nervous tension reigned in the assembly hall. Shouts of "It's time," "It's time to begin the meeting" were heard more and more often.

Only after I. G. Tseretelli appeared on the platform and explained the reason for the delay did quiet become established in the assembly hall.

At 3:25 P.M., the Presidium appeared and Chairman N. S. Chkheidze announced that the meeting was open.

. . .

Voting

N. S. Chkheidze announced the decision of the Presidium as to what questions would be put to a vote. But before proceeding to the voting on questions of the coalition, the question was raised as to what procedure of voting should be adopted on this question: A secret ballot or a roll call vote? Five hundred seventy-four persons voted in favor of a secret ballot; 660 persons voted for a roll call vote.

. . .

At 4:30 P.M., the Democratic Conference turned to a roll call vote on the question of "For or against the coalition."

---

[5] Zarudnyi, Peshekhonov, Avksent'ev, and Dan also spoke in favor of the coalition principle. Martov and Trotsky opposed a coalition.

Results of the Vote

The roll call vote on the first question lasted over five hours. At 9:10 P.M. the vote was ended.

The meeting was resumed, and Rudnev, the presiding officer, read the results [broken down] according to groups:

Soviets of Workers' and Soldiers' Deputies: in favor—83; against—192; abstained—4; *Soviets of Peasants' Deputies*: in favor—102, against—70; abstained—12; *economic and food supply organizations*: in favor—34; against—16; abstained—1; *trade unions*: in favor—32; against—139; abstained—2; *co-operatives*: in favor—140; against—23; abstained—1; *military organizations*: in favor—64; against—54; abstained—7; *nationality organizations*: in favor—15; against—40; *municipal self-governments*: in favor—114; against 101; abstained—8; *zemstvo and guberniya executive committees*: in favor—98; against —23; abstained—2; *other organizations*: in favor—84; against—30; abstained —1.

Total: in favor of the coalition—766; against—688; abstained—38.

Thus, by a majority of 78 votes, the Democratic Conference declared itself in favor of the coalition principle. In view of the fact that the Presidium still had not finally established the voting procedure for subsequent questions, it announced a half-hour break.

Amendments

The meeting was resumed under the chairmanship of Comrade Avksent'ev.

"A coalition with bourgeois elements is adopted," he reported. "Voting remains on the two amendments to this position, which have been submitted by the Presidium. The first amendment reads: 'Such elements of the Kadet [Party] as well as of other parties that were involved in the Kornilov plot shall remain outside the coalition.' The second amendment reads: 'The Party of the People's Freedom shall remain outside [the coalition].' The amendments shall be voted upon in the order in which they were read."

"In reverse order . . . Vote on it in the reverse order . . ," was demanded persistently from the benches of the Bolsheviks and the left Socialist Revolutionaries. . . .

A commotion arose in the assembly hall; persistent demands were heard for voting on the amendments in the reverse order, and the Chairman was forced to resort to a vote in order to determine the order in which the amendments should be voted upon.

By a significant majority, the meeting decided to vote in the order that was proposed by the Presidium.

"Thus, I put the first amendment to a vote," reported the Chairman.

. . .

By a majority of 798 [votes] to 139, with 196 abstaining, the first amendment submitted by the Presidium was adopted. Among those voting in favor of this amendment was V. M. Chernov.

The Exclusion of the Kadets from the Coalition

Next on the agenda was the second amendment, which read: "The Party of the Constitutional Democrats [People's Freedom] shall remain outside the coalition."

. . .

Avksent'ev reported the results of the voting: 595 [votes] in favor of the second amendment; 493 against it, with 72 abstaining. Thus, this amendment, too, was adopted.

The formula as a whole, together with the amendments, was put to a vote. Once again a large number of speakers gave their motives for their votes.

. . .

. . . Before announcing the results of the voting, Chairman N. D. Avksent'ev announced a forty-minute break for a conference of the Presidium, because certain new formulas were submitted, and requested that the members of the Conference remain within the building of the Aleksandrinskii Theater in view of the gravity of the situation. Then, N. D. Avksent'ev read the results of the vote.

Results of the Vote

In favor of the resolution as a whole—183 persons, against it—813, with 80 abstaining. Thus, the resolution as a whole was rejected by an enormous majority.

After this, a forty-minute break was announced.

. . .

Comrade Tseretelli took the rostrum.

"The Presidium has discused the situation which has developed after the voting," I G. Tseretelli reported, "and has come to the conclusion that this voting shows that in our midst, within the organized democracy, there is no agreement, no unity of will, which could be translated into reality by the forces of the whole democracy or by its greater majority. The Presidium therefore considers it necessary to suggest that this voting be regarded as an index of the attitude of the present meeting in order that individual groups and factions may take the mood into consideration in taking steps to reach mutual agreement, mutual concessions, and in forming a single will of the democracy.

"With this aim in mind, the Presidium suggests that all groups arrange a meeting together with the Presidium, at which steps will be taken for reaching an agreement within the democracy. . . ."

. . .

"At the same time, the Presidium has decided to submit to you the following resolution adopted unanimously by the Presidium:

" 'The All-Russian Democratic Conference resolves that it shall not disperse until such time as it establishes the conditions for the organization and functioning of governmental power in a form acceptable to the democracy.' " (*Applause from the whole audience.*)

"I remind you that this resolution has been adopted unanimously by representatives of all trends and groups represented in the Presidium," I. G. Tseretelli concluded his report.

The voting on the submitted resolution was next in order.

"Perhaps the Conference would like to adopt it without voting," the Chairman suggested.

The stormy applause from the whole assembly hall served as the best indicator that there were no objections to this resolution and that it was adopted unanimously.

The suggestion about organizing conferences, indicated in Comrade Tseretelli's report, was also adopted, together with the resolution.

Thereupon the meeting closed.

1357. CONFERENCE OF THE PRESIDIUM WITH REPRESENTATIVES OF FACTIONS, SEPTEMBER 20
[*Izvestiia*, No. 177, September 21, 1917, p. 2.]

All day yesterday the Presidium of the Democratic Conference was in session at the Smol'nyi Institute. The session was enlarged by the participation of representatives of groups from the Conference which were not heretofore represented in the Presidium, a well as representatives of political movements and of Central Committees of parties.

1358. RESOLUTION PRESENTED TO THE CONFERENCE BY THE PRESIDIUM AS A SOLUTION TO THE PROBLEM CREATED BY THE VOTE OF SEPTEMBER 19
[*Izvestiia*, No. 177, September 21, 1917, p. 4. Presented by Tseretelli.]

1. The Democratic Conference resolves that in settling the question of forming a strong revolutionary government, it is necessary to demand the realization of the August 14[6] program, an energetic foreign policy aimed at concluding a . . . general peace, and a government that is responsible to a representative body, which, pending the Constituent Assembly, would reflect the popular will.

2. In selecting from its membership a permanent representative body, the Conference shall instruct it to assist in forming a government on the above-mentioned conditions; should bourgeois elements be drawn into the . . . government, this body can and must be enlarged by inclusion of delegates from bourgeois groups. [It was called first the Democratic Council, then, when it was enlarged by the addition of bourgeois representatives, the Provisional Council of the Russian Republic.]

3. The predominance of democratic elements must be preserved in this body.

4. The government must be held accountable and responsible to this body.

5. The Conference instructs the Presidium to present to it by tomorrow a project for the election of a permanent institution whose members shall be drawn from the Conference, and, also, to elect five representatives from its own membership who would immediately take the necessary practical steps to aid in forming a government on the above-indicated principles. These representatives must report on their work to the above-mentioned representative body and must submit their decisions for its approval.

Voting

It was resolved to vote on the resolution according to its points. The first point was adopted by 1,150 votes to 171, with 24 abstaining.

---

[6] Chkheidze's declaration at the Moscow Conference, Doc. 1235.

The second point was adopted by 774 votes to 383, with 84 abstaining.
The third point was adopted by 941 votes to 8, with 274 abstaining.
The fourth point was adopted by 1,064 votes to 1, with 123 abstaining.
The fifth point was adopted by 922 votes to 5, with 233 abstaining.

1359. TSERETELLI'S REPORT TO THE ALL-RUSSIAN DEMOCRATIC COUNCIL ON ITS DELEGATION'S NEGOTIATIONS WITH THE GOVERNMENT
[*Izvestiia*, No. 180, September 24, 1917, pp. 3–4.]

The first session of the All-Russian Democratic Council was held yesterday in the Aleksandrovskii Hall of the Municipal Duma . . .

. . .

O. S. Minor's Motion

Minor opened the meeting and moved that it proceed directly to the matter at hand.

. . .

The Chairman's motion was accepted. A recess was announced and the members of the Council went into the room adjoining the Aleksandrovskii Hall where caucuses of individual factions and groups were opened.

The caucuses lasted for quite some time.

. . .

Elections of the Presidium

The meeting was resumed at 8:00 P.M. Minor served as Chairman and reported that N. S. Chkheidze was selected Chairman of the All-Russian Democratic Council.

A representative of the Bolsheviks challenged the nomination.

"Both at the Congress of Soviets of Workers' and Soldiers' Deputies and at the Democratic Conference," he elucidated, "Chairman Chkheidze did not exhibit impartiality with respect to our faction. The Bolshevik faction will therefore vote against the candidature of Chkheidze."

The meeting heard the Bolshevik challenge in silence. But, as though by way of answering it, the members accorded a noisy ovation to N. S. Chkheidze, who appeared in the assembly hall of the meeting. . . .

N. S. Chkheidze took over as Chairman and announced the membership of the Presidium elected by agreement of all the factions. . . .

. . .

Speech of I. G. Tseretelli

Next on the agenda was a report from the delegation that was authorized to conduct negotiations on the construction of the government.

A statement was received on behalf of the delegation requesting that this report be heard and discussed at a closed meeting. This request was adopted.

A recess was announced.

When the meeting was resumed, the Chairman gave the floor to I. G. Tseretelli.

I. G. Tseretelli began his speech by explaining the reasons that forced the delegation, authorized to conduct negotiations with the Provisional Government, to request a closed meeting. This request was based on consideration of the fact that the present meeting was called to resolve the fundamental question of the organization of power. In rendering an account of the negotiations with the Provisional Government, it will be necessary to touch upon questions that must not be made public for reasons of national expediency.

Emphasizing the fact that the delegation had adhered strictly to the scope of the powers with which it had been vested, I. G. Tseretelli reported that the first step of the delegation was to inform Kerensky of the decision of the Conference.

A. F. Kerensky firmly assured the delegation that he personally found the resolution of the Conference acceptable, but that he did not consider that he had the right to answer for the Government as a whole. He therefore suggested the organization of a joint session of the Provisional Government and the delegation . . . suggesting, incidentally, that representatives of bourgeois elements, with whom there had already been negotiations about their participation in the government, also be invited to take part in this joint conference.

The delegation accepted this suggestion and the joint session thus took place yesterday.

The beginning of the meeting was devoted to clarifying the question raised by the representatives of the bourgeoisie as to how the representatives of the democracy view the significance and the rights of the Democratic Conference. Do they consider it to be the only source of power, and do they recognize that the Provisional Government, and not some other organ, expresses the sovereign will of the Russian people?

The members of the delegation pointed out that, of course, the only source of power is the Russian revolution, that they recognize the full significance of the succession of power, but that at the same time they, as representatives of the Democratic Conference, are spokesmen for the All-Russian Democracy.

After clarifying this question, the meeting turned to the practical examination of the points of the program of August 14 and the addition to this program made by the Democratic Conference.

The nature of the foreign policy was the first question examined. The members of the delegation pointed out that the program of August 14 contained no indication for the necessity of pursuing an active foreign policy, but the international situation has now changed and an active struggle for peace must become the basis of foreign policy. As practical [measures], the members of the delegation proposed that the future Provisional Government take firm steps for convoking an interallied conference, at which the question would be raised of revising the agreements. The members of the delegation insisted that a representative of the democracy attend this conference, along with the representatives of the diplomatic corps.

This proposal did not meet with any particular objections and it was learned that an agreement on these grounds was possible.

As for questions of domestic policy, the great majority of points of the program of August 14 also drew no protests on the part of the bourgeoisie.

In the realm of financial legislation, the bills on a property tax and a property loan provoked objections on the part of the representatives of the bourgeois elements, but they were strictly of a technical nature and could not serve as an obstacle to an agreement. At the same time representatives of the bourgeoisie did not object to a revision of the financial legislation of the Provisional Government from the point of view of enlisting the propertied elements of the population to carry the burdens of war.

As for the nationality question, instead of the points in the August 14 program, which speak of the publication of a declaration of the Provisional Government on the recognition of the right to full self-determination for all peoples, to be realized by an agreement reached at the All-Russian Constituent Assembly, the representatives of the bourgeoisie proposed the following formula: "The publication of a declaration by the Provisional Government on the recognition of the right of self-determination of all peoples on the basis of principles to be worked out by the Constituent Assembly."

The most fundamental point of difference was not the August 14 program but the question of the preparliament and the responsibility of the Government. After lengthy and heated deliberations on this question, we found it possible to agree on the following position. The Democratic Conference [i.e., Provisional Council of the Republic] will be officially convoked and organized by the Government and it shall include bourgeois representatives, numbering approximately 100–120 persons. Both the bourgeoisie and the democracy will organize their own representation. This institution shall have the right to put questions to the Government, and the Government will be obligated to reply to them. The Government will not bear a formal legal responsibility to this Conference, but it stands to reason that no provisional government will, in fact, be able to exist without receiving a vote of confidence from the preparliament.

After concluding his report, I. G. Tseretelli supplemented it by answering a number of questions put to him. He declared categorically that reports on the progress of the meeting that have appeared in the press were distorted and did not correspond to reality.

In answer to the question of whether anything was said in the meeting about severing relations with the Bolsheviks, I. G. Tseretelli replied:

"We said at the Conference that, in so far as the Bolsheviks hamper the execution of the adopted program, we will fight them, but we will fight with political weapons, considering it inadmissible to use any other means in a political struggle."

At the end of the report a recess was announced, in accordance with Rozanov's motion, in order that the factions might clarify their attitudes toward the situation that had developed.

Debates

At 1:15 a.m. the meeting was resumed.

The first to speak was Trotsky from the Bolshevik faction, who declared that the delegation had exceeded its power, for, contrary to the vote of the Democratic Conference, it entered into an agreement with the Kadets, and also it had rejected—in essence—the principle of the responsibility of the government.

Further, Trotsky declared categorically that the agreement with the Kadets was a provocation to civil war and that, therefore, the Bolshevik Party, together with the overwhelming majority of all the Soviets, proposed that negotiations be broken off and that they proceed to the establishment of a popular government resting on the support of the Soviets.

The next was Karelin, speaking on behalf of the left Socialist Revolutionaries, who declared that the result of the negotiations had once and for all exposed the bankruptcy of the idea of the coalition.

Dan spoke on behalf of the Menshevik faction.

Arguing against Trotsky, Dan declared that the Mensheviks had never been supporters of a coalition at all costs.

"The results of the agreement far from satisfy us, either in substance or in form.

"However, we see no other way out except a coalition, because the democracy alone does not have sufficient strength to save the country."

Resolution

Dan read the following resolution:

"Having heard the report of Comrade Tseretelli, the Democratic Council considers the establishment of a preparliament, before which the government must hold itself accountable, to be a major step in the creation of a stable government and one that assures the implementation of the August 14 program, a policy aimed at the earliest achievement of a general democratic peace, and the convocation of the Constituent Assembly on the designated date.

"The Democratic Council finds it necessary to establish a formal responsibility of the government to the preparliament and, finding the agreement outlined by the delegation acceptable under the given conditions, declares that the power may belong to a government which enjoys the confidence of the preparliament."

After Dan, Rudnev spoke on behalf of the Socialist Revolutionaries, joining the resolution of the Mensheviks.

The resolution was passed [by a vote of 109 for, 84 against, 22 abstaining].

1360. *Russkiia Vedomosti* ON THE CONFERENCE
[No. 216, September 22, 1917, p. 3.]

The Petrograd Democratic Conference ended in complete failure. Its participants proved incapable of coming to any mutual understanding on the basic question which was the purpose of the meeting, namely, the question of the organization of the government. The Conference expressed itself first in favor of a coalition government and later against it. And the Presidium in its expanded membership vainly sought during the entire day to devise some formula round which the heterogeneous elements comprising the Conference could rally. A solution was eventually found, but an entirely artificial solution. The Conference resolved to appoint from its body a special representative organ (Council) which was entrusted with the organization of the government.

Essentially this was no decision, but at best a postponement of the decision. The newly created representative organ will have to deal, first of all, with the questions of whether or not the government should be a coalition cabinet or a homogeneous body and whether or not the K.D. can join the coalition. In other words, [it will have to deal with] the same questions the Conference struggled with for over a week, arriving at no definite decision . . . Viewing the sharp differences of opinion displayed within all factions and groups comprising the Conference and the complete disorder which reigned during the sessions of the Conference, about which the socialist papers complain bitterly, we get a clear picture of disorganized helplessness and breakdown with the democracy.

But this helplessness still remains not without some pretensions. Unable to come to an agreement among themselves on what the government should be, the Democratic Conference nevertheless elects a special council to organize power and demands that this power be responsible to the Council . . .

Further, on what grounds is the Conference demanding that the Provisional Government be responsible to the organ elected by the Conference? It goes without saying that there can be no question here about any formal considerations, because the Conference itself and the representative organ elected by it do not fall into any legal framework and nobody gave them the right to call the ministers to account. Nor are there any moral or political considerations for the establishment of such ministerial responsibility. The Conference itself has just given a picture of its helplessness, its complete disunity of political thought. Nevertheless the government must be responsible to the organ elected by this helpless assembly. But the majority of the participants in the Conference (Bolsheviks—for some considerations; the Cooperators—for other considerations) openly declared that the Conference does not reflect the will of the entire democracy; that it is disqualified to represent even the democracy as such, let alone the entire country, and yet the government is to be responsible to this disqualified assembly. In some instances the responsibility of the government increases it, raises its authority. But of course the assembly to which the government is responsible must itself possess authority. However, responsibility to an incidental assembly with its incidental balloting, capable of annulling immediately the decisions just adopted, can lead only to further weakening of the Provisional Government.

1361. *Den'* ON THE CONFERENCE
[No. 168, September 20, 1917, p. 1.]

Something much worse than could have been expected has happened. This is a collapse!

For five days political passions boiled around the issue of forming a government, for five days fifteen hundred people, who have arrived from all parts of Russia and have left important public matters, were deciding a question on which depends the future of the revolution and of Russia. And at the end of the first day it was clear that the Russian democracy was not in a position to solve this question, that the struggle of opposite political aspirations did not allow it to tell the exhausted nation anything else but the story of the deep and dangerous crisis which was undermining it.

This is a serious blow, and we do not know how the democracy will be able to cope with it.

The thoughtlessness of the group of politicians who have invented the absurd formula of a coalition without the Kadets has covered the Russian democracy with shame in the face of modern times and of history. . . .

There was something shameful observable in the very way in which the question of the coalition without the Kadets was brought up after the principle of coalition had been accepted in a general way. It was mockery, not only in respect to political logic, but also in respect to the political honor of the all-Russian democracy.

.   .   .

It cannot go on like this! Russia is perishing—and you took it upon yourself, you took it upon yourself with all confidence, pushing aside those who were doing what they could to give Russia a government, and you have given neither a government nor an opinion regarding the government.

It cannot go on like this! This could take place only in *émigré* circles while party matters were being decided, party matters which touched the small interests of small groups of people; but with Russia one cannot act in this manner.

We are facing a shameful collapse, and no words are strong enough to brand those who are guilty of it and those who are their witting or unwitting aides.

1362. *Volia Naroda* ON THE CONFERENCE
[No. 126, September 26, 1917, p. 1.]

The Democratic Conference has concluded. Through the efforts of the Presidium it was possible to forestall its complete collapse. This would have been a genuine disgrace to democracy. But the inner moral and political disintegration of the Conference was evident even from the second day. We had before us a building with a preserved, or rather artificially cemented, façade. This façade concealed the broken-off blocks. Compromise made it possible to bring the Conference to an end. The results show the compromise. But the compromise is so fragile that there is no reason for optimism.

. . .

The Democratic Conference was called in order to form a stable government. Through its discords, contradictions, and differences of opinion, showing complete disunion of democracy, it completely undermined the foundation of the present government. Will it succeed in creating something new and stable? This question could be answered with a definite "yes," had the Conference itself agreed beforehand upon some definite decision. But there was no such agreement.

1363. *Delo Naroda* ON THE CONFERENCE
[No. 162, September 23, 1917, p. 1.]

The Democratic Conference has ended.

We hailed its opening, and we hail its favorable conclusion. We say this with complete objectivity, calmly weighing the work completed by the revolutionary democracy.

Later we shall "add up the results," analyze what has been done by the Conference and point out what has not been done.

We do not shut our eyes to those serious differences of opinion within the democracy which were demonstrated again and again at the all-Russian tribune.

We do not view optimistically the immediate future and do not nourish unrealizable hopes in the "preparliament" to which the Conference gave birth.

We think that the work of the Conference was carried on far from smoothly, nor was it done with due energy and productivity.

We shall speak later about what divided the indivisible democracy at the Conference, and why!

We shall speak now about what united it.

The Conference was concluded with the singing of the "Internationale" and other hymns of the revolution.

And that was the concluding chord of the Conference!

A democratic peace to the entire world!—that is the slogan that united the entire Conference, all parties and all factions. The prophetic word about peace immediately created that enthusiasm which was lacking at the Conference during the entire time of its work.

The revolutionary democracy realizes that it is just this small word that holds its fate, its vital interests, and the solution of that great task it set itself before the entire world.

It is not discouraged by the failures on the difficult road of the struggle for universal peace; it has not lost faith in it. Perhaps it ceased to be that youthful, pure faith which dictated the famous appeal of the Soviet of Workers' and Soldiers' Deputies to the peoples of the world.

Experience proved that, in addition, heroic organized efforts are needed, also a colossal effort within the country, in order to make the slogans of Russian democracy a reality for the entire world.

And even greater opportunities are presented for this work.

In the name of peace we must make use of the future "preparliament." And the Constituent Assembly, which must convene on the appointed date, will afford to the revolutionary democracy unprecedented opportunities for an "active foreign policy" in the name of peace.

Gradually the revolutionary democracy now takes the matter of peace in its hands, and it alone will be responsible for it.

Responsible not only to the revolution and the country, but also to the democracies of the entire world which [made it known] through the representatives from the S.R. and S.D. that it places all of its hopes in the Russian comrades.

Thus the Russian revolutionary democracy is now the sole warrior for peace in the true sense of the word. Is it taking upon itself the cause of single combat with the yellow Internationale?

Has it faith in its strength?

It answered these questions with the closing chords of the Conference—the hymn of the red Internationale.

1364. LENIN ON THE CONFERENCE AND KERENSKY
[*Rabochii Put'*, No. 19, September 24, 1917, p. 3.]

The so-called Democratic Congress has ended. Thank God, one more comedy left behind. . . .

Kerensky as a Bonapartist exposes himself more and more. He was considered to be an S.R. Now we know that he is only an S.R. since March, having jumped to there from the Trudoviks for the sake of advertising himself. He is a partisan of Breshko-Breshkovskaia, who is the "Mrs. Plekhanova" of the S.R.'s, or a "Mrs. Potresova" in the S.R. *Den'*. The so-called "right" wing of the so-called "socialist" parties, the wing of the Plekhanovs, the Breshkovskaias, the Potresovs—that is where Kerensky belongs, and this wing does not differ seriously from the Kadets in *anything*.

The Kadets praise Kerensky, He makes *their* policy; *behind the backs of the people* he takes their advice and that of Rodzianko; he is exposed by Chernov and others of connivance with Savinkov, the friend of Kornilov. Kerensky is a *Kornilovist*, who *accidentally* quarreled with Kornilov, and he continues to be in intimate union with other Kornilovists. This is *a fact*, which has been proved both by the exposures of Savinkov and the *Delo Naroda* and by the continuing political game, the "leap-frogging" of ministers, which Kerensky plays with Kornilovists, bearing the name of the "commercial and industrial class."

Secret deals with Kornilovists, secret crony relations (through Tereshchenko and company) with "allied" imperialists, secret postponements and sabotage of the Constituent Assembly, secret deceit of the peasants in order to favor Rodzianko, that is, the *pomeshchiki* (doubling of prices on grain)—that is what Kerensky *in fact* does. Such is his *class* policy. In this consists his bonapartism.

. . .

The people are exhausted by hesitation and delays. Discontent grows openly. A new revolution is imminent. . . .

. . .

Ten earnest soldiers or workers from a backward factory *have a thousand times more value* than a hundred delegates sorted by the Lieber-Dans. Especially in revolutionary times the use of parliamentarism should not consist of losing precious time for the representatives of rottenness but *in teaching the masses by the example of rottenness.*

N. LENIN

BOLSHEVIK GAINS AND PROPAGANDA

1365. LENIN'S LETTERS OF AUGUST 30 AND SEPTEMBER 12–14 AND 13–14 TO THE BOLSHEVIK CENTRAL COMMITTEE ON THE UNEXPECTED AID GIVEN TO BOLSHEVISM BY THE KORNILOV AFFAIR AND URGING A SEIZURE OF POWER

[*Collected Works of V. I. Lenin: Toward the Seizure of Power*, XXI, Bk. I, 137–39, 221–29. All dates in the text are New Style. See *ibid.*, pp. 299–300, for a description of the reception of these letters by the Central Committee.]

A.

It is possible that these lines will come too late, for events are developing with a rapidity that is sometimes absolutely giddy. I am writing this on Wednesday, September 12, and the recipients will read it not earlier than Friday, September 15 [*sic*]. But in any case, on a chance, I consider it my duty to write the following:

Kornilov's revolt is an extremely unexpected (unexpected at such a moment and in such a form) and a downright unbelievably sharp turn in the course of events.

Like every sharp turn, it calls for a revision and change of tactics. And, as is the case with every revision, one must be extremely cautious lest one lose sight of principles.

It is my conviction that those who (like Volodarsky) roll down to defensism or (like other Bolsheviks) to a *bloc* with the S.-R.'s, to *supporting* the Provisional Government, are unprincipled. This is absolutely incorrect, this is unprincipled. We shall become defensists *only after* the passing of power to the proletariat, *after* peace has been offered, *after* the secret treaties and connections with banks have been severed, but *only after*. Neither the fall of Riga, *nor the fall of Petrograd* will make us defensists (I would like very much to have this read by Volodarsky). Until then we stand for a proletarian revolution, we are against the war, we are *not* defensists.

And *even now* we must not support Kerensky's government. This is unprincipled. One may ask: must we not fight against Kornilov? Of course we must! But this is not the same thing; there is a dividing line here; it is being stepped over by some Bolsheviks who fall into "conciliation," who allow themselves to be *carried away* by the flow of events.

We will fight, we are fighting against Kornilov, even *as Kerensky's troops do,* but we do not support Kerensky. *On the contrary,* we expose his weakness. There is the difference. It is rather a subtle difference, but it is highly essential and one must not forget it.

Wherein, then, consists the change of our tactics after Kornilov's revolt?

In that we are changing the *form* of our struggle against Kerensky. Without in the least relaxing our hostility towards him, without taking back a single word said against him, without renouncing the task of overthrowing Kerensky, we say: we must *take into account* the present moment; we shall not overthrow Kerensky right now; we shall approach the task of struggling against him *in a different way,* namely, we shall point out to the people (which struggles against Kornilov) the *weakness* and *vacillation* of Kerensky. That has been done even before. Now, however, it has become the main thing. Therein lies the change.

The change, further, consists in this, that the main thing is now to intensify our propaganda in favour of some kind of "partial demands" to be presented to Kerensky, demands saying: arrest Milyukov; arm the Petrograd workers; summon the Cronstadt, Vyborg and Helsingfors troops to Petrograd; disperse the State Duma; arrest Rodzyanko; legalise the transfer of the landowners' lands to the peasants; introduce workers' control over bread and factories, etc., etc. With these demands we must address ourselves not only to Kerensky, *not so much* to Kerensky, as to the workers, soldiers and peasants who have been *carried away* by the course of the struggle against Kornilov. Keep up their enthusiasm; encourage them to beat up the generals and officers who express themselves in favour of Kornilov; urge *them* to demand the immediate transfer of the land to the peasants; give *them* the idea of the necessity of arresting Rodzyanko and Milyukov, dispersing the State Duma, shutting down the *Ryech* and other bourgeois papers, and instituting investigations against them. The "Left" S.-R.'s must be especially pushed on in this direction.

It would be erroneous to think that we have moved *away* from the task of the proletariat conquering power. No. We have come tremendously nearer to it, though not directly, but from one side. *This very minute* we must conduct propaganda not so much directly against Kerensky, as *indirectly* against the same man, that is, by demanding an active and most energetic, really revolutionary war against Kornilov. The developments of this war alone can lead *us* to power, and we must *speak* of this as little as possible in our propaganda (remembering very well that even tomorrow events may put power into our hands, and then we shall not relinquish it). It seems to me that this should have been transmitted to the propagandists in a letter (not in the press); it should have been transmitted to propagandist groups, to the members of the party in general. As to phrases about the defence of the country, about a united front of revolutionary democracy, about supporting the Provisional Government, etc., we must fight against them mercilessly, since they are *phrases*. What we must say is that now is the time for *action;* you, Messrs. S.-R.'s and Mensheviks, have long since worn these phrases thread-bare. Now is the time for *action;* the war against Kornilov must be conducted in a revolutionary way by drawing in the masses, by arousing them, by inflaming them (as to Kerensky, he is *afraid* of the masses, he is *afraid* of the people). In the war against the Germans *action* is required right now; *immediate and uncon-ditional peace must be offered on definite terms.* If we do this we *can* attain either a speedy peace or a transformation of the war into a revolutionary one; otherwise all the Mensheviks and Socialist-Revolutionaries remain lackeys of imperialism.

P.S. Having read six copies of the *Rabochy after* this was written, I must say that there is perfect harmony in our views. I greet with all my heart the splendid editorials, press reviews and articles by V. M———n and Vol———y. As to Volodarsky's speech, I have read his letter to the editors, which "liquidates" my reproaches as well. Once more, best greetings and wishes!

Lenin.

B.

Having obtained a majority in the Soviets of Workers' and Soldiers' Deputies of both capitals, the Bolsheviks can and must take power into their hands.

They can do so because the active majority of the revolutionary elements of the people of both capitals is sufficient to attract the masses, to overcome the re-sistance of the adversary, to vanquish him, to conquer power and to retain it. For, in offering immediately a democratic peace, in giving the land immediately to the peasants, in re-establishing the democratic institutions and liberties which have been mangled and crushed by Kerensky, the Bolsheviks will form a government which *nobody* will overthrow.

The majority of the people is *with* us. This has been proven by the long and difficult road from May 19 to August 12 and September 25: the majority in the Soviets of the capitals is the *result* of the people's progress *to our side.* The vacil-lation of the Socialist-Revolutionaries and Mensheviks, and the strengthening of internationalists among them, is proof of the same thing.

The Democratic Conference does *not* represent the majority of the revolution-ary people, but *only the conciliatory petty-bourgeois top layer.* One must not let himself be deceived by the election figures; elections are not everything: compare the elections to the city councils of Petrograd and Moscow with the elections to the Soviets. Compare the elections in Moscow with the strike of August 25. Here we have objective data as regards the majority of the revolutionary elements that lead the masses.

The Democratic Conference deceives the peasantry without giving it either peace or land.

The Bolshevik government *alone* will satisfy the peasantry.

Why must the Bolsheviks assume power right *now*?

Because the impending surrender of Petrograd will make our chances a hun-dred times worse.

But to prevent the surrender of Petrograd while the army is headed by Keren-sky and Co. is not in our power.

To "wait" for the Constituent Assembly would be wrong. By surrendering Petrograd, Kerensky and Co. can always *destroy* the Constituent Assembly. Only our party, having assumed power, can secure the convocation of the Constituent Assembly; and, after assuming power, it could blame the other parties for delaying it and could substantiate its accusations.

A separate peace between the English and German imperialists must and can be prevented, but only by quick action.

The people are tired of the vacillations of the Mensheviks and S.-R.'s. Only our victory in the capitals will draw the peasants after us.

What we are concerned with is not the "day" of the uprising, not the "moment" of the uprising in the narrow sense of the word. This will be decided by the common voice of those who are in contact with the workers and soldiers, with the *masses*.

What matters is that now, at the Democratic Conference, our party has practically *its own congress*, and this congress must (whether it wishes to do so or not) decide the *fate of the revolution*.

What matters is that we must make the *task* clear to the party, place on the order of the day the *armed uprising* in Petrograd and Moscow (including their regions), the conquest of power, the overthrow of the government. We must think of *how* to make propaganda in favour of this without committing ourselves in the press.

We must recall and ponder the words of Marx on uprising: *"Uprising is an art,"* etc.

It would be naïve to wait for a "formal" majority on the side of the Bolsheviks; no revolution ever waits for *this*. Kerensky and Co. are not waiting either, but are preparing the surrender of Petrograd. It is just the miserable vacillations of the Democratic Conference that must and will cause the patience of the workers of Petrograd and Moscow to end in a violent outburst! History will not forgive us if we do not assume power now.

No apparatus? There is an apparatus: the Soviets and democratic organisations. The international situation *just now*, on the *eve* of a separate peace between the English and the Germans, is *in our favour*. It is precisely now that to offer peace to the people means to *win*.

Assume power at once in Moscow and in Petrograd (it does not matter which begins; perhaps even Moscow may begin); we will win *absolutely and unquestionably*.

N. Lenin.

C.

.   .   .

To show why this very moment must be recognised as the one when it is obligatory for the party to recognise the uprising as placed on the order of the day by the course of objective events, and to treat uprising as an art—to show this, it will perhaps be best to use the method of comparison and to draw a parallel between July 16–17 and the September days.[7]

On July 16–17 it was possible, without trespassing against the truth, to put the question thus: it would have been more proper to take power, since our enemies would anyway accuse us of revolt and treat us as rebels. This, however, did not warrant a decision to take power at that time, because there were still lacking the objective conditions for a victorious uprising.

1. We did not yet have behind us the class that is the vanguard of the revolu-

---

[7] The July Days and the Kornilov revolt.

tion. We did not yet have a majority among the workers and soldiers of the capitals. Now we have a majority in both Soviets. It was created *only* by the history of July and August, by the experience of ruthless punishment meted out to the Bolsheviks, and by the experience of the Kornilov affair.

2. At that time there was no general revolutionary upsurge of the people. Now there is, after the Kornilov affair. This is proven by the situation in the provinces and by the seizure of power by the Soviets in many localities.

3. At that time there were no *vacillations* on a serious, general, political scale among our enemies and among the undecided petty bourgeoisie. Now the vacillations are enormous; our main enemy, the imperialism of the Allies and of the world (for the "Allies" are at the head of world imperialism), has begun to vacillate between war to a victory and a separate peace against Russia. Our petty-bourgeois democrats, having obviously lost their majority among the people, have begun to vacillate enormously, rejecting a bloc, *i.e.*, a coalition with the Cadets.

4. This is why an uprising on July 16–17 would have been an error: we would not have retained power either physically or politically. Not physically, in spite of the fact that at certain moments Petrograd was in our hands, because our workers and soldiers would not have *fought and died* at that time for the sake of holding Petrograd; at that time people had not yet become so "brutalised"; there was not in existence such a burning hatred both towards the Kerenskys and towards the Tseretelis and Chernovs; and our own people were not yet hardened by the experience of the Bolsheviks being persecuted, while the Socialist-Revolutionaries and Mensheviks took part in the persecuting.

We could not have retained power July 16–17 politically, for, *before the Kornilov affair,* the army and the provinces could and would have marched against Petrograd.

Now the picture is entirely different.

We have back of us the majority of a *class* that is the vanguard of the revolution, the vanguard of the people, and is capable of drawing the masses along.

We have back of us a *majority* of the people, for Chernov's resignation, far from being the only sign, is only the most striking, the most outstanding sign showing that the peasantry *will not receive land* from a bloc with the S.-R.'s, or from the S.-R.'s themselves. And in this lies the essence of the popular character of the revolution.

We are in the advantageous position of a party which knows its road perfectly well, while *imperialism as a whole,* as well as the entire bloc of the Mensheviks and the S.-R.'s, is vacillating in an extraordinary manner.

Victory is assured to us, for the people are now very close to desperation, and we are showing the whole people a sure way out, having demonstrated to the whole people the significance of our leadership during the "Kornilov days," and then having *offered* the bloc politicians a compromise which they *rejected* at a time when their vacillations continued uninterruptedly.

It would be a very great error to think that our compromise offer has *not yet* been rejected, that the *"Democratic Conference" still* may accept it. The compromise was offered from *party* to *parties.* It could not have been offered otherwise. The *parties* have rejected it. The Democratic Conference is nothing but a *conference.* One must not forget one thing, namely, that this conference does not represent the *majority* of the revolutionary people, the poorest and most embittered peasantry. One must not forget the self-evident truth that this conference represents a *minority of the people.* It would be a very great error, a very great parliamentary idiocy on our part, if we were to treat the Democratic Conference as a parliament, for even *if* it were to proclaim itself a parliament, the sovereign parliament of the revolution, it would not be able to *decide* anything. The decision lies *outside* of it, in the workers' sections of Petrograd and Moscow.

We have before us all the objective prerequisites for a successful uprising. We have the advantages of a situation where *only* our victory in an uprising will put an end to the most painful thing on earth, the vacillations that have sickened the people; a situation where *only our* victory in an uprising will *put an end* to the game of a separate peace against the revolution by openly offering a more complete, more just, more immediate peace *in favour* of the revolution.

Only our party, having won a victory in an uprising, *can* save Petrograd, for if our offer of peace is rejected, and we obtain not even a truce, then *we* shall become "defensists," then we shall place ourselves *at the head of the war parties,* we shall be the most "warring" party, and we shall carry on a war in a truly revolutionary manner. We shall take away from the capitalists all the bread and all the shoes. We shall leave them crumbs. We shall dress them in bast shoes. We shall send all the bread and all the shoes to the front.

And then we shall save Petrograd.

The resources, both material and spiritual, of a truly revolutionary war are still immense in Russia; there are ninety-nine chances in a hundred that the Germans will at least grant us a truce. And to secure a truce at present means to conquer the *whole world.*

Having recognised the absolute necessity of an uprising of the workers of Petrograd and Moscow for the sake of saving the revolution and of saving Russia from being "separately" divided among the imperialists of both coalitions, we must first adapt our political tactics at the conference to the conditions of the maturing uprising; secondly, we must prove that we accept, and not only in words, the idea of Marx about the necessity of treating uprising as an art.

At the conference, we must immediately consolidate the Bolshevik fraction without worrying about numbers, without being afraid of leaving the vacillators in the camp of the vacillating: they are more useful *there* to the cause of revolution than in the camp of the resolute and courageous fighters.

We must compose a brief declaration in the name of the Bolsheviks in which we sharply emphasise the irrelevance of long speeches, the irrelevance of "speeches" generally, the necessity of quick action to save the revolution, the absolute necessity of breaking completely with the bourgeoisie, of completely ousting the whole present government, of completely severing relations with the Anglo-French imperialists who are preparing a "separate" partition of Russia, the necessity of all power immediately passing into the hands of *revolutionary democracy headed by the revolutionary proletariat.*

Our declaration must be the briefest and sharpest formulation of this conclusion; it must connect up with the points in the programme of peace to the people, land to the peasants, confiscation of scandalous profits, and a halt to the scandalous damage to production done by the capitalists.

The briefer, the sharper the declaration, the better. Only two more important points must be clearly indicated in it, namely, that the people are tired of vacillations, that they are tortured by the lack of decisiveness on the part of the S.-R.'s and Mensheviks; and that we are definitely severing relations with these *parties* because they have betrayed the revolution.

The other point. In offering an immediate peace without annexations, in breaking at once with the Allied imperialists and with all imperialists, we obtain either an immediate truce or a going over of the entire revolutionary proletariat to the side of defence, and a truly just, truly revolutionary war will then be waged by revolutionary democracy under the leadership of the proletariat.

Having made this declaration, having appealed for *decisions* and not talk; for *actions*, not writing resolutions, we must *push* our whole fraction *into the factories and barracks*: its place is there; the pulse of life is there; the source of saving the revolution is there; the moving force of the Democratic Conference is there.

In heated, impassioned speeches we must make our programme clear and we must put the question this way: either the conference accepts it *fully*, or an uprising follows. There is no middle course. Delay is impossible. The revolution is perishing.

Having put the question this way, having concentrated our entire fraction in the factories and barracks, *we shall correctly estimate the best moment to begin the uprising*.

And in order to treat uprising in a Marxist way, *i.e.*, as an art, we must at the same time, without losing a single moment, organise the staff of the insurrectionary detachments; designate the forces; move the loyal regiments to the most important points; surround the Alexander Theatre; occupy Peter and Paul Fortress; arrest the general staff and the government; move against the military cadets, the Wild Division, etc., such detachments as will die rather than allow the enemy to move to the centre of the city; we must mobilise the armed workers, call them to a last desperate battle, occupy at once the telegraph and telephone stations, place *our* staff of the uprising at the central telephone station, connect it by wire with all the factories, the regiments, the points of armed fighting, etc.

Of course, this is all by way of example, to *illustrate* the idea that at the present moment it is impossible to remain loyal to the revolution *without treating uprising as an art*.

N. LENIN.

1366. REGULATIONS ON THE WORKERS' MILITIA
[*Izvestiia*, No. 162, September 5, 1917, p. 4.]

Confirmed by the Committee for the People's Struggle Against Counterrevolution attached to the Central Executive Committee of the Soviet of Workers' and Soldiers' Deputies.

I. Aims

1. The Workers' Militia shall be entrusted with: (a) the protection of mills, factories and workshops, barracks and workers' quarters in the industrial districts where such exist; (b) the maintenance of peace and order in the industrial district in the face of counterrevolutionary actions and the protection of public safety ([security of both] person and property) ; (c) rendering aid and assistance to military units and officers of the city militia when the circumstances so require, at the request of the commissar of the local district; (d) . . . guard, postal, and patrol duties shall be assigned to the Workers' Militia only in the industrial district and in those areas where such have not been assigned to military units or

the city militia; (e) all arrests, searches, seizures, requisitions, and other [forms of] security measures and measures for suppressing crime may be carried out by members of the Workers' Militia only by lawful means and in no [cases] other than at the request of the Committee for the Struggle Against Counterrevolution or the municipal commissars.

II. Personnel

.   .   .

3. The personnel of the militia shall be selected at the recommendations of socialist party and trade organizations, screened by factory committees and confirmed by the District Soviets of Workers' and Soldiers' Deputies.

4. During the initial period, the number of armed militia [men] for Petrograd must not exceed 8,000 persons;

.   .   .

8. The Chief of the Workers' Militia, [to be] elected by the district chiefs of the militia and confirmed by the Committee for the Struggle Against Counterrevolution, shall be in charge of the entire Workers' Militia.

9. The Committee of the Workers' Militia shall consist of two representatives each from the All-Russian Central Executive Committee, the Petrograd Executive Committee of the Soviet of Workers' and Soldiers' Deputies, the Central Council of Factory Committees, the Petrograd Council of Trade Unions and the Inter-district Council, and one representative each from the Headquarters of the Petro-grad Military District, the Municipal Duma, the Commissar in charge of the affairs of the former prefecture, and the Central Bureau of the City Militia.

.   .   .

11. All arms shall be listed, marked numerically, and kept in the District Soviets of Workers' and Soldiers' Deputies.

12. All arms kept in the Soviets shall be registered with the Committee for the Struggle Against Counterrevolution.

1367. STATEMENT OF THE PUBLIC PROSECUTOR ON THE CASE OF THE BOLSHEVIKS
[*Izvestiia*, No. 163, September 6, 1917, p. 4.]

In view of the release of a number of Bolsheviks involved in the armed demonstration of July 3–5, members of the press turned to the Public Prosecutor of the Petrograd Court of Appeals, S. V. Karchevskii, with the question: Is this release the result of an admission by the Prosecutor's Office of its mistake with regard to the Bolsheviks' case and a change in the opinion of the prosecution with regard to the very legitimacy of instituting these proceedings?

In answer to this, S. V. Karchevskii stated that he asked them to emphasize that the prosecuting magistracy's opinion on the Bolsheviks' case has not changed a whit with the resignation of N. S. Karinskii.

S. V. Karchevskii holds to the same views as those of his predecessor, N. S. Karinskii.

"The Prosecutor's Office," said S. V. Karchevskii, "has all the evidence for drawing up a well-grounded bill of indictment."

All the arrests were carried out as a necessary measure of suppression, and when it was later established that, with respect to some of the persons [involved], their release could not be used for covering up the tracks of their crime, they were set at liberty. L. Trotsky was released under this procedure. The question of releasing "all the Bolsheviks" as reported in the press was never raised.

1368. COMMENT OF *Volia Naroda* ON THE SOVIETS' ACTIVITIES
[No. 113, September 8, 1917, p. 1.]

. . .

From the early part of May, the Soviets, both the Petrograd and the All-Russian Soviet of W. and S.D. and the Moscow and the All-Russian Soviet of Peasants' Deputies, constantly exhibited a consistency and firmness in their line of conduct. Without succumbing to the psychology of panic and confusion, they firmly followed a definite course, not fearing attacks from the right or the left. The firmness and conviction of the policy of the Soviets reached a climax on July 3–5.

These were the days of difficult examination of the Soviets' political maturity. And the Soviets passed this test brilliantly. Neither the threat of bayonets nor the danger of arrest forced them to abandon their line of conduct. To the importunities of the mob, the Soviets replied with a refusal; to the threats of the Bolsheviks, with the reaffirmation of their unchanging line of conduct.

Such also was the policy of the Soviets later.

But something different is observed following the Kornilov action.

The easy victory over this counterrevolutionary attempt turned the head of part of the democracy.

. . .

. . . Following the Kornilov days the Petrograd Soviet of W. and S.D. adopts by an overwhelming majority a purely Bolshevik resolution. Yesterday's papers report that the Moscow Soviet of W. and S. Deputies has also adopted the same resolution.

Moreover, the same vacillation is observed both in the Central Committee of the All-Russian Soviet of Workers' and Soldiers' Deputies and partially in the Executive Committee of the All-Russian Soviet of Peasants' Deputies. The Menshevik faction, which up to this time adhered strictly to the principle of coalition, passes a vague resolution which may be interpreted in favor of as well as against coalition.

The Socialist Revolutionary faction gives a picture of the struggle of two currents and comes to no decision.

Moreover, events obviously turned the majority of the Soviets, and even entire currents such as that of the Mensheviks, to the side of bolshevism. Nothing else could explain a number of acts committed by the Central Executive Committees of the Socialist Revolutionaries and the Social Democrats recently.

Among such acts is the order by the Central Committee against the disbandment of the revolutionary organizations which came to life in connection with the suppression of the Kornilov revolt. As is known, these organizations took into their own hands purely governmental commissions during the days of the Kornilov movement. Such seizure at the time was desirable. Now however, after the Kornilov revolt has been suppressed, it is obvious that these organizations cannot enjoy the rights of official organs of government. . . .

It was in this connection that A. F. Kerensky issued an appeal to the revolutionary organizations, pointing to the necessity of transferring their functions to the government organs.

It would seem quite clear. Nothing, it would seem, could be more clear and necessary than this order.

.   .   .

But, alas! The Central Executive Committee saw in this order some sort of trick; it was suspicious of it, and, what is more, it issued a counterorder "not to dissolve the arbitrary revolutionary organizations," that is, they should not surrender their commissions. A counterorder has been issued. Thus the Soviet attempts to annul the government order.

The same vagueness and trickery is also seen in this government order by *Rabochaia Gazeta* in its vigorous attack against it and insistence that it be annulled.

Frankly, such interpretation of the government act could be accounted for only by the bustle of public confusion. Frankly, only by succumbing to the psychology of bolshevism could one accept such suspicions and such steps as both the Soviet and the *Rabochaia Gazeta* entertained.

In a sound social atmosphere such counterorders would have been impossible. They would be impossible, the more since *Rabochaia Gazeta* itself anticipates all the dangers of further exercise of governmental functions by the revolutionary organizations.

"The revolutionary democracy should be more cautious and wary. It is dangerous to play with fire. If today generals or commissars may be replaced and arrested by the Soviet of Workers' Deputies or its Committee to combat counterrevolution, tomorrow this right will readily be adopted by the company committee or regional food board, and day after tomorrow, by any group of workers or soldiers. And from here is but one step to lynchings."

It would be difficult to speak more convincingly in favor of the order by the Provisional Government and against what the *Rabochaia Gazeta* itself advocates.

But apparently in the state of social confusion all logic is lost. It is replaced by irresponsible impulses and thoughtless acts.

1369. The Bolsheviks Take Over Direction of the Petrograd Soviet

[*Izvestiia*, No. 167, September 10, 1917, pp. 4–5. As a result, a predominantly Bolshevik Presidium was named and Trotsky was elected President. The vote of September 9 resulted from the split in the S.R. Party as well as from growing Bolshevik strength. The Moscow Soviet was taken over by the Bolsheviks at about the same time.]

On September 9 the Petrograd Soviet of Workers' and Soldiers' Deputies held a session in the assembly hall of the Smol'nyi Institute.

.   .   .

The session was very late in starting. N. V. Chkheidze arrived at the Presidium only at 7:40 P.M. and was met with a storm of applause. He announced the session opened. . . .

Comrade Chkheidze

Comrade Chkheidze stated that the Presidium had decided to resign—which fact has already been announced in the newspapers—and that he now officially confirmed this on behalf of his comrades: Tseretelli, Chernov, Lieber, Dan, Gots, and Skobelev. In stating the reasons for the resignation of the Presidium, N. S. Chkheidze declared that the Presidium had expressed the will of the vast majority of the Soviet and that this reason alone had enabled it to remain in office.

"But at the last session [August 31]," he said, "a resolution was adopted which the Presidium fundamentally rejects. In addition, it was established that only a bare minimum was present to form a quorum.

"This means that either it was a fortuitous session or a vast majority of the Petrograd Soviet adheres to this position; if the latter is true, then the Presidium cannot act as spokesman for this will.

"It is physically impossible for the Presidium to remain, and, having resigned all its powers," said N. S. Chkheidze, "it suggests that a Presidium be elected which would represent the majority present here."

Comrade Kamenev

"Comrade Chkheidze has informed you of the resignation of the Presidium, explaining this step by the fact that the resolution adopted at the preceding session repudiated the tactics pursued by the majority of the Soviet. I think that these tactics are repudiated, not by that resolution, but by that policy of conciliation which was pursued by the Presidium. On behalf of the faction I declare that the Petrograd Soviet must have a Presidium which is based on proportional representation, in view of the fact that one trend, namely, the party of the Bolsheviks and the Mensheviks-Internationalists, has not had a single representative up to the present time."

. . .

[Short speeches by Comrades Bronzov, Martov, Kaplan, Bogdanov, Tseretelli, Trotsky, and Chkheidze followed.]

Comrade Weinstein

Comrade Weinstein, speaking on behalf of the faction of Mensheviks and Socialist Revolutionaries, read the resolution on the question of the Presidium. When Comrade Weinstein enumerated the names of the members resigning from the Presidium, he did not mention Kerensky's name.

The next speaker, Comrade Kamenev, noted this circumstance immediately and declared that evidently the Presidium earlier had excluded Kerensky's name from its membership, not finding him to be a worthy member of the Presidium of the Petrograd Soviet.

The floor was given to Comrade Tseretelli for a clarification of facts.

Tseretelli declared that [the reason that] Kerensky's name was not included in the [list of] members of the Presidium mentioned in Comrade Weinstein's resolution was of course not at all because the Presidium had taken this or that decision with respect to Kerensky, but because Kerensky was not in Petrograd at the moment "and we had no opportunity of contacting him and finding out his view on this matter," declared Comrade Tseretelli.

"But, personally, I am certain," said Comrade Tseretelli, "that, were Comrade Kerensky here, he would act in exactly the same way."

After a few speakers had explained their motives for the vote, Chairman N. S. Chkheidze informed the meeting that there were two resolutions on the question at hand: the resolution of Comrade Weinstein and the resolution of Comrade Kamenev. N. S. Chkheidze placed the [following] question before the meeting: Which resolution will the meeting choose for its basis of action? The voting began.

Volodarskii, representative of the Bolshevik faction, insisted on a roll call vote. This motion was adopted by the meeting.

A break was arranged for this purpose.

After the break, N. S. Chkheidze read the results of the roll call vote. They revealed that the resolution submitted by Weinstein received 414 votes, while the resolution submitted by Kamenev received 519. There were 67 abstentions.

The Resolution of the Bolsheviks

"We propose to re-elect the Presidium on the basis of [a system of] proportional representation, i.e., to supplement the present Presidium with the proper number [of representatives] of [heretofore] unrepresented factions."

"Thus, there is no Presidium," declared N. S. Chkheidze. "We ask the Presidium of the Soldiers' and Workers' Sections to take the place of the Presidium." N. S. Chkheidze left the Chairman's seat and went out of the assembly hall. Comrades Tseretelli, Dan, and others left with him.

.   .   .

1370. Resolution of the Petrograd Soviet of September 11
[*Izvestiia*, No. 169, September 13, 1917, p. 4.]

After the speeches of [Comrade Dan and] Comrade Trotsky, Comrade Zeiman, representative of the Socialist Revolutionary faction, gave a speech on the program. In conclusion, he read a resolution consisting of two sections: on the program and on the motives.

The section of the resolution that dealt with the program was adopted by an overwhelming majority. It may be summed up as follows: 1) quick and ruthless liquidation of the Kornilov revolt; 2) abolition of the death penalty; 3) exertion of every effort toward the earliest achievement of universal peace based on the formulas of the Russian revolution; 4) convocation of the Constituent Assembly at the appointed time; 5) immediate dissolution of the State Duma and the State Council; 6) transfer of all land to the temporary jurisdiction of the land committees pending the decisions of the Constituent Assembly; and 7) on the labor question: introduction of nationwide control over production with the assistance of workers' organizations; realizations, in practice, of the eight-hour day; resolute struggle against malicious shutdowns of enterprises, exorbitant capitalist profits, and mass unemployment; in the army: a radical purge in the officers' corps of all persons, from top to bottom, who are not thoroughly imbued with the spirit of the new democratic army and who are unwilling to cooperate with soldiers' organizations.

The Soviet further decided that, basically, it is impossible to have a coalition with the bourgeois elements. The membership of the new government must be strictly socialist.

The session then turned to elections to the Democratic Conference.

.   .   .

1371. The Petrograd Soviet Resolution in Favor of Calling an All-Russian Congress of Soviets
[*Izvestiia*, No. 178, September 22, 1917, p. 4.]

The Petrograd Soviet of Workers' and Soldiers' Deputies, having deliberated in a special session on the critical state of affairs which has developed, considers:

1) That the country is confronted with the threat of a new danger from the direction of the counterrevolutionaries.

International imperialism, in close alliance with the Russian bourgeoisie, is preparing to crush the revolutionary workers, soldiers, and peasants.

Counterrevolutionary organizations of the capitalists are still in existence and are in session even now in Moscow at the so-called Conference of Public Leaders, which was the center of the Kornilov movement. From a number of its orders, it is clear that the Provisional Government is striving to undo the revolution.

All these conditions have brought about an extremely strained situation, and confront the proletariat, the peasants, and the soldiers with the question of repulsing in the near future a possible counterrevolutionary attempt.

2) The artificially concocted Democratic Conference did nothing to improve the confused situation. On the contrary, this body was incapable of resolving the question of a revolutionary government precisely because of the artificial selection of its members and gave the impression of impotence of the revolutionary democracy. At the same time, it embodied and rallied the essentially antidemocratic elements of the right wing, which threaten the revolutionary democracy with their readiness at any moment to go over to the camp of open counterrevolutionaries.

The so-called preparliament is in fact turning into an organization where the deciding voice is reserved to the more conservative sections of the democracy at the expense of the revolutionary organizations of workers, soldiers, and peasants. Such a preparliament threatens to become a screen for new bargains with the bourgeoisie, for new postponements of the Constituent Assembly, and for the continuation of an imperialistic policy which signifies further disorganization of the national economy.

3) Therefore, the counterrevolution can only be repulsed by the organized centers of the revolutionary democracy—the Soviets of Workers', Soldiers', and Peasants' Deputies, and comparable organs.

4) The Soviets should immediately mobilize all their forces so as not to find themselves unprepared or caught unawares by a new wave of counterrevolution. Wherever they have full power, under no circumstances should they relinquish it. The revolutionary committees, formed during the days of the Kornilov affair, must keep their whole apparaus alerted. Wherever the Soviets do not have full power, they must do their utmost to strengthen their positions, keep their organizations in a state of alertness, create special organs as the need arises for combating the counterrevolution, and keep a close watch over the organized strength of the enemy.

5) In order to unify and coordinate the actions of all the Soviets in their fight against imminent danger and in order to resolve the questions pertaining to the organization of revolutionary government, it is necessary at once to convene the Congress of Soviets of Workers', Soldiers', and Peasants' Deputies.

1372. A BOLSHEVIK EXPOSITION OF THE AIMS OF THE REVOLUTION
[*Rabochii Put'*, No. 20, September 26, 1917, p. 3; and No. 21, September 27, 1917, p. 2.]

. . . .

. . . The misery of the poorest peasants, the horrors of war, the horrors of famine—all this makes it more and more clear to the masses that the proletarian road is the right one, that it is necessary to sustain the proletarian revolution.

The "peaceful" petty bourgeois hopes of a "coalition" with the bourgeoisie, of an agreement with it, of the possibility of "calmly" awaiting an "early" Constituent Assembly, and so forth—all this is being mercilessly, cruelly, inexorably smashed by the course of the revolution. The Kornilov movement was the last cruel lesson . . .

Discontent, indignation, anger at the army are growing among the peasantry and the workers. The "coalition" of the S.R.'s and the Mensheviks with the bourgeoisie, which promises everything and does not fulfill anything, excites the masses, opens their eyes, incites them to rebellion.

Opposition among the S.R. of the left (Spiridonova and others) and among the Mensheviks (Martov and others) is growing, reaching already 40 per cent of the Soviet and of the "congresses" of these parties. And *below,* among the proletariat and especially among the poorest peasantry, the *majority* of the S.R. and of the Mensheviks are of the "left."

The Kornilov movement teaches us. The Kornilov movement has taught many things.

It is impossible to know whether the Soviets can now go further than the leaders of the S.R. and of the Mensheviks, guaranteeing thereby the peaceful development of the revolution, or will again only shift from one foot to another, making thereby a proletarian uprising inevitable.

This is impossible to know.

Our business is to make everything possible in order to guarantee "the last" chance of peaceful development of the revolution, contributing to this by our program . . .

The following lines represent an attempt to disclose this program.

Let us spread it among the "lower" strata, among the masses, among the employees, the workers, and the peasants, and not only among our own, but especially among those of the S.R., among the nonparty ones, among the ignorant ones . . .

. . .

The Fatal [Consequences] of an Agreement with the Capitalists

1. To leave in power the representatives of the bourgeoisie, even in a small number; to leave such obvious Kornilovists as Generals Alekseev, Klembovskii, Bagration, Gagarin, and so forth, or such people who, like Kerensky, have proved their complete impotence against the bourgeoisie and their ability to act as a Bonaparte, would mean to open wide the doors to famine and to an inevitable economic castastrophe (which the capitalists wittingly speed up and render more acute) on the one hand, and to a military catastrophe on the other, because the army hates Stavka and cannot participate with enthusiasm in an imperialistic war. Besides, the Kornilovist generals and officers, while remaining in power, will beyond doubt wittingly open the front to the Germans, as they did in Galicia and Riga. Only the formation of a new government on new principles exposed hereunder could prevent this. After everything that has happened since April 20, to continue any kind of agreement with the bourgeoisie would be not only a mistake on the part of the S.R.'s and the Mensheviks but a direct betrayal of the people and of the revolution.

Power to the Soviets

2. All power in the country must be transferred entirely to the representatives of the Soviets of the Workers', Soldiers', and Peasants' Deputies on the

basis of a definite program and with the complete responsibility of the government to the Soviets. . . .

The arming of workers and revolutionary troops—that is, troops that have proved in action their ability to suppress Kornilovists—should be carried out without fail and everywhere with full assistance on the part of the government.

Peace to the Peoples

3. The Soviet government must immediately propose to all the belligerents (that is, to the governments and to the working and peasant masses at the same time) the conclusion now of a general peace under democratic conditions and also the conclusion immediately of an armistice (even if for only three months).

. . .

While proposing these conditions of peace, the Soviet government must immediately begin to realize them in action by publishing and canceling the secret pacts by which up to now we have been bound, which were concluded by the Tsar and which hold for the Russian capitalists the promise of plundering Turkey, Austria, and so forth. Then we must immediately satisfy all the conditions of the Ukrainians and the Finns, guaranteeing them and to all the nationalities of Russia complete liberty up to and including [the right of] separation . . .

. . .

If the least probable should occur—that is, if not one of the belligerents would accept even an armistice—then, on our part, war would become really forced, really just and defensive. . . .

. . .

[September 27]

4. The Soviet government must immediately declare all [rights of] private property for *pomeshchik* lands canceled without compensation and it must immediately transfer these lands to the jurisdiction of the peasant committees . . .

. . .

The Fight Against Famine and Disorder

5. The Soviet government must immediately place workers' control over production and consumption on a national scale. . . .

The immediate nationalization of banks and of insurance businesses and also of the main branches of industry (oil, coal, metallurgy, sugar, and so forth) is essential . . .

These measures, without reducing by one kopek the property of the average peasants, Cossacks, or small craftsmen, are beyond doubt fair for the purpose of spreading equally the hardships of war, and are urgently needed for the purpose of fighting famine. . . .

. . .

Fight Against the Counterrevolution of the Pomeshchiki and the Capitalists

6. The Kornilov and Kaledin rebellions were sustained by the whole class of the *pomeshchiki* and the capitalists, with the K.D. ("People's Freedom") Party at their head. This is already proved beyond doubt by facts published in the *Izvestiia* of the Central Executive Committee.

But nothing has been done either for the suppression of this counterrevolution or even for its investigation, and nothing serious can be done without the transfer of the government to the Soviets. No commission which does not possess governmental authority has the power to carry out a complete investigation, to arrest those guilty, and so forth. Only a Soviet government can and must carry it out. Only a Soviet government, by arresting the Kornilovist generals and the leaders of the bourgeois counterrevolution (Guchkov, Miliukov, Riabushinskii, Maklakov and Company), by dissolving the counterrevolutionary organizations (the State Duma, the Officers' Unions, and so forth), by placing their members under the supervision of the local soviets, by disbanding counterrevolutionary units, will guarantee Russia against an inevitable repetition of "Kornilovist" attempts.

Only a Soviet government can create a commission for a full and public investigation of the case of the Kornilovists and also of all other cases, even those started by the bourgeoisie, and the party of the Bolsheviks would call the workers to show full obedience and assistance only to such a commission.

Only a Soviet government could successfully fight such an obvious injustice as the seizure by the capitalists, with the help of millions plundered from the people, of the largest printing houses and of the majority of the newspapers. It is necessary to close the bourgeois counterrevolutionary newspapers (*Rech'*, *Russkiia Slovo*, and so forth), to confiscate their printing houses, to declare private ads in the newspapers a monopoly of the state, to transfer them to the newspaper of the state, which would be published by the Soviets and would tell the truth to the peasants. Only thus can one knock out of the hands of the bourgeoisie a powerful weapon of unpunished falsehood and smear, a weapon for deceiving the people, for confusing the peasantry, and for preparing counterrevolution.

The Peaceful Development of the Revolution

7. A possibility, which very seldom arises in the history of revolutions, of guaranteeing the convening of the Constituent Assembly at the date set without new delays, the possibility of saving the country from a military and economic catastrophe, the possibility of guaranteeing a peaceful development of the revolution, is now opened before the democracy of Russia, before the Soviets, before the parties of S.R. and of the Mensheviks.

If the Soviets would now take into their hands completely and entirely the national government in order to implement the aforesaid program, not only could the Soviets be guaranteed the support of nine-tenths of Russia's population, of the working class, and of the overwhelming majority of the peasantry; the Soviets would also be sure of the greatest revolutionary enthusiasm of the army and of the majority of the people, of that enthusiasm without which it is impossible to vanquish famine and war.

There could be no question as of now of any resistance to the Soviets, provided there is no hesitation on their part. . . .

.   .   .

If this possibility is missed, then the course of the revolution's development, beginning from the movement of April 20 and ending with the Kornilov movement, indicates the inevitability of a very acute civil war between the bourgeoisie and the proletariat. An inevitable catastrophe will bring this war nearer. As all the data and considerations conceivable to the mind of man indicate, it would end by a complete victory of the working class, by the poorest peasantry supporting the latter for the purpose of implementing the aforementioned program, but it may prove extremely painful, bloody, costing the lives of tens of thousands of *pomeshchiki*, capitalists, and officers sympathizing with them. The proletariat will not stop short of any sacrifices in order to save the revolution, which is impossible to do outside of the aforesaid program. The proletariat would give its entire support to the Soviets, provided the latter seize their last chance [of securing] a peaceful development of the revolution.

1373. *Delo Naroda* WARNS OF THE DANGERS IN GROWING BOLSHEVIK
STRENGTH AND IN POPULAR APATHY
[*Delo Naroda*, No. 165, September 27, 1917, p. 1.]

. . .

Yes, bolshevism is gaining ground in factories and in the Soviets of Workers' Deputies. Bolsheviks are elected to volost committees, to municipal dumas. They and the "left S.R.'s" succeed, and sometimes with no special effort, in passing their "left" resolutions: "all power to the Soviets," "peace on all fronts." All this is indisputable. But along with this weariness and apathy of the popular masses is growing, at the same time, another wing—the right, the counterrevolutionary wing—and even pogrom tendencies are ripening. In Moscow, which but recently was regarded as [dominated by the] S.R.'s, thanks to the brilliant victory of the S.R.'s during the elections to the central municipal duma—in this Moscow, according to recent reports, at the elections to district [municipal] dumas, the Bolsheviks took first place, the K.D. second, the S.R. third, and the Mensheviks fourth.[8] Moreover, the number of voters dropped 50 per cent. The Petrograd Soviet of Workers' Deputies goes over into the hands of the Bolsheviks, and Trotsky is elected president in place of Chkheidze. And, moreover, of the one thousand members, only four hundred participate in the elections. At the Obukhovskii factory where the S.R.'s were formerly in complete control, now after the re-elections to the Soviet of Workers' Deputies 11 Bolsheviks and 2 syndicalists are elected, but not one S.R. and not one Menshevik. And, moreover, only an insignificant number of workers participate in the elections. Meetings formerly thronged by thousands are now attended only by hundreds. In villages insignificantly small numbers participate in volost elections—from 3 to 10 per cent of the total population go to the elections. The circulation of socialist papers in many places drops; the circulation and influence of the yellow press, on the other hand, increases. Among the popular masses a weariness is observed from conferences, voting, and resolutions. Here and there pogroms flare up. Anarchical speeches begin to sound loudly, such as anarchist Bleikhman's recent appeals in the Kronstadt Soviet of Workers' Deputies for assassinations, and settling of accounts with "the whole 'Kornilovshchina,' beginning with Kerensky and Tseretelli," with the whole "Kerenshchina or Chernovshchina"—"Kerensky and his entire company are still alive" . . .

With a background of such phenomena the "country's tendency toward the left" assumes an entirely special character and meaning. We must talk not of the country's leaning toward the left but about the damage to the revolution. Only blind people and fanatics could evaluate these phenomena in any other way. And

[8] The Bolsheviks received 51 per cent of the vote as opposed to 11 per cent in July (Oliver Henry Radkey, *The Election to the Russian Constituent Assembly of 1917*, p. 53).

to all genuine revolutionaries, to whom it should be clear that a revolution can be created only by the will of all the working people, [to all of them] the meaning of the indicated phenomena is also clear. They conceal menacing forebodings for the revolution. If this process of the country's tending toward the left continues to go further, the revolution risks being no better off than at the start. The Bolsheviks and the "left S.R.'s" are already proving not to be left enough . They are replaced by the anarchists and syndicalists, on the base of the apathy and inertia of the popular masses. What does the Constituent Assembly promise us under such circumstances? What surprises has it in store for us from the point of view of its composition?

What deductions are we to make from the above? What is the solution?

We must, first of all, become aware of our responsibility to the revolution. This appeal must be addressed both to the country and to the Government. We must call to order all those who in the heat of political struggle are satisfied with the problems of today, forgetting about those of tomorrow. It is necessary to warn those who, carried away first of all by the struggle with political opponents, forget the positive problem of the revolution and democracy. We must be concerned now not with expanding the revolution but with deepening it, with sound creative work into which the popular masses should be drawn. Only under these conditions can the Russian revolution win; only then will the Constituent Assembly be able to work profitably for the creation of a new people's Russia.

1374. The Official Call for the Congress of the Soviets
[*Izvestiia*, No. 184, September 29, 1917, pp. 1–2.]

The Bureau of the Central Executive Committee has resolved to call the All-Russian Congress of Soviets of Workers' and Soldiers' Deputies around October 20. . . .

. . .

The decision to call the Congress of Soviets of Workers' and Soldiers' Deputies was dictated by the fact that, according to the bylaws, the Central Executive Committee has to start preparations for the convocation of the second Congress three months after the first Congress. This work has now been started and it must be assumed that the Congress will convene approximately four weeks hence.

The question of the Congress, however, cannot be decided in a strictly formal manner. And now, when the requirements of the bylaws have been fulfilled, one has to be clearly cognizant of the *political* significance of the Congress and to have a clear conception as to what specific questions the Congress will take up.

The Congress will convene around the 20th of October and will remain in session until the beginning of November. In the very heat of the election campaigns to the Constituent Assembly (the elections have been set for November 12), hundreds of valuable workers from socialist parties will have to leave their places: it stands to reason that an organization of the Congress by means of "transforming the mandate" to the Petrograd comrades would rob the Congress of any meaning! Consequently, the absence of hundreds of workers is absolutely inevitable.

But if the revolutionary democracy is making this big sacrifice, then it is necessary that every effort be exerted to prevent the sacrifice from being fruitless. This means that one must first come to a clear agreement on the political significance of the Congress and on the program of its sessions.

1375. "THE CONGRESS OF THE SOVIETS"
[Editorial in *Rabochii Put'*, No. 27, October 4, 1917, p. 1.]

Let us imagine that the elections to the Constituent Assembly are guaranteed; let us imagine that the elections to the Constituent Assembly have taken place. What! In this case the Soviets will no longer be necessary and we will have to dissolve them? Certainly not!

In the Constituent Assembly the *pomeshchiki* and the bourgeoisie will be in the minority. Do you think that they will bow before the decisions of the Constituent Assembly if there does not exist a *factual force* which will compel them to do so? . . .

It would be a complete idiocy of parliamentarianism to believe that the bourgeoisie and the *pomeshchiki* would give away the *pomeshchik* lands at the disposal of the Constituent Assembly without fighting, if the Assembly did not have the actual force *to compel* them to do so. One must fight with the spreading of *mystical* views on the Constituent Assembly. The Constituent Assembly will be strong only inasmuch as the *actual relationship of forces* is in its favor. If it does not have an apparatus in the provinces, if it does not possess an organized force in the army, among the workers, among the peasants, can one guarantee that the *pomeshchiki* and the capitalists will not mock the Constituent Assembly and simply dissolve it as the Tsar dissolved the first two Dumas? And what other apparatus can the Constituent Assembly have in the localities except the Soviets?

. . .

CHAPTER 30

October

THE FORMATION OF THE LAST MINISTRY

1376. DECLARATION OF THE THIRD COALITION GOVERNMENT, SEPTEMBER 25, 1917

[*VVP*, No. 163, September 28, 1917, p. 1. The membership of the new government was as follows: A. F. Kerensky, Minister-President; A. I. Verkhovskii, Minister of War; D. V. Verderevskii, Minister of the Navy; A. M. Nikitin, Minister of the Interior and Post and Telegraph; M. I. Tereshchenko, Minister of Foreign Affairs; S. N. Prokopovich, Minister of Food; M. V. Bernatskii, Minister of Finance; S. S. Salazkin', Minister of Education; A. V. Liverovskii, Minister of Transport; A. I. Konovalov, Minister of Trade and Industry; N. M. Kishkin, Minister of Welfare; P. N. Maliantovich, Minister of Justice; K. A. Gvozdev, Minister of Labor; S. L. Maslov, Minister of Agriculture; A. V. Kartashev, Minister of Confessions; S. A. Smirnov, State Controller; and S. N. Tret'iakov, Chairman of the Economic Council.]

Profound discord has come once more into the life of our country. Notwithstanding the swift suppression of the revolt of General Kornilov, the repercussions caused by it are threatening the very existence of the Russian Republic.

Waves of anarchy are sweeping over the land, pressure from the foreign foe is increasing, counterrevolution is raising its head, hoping that the prolonged governmental crisis, coupled with the weariness that has seized the entire nation, will enable it to crush the freedom of the Russian people.

The Provisional Government has a great and unusual responsibility to the people. History has entrusted it with the obligation to lead Russia to the Constituent Assembly. This responsibility is made bearable by the sincere belief that, united in the general desire to save the country and guard the conquests of the revolution, the representatives of all classes of the Russian people will understand the common task of cooperating with the Provisional Government in establishing a strong authority, capable of solving by earnest work the State problems as they come up, and leading the country, without more shocks, to the Constituent Assembly, the summoning of which, according to the profound conviction of the Provisional Government, cannot be postponed a single day.

Leaving to the Constituent Assembly, as the sovereign of Russia, the final determination of all important questions on which the welfare of the Russian people depends, the Provisional Government, as now completed, is of the opinion that only by carrying on with energy a series of measures in different spheres of State activity can it fulfill its duty and satisfy the pressing national needs.

The Provisional Government believes firmly that only the blessings of a universal peace will enable our great country to develop its creative forces. It will continue, therefore, its active foreign policy in the spirit of the democratic principles proclaimed by the Russian revolution, which has made them a national possession and which has for its object the attainment of universal peace, peace without violence on either side.

The Provisional Government, working in full agreement with the Allies, will, in the near future, take part in the interallied conference. At this gathering the Government will have among its plenipotentiaries someone who has the special confidence of the democratic organizations.

At this conference, where general war questions common to all the Allies will be decided, our delegates will also strive to come to an understanding with the Allies on the basic principles laid down by the Russian revolution.

While striving for peace, the Provisional Government will, nevertheless, with all its might defend the common Allied cause, protect the country, resist all attempts to take national territory and impose a foreign yoke, and will drive the enemy's troops from the borders of our native land.

In its efforts to raise the fighting efficiency of the army, the Provisional Government will follow the democratic way, which is the only one that can give successful results and which has already been announced in the order of the Supreme Commander and proclaimed by the Minister of War, in the name of the Provisional Government. The selection of the commanding officers will be based on their technical preparation to handle the problems of the present war, as well as on their loyalty to the republican form of government and on their ability to cooperate closely with the commissars and army and navy organizations in the rear and at the front. By means of these measures the necessary military discipline will be restored, without which a mighty army is impossible. In a special law that is to follow, the status, rights, and obligations of army and navy organizations will be carefully defined. Among the necessary measures that are most essential for raising the fighting efficiency of the army is the reduction in size of the various units in the rear, which have increased out of proportion, by demobilizing at first the older soldiers. To keep them longer in service would throw an additional load on the army, a heavy burden on the State treasury, and would be a loss to the national economy.

In order to keep indissoluble the bond between the rear and the front, to guard the national economy from further disorganization, to decrease those sufferings which lie so heavily on the shoulders of the laboring masses, the Provisional Government has been moved to undertake without delay the implementation of the following measures, which supplement and develop what has already been done by the Government.

1. National Economy

The Provisional Government will strive to set fixed prices on the basic articles of industry, and at the same time regulate the mutual relations of capital and labor, wages and hours of work. It will make wide use of the cooperatives, under general State control, in the preparation, production, and distribution of agricultural and all kinds of industrial products. It will also make wide use of private trade, under direct State supervision. It will introduce special legislation relative to State control over industry, with the participation of the laboring and industrial classes and active interference in the management of enterprises, with the object of increasing their productivity. It will further increase the number of labor exchanges and chambers of arbitration to protect the right of all kinds of labor to organize and will guard the technical personnel against all lawless attacks. It will prepare measures for the gradual and painless demobilization of the national economy and will reduce the misery due to unavoidable unemployment. It will, in particular, work out a plan for public works, having for its object the reconstruction of regions devastated by the war.

2. Land Relations

The immediate improvement of land relations should be entrusted to the land committees. In order to make the greatest use of lands and thus save the national economy from complete ruin, lands designed for agriculture should be placed under the jurisdiction of land committees by a special law about to be passed. However, the existing forms of land ownership should not be violated.

3. Finance

It will strive to reform the assessment of the inheritance tax, introduce a tax on surplus profits, on luxuries, and on property; increase in the necessary proportion the indirect taxes; and introduce new indirect taxes in the form of financial monopolies, with the participation of cooperatives and other public organizations in the distribution of monopolistic goods. It will reform the taxation machinery and introduce a system of inspection, so that no one shall evade the proper payment of tax. It will strive for strict economy in the expenditures of the State treasury and the elimination of all useless expenses. It will attract deposits into the State Bank through mutual loan and savings banks and other cooperative institutions and have State supervision over private credit institutions.

4. Local Government

It will put into force and further develop the democratic laws on local self-government, with a view to gradually transferring all the functions of local government to the organs of local self-government, while reserving the right for the Government commissars to watch over the legality of public acts of local self-government, and bring to an end the authority of executive committees, at the moment of the election of the local organs of self-government.

5. Nationality Question

It will recognize for all nationalities the right of self-determination on such principles as the Constituent Assembly shall determine. It will work out and issue laws that will give minorities, in places of their permanent residence, the right to use their native languages in schools, courts, institutions of self-government, and in their dealings with the local State organs. It will establish, attached to the Provisional Government, a council on nationality affairs, in which all the nationalities of Russia will be represented for the purpose of preparing material on the nationality question for the Constituent Assembly.

In setting itself these objectives, the Provisional Government realizes that not all of them can be carried out in the short time that still remains before the meeting of the Constituent Assembly. But the very attempt to carry them out will facilitate the work of the Constituent Assembly and will give the Government solid support in the field of national defense and the reconstruction of the national economy, as well as in its energetic, determined, and systematic struggle with all counterrevolutionary and anarchical attempts which ruin the country and the revolution.

In this struggle, as in all its activities, the Provisional Government, being the spokesman of the will of the revolutionary people, will collaborate closely with the organizations of the people. It sees in this collaboration the best means for solving some of the problems before the country.

In order that the revolutionary government may be closely in contact with the organized public forces and thereby gain the necessary stability and strength, the Provisional Government will, in the very near future, work out and publish a statute about a Provisional Council of the Republic, which will function until the meeting of the Constituent Assembly. This Council, made up of representatives of all elements of the population, *including those delegates already chosen at the Democratic Conference,* will have the right to ask questions of the Government and to receive answers by a certain time, to work out legislative measures, and to deliberate on all questions that may be laid before it by the Provisional Government, or that may arise from its own initiative. Drawing strength from such a council, the Government, preserving in accordance with its oath the inviolable unity and succession of State power created by the revolution, regards it as its duty in all its activities to take into consideration the important public significance of the Council, until the Constituent Assembly shall give full and complete representation to all elements of the population of Russia.

Firmly supporting this program which expresses the aspirations of the people, and calling on everyone for active and immediate participation in the preparation for the calling of the Constituent Assembly in the shortest possible time, the Provisional Government trusts that all Russian citizens will rally around it in the spirit of friendly cooperation in the name of the fundamental and urgent problems of our day—defense of our native land against the foreign foe, restoration of law and order, and guidance of the country to the sovereign Constituent Assembly.

A. KERENSKY, Minister-President

1377. *Den'* ON THE NEW GOVERNMENT AND THE DECLARATION
[No. 174, September 27, 1917, p. 1.]

Officially the government crisis has been solved. The Provisional Government in its new composition has started working and has published its program.

The contents of this program are already known to us through the negotiations which have been carried out between the representatives of the bourgeoisie and the democracy.

It is not necessary to dwell at length upon it, and it would be sufficient to repeat what we have already often indicated: the essence is not in the broad program embracing all sides of national life, which is obligatory for any government; the essence is not even in the narrower, practical program, which in view of existing conditions the Government has put into effect immediately. The essence is in the good will of the contracting parties.

And in this instance the contracting parties are not the representatives who have gathered within the cabinet, but the classes which have delegated them. Coalition is based on compromise, that is, on self-restriction; a coalition presupposes the collaboration of antagonistic forces.

A certain level of political development of the coalition elements is essential in order to create in practice an honest coalition.

It is true that life has brought us to a point where even a minimum level is sufficient.

We have to defend the most elementary conditions of national existence. The declaration of the Government quite rightly brings forward the issues of raising the fighting capacity and the discipline of the army for the purpose of defending the country from the enemy, or, let us be more precise, still more for the purpose of defending the country against itself during demobilization; also for the purpose of fighting anarchy and restoring basic lawfulness. We will have to conduct an active foreign policy in the sense of taking realistic steps for the purposes of achieving peace and for the active defense of Russia from attempts against Russian territories during the peace [negotiations]; [furthermore,] it is essential that we should carry out the electoral campaign for the Constituent Assembly.

To anyone who is not blinded by passion it is quite clear that precisely those questions are urgent on which the divergency is the least; this has been proved by the negotiations.

At the same time, the present coalition differs to its advantage from the previous coalition because in this instance both sides have made concessions.

Finally, the previous experience has shown that even a poor peace is a better guarantee of calm for the country than the prospect of an obviously evil quarrel.

The conditions for preserving the coalition for a short period are objectively present.

But let us have no illusions. The coalition will face difficult days, because, not statesmanlike wisdom, but the elements of class passions and of mutual hatred will have to save their imperious words.

If fate decides that we will lead the country safely to the Constituent Assembly, it will be the result of the unceasing struggle of all the statesmanlike elements of the country, and first of all of democracy against the raging anarchy.

In this connection, the newly organized Council of the Republic will perhaps play the role of a buffer, and then, in spite of all its defects, it will have an enormous historical significance.

The present coalition was born in the throes of suffering, and those elements of the democracy that from the first days of the Kornilov rebellion have preserved their clarity of mind and the firmness of their will may say with satisfaction that their systematic struggle against the elements of disorder has been successful. They will find in this fact a new inspiration, permitting them, united within the Soviet and in the country, to create by their active support of the Government an atmosphere that would give the Government the force to lead boldly and straightforwardly the ship of state, when necessary [even] against the elements raging around it.

1378. *Delo Naroda* ON THE NEW GOVERNMENT AND THE DECLARATION
[No. 166, September 28, 1917, p. 1.]

Both the composition and the declaration of the new, third-in-succession, coalition government are published. Except for some digressions, the declaration represents, according to the agreement made between the revolutionary democracy and bourgeois Russia, a brief—in places verbatim—statement of the program of August 14. The forced establishment of industrial trusts and mergers as one of the means of establishing state control over production is omitted. Likewise the forceful subscription to the loan is deleted. Some softening, as compared with the program of August 14, in the formulation of measures proposed in the field of land relations is of no essential significance.

On the whole the declaration made public coincides with this program. And the revolutionary democracy could welcome the platform of action by the new Government, had it the assurance that it would be *implemented*. After all, we did have a program of May 6 [*sic*], and a program of July 8, and yet of those high-sounding promises [only a small part (?—illegible)] was actually realized.

. . .

. . . We have no assurance that the declaration will not remain on paper and that, finally, that bold and resolute creative sweep will be born which alone can convert the word into deed.

The cause of this, first of all, is the *composition* of the new Government. We fail to see in it the leaders of those parties and classes of the population who joined the coalition, destined leaders of the country whose energy and loyalty would guarantee the realization of the program.

. . .

Who is to blame for this? First of all and above all, the revolutionary democracy itself. It suffers from some sort of fear of authority, some sort of absence of will to action, to national creativeness. Instead of sending its best men into the coalition government that it formed and according to its own plan, it is satisfied to leave the decision of the composition of the Ministry entirely to the Minister-President, whom it deprives at the same time of its most creative forces. What is it—apathy, helplessness, or fear of responsibility?

Be that as it may, with the present composition of the government the sole guarantee of realizing the program declared by it is the work of the future Provisional Council. It must immediately begin earnest, organic work. Draft laws designed to implement the program of August 14 must be worked out in the commissions at the earliest possible time. And the Council must, with all the strength of its authority and its organized pressure, insist on making laws of these draft laws immediately.

Let there then awaken in the ranks of the revolutionary democracy gathered at the "preparliament" a thirst for creative work, energy for tireless state labor, a desire to turn the word into deed. Only by this awakening to reality can democracy justify that coalition "combination" which it created after a month-long painful "crisis of power" and which, it triumphantly promised the country, could bring us to the Constituent Assembly.

1379. *Izvestiia* ON THE NEW GOVERNMENT
[No. 181, September 26, 1917, p. 1.]

The new government has been formed. It was formed on the basis of a compromise, and therefore, as any compromise, it can be criticized as sharply as one pleases, to one's heart's content.

One can be especially critical now, when life is so difficult for the workers, the peasants, and the soldiers, when their demands are so legitimate and . . . when the possibility of satisfying them is so remote.

But criticism of this nature, regardless of how brilliant it may be, is completely unproductive. More than that, it is extremely harmful because it suggests to workers, peasants, and soldiers the thought that another government will assume power—a democratic or a soviet government—and that the land will start flowing with milk and honey.

No, comrades! There is no government now that could give you this milk and honey. Until we achieve a universal peace—a peace that would not weigh us down with new burdens—and until we heal, by long and persistent labor, all the grave wounds inflicted by the war, life in revolutionary Russia will not resume its normal course. Until then we are forced to carry the cross laid on the people's shoulders by the Tsar on the day he plunged Russia into war.

And we must think only of ways of mitigating national calamities, of preventing unnecessary bloodshed among the people, and of not destroying the cause of revolution.

These are the considerations that dictated the decision of the Democratic Council to recognize as acceptable the compromise that has been reached.

.   .   .

[The democracy] has agreed to this [compromise] because the preparliament will enable it to fight for the realization of its demands by peaceful methods, and not by revolts or uprisings which would bring utter ruin to the revolutionary country.

But they say that the preparliament will be a "talking shop," because the government is not held formally responsible to it.

Comrades! It is up to you to convert this responsibility, which does not exist in writing, into a reality.

.   .   .

The fate of the preparliament, as also of the whole Russian revolution, is in your own hands, comrades!

The program of the new government—study it carefully, comrades!—meets the demands of the democracy in many, very many, respects. The preparliament offers you a means of achieving the practical realization of this program and of seeing to it that it is carried out in a democratic spirit.

Then let us take up the work together and try to lead the country, by peaceful means, to the Constituent Assembly, which will be born of universal suffrage and will indisputably express the will of the people.

1380. Adverse Comment by *Novaia Zhizn'*
[No. 138, September 27, 1917, p. 1.]

"The king is dead, long live the king!" The coalition of representatives of the democracy with the nonparty bourgeois and Kadets . . . this hopelessly compromised and apparently entirely buried coalition has again been resurrected in its original form. . . .

But we did not simply go back. Recent events have clarified what to many was a secret not so long ago, and, on the basis of new evidence, we can foretell for the new coalition an even less glorious fate than the one that befell the previous coalitions.

. . .

Upon whose backing can the new ministry then count? Where is its social support?

The Kadets speak of the new ministry with great reservation. . . . On the other hand, the Bolsheviks look upon the new coalition as an openly provocative action and strongly advocate the idea of a "second revolution." It is curious that even the Mensheviks and the S.R.'s, the true spiritual fathers of the coalition, did not contribute to it a single outstanding party leader, so little confidence did their own child inspire in them.

Under such circumstances the new coalition will hardly be able to preserve even that unstable balance that the old coalition barely managed to do. With every day it grows clearer and clearer that only a revolutionary power supported by a bloc of democratic parties can serve as a stronghold against counterrevolution. Attempts to follow a middle course have already been overcome by the Russian revolution.

THE PROVISIONAL COUNCIL OF THE RUSSIAN REPUBLIC

1381. *Den'* ON THE TASKS OF THE COUNCIL
[No. 182, October 6, 1917, p. 1.]

The Provisional Council of the Russian Republic starts its work in the most difficult moment of the Russian revolution.

The enemy attempts [to seize] the last defensive lines standing on his way to Petrograd. What has been expected from the very beginning of the war with so much alarm—a struggle between our forces and German forces on the sea— becomes an actual possibility. The threat to Petrograd ceases to be mere words or rumors.

Apparently the Government will be compelled to leave the capital, which, by the force of military events, is being included in the theater of military operations.

In these alarming days an economic catastrophe is coming over the country, already flooded by the waves of anarchy. The agrarian movement in the villages and banditry in the cities are threatening all the population with famine; the industrial crisis creates huge cadres of unemployed. A new hour of trial, the most difficult, the most gloomy, and the most fatal for all the revolution, is at hand.

And in this moment a national institution starts its activity, an institution whose intended purpose is to support and aid the revolutionary government. The Council of the Russian Republic was created in order to relieve the revolutionary government of the impossible burden of irresponsibility and to give the whole nation the possibility of sharing with the Government the responsibility for the fate of the country.

That for which the revolutionary government is now carrying the full responsibility for the country bears only one name—"defense." In this single word all the tasks standing before the Government and before the country embodied in the Council of the Republic are included.

. . .

The Council must call the whole country to order, to that revolutionary democratic order that is based on the inner consciousness of the necessity to save a freedom acquired at such a high price and on the independence of the whole people; it should also call for respect toward the authority of a government that strictly safeguards its own prerogatives.

The first immediate task of the Council is to imperiously raise its voice in favor of the "defense of the homeland"—the justification of which is still required in our country—an effective support in this matter of a government consecrated by the authority of the Council of the Republic.

The foremost duty of the Council of the Republic is to breathe a living soul into the exhausted nation, to light a new fire of revolutionary inspiration, to inspire consciences [with the idea] that the defense of the country is required for the sake of the revolution's victory.

It was said about the great French revolution that it kindled a guiding light in the gloom of the graves.

If the Council of the Russian Republic also lights its candle and dispels by the flame of its revolutionary enthusiasm [for the cause] of the country's defense the deathly gloom and cold which are invading the country, then it will perform all that is now needed to save the country and the revolution.

1382. *Izvestiia* ON THE ROLE OF THE COUNCIL
[No. 188, October 4, 1917, p. 1.]

The statute on the Provisional Council of the Russian Republic has finally been published.

. . .

The country is in extreme danger. A formidable foe is pressing on it from without. Within the country there is a bloody upsurge of pogroms and anarchy. All the open and concealed enemies of the revolution are persistently trying to make use of the misfortunes of our native land to provoke a civil war, to drown the revolutionary democratic classes in blood, and thus to establish the rule of a counterrevolutionary dictatorship. And there are sufficient passionate but unreasoning heads among the toiling masses who are throwing themselves, with their eyes closed, into the skillfully spread net.

Under such circumstances, the functioning of a representative body in which all classes, all parties and factions, must publicly and openly conduct their political work is the best possible means of organizing and consolidating all the forces of the country to repel the external and domestic enemies and, at the same time, to prevent a civil war and introduce a genuine revolutionary order. Every unnecessary day of delay, therefore, carries the threat of the greatest dangers, and no questions of prerequisites, and so forth, can justify this delay. In any case, attempts, based on any considerations whatsoever, to postpone once again the convocation of the Council would constitute a real crime.

As for the actual statute on the Provisional Council of the Republic, it stands to reason that the rights granted to the institution are extremely far removed from what the democracy demands for any parliament, from the rights with which the Constituent Assembly will be vested. But it must be remembered that the Council of the Republic is not a parliament; that the period of its existence is calculated for only one and a half months until the convocation of the Constituent Assembly; that during this short period it will at any rate be unable to initiate any extensive legislative work; that its principal task will be effecting supervision and control over the actions of the Provisional Government and giving to the Government guiding instructions for its activity in all spheres of national life.

. . .

The work in the Council of the Republic must serve the democracy as the best preparation for the immense revolutionary work in state construction, which will comprise the task of the future All-Russian Constituent Assembly.

1383. THE ATTACK OF *Rabochii Put'* ON THE COUNCIL
[No. 30, October 7, 1917, p. 1.]

Today the Provisional Council of the "Republic" opens, constituted of persons graciously "invited" by the ruling Bonapartist clique, with Kerensky at its head. Entrance tickets to this assembly of lackeys were also offered to us Bolsheviks— we threw them into the faces of the Kornilovists and half-Kornilovists gathered for the purpose of impersonating "the representatives of democracy."

The whole power is in the hands of counterrevolution, in the hands of the clique "responsible" to the Anglo-American and French banking concerns, and "irresponsible" to hundreds of millions of peasants, soldiers, and workers of Russia.

The dictators of the Russian "Republic" are themselves ashamed of their naked imperialistic indecency. They are willing to surround themselves with "socialistic menials" dressed up in embroidered "socialist" liveries. They are willing, together with "the leaders of the revolution" (Tseretelli and company), who have passed to the bourgeoisie, to carry out hastily a "business" program.

And the government of capitalistic autocracy does have a lot of "business": first of all, it is necessary to *pacify* the peasants and to feed the famished villages with lead; it is necessary to *pacify* the aroused city population, which is hungry, while on the large estates lies the grain of last year's crop, held in the expectation of a new doubling of grain prices; it is necessary *to cope* with the Baltic sailors, who are "mad enough" to demand elected commissars; it is necessary *to run away* from Petersburg to "quiet" Moscow, and, leaving Petrograd in the hands of military authorities, "to calm down" the Petrograd Soviet of Workers' and Soldiers' Deputies; it is necessary once again *to postpone* the Constituent Assembly, *substituting for it* "for the time being" *a preparliament* of Kerensky's "menials"!

. . .

The petty bourgeois leaders, drawing along with them part of their partisans inclined toward the bourgeoisie, have once again shamelessly *betrayed,* have once again dishonorably *betrayed,* and, violating the mandates of those who had delegated them, have come to an agreement with the Kadets; have surrendered to the mercy of an *irresponsible* dictatorial government, laying down at its feet the rights of their own democratic Soviet. . . .

There is no place on the revolutionary front for the heroes of compromise and betrayal. The revolution will win in spite of them and against them.

. . .

The government of the counterrevolutionary dictatorship, together with its "republican" advisers, will be unable to restrain it either through violence or through deceit!

1384. The Opening of the Council

[*VVP*, No. 172, October 8, 1917, p. 3; *Rech'*, No. 237, October 8, 1917, p. 3.]

The opening of the Provisional Council of the Russian Republic took place at 5:00 P.M. on October 7.[1] Present at the opening were members of the Provisional Government, headed by the Deputy Minister-President and Minister of Trade and Industry, A. I. Konovalov, representatives of the diplomatic corps from Great Britain, France, and Italy, the Ambassadors of the United States and Japan, the Belgian and Serbian Ministers, and representatives of neutral countries.

At 5:00 o'clock the Supreme Commander and Minister-President, A. F. Kerensky, took the chair, declared the session of the Provisional Council of the Russian Republic open, and addressed the following speech to the session:

"On behalf of the Provisional Government of the Russian Republic, I declare the Council of the Russian Republic open. For the first time since the great Russian revolution, the Government has received the opportunity to meet and work together with representatives of the organized forces of the Russian people. This first session is being opened here, in this hall, which, for many decades, represented the stronghold of tyranny and autocracy. We can, and must, see this as a bright symbol of the future. Permit me to express our common sentiments and proclaim: 'Long live our common native land, henceforth and forevermore free.' Never will the destructive autocracy be resurrected, nor will anyone—be it a person or a group, dare to attack the sovereign will of the Russian people, which will speak its decisive word at the forthcoming Constituent Assembly. The Provisional Government of the Russian Republic, invested by the revolution with full power, is bound by oath to transfer this power to a plenipotentiary organ of the peoples of Russia—the Constituent Assembly. It is precisely in this that [the Provisional Government] has until now seen one of its chief tasks—to defend the will of the people against any encroachments on it, regardless of the origin. Resting on [the support of] all the broad, responsible elements of the Russian population, the Provisional Government has twice already succeeded in nipping in the bud such pernicious, criminal attempts. Today the Provisional Government is confident that the present session of the Council of the Russian Republic will assist and support the Provisional Government in this task of safeguarding the rights of the Constituent Assembly and [assuring] the earliest possible commencement of its work.

. . .

". . . There are three tasks that must now command the full attention of the Council, just as they command the full attention of the Government; they are very simple, but [at the same time] infinitely difficult [to carry out]: the defense of

[1] On October 6, 1917, the Government issued a law dissolving the Fourth Duma and terminating the commissions of its members. *Sob. Uzak.*, I, 2, No. 1846.

the country and the restoration of the combat potential of the army, enabling it vigorously to repulse beyond our national frontiers the enemy, which is becoming more and more audacious and, I might say, more and more arrogant. I am saying so, not because his success stems from his own strength, but, rather, from our impotence. It is precisely this knowledge that the Provisional Government will impart to you at one of its next sessions; it is this knowledge that gives us the firm assurance that, in spite of the full gravity of the present situation, if the Russian people are willing, they will be able to find a way out of this difficult situation sooner than their enemies think. It is with the deepest reverence and the deepest satisfaction and enthusiasm that I, as Supreme Commander, must testify here before you, before the whole country and the world, about the inimitable examples of heroism and the feats that are now being performed by our sailors perishing in an unequal fight against an enemy ten times as strong as they. The great sense of responsibility to our native land and the conditions of combat have forged a united family out of all the fighters at sea, and, headed by their astoundingly courageous officers, the Russian seamen are every day performing legendary feats. I cannot say the same about our land forces. I do not feel I have the right to conceal the truth, and I never have, at any place, concealed it. . . . The vast ignorance of the people, a legacy we received from the old regime, and that unbridled agitation and propaganda that have forgotten about responsibility to our native land, which are now being carried on among the most ignorant masses of the army—that is where the responsibility lies for the disgrace and the misfortunes we are now experiencing. The Provisional Government is adopting every possible measure to avert the great danger which threatens the capital, the vital nerve center of the State. . . . The Russian revolution and the free Russian people have stated their tasks and aims of war completely, clearly, definitely, and in terms understandable to everyone. What the great Russian people and the great Russian democracy desire are not battles and annexations, but peace and the earliest possible return to peaceful cooperation among nations.

". . . We are confident that the delegation from the Provisional Government, which includes a representative of the Russian democracy, that is going abroad in the very near future will establish our position at the present difficult and crucial moment of the war clearly, explicitly, and in a befitting manner. . . . The Provisional Government believes that it has the right to turn to the members of the Council gathered here, not only with a request, but with a demand in the name of the country. We ask and we demand that all the energies and initiatives of the public be directed at putting a stop to those scandalous events in public life that are destroying our State. . . . Elementary law and order must be established in Russia, the right of every person to personal inviolability must be restored in Russia, the domicile of every person must be protected against unlawful entry, and the very life of every citizen of the state of Russia—regardless of the party or class to which he may belong—must be made secure. It is necessary to restore industrial production, and, most important and most fundamental of all, it is necessary to fully restore the fighting capacity of the Russian army. And only after fulfilling the first two tasks will we be able to achieve the third.

"On behalf of the army, on behalf of all the commanders who are leading the armed forces, on behalf of army and other committees, I can state with absolute certainty that at the present time the army is waiting for only one thing— that the rear just as calmly perform its duty to the end, and return to productive labor to save our native land. In particular, I cannot help but dwell on the food question. I hope that the representatives of the Russian peasantry present here will, in the very near future, be able to give the army the full support that it needs. The food situation on the front is growing worse by the day, and the consequences that can ensue from hunger on the front are becoming more and more real and more and more threatening with every passing day. The great aspirations with which we are approaching the Constituent Assembly for a new and final decision of the question include not only the question of the will of the country but also the land question, a question that is of closest concern to those who, should the Russian revolution and Russian freedom be destroyed, will once again lose every possibility of stepping into the broad field of creative work in agriculture. . . . Allow me then, gentlemen, members of the Provisional Council of the Russian Republic, to welcome you once again on behalf of the Provisional Government. . . .

". . . We ask only one thing of you: let there be but one desire at the basis of your work—to give everything for the sake of the good of the State, the desire to forget everything for the sake of saving our native land, and the desire, even in this terrible hour in the history of the Russian State, to remember that we are all brothers in one and the same country, and that without depending upon each other in this unequal fight we will not be able to reach the bright road which has been the dream of endless generations of Russian peoples. We, the Provisional Government, invested with full power, we are only servants of the country, and we ask you to tell us the truth, but only the truth—in all honesty and honor."

The Minister-President's speech was often interrupted by loud expressions of approval from the members of the Council.

After his speech, the Supreme Commander and Minister-President offered the presidential chair to E. K. Breshko-Breshkovskaia, the senior member of the Provisional Council of the Russian Republic.

After the welcoming speech of E. K. Breshko-Breshkovskaia, [the Council] proceeded to the election of a Chairman of the Provisional Council of the Russian Republic. N. D. Avksent'ev, President of the Executive Committee of the All-Russian Soviet of Peasants' Deputies, was elected Chairman [and spoke as follows]:

. . .

"In commencing its work, I am confident that the Council of the Russian Republic will set as its aim the earliest possible achievement of a universal, democratic peace, with the recognition of the right of nations to self-determination. We know that all the peoples in the world, having suffered over three years in this great war, are aspiring for the same [goals], but, at the same time, free Russia will not for a minute abandon her great concern over the defense of the country. . . . Therefore our first slogan must now be: All our strength for saving the freedom of our native land, for defense, and for saving the gains of the revolution. While we have assembled here, out there—at the front and on the seas— soldiers [and sailors] of the revolutionary army and navy are heroically dying in defense of free Russia. According to reports from naval authorities, our navy is fighting a fearless and unequal battle against a most powerful foe . . . in the Gulf of Riga, and it prefers to die rather than surrender. Our first thoughts should be devoted to them—to the sailors and officers.

"To the army and navy go our first thoughts, our admiration, our anxiety, and our blessings, but, most important, our unfailing thoughts about them, and our active, immediate assistance. The organized public, as represented by us, and the Government power must combine all their efforts in active work, in organizing the rear, in making sacrifices for the army. However difficult our position is at the present, we must look for assurance in other things besides. The great peoples of our Allies are always with us; they are united with us through blood; they are merged with us in both fortune and misfortune through their yearning for the earliest possible conclusion of a dignified peace. We send them our warm, fraternal greetings. Our alliance with the fraternal peoples, and the desire for freedom, for the self-determination of nations, cannot be destroyed; it is by nature indissoluble.

"But if our external position is difficult, then no less difficult is the situation within the country. The internal conditions of the country are no less of a threat to her freedom and to the gains of the revolution than is the external position. The economic chaos, the disorganization of transport, the financial difficulties, and the shortage of food supplies—all these undermine the existence of the young freedom, give birth to dissatisfaction, destroy the strength of the front, and breed and increase anarchy. . . .

"Citizens, what I have just said is well known to all of you. The difficult position in which Russia finds herself both in foreign and internal affairs, the state of disorganization and weakness which we now observe, is not something new for any of us. This state is inscribed in heavy, bloody letters on the heart of every Russian citizen. But, citizens, this is not the only guidepost in our work. . . . There must also be a great faith which each one of us should have, a faith in the destiny of our native land. . . . Citizens, many of you present here have long been waiting for this freedom, have long been calling for it. Citizens, many of you present here have accepted suffering in the name of this freedom; you have believed in it; you believed in the emancipated people. Can it really be that six months after the attainment of this cherished freedom, six months of horrible ordeals, when it was difficult for the people to get back on their feet, to become organized quickly—can it really be that this can kill your faith? Never! I assume that when I say 'never' I am expressing the unanimous sentiment and the unanimous faith of the whole assembly.

"The Provisional Council of the Russian Republic is the name for a newly established state institution. It will be in existence for less than three months, because in two months, finally, will come the true lord of the Russian land—the All-Russian Constituent Assembly, for which Russia is waiting and preparing herself as she would for a great celebration. The Provisional Government has promised not to delay its convocation for a single day, for a single hour, and to exert all its efforts and adopt every measure to assure this convocation. The Council of the Russian Republic must strive tirelessly and unremittingly for the same end, bringing all its influence to bear on the country and the governmental authorities toward realizing it. . . . Permit me to express my deep assurance that the Russian public will be able to carry out this task, and permit me with all my heart to wish you success in the responsible work of the Council. Permit me, in opening our session, to invite you to join me in my cry: 'Long live our native land, long live Free Russia.' "

N. D. Avksent'ev's speech was met with loud applause from the members of the Council.

. . .

[Declaration of the Bolsheviks]

N. D. Avksent'ev announced that he had received a statement from the Bolshevik faction requesting the floor for reading a declaration which defined its attitude toward the Council. According to regulations, the right to permit such a reading of the declaration belongs to the Chairman. N. D. Avksent'ev announced that he was granting the request, but warned that the declaration must be limited to ten minutes and that there could be no debates on the subject.

L. Trotsky was recognized . . .

"The official purpose of the Democratic Conference," L. Trotsky began, "summoned by the Central Executive Committee of the Soviet of Workers' and Soldiers' Deputies, was the removal of the irresponsible personal regime which bred the Kornilov affair, and the establishment of a responsible government, capable of liquidating the war and assuring the convocation of the Constituent Assembly at the appointed time. In the meantime, behind the back of the Democratic Conference, by means of behind-the-scenes deals between Kerensky and the leaders of the Socialist Revolutionaries and the Social Democratic Mensheviks, a result has been reached which is in direct contradiction to the officially announced aim; in short, a power has been created in which and around which open and concealed Kornilovites are playing the leading roles. The irresponsibility of the Government is henceforth assured and officially proclaimed. The Council of the Republic has been declared a deliberative body. In the eighth month of the revolution, the irresponsible government is creating for itself a cover out of a new edition of the Bulygin Duma.[2] The bourgeois elements have entered the Council in numbers to which, as the elections show, they had no right whatsoever. In spite of all this, it was precisely the Kadet Party which succeeded in obtaining an irresponsible government, even before the preparliament, which was unrepresentative, in favor of the bourgeoisie. That very same Kadet Party, which had insisted on the dependence of the Provisional Government upon the President of the State Duma, Mr. Rodzianko, has succeeded in achieving the independence of the Provisional Government from the Provisional Council of the Republic. The bourgeois elements will occupy a less auspicious position in the Constituent Assembly than they do in the Provisional Council. And if the bourgeois elements were really preparing themselves for the Constituent Assembly a month and a half hence, they would have no motives for defending the irresponsibility of the present Government. But the whole point is that the bourgeois classes, who do not reveal [their] policy, have set for themselves the aim of frustrating the Constituent Assembly. (*Noise from the right, cries:* "Lie!") In the fields of industry, agriculture, and food [supply], the policies of the Government and the propertied classes are intensifying the natural disorganization engendered by war. The bourgeois classes, who are provoking a peasant uprising (*strong commotion and protests from the right; cries:* "Lie!"), who are provoking a civil war, are now undertaking to suppress it and to steer the course openly toward the bony hand of hunger, which must strangle the revolution and, first of all, the Constituent Assembly.

"No less criminal is the foreign policy of the bourgeoisie and its government. After 40 months of war, a mortal danger threatens the capital. The thought of

[2] A very limited national assembly proposed by Minister of the Interior Bulygin in the summer of 1905.

surrendering the revolutionary capital to the German forces does not in the least arouse the indignation of the bourgeois classes. (*Noise and protests.*) On the contrary, this is accepted as a natural link in the general policy which must facilitate a counterrevolutionary plot. In response to the danger, a plan has been advanced for transferring the Government to Moscow; instead of recognizing that the salvation of the country lies in the conclusion of peace, instead of proposing an immediate peace directly to all the exhausted peoples over the heads of all the imperialist governments and the diplomatic corps, thus making it virtually impossible to continue the war, the Provisional Government, under orders of the Kadet counterrevolutionaries and Allied imperialists, is prolonging the devastating war without reason, without purpose, and without plan, dooming to senseless death new hundreds of thousands of sailors and soldiers, and is preparing for the surrender of Petrograd and the downfall of the revolution, while the sailors and the Bolshevik soldiers are perishing, together with other soldiers and sailors, as a result of someone else's mistakes and crimes. (*Loud commotion and protests in the center and on the right.*) The so-called Supreme Commander is continuing to raid the Bolshevik press. The leading party in the Provisional Council serves voluntarily as a screen for this whole policy. We, the Bolshevik faction of the Social Democrats, declare: With this government of betrayal of the people——" (*strong commotion on the right and in the center; cry:* "Scoundrel!").

The Chairman [tried] to call Trotsky to order, but his voice could not be heard in the general commotion.

TROTSKY. "With this Council of counterrevolutionary connivance——"(*loud noise and shouts:* "Get out; away with him!" "Citizen Trotsky, you have paved the way for the surrender of Petrograd!" *a shout is heard from the center*).

CHAIRMAN. "I have called the speaker to order and I request that the assembly calmly hear out his statement."

"We can't listen to him calmly!" cries were heard.

The Chairman called upon the assembly to maintain dignity, and asked Trotsky to continue.

"We have nothing in common," Trotsky declared, "with that unofficial work, devastating to the people, which is being carried on behind the scenes. The revolution is in danger. At a time when Wilhelm's troops are threatening Petrograd, the Government of Kerensky and Konovalov is preparing to run from Petrograd in order to turn Moscow into a stronghold of the counterrevolution. We are appealing to Moscow workers and soldiers for vigilance. In leaving the Provisional Council (*loud noise in the center*), we are appealing to the workers, soldiers, and peasants of all Russia for vigilance and fortitude. ("The German [workers, soldiers, and peasants] and not the Russian!" *a cry is heard.*)

"Petrograd is in danger." L. Trotsky continued, "The revolution and the people are in danger. The Government is intensifying this danger, and the ruling parties are helping it. Only the people can save themselves and the country. We address the people: "Long live an immediate, honest, democratic peace. All power to the Soviets, all land to the people. Long live the Constituent Assembly. (*Applause from the benches of the Bolsheviks.*)

"Apart from the members of the Bolshevik faction," Trotsky concluded, "this statement is supported by the delegate of the 2nd Army, the delegate of the Railroad Union, Mamaev, and the delegates of national organizations, Stuchko and Bul'shii."

After Trotsky read the declaration, the Bolsheviks stood up and walked out of the assembly hall, accompanied by noise and sarcastic cries from different places.

"Go to your German trains!" somebody shouted from the audience.

　　　　．　　．　　．

1385. SPEECH OF KUSKOVA

[Delivered October 12. *Russkiia Vedomosti*, No. 234, October 13, 1917, p. 4. The cooperatives, at their congress earlier in the month, had decided to participate directly in the political campaigns for the Constituent Assembly. *Vlast Naroda*, No. 136, October 7, 1917, p. 2.]

E. D. Kuskova, representative of the group from the cooperatives, mounted the rostrum. All newspapers were once again put aside in the auditorium, and the delegates followed the address with mounting interest.

"The cooperatives," said E. D. Kuskova, "from the very onset of the war took the irrevocable position for the defense of the country, the most naked, unadorned self-defense. Thanks to the cooperatives, the profound food crisis was felt in our country only in the third and even the fourth year of the war, and not earlier. And at the present time, convinced that economic ruin is now possible on a wide national scale, the cooperatives have now entered the political and public arena with a cause entirely foreign to them.

"But we came here in the interests of a great work. However, the early days of our work in the preparliament failed to satisfy us on two scores. Those very same defense forces, without whose union defense is unthinkable, began, first of all, by demonstrating their views and by disputes. Moreover, during these past seven months all we did was argue and demonstrate our views. Is it possible that we came here also to do the same? . . . In this respect we were not satisfied with the report by the representative of the Government, which we support whole-heartedly. It was not too easy to listen to Kerensky dissipate his strength and oratory to convince the representatives-internationalists. (*Voices from the right:* "Correct.") No persuasion by word of mouth will teach those who have not learned from everything we have experienced and have seen. (*Voices from the center:* "Correct." *Protests from the left.*) They can call me any name they wish," continued Kuskova; "this has long since ceased to bother me. (*Applause from the right.*) We would like to see the government take a firm stand against those aspects of our life that concern all of us. This would help us in discussing certain practical problems. Leiber, for instance, demands the repeal of the death penalty. Of course there would not be found a single person in this auditorium who would demand the death penalty. (*Voices from the right:* "Correct.") But we wanted the government to tell us whether it had first exhausted all other means of struggle before arriving at the death penalty. What interests us more than anything else at the moment is the expediency of those measures that should be pursued.

　　　　．　　．　　．

"We live at such a moment," continued the speaker, "that we cannot talk about the safety of the army without talking of the anarchy in the rear, because, with the anarchy which now develops in the country, there unquestionably can be not only no defense of the country but also no defense of the revolution. (*Voices:* "Correct." *Applause.*) We lost the revolution of 1905 because of this anarchy.

The question of combating anarchy is equally acute for all of us. (*Voices from the right and the center:* "Correct.") Let there be different interests, but at the moment not one question can be solved without first establishing order in the country. Call it what you wish—Kornilov or revolutionary order. But neither the work of the Constituent Assembly nor the defense of the country is possible without first installing order in the country. . . .

"But if we actually see miserable and tormented masses, who under the autocratic rule unfortunately grew to be licentious, we must say that all means should be exhausted immediately, down to coercion, in order to channel the masses into an arm of organized defense of their motherland. (*Loud applause from the right and shouts:* "Correct!") Has there ever been for any socialism in the world any other way of upholding the interests of the masses than the way of ("Compulsion," *ironically prompted from the left*) organization? There can be no firm authority unless the authority knows upon whom it can depend and who supports it. To our great misfortune we have no such support as yet. (*Voices from the left:* "Correct.") The Internationalists and the Bolsheviks were able to organize a hundredfold stronger than those who maintain that they stand on the platform of defense. And we have gathered here to determine this middle course which would enable the authority to orient itself as to the forces it deals with and [to see] what agreements are possible between the varied interests which tear the country apart. Many may tell me that this is complacency, but this complacency has already been accepted by all Western countries. . . .

"The government must come here with entirely definite tasks which it understands better because of its experience of seven months' work. And our responsibility is to do everything possible in order that the masses and the army do not suffer from the breakdown and devastation of war and go to the front with a curse. This responsibility to give first attention to the condition of the masses will under no circumstances be repudiated, even by those of the right wing who have gathered here. (*Applause from the right.*) But the Soviet of Workers' and Soldiers' Deputies also, particularly of the Donets Basin, must call to order the miners who, after an appreciable raise in wages, produce but 10–12 carloads per month. We must give most serious attention to the productivity of labor. The Moscow department of labor stated that out of 160 enterprises of the Moscow region which it surveyed, only four can exist without a deficit as a result of a tremendous rise in the price of labor, raw material, materials, fuel, etc. And again in the name of defense, in the name of the organization of the masses, reforms come, not with an empty slogan—'Down with capitalism'—but with an analysis of those conditions in which we are just as much interested as they are. Only in the event that everything is done on each side equally to give the maximum of work and maximum of wages will we be able to solve the economic problem during the war. . . .

"At the moment when it is a question of defending the city where we are accustomed to carry on our disputes, in the name of the cooperatives I would like to appeal to you not only with a request but with a plea to put aside declarations, or at least transfer them to other tribunes, and in the name of—I shall not say the motherland, because this word could not be repeated—I would call upon you to make this revolutionary preparliament a businesslike institution where we should not have to hear that only German bayonets will calm us down. (*Loud applause from the right and shouts:* "Bravo!" *Movement throughout all the benches.*) The masses are dreadfully tired of what we, their intelligent leaders, are doing. In Moscow I was amazed by the phenomenon that the queues that left churches were just as long as those from bakeries. And when, out of curiosity, I visited several churches, I heard that the people there prayed passionately for Russia's deliverance, not from the external, but from the internal enemy. (*Agitation on all the benches.*) We must do everything so that the masses have faith in us. Without such faith it is also impossible to raise the combat effectiveness of the army. It is urgent that the people believe that their leaders want only the salvation of the motherland. (*Voices from the right:* "How can we believe the Zimmerwaldists?") The shout we have just heard may perhaps bring greater ruin among the masses than the Zimmerwald words, because the old, grease-stained Zimmerwald proclamations, which we chewed back in the days of autocracy and which we have not swallowed yet, we shall be swallowing in the course of defense. Such is our fate. (*Voices from the right:* "A melancholy fate.")

"But your fate (*says the speaker, turning to the right*) is different. You are famous for your cultural strength. You say that you are the cleverest, the most cultured party. You carried on your work in the light of day, even under autocracy. But the left faction carried it on then under totally different circumstances. Small wonder, then, that we have not as yet put away our school notebooks of public work. We shall put them away today. But we need great understanding in our work. Recall that the property-owning class abroad knows how to extend this support to the struggling working classes. Not only does it not condemn them; it offers them, as in Belgium, the general right of election.

"Once more I appeal to you to find those points of unity that would really ensure the defense of the country and the State from devastation. Only after we exhaust all means of search and find that there is no mutual point of contact, only then shall we leave this auditorium for independent, separate actions. But if we have these points of contact, we must bring them to light at the earliest possible moment. We shall transfer our disputes to the tribune of the Constituent Assembly. But we must make this, our preparliament, strictly a defense union to defend our motherland." (*Tempestuous, prolonged applause from the benches to the right and part of the center.*)

A. S. Zarudnyi, greatly moved, approached Kuskova and kissed her hand. Almost the entire right wing arose and applauded loudly.

1386. THE GOVERNMENT AND THE COUNCIL ON THE EVACUATION OF PETROGRAD

[Session of October 13. *VVP*, No. 177, October 14, 1917, p. 3.]

Having heard the Provisional Government's report on the strategic position of the Northern Front in connection with the possible evacuation of Petrograd, the Provisional Council of the Russian Republic states: 1) that the Provisional Government has announced its intention to defend Petrograd to the last; 2) that, in the present difficult position of the country, the Provisional Government considers it necessary to remain in Petrograd until such time as there is a direct threat of military danger to the capital; 3) that not only is the Provisional Government itself remaining in Petrograd, but it also intends to convoke the Constituent Assembly in Petrograd.

Concurring completely with the opinion of the Provisional Government, the

Provisional Council urges the Government to issue at once a similar statement to the population . . .

1387. THE FAILURE OF THE COUNCIL TO ACHIEVE A MAJORITY FOR ANY OF THE RESOLUTIONS PROPOSED ON NATIONAL DEFENSE
[*Russkiia Vedomosti*, No. 240, October 20, 1917, p. 3.]

Three days ago, speaking of the K.D. Party Congress and its attitude toward the preparliament, we pointed out that the speeches made in the Provisional Council, even by those S.R.'s and S.D.'s who consider themselves to belong to the "defensist" camp, gave little hope that a majority ready to firmly support the implementation of statesmanlike principles in governmental policy could be formed. The results of these debates on the question of the country's defense have definitely confirmed our doubts. It disclosed even something more: the complete lack of any kind of definite majority within the Council of the Republic. All the resolutions proposed were rejected one after another [on October 18]. Faced by the enemy invasion directed against the capital, the assembly, to which the representatives of "revolutionary democracy" aspire to give the character and the rights of a parliament, proved to be powerless to express itself on the most important of all the national issues of the moment—on the issue of the country's defense.

It would be incorrect to consider that all the parties and groups of the parliament are equally responsible for this sad outcome. But all of them have demonstrated party intransigency. On the right and in the center, energetic attempts had been made in favor of unity. The resolution proposed by N. V. Chaikovskii represented the fruit of an agreement entered upon beforehand by a number of heterogeneous groups: by the cooperatives, by the Popular Socialists, by the "Edinstvo," by the Peasant Union, by the Party of the People's Freedom, by the Cossacks, by the Radical Democratic Party, and by the industrial group. The representatives of the Moscow Congress of Public Leaders adhered to it, although with certain reservations, and voted for it. Of all the resolutions, the resolution of this coalition gathered the greatest number of votes, and during the first voting was even approved by a small majority.

But this resolution also was to be rejected by several votes when the voting was verified by means of a division.

Among the resolutions opposing it, the resolution of the S.R.'s of the right had the greatest relative success, with the representatives of the other groups on the left side of the hall voting for it also, but it received many fewer voices than the resolution of the right-center bloc.

What is the essence of the discord which has divided the preparliament into two approximately equal halves?

. . .

Why did the "defensists" from the S.R. and S.D. parties vote against the resolution of N. V. Chaikovskii? This is easy to find out by comparing it with the resolution of the S.R.'s proposed by P. Sorokin. The resolution of Chaikovskii in its wording wholly corresponds to the substance and the significance of the question it touches. It does not attach extraneous controversial issues to the basic issue and it does not convey under the banner of defense any kind of party "smuggling." It places the interests of defense in the foreground, subordinating to it all the other issues of the moment.

The spirit of Sorokin's resolution is absolutely antipodal. Instead of a direct and unconditional appeal for defense, here in the foreground are placed the *conditions* which accompany this appeal, and, among these conditions, the main role is played by two demagogic slogans, which have already played a fatal role in the destiny of our revolution.

Mr. Sorokin and his adherents believe that, in order to raise the fighting capacity of our army, there is needed, first, "an energetic and open policy," striving for the earliest possible conclusion of a "peace without annexations and indemnities on the basis of the self-determination of peoples," and, second, the transfer of agricultural lands to the land committees. . . .

. . . First formulas, then defense! They cannot be moved from this. They have not forgotten anything or learned anything.

And when, at the sight of the powerlessness and the discord which the pre-parliament has disclosed in the very first steps of its activity and which do not bode for it a brilliant future, thoughts turn to the circles of the "revolutionary democracy," on whom depends the success of making the preparliament the center and the support of a unifying, statesmanlike idea, then one cannot fail to come to the sad conclusion that not everyone who repeats the words "defense" and "defensism" actually serves the tasks of the country's defense. Even in this hard and awe-inspiring hour these words, as before, are being used in vain by those in whom a blind faith in hackneyed phrases has killed the capacity to act.

1388. The Government's Recommendations for Legislation by the Council

[*Ekon. Polozhenie*, I, 310–11.]

October 19, 1917

Dear Nikolai Dmitrievich [Avksent'ev]!

Referring to your letter of October 16, . . . with regard to the list of legislative measures which the Provisional Government proposes to submit for examination to the Provisional Council of the Russian Republic, I wish to state the following:

During the preparatory period for the opening of the Council of the Republic and in the first days of its work, the Provisional Government directed its chief attention to a general consideration of the most important aspects of our state life which were contemplated and in part already accomplished. It did not prepare in advance a final list of government draft laws which could be made the subject of discussion by the Council. The Government thought that the question about this aspect of the Council's activity would be decided gradually as the appropriate materials were prepared by the departments in the light of a preliminary appraisal by the Provisional Government and in connection with the country's needs at the given moment.

Nevertheless, at the present time, after examining the information submitted by the departments about the important work they are doing, the Provisional Government has outlined, in regard to the more urgent matters that would be desirable to submit for examination to the Council of the Republic, the suggestions now in the process of preparation by the departments on the following questions:

I. In the Ministry of Finance: 1) taxation of inheritance, 2) property taxation, 3) tea monopoly, 4) the establishment of other state monopolies.

II. In the Ministry of Trade and Industry: 1) abolition of the merchant estate [*soslovie*], 2) separation of the right to exploitation of the mineral resources from those on the surface.

III. In the Ministry of Labor: 1) the question of freedom of organization, 2) introduction of compulsory arbitration between employers and workers.

IV. In the Ministry of Justice: 1) change in some articles of criminal laws with a view to intensifying the warfare against drunkenness, 2) increasing the penalty for desertion . . . , 3) establishment of a central committee and special guberniya and municipal commissions to clarify the extent of damage suffered by institutions, organizations, corporations, and individuals during the revolution of 1917, 4) restrictions with regard to the law of inheritance, 5) abolition of the law regarding the drafting for military service of persons under trial, also those who are serving a sentence, 6) the procedure for issuing birth and death certificates to persons who profess to be freethinkers, 7) legalizing in Russia of civil marriages of Russian *émigrés* abroad, 8) establishment of local courts in Siberia and in Arkhangel'sk guberniya, 9) establishment of local courts in the Turkestan krai, 10) establishment of local courts in those parts of Vil'na and Kovno guberniyas that are unoccupied by the enemy.

Of the enumerated draft laws the one of the Ministry of Finance on the inheritance tax has already been subjected to a preliminary study by the Provisional Government and transmitted for discussion to the Council of the Republic.

I beg you, dear sir, to accept my assurances of sincere respect and devotion.

KERENSKY

1389. VERKHOVSKII'S TESTIMONY RECOMMENDING PEACE NEGOTIATIONS BEFORE THE JOINT SESSION OF THE COMMITTEES ON DEFENSE AND FOREIGN AFFAIRS OF THE COUNCIL, OCTOBER 20, 1917

[*Byloe*, 6 (June 1918), 28–41. See also A. I. Verkhovskii, *Rossiia na Golgofe*, p. 130; V. Nabokov, "Vremennoe Pravitel'stvo," *ARR*, I (1921), 80–83; and P. N. Miliukov, *Istoriia vtoroi russkoi revoliutsii*, I, vypusk, 3, 171–73.]

Having opened the session at 9:30 P.M., the Chairman of the Committee on Foreign Affairs, M. I. Skobelev, pointed out that in view of the particularly close connection . . . between questions of defense and those of foreign policy, he considered it necessary, with the consent of the Presidium of the Committee on Defense, to call the present joint session of the committees. At the same time, bearing in mind that a very secret report by the Minister of War was about to be heard, he proposed that the meeting be considered completely closed, even for members of the Council who did not belong to the committees or to the Presidium of the Council.

The committees accepted M. I. Skobelev's proposal for announcing the meeting strictly closed.

The Minister of War, A. I. Verkhovskii, who then took the floor, declared that he intended to give to the Committee a frank and exhaustive report on the condition of the army. Pausing on the material side of the question and turning, first of all, to the numerical [strength] of our forces, the Minister of War pointed out that this [strength] is expressed in a figure of 10.2 million, of which 6 million apply to the front and the immediate rear [lines], 3 million to various wartime institutions, and 1.2 million to the rear, in the strict sense of the word. Of the above-mentioned total, there are slightly under 5 million actual fighters, i.e., persons armed with guns, machine guns, and cannons. Two hundred thousand men are diverted to organizations of the zemstvo and town unions, 100,000 to the Red Cross, and 600,000 to the construction and operation of railroads.

As was recognized back in August, it is beyond the means of the State to maintain an army of such enormous size at the present time. . . .

As a result, all feasible reductions will add up to no more than 1.2 million; i.e., the army will be cut down to 9 million. However, according to the statement of the Minister of Food, it is possible to feed only 7 million. But Stavka does not agree to a reduction of this size, considering the figure of 9 million to be the absolute minimum for holding the front.

Turning next to the cost of the war, the Minister of War pointed out that it is now costing 65–67 million [rubles] per day. Of this, 8 million is actually spent on war needs, 23 million on allowances of all types, 25 million on artillery, technical orders, and railroads, and 10 million on rations for families of servicemen. In addition, expenses are constantly increasing; in 1914 they amounted to 4 billion, in 1915 to 11 billion, in 1916 to 18 billion, and in 1917 an overexpenditure of 8 billion is anticipated. At the insistence of the Minister of Finance, work was commenced on reducing the military budget, but it turned out that it was only possible to decrease it by 5 million per day, which is obviously insufficient.

Concerning the supply of food to the army, the following figures, cited by the Minister of War, will give an idea of the gravity of the situation. In September the delivery of flour to all the fronts did not exceed 26 per cent of the requirement, and [the delivery] of grain forage, 48 per cent. The bread ration on the Western Front was reduced to 1 pound, and sugar to $1\frac{7}{8}$ pounds; there are not more than 20 cars being delivered at the present time, instead of the required 122. The situation on the Northern Front was so critical that passenger cars were required to deliver provisions; in spite of this, the front is already beginning to experience hunger, especially since there are fears of a meat shortage, as the deliveries of meat have been running 50 per cent short of the orders. The situation is also very dismal in the military districts of the rear; the Moscow Military District lives from day to day, often resorting to force of arms to obtain supplies.

The procurement of footgear is far behind the requirements, which have been set at $2\frac{1}{2}$ million pairs per month. Back in January 1,300,000 pairs were procured, but in September this figure fell to 900,000. Neither are the large orders placed abroad of any help. England has already refused to deliver $2\frac{1}{2}$ million pairs of boots. America has undertaken to procure $3\frac{1}{2}$ million, but the delivery date has been postponed and only 116,000 [pairs] have been received to date. The situation is relatively better in Japan, which has already delivered 200,000 pairs out of the 700,000 pairs ordered for January 1, 1918.

With respect to warm clothing, up to 3 million sheepskin coats have been procured, but only half of these have been issued because of the impossibility of their delivery; undershirts, jerseys, and breeches are available for all, but even here one comes up against the difficulty of delivery. As for warm underclothes, the army is provided with them.

The grievous condition of the dying air force was discussed at the Moscow Conference; the automobile business is in the same situation. There is no concern as yet over armaments, because there is a sufficient quantity of both artillery supplies and rifles from the standpoint of strategic tasks.

Such are the facts about the material condition of the army. Turning to a description of the morale factors, the Minister of War emphasized that in this respect the situation is even more discouraging. The prime mover of the war—the authority of the commanders and the subordination of the masses—has been thoroughly uprooted . . . Elective committees—army committees, in particular—could play a certain role, and they still have influence in some places, but their influence is declining as they adopt a statesmanlike point of view, thereby divorcing themselves from the masses, to whom this point of view is beyond comprehension. Thus, in the 5th Army, Bolshevik propaganda has already gained the upper hand over the more moderate trends.

There is no training whatsoever at the front. Of the commanding officers, [only] the older men—and this includes commanders of battalions—can still satisfy combat requirements; but the younger officers, especially the postrevolutionary ones, have had only the most superficial training.

General disintegration gained momentum and spread, particularly under the influence of the Kornilov affair. As far as a way out of this grave situation is concerned, strictly speaking, it does not exist. Nevertheless the Minister of War conscientiously considered [the situation] and is carrying out all measures to improve the fighting capacity of the army by the spring of 1918.

The general plan of these measures is divided into several parts. First, in connection with the reduction of the armed forces mentioned earlier, it is planned to call up the recruits for the year 1920, enrolling them in the best available cadres, where they can escape corruption.

Second, serious attention is being given to the improvement of discipline in the rear. The principle of subordination of the rear to the front is being introduced for this purpose; thus, all the active [field] units will have corresponding reserve units at their complete command, which will include the right of imposing punishments. In this connection one should bear in mind that the present discord between the front and the rear might play a certain role in this: many of the front units have definitely declared that they would even be willing to use force in bringing the rear into submission.

On a level with this, measures are being adopted for combating anarchy in general. For this purpose, the War Department is willing to spare 100,000 to 150,000 combat soldiers and officers capable of forming reliable cadres of the militia; negotiations with zemstvo and town self-governments have already been started in this direction. That such a measure is more than necessary and timely is evident from the ever-increasing disintegration in the rear. It suffices to say that no less than 2 million deserters have been estimated whom there is no possibility whatsoever of catching. With all our endeavors, we have succeeded in rounding up not more than 200,000 deserters to date, but this proved to be useless, because returning corrupted elements of this kind to the front has served only to promote and accelerate its disintegration.

To the third category of measures belong the regulating of the rights and duties of commissars and their relations with commanders; rules to this effect will soon be published.

. . .

With respect to an immediate strengthening of discipline, A. I. Verkhovskii believes that the existing disciplinary courts, which function extremely slowly and inadequately, must be the first to undergo reform. In order to remove this evil, it is intended to decree that if such a court does not pass judgment within 48 hours, the penalty will be imposed personally by the commander. Likewise, the latter shall be granted full powers in areas where there are no courts at all.

Furthermore, it is intended to form special penal regiments subject to collective penalties in the form of deprivation of leaves, allowances, and so forth.[3]

. . .

In conclusion, it is necessary to make a note of the measures designed to improve the very difficult material position of the officers at the present time.

The above-mentioned program of reorganization was, by the way, submitted to Allied military representatives and it met with their complete approval and support; they could not suggest any supplementary measures.

Having concluded the account of his program, the Minister of War found it necessary to place particular emphasis on the corrupting influence of the Bolsheviks on the army. Ideological bolshevism, strictly speaking, does not exist at all in the army; the Bolshevik slogans are accepted only as a cover for an opportunity not to perform one's duty, and all the so-called *shkurniki* [self-seekers] make use of them. Under such conditions, any appeal for organization or self-denial is rejected by the soldiers, who do not understand what they are supposed to be fighting for. Any struggle against this phenomenon is doomed to failure before it is attempted. Only drastic measures could be of help, such as the complete exclusion of politics from the army, but [the command] cannot bring itself to adopt them; and even if officers were found who were willing to implement such measures, they would be murdered immediately. The army organizations are completely helpless in this respect; either they are losing more and more of their authority or they are changing their own colors to bolshevism.

In summarizing the contents of his report, the Minister of War once again emphasized the following basic facts: 1) the reduction of the army to a desirable size cannot be carried out for strategical reasons; 2) under these conditions the army cannot be fed; 3) similarly, it cannot be properly clothed . . . ; 4) there is no one to take command; 5) bolshevism is continuing to corrupt our combatant forces.

The objective data indicated above force us to acknowledge plainly and frankly that we cannot fight. At any rate, A. I. Verkhovskii announced without a moment's hesitation that he does not feel he has the strength to continue working under the present conditions and has already asked the Minister-President to find someone to succeed him. His plan for restoring our combatant strength is good by itself, but A. I. Verkhovskii does not believe in it, since it is only a palliative and cannot overcome the ever-expanding and corrupting [influence] of the propaganda for peace. Reports have already been received that some of the units have decided to leave the trenches without waiting for winter. The Congress of Soviets is going

[3] See Doc. 1326.

to be held in the very near future, and it will not fail to intensify this mood and the general craving for peace. If the Bolsheviks have not as yet come forward to seize power, it is only because delegates from the front have threatened to suppress them. But who can promise that this threat will still be in force in five days' time, and that the Bolsheviks will not take action? Nor must one forget that the propaganda for peace is supported energetically by Germany, *and the Minister knows from reliable sources that two of the newspapers published here are receiving funds from the enemy.* The only possibility of fighting against all these noxious and corrupting influences is by cutting the ground from under them—in other words, by taking the initiative in raising at once the question of concluding peace. The real data on which we may base ourselves in this connection consist of [the following]: first, in spite of all our weakness, we are holding 130 enemy divisions on our front, and second, our indebtedness to the Allies, which has reached the sum of 20 billion [rubles]. Arguments of this nature are quite sufficient to induce the Allies to . . . terminate this debilitating war, which they alone need, but which is of no interest to us. At the same time, there is no doubt that news of an early peace will at once introduce healthy principles into the army, which will provide the opportunity of suppressing anarchy both at the front and in the rear with the support of the more reliable units. And since the conclusion of peace will itself require considerable time for negotiations, one can count on restoring the combatant strength of the army by this time, which, in turn, will reflect favorably on the actual terms of the peace treaty.

Once again directing attention to the closed nature of the meeting, Chairman M. I. Skobelev pointed out that the report of the Minister of War should be regarded as material for forming judgments on foreign policy; but before turning to foreign policy he considered it appropriate to give an opportunity to those who wished to ask the Minister of War some brief questions about the statements he had made.

The Minister of Foreign Affairs, M. I. Tereshchenko, asked the Minister of War to clarify, in connection with the question of feeding the army, whether the figure of 9 million—which, according to A. I. Verkhovskii, constituted the numerical strength of our military forces—is an estimate or the actual number; in other words, does it include the 2 million deserters? Further, it appears important to know about the organization of food supply to the army in the preceding year. Concerning the general conclusions of the Minister of War, the [following] questions . . . suggested themselves: Does the Minister of War really believe that one could successfully counteract the German propaganda for peace by a proposal designed to realize the very aims which the German propaganda has set for itself? Then, why should peace be advantageous to the rear units—for example, to the Petrograd garrison—and how is one to account for the fact that the front, which, seemingly, is enduring greater suffering from the war than is the rear, still finds the strength to undertake the suppression of the idle rear?

The Minister of War replied that the figures he quoted were not fictitious, but they represented the actual number of persons receiving state rations. One cannot vouch for their complete accuracy; this requires verification by taking a census of the army, which has already been started by the supply corps. At any rate, it is known that the army has 2 million persons in excess of the number of persons that can be fed by the State. As for the data for last year, the Minister cannot provide this information at the present time. The Minister of Foreign

Affairs remarked that, according to his information, last year's shortage was as high as 47 per cent [of the orders placed], but the army had nevertheless held its ground. Then M. I. Tereshchenko stated that he still had not received a reply to his main questions: about the reasons for the difference in attitudes between the rear and the front, and about the expediency of counteracting German propaganda by fulfilling its aims.

The Minister of War pointed out that the question about the difference between the attitudes of the rear and the front is not of material importance, especially after the recent subordination of reserve units to field divisions, so that the latter can at any moment demand replacements from the former. To the second question, A. I. Verkhovskii said that he has a much broader view of the question than has M. I. Tereshchenko. We are not talking about realizing German claims, but about saving the State, i.e., about preserving as much of it as possible according to the actual correlation of forces. And only by immediate, energetic action in favor of peace can this aim be achieved. In the opposite case, if the war is continued, by spring the situation will be worse and anarchy will grow, especially if there is a poor harvest.

Chairman M. I. Skobelev asked the Minister of Foreign Affairs to proceed with his report on foreign policy.

. . .

Martynov wanted to know whether the conclusions of the Minister of War were discussed in the Provisional Government; and, if so, how did the Government react to them? In particular, did it have in mind any methods for restoring the fighting capacity of the army?

The Minister of Foreign Affairs stated that the views of the Minister of War were never reported to the Provisional Government, and that he was hearing them for the first time.

The Minister of War formally confirmed the statement of the Minister of Foreign Affairs, but indicated, at the same time, that the substance of his views was long known to the Provisional Government. As far as other plans for re-establishing our fighting strength were concerned, such have not been brought up in the Provisional Government.

. . .

A. I. Verkhovskii expressed his conviction that news of a decision in favor of peace would cause an immediate upsurge of energy in the army. Then units will be found which, in the name of preserving the country for the coming of peace, will undertake to suppress anarchy and corruption both at the front and in the rear. As a result, when the time comes for concluding peace, order in the country will be re-established, the army will be [brought back to normal conditions], and, consequently, we will have a real force at our command.

. . .

The Minister of War replied that he is interested, not in the gains of the revolution, but in the salvation of the country.

N. K. Kul'man expressed his perplexity at how peace with annexations to the advantage of Germany could be considered the salvation of the country.

The Minister of War believed that the time had come to turn from loud and eloquent speeches to a sober evaluation of the situation. We must decide what we can afford and what we cannot afford. If we do not have the means for a better peace, we must conclude the kind of peace that is now possible. In the opposite case, the situation would only deteriorate.

E. D. Kuskova asked the Minister of War to answer the following questions: First, did the Minister know about the state of the army when he assumed office? Second, was he speaking today as a private person or as a representative of the Provisional Government? This formal question is of great importance in view of the fact that, according to the Minister of Foreign Affairs, the data presented by the Minister of War, and especially the conclusions he reached from the data, have not been discussed in the Provisional Government. And finally, third, how concretely does the Minister visualize the formula for peace under the present conditions—has he had discussions on this subject with Allied representatives?

The Minister of War replied that during his tenure as commander . . . of the Moscow Military District, he already had an over-all idea of the situation, of course, but on entering the office of Minister he was not able to grasp at once all the questions involved, because of the inadequate machinery for transmitting information within the Ministry. Now, having familiarized himself with the whole picture of army life, he had come to the conclusion he mentioned about peace. This question is a heavy, personal drama for him, since, on the one hand, to resign in connection with the question of peace would mean to provoke an outburst in the army, and, on the other hand, he does not wish to be a passive participant in the disintegration of the army. As for raising the question of peace, the Minister believes that appropriate steps must be taken conjointly with the Allies.

E. D. Kuskova said that the explanations offered by the Minister have complicated the matter even more by failing to clarify a number of contradictions. On the one hand, the army is considered incapable of fighting; on the other hand, the Allies may well refuse to conclude peace at the present time. What is the logical way out of this situation, and what kind of peace is possible under the circumstances? Does this not mean that we must simply surrender ourselves to the mercy of the enemies and the Allies?

The Minister of War rejoined that to date no one has given a frank elucidation of the position of our army to the Allies, and this has created an illusion among them that the army will be useful for something, at least, according to the proverb "One can at least get a tuft of wool from a mangy sheep." Meanwhile, there can be no doubt that by spring we will not even be in a position to hold the line against 60 enemy divisions. This must be told bluntly to the Allies and then they will take the matter much more seriously, especially after the recent defeat in Italy. E. D. Kuskova emphasized her dissatisfaction with the Minister's explanation, which contained no answer to the question about a concrete, practical formula for peace.

Malevskii inquired what would happen if the Allies reject our proposal for concluding peace.

The Minister of War pointed out that in that case, being bound by certain commitments, we would have to submit to fate, i.e., go through such trials as a Bolshevik uprising, which, in the event of success, would likewise be incapable of establishing a firm power in the absence of organized forces, anarchy, and all the repercussions that follow from it.

.   .   .

Dmitrenko raised a question about the possible forms of technical assistance from the Allies.

The Minister replied that assistance is primarily needed in the form of supplying rolling stock for our railroads. However, [technical assistance] is proving to be far from adequate, and a certain evasiveness has even been noticed among the Allies in fulfilling their promises. Thus, of the 2,375 locomotives ordered from America, only a small number have been delivered—and with such delay that the very assistance is losing its meaning, since it does not cover the losses from wear and tear. Similarly, the assistance of American engineers in increasing the traffic capacity of the Siberian Railroad has yielded nothing. As for artillery and munitions, in this respect England is meeting our [needs] reluctantly, stating that the arms she delivers could easily fall into the hands of the Germans, considering the present state of the Russian army. Meanwhile, we have surrendered only 12 British cannons at Ternopol', whereas Italy lost all of 300 during these days. The position of the air force is very distressing; it is dying out completely in the absence of adequate deliveries of aircraft machinery from abroad. Only recently did the situation improve after we offered compensation in the form of cast iron and charcoal.

The Minister of Foreign Affairs remarked that, according to the figures available to him, the American engineers have succeeded in increasing the traffic capacity of the Siberian Railroad five times.

. . .

Supporting P. B. Struve's motion to postpone the debates, the Minister of Foreign Affairs declared that, on his part, he was unable to speak on behalf of the Government at the present session, in view of the difference of opinion which had suddenly arisen with the Minister of War, who did not report to the Government on the conclusions which he reported today and which fundamentally contradict the whole preceding policy of the Government.

The Chairman suggested hearing the last speaker who signed up for the question period before turning to the next item on the agenda.

Yu. O. Tsederbaum (Martov) asked the Minister of War whether he should understand his statement about suppressing anarchy within the country to mean the establishment of a dictatorship.

The Minister of War replied that the point is not the name [by which you call it]. But in order to fight anarchy a strong personal power is just as necessary as it is for commanding an army, and in this sense the power referred to may be considered a dictatorship.

When the list of speakers was exhausted . . . the Chairman proposed to turn to a clarification of the subsequent order of discussion.

. . .

The joint meeting of the committees resolved by a majority of votes to examine the technical data in the Minister's speech at a special session of the Committee on Defense, and to set a date for another joint session to discuss questions of defense and foreign policy in their full scope.

At 12:10 A.M. the meeting was closed by the Chairman.

1390. BURTSEV'S CHARGES AND THE LEAVE OF ABSENCE OF GENERAL VERKHOVSKII

[*Delo Naroda*, No. 187, October 22, 1917, p. 2; and "Stavka 25–26 Oktiabria 1917," *ARR*, VII (1922), 281–83. On the same day, the Government announced the closing of *Obshchee Delo* and the departure of General Verkhovskii for a two weeks' leave of absence because of illness. Kerensky took over his duties as Minister of War. *Russkiia Vedomosti*, No. 243, October 24, 1917, p. 5, reported that it was not Verkhovskii's views on peace that the Government objected to, but rather his comments on the need for an authoritarian rule. Verkhovskii, in his *Rossiia na Golgofe*, p. 137, claimed that his proffered resignation was not accepted because the Government did not want to appear opposed to peace.]

A.

Regarding the notice that appeared in yesterday's issue of *Obshchee Delo*, alleging that the Minister of War, General Verkhovskii, had proposed the conclusion of peace in secret from our Allies, the Minister of War, in an interview with representatives of the press, has made the following declaration:

"Objecting with all my soul to the conclusion of a shameful separate peace, I objected—and object—to the defeatist agitation which has intensively developed during the days of the military operations with which the enemy hoped to create a psychological reaction among the people, calculating that the hearts of the cowards would falter and they would sign a shameful peace.

"Thus I spoke in the Central Executive Committee of the Soviet of Deputies and in the Council of the Republic.

"At the same time, taking into account the degree of disintegration brought about on the front by the replacements arriving from the rear which had been subjected to defeatist propaganda, I indicated the necessity of taking resolute measures in order to combat destructive activities in the rear. A series of my orders bears witness to these measures.

"The fact that intentions are being ascribed to me that are absolutely contrary to and do not in the least correspond to anything I have done or do as Minister of War can be explained only by a wish to misunderstand me. On the other hand, the fact of ascribing to me a proposal to conclude a separate peace and to inflict a blow upon the army can only contribute to developing that against which I am fighting, i.e., defeatism. Also, this was not understood by Burtsev."

In conclusion, the Minister of War declared emphatically that he has never and nowhere spoken in favor of a separate peace.

"No. 23 of the newspaper *Obshchee Delo*, in a notice signed by V. L. Burtsev, reported that at the session of the Committee on Defense of the Council of the Republic the Minister of War, General Verkhovskii, proposed the conclusion of peace with Germany in secret from the Allies.

"We deem it necessary to declare that neither in the Committee on Defense nor in the joint session of the Committees on Foreign Affairs and on Defense did General Verkhovskii make such proposals.

> "M. SKOBELEV
> "Chairman of the Committee on Foreign Affairs
> "F. ZNAMENSKII
> "Chairman of the Committee on Defense"

The Minister has started prosecution against the editor of the newspaper *Obshchee Delo*, Burtsev, for having inserted in the issue of October 21 a notice which is of obviously libelous nature.

B. *Conversation Between A. F. Kerensky and N. N. Dukhonin During the Night of October 21–22, 1917* *

[DUKHONIN] The Chief of Staff of the Supreme Commander is at the apparatus.

[KERENSKY] Hello, Nikolai Nikolaevich.

[DUKHONIN] I greet you, Aleksandr Fedorovich. What are your orders?

[KERENSKY] I regret that unexpected circumstances have delayed my arrival; in general, I wish to inform you so there will be no misunderstandings. In short, my arrival was in no way delayed by fear of some kind of unrest, rebellions, and the like; it is possible to cope with this sort of thing without me, because everything is organized. I was detained by the need to reorganize hastily the higher administration of the War Ministry because General Verkhovskii is going on leave today, and, as a matter of fact, he will not return to his post; this departure is caused by his exhaustion, which caused him recently to make a few speeches which are difficult to explain and which he himself later on admitted to be tactless. The situation became absolutely impossible after his declaration made at a secret session of the Foreign Affairs Committee of the Council of the Republic with regard to the fighting capacity of the army and to the possibility of continuing the war, and also with regard to the reorganization of the Government for the purpose of fighting anarchy, with suggestions as to the necessity of strengthening the principle of personal [leadership]. These speeches have caused enormous misunderstanding and even alarm because they were completely unexpected, even to the members of the Provisional Government who attended the session. The situation had become hopeless for Verkhovskii. I had to undertake as painlessly as possible the quickest possible liquidation of this episode because these declarations could have been used by the extreme elements on both sides. Burtsev has already attempted to do it, naturally distorting the facts, while on the other side the Bolsheviks are attempting to do it. Temporarily, because of his departure on leave, the Minister of War is relieved of all his duties; General Manikovskii is appointed Acting Minister of War, while the general leadership, especially for the political side, is being transferred to the Minister-President. Thus the policy of the War Ministry remains completely democratic, and the Commissar at Stavka should be informed of this so as to enable him to inform the front in good time, putting an end to possible attempts to use the departure of the Minister of War for antinational goals. This is the main thing. Second, it is necessary in the shortest time possible to select and direct to Petersburg at the disposal of Prince Eristov, Chief of the Administration of the Militia at the Ministry of the Interior, some 150 officers who are now in the reserve and not on active duty, in order to prepare them and put them in all haste at the disposal of the guberniya commissars for the purpose of assisting in the organization of the militia and in general for assisting the Administration in its fight against anarchy. Naturally you must call those who wish to volunteer, but not the former *gendarme* and police officers, and also you must select the best. This should be done as quickly as possible. I have not replied to a series of telegrams because I expected to arrive before

---

* The date is ascertained by the official German communication cited in the text.

Saturday. The main thing is that everyone in the Provisional Government is interested and concerned about the size and the speed of a possible reduction in the army and about its reorganization; the Ministries of Finance and of Food urge us very energetically in this regard. Are you aware of the order of the Minister of War regarding the supervision of front divisions over their reserve regiments? I think that this should be put into effect as soon as possible. . . .

[DUKHONIN] The order of the Minister of War is known and has been communicated for immediate implementation. Today I have received from the Minister of War a further—I think already a third—wording of a regulation for the army committees. After being again reviewed in the political section and by the representatives of the Democratic Conference [Provisional Council], it is still unacceptable to the army because it does not correspond with the efforts to increase the fighting capacities of the army and to raise the authority of the commanders, and, in this sense, it is much less satisfactory than the previous wordings. The opinion of the representatives of the front and the basic theses of our program are not taken into consideration; only the interests of the committees are being taken care of, and the approval of the commanders by the committees is being introduced in full in a secret way. The Commissar at Stavka has sent a circular to the commissars of the front—a proposal which has been communicated to me in copy —to work out jointly, by agreement between the Commanders in Chief and the committees, lists of approved officers for promotion to responsible command positions; attached to the circular is an instruction regarding the order of appointment of officers up to and including the commanders of divisions; at the same time certain stages of service are being fixed for various positions. . . . Regarding the reduction of the armies, everything possible is being done in this respect, [but] to increase the tempo of the reduction is absolutely impossible without serious damage to the fighting capacities of the army and especially in view of the free electoral campaign. All the reserve . . . regiments that are subject to disbanding send petitions that it be started after the end of the elections, and on these grounds there is unrest. Under these conditions disbanding should be done with extreme caution; on all fronts committees for the reduction are at work. . . .

.   .   .

THE CONGRESS OF PUBLIC LEADERS AND THE
TENTH CONGRESS OF THE KADET PARTY[4]

1391. THE MOSCOW CONGRESS OF PUBLIC LEADERS
[*Russkiia Vedomosti*, No. 234, October 13, 1917, p. 5; and No. 235, October 14, 1917, p. 5.]

Yesterday the Congress of the Public Leaders opened in the Ars movie theater. The basic membership of the Congress is the same as in August. But even a superficial observer sees some differences. Thus the army, and, in particular, the high commanding personnel, is less represented. As at the last Congress, in the

[4] The dates of these Congresses should be noted in relation to the sessions of the Provisional Council of the Russian Republic covered in the preceding section.

first rank in the center sits the former Supreme Commander, General Brusilov; beside him is General Ruzskii, who even before the beginning of the Congress, at his appearance in the hall of the Ars theater and then later when he entered the hall of the Congress, was the subject of loud, friendly ovations. Replying to them, General Ruzskii twice addressed short speeches to those who greeted him, saying that he attributed these ovations to the fact that in its time—these words he stressed with particular intonation—the Russian army had so valorously defended the liberty of Russia. During the speech of Prince E. N. Trubetskoi there was again a loud ovation addressed to the two leaders of our army. And the ovations addressed to the officers, when Prince Trubetskoi spoke of the great and unexampled heroism of the Russian officer, seemed still stronger and longer. This time the clergy, absent at the First Congress, was represented quite substantially. Both the orthodox and the Old Believer clergy were represented. The cooperatives, the merchants, the craftsmen were more extensively represented.

As in August, the presidential chair was occupied by M. V. Rodzianko, who opened the Congress and who was elected by acclamation and with loud cheers as Chairman of the Congress. Prince E. N. Trubetskoi, A. A. Evdokimov, P. D. Dolgorukov, and S. I. Chetverikov were elected by the Congress as his deputies.

"During the two months that divide this Congress from the first one," said M. V. Rodzianko in his speech of introduction, "the political horizon of our country has become still darker, still more gloomy, still more threatening. But this should not fill us with a feeling of hopelessness or despair. On the contrary, our conviction that our homeland will not perish, that she will save herself, is only the deeper. There is much to sustain and to deepen this faith; there are many signs that a salutary change is near, that [perhaps] it has come already, that the necessity of working for the precious cause of Russia's salvation is [understood] more widely. And this consciousness speaks ever more clearly and strongly, not only within the so-called bourgeois strata but also in the socialist strata of Russian society. This is a fortunate token. The danger and threat to the unity of the country, drawing so rapidly nearer, cannot but awaken the country, cannot fail to make it shed the ugly forms of faintheartedness and apathy, and cannot fail to give birth in everyone to a readiness to sacrifice his life for the homeland. There is no reason to consider the situation hopeless; there is no reason to assert that it is already too late to save it. By harmonious, common efforts she will be saved."

Further, M. V. Rodzianko outlined the basic tasks before the Congress in connection with the difficult situation experienced by the country, and he dwelt in detail on the question of the possibility of achieving peace in the near future; within Russian society the belief grows that such a peace is an inevitable calamity: Russia cannot continue the war, and therefore peace, even a shameful or ruinous one, is necessary. It is necessary to protest very resolutely against such thinking. And not only against a separate peace, which would be an unheard-of betrayal of our valorous Allies who show such an indulgent attitude toward our present-day political illness, but also against a general immediate peace, now when we are the defeated side—which is unthinkable and unpermissible—because it would certainly be linked with a partition of Russia in one form or another and accompanied beyond any doubt by our economic subjugation. This peace would bring a return of the hated past because Wilhelm would not permit the consolidation of our liberties, which are so dangerous for him. Peace will become possible only when we again become strong. This should be proclaimed loudly.

A. F. Belorussov, who described what the Council of the Congress had done since its first meeting in August with regard to the participation of the representatives of the Congress in the preparliament and with regard to the current tasks now standing before the Congress, submitted the first report. The first and basic task is to strengthen the organization of those elements that are united within the Congress, to transform the embryo now existing into a close network covering the whole country and uniting all the statesmanlike and nationally thinking [people]. It is necessary to develop the self-activity of the public; it is necessary that a reaction against the revolutionary democratic organizations which now enjoy authority and power should come into being. Such an organization is necessary in order to fight not only against the danger from the left, on which the main attention of the Congress is now focused, but also against a probable danger from the right. . . . A wave of reaction could also wipe us out, wipe out the new democratic Russia; and this Russia is more precious to us than anything else, because our loftiest wish, the object of our ancient dreams and cares, of our struggles, is a democratic Russia, free, self-governing, and self-activated. . . . We are called reactionaries, we are called Kornilovists. No, our aim is a counterreactionary struggle against reaction. As to being called Kornilovists, we could be only in the sense that we value what is sound in an action directed toward making Russia come back from the road of anarchy, in the sense that this aspect of the action can arouse our sympathy.

The Report of P. I. Novgorodtsev

The main event of the first day of the Congress was the report of P. I. Novgorodtsev, who started by giving a description of the existing situation in Russia. The edifice of the Russian state, said the reporter, is in a state of disintegration; the secular supports are shattered and falling to pieces. . . . And when one compares what is going on now with the bright enthusiasm of the first revolutionary days, the heart becomes heavier, the feeling of pain still more acute and insufferable. How did it all happen; how were we brought to these conditions? And where is the limit to disintegration? The answer lies in understanding the difference existing between our revolution and all the other revolutions. And such a difference exists. It lies in the fact that from the very first days of the revolution its leaders were dominated by fear of counterrevolution. And this fear has poisoned their faith in the Russian revolution. Because of it the controlling organs of the revolutionary democracy were placed above the revolutionary government everywhere—at the front and in the rear, at the center and in the provinces. These omnipresent organs entangled and tied up, as in a net, the normal activities of the Government. Thus was created that fatal dual power which gradually decomposed the Russian national [organization]. . . . It is true that as soon as the socialists come closer to power they begin to realize that these principles are unsuitable; they begin to see through them. But along with them remain those who were blinded and who have a great influence on the masses. . . . The Government was not sufficiently strong to withstand this influence. Therefore we have heard only many words about a firm government, but we have seen a government which resorted solely to admonitions, which is able only to make concessions to both sides, which operates by compromises—the latter very soon ceasing to satisfy those for the sake of whom they were made. Instead of a policy of vivid action, we see only rhetoric of vivid words. . . . Salvation lies . . . in uniting those who are capable of uniting on a higher level than that of class interests. And in this new unity, based on national [interests], there can be no place for defeatists or internationalists. . . .

. . . Everything indicates that a salutary shift is taking place in the course of the revolution; that, instead of a united revolutionary front, the foundations of national unity are being laid.

.   .   .

Prince E. N. Trubetskoi characterized what is happening in Russia as only a transitory disease, as an epidemic which has its usual course, and its term. The term is already ending, the signs of future recovery are already present. The very growth of bolshevism is such a symptom. Everything that is in the middle fails; there remains only what is sound or what represents a putrefied and therefore dead mass. Bolshevism is such a mass. And its death is unavoidable.

The speech of A. A. Kizevetter was devoted exclusively to bolshevism. He argued that now bolshevism and its successes are only a mirage, only an illusion. And the proof that this success is not lasting lies in the fact that bolshevism pretends to be what it is not; it tries to camouflage itself in the feathers of others. It thinks of itself as being the sole democratic element, arbitrarily calls itself thus; but in reality it represents only a pseudo-democracy, a false democratism, the distortion of democratic principles. And as falsely it asserts that it alone deploys in all its purity and fullness the revolutionary banner. All of it is permeated through and through precisely with the poison of the old order, and this order, which legally has been destroyed, lives in the heart of the Bolshevik, in his manners, in his methods and struggles, and so forth. As that old order . . . invented plots where they did not exist, likewise the Bolshevik invents counterrevolution so that his struggle against it can constitute a basis and a justification for himself and for his methods. As the old order did not trust the Russian people and was afraid of it, bolshevism likewise does not believe in and therefore is afraid of a strong army, because it believes that a strong army would unfailingly be a support of the reaction. The speaker concluded by invoking genuine democracy against bolshevism, true liberty against Bolshevik false liberty, and faith in the Russian people against the Bolshevik smears against it and against its army.

.   .   .

Radionov violently attacked the Government which has introduced into the administration of the country the mentality and the habits of the underground. Assistant Professor Il'in asserted that now there were only two parties in Russia, the party of order and the party of disintegration, and that the last was headed by A. F. Kerensky because he covered everything by his eloquence. The speaker argued that Kornilov could have been the leader of the party of order. The revolution in its present stage could be characterized as an "egotistic plunder."

A. D. Alferov objected, pointing out that one cannot aspire for strong government and shatter it at the same time. The task of the Congress consisted, not of such steps, but of the practical matter of the speediest possible creation of a wide organization in local areas. . . .

. . .

The Evening Session

. . .

The Debates

The debates that took place after the report bore a general character, although M. V. Rodzianko, who was presiding, proposed to discuss along with them those reports that were submitted in the morning. However, apparently sufficient unto the day was the evil thereof. A series of speakers passed in turn before the Congress. But the tone of the speeches was always the same, the themes were monotonous: they consisted of appeals to save the country from the gloomy sights of disintegration and anarchy reigning in the country, to struggle against bolshevism.

Only two moments caused animation: one, if one may say so, positive, and the other, negative, undesirable. Two speeches were delivered. One was the emotional speech of the peasant worker E. B. Surin, who took the rostrum in order to say that here for the first time he heard words of truth. "As we live now," said he, "we cannot live any longer. Before, an old and cruel government was dominating us. Now we are dominated by impotence and arbitrariness."

This speaker left the rostrum under a thunder of applause, which turned into an ovation.

Incident

In a different way the meeting was stirred up by another speech, also by a representative of the lower strata, a Kuban Cossack. This speech, incoherent and full of anger, full of attacks against the Jews, whom the speaker considers to be guilty of all the calamities that befell our country, provoked protests and even audible hissing from the Congress; neither did he spare A. F. Kerensky, ascribing to him a Jewish origin.

. . .

The Speech of General Brusilov

"In order to answer why what happened to the army did happen," said the former Supreme Commander, beginning his long speech, "one should look at what the Russian soldier was before the upheaval, what his mentality was. Then his world outlook was based on three wholes—the faith, the Tsar, the motherland. He stood very firmly on this. In preparing to fight, he used to put on clean underwear, pray to God, and say: 'I am going to my death to save the motherland.' He went and he died. He was not interested in any kind of politics, in what was going on in the rear; he was not interested and understood it poorly. If anybody was interested in it and suffered over it, it was the officer, who was apprehensive for the destinies of his motherland, who cursed a situation that was leading it toward ruin. Before the upheaval, not the soldier but the officer had revolutionary inclinations. This is why in the first moments of the upheaval it was precisely the officer [who] showed the greatest sympathy toward it. But then, how could it happen that it was precisely the revolutionary upheaval that split the army in two, into soldiers and officers? The answer should be found in the memory that persisted in our leftist parties after the unsuccessful revolution of 1905. Then it did not succeed because of the loyalty of the army toward the old regime.

And from this alarming recollection was born the idea that the army should be destroyed in order to ensure the revolution. Thus came to life the notorious Order No. 1—which one of the preceding speakers called 'Cain's document.' Delegates from Petrograd started slipping to the front, and from the front delegates slipped to Petrograd. Poison flowed like a river.

"Salvation lies in the restoration of discipline, but of a genuine discipline and not of some kind of democratic revolutionary discipline," continued General Brusilov. "The words that are said about the latter are just an odious lie. There is and has been but one discipline—military discipline—and it exists also in the republican armies, in the French and American armies, and in the army of free England, everywhere in every army that has ever anywhere existed."

Further General Brusilov touched on the question of the committees. He cannot agree with those who are for their complete and immediate destruction. The committees were the result of the introduction of politics into the army. . . .

"Everyone speaks," continued General Brusilov, "of a strong government. But a strong government will appear only when the majority of the people and of the army feel the depths of the country's downfall, when they will say: We have enough of disintegration, we wish order, we wish to avail ourselves of liberty and not of anarchy. When this happens, a strong government will arise also. Then too the Minins and the Pozharskiis will appear. We have already had an untimely Pozharskii," exclaimed General Brusilov under a thunder of applause, "Kornilov. But he did not appear in time; he appeared at a moment when Pozharskii could not yet appear and nobody followed him. Had Minin appeared too, he would also be sitting in Bykhov, and perhaps something even worse would have happened to him. When the people demand it in earnest, when it becomes necessary, the Pozharskiis and the Minins will be found. And then they will be strong; then they will be followed. The French revolution led to Napoleon. All of us Russians, we should wish one thing, that there be no Napoleons, but as many Pozharskiis and Minins as possible. They are Russian and good creations, while Napoleon is a French invention and let him remain there."

.   .   .

The Speech of General Ruzskii

The last to speak on military questions was General Ruzskii, who devoted the first words of his speech to refuting the fiction of Germany not being responsible for starting the war. . . . Further, General Ruzskii revealed a series of facts proving that attempts to disintegrate our army began much before the upheaval. The propaganda to this end was started in the middle of 1915 after our defeats in Galicia . . . But then this propaganda went on secretly, from the underground, from where within the trenches suddenly appeared proclamations calling for no advance, no fighting. There were cases of refusal to obey orders to attack, to carry out a given operation. . . . But with the coup d'état it was conducted quite openly. The very next day after the upheaval all sorts of agitators flooded in *en masse*. Attempts to place even a few obstacles against this flow were not successful. We were prevented from taking measures along these lines. This propaganda was the first cause of the army's disintegration. The second cause was Order No. 1, and the third was the Declaration of Soldiers' Rights. All this juggling with the term "revolutionary army" finally led the soldiers' minds astray. Finally, the fourth cause of the army's disintegration at the front was the rear of the army, which in its turn was subject to the propaganda of the deserters. . . .

How should one fight against disintegration? General Ruzskii recalled the conference at Stavka on June 16, which he attended. . . . The generals were told that the measures proposed by the senior commanders would be accepted, but they were asked only not to insist upon their immediate realization in full. Since then months have passed and nothing of what was proposed has been realized. In this General Ruzskii sees the source of that feeling of desperation that seized Kornilov. . . .

Is there still hope, is there a hope of recovery? The main elements in the army's existence, its military spirit, its very soul, have been extinguished. But there still remain vital forces, and they could arise. If this happens, if we are able to do it, then the army will be saved; Russia will be saved.

"I do not want to think, I cannot think," exclaimed General Ruzskii with force, "that we will not manage it, that there is no hope. There exists an exaggerated pessimism. The means have been indicated and they are the only ones." While in complete agreement with General Brusilov regarding the impossibility of now dispensing completely with the military committees, while agreeing with him with regard to the way this institution is set, General Ruzskii disagrees with the former Supreme Commander as regards the commissars, those "eyes of the revolution" which they claim to be. He considers it absolutely harmful to preserve this institution . . . A commander should be trusted or distrusted. And if trust exists, then there is no place for control over him. The commissar is merely harmful.

Agreeing with General Brusilov, General Ruzskii expressed himself very categorically in favor of expelling politics from the army. Until this is done, no goals of recovery, of restoration of fighting capacities, can be achieved. Like General Brusilov, General Ruzskii concluded his speech by an ardent appeal for the unity of all to whom the homeland is precious, who wish its salvation.

.   .   .

The Evening Session

The evening session was also devoted exclusively to the question of the army. A long line of speakers passed, attempting to solve all those "accursed questions" of the army and its disintegration, pointing out the concrete measures that could lead the army out of this state of disintegration.

.   .   .

. . . A. S. Belorussov reported the project of the draft resolution proposed by the Presidium. The resolution met no objections and was unanimously approved.

The Resolution

"The Moscow Congress believes," the resolution states, "that in order to stop the national disintegration, it is necessary, first of all, to resolutely fight anarchy in all its manifestations, a step that the government will finally be obliged to take; and second, that that part of the people whose ideology is national and statesmanlike, united in its devotion to the great national ideals, to the democratic principles of the new free Russia and the recognition of the necessity of wide social reforms, should show initiative [and] activity.

"But in order to become actually strong, and therefore influential also within the government, the national democracy of Russia should be organized. The Moscow Congress of Public Leaders contemplates this organization in the form of an association or of a union which would join together entire parties or groups as well as individual citizens sharing [the ideas expressed in] the decisions of the First and Second Moscow Congresses. This association does not pursue any kind of class or party interest; it does not encroach upon the independence or the internal life of the organizations that enter into it.

"Passing to the questions of the current moment, the Moscow Congress believes:

"1) Regarding the role of its deputies in the preparliament, it is advisable that the deputies of the Congress, as representatives of an association of the statesmanlike thinking elements of the country, be the defenders of the leading ideas of the association in the Provisional Council. The Government should become conscious of the fact that within the ranks of the defenders of right and order there is no dissent on basic national issues. At the same time the Congress expresses the conviction that its participants and the members of its Council who are members of the Government will direct all their efforts toward an unswerving realization of the theses of the Moscow Congress.

"2) Regarding the question of the Constituent Assembly, in spite of all the apprehensions arising about the conditions under which the elections to the Constituent Assembly will be held, it is essential that the organizations that are close to the Congress assist the elections by supporting the lists of those groups that stand on a national statesmanlike platform.

"In case the organizations associated at the Moscow Congress of Public Leaders present several separate lists, it is advisable that the widest possible agreement exist among them on merging these lists according to the procedure established by law.

"It is not only admissible but desirable to associate with the group of Popular Socialists and the group of the 'Edinstvo,' with the understanding that the latter, in this moment of responsibility for the Russian public, abandon class struggle and adhere to the ideal of national unity and collaboration.

"In the Constituent Assembly itself, the national and statesmanlike elements should create a common front in order to undertake firm and systematic organizational work with a view to establishing the Russian State on the principles of liberty, social justice, and the national unity of Russia.

"Considering that organic work within the Constituent Assembly should be based on a national platform, the Congress believes that in order to complete this task successfully and also in order to implement the new legislation, the Government should finally create an apparatus of power and of national administration.

"3) Regarding the question of peace and war, the Congress considers it timely and necessary now to declare that, in spite of the triumph of the German fleet in the Baltic Sea and in spite of a very definite threat to Petrograd, the public conscience excludes the very thought of betraying our Allies and of a separate peace. Such a peace would represent the most severe blow to our national honor and dignity and would reflect fatally on the whole future of Russia. The Congress firmly believes that the Russian people will find in itself sufficient strength to bring the war to a peace which will correspond to the interests, honor, and dignity of Russia."

. . .

1392. *Rech'* ON THE CONGRESS
[No. 243, October 15, 1917, p. 1.]

While the Council of the Republic is in session in Petrograd, a second Congress of Public Leaders has opened in Moscow. According to the conventional terminology, this is a meeting of bourgeois elements, although it is difficult to ascertain what many *pomeshchiki* have preserved, now that the work of the "peasant" Minister has produced its fruits; likewise it is hardly possible convincingly to explain why, for instance, the professors who participate at the conference and who have received pitiful raises in their pay represent bourgeois elements while the longshoremen of the Volga who strive to increase their pay up to 280 rubles a day proclaim themselves to be the revolutionary proletariat.

So the bourgeois elements have again gathered in Moscow together with military representatives of the commanding personnel who have been dismissed as useless. Thus this Congress is, as it were, set against the Democratic Conference which was held here, and a comparison between the two becomes unavoidable. As it will be easy to remember, that Conference turned into a court [judging] the bourgeois elements and the Kadets. The court was held in the absence of the accused; therefore only words of accusation were heard. All the guilt and all the responsibility were placed on those absent; there were appeals for a rupture and for the unification of the democratic front.

In Moscow at the congress of the bourgeois elements there is also talk of those absent, not in order to judge them and condemn them but to urge for the sake of saving Russia the most extensive and deep unity with the democracy.

At the Democratic Conference all those who were not present were declared counterrevolutionaries and rebels. At the Moscow Congress they speak of the necessity of fighting against counterrevolution from the right, should this, as is unfortunately quite possible, become necessary.

. . .

However, here we would like to stress something else; we would like to draw attention to the restraint, the equanimity, and the calm of the Moscow Congress; we do not do it in order to offer comparisons but in order to stress that a lack of hatred and a sober attitude toward reality, the preservation of a deep faith in tomorrow in spite of the painful disorganization of today, constitute without doubt a comforting sign.

On the other hand, if one compares this symptom with those signs of change of attitude within the active army of which the newspapers write daily and with the recovery which, for the time being still very modestly, begins to be outlined within the country, then one must recognize that these symptoms are not accidental but bear witness to a genuine inner process now under way.

. . .

Now along with the Provisional Government another national institution has been formed—the Council of the Republic. The latter should pay attention to the favorable symptoms we have mentioned and should assist in consolidating and uniting them into one single whole, thereby making them powerful. Up to now the Council has not done anything in this direction; on the contrary, there has appeared merely a new rostrum for old arguments, which bore everyone and which no one wishes to hear. It would be extremely sad if the Council did not attempt to use the possibilities that are being opened before it and that put into its hands [the opportunity to play] a serious role in the course of our revolution.

1393. "THE COUNCIL OF COUNTERREVOLUTION"
[Editorial in *Delo Naroda*, No. 181, October 15, 1917, p. 1.]

Its meeting takes place now in Moscow. It includes "everybody, except those whom they call *tovarishchi*."

This is literally what A. S. Belorussov said in his speech.

The same speaker characterized the members of the Congress in the following words:

"Let them call us reactionaries and Kornilovites!"

And the lecturer, I. A. Il'in, exclaimed:

"The time has come to say that we are now counterrevolutionaries. We are Kornilovites and counterrevolutionaries!"

Under a thunder of applause the learned Kornilovite further said:

"The party of disorder has its leader, A. F. Kerensky."

Here Orlov, a Cossack, completed the picture. He asserted that the cause of Russia's disintegration lies in the German agents and the Jews. At the head of the latter stands the "pure-blooded or half-breed Jew Kerensky."

This orator was not thrown out of the hall. He was merely "denounced."

Such are the data. They sum up what takes place in Moscow now under the banner "Congress of Public Leaders."

Gathered there were generals (former Minister of War Polivanov, who demanded the reinstatement of Kornilov to the post of Supreme Commander), members of the dissolved Duma with Kammerherr Rodzianko at their head, the Moscow Metropolitan, Archpresbyter Shavel'skii, professor-idealists and philosophers, Prince Trubetskoi, Novgorodtsev, and finally, as the last stroke of the picture, an incidental figure of the revolution, the sailor Batkin.

And so, the gauntlet has been thrown down.

Minins and Pozharskiis, according to the characterization of Prince Trubetskoi, have gathered in Moscow in order to carry out the principles of Kornilov.

They know how revolutionary Russia in the rear and at the front met the plot of Stavka, how close we were to fratricidal slaughter. And in spite of this, perhaps because of this, they propose Kornilov as their leader, and his "principles" as their banner.

They look for a cause to rouse the irreconcilable passions; they, saviors of the fatherland, in the grave hour in its history, in the face of the foreign enemy, provoke an internal bloody conflict. They need blood; they need total darkness, total animosity; and, while diverting attention from the basic aims of the revolution, they need to trample, suffocate, and put it out of existence.

It is the same question.

It has to do with "arbitrary organizations"—that is, organs expressing the will of the revolutionary democracy—with enslaving the working class, with the death penalty in the rear, and finally with the idea of making the peasants give up their hopes for land.

And that is why professor-idealists, generals, metropolitans, shady characters, and pogromists are so touchingly united at the council of the counterrevolution.

They were welded by hatred of the revolution and fear of the forthcoming Constituent Assembly.

And in their class animosity they reveal the cards of their Petrograd allies— the diplomatic speech of the Kadet Adzhemov in the Council of the Republic had the same source and pursued the same aims:

"Down with Kerensky, and hail Kornilov!"

Do they really believe that from the end of August to the end of October the situation changed in their favor?

Or are they impatient? Or, in the heat of players who have lost, do they stake everything—do they stake blood?

Playing with fire is dangerous for those who start the fire.

1394. The Kadet Congress

[From *Rech'*, No. 243, October 15, 1917, p. 3; and *Russkiia Vedomosti*, No. 236, October 15, 1917, p. 5; and No. 237, October 17, 1917, p. 5. In his *Istoriia vtoroi russkoi revoliutsii*, I, vypusk 3, 145–46, Miliukov outlined again his reasons for opposing any further alliance with the moderate socialists and for following an unconciliatory Kadet Party line. He adds that though a majority of the Central Committee and the Duma faction was in favor of an agreement, the "overwhelming majority of the Congress declared itself in favor of P. N. Miliukov's tactics—and was prepared to go even further."]

Today the All-Russian Congress of the Party of the People's Freedom began its work, being called chiefly in view of the elections to the Constituent Assembly to be held in the near future . . .

· · ·

The first report was submitted by V. D. Nabokov. He gave the characteristics of the situation created after the split within the Government at the end of August in connection with the Kornilov events and the formation of the new cabinet and the preparliament.

"At that moment," said Nabokov, "three solutions of the existing governmental crisis seemed plausible: the first solution, the formation of a homogeneous, so-called bourgeois government; a second solution, the formation of a homogeneous, purely socialistic government without an admixture of bourgeoisie; and the third, the creation of a mixed government, a coalition cabinet.

"Was the first issue practicable? Remembering the situation created in connection with the Kornilov episode, remembering what an uncompromising attitude the democratic circles took then with regard to the bourgeois circles, especially in respect to the K.D., it becomes evident that this method of solving the crisis was not possible. . . .

"Also the second solution, that of a homogeneous socialist cabinet, seemed as impracticable. The socialists themselves, except for the Bolsheviks, were against it, fully realizing that such a step would be fatal for the country. Furthermore, the Democratic Conference proved clearly that a united democratic front did not exist, that it was disintegrating.

"Finally, the third solution, the formation of a ministry of socialist and non-socialist elements, i.e., a return to the principle of coalition, was recognized as the only one acceptable.

"What was the position of the K.D., and was it well founded? The Party also was facing only two roads: either agreement with a coalition or a resolute refusal to participate in the government, a resolute rupture with the democracy. . . . Having once recognized that a homogeneous socialist government at that moment was impossible, would not our decision have threatened the country with remaining entirely without a government? Or a homogeneous socialist government might have been formed with all the fatal consequences we foresaw . . . Our refusal would have been a sort of invitation for such a government.

"It is true that there was a point of view that this was precisely what should have been attempted. As the abscess was ripe and as anyway it was necessary to pass through the difficult operation of lancing it, then let that operation come as soon as possible. . . . We do not know whether we would have been able to clear the Party of the responsibility for what might have resulted from our refusal to participate in the coalition, from its responsibility for the consequences of our step.

"Therefore there remained but one solution: our representatives had to enter the cabinet.

. . .

"It is necessary to give the Government a reliable basis. This is the goal. There is hope that it may be reached. The preparliament possesses elements for this purpose; there is patriotism, there are statesmanlike points of view. Now, as we meet our opponents face to face there, the chances of our moral victory increase at every encounter. And this is recognized; this is also felt by our opponents.

". . . Since the formation of the new government and of the Council of the Republic, only a few days have passed, but these days have brought inspiration, optimism, and hope," V. D. Nabokov concluded.

. . .

The Report of P. N. Miliukov

. . .

Speaking . . . of what the Party of the People's Freedom should stand for in the electoral campaign, P. N. Miliukov established the following platform:

1) The war to the end in agreement with the Allies. The rejection of the democracy's views on the subject as reflected in the mandate to Skobelev.

2) The restoration of the fighting capacities of the army; the way to do it—to reduce the functions of the committees to those of economic welfare and cultural enlightenment; the re-establishment of the disciplinary authority of the commanders.

3) The unity of power.

4) The strength of the Government.

5) The restoration of authority in the provinces.

6) Independent courts.

. . . P. N. Miliukov proposed to the Congress the approval of the following three theses, which define the line of conduct of the Party:

1) The Congress of the Party of the People's Freedom approves the actions of the representatives of the Party both during their participation in the Government in its former membership and during the negotiations which concluded with the formation of the new Provisional Government and the establishment of the Council of the Republic.

2) Being the direct continuation of all the former activity of the Party during the revolution, the activity of the group within the Council should consolidate in the consciousness of the masses a firm and definite view on the way to save the homeland, the view that found its expression in a series of party decisions and that has already united around it various elements and public groups which become more and more numerous.

3) The Congress believes that the immediate task of the Party within the Council should be an endeavor to form in it a leading center of statesmanlike thinking uniting the sound political elements, which would give the Provisional Government the opportunity to rely on them in the accomplishment of the urgent and vital tasks imposed on it, and which would direct the Government along an unswerving path toward the realization of these tasks.

The Speech of M. S. Adzhemov

. . .

"I pass," continued M. S. Adzhemov, "to the point of view that is defended by P. N. Miliukov. He approves the formation of a coalition government. Here there is no dissent between us, but P. N. Miliukov believes that our activity in the Provisional Council should be of a party nature, that we must use the rostrum of the Council in order to maintain all our positions. But if we strive to keep our principles pure, we shall not do anything for the country. And in the meantime the democracy has split. There are democratic masses which have moved away from bolshevism. The proletarian masses which strive for a social revolution become more and more isolated. We should interfere in this process. We should find common roads with the huge masses which have moved away from the Bolsheviks; by pushing them from us we would pour water over the Bolshevik mill wheel.

"It is said that without sharply defining our attitude toward the Government we would obscure [in the eyes] of the voters the image of our party; but the voter does not reckon with speeches, however brilliant they be, but with actions. He will know that we participate because our conscience forces us to take upon ourselves this work which is necessary for the country; [he will know that our work] demands that we not leave the Government to inexperienced people.

"All the history of our participation in the Government," continued M. S. Adzhemov, "speaks against those who manifest such sharp criticism of its activity. As you remember, when Miliukov withdrew from the first cabinet, we nevertheless left our representatives there. At the same time this cabinet was marked by a trait that P. N. Miliukov defined as 'Tolstoyism.' For it is we who organized the land committees. And we, as a strong party, should not be afraid to hear the truth. Furthermore, we withdrew from the second cabinet because the Ukrainian bill was approved, but we re-entered it later, and specifically F. F. Kokoshkin, who was an enemy of the bill, joined it. Why? Because this was a period of rupture with the Soviets. We joined the third cabinet also, and this was done with the approval of P. N. Miliukov.

"It is an extraordinary thing," exclaimed the speaker, "that our comrades, the former ministers, have taken the most uncompromising position with regard to the Government; here they represent the wing most to the right. For the second day we are busy trying to destroy the coalition. But today there can be no other coalition.

"If in the preparliament," M. S. Adzhemov concluded his speech, "we are preoccupied only with preserving the purity of our tactics, we will not create anything."

The Reply of P. N. Miliukov

P. N. Miliukov began by pointing out that the opinion defended by M. S. Adzhemov was the opinion of the majority of the Central Committee and not the opinion of its minority, to which, remarked the speaker, "I belong." . . .

"Adzhemov has formulated our dissent," said P. N. Miliukov further, "as if in general our activity in the preparliament also should have a party nature. This expresses my thought quite inexactly. The six points which I read here yesterday contain no party demands. They are national and therefore they are compulsory for everybody. The question is whether we can make any concession in respect to some of them. For me it is clear that we cannot. M. S. Adzhemov said that our line of behavior to be taken in the Council should depend on the line that we will take during the elections to the Constituent Assembly. This argument is not only erroneous but also dangerous. We were in the Fourth Duma in a bloc with the Nationalists, but I would never have said that at the elections to the Fifth Duma, if they had taken place, we would have to preserve this bloc. For the same reason we cannot beforehand define our attitude toward parties that will participate in the elections to the Constituent Assembly. The problem of the current moment consists for us in influencing the voting in a favorable sense, because I believe that if the membership of the Constituent Assembly should be the same as that of the Council it would mean the ruin of Russia. A process of disillusionment in the slogans brought forward by the extreme parties is now taking place, and we should speed up this process. Our activity is not an introduction to the work in the Constituent Assembly but an introduction to the elections.

"We are witnessing a split in the democracy and we should take advantage of this split. What is the essence of this split? The center of the democracy, rejected from its political and social bases at the auction where the extreme leftists have increased the prices, finds itself in a kind of state of meditation. This perhaps draws it closer to us. But it is powerless and therefore useless. So why should we support with our clear slogans its false phraseology, what I have called its official hypocrisy?

"My opponent," continued P. N. Miliukov, "in order to defend his position, tries to find arguments in our past. He dabbles in psychology. He says that the most uncompromising opponents of the Government are our comrades who have headed ministries. To this I can answer only thus: I do not know to what degree this answer could wound anybody, but it convinces me of only one thing—that one must have participated in our Government to be convinced of how hopeless it is there. M. S. Adzhemov further recalls that during the period of the first cabinet we did not speak of a strong government, although there also was the

'Tolstoyism' of L'vov. I must say that we continuously struggled against it and were in the minority."

Passing to the remarks made by V. D. Nabokov regarding the creation within the parliament of a unifying center, regarding the creation of a majority, P. N. Miliukov said that he was far from being in principle an opponent of creating such a majority; he only feared that, by seeking such a majority, the six points which were the national program would be dimmed.

"Such," P. N. Miliukov concluded his objections, addressing himself to the Congress, "are our dissents, which we bring out for your solution. We should preserve the unity that we have found in these theses. And you will preserve it by approving them."

. . .

1395. *Russkiia Vedomosti* ON THE TWO CONGRESSES
[No. 237, October 17, 1917, p. 3.]

In the midst of the stupendous breakdown of our internal state life, in the face of the menacing outward danger that approaches from the Northwestern Front, there is a growing need for organization of the elements of the country that have not lost their national feeling. There is need also of presenting on a broad scale to the public those elementary and, moreover, urgent problems, the quick solution of which is indispensable to save us from defeat at the front and hopeless anarchy within. The loud and insistent voice of this need rings clearly in the debates and resolutions in those congresses which succeeded each other or took place simultaneously in Moscow recently.

The second meeting of the Congress of Public Leaders, which adjourned Sunday, showed that it was not a transitory need of the moment, but one of lasting significance which gave birth to this organization.

. . .

In particular, one of the most valuable characteristics of the Congress was the active participation in it of authoritative and outstanding specialists on military questions. At the present moment when all along the line utopian ideas triumph about the "democratization" of the army, nonexistent in any democracy of the world, it was more important than ever for the Russian public to hear the last-hour warning about the dying army, which rang with acute pain and concern in the speeches of Generals Ruzskii and Brusilov.

Almost simultaneously with the nonparty "conference" designed to unite all the nationally aware elements of the country, there was in session the All-Russian Congress of that party, which, among the mentioned elements, undoubtedly represents the largest organized force and, one could say even more, which at the present time, with the split as revealed among the socialist groups, is almost the only important party in Russia that has preserved unity, inner solidarity, and discipline.

. . .

In view of the approaching elections to the Constituent Assembly, the chief subject of attention of the Congress would apparently have to be the forthcoming pre-election campaign. But the extraordinary conditions of the present time had the same effect on the mood of the Congress as they had on the sentiment of all of Russia; the interest in the forthcoming elections was, to a large extent, over-shadowed by a yet more acute interest in the current moment. The center of gravity of the general political speeches and debates was the tactics not of to-morrow but of today—the question of the position of the party in the preparlia-ment and the Government.

Two main currents were revealed at the Congress as well as in the Central Committee of the Party with respect to this question. One of them, which found its expression in the speeches of V. D. Nabokov and M. S. Adzhemov, saw as the immediate aim the strengthening of the coalition government by means of creating in the preparliament a bloc with the more moderate socialist groups. The other, expressed most clearly in speeches by P. N. Miliukov and P. I. Novgorodtsev, emphasized the necessity of preserving complete consistency and firmness in defending those minimum demands of statehood that, because of their elementary nature, tolerate no compromises. It treated skeptically the possibility of creating a majority in the preparliament, ready to support without any deviations these demands. The first tendency, according to the statement by P. N. Miliukov, tri-umphed at the Petrograd session of the Central Committee, which preceded the Congress. But at the Congress itself the second tendency clearly predominated. The difference of opinions was resolved by including in the tactical resolution of the Congress a conciliatory formula.

Thanks to this formula, the question about the tactics of the K.D. faction in the preparliament remained to a certain extent open. But there is no doubt that it will resolve itself in the very near future. We shall see very soon whether or not it is possible to hope for the formation in the preparliament of a majority for a steadfast implementation of those national beginnings which, according to the just remark of the leader of the K.D. Party, are "not disputed anywhere except in Russia." We must say frankly that the first statements at the Provisional Council by the representatives of the S.D. and the S.R. of the "defensive" tendency hold little hope for this. The education in statehood of the predominating elements in the Soviet proceeds slowly. And compared with the terrifying rapidity of events, this slowness assumes a truly fatal significance.

1396. *Vlast' Naroda* ON THE TWO CONGRESSES
[No. 144, October 17, 1917, p. 2.]

Two trends were competing at the Congress of the K.D. Party. One of them could, with good reason, be called Kadet bolshevism. It opposed "conciliation," which was proposed between the K.D. and the revolutionary state groups in the Council of the Republic. It would like to maintain in the maximum degree the purity of party principles. The fanaticism and intolerance of Leninist bolshe-vism were thus opposed by the same fanaticism and intolerance of the adherents of the constitutional regime . . .

The other tendency at the Congress of the K.D. Party, that of coalition and "conciliation," although it followed the course already marked in the very first steps of the practical work in the preparliament, suffered by one quite serious defect: inability or deliberate unwillingness to define with sufficient clarity the limits of coalition and conciliation to be allowed to the K.D.

In the official resolution of the Congress it says that the "immediate task of the Party in the Council should be an endeavor to form in it a leading center of statesmanlike thinking uniting the sound political elements" . . . What elements must we, according to this resolution, consider sound? The answer to this question gained from the debates in the Congress is quite vague.

.   .   .

P. I. Novgorodtsev defined quite mildly the group of public leaders who rallied around their Congress. "They are more to the right than we are," that is, the Kadets, he said. But with respect to Orlov and Il'in, the melancholy heroes of the recent Congress of Public Leaders, this quantitative difference must be replaced by a qualitative one: they should be purely and simply recognized as counterrevolutionaries. To include them in the orbit of Kadet influence is useless, to say the least.

This is not enough. What becomes clear with regard to Il'in and Orlov is effaced and grows dim in other characteristic nuances of the Congress of Public Leaders, as well as the Congress of the K.D. Party. They are of course ashamed of Il'in and Orlov, and they will not risk including them among the sound, statesmanlike elements. But as for General Kornilov, who raised the banner of revolt, he was raised to a martyr and hero both at the Congress of Public Leaders and at the Congress of the Kadet Party. Is Kornilov then also a representative of the sound elements?

The vague and elastic formula of the K.D. resolution can supply us with no answer to this question. Consequently, if the K.D. really wanted to assist in implementing the idea of general national and state ideas, they should have first of all outlined quite definitely the limits of the leading center of the state which they had in mind. For us these limits had been marked out long ago: they start from the revolutionary-state socialists, through the yet unformed democratic groups, down to the representatives of industry and the K.D. Party—and not one step farther, either to the left to anarcho-bolshevism, or to the right to those whom Prof. Novgorodtsev so mildly defined with the words "more to the right than the K.D."

And as long as the Kadets continue to gloss over the dividing line separating the coalition from the right, so long will the distrustful attitude toward them continue. In the interests of the coalition and the struggle against anarchy, they must once and for all cut themselves off not only from the Il'ins but from the Kornilovs as well.

THE BOLSHEVIK SEIZURE OF POWER
AND THE LAST STAND OF THE PROVISIONAL GOVERNMENT[5]

1397. EDITORIAL IN *Rabochii Put'* PROMISING THAT THE CONVOCATION OF THE CONSTITUENT ASSEMBLY WILL BE ASSURED IF ALL POWER IS TAKEN BY THE CONGRESS OF SOVIETS

[No. 26, October 3, 1917, p. 1. At the same time, Lenin was writing the Central Committee of the Bolshevik Party that the moment was ripe for the seizure of power and

---

[5] It should be re-emphasized here that this section especially makes no attempt at an extensive coverage of the events of the October revolution, which are carefully documented in the Hoover Institution's publication *The Bolshevik Revolution*, by Bunyan and Fisher. Their volume is indispensable for a study of this period.

that they had "no right to wait for the Congress of Soviets; they must *take power imme-diately.*" *Collected Works of V. I. Lenin: Toward the Seizure of Power,* XXI, Bk. II, 69. See also Lenin's remarks on the Constituent Assembly in the next document.]

Since the first day of the revolution the capitalists and the *pomeshchiki,* agree-ing to the convening of the Constituent Assembly *in words,* have sabotaged it *in fact* by postponing under various pretexts the date of its convening "until better times." . . .

[Besides Tseretelli,] other representatives of the "revolutionary democracy" argue in the same fashion.

.   .   .

Now again "for the sake of the Constituent Assembly" the defensists have started a campaign against the Congress of the Soviets.

.   .   .

Our duty, the duty of the proletariat's party, is to tell all the people: While power is in the hands of the bourgeoisie and the *pomeshchiki* (and now it is *entirely* in their hands), the convening of the Constituent Assembly is in no way guaranteed. . . . That is why we say to the people: In order for the Constituent Assembly to take place, in order for the popular masses to participate intelligently and freely in the elections, in order for the decisions of the Constituent Assembly to become really valid, it is necessary that an end be put to all the intrigues, all the conspiracies of the counterrevolution; that the Congress of the Soviets of the revolutionary soldiers and peasants take into its hands, along with power, the fate also of the Constituent Assembly.

If the power is transferred to the Soviets, the fate of the Constituent Assembly will be in good hands. If the bourgeoisie succeeds in hindering the transfer of the power to the Soviets, it will break the Constituent Assembly.

.   .   .

1398. The Meeting of the Central Committee of the Bolshevik Party on the Night of October 10, and the Decision to Seize Power

[This excerpt from the minutes is taken from the *Collected Works of V. I. Lenin: Toward the Seizure of Power,* XXI, Bk. II, 106–7. Dates are New Style. A more com-plete account is published in *ibid.,* pp. 326–28, and in Bunyan and Fisher, pp. 56–58. Lenin had returned from Vyborg in disguise the day before in order to personally plead his case for immediate seizure of power before the Committee. On the previous day, the Military Revolutionary Committee of the Petrograd Soviet, which was to act as the general staff of the uprising, was organized under the direction of Trotsky. *Ibid.,* pp. 68–69. See Trotsky's account of the October 10 meeting in "Vospominaniia ob oktiab'rskom perevorote," *PR,* No. 10 (1922), p. 58.]

I

Lenin states that since the beginning of September a certain indifference towards the question of uprising has been noted. He says that this is inadmissible, if we earnestly raise the slogan of seizure of power by the Soviets. It is, therefore, high time to turn attention to the technical side of the question. Much time has obviously been lost.

Nevertheless, the question is very urgent and the decisive moment is near.

The international situation is such that we must take the initiative.

What is being planned, surrendering as far as Narva and even as far as Petrograd, compels us still more to take decisive action.

The political situation is also effectively working in this direction. On July 16–18, decisive action on our part would have been defeated because we had no majority with us. Since then, our upsurge has been making gigantic strides.

The absenteeism and the indifference of the masses can be explained by the fact that the masses are tired of words and resolutions.

The majority is now with us. Politically, the situation has become entirely ripe for the transfer of power.

The agrarian movement also goes in this direction, for it is clear that enormous efforts are needed to subdue this movement. The slogan of transferring the entire land has become the general slogan of the peasants. The political background is thus ready. It is necessary to speak of the technical side. This is the whole matter. Meanwhile we, together with the defensists, are inclined to consider a systematic preparation for an uprising as something like a political sin.

To wait for the Constituent Assembly, which will obviously not be for us, is senseless, because it would make our task more complex.

We must utilise the regional congress and the proposal from Minsk to begin decisive action.

II

Resolution

The Central Committee recognises that the international situation of the Russian Revolution (the mutiny in the navy in Germany as the extreme manifestation of the growth in all of Europe of the world-wide Socialist revolution; the threat of a peace between the imperialists with the aim of crushing the revolution in Russia) as well as the military situation (the undoubted decision of the Russian bourgeoisie and of Kerensky and Co. to surrender Petrograd to the Germans) and the fact that the proletarian parties have gained a majority in the Soviets; all this, coupled with the peasant uprising and with a shift of the people's confidence towards our party (elections in Moscow); finally, the obvious preparation for a second Kornilov affair (the withdrawal of troops from Petrograd; the bringing of Cossacks to Petrograd; the surrounding of Minsk by Cossacks, etc.)—places the armed uprising on the order of the day.

Recognising thus that an armed uprising is inevitable and the time perfectly ripe, the Central Committee proposes to all the organisations of the party to act accordingly and to discuss and decide from this point of view all the practical questions (the Congress of the Soviets of the northern region, the withdrawal of troops from Petrograd, the actions in Moscow and in Minsk, etc.).

1399. EDITORIAL IN *Rabochii Put'* ON "ALL POWER TO THE SOVIETS"
[No. 35, October 13, 1917, p. 1.]

. . .

All power to the Soviets—it means a basic purge of each and every governmental institution in the rear and at the front, from top to bottom.

All power to the Soviets—it means the election, and the possibility of replacing each and every "chief" in the rear and at the front.

All power to the Soviets means the election, and the possibility of replacing "the representatives of authority" in the cities and in the villages, in the army and in the fleets, in the "administrations" and "institutions," on the railroads and in the post and telegraph offices.

All power to the Soviets means the dictatorship of the proletariat and of the revolutionary peasantry.

.   .   .

The dictatorship of the proletariat and of the revolutionary peasantry means the dictatorship of the toiling majority over the exploiting minority, over *pomeshchiki* and capitalists, over speculators and bankers, for the sake of a democratic *peace*, for the sake of workers' *control* over production and distribution, for the sake of *land* for the peasants, for the sake of *bread* for the people.

The dictatorship of the proletariat and of the revolutionary peasantry means an open dictatorship, a mass dictatorship accomplished in the eyes of everybody without conspiracy or work behind the scenes. . . .

The dictatorship of the proletariat and of the peasantry means a dictatorship that would not use violence against the masses; it means a dictatorship by the will of the masses, a dictatorship tending to curb the will of the enemies of these masses.

.   .   .

The moment has arrived when the revolutionary slogan "All power to the Soviets" must finally be realized.

1400. *Delo Naroda* on the Bolshevik Preparations for an Uprising
[No. 181, October 15, 1917, p. 1.]

The Bolsheviks are getting ready for action. This is a fact. Moreover, we have reason to assert that this action is intended to be an armed one.

"The country is ripe for a dictatorship of the proletariat and the revolutionary peasantry. The moment has arrived when the revolutionary slogan 'All power to the Soviets' must finally be realized." Thus writes *Rabochii Put'*.

At the self-appointed Congress of the Soviets of the Northern Region, which the Bolsheviks look upon as the "forerunner of the All-Russian Congress of the Soviets," Trotsky protested against the withdrawal from Petrograd of the revolutionary troops for his protection, counting precisely on the aid of the Petrograd Garrison to realize "immediately" the creation of a Soviet government and an "immediate" proposal of peace on all fronts. "The time for words is past. The hour has struck when by a decisive and united action of all the Soviets the country and the revolution may be saved and the question of central power decided . . ." "If the workers, if the soldiers and peasants *endure* and *wait*, they will wait in vain to see the Constituent Assembly, just as they have waited until now in vain to see the land. Each day brings new dangers. All strength in the struggle for final victory over the traitors and betrayers of the revolution; the Petrograd proletariat and garrison—the fate of the revolution—are in your hands! . . ."

This is the way the Bolsheviks appeal for a "new revolution," for an insurrection in the next few days.

This call is heard in the days of our heaviest defeats on the front, which is almost at Petrograd; when the crucial question is defense from the external enemy, who is at the very approaches to Petrograd. We hear the call to insurrection and civil war when it is clear to all who love their motherland and who want to defend it from the external enemy that now, more than ever, we need the unity of the revolutionary front. The demand to form a new central power by the Soviets is heard actually on the eve of the convening of the Constituent Assembly, whose plenary powers to solve this question are not shared by any other institution.

All means are employed by the Bolsheviks to arouse the masses and prepare an insurrection: demagogic flattery of the masses, whipping up of all elements, slanders, lies.

The Bolshevik press had been speculating for some time with rumors about the evacuation of Petrograd, assuring the masses that the Government is fleeing, having betrayed and sold revolutionary Petrograd. The Bolsheviks do not wish to repudiate this slander even after the official denial of this rumor. "The Provisional Government," asserts *Rabochii Put'*, "fools the Petrograd workers and soldiers by inflated assurances that it has declined [to accept] the decision to move." Now the Bolsheviks have gone even further and accuse the Government of . . . defeatism. . . .

The Bolsheviks are hurrying. They already sense that a new change in mood is ripening among the masses, that their present dominant influence will lessen. And they want to make use of the profitable moment as soon as they can. . . .

Our memory is too short. We often forget that the Kornilov movement came after the days of July 3–5. What will come now after the new action by the Bolsheviks? The second Kornilov affair may prove to be more dangerous than the first, especially with the growth of the dark instincts among the masses aroused by the pogrom leaflets.

The revolution should muster all its forces against the announced march of the Bolsheviks. Let a menacing and united rebuff be the answer to the appeal for a criminal action in this grave moment for our country.

1401. *Izvestiia* ON THE BOLSHEVIK USE OF AND ACTIVITIES IN THE SOVIETS

[No. 200, October 18, 1917, p. 1.]

One can no longer close one's eyes to the fact that the Bolshevik Party has brought about a deep split in our democratic organization. Since this party obtained a majority in the Petrograd Soviet, it has converted it into a party organization of its own and, leaning on its [support], launched a party struggle to seize [control] of all the Soviet organizations throughout Russia.

. . .

There is a very fundamental difference between the Bolsheviks and the rest of the parties included in the organization of the Soviets. They have consistently opposed the slogan of national defense, while the others supported this defense in every way. A conflict, which is most unfortunate for the future of democracy, was disclosed on these grounds between the front and the rear, which the front did not support: the Bolsheviks were, and have remained, on the side of the rear. A split is being introduced into the army: read the recent announcements of the 12th Army or the resolution of the Luga Soviet and you will see that here, too, the split is complete. The Bolsheviks are in favor of seizure of power by the Soviet, while the rest of the parties are opposed to this. Nevertheless, the Bolsheviks want to foist this tactic on the All-Russian Congress, and in order to make this easier to achieve they have taken it upon themselves to convene the Congress by circumventing the Central Executive Committee.

. . .

The Bolsheviks want to overthrow the Provisional Government; they want to overthrow the Central Executive Committee; they want to disperse the Council of the Republic, which has just begun to function; they even want to forestall the Constituent Assembly by [convoking] the Congress of Soviets (which also means to overthrow it, only in a veiled form), and they even want to overthrow the Congress of Soviets itself, convoking it contrary to the [provisions of] the Bylaws. Is there not too much of overthrowing, and might not the result of all this be their own overthrow?

. . .

In so far as possible, *Izvestiia* has always refrained from [pursuing] any party policy in an open or concealed form, and it will continue to uphold these traditions in the future, ignoring the vulgar harangue of certain extremist organs.

But in the present case it is a question of a split within the entire organization of the Soviets, which has, until now, safeguarded the revolution and which, in spite of many instances of decline, still carries immense significance. We cannot fail to warn against a split in this organization. A split never brings strength, it only weakens, and it can only benefit the enemies of democracy.

1402. Maksim Gorky Urges the Bolsheviks to Deny that They Are Planning an Uprising
[*Novaia Zhizn'*, No. 156, October 18, 1917, p. 1.]

Rumors that the "action of the Bolsheviks" is anticipated on October 20 are becoming more insistent. In other words, the ugly scenes of July 3–5 may be repeated. . . .

An unorganized mob will pour out into the streets, not knowing what it wants, and adventurers, thieves, professional murderers, using it as a shield, will begin to "make the history of the Russian revolution."

In other words, there will be a repetition of that bloody, senseless slaughter which we have already seen and which undermined throughout the country the moral meaning of the revolution, shook its cultural import.

It is very probable that this time events will assume an even bloodier pogrom character and cause an even greater blow to the revolution.

Who needs all this? And to what end? The Central Committee of the Social Democratic Bolsheviks apparently is not participating in the planned adventure, because up to this time it has in no way confirmed the rumors of the proposed action, but neither does it deny them.

It is not out of place to ask: Is it possible that the adventurers, seeing the decline of the revolutionary zeal on the part of the thinking proletariat, hope to stimulate this zeal by abundant bloodletting?

Or do these adventurers wish to hasten the blow of the counterrevolution and for this purpose try to disorganize the forces which were so hard to organize?

The Central Committee of the Bolsheviks is obliged to deny the rumors about the action of the 20th. It must do so if it is really a strong and free-acting political organ, capable of guiding the masses, and not a weak-willed plaything of the wild mob's mood, not a tool in the hands of the most shameless adventurers or insane fanatics.

1403. TROTSKY'S DENIAL

[*Izvestiia*, No. 201, October 18, 1917, p. 5. Made before the Petrograd Soviet.]

Comrades, during the past days all the press has been full of reports of rumors and articles concerning the coming alleged demonstrations attributed sometimes to the Bolsheviks, sometimes to the Petrograd Soviet.

I must make the following statement on this subject on behalf of the Petrograd Soviet:

"The decisions of the Petrograd Soviet are published for public information. The Soviet is an elective institution; every deputy is responsible to his electors. This revolutionary parliament cannot adopt decisions that would be withheld from the knowledge of all the workers and soldiers.

"All those persons from the bourgeoisie who consider that they have the right to question us regarding our political plans we can refer to our political decisions, which are known to all.

"If the Petrograd Soviet finds it necessary to call a demonstration, then it will do so.

"But I do not know where and when these demonstrations were decided upon. The bourgeois press says that a demonstration has been set for October 22. But October 22 was unanimously set by the Executive Committee as a day of propaganda, of agitation, and for raising funds.

"It was also pointed out that I, as President of the Soviet, had signed an order for 5,000 rifles. By virtue of the decision of the Committee for the People's Struggle Against Counterrevolution, even back in the Kornilov days, it was decided to form a workers' militia and arm it. It was in execution of this decision that I ordered 5,000 rifles from the Sestroretskii factory.

"Another important question concerns the convocation of the Congress. They [the bourgeoisie] want at this time to clear Petrograd of its garrison. This is perfectly understandable, because they know that the Congress will definitely pass a resolution on transferring the power to the All-Russian Congress of Soviets, for the immediate conclusion of truces on all fronts and for the transfer of all land to the peasants. The bourgeoisie knows this and, therefore, wants to arm all the forces that are subordinate to it against us.

"This lie and slander is, in fact, the preparation for an attack against the Congress.

"It is known to all honest people that the Petrograd Soviet has not set a date for an armed demonstration, but if it does so, the entire Petrograd Garrison and the proletariat will follow under its banner. At the same time, we declare to the workers and soldiers that the attack in the bourgeois press against the Soviets is in preparation for a conflict, a mobilization of all the forces against the workers and soldiers.

"We have still not set a date for the attack. But the opposing side has, evidently, already set it. We will meet it, we will repel it duly, and we will declare that at the first counterrevolutionary attempt to hamper the work of the Congress we will answer with a counteroffensive which will be ruthless and which we will carry out to the end."

1404. Dan's Remarks Before a Meeting of Representatives of Regimental and Company Committees

[*Izvestiia*, No. 202, October 20, 1917, p. 5. Meantime, Bolshevik representatives of the Military Revolutionary Committee were working to gain the allegiance of the Petrograd Garrison in anticipation of the uprising.]

A meeting of representatives of regimental and company committees, called at the initiative of the Central Committee, was held yesterday in the Smol'nyi Institute.

Comrade Dan [spoke] in connection with rumors about a demonstration that is being prepared and gave a report on the Congress of Soviets.

He pointed out that if the demonstration takes place, it will undoubtedly have disastrous consequences for the gains of the revolution.

. . .

"This is the most unpropitious moment for a demonstration, and it would be difficult to render a greater service to the Germans than by staging a demonstration at this time. In order to prevent any demonstrations, it is necessary to organize the regiments, close their ranks in the combatant sense, create a definite force for anticipating a German onslaught and a counterrevolution, and restrain the soldiers from [staging] an armed demonstration which can only play into the hands of the counterrevolution.

"One cannot settle the question of power by [resorting to] force of arms only a few days before the [convocation of the] Constituent Assembly—the plenary lord of the Russian Land."

Then Comrade Dan gave a report on the reaction of the provinces to the Congress of Soviets.

Until now, only 50 Soviets have agreed to send their delegates to the Congress. The total number of Soviets, however, is 917. Almost the entire front has declared itself opposed to the Congress. But the Central Executive Committee has nevertheless taken every measure [to assure] that the Congress will convene and that as many representatives as possible will assemble.

Comrade Smirnov described the mood of the front on the basis of telegrams that have been received from there. The front considers that a demonstration at the present time would be a betrayal of the cause of the revolution.[6] At the same time, the front appeals for calmness and expresses confidence that comrade workers, soldiers, and peasants will refrain from [staging] any demonstrations and will not want to destroy the long-suffering army and the freedom that was won. After a number of speeches from representatives of the Petrograd Garrison and the front, Comrade Trotsky stepped forward with his objections to Comrade Dan.

He believed that the Congress would not detract from the work on the elections to the Constituent Assembly, and that it would create a revolutionary power. In addition, he declared that the Petrograd Soviet is not appealing for demonstrations, and he proposed that the meeting adopt three resolutions: on the demonstration, on the convocation of the Congress, and on the general political situation.

In view of the many speeches by delegates from the front as well as by the

---

[6] See, for example, the protest against an armed demonstration from the Executive Committee of the Southwestern Front in *Izvestiia*, No. 203, October 21, 1917, p. 6.

representatives of all the units of the Petrograd Garrison, the meeting lasted until late at night.

The Chairman suggested proceeding to vote on the resolutions submitted by Comrade Trotsky. However, Comrade Lazimir declared that the present meeting was called by the Central Executive Committee without the [sanction of the] Military Section of the Petrograd Soviet; he therefore considered that it was not competent and proposed that it not pass any resolutions.

The meeting concurred with the opinion of Comrade Lazimir and closed without passing any resolutions.

1405. *Rech'* ON THE BOLSHEVIKS AND THE OTHER SOCIALIST PARTIES
[No. 248, October 21, 1917, p. 1.]

There is no doubt that bolshevism is undergoing a severe crisis. Whether action will take place or not is now a matter of indifference. If it takes place, it will be crushed and will cause a severe reaction which will bring upon the Bolsheviks the curses of all those whom they have lured from the [right] path. If the action does not take place, they will lag behind the moods which they themselves have kindled, and their credit will be undermined. Feeling their critical situation, the Bolsheviks have decided to stake everything and to go banco. . . .

In such a moment what should be the attitude of the revolutionary democracy toward bolshevism? Without any exception, not even up to and including *Novaia Zhizn'*, it severely condemns the behavior of the Bolsheviks, considers it fatal for the revolution, sees in it betrayal. . . .

To put it briefly, the rupture is complete, and with such relations the revolutionary democracy should only take care to isolate the Bolsheviks, who inevitably will be severely compromised in the eyes of the masses. It should take care not to permit democracy and bolshevism to be confused, so that the democracy will not share the responsibility for the excesses of the latter. As a matter of fact, the *Rabochaia Gazeta* seems to understand this. Yesterday, with regard to the forthcoming Congress of the Soviets, the Menshevik organ stated:

"When the majority of the Bureau of the Central Executive Committee of the Soviet of Workers' and Soldiers' Deputies decided to convene a Congress of the Soviets at the end of October, it was undoubtedly the victim of Bolshevik blackmail. It is only too obvious that the convening of a Congress on the eve of the elections to the Constituent Assembly, when the political parties are so busy in their localities and have so few workers, was senseless!"

. . .

If the Mensheviks were not lagging behind the Bolsheviks, their change of mood would attract the proletariat to their ranks and would give them victory. But if they behave as half-Leninists, if they, according to their own admission, succumb to the Bolshevik blackmail, then no change of mood will help them. The workers whom they quite unjustly confuse with the Bolsheviks will pass them by . . .

Therefore, there is not the slightest exaggeration in asserting that the half-Leninists are more dangerous than the Leninists, and that on them falls no less responsibility for the confusion which we experience now.

1406. THE CONFLICT BETWEEN THE PETROGRAD SOVIET AND THE
PETROGRAD MILITARY DISTRICT HEADQUARTERS

[*Izvestiia*, October 24, 1917, p. 5.]

A sharp conflict developed between the Petrograd Soviet of Workers' and
Soldiers' Deputies and the Petrograd Military District Headquarters on the
grounds that the Petrograd Soviet of Workers' and Soldiers' Deputies organized
a Military Revolutionary Committee for controlling the actions of the Petrograd
Military District Headquarters.

To this day, alongside the Petrograd Military District Headquarters, there
exists a special council [made up of] members of the Military Section of the
Central Executive Committee and the Soldiers' Section of the Petrograd Soviet.
The Petrograd Soviet raised the question of organizing a Military Revolutionary
Committee with the right to control and even countermand such decisions of the
Petrograd Military District Headquarters as it finds unfavorable to the Soviet.

On October 21, the Petrograd Soviet recognized the Military Revolutionary
Committee as the leading organ of the troops of the capital.

On the night of October 22, the members of the Military Revolutionary Committee presented themselves at District Headquarters and demanded that they be
permitted to control the orders of the Headquarters with the right to a deciding
voice.

Colonel Polkovnikov, the Commander of the troops, replied to this demand
with an emphatic refusal.

The Petrograd Soviet then called a meeting of representatives of regiments,
[to be held] at Soml'nyi Institute. From this meeting telephoned telegrams were
dispatched to all units [stating] that the Headquarters has refused to recognize
the Military Revolutionary Committee and, by so doing, has severed [relations]
with the revolutionary garrison and with the Petrograd Soviet of Workers' and
Soldiers' Deputies, and has become a direct instrument of the counterrevolutionary forces.

"Soldiers of Petrograd," the telephoned telegram read, "the protection of
the revolutionary order against counterrevolutionary attacks falls upon you
under the leadership of the Military Revolutionary Committee. Any orders to
the garrison that are not signed by the Military Revolutionary Committee are
not valid. All orders of the Petrograd Soviet for today, the day of the Petrograd
Soviet of Workers' and Soldiers' Deputies, shall remain in full force. It is the
duty of every officer of the garrison to exercise vigilance, self-control, and strict
discipline. The revolution is in danger. Long live the revolutionary garrison."

The Commander of the [Petrograd] Military District called a separate meeting, with the participation of representatives of the Central Committee and the
commissar attached to the [Petrograd] Military District Headquarters. Representatives of the Petrograd Garrison were called out from the Smol'nyi Institute
to attend the same meeting. A delegation, headed by Second Lieutenant Dashkevich, came to the District Headquarters. Dashkevich announced that he was
authorized by the garrison to inform the District Headquarters that henceforth
all the orders issued by it must be countersigned by the Military Revolutionary
Committee of the Petrograd Soviet. To this, Second Lieutenant Dashkevich
added that he had not been authorized to say anything more, and the delegation
departed.

In connection with the conflict, General Cheremisov, the Commander of the Northern Front, was urgently summoned to Petrograd. He arrived in Petrograd yesterday and conferred at great length with the Minister-President concerning both the situation at the front and the conflict between the Petrograd Military District Headquarters and the Petrograd Soviet.

Without entering into an appraisal of the conflict and without expressing himself on the point, General Cheremisov insisted on some form of measures to be taken for preparing the Petrograd Garrison to meet the enemy, which is making preparations for a large-scale campaign on the Northern Front. Referring to the resolutions given to him by the army, General Cheremisov spoke of the necessity of replacing the regiments at the front by regiments from the Petrograd Garrison. General Cheremisov said that if the Military Revolutionary Committee insists that these regiments not be moved, then he would register a categorical protest on behalf of the armies under his command.

1407. The Mensheviks of the Petrograd Soviet Appeal to the Workers and Soldiers Not to Heed the Bolshevik Call for a Seizure of Power

[*Izvestiia*, No. 205, October 24, 1917, p. 1.]

In this portentous hour of the Russian revolution, when the enemy stands at the gates of Petrograd, when a wave of pogroms is sweeping over all Russia, and when the counterrevolution has mobilized all its forces, the Bolshevik Party wants to call you out into the streets to overthrow the Provisional Government and seize power.

Comrade workers and soldiers, your demonstration will [spell] the triumph of the counterrevolution!

The organized dark elements, led by an experienced hand, are waiting for your demonstration in order to convert it into a pogrom and frustrate the Constituent Assembly.

Comrades, think [carefully] about the outcome of your demonstration!

All the monarchistic and Black Hundred gangs will be able to take advantage of any demonstration to drown the Russian revolution in torrents of blood.

The slightest disruption in the regularity of streetcar and railroad services will leave the town and the army in the field without bread or other food supplies.

Your demonstration will cause a split in the ranks of the army and the navy, and will give the enemy an opportunity to capture revolutionary Petrograd with ease.

Your demonstration will give rise to a civil war in the ranks of the democracy and it will bring nothing but harm to the cause of revolution and socialism.

Comrade soldiers and workers! Raise the question of the demonstration in all factories, plants, and barracks; explain its danger to the cause of the revolution and appeal persistently for a refusal to demonstrate.

Let no one betray the cause of the revolution at this alarming moment! Let each one of you exert every effort to calm down the masses, which have been aroused by demagogic and criminal slogans!

Let everyone rally to the cause!

Remember your revolutionary duty!

Long live the Russian revolution!

Long live the proletariat and the revolutionary army!
Long live the Constituent Assembly.

1408. KERENSKY'S SPEECH BEFORE THE COUNCIL OF THE REPUBLIC, OCTOBER 24, 1917

[*Rech'*, No. 251, October 25, 1917, p. 2.]

Attempts to Thwart the Constituent Assembly

The Provisional Government has authorized me to make the following statement. Of late, the nearer we come to the day of the convocation of the Constituent Assembly—which will establish forever a free, democratic system of government in Russia, an achievement of the great Russian revolution—the more persistent, arrogant, and insolent become the attempts of the two wings of Russian public opinion to block and eliminate the possibility of convoking the Constituent Assembly. At the same time, attempts to disorganize the defenses of the Russian State and to betray the liberty and independence of Russia [into the hands of] a ruthless and relentless foe who is advancing on our capital are becoming increasingly persistent. The Provisional Government, as I have repeatedly stated, considers it its duty to safeguard the freedom of every citizen . . . in the exercise of his political and civil rights, and has therefore remained apparently indifferent to the violent attacks to which it has been subjected in the press, at meetings, and at public gatherings. Lately, all of Russia, and the . . . capital in particular, has become alarmed . . . by those open appeals for insurrection which come from an irresponsible—I would not say extremist, in the sense of [political] trends, but extremist in the sense of absence of reason—section of the democracy which has split off from the revolutionary democracy. At the same time another section of the press was also agitating and conducting propaganda for supplanting the Provisional Government . . . immediately by a dictatorship. (*Voices from the right:* "By a strong government!") This has been published recently in the newspapers *Novaia Rus', Zhivoe Slovo, Obshchee Delo.* On the other hand, appeals for insurrection have appeared daily in the newspapers *Rabochii Put'* and *Soldat.* At the same time, preparations have been started recently for actually overthrowing the present state system by means of an armed uprising.

The Proclamation of Ul'ianov-Lenin

In order to substantiate my statements and in order to prevent anyone from reproaching the Provisional Government with making false accusations or malicious fabrications about any party, I consider it my duty to cite here a few of the more explicit passages from a number of proclamations published in the newspaper *Rabochii Put'* by a wanted offender against the state, Ul'ianov-Lenin, who is now in hiding. Thus, in one of the issues containing a number of these proclamations, Ul'ianov-Lenin wrote: "On the morning of October 16, I learned that . . . the idea of an uprising was discussed in detail at a very important Bolshevik meeting in Petrograd. All the most influential individuals from every branch of Bolshevik work in the capital were represented at the meeting, and only the most insignificant minority—two comrades—took a negative stand on this question. Their arguments must be analyzed and their hesitation revealed in order to say how disgraceful they are." The proclamation ends with the words: "What are you waiting for? Are you waiting for a miracle? Are you waiting for the Constituent Assembly? Wait, you starvelings! Kerensky promised to convoke the Constituent Assembly." In the next appeal, the same Ul'ianov speaks explicitly about the necessity for an immediate uprising, and says: "Any delay of the uprising is tantamount to death."

Destructive Movement

At the same time as these appeals were being made, other leaders of the Bolshevik Party were appealing at various meetings and public gatherings for an immediate, open, armed uprising. Especially noteworthy in this respect was the speech of the present President of the Soviet of Workers' and Soldiers' Deputies in Petersburg, Bronstein-Trotsky, as well as the speeches of several other key organizers of the uprising. Proclamations and appeals of a similar type, weighted down, in addition, with an appeal for disobeying combat orders and insubordination to military authorities, were published in yet another organ of this party—the newspaper *Soldat*—which was aimed especially at soldiers and which was supposed to destroy the noxious influence of the publication *Golos Soldata*, an organ of the Central Committee of the Soviet of Workers' and Soldiers' Deputies. I am not going to cite here from newspapers of the opposite trend, which were also closed last night by my order. I merely want to point out—and this is extremely important—the completely clear, definite, and indissoluble connection between the actions and statements of the two [extreme] wings. I must also point out that a whole series of articles in *Rabochii Put'* and *Soldat* coincide with articles in *Novaia Rus'*, even with respect to style and the words used. I want to emphasize this in order to make it absolutely clear to the Council of the Republic that we are now dealing not only with the actions of this or that political party, but with an organized attempt to exploit foolish oversights or offenses of individual political parties in the interest of an organization that is striving at all costs to provoke an enormous, spontaneous, destructive movement in Russia. (*Voice from the right:* "This has already been done!") . . . Considering the present mood of the masses and the events that have already taken place in the provinces, an open movement in Petersburg inevitably would be accompanied by the heaviest incidence of pogroms, disgracing forever the name of free Russia. Simultaneously with all the phenomena which I have pointed out and which the Provisional Government and the military authorities, in particular, have been watching closely, a number of preparations have been started for active demonstrations.

Betrayal and Treason

Very characteristic and very important is the admission by Ul'ianov-Lenin, himself the organizer of the uprising, that "the position of the extreme left Russian social democratic wing is particularly favorable." "Just think," Lenin writes; "the Germans only have Liebknecht, without newspapers, without freedom of assembly, without soviets; with the incredible hostility of all classes of the population, down to the last well-to-do peasant; with the excellent organization of the imperialist bourgeoisie. And yet the Germans are making some attempts to agitate, while we, having dozens of newspapers, freedom of assembly, with a majority in the Soviets, we who are the best organized proletarian Internationalists in the whole world—can we refuse to support the German revolutionaries and the revolutionary organizations?" Thus, the organizers themselves are admitting (this is extremely important for me to note) that the political conditions for the free activity of all political parties are perfect at the present time under the present Provisional Government, which is headed, in the opinion of the Bolshevik Party, "by a usurper, a man who has sold himself out to the bourgeoisie—Minister-President Kerensky." I find it necessary to point this out so that everyone will clearly understand that by organizing an uprising . . . by disorganizing the defensive capacity and the vital capacity of the country—intentionally or unintentionally— (*voices from the right:* "Intentionally") the organizers of the uprising are assisting not the proletariat of Germany, but . . . the ruling classes of Germany; they are opening Russia's front to the armored fist of Wilhelm and his friends. (*Prolonged applause from the right and the center. Cries from the right:* "True!")

The motives are quite immaterial to the Provisional Government; it is immaterial whether this is being done intentionally or unintentionally. But in full awareness of my responsibility, I proclaim from this platform that such actions by a Russian political party constitute treason and betrayal of the Russian state. (*Cries from the right:* "Name the accomplices!" *Noise from the left, and cries:* "They are in your midst!") In addition, I must point out that the attempt to thwart the organized movement of the free Russian people toward the Constituent Assembly is occurring just at a time when the Provisional Government, after a series of preparatory measures, is discussing the final aspects of the procedure by which land shall be transferred temporarily, pending the Constituent Assembly, to the disposal and management of land committees. (*Loud applause in the center and from the left.*) This is occurring just when the Provisional Government—in accordance with the obligations it has assumed and its own convictions, and in spite of all the difficulties that confront it in foreign policy due to the disorganization and corruption of the army, which have come about not without the participation of supporters of immediate peace—when the Provisional Government was planning to send its delegation to the Paris Conference in the next few days in order to direct the attention of the Allies—among other matters relating to its convictions and its program—to the necessity of defining explicitly the tasks and aims of war and to measures for hastening the conclusion of the war, i.e., peace. (*Loud applause from the left and the center.*) If you take into account that all this is occurring less than three weeks before the elections of members of the Constituent Assembly, i.e., three weeks before elections to the Constituent Assembly, . . . then you will understand the actual aims of the real enemies of the people and of Russian freedom. (*Loud applause from the right and the center.*)

The Beginning of the Uprising

Thus, after open preparations of this kind and propaganda for an uprising, the group that calls itself Bolshevik has come to the point of carrying this [uprising] out. For instance, in the afternoon of the day before yesterday the troops of the Petersburg [Military] District received an order not to obey [their] commanders or [any] military authorities unless the orders were countersigned by the commissars of the Petersburg Revolutionary Staff [*sic*] who were arbitrarily sent to the regiments. This was done at a time when, according to general regulations, commissars of the Provisional Government, appointed in agreement with the Central Committee, existed in both the army and the Petersburg Garrison. The military authorities viewed this action of the Revolutionary Staff [*sic*] to be not only unlawful but patently criminal. (*Cries from the right:* "Right!") And it therefore demanded an immediate rescindment of this order, a recognition that no one but the lawful authorities has the right to command the troops, and a notification of commissars of the Provisional Government who were assigned to the troops for the purpose of seeing to it that the actions of individual military commanders were proper in the political sense. I must note that the Central Committee adopted the same point of view in considering the action of the Revolutionary Staff [sic] as being completely inadmissible. But although there was every reason for adopting immediate, decisive, and vigorous measures, the military authorities, following my instructions, believed it necessary first to give the people the opportunity to realize their own intentional or unintentional mistake. (*Cries from the right:* "That is what's bad!") And they granted them time to retract [their stand] upon seeing their mistake. We had to do this also because no tangible results of this order were evident during the first few days after the announcement was made among the troops. I would prefer, in general, that authorities act more slowly, but more surely and, when the time calls for it, more resolutely. (*Applause from the left, cries:* "Right!") In spite of numerous attempts to ward off the obvious uprising, with all its consequences threatening to bring even greater difficulties to the people and the country, difficulties that are heavy to bear not for the leaders who have the custom and an extraordinary talent for going into hiding (*loud applause from the right*) but for the masses whom they are leading at . . . their own responsibility; in spite of the numerous measures adopted, the speeches, persuasions, and proposals which have come from various public organizations; in spite of the very impressive statement that was made yesterday by the delegates who arrived here from the front—the Government did not receive any statements retracting the orders that were issued. Not until 3:00 A.M. were we informed that all the points presented in the form of an ultimatum by the military authorities were acceptable in principle. Thus, at 3:00 A.M. the organizers of the uprising were compelled to announce officially that they had committed an unlawful act which they now wished to retract. (*Miliukov from his seat:* "How original!") But, just as I expected—and, in fact, as I was sure from all the preceding tactics of these people—this was but another case of the usual delaying [tactics] and a deliberate deception. (*Cries from the right:* "So you have finally learned this!") At this moment the period of grace has expired, and we do not as yet have the declaration that was supposed to have been issued [by the Military Revolutionary Committee] to the regiments. What we have is just the contrary, namely, an unauthorized distribution of arms and ammunition; and, in addition, two companies have been summoned to the aid of this Revolutionary Staff [sic]. Thus, it is my duty to establish before the Provisional Council that the obvious, definite, over-all condition of a certain part of the population of Petersburg [must be termed] a state of insurrection. (*Voice from the right:* "That's what it has come to!") This is the situation from the legal standpoint, and I have proposed that judicial investigations be started immediately. (*Noise from the left.*) Arrests have also been ordered. (*Protests from the left.*) Yes, yes, listen, because at the present time, when the State is imperiled by deliberate or unwitting betrayal and is at the brink of ruin, the Provisional Government, myself included, prefers to be killed and destroyed [rather than to betray] the life, the honor, and the independence of the State. (*Loud, prolonged applause. All the members of the Council, with the exception of the Internationalists, and the audience, which includes many military men, rise from their seats and accord the Minister-President a stormy ovation.*)

ADZHEMOV (*from his seat*) : Take a photograph of these people [to show that they remained] seated. (*Loud cries from the left.*)

CHAIRMAN: I call the meeting to order.

LAPINSKII *and* MARTOV *are shouting something from their seats, but their words cannot be heard on account of the noise.*

CHAIRMAN: Member of the Council Martov, I call you to order.

MINISTER-PRESIDENT: The Provisional Government might be reproached——

MARTOV (*from his seat*) : With confusion.

CHAIRMAN: Member of the Council Martov, I again call you to order.

The Attitude of the Front

MINISTER-PRESIDENT: The Provisional Government can be reproached with weakness and extraordinary tolerance, but, at any rate, no one has the right to say that the Provisional Government, in all the time that I have stood at the head of it, and even before that, has ever resorted to any kind of repressive measures until there was a threat of immediate danger and peril to the State. (*Loud applause from the center and the right.*) . . . And I believe that our task of strengthening freedom and our tactics give us the right and the grounds to demand that the country support our decisive measures in a time of need, since no one can suspect us of undertaking these measures for any purposes other than the necessity of saving the State. (*Loud applause from the center.*) I have to say that the attitude of the front toward the events . . . in the rear, and especially in Petersburg, is completely clear. . . . I consider it my duty to read only the resolution of the Joint Army Committees located at Stavka: "The Army," it is stated in this resolution, "urges all citizens of the Republic to make the utmost sacrifices in the name of the earliest peace which will bring justice to all the toilers of the world and well-being to all the nations. [The Army] therefore insists upon the strictest adherence to the will of the organized majority of the people. It urges the Provisional Government, in agreement with the Provisional Council of the Republic and the All-Russian Central [Executive] Committee, to put a stop at once to the savage military pogroms in towns and villages, and to suppress as resolutely and energetically as possible every form of excess and license. In exercising restraint against all accomplices of the destruction of national integrity, the Government will be supported by the Army, [which will fight] with all its strength as though it were fighting against the enemies of the people." (*Loud applause from all the benches, with the exception of the Internationalists.*)

In a State of Insurrection

(*[At this point] A. I. Konovalov, Deputy-Minister-President, approached A. F. Kerensky and handed him a note. There was a long pause. Having read the note, A. F. Kerensky continued.*)

I have been given a copy of the document that is now being sent to the regiments: "The Petrograd Soviet is in danger. I hereby order the regiments to be in complete readiness for action and to await further instructions. Any delay or failure to execute the order will be considered a betrayal of the revolution. Signed for the President, Podvoiskii. Secretary, Antonov."[7] (*Cries from the right:* "Traitors!") Thus, the present situation in the capital is one that in the language of law . . . is called a state of insurrection. (*Voices from the right:* "Traitors!")

[7] See Bunyan and Fisher, p. 86.

This is an attempt to incite the rabble against the existing order; it is an attempt to block the Constituent Assembly (*cries from the center and the right:* "Right!"), and to expose the front to the serried ranks of Wilhelm's concentrated forces. (*Cries from the center and the right:* "Right!" *Noise from the left, and cries:* "Enough!"*) I use the word "rabble" deliberately, because all the responsible elements of the democracy and its Central Executive Committee, all the army organizations, and all that free Russia can and must be proud of—the reason, the conscience, and the honor of the great Russian democracy—all protest against this . . . (*stormy applause on all the benches, with the exception of the Internationalists*) . . . They understand perfectly well that the objective danger of this demonstration does not lie in the fact that a part of the local garrison might seize power, but in the fact that this movement, just as in the month of July, could serve as a signal for the Germans at the front to deliver a new blow on our borders, and it could provoke a new [counterrevolutionary] attempt, even more serious, perhaps, than that of General Kornilov. Let everyone recall that Kalushch and Ternopol' coincided with the July uprising. Let everyone remember that only recently I said from this rostrum that the danger which we consider to be serious today could flare up tomorrow if the political situation gives the enemy forces an opportunity to attempt a new adventure. And I . . . assert that if a new military catastrophe occurs we will not need to look for the culprits—they are present. (*Cries from the right:* "Right!" *Cries from the benches of the Internationalists:* "The guilty ones are they who are prolonging the war behind the backs of the democracy!"*)

Address to the "Internationalists"

I believe (A. F. Kerensky addressed the Internationalists) that everyone at the present time must decide whether he is on the side of the Republic, freedom, and the democracy, or against these. (*Prolonged applause on all the benches, with the exception of the Internationalists.*) And if there are people who believe that the truth is on the other side, then they must manfully take their place in those ranks, and not behave themselves as they do now. (*Storm of applause from the right and the center; noise from the left.*)

Appeal for Support

. . . I have come to call upon you for vigilance, for the defense of all the gains of freedom won by the many sacrifices, by the blood and the lives of many generations of free Russian people. I have come here not with a request, but with the conviction that the Provisional Government, which is now defending this new freedom, and the new Russian State, born to a great future, will receive the unanimous support of everyone, with the exception of those people who can never bring themselves to speak the truth openly and courageously; [that it will receive] the support not only of the Provisional Council but of the whole Russian State. (*Storm of applause on all the benches, with the exception of the Internationalists.*) . . . And I was authorized to declare on behalf of the Provisional Government that the Provisional Government has never infringed on the rights of the citizens of . . . Russia to enjoy complete political freedom. Proceeding from a definite point of view on the current situation, the Provisional Government believes that one of its most important duties is to avoid provoking any sharp critical disturbances before the convocation of the Constituent Assembly. Now, however, in full awareness of its responsibility to the state and to the future of the country, the

Provisional Government makes [the following] declaration: All elements of Russian society, those groups and those parties which have dared to raise a hand against the free will of the Russian people, threatening at the same time to expose the front to Germany, are subject to immediate, final, and definite liquidation. (*Storm of applause from the center and from part of the left. Laughter on the benches of the Internationalists.*) Let the people of Petrograd know that they will meet with a power that is resolute; and perhaps, in the last hour or in the last minute, reason, conscience, and honor will prevail in the hearts of those who have still preserved some of these values. (*Applause from the right and the center.*) I ask for the sake of the country—and let the Provisional Council of the Republic forgive me—I *demand* that this very day, at this afternoon's session, the Provisional Government receive your answer as to whether or not it can fulfill its duty with the assurance of support from this exalted gathering.

.   .   .

(*A. F. Kerensky's speech was drowned in loud, prolonged applause on all the benches with the exception of the Internationalists. All the members of the Council, with the exception of the Internationalists, and the audience rose from their seats and once again accorded a stormy ovation to the Minister-President. General commotion.*)

1409. Dan's Speech Before the Council
[*Rech'*, No. 251, October 25, 1917, p. 2.]

The floor was given to Gurvich-Dan, who spoke on behalf of the Mensheviks.

I agree with the Minister of Labor, Gvozdev, [Dan said,] that what we observe in Petrograd is not a demonstration of the revolutionary proletariat and the revotionary army in defense of freedom. The working class, as a whole, will not go for this criminal venture into which the Bolsheviks are pushing it. (*Applause from the left.*) There is no doubt in my mind that the demagogic agitation and the incredible actions which the Bolsheviks permit themselves are truly criminal in nature and are aimed against the revolution. (*Applause on all the benches.*) But, while I have wanted to fight against bolshevism as vigorously as possible, I do not want, nor have I ever wanted, to become an instrument in the hands of counterrevolutionaries. (*Applause from the left.*) There is no doubt in my mind that the Bolsheviks have taken advantage of all the misfortunes that have befallen our native land. If we want to avert the catastrophe that threatens our country, then we must adopt the necessary measures, but not look for the solution in a resort to arms. (*Storms of applause from the left.*) For if the Bolshevik uprising is drowned in blood, then whoever wins—be it the Provisional Government or the Bolsheviks—it would mean a triumph for a third force, which would sweep away both the Bolsheviks and the Provisional Government, and the whole democracy. (*Applause from the left; cries from the right:* "Tell this to the Bolsheviks and not to us!") The Bolsheviks have only taken advantage of the real dissatisfaction among the broad masses, whose needs have not been met. The satisfaction of these needs is obstructed by classes whose representatives are sitting on the right side. (*Applause from the left.*) First of all, one must satisfy the people's cry for peace. (*Applause from the left.*) Not out of weakness, but out of revolutionary strength, pride, and the desire to preserve the revolution, we must say that we demand immediate negotiations for peace. (*Applause from the left.*) Yesterday's speech of the Minister of Foreign Affairs played a fatal role in all the events of the past day. He did not say a single word about raising the question of peace negotiations at the Allied Conference. Furthermore, apart from the question of peace, it is necessary to formulate the land question in such a way that no one would have any doubts that the Government is taking firm steps in the direction of satisfying the needs of the people. We, Mensheviks, do not want a government crisis, we want to defend this Provisional Government. But let us make it possible for the whole democracy to rally around it.

1410. MARTOV'S SPEECH AND THE RESOLUTIONS OFFERED TO THE COUNCIL
[*Rech'*, No. 251, October 25, 1917, p. 2.]

Following Dan, L. Martov spoke on behalf of the Internationalists. He declared that the Internationalists will not stand in the same ranks with the Kornilovites, and that if a conflict becomes unavoidable as a result of the policy which has been pursued to date, they will not be able to suppress the uprising. (*Applause from the left.*) "The language of Kerensky, who spoke about the movement of the rabble when the question concerned the movement of a significant part of the proletariat and the army, cannot be called anything else but a language of challenge to civil war. Only a government that is guided by the interests of the democracy can deliver the country from the horrors of a civil war." (*Applause from the left.*)

. . . After the recess, A. V. Peshekhonov, presiding, stated that two [resolutions] . . . had been submitted. The first formula, submitted by the Mensheviks, the Internationalists, the left Socialist Revolutionaries, and the Socialist Revolutionaries, read [as follows]: "The recently developing revolutionary movement with the aim of seizing power threatens to provoke a civil war and create favorable conditions for pogroms and for the mobilization of Black Hundred counterrevolutionary forces. It will have the inevitable result of frustrating the Constituent Assembly and of bringing about a new military catastrophe and the collapse of the revolution under conditions of economic paralysis and the complete disintegration of the country. The success of the aforesaid agitation is due not only to the objective conditions of war and disorder, but also to the delay in carrying out urgent measures, and therefore it is, above all, necessary to issue a decree on the transfer of land to the jurisdiction of land committees, and to take a vigorous stand in foreign policy, proposing that the Allies proclaim the conditions of peace and enter into peace negotiations. In order to combat manifestations of anarchy and [to prevent] an outbreak of pogroms, it is necessary to adopt immediate measures for their liquidation and to create for this purpose, in Petrograd, a Committee of Public Safety consisting of representatives of municipal governments and of organs of the revolutionary democracy, acting in contact with the Provisional Government."

The second formula was submitted by the cooperative organizations and the Party of the People's Freedom. This formula read: "Having heard the report of the Minister-President, the Provisional Council of the Russian Republic declared that, in the struggle against traitors to the native land and to the cause of the revolution who have resorted to the organization of an open revolt in the capital, in the face of the enemy and on the eve of the Constituent Assembly, the Provisional Council will give its full support to the Government and urges that the most decisive measures be adopted for suppressing the revolt . . ."

. . .

The first resolution received 123 votes for and 102 against, with 26 abstentions. . . . The session closed at 8:30 P.M.

1411. Stankevich's Account of the Voting in the Council and the Events of the Night of October 24
[V. B. Stankevich, *Vospominaniia, 1914–1919 g.*, pp. 258–61.]

On October 24, I came to Petrograd with a quantity of all sorts of reports and materials. Kerensky met me in high spirits. He had just come back from the Council of the Republic, where he had delivered a strong speech against the Bolsheviks and was met with the usual unanimous ovations.

—Well, how do you like Petrograd? he asked, meeting me.

I expressed my perplexity.

—Don't you know that an armed uprising is going on here?

I laughed, because the streets were absolutely calm and there was no word of any kind of uprising. Although preoccupied, he also had a somewhat ironical attitude toward the uprising. I told him that an end should be put to these eternal shocks within the country and that the Bolsheviks should be checked by resolute measures. He answered that his opinion was the same as mine and that now no kind of Chernovs could help either the Kamenevs or the Zinovievs . . . if one could only manage to cope with the uprising. But on the latter there was so little doubt that Kerensky immediately agreed that I should summon Dukhonin to Petrograd, and I immediately sent the necessary telegram.

Kerensky asked me to go to the Council of the Republic in order to see what was going on and to negotiate with the leaders regarding the finality and firmness of the resolution.

The Mariinskii Palace was overflowing. Besides the members of the Council there were many representatives of the "world of officialdom" and of the military in the foyers and in the boxes. There was excitement. The parties conferred within their groups, trying to come to an agreement among themselves . . . but without results because the S.R.'s censored in their own group a fifth resolution and apparently were losing hope of agreeing on anything. Among other things, I started to speak of the necessity of organizing a civil defense with students, but the Mensheviks recoiled from me as if I were contaminated.

—The Government has already committed a lot of stupidities, and you even wish to organize a white guard.

Then the voting on the resolutions began, a blind voting, without preliminary agreements. A resolution worked out by Dan, stating that the Soviet held both the Government and the Bolsheviks responsible for the Bolshevik uprisings and proposing to transfer the matter of defending the country and the revolution to some kind of committee of safety composed of representatives of the Municipal Duma and of the parties, turned out to be adopted. I immediately came to the conclusion that such a resolution was nothing but a refusal to support the Government, and I expressed the supposition that the Government would resign. Having advised Kerensky of the resolution by telephone, I immediately went myself to the Winter Palace. Kerensky was astounded and excited and declared that under such conditions he would not remain one single moment at the head of the Government. . . .

. . .

However, next morning it became clear that the events had taken such a turn that the crisis of the Government could not be solved in the usual manner: almost the whole town was in the hands of the insurrectionists. I found Kerensky at the [Military District] Headquarters. He had not slept the whole night and now intended to leave. We accompanied him. He went in his own car with his a.d.c.'s in full military dress. The Government and a small and increasingly thinning group of military from the Staff remained in the Winter Palace and at the Headquarters. I sat down to write a proclamation to the army. The Government, under the chairmanship of Konovalov, which was in session at the Winter Palace, approved my text. I immediately went myself to the telegraph and sent the proclamation to Stavka. Besides, I contacted Dukhonin, who during the night had already received from the Headquarters news of the uprising. Dukhonin assured me that all necessary measures had been taken for sending troops to Petrograd and that several units should begin to arrive immediately. I returned to the Government and reported my negotiations. The Government discussed the question of whom to select as Governor General of Petrograd. After a few arguments and hesitations, Kishkin was selected. The latter immediately began to confer with [General] Bagratuni [Commander of the Petrograd Military District] and Pal'chinskii [Assistant Minister of Trade and Industry].

All this time, sad and alarming news was coming in by telephone. The stations were occupied. The telegraph and the telephone exchange were occupied. The Mariinskii Palace was occupied, and the members of the Council who gathered there—a session being intended for the purpose of reviewing yesterday's resolution—were thrown out.

. . .

1412. Dan on the Resolution and Its Presentation to Kerensky
[F. Dan, *Letopis' revoliutsii*, Bk. I, pp. 167–75.]

. . .

. . . For us it was axiomatic that to try fighting the Bolsheviks by purely military means was absurd not only because of the "confused" considerations, which, according to the assertions of Kerensky, "were incomprehensible in their essence to simple mortals," but also because of the simple fact that the Government did not and could not dispose at the time of such means. For us it was axiomatic that if one had to counteract the Bolsheviks in one way or another, with any hope of success, it could only be by realizing a definite policy which would assemble around the Government the forces that it was lacking and that would allow it to counteract the violence of the Bolsheviks with their assistance.

. . .

. . . In no case could we reduce this "assistance" to consolidating the Government in its blindness and to pushing it with our own hands toward the abyss into which it was already rolling all too quickly even without that. Quite the contrary. We considered it our duty once again to point out to the Government in this final moment the road that could lead it to salvation (if any could) and to confirm to it that we were actually ready to go with the Government to the very end of this road.

In this sense I compiled a draft resolution . . .

. . .

In our group . . . it was accepted also by the Menshevik Internationalists (Martov's group), which was then taking an isolated stand.

Matters were different in the other groups. . . . In particular, the opposition was strong in the group of the S.R., where quite a large wing was ready to meet the demands of Kerensky. However, another part of the S.R. group, with A. R. Gots at its head, fought tenaciously for the point of view that was formulated in our resolution.

. . . At the insistence of Gots, I was invited to make a report in the S.R. group regarding the crisis that was going on and to justify the draft resolutions proposed by me. . . .

As the result of all this struggle within the Council, which actually occupied the whole day and a part of the evening, the resolution was approved by an insignificant majority. . . .

As soon as the resolution was adopted, the question arose what to do later on, because it was clear that every minute was precious and that no time should be lost.

It was my idea to go immediately to the session of the Provisional Government and to demand on behalf of the majority of the Council of the Republic the immediate publication [of the resolution], putting up that very night all over the city posters stating that the Provisional Government: 1) has turned to the Allied powers with the demand for an immediate proposal to all the belligerents to stop military operations and to start negotiations for a general peace; 2) until the final solution of the agrarian question, has ordered by telegram the transfer of all *pomeshchik* lands to the jurisdiction of the local land committees; 3) has decided to hasten the convening of the Constituent Assembly, setting it for some date which I do not remember exactly.

Gots, whom I made party to my idea, willingly accepted it. We decided that N. D. Avksent'ev, President of the Council of the Republic, as a person who was officially required to express the opinion of the preparliament as defined in the resolution that had just been adopted, should join us. Avksent'ev tried in every way to avoid this; essentially he did not share the point of view expressed in the resolution, and therefore he was obviously very little inclined to defend it, especially in the unusual form that we were proposing. Yielding only to our insistence, to the reference of Gots to party discipline, and to his official duties as President, he unwillingly went along with us.

Such was "the delegation of the socialist groups," with regard to the membership of which A. F. Kerensky is for some reason silent. I would add that in the course of the conversation of the delegation with Kerensky, Avksent'ev, in accordance with his general outlook, scarcely spoke; he only intervened with sporadic remarks which mainly had for their purpose mitigating the sharpness of our standpoint and voicing support of Kerensky. . . .

· · ·

I have already said that we came to the Provisional Government with a very definite and complete proposal: to adopt immediately very important decisions with regard to the issues of war, of land, and of the Constituent Assembly, and to announce immediately these decisions to the population through telegrams and posters. We insisted that it should be done, at all costs, that very night so that in the morning every soldier and every worker would know about the decisions of the Provisional Government. . . .

· · ·

. . . Kerensky, who gave the impression of a man completely exhausted and worn out, seemed to be extremely aggravated by our arguments, and at the end he haughtily declared that the Government had no need for admonitions and instructions; that now was the time for action and not for conversation.

However, this did not appease us. We demanded that Kerensky report to the Government, which was still in session, on the resolution of the Council of the Republic and our proposal and on our desire to be admitted to the session of the Government and to be heard. Kerensky sharply turned away and went into the next hall, where the session was in progress.

In a few minutes he returned and drily declared that the Government took into account our refusal to grant it our unconditional assistance, that it had no need of advice from strangers, and would act itself and would cope itself with the rebellion.

We answered immediately that by its action the Government would not only destroy the revolution and itself, but deprive us and the parties that we represented of the possibility of showing our solidarity and of rendering it effective support.

. . . The die was cast. Much of the later behavior—on October 25, that of the Presidium of the Central Executive Committee then in existence, as well as our further attitude toward the episodes of the struggle between the Provisional Government and the Bolsheviks—was already outlined in this nocturnal conversation.

· · ·

F. DAN

1413. *Rech'* ON THE COUNCIL'S ACTION
[No. 251, October 25, 1917, p. 2.]

Quite unexpectedly today's session turned into a "great parliamentary day." . . . But following the Minister of Interior, A. M. Nikitin, who gave very thorough explanations regarding the seizure of food freight, the rostrum was taken over by Minister-President A. F. Kerensky, who concentrated all the attention of the Council of the Republic on the events that are now taking place in Petrograd. A. F. Kerensky described in very strong language irresponsible actions undertaken by the Bolsheviks . . . The speech of A. F. Kerensky, which appealed for support for the Provisional Government in an energetic suppression of the rebellion, evoked stormy and continued applause from all the benches of the Council, with the exception of an insignificant group of Menshevik-Internationalists and left S.R.'s. It seemed that the Government had finally united an overwhelming majority of the Council of the Republic, which would be ready to give it decisive and energetic support for the liquidation of the Bolshevik uprising. But immediately after that, something utterly incomprehensible and absurd happened. After A. F. Kerensky's speech, a recess was announced which lasted till 6:00 P.M. During the recess, consultations took place among all the factions. From the very beginning the cooperative representatives and the K.D.'s proposed that all the factions, with the exception of the Internationalists, join in a single resolution, expressing, in the present difficult moment, their readiness to support the Provisional Government in suppressing the Bolshevik uprising. But once again the Mensheviks and the S.R.'s manifested in full measure their half-way policies. The S.R.'s worked out the original resolution, which spoke of supporting the Provisional Government but which, at the same time, indicated the urgent necessity of putting into practice a decree regarding the transfer of all the lands into the hands of the land committees. The Mensheviks went still further. They started negotiations with the Menshevik-Internationalists, i.e., with that part of the Council that had occupied a completely isolated position during the speech of the Minister-President and whose behavior provoked stormy protests not only from the right but also from the center . . . As the session was resumed, the President had three resolutions . . . : [those] of the S.R.'s, of the Mensheviks, and of the cooperative representatives, in the last of which also the K.D.'s joined. However, during the session, the S.R.'s changed their mind and demanded . . . [a recess. A new recess was] announced, and, after consultation, the S.R.'s decided to withdraw their resolution and to join in the formula of the Mensheviks and Menshevik-Internationalists. The change of the S.R. position confused some of the cooperative representatives. They intended to abstain during the vote on the S.R. resolution, but as a common resolution was submitted on behalf of the S.R. and the Mensheviks [and] was the first put to vote, some of the cooperative representatives and Popular Socialists, having failed to grasp the essence of the change that took place, abstained from voting. As a result, the resolution of the S.R.'s and of the Mensheviks was accepted by a majority of 123 to 102, with 26 abstaining (the cooperative representatives, Popular Socialists, and zemstvo representatives). The acceptance of this resolution was a complete surprise to the majority of the Council, and after the close of the session, heated arguments took place in the Mariinskii Hall as to the position that the Government must now assume, in view of the acceptance of a resolution that speaks not so much of readiness to support the Provisional Government in fighting the Bolshevik uprising as of the necessity of transferring the land into the hands of the land committees, of raising the question of peace, and of forming in Petrograd a committee of public safety. Some were even found to say that after the acceptance of this resolution the only thing that remains for the Provisional Government is to abdicate its authority. The representatives of the groups whose resolution was accepted had another point of view. They argued that the accepted resolution, in which the Bolshevik uprising was clearly condemned, gives the Provisional Government the possibility of liquidating the uprising, provided, to be sure, it takes the path indicated in the resolution. In connection with the resolution's acceptance, in certain bourgeois circles the question has even been raised of leaving the Council's membership; but, for the time being, the question remains open.

1414. *Den'* on the Council's Action
[No. 198, October 25, 1917, p. 1.]

I do not know how Lenin and Trotsky will be engraved on the pages of history. I think that history will find few tender words for them and will not include them among its heroes.

But I know one thing—the leaders of the Russian preparliament are guaranteed the immortality of comic characters.

It is true that [their situation] is funny [only] in the eyes of an executioner, but this will not render them more respectable in the eyes of history. It will record them as the most perfect expression, as the climax of that type of Russian public man who long ago found his original prototype in the famous fable about the philosopher who fell into a pit.

"The philosopher" had a chance of getting out of this pit. A rope was handed down to him. He was told to get out. But the philosopher, precisely because he was a "philosopher" and, as such, unable to act obeying the orders of common sense and of impulsive feelings, did not get out of the pit.

. . .

It would seem that [the situation] was clear: cries of help were addressed to you. You were asked to come to the rescue, while somebody was already trying to seize by the throat those who were invoking your help. You had but two alternatives—either to make every effort to save those who invoked your help, or to join those who were seizing them by the throat.

But instead of responding spontaneously in this terrible moment, which will cost human sacrifices, you took accounts from your notebooks to present to those who were calling for help. You will be equally despised both by those who invoked your help and by those who wanted to strangle them.

And, on its part, history will give you a kick and will say: You were contemptible!

1415. Resolution of the Central Committees of the Soviets of Workers', Soldiers', and Peasants' Deputies Against the Bolshevik Action, Night of October 24

[*Izvestiia*, No. 207, October 26, 1917, pp. 2–3. On the same evening, Lenin wrote the Central Committee of his party that to delay "the uprising now really means death. . . . [T]he matter must absolutely be decided this evening or tonight. . . . If we seize power today, we seize power not against [the Congress of] Soviets but for them." *Collected Works of V. I. Lenin: Toward the Seizure of Power:* XXI, Bk. II, 144–45.]

Having examined the situation that has developed in Petrograd, the Joint Session of the Central Executive Committee of the Soviets of Workers' and Soldiers' Deputies and the Central Committee of the Soviets of Peasants' Deputies declared that:

1) An armed clash on the streets of Petrograd would untie the hands of the lurking bands of hooligans and pogromists.

2) It would inevitably lead to the triumph of counterrevolutionary elements which have already mobilized their forces for crushing the revolution and would thereby thwart the Constituent Assembly.

3) By disrupting transport and supplies, it would doom Petrograd and the army to starvation.

4) Finally, it would greatly increase the danger of the enemy's capture of the revolutionary capital.

Therefore, the Central Executive Committee of the Soviets of Workers' and Soldiers' Deputies and the Central Committee of the Soviets of Peasants' Deputies call upon the workers and soldiers of Petrograd to preserve complete calm and not to respond to appeals for armed demonstrations which can only lead to disaster.

In the interest of combating any subversive activities and counterrevolutionary attacks, the Session has found it necessary to form at once a Committee for Public Safety which shall have the participation of representatives from local self-governments, organs of the revolutionary democracy, and soldiers' parties.

In the meantime, it wishes to emphasize that the present movement in Petrograd is rooted in a feeling of deep dissatisfaction among the broad popular masses, which was bred by the war, by economic chaos, and by the vacillating policy of the Provisional Government.

The Session declares that the plenary organs of the revolutionary democracy will apply all their energies to continue the struggle to satisfy the needs of the people. The Session is giving priority to demands for having the Provisional Government publish a decree on the transfer of land to the land committees, and for having the Provisional Government propose to the Allies at once that they proclaim their peace terms and enter into peace negotiations.

The Central Executive Committee of the Soviets of Workers' and Soldiers' Deputies and the Central Committee of the Soviets of Peasants' Deputies appeal to all the revolutionary democratic forces in the country for their organized support in this struggle.

The resolution was adopted by a majority of votes.

The session closed around 4:00 A.M.

1416. The Government's Decision to Remain at Its Post and the
Difficulties in Sending Troops to Its Aid
["Stavka 25–26 Oktiabria 1917," *ARR*, VII (1922), 294, 296.]

October 25, 1917

A

To the Chief of Staff of the Supreme Commander:

The Petrograd Soviet of Workers' and Soldiers' Deputies has declared the Government deposed and has demanded the transfer of power by threatening the Winter Palace with bombardment from the guns of the Peter and Paul Fortress and of the cruiser *Aurora*. The Government can transfer its power only to the Constituent Assembly. It has decided not to surrender, and to place itself under the protection of the people and of the army. Hasten the dispatch of troops. October 25. No. 11690.

Deputy Minister-President Konovalov

B

To the Deputy Minister-President Konovalov:

[Replying] to 11690. Measures for the earliest arrival of the troops are being taken. First Lieutenant Danilevich has been informed of the expected time of the arrival of the units, but I consider it my duty to report that in the region nearest to Petrograd, independently from us, the movement is being hindered. 7927. DUKHONIN.

1417. THE SURRENDER OF THE MILITARY DISTRICT HEADQUARTERS AND THE SIEGE AND CAPTURE OF THE WINTER PALACE

[*Izvestiia*, No. 208, October 27, 1917, p. 5; and No. 207, October 26, 1917, pp. 3–4. An excellent account of the siege, which includes translations from Maliantovich's description, may be found in David Shub, *Lenin*, pp. 247–51. See also Dr. David Soskice's article in the *Manchester Guardian*, November 14, 1957, p. 7, which first appeared in the same newspaper in 1917, and S. L. Maslov's account translated in Bunyan and Fisher, pp. 116–18.]

In the Headquarters of the [*Petrograd*] *Military District*

In the evening of October 24, the Provisional Government's position in the conflict with the Military Revolutionary Committee was quite auspicious. It still seemed that the Military Revolutionary Committee in the garrison had only a numerical superiority, whereas the Government authorities had a qualitative superiority. However, the turn of events on the night of October 24–25 demonstrated that this view was not well founded. The actions of the Military Revolutionary Committee, as they unfolded, were very systematic; step by step, the Committee enlarged on its successes. The Headquarters of the Military District found itself unable even to implement its order on raising bridges, since the Nikolaevskii Bridge was lowered once again by the Red Guards, and the 32 shock troopers who were sent out to raise the bridge for the second time encountered . . . over 200 armed sailors and Red Guards on the bridge and, therefore, could not fulfill their mission.

. . .

Between 3:00 and 4:00 A.M. the Supreme Commander and Minister-President, A. F. Kerensky, arrived at the Headquarters of the Military District. A conference was called at which it was decided to inquire into the Cossacks' attitude toward these events. Orders were immediately telephoned to the 1st, 4th, and 14th Don Cossack Regiments. In addition, the following telegram was sent immediately to the regiments: "In the name of freedom, honor, and the glory of our native land, the Supreme Commander has ordered the 1st, 4th, and 14th Don Cossack Regiments to come to the assistance of the Central Executive Committee, the Soviets of the Revolutionary Democracy, and the Provisional Government, for the salvation of imperiled Russia." The telegram was signed by Major General Bagratuni and was countersigned by Malevskii, Commissar of the Central Executive Committee.

On receiving the order to advance, the Cossacks did not do so . . . but entered, instead, into negotiations. They asked whether the infantry would advance along with them and, in the end, announced that they would not advance alone, that they did not want to act as human targets, and that they were therefore refusing to advance. It was later learned that several military schools asked the Cossacks whether they intended to advance; in the end, they remained on their premises, whereas the Pavlovskoe Military School announced that it could not come forward for fear of the Grenadier Regiment.

. . .

In the morning, sailors from Kronstadt arrived on several transports and began to disembark on the Nikolaevskaia Quay. The cruiser *Aurora*, the battleship *Zarai Svobody*, and two destroyers arrived with them. At the same time, news was also received that the armored cars had started to go over to the side of the Petrograd Soviet.

At 12:00 NOON, A. F. Kerensky, accompanied by Captain Kuz'min, Assistant Commander of the Military District, and the adjutants left in an open automobile for one of the stations in order to meet the troops that Kerensky had called from the front for suppressing the movement. In the evening no news had yet been received about the destination of Kerensky. In the afternoon, armed cadets from the Mikhailovskii Artillery School arrived at the Winter Palace, but when it became dark they went back.

At 6:40 armored cars from the Military Revolutionary Committee appeared in the Palace Square, and occupied all the entrances and exits to the square. . . .

At 6:30 P.M. two motorcyclists arrived at the Headquarters of the Military District by authorization of the committee of the Fortress of Peter and Paul and presented an ultimatum to the Headquarters. The ultimatum stated that if the Headquarters of the Military District did not surrender, the Fortress and the battleships standing across the Nikolaevskii Bridge would open fire on them. . . . Present at the Headquarters of the Military District at this time were the [following] persons: N. M. Kishkin, who was commissioned to restore order in Petrograd; his assistants, engineers Rutenberg and Pal'chinskii; the commander of the Military District, Major General Bagratuni; Quartermaster General of the Staff, Paradelov; Assistant Director of the Political Department, Count Tolstoi; and others. The conference in the Headquarters of the Military District did not produce any definite results and the Commander of the Military District, together with an authorized representative and his assistant, went to the Winter Palace to confer with the Provisional Government. When the 20-minute period was up, one of the delegates was sent back to the Fortress with instructions from the Staff to request that it be given an additional 10 minutes. In these 10 minutes the 1st Quartermaster General, N. M. Paradelov, who remained at the Headquarters, was to have received a definite reply from the Winter Palace. The new 10-minute period elapsed, and since there was no answer from the Winter Palace, the detachment of Red Guards, sailors, and soldiers posted at the gates to the building of the Headquarters, under the command of an ensign from the Pavlovskii Regiment, occupied the Headquarters. General Paradelov, who was left not only without soldiers at his disposal, but even without officers, had no choice, and at 7:40 he surrendered. The Headquarters of the Military District was occupied by the troops of the Military Revolutionary Committee.

In the Winter Palace

. . .

On the morning of October 25, the Provisional Government held a session under the chairmanship of A. I. Konovalov [Kerensky having departed for the front], who announced that the session . . . was continuous.

N. M. Kishkin was appointed Governor General of Petrograd with command over all the military and civil authorities.

The Provisional Government decided to address a special appeal to the front in connection with the present events.

At 8:30 P.M., the Provisional Government at the Winter Palace received an ultimatum signed by the Petrograd Soviet of Workers' and Soldiers' Deputies, according to which the members of the Government were given 20 minutes in which to surrender with the least bloodshed possible, threatening, in the event of a refusal, to occupy the Winter Palace by force of arms [directed at it] from the Peter and Paul Fortress and the cruiser *Aurora*.

The Provisional Government, which was in full complement [*sic*] at the Winter Palace, refused to enter into any negotiations and gave no direct reply to the ultimatum.

After receiving the ultimatum in the corridor of the Winter Palace, the cadets, posted in the palace for guard [duty], were assembled, and Ministers Maslov, Kishkin, and Maliantovich delivered speeches in which they pointed out the groundlessness of the Bolshevik demands and condemned the action of the Bolsheviks on the eve of the convocation of the Constituent Assembly.

. . .

Appeals from the Provisional Government

I

Ominous events are coming to a head in Petrograd. Immediately following the orders to the troops of the Petrograd Garrison to leave for the front in order to defend the capital against the advancing enemy, persistent agitation was begun in the regiments and the factories against the Provisional Government and the Central Committee of the Soviets of Workers' and Soldiers' and Peasants' Deputies. Under the influence of this agitation, a Military Revolutionary Committee was arbitrarily formed, which, independently of the Petrograd Military District Headquarters, began to give orders to the troops and even tried to paralyze the whole complicated and responsible military work by demanding that no order issued by the Headquarters be executed without a confirmation by the Committee. This forced the Provisional Government to adopt resolute steps to combat such occurrences, which threatened to stop the whole work on the defense of the capital. Resting on the support of the Central Executive Committees and the Council of the Republic, it issued an order for closing down the newspapers that have openly been advocating civil war and for the arrest of the chief agitators, who have been calling upon the troops to rise against the State power and the highest organs of the revolutionary democracy.

However, in view of the instability and indecisiveness of a section of the Petrograd Garrison, not all of the orders of the Provisional Government were executed, and Petrograd is in danger of finding itself in the hands of the raging elements of civil war and anarchy. At the same time, there is the threat of the termination of the activities of the State organism, the termination of the diplomatic work which has as its aim the hastening of peace, the termination of work on the convocation of the Constituent Assembly, the termination of the supply of provisions, clothes, and ammunition to the army.

The time for the struggle has come. The army in the field, languishing under the intolerable conditions of military life, cannot permit a treacherous stab in the back from the home front. The units that have been holding in check the iron hordes of the invaders must not permit their rear units, which have not yet known the burdens of war, to refuse to obey combat orders and leave the front without support. The army in the field cannot permit the complicated work of international relations, guaranteeing the hastening of peace, to be thwarted at the most crucial time. The front must use the full force of its authority and the force of arms to support its wrathful demands on the rear which have been unanimously announced by all the army committees. Rally around the Provisional Government and around the central organs of the revolutionary democracy. Give a firm rebuff to the treacherous agitation and stop the outrages in the rear.

A. KONOVALOV, Acting Minister-President

II

Citizens, save the native land, the Republic, and freedom. Madmen have stirred up a rebellion against the only State power established by the people pending the Constituent Asssembly—against the Provisional Government. The members of the Provisional Government are performing their duty; they are remaining at their places and they will continue their work for the good of the country, for the restoration of order, and for the convocation, at the appointed time, of the Constituent Assembly, the future authorized master of the Russian land and of all the peoples that inhabit it.

Citizens, you must help the Provisional Government. You must strengthen its power. You must hinder the madmen who have been joined by all the enemies of freedom and order, the supporters of the old regime, in their attempt to thwart the Constituent Assembly, destroy all the gains of the revolution, and the whole future of our dear, native land.

Citizens, organize around the Provisional Government for the defense of its temporary power in the name of the order and the happiness of all the peoples of our great native land.

October 25, 1917

The Arrest of the Members of the Provisional Government

On October 26, at 2:10 A.M., Antonov, a member of the Temporary Revolutionary Committee of the Executive Committee of the Soviet of Workers' and Soldiers' Deputies, arrested [the following members of the Provisional Government] by order of the Committee: Rear Admiral Verderevskii; Minister of Welfare Kishkin; Minister [of Trade and Industry and Deputy Minister-President] Konovalov; Minister of Agriculture Maslov; Minister of Transport Liverovskii; Acting Minister of War Manikovskii; [Minister of Labor] Gvozdev; [Minister of Justice] Maliantovich; [President of the Economic Council] Tret'iakov; General for Special Assignments Borisov; State Controller Smirnov; Minister of Education Salazkin'; Minister of Finance Bernatskii; Minister of Foreign Affairs Tereshchenko; Assistant to the Special Commissioner of the Provisional Government Rutenberg; Minister of Post and Telegraph Nitikin; Minister of Confessions Kartashev; [Assistant Minister of Trade and Industry] Pal'chinskii. Other officers and cadets were disarmed and released. Three files and the portfolio of the Minister of Education were seized.

1418. The Dispersal of the Council of the Republic

[*Izvestiia*, No. 207, October 26, 1917, pp. 4–5.]

Yesterday at 11:30 A.M. everything outwardly in the Mariinskii Palace resembled an ordinary parliamentary day, not "a big day" but just a usual one. There were a few Council members in the Assembly Hall; there were a few more members in the lobbies, but still few in number.

However, the outward appearance of the Palace was completely incongruous with the mood of the members of the preparliament and the journalists as well as the small number of people in attendance. They were not waiting for the session. It was clear to everyone that regular work of the Council of the Republic was out of the question.

After 12:00 o'clock, most of the factions were holding short improvised meetings in their rooms. At just that time armed soldiers entered the premises of the Palace. They lined up all along the main stairway. Reinforced sentries were stationed at every entrance. News spread quickly throughout the Mariinskii Palace that soldiers were demanding that the premises of the Palace be cleared.

The Presidium urgently summoned the *Senor'en konvent*. N. D. Avksent'ev personally made the rounds of the rooms of the factions, requesting the members of the *Senor'en konvent* to appear immediately at a conference. Ten to fifteen minutes later the decision of the *Senor'en konvent* was already known: to issue a protest against coercion, to submit to force, and to instruct the President of the Council of the Republic to resume the work of the Council at the earliest time.

There was some confusion—some of the members of the Council assumed that this concluded [the session] and left the Mariinskii Palace. In the meantime, it was decided to open the session.

A little over a hundred seats were occupied in the Assembly Hall. N. D. Avksent'ev opened the session. In five or ten minutes the list of speakers was already exhausted.

It was unanimously resolved to issue a protest against the use of violence, and it was decided, by a majority of 56 votes to 48 votes, with 2 abstaining, to close the session.

In declaring the session closed, N. D. Avksent'ev announced that the members of the Council of the Republic would be notified about the date of the next session.

. . .

1419. Protest of the Council of the Republic

[*Delo Naroda*, No. 192, October 28, 1917, p. 2.]

To All, All, All!

Citizens of Russia!

The Provisional Council of the Russian Republic, yielding to the pressure of bayonets, was compelled to disperse on October 25 and to temporarily interrupt its work.

Those who have seized power with the words "liberty and socialism" on their lips are perpetrating violations and arbitrary acts. They have arrested and jailed in the tsarist prison the members of the Provisional Government, the socialist ministers being within their number. They have closed the newspapers, seized the printing houses, and have subjected to censorship even the socialist organs of the press. They have dispersed the Provisional Council of the Republic, whose membership includes representatives of all strata and classes of the Russian population, and the representatives of all the democratic revolutionary parties, with the exception of the Bolsheviks and anarchists.

The rebellion which was raised in Petrograd has already caused bloodshed on the streets of the capital. A civil, internecine war threatens to overflow in a wide wave over the whole country. Blood and anarchy threaten to choke the revolution, to sink liberty and the Republic, and to bring on their crest the restoration of the old regime.

By organizing an armed plot behind the backs of the democracy at a moment of mortal danger when country and freedom are in danger owing to the onslaught of imperialistic armies from the outside, those who have seized power have violated all the rights and laws of the revolution and of the democracy and have thereby placed themselves outside of the revolution and outside of the democracy.

A power which was conceived in blood and crime, which actually betrays the interests of the homeland and of the revolution, which is relying on the bayonets of the soldiers and on the base instincts of the ignorant masses exhausted by war and by the tsarist regime; a power which tempts that part of the democracy that lacks consciousness by the deceitful mirage of an "immediate" conclusion of the long-awaited peace; a power which consciously deceives the people by promises of an "immediate" satisfaction of its craving for land and food, of an "immediate" reorganization of Russia on the basis of socialist principles; a power which under the pretext of an immediate convening of the Constituent Assembly shamelessly and obviously to everyone sabotages the elections set for November 12, and which in fact delays [the convening of] the Constituent Assembly for an undetermined period—such a power not only cannot inspire confidence but cannot be [even] recognized as a democracy. It should be isolated from the democracy and from all those for whom the homeland and the revolution are dear.

Such a power should be recognized as the enemy of the people and of the revolution; it is necessary to fight against it, it is necessary to overthrow it.

Also the Provisional Council of the Republic appeals to all the citizens of Russia, whatever their convictions, not to recognize the newly-appeared power in Russia of the Bolshevik plotters and rebels against democracy and the revolution.

The Provisional Council of the Republic calls upon all the citizens of Russia to refuse their obedience and not to execute the orders and the interdictions of the Bolshevik power.

The Provisional Council of the Republic, prior to resuming its work, calls upon the citizens of the Russian Republic to stand around their organs of local self-government elected on the basis of universal suffrage and around the all-Russian and the local committees to save the fatherland and the revolution, which are organizing the overthrow of the power of the Bolsheviks and the re-establishment of a government that will be capable of bringing the tormented country to the Constituent Assembly.

THE PRESIDIUM OF THE PROVISIONAL COUNCIL OF THE RUSSIAN REPUBLIC

October 27, 1917

1420. Lenin's Speech Before the Petrograd Soviet and the Opening of the Second All-Russian Congress of Soviets of Workers' and Soldiers' Deputies, Night of October 25–26

[*Izvestiia*, No. 207, October 26, 1917, pp. 5–7; and No. 208, October 27, 1917, p. 3.]

A. Lenin's Speech Before the Soviet at About 3:00 p.m.

"Comrades, the workers' and peasants' revolution, about the necessity of which the Bolsheviks have been speaking all the time, has come to pass.

"What is the significance of this workers' and peasants' revolution? First of all, the significance of this revolution is that we shall have a Soviet Government, our own organ of power, without the participation of any bourgeois. The oppressed masses will form a government themselves. The old State machinery will be uprooted and a new machinery of government will be created, embodied in the Soviet organizations.

"This is the beginning of a new period in the history of Russia, and the present, third Russian revolution must ultimately lead to the victory of socialism.

"One of our immediate tasks is the necessity of ending the war at once. But in order to end this war, which is closely bound up with the present capitalistic system, it is clear to all that it is necessary to overcome capitalism itself.

"We will be aided in this work by the world workers' movement, which is already beginning to develop in Italy, England, and Germany.

"A just and immediate offer of peace by us to the international democracy will find everywhere a fervent response among the masses of the international proletariat. In order to strengthen this confidence of the proletariat, it is necessary to publish at once all secret treaties.

"An enormous part of the peasantry within Russia has said: enough of playing games with the capitalists—we will go with the workers. We shall win the confidence of the peasantry by one decree, which will abolish *pomeshchik* land-ownership. The peasants will understand that their only salvation lies in an alliance with the workers.

"We will institute real workers' control over production.

"You have now learned how to work together in harmony, as evidenced by the revolution that has just occurred. We now possess the strength of a mass organization, which will triumph over everything and which will lead the proletariat to world revolution.

"In Russia we must now devote ourselves to the construction of a proletarian socialist state.

"Long live the socialist world revolution." (*Storm of applause.*)

It was decided not to open debates on Lenin's speech. . . .

B. The Opening of the Congress

Statement by Dan

"Comrades, the Congress of the Soviets of Workers' and Soldiers' Deputies is meeting at such an exceptional moment, under such exceptional circumstances, that you will understand why the Central Executive Committee considers it superfluous to open the meeting of the Congress with a political speech. At this very moment as I, a member of the Presidium of the Central Executive Committee of the Soviets of Workers' and Soldiers' Deputies, am speaking to you, our comrades in session at the Winter Palace are under fire. This is not the time for political speeches.

"I announce the first meeting of the Congress of the Soviet of Workers' and Soldiers' Deputies opened.

"I propose that we proceed to the elections to the Presidium. Please submit your motions accordingly."

Statement by Avanesov

"Comrades, in agreement with the Bureaus of the Bolshevik, Socialist Revolutionary, Menshevik and Internationalist factions, it was resolved to elect the Presidium from members of Soviets present here on the basis of proportional representation. Five hundred and fifteen delegates were registered at the opening of the Congress. Now there are several more, but they have not been entered on the lists."

Then Avanesov read the list from the Bolshevik faction: Lenin, Zinoviev, Kamenev, Lunacharskii, Kollontai, and others—14 persons in all.

The Socialist Revolutionaries were given seven seats, the Mensheviks three, the Internationalists one.

The Socialist Revolutionary faction was represented by Kamkov, Spiridonova, Kakhovskaia, Mstislavskii, Karelin, Zaks.

Then the right-wing faction of the Socialist Revolutionaries and Mensheviks announced their refusal to submit their lists.

The Menshevik-Internationalist faction declared that it was refraining, for the time being, from entering its candidate to the Presidium.

The submitted lists were approved and the Presidium took its place amidst applause.

The Program for the Day

Kamenev read the following agenda: 1) the organization of a government, not organization of power, 2) war and peace, 3) the Constituent Assembly.

. . . .

Martov's Motion

On behalf of the Menshevik-Internationalist faction and the Jewish Social Democratic Workers' Party, Martov moved to place as the first point on the agenda the question of a peaceful solution to the present crisis.

Martov declared that the Menshevik-Internationalist faction did not find it possible to assume political responsibility for the venture embarked upon by the Bolsheviks.

"Measures must be adopted," the speaker said, "to stop military action on both sides." Martov insisted that the question of a peaceful solution of conflicts be given priority at the Congress, because the question was far too serious and civil war had already started."

All the factions supported Comrade Martov's motion.

On behalf of the Bolsheviks, Lunacharskii declared that the Bolshevik faction had no objections to giving priority to this question.

Kharash's Statement, Made Out of Order

Kharash [12th Army], representing the faction of [right] Socialist Revolutionaries and Mensheviks, was given the floor.

"Comrades, now, when the Winter Palace is under fire, at a moment when representatives of the socialist parties, not recalled by their parties, are in session in the Winter Palace, at this moment the Congress opens its meeting.

"A criminal political venture has been going on behind the back of the All-Russian Congress, thanks to the political hypocrisy of the Bolshevik Party.

"On behalf of the Menshevik and Socialist Revolutionary faction, I categorically protest against these criminal actions and declare that we will do everything in our power to counteract this political venture."

Statement by the Front Group

Kuchin appeared on the rostrum on behalf of the Front Group.

"Comrades, the convocation of the present Congress was preceded by discussions regarding its necessity in all army organizations, and for a number of grave political reasons, all the army organizations have found the Congress untimely.

"After the resolution of the Central Executive Committee favoring the convocation of the Congress, some of the army organizations sent their representatives to the Congress, but there are also some, quite a few in number, that did not send [their representatives].

"The army is not fully represented at this Congress and, consequently, [this Congress] cannot be considered competent. (*Voice from the audience:* "On whose behalf are you speaking?")

"On behalf of the following army committees: [those of the] 2nd, 3rd, 4th, 6th, 7th, 8th, 9th, 10th, 11th, 12th [armies], the Special Army, the Caucasian Army, and the committees of all the fronts. (*Voice from the audience:* "You are not a representative of the army.")

"I was elected by the Army Congress at the beginning of October.

"As concerns the seizure of power, all the above-enumerated organizations have declared themselves against this seizure.

"The Congress was called primarily to discuss the question of forming a government, and what has happened? This adventure of seizing power has already occurred and the will of the Congress has been decided beforehand.

"We declare that the civil war brought about by the Bolshevik adventure is a stab in the back of the army. It is necessary to save the revolution from this mad attempt, and in the name of saving the revolution, we will mobilize all the revolutionary responsible forces in the army and in the country.

"The Front Group has set this task for itself; it declines all responsibility for the consequences of this adventure, and it is leaving this Congress.

"From now on the arena of the fight is transferred to the local areas."

Comrade Kuchin's statement was met variously by disapproving shouts from one part of the audience and by applause from the other.

Statement by Khinchuk

Comrade Khinchuk made the following statement on behalf of the united Social Democratic factions:

"Taking into consideration:

"1. That the military plot was conceived and carried out by the Bolshevik Party in the name of the Soviet behind the backs of all the other parties and factions represented in the Soviets;

"2. That the seizure of power by the Petrograd Soviet on the eve of the Congress of Soviets represents a subversion and a break-up of the whole Soviet organization and has undermined the significance of the Congress as a plenary representative of the revolutionary democracy;

"3. That this plot is plunging the country into civil war, is thwarting the Constituent Assembly, threatens a military catastrophe, and leads to the triumph of counterrevolution;

"4. That there remains only one possible peaceful way out of the situation— negotiations with the Provisional Government on forming a power that would rest [on the support of] all the elements of the democracy;

"5. That the United Russian Social Democratic Workers' Party considers it its duty to the working class not only to decline all responsibility for the actions of the Bolsheviks, who are shielding themselves with the Soviet banner, but also to warn the workers and the soldiers against the opportunistic policy fatal to the country and to the revolution;

"The faction of the Russian Social Democratic Workers' Party (United) is leaving the present Congress, and invites all other factions who likewise refuse to bear the responsibility for the actions of the Bolsheviks to meet at once to discuss the situation."

The Declaration of the Socialist Revolutionary Faction

Next, Gendel'man made the following statement on behalf of the Socialist Revolutionary faction.

"The Socialist Revolutionary faction at the All-Russian Congress of Soviets of Workers' and Soldiers' Deputies, in agreement with the Central Committee of the Socialist Revolutionary Party, makes this announcement:

"1. The seizure of power by the Bolshevik Party and the Petrograd Soviet of Workers' and Soldiers' Deputies, on the eve of the Constituent Assembly and one day before the opening of the All-Russian Congress of the Soviets of Workers' and Soldiers' Deputies, is a crime against the country and the revolution. It signifies the beginning of a civil war and the thwarting of the Constituent Assembly, and threatens to ruin the revolution.

"2. Anticipating an outburst of popular indignation, which will inevitably occur following the unavoidable discovery of the bankruptcy of Bolshevik promises, which are obviously impossible to fulfill at the present time, the Socialist Revolutionary faction is calling upon all revolutionary forces of the country to become organized and stand on guard over the revolution so that when the imminent catastrophe occurs, by taking the fate of the country into their hands and preventing the triumph of a counterrevolution, [they can] realize the earliest possible conclusion of a general democratic peace, the convocation of the Constituent Assembly at the appointed time, and rationalization of land.

"3. The Socialist Revolutionary faction, taking cognizance of the seizure of power by the Bolshevik Party and its leader, the Petrograd Soviets of Workers' and Soldiers' Deputies, is holding them fully responsible for the consequences of their insane and criminal action, and, having established the consequent impossibility of collaboration with them, is leaving the Congress."

Resolution of Martov

Comrade Martov submitted the following resolution.

"Taking into consideration:

"1. That the coup d'état, transferring the governing power in Petrograd to the Military Revolutionary Committee one day before the opening of the Congress, was engineered by the Bolshevik Party alone, by a purely military plot;

"2. That this coup d'état threatens to bring about bloodshed and civil war and the triumph of a counterrevolution which would suppress in blood the whole movement of the proletariat and, at the same time, destroy the gains of the revolution;

"3. That the only way out of this situation, which could still arrest the development of a civil war, might be an agreement between the insurgent elements of the democracy and the rest of the democratic organizations on forming a democratic government that is recognized by the entire revolutionary democracy and to which the Provisional Government could painlessly surrender its power;

"The Menshevik faction proposes that the Congress pass a resolution on the necessity of a peaceful settlement of the present crisis by the formation of an all-democratic government. The Menshevik-Internationalist faction proposes that the Congress appoint a delegation for this purpose for entering into negotiations with other democratic organs and all the socialist parties.

"The Menshevik-Internationalist faction proposes that the Congress discontinue its work pending the disclosure of the results of the work of this delegation."

Late at night the Menshevik-Internationalists left the assembly hall of the meeting. The Peasants' Deputies also left the Congress.

All those who left the Congress went to the Municipal Duma.

Representatives of the cruiser *Aurora* and the destroyer *Zabiiaka* spoke at the Congress, declaring that they only fired blank shots at the Winter Palace. One person was accidentally killed on the cruiser.

The left Socialist Revolutionaries asked for a recess to discuss the question of their further attendance at the Congress.

It was decided to announce a recess of the Congress.

A further account of the meetings will be given in tomorrow's issue.

Proclamation of the Congress on the Assumption of Power[8]

To All Workers, Soldiers, and Peasants:

The second All-Russian Congress of Soviets of Workers' and Soldiers' Deputies has opened. It represents the great majority of the Soviets, including a number of deputies of peasant Soviets. The prerogatives of the Central Executive Committee of the compromisers are ended.

Supported by an overwhelming majority of the workers, soldiers, and peasants, and basing itself on the victorious insurrection of the workers and the garrison of Petrograd, the Congress hereby resolves to take governmental power into its own hands.

The Provisional Government is deposed and most of its members are under arrest.

The Soviet authority will at once propose a democratic peace to all nations

---

[8] Passed in the early morning after the recess. This translation is from Bunyan and Fisher, pp. 121–22.

and an immediate armistice on all fronts. It will safeguard the transfer without compensation of all land—landlord, *udel,* and monastery—to the peasant committees; it will defend the soldiers' rights, introducing a complete democratization of the army, it will establish workers' control over industry, it will insure the convocation of the Constituent Assembly on the date set, it will supply the cities with bread and the villages with articles of first necessity, and it will secure to all nationalities inhabiting Russia the right of self-determination.

The Congress resolves that all local authority shall be transferred to the Soviets of Workers', Soldiers', and Peasants' Deputies, which are charged with the task of enforcing revolutionary order.

The Congress calls upon the soldiers in the trenches to be watchful and steadfast. The Congress of Soviets is confident that the revolutionary army will know how to defend the revolution against all imperialistic attempts until the new government has concluded a democratic peace which it is proposing directly to all nations.

The new government will take every measure to provide the revolutionary army with all necessities, by means of a determined policy of requisition from and taxation of the propertied classes. Care will be taken to improve the position of the soldiers' families.

The Kornilovists—Kerensky, Kaledin, and others—are endeavoring to lead troops against Petrograd. Several regiments, deceived by Kerensky, have already joined the insurgents.

Soldiers! Resist Kerensky, who is a Kornilovist! Be on guard!

Railwaymen! Stop all echelons sent by Kerensky against Petrograd!

Soldiers, Workers, Employees! The fate of the Revolution and democratic peace is in your hands!

Long live the Revolution!

THE ALL-RUSSIAN CONGRESS OF SOVIETS OF
WORKERS' AND SOLDIERS' DEPUTIES
DELEGATES FROM THE PEASANTS' SOVIETS

1421. EDITORIAL IN *Rech'*
[No. 252, October 26, 1917, p. 1.]

Thus the die is cast. A country which is exhausted and tormented by three years of war, which has experienced the convulsions of a revolution, which is reduced to misery, which has reached the last degree of economic and industrial disintegration, a country deprived of a firm and solid government, a country which has become the arena of anarchic and pogrom movements—this unfortunate, perishing country will have to undergo a new stage on her road to Golgotha. We have already entered an era of new vivisectional experimentation over her. As these lines are being written, we do not as yet know whether this experiment has been completed, whether actually all the power has passed to the Soviets— either to the Soviets or to their candidates—whether the reins of government have already been seized by Messrs. Lenin and Trotsky. We do not know whether there is still a government in Russia. But already we know one thing: a new, deep shock has taken place and its consequences for the internal and international situation of the country are incalculable.

Up to this time we did not want to lose hope that the cup of new trials would pass from our homeland. However small this hope, it nevertheless seemed to us that blind party fanaticism also had limits, beyond which one would feel the [oncoming] ruin of the whole country and those "conquests of the revolution" of which so many high-sounding but dead words were said during these last eight months. These hopes were not to be realized. Evidently history repeats itself, and we will not be able to forget any of its gloomy and bloody pages.

Whatever tomorrow brings us, whatever form the government takes, into whatever hands it passes, it is absolutely clear that before this government, before any government, the same problems will arise. They are dictated by the whole complex of conditions under which we are living, by our international situation, by the state of our army, of our finances, of our food problem. They are inescapable; they cannot be got rid of by the cheap rhetoric of idle talk at meetings; deceitful and unrealizable promises cannot be substituted for them. They will arise also before Messrs. Lenin and Trotsky if their rebellious plot succeeds. Then the country will have to suffer new convulsions, to taste the bitter fruits of political senselessness and adventurism; and who knows whether it will be able to recover from these new doses of poison.

Up to the last moment the Provisional Government did not consider that it had the right to throw from its shoulders the burden of heavy historical responsibility for the fate of the country. We welcome its valorous firmness. In spite of all the horrors of a situation without solution in which it found itself because the units of the Petrograd Garrison had forgotten their duty to the country, the Government did not capitulate before violence. Up to the last minute, it believed in the patriotism, the conscience, and the wisdom of the wide circles of the population, and addressed itself to them for support. And if these appeals prove vain, if the legitimate government recognized by the whole country in the first days of the February upheaval is overthrown, then let all responsibility for future tragic events fall on the heads of those who in the days of the greatest mortal danger for their homeland threw her into the abyss of new tempests and agitations.

1422. THE ALL-RUSSIAN EXECUTIVE COMMITTEE OF PEASANTS' SOVIETS TO ALL THE PEASANTS

[*Delo Naroda*, No. 191, October 28, 1917, p. 3.]

Comrade peasants!

All the liberties gained with the blood of your sons and brothers are now in terrible, mortal danger.

The revolution is perishing! The homeland is perishing!

Again, fraternal blood is being shed on the streets of Petrograd. Again the whole country is thrown into an abyss of confusion and disintegration. Again a blow is being inflicted in the back of the army, which defends the homeland and the revolution from external defeat.

On October 26 the Party of the Social Democrats–Bolshevik and the Petrograd Soviet of Workers' and Soldiers' Deputies, which is led by it, seized power in their hands. They have arrested, in the Winter Palace after artillery and machine-gun fire and jailed in the Peter and Paul Fortress, the Provisional Government and the socialist ministers, among whom were the members of the Executive Committee of the All-Russian Soviet of Peasants' Deputies, S. L. Maslov and S. S. Salazkin'. They have dispersed by armed force the Provisional Council of the Russian Republic, elected for the supervision of the activity of the Provisional Government until [the convening] of the Constituent Assembly. Finally, they have declared the Minister-President and Supreme Commander, A. F. Kerensky, a state criminal.

Incalculable are the calamities which these actions bring on Russia; immeasurable is the crime against the people and the revolution of those who have raised the rebellion and have sown confusion within the country. First they divide the forces of the toiling people by bringing within their ranks confusion and discord and by facilitating for the external foe the possibility of completely routing and conquering our country.

A blow against the army is the first and the worst crime of the Bolshevik Party!

Second, they have started a civil war and have seized power by violence at the very moment when the Provisional Government, by completing the working out of the law regarding transfer of all the land into the hands of the land committees, was accomplishing an action desired by all the toiling peasantry, and when there remained only the advent of the fully empowered master of the Russian land—the Constituent Assembly. They are deceiving the country by calling the Congress of the Soviets gathered in Petrograd the voice of the whole people, of the whole democracy, whereas all the representatives of the front, of the socialist parties, and of the Soviets of Peasants' Deputies have withdrawn from it. Taking advantage of a few peasants who turned out to be at this Congress in spite of the decision of the Committee of the All-Russian Soviet of Peasants' Deputies and of the Congress of the representatives of the guberniya soviets of peasants' deputies, they have the daring to state that they are relying on the Soviets of Peasants' Deputies. Without possessing any power in this respect, they speak on behalf of the Soviets of Peasants' Deputies. Let all toiling Russia know that this is a lie and that all the toiling peasantry—the Executive Committee of the All-Russian Soviet of Peasants' Deputies—indignantly rejects any kind of participation of the organized peasantry in this criminal violation of the will of all the toilers.

The Bolsheviks promise the people immediate peace, bread, land, and freedom. All these promises, which take into account the exhaustion of the popular masses and their lack of consciousness, are [mere] lies and bragging. They are to be followed not by peace but by slavery. It is not bread, land, and liberty that they will bring, but by increasing the confusion and by aiding the dark forces to re-establish the accursed tsarist regime, they will bring civil war, blood, the same want of land as before, and the triumph of the knout and of the *nagaika*.

Therefore, considering that the upheaval which has taken place threatens the army and the country with an immediate rout, that it delays the convening of the Constituent Assembly and cannot create a government which would enjoy the recognition of the whole nation, the Executive Committee of the All-Russian Soviet of Peasants' Deputies deems it its sacred duty before its own conscience and before all the country to declare that it *does not recognize the new Bolshevik power* as the government of the nation, and calls upon the local Soviets of Peasants' Deputies, upon the organs of local self-government, and upon the army not to obey this power created by violence, and to maintain at the same time complete order and guard the country against external defeat. The Executive Committee of the All-Russian Soviet of Peasants' Deputies has undertaken the following tasks:

1) The re-establishment of a government enjoying general recognition, and one that can bring the country to the Constituent Assembly.

2) The convening of the Constituent Assembly without any alteration of the electoral law.

3) The transfer of all the lands to the jurisdiction of the land committees.

THE ALL-RUSSIAN EXECUTIVE COMMITTEE
OF PEASANTS' SOVIETS

1423. *Izvestiia* ON THE SEIZURE OF POWER

[No. 207, October 26, 1917, p. 1. The last issue published before the Bolsheviks seized the newspaper.]

Yesterday we called the Bolshevik uprising an insane venture. Today, when the attempt was crowned with success in Petrograd, we have not changed our mind. We repeat that this is not a transfer of power to the Soviets, but a seizure of power by one party—the Bolsheviks. Yesterday we were saying that this means the thwarting of the greatest gain of the revolution—the Constituent Assembly. Today we must add that it means the thwarting of the Congress of Soviets and, very probably, of the whole Soviet organization. These are the facts: the Socialist Revolutionary Party and the Mensheviks of the Social Democratic Party (the defensists as well as the Internationalists) have found it impossible, under the present circumstances, to participate in the Congress. The representatives from the front adhere to the same opinion. When these factions depart from the Congress, it will be left only with what it should have been left as a result of a complete Bolshevik overthrow, i.e., with only the Bolsheviks. They can call themselves whatever they please, but this will not alter the fact that the Bolsheviks alone participated in the uprising. All the other socialist and democratic parties are protesting against it.

We do not know how the situation will develop. But we do not expect anything good. We are absolutely certain that the Bolsheviks will not be able to organize state power. And as yesterday, so also today, we repeat that what is happening will react worst of all on the cause of peace. Only yesterday the Council of the Republic adopted a resolution calling for a vigorous policy of peace. Today the Council of the Republic was to vote on a special resolution on this question. But the Mariinskii Palace was occupied by the Temporary Revolutionary Committee, and the session did not take place. Of course, the contemplated departure abroad within the next few days of the Russian delegation will not take place either, and consequently all the steps that have been undertaken in the direction of peace have been stopped by the action of the Bolsheviks. What other steps can the Bolsheviks themselves take? They have no possibility now of undertaking anything whatsoever, and they will not have this possibility, simply because they are not recognized by a single government: by either the Allies or the Germans.

But it is still premature to speak of this. To date, the Bolsheviks have seized Petrograd but not all of Russia. The danger of a bloody civil war is threatening. Bloodshed and pogroms—this is what we must prepare ourselves for. This can only be averted, if it is not already too late, by one event: if a democratic government, recognized by all democratic elements and parties, is formed anew, and if the Bolsheviks agree to submit to such a government.

The entire responsibility for the future of the country now falls on them alone.

1424. CONVERSATION BY DIRECT WIRE BETWEEN GENERAL BARANOVSKII AND
FIRST LIEUTENANT DANILEVICH OF OCTOBER 26, 1917, REGARDING
THE EVENTS IN PETROGRAD AND KERENSKY'S MOVEMENT
TOWARD THE CAPITAL WITH TROOPS

["Oktiabr' na fronte," *KA*, XXIII (1927), 157–60].

Danilevich is at the apparatus.

I am listening. What will you tell me, my dear fellow?

Good day, Vladimir L'vovich. I want to inform you about the real situation
in Petrograd. In the morning of the 25th, and still at a moment when the question
of the overthrow of the Provisional Government was not an actual threat and in
Petrograd everything was quiet, the Bolsheviks issued a newspaper, *Rabochii Put'*,
in which the deposition of the Government was announced as an accomplished fact.
Around 11:00, A. F. [Kerensky] left in the direction of Luga for the purpose of
meeting the motorcyclists. In his absence the remaining members of the Provisional Government were in session and talking, as is their habit. The Petrograd
Headquarters were inactive. It was decided to transfer power in Petrograd to
Kishkin and to Pal'chinskii and Rutenberg as his assistants. The latter naturally
did what they could, but being civilians they did not even take care of organizing
those numerous troops in the Ensigns' Schools that were faithful to the Government. . . .

.   .   .

[BARANOVSKII] Is there anybody beside you?

[DANILEVICH] I am alone with a telegraph employee.

[BARANOVSKII] I can tell you that Kerensky with a cavalry corps proceeds to
Petrograd. The order to continue the movement of the troops was given today
at around 11:00 o'clock. A. F. spent the night at my place awaiting the arrival of
General Krasnov, with whom he went to Ostrov.

.   .   .

1425. THE FAILURE OF ATTEMPTS TO RE-ESTABLISH THE PROVISIONAL
GOVERNMENT IN MOSCOW

[P. N. Miliukov, *Istoriia vtoroi russkoi revoliutsii*, I, vypusk 3, 295–96.]

There was still another force which under different circumstances could have
played a role in the struggle [against the October uprising]: it was the representatives of the government overthrown in Petrograd. During these days the
opponents of the Bolsheviks could not but envisage them as the only representatives of the legitimate authority. S. N. Prokopovich was the only Minister who
was not arrested in the Winter Palace. He was arrested on his way there at 10:00
o'clock in the morning, but around 5:00 P.M. he was freed from the Smol'nyi.
During the day of October 26 a conference of the assistant ministers who were in
Petersburg was held under his chairmanship. In the words of S. N. Prokopovich,
"he pointed out at this conference the necessity, after losing Petersburg, to organize resistance at Moscow and asked to be invested with such powers." Having
received these powers, he arrived in the morning of the 27th in Moscow and drove
directly from the station to the Municipal Duma, where the public committee was
in session; his colleagues Khizhniakov and Kondrat'ev were with him. At the
Duma they proposed to "co-opt" the committee into the Provisional Government.

But the authority of the Provisional Government, as we have seen, was low, and to accept its trademark in Moscow would not have meant to ease the struggle. S. N. Prokopovich himself recalls that "in Moscow the rightists said openly: 'Only let the Bolsheviks overthrow the power of the Provisional Government and then it will be easy [for us] to cope with them.'" S. N. Prokopovich adds: "In the camp of both the rightists and the leftists I saw during these days almost open rejoicing over the boldness of the Bolsheviks."

With such moods the proposal of Prokopovich with regard to "co-option" received a less than reserved welcome in the Duma. Apparently the powers granted by the assistant ministers in Petrograd had lost their validity in Moscow. Thus, the idea of Prokopovich and of his comrades to create in Moscow a substitute for the Provisional Government could not be realized.[9]

. . .

1426. The Situation on the Northern Front on October 26

["Stavka 25–26 Oktiabria 1917," *ARR*, XII (1922), 313. At Pskov, the Headquarters of the Northern Front, where Kerensky arrived on the night of October 25, he found that the Commander in Chief, General Cheremisov, had countermanded his order to send troops to the capital to put down the uprising. Early the next morning, Kerensky ordered the advance resumed and proceeded toward Petrograd with General Krasnov. See Bunyan and Fisher, pp. 140–45.]

October 26, 1917

The office of the Commissar of the Northern Front; the Commissar of the Northern Front is at the apparatus.

Is the Commissar of the Northern Front at the apparatus?

Yes, he is.

The Deputy Chief of Staff of the Supreme Commander Vyrubov is at the apparatus. I ask you to inform me of the situation in Pskov. At 13 hours and a half I talked with Ensign Tolstoi and through him I received by apparatus the order of the Supreme Commander given in Pskov on the 25th. This order has not been received from Pskov. Tell me—where is the Supreme Commander? Is he expected at some time in Pskov?

[VOITINSKII] I am communicating very secretly that tonight the Supreme Commander was in Pskov; from Pskov he left with General Krasnov for Ostrov, where he has taken the command of a cavalry division with which at the present time he is proceeding in the direction of Petrograd. The first echelon, in which the Supreme Commander and Krasnov are, has already passed Pskov and with great precautions is moving farther. I report with regard to the situation: [in the] 12th Army a detachment is being prepared to be sent to Petrograd, where Mazurenko and Fomin have gone from the Central Executive Committee; probably they will be entrusted with the leadership of the detachment. In the 1st Army matters are bad; there the army committee has proclaimed itself a military-revolutionary committee and has demonstrated its energy by sending away the temporary acting commissar, Smaltovskii. . . . In the 5th Army matters are more or less the same—exact information will be received from there later on. In the

[9] For additional materials on the activities of the truncated and semi-illegal Provisional Government after October 25, see M. Fleier, "Vremennoe Pravitel'stvo posle oktiabria," *KA*, VI (1924), 195–221.

Cossack units spirits are high—maybe even too high. In Pskov a bloodless war-fare is at present being waged between myself and the Military Revolutionary Committee, which has established control over the apparatuses with the exception of mine. They try to stop the echelons and intend to arrest me; nevertheless I managed to print several thousand copies of the order and of the proclamation. We have also managed to maintain contact with Petrograd and with all the parts of the front, and in the near future we think that we will manage also to get rid of the observation at the apparatuses. Contact has been established with the Luga Garrison, which has itself offered assistance; we managed to send the proclama-tion and the order by open radio-telegram. This, I think, is everything.

[VYRUBOV] Perekrestov, President of the All-Army Committee at Stavka, was present with me at our conversation.

1427. TELEGRAM FROM GENERAL DUKHONIN TO KERENSKY ON THE ORGANIZATION OF THE ARMED FORCES FOR THE SUPPRESSION OF THE REBELLION

["Oktiabr' na fronte," *KA*, XXIII (1927), 162.]

To the Supreme Commander Kerensky. Copy to the Commander in Chief of the Northern Front.

340. All the orders have been given. I have personally confirmed to the Com-mander in Chief of the Northern Front today the necessity for the exact execution of your Order No. 315. On the other fronts the attitude is calm. Together with the committees and the commissars we organize a further strengthening of our resources. October 27. 7962. DUKHONIN

1428. TELEGRAM FROM GENERAL V. A. CHEREMISOV RECOMMENDING THE NONINTERVENTION OF THE ARMY IN THE POLITICAL STRUGGLE

["Oktiabr' na fronte," *KA*, XXIII (1927), 176.]

To the Commanders of the 1st, 5th, 12th Armies, to the Commander of the 42nd Corps, to the Commander of the Fleet, to the Chief of the General Staff, to the Chief of Staff of the Supreme Commander.

The political struggle which takes place in Petrograd should not touch the army, whose task remains the same as before—to solidly hold the positions now occupied, maintaining order and discipline. October 27. No. 2003. CHEREMISOV.

1429. THE DON COSSACKS OFFER KERENSKY AND THE COUNCIL OF THE REPUBLIC ASYLUM AND SUPPORT IN THE STRUGGLE AGAINST THE BOLSHEVIKS

[*Razlozhenie armii*, p. 157.]

Stavka. To the Supreme Commander. To all armies, corps, and divisions.

The Don Cossack *Voisko* invites the Provisional Government and the members of the Council of the Republic to come to Novocherkassk, where it is possible to organize a struggle against the Bolsheviks, and where the personal safety of both is guaranteed. The Fourth Cavalry Corps, consisting of Terek and Kuban' Cossacks, welcomes the initiative of the Don Cossacks and offers its forces for the struggle against the Bolsheviks and the anarchy which reigns in the country; they are ready to sacrifice their lives for the salvation of the fatherland.[10]

BASHMAKOV, Commissar of the Corps
TARASOV, Chairman of the Corps Committee

October 27, 1917. No. 62.
[Received October 29.]

1430. PROCLAMATION FROM THE MILITARY REVOLUTIONARY COMMITTEE
"TO ALL THE PEOPLE"
[*Izvestiia*, No. 210, October 29, 1917, p. 2.]

Former Minister Kerensky, overthrown by the people, refuses to submit to the decision of the All-Russian Congress of Soviets and is making a criminal attempt to oppose the legal government, elected by the All-Russian Congress, the Soviet of People's Commissars. The front has refused to support Kerensky. Moscow has joined the side of the new government. In a whole series of other towns (Minsk, Mogilev, Khar'kov) the power has been transferred to the Soviets. Not a single infantry unit is opposing the workers' and peasants' government, which, in harmony with the adamant will of the army and the people, has entered into peace negotiations and has transferred the land to the peasants.

Like General Kornilov, the criminal enemy of the people has mustered only a few echelons of confused Cossacks and is attempting to deceive the people of Petrograd by fraudulent manifestoes.

We make a public announcement: If the Cossacks do not arrest Kerensky, who has deceived them, and continue to move toward Petrograd, the troops of the revolution will advance with full force in defense of the precious conquests of the revolution—peace and land.

Citizens of Petrograd! Kerensky has run out of town, abandoning you to the care of Kishkin, who once advocated the surrender of Petrograd to the Germans; to the care of Rutenberg, a Black Hundredist who sabotaged the food supply of the city; to the care of Pal'chinskii, who aroused the unanimous hatred of the whole democracy. Kerensky ran, dooming you to surrender to the Germans, to starvation, to a blood bath. The insurgent people arrested Kerensky's ministers and you have seen that public order and the food situation in Petrograd have only benefited from this. At the demand of the *pomeshchiki*, the capitalists, and the speculators, Kerensky is marching against you in order to return the land to the *pomeshchiki*, in order to resume the perilous, abhorred war. Citizens of Petrograd, we know that the vast majority of you are in favor of the government of the revolutionary people and are against the Kornilovites, led by Kerensky. Do not let yourselves be deceived by fraudulent declarations of the helpless bourgeois conspirators, who will be ruthlessly crushed.

Workers, soldiers, peasants, we demand of you revolutionary vigilance and revolutionary discipline.

The millions of the peasantry and of the army are with us.

The victory of the people's revolution is assured.

MILITARY REVOLUTIONARY COMMITTEE OF THE PETROGRAD
SOVIET OF WORKERS' AND SOLDIERS' DEPUTIES

Petrograd, October 28, 1917

[10] Kerensky received a similar personal telegram from the Acting Ataman of the Don Cossacks, Mitrofan Bogaevskii, inviting him to come to Rostov.

1431. Telegram from General Baranovskii to Kerensky on the Impossibility of Stopping the Movement of Troops Proceeding from
Finland to the Assistance of the Bolsheviks
in Petrograd
["Oktiabr' na fronte," *KA*, XXIV (1927), 79–80.]

To Gatchina. To the Supreme Commander.

162. The Staff of the Northern Front cannot take measures against the movement of rebellious troops from Finland because there is no contact with Finland.
Everywhere in Finland the Bolshevik revolutionary committees act. I suppose
that the detachments of the 428th Regiment will disperse in the same way as the
Petrograd detachments. Can you not attempt to direct an armored train to Finland
for the purpose of temporarily damaging the tracks, or take some other measures
by acting through Petrograd? Pskov. October 29. No. 2017. Baranovskii.

1432. Queries of the Commissar of the Northern Front Concerning
the Movement of Troops Directed to Be at the
Disposal of Kerensky at Gatchina
["Oktiabr' na fronte," *KA*, XXIV (1927), 80–81.]

Voitinskii, Commissar of the Northern Front, is speaking. Transmit, if possible immediately, to General Kondrat'ev the request of the Supreme Commander
to explain where the echelons of the 17th Corps of General Schilling are located,
and how many of them are on the way. Telegraph detailed information to Tsarskoe
as soon as possible. At the same time, take all necessary measures in order to
hasten the movement of the echelons. There is reason to fear that railway traffic
may stop; therefore it is necessary to hasten with the concentration of the troops.
In case of cessation of traffic, I request you to take in advance measures without
stopping at anything to guarantee the forward movement of our echelons. Send
a copy of this telegram to Baranovskii. Execute it immediately. [October 30.]
Voitinskii.

1433. "In Tsarskoe Selo and Gatchina"
[V. B. Stankevich, *Vospominaniia, 1914–1919 g.*, pp. 267–81.]

The next evening the news burst that Kerensky with troops was approaching
Petrograd. He was in Luga. He was in Gatchina. He was in Tsarskoe Selo. He
had already spoken by telephone with Petrograd. The news raised the spirits of
political circles. Animated attempts to organize the struggle against the Bolsheviks
were started. The same rumors were reflected by the extremely low spirits of the
Bolsheviks—as was demonstrated by their patrols in the streets; there were cases
of ladies disarming soldiers. The conviction of an early liquidation of the Bolsheviks grew with every hour—all the more so as news began to arrive from the
barracks regarding the discontent of the garrison with their new masters. Proposals to participate in an armed action against the Bolsheviks began literally to
pour in. There was information regarding the confusion in the midst of the
Military Revolutionary Committee itself. The Municipal Duma and the quarters
of the Peasant Union in the School of Law were entirely in our hands and constituted the center where public and armed action against the Bolsheviks was
being prepared.

On October 26 an engineer from the group of the "Edinstvo" who was unknown to me proposed that we attempt going by car to Kerensky. At first I looked upon this project as a [reckless] venture. But having thought over the situation and studied the map, I decided that the matter was not hopeless. With revolvers in our pockets, we drove through Kolpino to Tsarskoe Selo. . . .

. . .

We took a car and went to look for Kerensky. Immediately beyond Tsarskoe Selo we came across a cavalry detachment. At the sight of the silently irresolute appearance and attitude of the Cossacks my spirits sank at once. Moreover, the officers immediately requested me to speak to the Cossacks and to tell them that as yet not everyone in Petrograd was on the side of the Bolsheviks and that the Cossacks were not going against the whole people. . . .

After my speech, which was heard in silence, I was taken to Kerensky. He was with Krasnov in a hut, in a room where a sick woman was lying on the bed. My news regarding Petrograd—undoubtedly too optimistic, but it corresponded to all the data in our possession—gave courage to both Kerensky and Krasnov. Krasnov asked whether he could wait at least one more day before his further advance, because his Cossacks were tired and it was essential for him to await the infantry. My opinion was that if the forces were insufficient for an immediate offensive, it was possible to wait. I did not consider myself entitled to ask for detailed [information] as to the condition of the detachment, because the conversation was held in the presence of too many people. But I myself then had the impression that Krasnov had in his hands, in any case, the whole cavalry corps.

Having personally ascertained that Kerensky was near Petrograd, I returned and reached Petrograd only late in the evening [October 28]. I went immediately to the Committee to Save the Fatherland and the Revolution and was very pleased that during the day the organizational work had progressed immensely. The military committee had contacted almost all the units and considered itself to be the leader of a very considerable armed force. The question of action within the city was raised. But it was unanimously decided to wait at least one more day: every hour increased our strength and our organization, and, besides, my news that Kerensky's detachment would apparently start an offensive on Petrograd in a day also inclined in favor of waiting in order to deliver a coordinated blow.

I went home, leaving the military committee to decide organizational questions. Next day I learned that after my departure Polkovnikov and someone else came to the committee and brought the news that the Bolsheviks had set the disarmament of the junkers [military cadets] for the next day; that is, they intended to deliver a blow on our main forces. It was natural to prevent the blow. Therefore it was decided to start action immediately.

And actually from early morning [October 29] both rifle and artillery fire continued everywhere, especially near the Pavlovskii and Nikolaevskii Military Schools; this was the execution of the Bolshevik plan. Also the anti-Bolshevik forces developed their plan—for a time the telephone exchange and the telegraph were occupied and certain forces were grouped around the Mikhailovskii Engineering School, in the Engineer Fortress, where the center of the anti-Bolshevik uprising was located. But toward midday the Schools were routed, and the forces of the uprising, deprived of the support of their main cadres, the junkers, began noticeably to thin. Toward evening the failure of the uprising was obvious—already by around 4:00 o'clock I did not find anyone in the Mikhailovskii School, The failure of the uprising, the unexpected weakness of our forces, and the unexpected energy shown by the Bolsheviks seemed to us astounding. At any rate, the only hope that remained was in Kerensky's detachment.

. . .

Next day I decided to go again to Kerensky. A. R. Gots joined me. By the same road and with the same ventures we groped our way up to Tsarskoe Selo.

. . .

As Krasnov's staff was located in Tsarskoe, we first of all dropped in to see him. Krasnov did not say one word about the defects of Kerensky and only mentioned that Kerensky hurried him too much, since he could not start a further movement forward owing to lack of forces. The infantry was still absent and the Cossacks so few that Krasnov could not even take away with him the weapons which the garrison of Tsarskoe Selo had left in the barracks. But the main thing on which Krasnov insisted was the absence of infantry.

—The Cossacks don't want to go because they think they are being led against the people, as there is only infantry against them. Take what measures you want, but give us infantry; with just one battalion we can show them.

From the entourage of Krasnov we learned that Savinkov was carrying on an intensive agitation against Kerensky among the detachments.

Kerensky was in Gatchina, in the calm and hospitable palace. He was extremely pleased at our arrival and insisted that some of us remain with him.

—Because there is no one with me, except my young a.d.c.'s. And often it is necessary to make very responsible decisions.

Then he began to tell us of the deputation from Vikzhel'[11] which had just left him. With special indignation he recalled Planson, who had found it appropriate at this moment to catechize Kerensky and to enumerate his guilts and sins.

. . .

Animation reigned throughout the entire night in the Gatchina Palace. Krasnov's whole staff arrived; Savinkov arrived. Sessions between officers were taking place. Kerensky learned with displeasure that Chernov, who before that toured the Northern Front with great success, was arriving in Gatchina. Kerensky asked me to meet Chernov and to convince him to proceed farther immediately, if possible without coming to the Palace, in any case without trying to play any kind of role in Gatchina. This seemed to me to be superfluously suspicious and distrustful. I put Chernov in my room and even insisted that Kerensky should receive him. The conversation did not last long, but was very calm.

We hardly had time to return with Chernov to my room when Kerensky again summoned me. Savinkov was with him. It turned out that Savinkov came from an officer assembly of the Gatchina detachment with the proposal to confirm him as the commissar of the detachment. Kerensky asked me what I thought about it. I said that in my opinion this appointment was undesirable because we had a great many difficulties already and were not succeeding in getting any infantry. On the other hand, the name of Savinkov was so unpopular in the leftist circles

11 Vikzhel' attempted to bring about the formation of a socialist coalition government and threatened a railroad strike if the civil and armed struggle continued.

and committees that the news of his playing an active role in the detachment could definitely deprive us of all hopes [of getting] any infantry. Savinkov disagreed with me and tried to prove that the essential thing was to draw to our side the officer class which was on the side of Savinkov, as proved by his recent election. Kerensky interrupted our rather singular discussion, declaring that he confirmed Savinkov.

In my room I found Voitinskii, Semenov,[12] and a kind of suspicious-looking officer with a bandaged cheek, who asserted that the officers of the Gatchina Palace had organized a conspiracy against Kerensky, that he allegedly heard with his own ears how they said that at the first attempt of Kerensky to leave they would shoot him in the head. Naturally, I took it to be a complete absurdity and did not even tell Kerensky of it. But it describes the atmosphere in the Gatchina Palace.

. . .

Kerensky decided to call a conference [consisting of] Krasnov, Savinkov, the chief of staff of the detachment, the chairman of the Cossack Division Committee, and some others. The line of the controversy was immediately obvious. Savinkov insisted on fighting at all cost, agreeing as the last resort to negotiations only as a stratagem in order to gain time. At that time he was carried away by the idea of calling for help from the Poles of Dobvor-Musnitskii's corps. I developed the opposite point of view, trying to prove that a further continuation of the struggle would involve the complete disintegration of the front; one should find a working agreement at the expense of the maximum concessions possible. Krasnov did not show much interest in broad political prospects: he needed an armistice at all cost in view of the conditions of his detachment. The rest of the military expressed themselves firmly in the same sense. Kerensky was bowing to the inevitable and apparently agreed with me. The representatives of the Cossacks supported Krasnov. Anyway, whether as a stratagem or for the beginning of negotiations, the necessity of an armistice was indisputable and it was decided immediately to make such a proposal to the Bolsheviks. We started the compilation of the respective documents which on behalf of Krasnov were to be sent to the "headquarters of the mutineers," as Krasnov stubbornly called the Bolsheviks in his messages. I refused to go to the Bolsheviks with a white flag, because, with Kerensky, I considered that only military authorities could enter into negotiations forthwith. As for Kerensky himself, he was to secure the consent of the political groups. Therefore it was decided that I should immediately go secretly to Petrograd in order to carry on the negotiations. On the other hand, Kuz'min was to go with the white flag to the Bolsheviks.

. . .

1434. Kerensky Appoints Avksent'ev His Successor in Case of
"Possible Necessity"
[Alexander F. Kerensky, *The Catastrophe*, p. 359.]

. . .

On the same evening of November twelfth [N.S.], taking advantage of the arrival of a group of friends from Petrograd, I gave them a letter addressed to

---

[12] See G. Semenov's account of Gatchina and Kerensky's escape in his "Vospominaniia byvshego Esera," *Prozhektor*, Nos. 8-9 (1923), 28–31; also the account of V. A. Veiger-Redemeister in his "S Kerenskim v Gatchine," *PR*, IX (1923), 79–95.

N. D. Avksentieff, President of the Council of the Republic, transferring to him, in the event of "possible necessity," the rights and duties of premier of the Provisional Government, suggesting also the immediate filling of vacancies.

1435. The Decision to Arrest Kerensky, and His Escape

[N. Avdeev, "Vokrug 'Gatchiny,'" *KA*, IX (1925), 173, which includes a valuable collection of documents on Gatchina.]

. . . General Krasnov organized a delegation to Krasnoe Selo for the purpose of concluding an immediate armistice on the front until the result of Stankevich's mission were known. The delegation was composed exclusively of Cossacks, who in the evening [October 31] left for Krasnoe Selo. These delegates returned to Gatchina in the morning of November 1 . . . together with a delegation of sailors headed by Dybenko. The basic demand of the sailors was that Kerensky be surrendered unconditionally for the disposal of the Bolshevik authorities. The Cossacks agreed to this demand, because even before the return of their delegates during the night of October 31–November 1 . . . they decided to arrest Kerensky and had placed him under secret surveillance. Did the officers take part in deciding the question of Kerensky's arrest? Ensign Breze testified during his interrogation that the decision to arrest Kerensky had been taken by the Cossack committees, while Ensign Miller testified that the decision to arrest him was taken by the officers and soldiers of the Krasnov detachment.

Kerensky managed to escape from the Gatchina Palace dressed in the uniform of a sailor. In the materials which we are printing we find only a short notice to the effect that Kerensky fled from the Gatchina Palace around 3:00 P.M. on November 1 . . . but how he did it remains unknown. Regarding the circumstances of Kerensky's escape, the arrested General Krasnov gave interesting written testimony on November 1. . . .

1436. Krasnov's Account of Kerensky's Escape, Written November 1, 1917

[Submitted to the Bolsheviks after his arrest. L. D. Trotskii, *Oktiabr'skaia Revoliutsiia*, pp. 90–91.]

1917, November 1, 19 hours.

Today at about 15 hours the Supreme Commander (Kerensky) summoned me to him. He was very excited and nervous.

—General, he said, you have betrayed me . . . Here your Cossacks say definitely that they will arrest me and hand me over to the sailors . . .

—Yes, I answered. There are conversations on the subject and I know that there is no sympathy for you anywhere.

—But the officers say the same thing?

—Yes, the officers are especially dissatisfied with you.

—What should I do? I am compelled to suicide.

—If you're an honest man, you will go immediately to Petrograd carrying a white flag, and you will present yourself to the Revolutionary Committee, where you will negotiate as head of the Government.

—Yes, I will do it, General.

—I will give you an escort and will request that a sailor go with you.

—No, only not a sailor. Do you know that Dybenko is here?

—I do not know; who is Dybenko?

—He is my enemy.

—Well, what can we do? As you are playing a big game, you have to respond.

—Yes, but I will leave only by night.

—Why? This would be running away. Go calmly and openly, so that everybody can see that you are not running away.

—All right. Only give me a reliable escort.

—All right.

I went, summoned a Cossack of the 10th Don Cossack Regiment, Russkov, and ordered him to assign eight Cossacks for the escort of the Supreme Commander.

In half an hour the Cossacks came and said that Kerensky was absent, that he had run away. I gave the alarm and ordered that he be found; I suppose that he could not have run away from Gatchina and is concealed somewhere here.

MAJOR GENERAL KRASNOV
Commander of the Third Corps

1437. KRASNOV'S LATER ACCOUNT OF KERENSKY'S ESCAPE

[P. N. Krasnov, "Na vnutrennem fronte," *ARR*, I (1922), 172–74.]

. . .

In the morning of November 1 the negotiators came back and with them a crowd of soldiers. Our armistice was accepted and signed by the representative of the sailors, Dybenko, who came to visit us himself. Of enormous height, a handsome man with waving black curls, a black moustache, and a youthful beard, with large languid eyes and a rosy complexion, infectiously gay, his white teeth flashing, a joke always ready on his laughing lips, physically an athlete, with a flair for noble attitudes, he charmed in a few minutes not only the Cossacks but even many officers.

—Give us Kerensky and we will deliver Lenin to you. Let us exchange one ear for another! he said, laughing.

The Cossacks believed him. They came to me demanding the exchange of Kerensky for Lenin, whom they would immediately hang here near the Palace.

—Let them bring Lenin here and then we will speak, I said to the Cossacks and sent them away. Around midday Kerensky summoned me. He had heard of these conversations and was alarmed. He asked that the Cossack sentry post at his doors be replaced by a sentry post of junkers.

—Your Cossacks will betray me, said Kerensky with grief.

—They will betray me first, I said, and ordered the Cossack sentry post removed from the doors of Kerensky's apartment.

Something odious was going on. It stank of foul treason. The Bolshevik contamination had only touched the Cossacks, but they had already lost all notions of right and honor.

At 3:00 P.M. the committee of the 9th Don Regiment with Lieutenant Colonel Lavrukhin burst into my room. The Cossacks hysterically insisted on the surrender of Kerensky, whom they would take themselves under their own escort to Smol'nyi.

—Nothing of this will happen. We will not allow one hair on his head to be touched.

Evidently it was the demand of the Bolsheviks.

—Are you not ashamed, Cossacks? I said. You have already many crimes on your conscience, but the Cossacks have never been betrayers. Remember how your forefathers replied to the Tsars of Moscow: There is no handing over from the Don! Whatever he is, he will be judged by our Russian court and not by Bolsheviks.

—He is a Bolshevik himself!

—This is his business. But to betray a man who has put himself under our protection would be base, and you shall not do it.

—We will set our own sentry posts around him so that he will not escape. We will choose reliable people whom we can trust! shouted the Cossacks.

—All right, set them, I said.

When they left I went to see Kerensky. I found him deathly pale in a remote room of his apartment. I told him that the time had come for him to leave. The yard was full of sailors and Cossacks, but the Palace had also other exits. I pointed out that the sentinels stood only at the main entrance.

—However great your faults before Russia, I told him, I do not consider myself entitled to judge you. I guarantee you half an hour of time.

Leaving Kerensky, I arranged through reliable Cossacks that the sentry post not be assembled for a long time. When it appeared and went to inspect the quarters of Kerensky, Kerensky was not there. He had fled.

The Cossacks rushed to me. They were terribly aroused against me. There were voices calling for my arrest, saying that I had betrayed them by giving Kerensky the opportunity to escape.

．　．　．

1438. Miliukov's Assessment of the Conflicting Accounts

[P. N. Miliukov, *Istoriia vtoroi russkoi revoliutsiia*, I, vypusk 3, 276–77. See also N. Avdeev's similar comments in his "Vokrug 'Gatchiny,'" *KA*, IX (1925), 174.]

In his memoirs Kerensky asserts that "all this is absurdity and invention," and that he had not had any interview with Krasnov immediately before his flight.[13] The assertions of Kerensky are confirmed not only by the suspiciously theatrical tone of the harangue, which characterized also a part of the foregoing conversation, but also by the circumstance that in his original account, compiled when his memory was fresher, Krasnov did not say anything regarding his second conversation with Kerensky. There he told of Kerensky's flight as having been completely unexpected for him also. He described how, after the conversations cited above, which took place around midday, he had hardly the time to receive information with regard to the negotiations with the Cossacks, to send a telegram to Stavka, and to summon to the apparatus the Cossack commissar at Stavka, when in the room of the staff officers he met perplexed Cossacks and officers who told him that Kerensky had fled. "This news seemed to me completely incredible,"

---

[13] A. Kerenskii, "Gatchina," *Izdaleka*, p. 224 n. Although this earlier article is essentially the same as Chapter XVIII of his *The Catastrophe*, there is some material in each not included in the other.

said Krasnov in his original "Description."[14] "It was broad daylight, this corridor of the palace (the apartment of Kerensky faced two corridors; one exit was guarded, the other locked), the yard of the Palace and the square in front of it swarmed with Cossacks and soldiers. How was it possible for such a physically distinctive person as A. F. Kerensky to escape through all this swarm of people?" By his questioning Krasnov found out that Kerensky "left in a sailor jacket and blue spectacles."

Apparently [wishing] to cover himself before his superiors, Krasnov telegraphed to General Dukhonin at Stavka: "I ordered the arrest of the Supreme Commander; he managed to escape."

Obviously, from an order to arrest to assistance to escape there is a very long distance; and the only way out of this series of General Krasnov's inner contradictions is to recognize the account of Kerensky—which coincides with the original testimony of Krasnov himself—as the more correct. . . .

. . .

1439. TELEGRAM FROM VOITINSKII TO THE NORTHERN FRONT ANNOUNCING
THE DEPOSITION OF KERENSKY

["Oktiabr' na fronte," *KA*, XXIV (1927), 90. A similar telegram was sent by Dukhonin on the same day to all military and naval forces, announcing he had temporarily taken over the duties of Supreme Commander and calling upon the armed forces to remain at their posts and defend the country from the enemy pending settlement of the political crisis. See Bunyan and Fisher, p. 173.]

To Pskov—To the Commander in Chief of the Northern Front, to the Chief of Staff of the Northern Front, to the Deputy Commissar of the Northern Front, to the Chief of Military Communications of the Northern Front, to the Commissariat of the Northern Front.
November 1, 1917. From the 3rd Cavalry Corps.

An agreement has been reached between the troops concentrated near Petrograd and the representatives of the Petrograd Garrison on the basis of the deposition of Kerensky. Immediately instruct all the echelons moving to Petrograd to stop and to cease any kind of operations connected with the formation of Kerensky's detachment. VOITINSKII.

---

[14] In a footnote on pp. 241–42, Miliukov wrote: "An earlier account was printed by Krasnov in Velikie Luki in 1917 under the title 'Description of the Operations of the Third Cavalry Corps Against the Soviet Troops Near Petrograd.' A copy of this 'Description' was given to me by the author himself during the autumn of 1918 in Rostov; it was used by me in order to compile the text of my history and was left by me in Kiev when I left for Yassy in November 1918. Unfortunately, according to the words of General Krasnov, this copy was unique. Another account more detailed and picturesque but less documented and authentic was printed by Krasnov in the first volume of *Arkhiv Russkoi Revoliutsii*. . . ."

Source Abbreviations

Adamov, *Evropeiskie derzhavy i Gretsiia* — E. A. Adamov (ed.), *Evropeiskie dershavy i Gretsiia v epokhu Mirovoi Voiny po sekretnym dokumentam b. ministerstva inostrannykh del*

Adamov, *Konst. i prolivy* — E. A. Adamov (ed.), *Konstantinopol' i prolivy po sekretnym dokumentam b. ministerstva inostrannykh del*

Adamov, *Razdel* — E. A. Adamov (ed.), *Razdel Asiatskoi Turtsii po sekretnym dokumentam b. ministerstva inostrannykh del*

ARR — *Arkhiv Russkoi Revoliutsii*

Avdeev — N. Avdeev and others, *Revoliutsiia 1917 goda (Khronika sobytii)*

Dimanshtein — S. M. Dimanshtein (ed.), *Revoliutsiia i natsional'nyi vopros*

Ekon. Polozhenie — *Ekonomicheskoe Polozhenie Rossii Nakanune Velikoi Oktiabr'skoi Sotsialisticheskoi Revoliutsii*

For. Rel. of U.S. — *Papers Relating to the Foreign Relations of the United States*

GFO — Records of the German Foreign Office received by the Department of State

Golder — Frank Alfred Golder, *Documents of Russian History, 1914–1917*

Gos. Sov. — M. N. Pokrovskii and Ya. A. Yakovlev (eds.), *1917 god v dokumentakh i materialakh.* Vol. IX: *Gosudarstvennoe Soveshchanie*

KA — *Krasnyi Arkhiv*

Krest'ianskoe dvizhenie v 1917 godu — M. N. Pokrovskii and Ya. A. Yakovlev (eds.), *1917 god v dokumentakh i materialakh.* Vol. V: *Krest'ianskoe dvizhenie v 1917 godu*

Lozinskii, *Ekonomicheskaia Politika* — Z. Lozinskii, *Ekonomicheskaia Politika Vremennago Pravitel'stva*

Nikolaevskii — B. I. Nikolaevskii (ed.), "A Collection of Extracts from Menshevik Newspapers, 1917–1920"

Osobyi Zhurnal — *Osobyi Zhurnal Zasedanii Vremennago Pravitel'stva*

Padenie — *Padenie tsarskogo rezhima*

PR — *Proletarskaia Revoliutsiia*

Protokoly — M. N. Pokrovskii and Ya. A. Yakovlev (eds.), *1917 god v dokumentakh i materialakh.* Vol. I: *Petrogradskii Sovet Rabochikh i Soldatskikh Deputatov; Protokoly zasedanii Ispolnitel'nogo Komiteta i Biuro I.K.*

Rabochee dvizhenie v 1917 godu — M. N. Pokrovskii and Ya. A. Yakovlev (eds.), *1917 god v dokumentakh i materialakh.* Vol. VII: *Rabochee dvizhenie v 1917 godu*

Razlozhenie armii — M. N. Pokrovskii and Ya. A. Yakovlev (eds.), *1917 god v dokumentakh i materialakh.* Vol. VI: *Razlozhenie armii v 1917 godu*

Reports to the Department of State — North Winship, "U.S. Consulate Reports: Petrograd Revolution, Mar.–July, 1917"

Sb. Tsirk. MVD. — *Sbornik Tsirkuliarov Ministerstva Vnutrennikh Del za period Mart-Iiun' 1917 goda*

Sbor. Ukaz. — *Sbornik Ukazov i Postanovlenii Vremennago Pravitel'stva*

Sbornik sekretnykh dokumentov — *Sbornik sekretnykh dokumentov iz arkhiva byvshago ministerstva inostrannykh del*

Sob. Uzak. — *Sobranie Uzakonenii i Rasporiazhenii Pravitel'stva*

VVP — *Vestnik Vremennago Pravitel'stva*

Z Dok. Chwili — *Z Dokumentow Chwili*

Zhurnaly — *Zhurnaly Zasedanii Vremennago Pravitel'stva*

Glossary

Appanage lands	See *udel* lands.
Chin	Rank or grade in the Table of Ranks established by Peter the Great. All offices in the military or civil service were arranged in a hierarchical order of 14 classes. The first eight grades in the civil service conferred hereditary nobility, which was granted with the attainment of lowest commissioned rank in the military service.
Dessiatine	A Russian unit of area equal to 2.7 acres.
Duma	The Imperial State Duma was the national assembly created in 1906, and elected by limited suffrage. Four Dumas were elected before the February revolution. The municipal dumas were town councils, also chosen by limited suffrage. In the larger cities there were district dumas as well.
Gendarme Corps	A special police corps directly under and responsible to the Ministry of the Interior at the call of civil authorities for maintaining order. Also investigated political crimes, acted as railroad police, and supervised political prisons.
Gradonachal'nik	Town governor, or prefect, principally in charge of police matters, appointed only to the capitals and several other cities or areas.
Guberniya	A major administrative division of the Empire. Subdivided into uezds.
Hectare	A unit of area equal to 2.471 acres.
Inorodtsy	Russian subjects belonging to the following groups: the mountain peoples of the northern Caucasus, all Jews, the Siberian nomads, the Samoeds, the nomads of Stavropol' guberniya, natives of the Komandorskie Islands, the Kalmyks, and the Ordynsty of the Transcaspian oblast.
Kabinet	His Imperial Majesty's *Kabinet*. A section of the Ministry of the Imperial Court that was in charge of the Emperor's property, including lands, thus, *Kabinet* lands.
K.D.'s	Constitutional Democrats.
Khutor	Settlement on self-contained enclosed holdings, including the house and farm buildings of the peasant. The final step in the Stolypin agrarian program to abolish the commune in favor of individual farms.

Krai	A large administrative unit on the borderlands, composed of several guberniyas or oblasts and headed by a Governor General, as, for example, the Turkestan Krai.
Krug	Elected council of the Cossack *Voisko*.
Mezhduraionyi	The *Mezhduraionyi Komitet* was an autonomous organization of workers and professional revolutionaries in Petrograd, which included Trotsky, Lunacharskii, and Riazanov and which joined the Bolsheviks in July.
Oblast	A large administrative division, in the Caucasus, Central Asia, and the Far Eastern territory.
Obshchina	The peasant commune, sometimes called the *mir*.
Okhrana	The tsarist secret police.
Order of St. George	Founded by Catherine II for military service on land and sea. Had four classes, including one for noncommissioned officers, the St. George Cross.
Otrub	The consolidation of the individual strips belonging to a peasant, with the exception of his village plot and house. A step in the Stolypin reform to abolish the commune and establish individual peasant farms.
Pomeshchik	Originally a person granted land by the Tsar in return for service to the state. By 1917 used loosely to denote any landowner of the gentry class.
Pood	A Russian weight equivalent to 36.1 pounds avoirdupois.
Possessional lands	Term used to designate Tsar's lands in the western part of Russia (Poland and Belorussia) which were rented.
P.S.R.	Party of the Socialist Revolutionaries.
S.D.'s	Social Democrats. The two main branches of the Social Democratic Workers' Party were the Mensheviks and the Bolsheviks.
Sen'oren konvent	The Council of Elders or steering committee of the State Duma and later of the Provisional Council of the Russian Republic. Composed of the leaders of each of the parliamentary factions.
Sosloviia	Social classes or estates, see p. 210n.
S.R.'s	Socialist Revolutionaries.
State Control	A ministry which checked all ministerial estimates and audited the books of government institutions, with some few exceptions.
Stavka	The Headquarters of the Supreme Commander.

Trudoviks	The Trudovik Group was organized in the First Duma and included peasant deputies, radical intelligentsia, members of the Peasant Union, and the Socialist Revolutionaries. Had a definite agrarian program. Kerensky was the leader of the Group in the Fourth Duma.
Tsenzovyi	From *izbiratel'nyi tsenz*, literally "electoral qualification." See p. 131n.
Udel lands	Lands which provided financial support for members of the Imperial family other than the immediate family of the Tsar. Administered by a department under the Ministry of the Imperial Court.
Uezd	An administrative subdivision of the guberniya.
Verst	A Russian measure of distance, about two-thirds of a mile.
Voinskii nachal'nik	An officer in charge of the district military administrative office.
Voisko	A Cossack army or host, included civil as well as military institutions.
Volost	A peasant administrative division of the uezd, which usually included several communes.
VTsIK	All-Russian Central Executive Committee of the Soviets of Workers' and Soldiers' Deputies.
Zemgor	The joint Committee of the Unions of Zemstvos and of Towns for the Supply of the Army, organized in July 1915.
Zemskie nachal'niki	Agents of the central government, appointed from the gentry class, with judiciary and administrative authority over the peasants.
Zemsoiuz	The Union of Zemstvos.
Zemstvo	The elective assembly of the guberniya and uezd in which all classes were to some extent represented. It elected an executive board (*uprava*). Created by the local government reform of 1864.

Chronology

(All dates are Old Style)

1916. NOVEMBER

1   Opening of the Fifth Session of the Fourth Imperial State Duma.

1   Miliukov's speech in the Duma.

10   Stürmer's resignation and the appointment of Trepov as Chairman of the Council of Ministers.

19   Speech of Purishkevich in the State Duma.

DECEMBER

16–17   Assassination of Rasputin.

27   Nomination of Prince Golitsyn as Chairman of the Council of Ministers.

1917. JANUARY

26   Arrest of members of the Workers' Group in the Central War Industry Committee.

31   Strikes and meetings in factories in Petrograd.

FEBRUARY

1   Continued strikes and meetings in Petrograd factories.

5   Order separating the Petrograd Military District from the Northern Front and subordinating it to General Khabalov, who is invested with special powers to maintain order.

10   Last report by the President of the Duma, M. V. Rodzianko, to the Tsar on the situation in the country and the need for a new ministry based on public confidence.

14   Duma resumes sessions after Christmas recess.

15   25,000 workers in Petrograd on strike in 15 plants. Demonstrations of workers.

18   Strike in the Putilov factory begins.

19   Beginning of bread shortage in Petrograd.

22   Lockout of workers of the Putilov works. Tsar leaves for Stavka.

23   General Khabalov announces there should be no bread shortage. Emergency conference in Mariinskii Palace of the Presidium of the Duma,

ministers, and representatives of the Petrograd municipality on the food shortage. Strikes spread to more plants. Demonstrations. Streetcar transportation disrupted. First clashes with the police.

24 About 200,000 workers on strike in Petrograd. Demonstration on the Nevskii Prospekt. First shots near Liteinyi Prospekt and near Znamenskaia Square. Cossacks called out.

25 General strike in Petrograd. Troops and Cossacks guard streets. Schools closed. Shooting in many parts of the city. Newspapers shut down.

26 Number of demonstrators mounts. Government occupies bridges across the Neva, places machine guns on roofs, and barbed wire in the streets. Some casualties. Rodzianko telegraphs Emperor reporting rioting in capital and urging the formation of a government of confidence. Late in the evening Rodzianko receives an Imperial ukase dissolving the Duma.

27 Mutiny of the Guards reserve regiments, which then occupy the Arsenal and the Peter and Paul Fortress and march to the Duma. The Duma accepts prorogation but decides not to disperse. Delegations from various regiments pledge loyalty to the Duma. Second telegram from Rodzianko to the Emperor. Conference of members of the Duma resolves to form a Temporary Committee. Formation of Petrograd Soviet of Workers' Deputies. Imperial ministers and other high officials arrested. Khabalov informs Stavka he cannot restore order.

27 Prince Golitsyn resigns. Temporary Committee of the Duma announces it has taken power to restore state and public order.

28 Emperor leaves Stavka for Tsarskoe Selo, but by orders of Temporary Committee to railroad employees he is forced to turn back. Orders his train rerouted to Pskov. Admiralty with rest of loyal troops capitulates. Formation of a Military Commission. Joint Food Commission of Duma and Soviet is formed and issues bread ration cards for Petrograd. Appointment by Temporary Committee of special commissars to ministries. Formation of Moscow Soviet.

MARCH

1 Executive Committee of the Petrograd Soviet votes not to participate in the new government. Beginning of negotiations between Duma and Soviet representatives on the bases of new government. Order No. 1 published by the Soviet. British and French ambassadors recognize the authority of the Temporary Committee *de facto*.

2 Tsar abdicates for himself and his son in favor of his brother Grand Duke Mikhail Aleksandrovich. Provisional Government formed and its program agreed upon with the Soviet.

3 Grand Duke Mikhail Aleksandrovich refuses to accept the throne. Provisional Government publishes its program. Soviet demands the immediate arrest of members of the Romanov family.

4 Formation of Ukrainian Central Rada in Kiev. Ukase on abolishing courts with estate representatives. Abolition of Gendarmes Corps and

the Okhrana. Law establishing an Extraordinary Commission to investigate malfeasance of officials of the old regime. Removal of Imperial governors and vice-governors and the designation of chairmen and vice-chairmen of guberniya zemstvo boards as commissars of the Provisional Government. Abolition of Jewish quotas in educational institutions and the restoration of rights of former students dismissed for political reasons.

5 Petrograd Soviet authorizes the cessation of strikes and the return to work. Appointment of a special commissar to guard Imperial family at Tsarskoe Selo. War Ministry Order No. 114 abolishing certain restrictions on soldiers.

6 War Ministry order establishing Polivanov Commission. End of strikes in Petrograd. Ukase on amnesty for political prisoners.

7 Restoration of the Constitution of the Grand Duchy of Finland. Government decrees arrest of the former Emperor and Empress.

8 Establishment of the Liaison Commission. Arrest of the Emperor in Mogilev and the Empress at Tsarskoe Selo.

9 Establishment of the Special Transcaucasian Committee. Arrival of Nicholas II at Tsarskoe Selo. Holy Synod appeals to the people to support the new government. Recognition of the Provisional Government by the United States. State Committee on Food Supply formed.

10 Abolition of the Department of Police and creation of a temporary office to replace it. Agreement between Petrograd manufacturers and the Soviet introducing the eight-hour day and factory committees.

11 Recognition of the Government by France, Great Britain, and Italy. Dismissal of Grand Duke Nikolai Nikolaevich as Supreme Commander and the appointment of General Alekseev.

12 Stalin returns from Siberian exile. Abolition of the death penalty.

13 Abolition of field courts-martial.

14 Authorization of the use of the Ukrainian language for instruction in the schools of the Ukraine. Order to re-establish Cossack self-government. Appeal of the Soviet "To the Peoples of All the World" on the struggle for peace.

16 Transfer of the properties of the Imperial family to the State. Proclamation on the independence of Poland.

17 Mitigation of the punishments for common crimes committed before the revolution. Abolition of brutal prison practices.

19 Law on the preparation for the land reform.

20 Law removing all restrictions on cooperatives and their unions. Suspension of the activities of the *zemskie nachal'niki*. Abolition of all religious and nationality discriminations.

22 Battle of Stokhod. Establishment of the Juridical Council.

23 Funeral in Petrograd for victims of the revolution.

24 Introduction of bread rationing in Petrograd.

25 Law on the formation of the Commission for the restoration of the Judicial Charters of 1864. Establishment of a Special Council to draft the electoral law for the Constituent Assembly. Establishment of the grain monopoly and local food supply committees. Seventh Congress of the Party of the People's Freedom votes for a democratic republic.

27 Declaration of the Government on war aims. Law on the Liberty Loan of 1917. Law on the autocephaly of the Georgian Orthodox Church.

29 Opening of the Finnish Sejm. Opening of the All-Russian Conference of Soviets of Workers' and Soldiers' Deputies.

30 Law on local self-government in Estonia.

31 Arrival of the French and English socialists in Petrograd.

APRIL

1 Resolution of the All-Russian Conference of Soviets to support the Provisional Government in so far as it fulfills its democratic program.

3 Arrival in Petrograd of Lenin, Zinoviev, and others from Switzerland via Germany.

4 Unity conference of Bolshevik and Menshevik factions of the Social Democratic Party is unsuccessful. Lenin announces his April Theses. Ukase of the Government to prosecute deserters unless they return to duty voluntarily by May 15.

7 Publication of Lenin's April Theses. Congress of Railroadmen to organize All-Russian Railroad Union.

8 Government authorizes the use of troops to put down agrarian disorders.

9 Arrival of Albert Thomas in Petrograd.

11 Law on the protection of crops.

12 Law on the freedom of assembly.

15 Law on elections to municipal dumas and the organization of district dumas in large cities. April 18 (May 1) declared an official holiday.

16 Order on the status of army committees and on military disciplinary courts.

17 Law on the formation of the militia.

18 Miliukov sends the Allies the text of the Government's declaration on war aims of March 27 with an accompanying note.

20 Workers' and soldiers' demonstrations in Petrograd against Miliukov's note. Counterdemonstration by Miliukov's supporters.

20-21 Government and Soviet negotiate and agree on a supplemental explanation of the Miliukov note.

21 Resolution of the Petrograd Soviet to stop all demonstrations. Law on the formation of land committees.

22 Petrograd Soviet votes to support the Liberty Loan.

23 Law on factory committees.

24 All-Russian (April) Conference of Bolsheviks opens. Law on the establishment of coeducational *gymnasia, pro-gymnasia,* and *real* schools.

26 Government's declaration on the state of the nation and on the necessity for expanding its membership to form a coalition. Publication of Kerensky's letter on a coalition. Law abolishing deportation to Siberia.

27 Prince L'vov's letter to Chkheidze and Rodzianko on a coalition government. Law on the freedom of the press. Meeting of the members of the four Imperial State Dumas.

MAY

1 Resignation of Guchkov as Minister of War. Executive Committee of the Soviet votes to approve participation of representatives of the socialist parties in the Government.

3 Miliukov resigns.

4 Opening of the All-Russian Congress of Peasants' Soviets.

5 Formation of the first coalition Provisional Government. Laws on the founding of the Don University, the Tiflis Polytechnical Institute, and Perm' University. Establishment of the Ministries of Food, Labor, Welfare, and Post and Telegraph.

6 Publication of the declaration of the new government. Ukrainian Military Congress declares for the autonomy of the Ukraine.

7 The All-Russian Conference of the Social Democratic Party (Menshevik) votes to support the coalition government.

9 Eighth Congress of the Party of the People's Freedom. Law on an all-Russian agriculture and land census and on an urban census. Grant of academic autonomy to the Academy of Science.

11 Declaration of Soldiers' Rights.

16–25 Kronstadt Soviet refuses to recognize the authority of the Government, but agreement is reached after the mission of Tseretelli and Skobelev to the fortress.

20 Minister of Trade and Industry Konovalov resigns. Arthur Henderson arrives in Petrograd.

21 Law on elections of guberniya and uezd zemstvo members. Law on volost zemstvos.

22 General Brusilov appointed to succeed General Alekseev as Supreme Commander.

25 Opening of the Special Council to draft an electoral law for the Constituent Assembly. Opening of the Third Congress of the Socialist Revolutionary Party.

26 Disbandment of four regiments for their refusal to go into action.

28 Law introducing juries in military courts.

30   All-Ukrainian Peasant Congress declares for a federated Russian republic and Ukrainian autonomy. First Petrograd Conference of Factory Committees supports introduction of workers' control in production and distribution of goods.

31   Arrival in Petrograd of the Root Mission from the United States. Tereshchenko sends note to the Allies proposing a conference to re-examine war aims.

JUNE

1   Admission of women to the bar.

2   Government orders the deportation of the Swiss Socialist Robert Grimm.

3   First All-Russian Congress of Soviets of Workers' and Soldiers' Deputies opens in Petrograd.

6   Central Committee of the Black Sea Fleet demands the resignation of the Commander of the Fleet, Admiral Kolchak.

7   All-Russian Cossack Congress opens in Petrograd. Law on the All-Russian Zemstvo Union.

9   Congress of Soviets forbids the demonstration called by the Bolsheviks for June 10.

10   First Universal of the Ukrainian Rada.

12   Enactment of an extraordinary income tax levy and an increase in the rates of the income tax.

14   Government sets August 17 for elections to the Constituent Assembly and August 30 for its convocation.

16   Kerensky's order on the offensive.

17   The extension of zemstvo institutions to the oblasts of Akmolinsk, Semipalatinsk, Semirechensk, Turgaisk, and Uralsk, the guberniya of Arkhangel'sk, and Siberia.

18   Russian offensive begins. Early successes. Soviet demonstration in Petrograd, in which Bolshevik slogans predominate.

19   Congress of Soviets passes resolution supporting the offensive.

21   Establishment of the Economic Council and the Central Economic Committee by the Provisional Government. All-Russian Conference of Trade Unions opens in Petrograd.

22   Circular of the Minister of Education on the gradual reform of Russian orthography.

24   Introduction of student self-government in institutions of higher learning.

25   Elections to the Moscow Municipal Duma.

27   Appeal of the Minister of Labor to the workers to refrain from arbitrary actions.

JULY

1   Delegation from the Government consisting of Kerensky, Tseretelli, and Tereshchenko reaches agreement in Kiev with the Ukrainian Rada on regional self-government. Introduction of zemstvo institutions in the oblasts of Transcaspia, Samarkand, Syr-Dar'ia, and Ferghana, in the Kalmyk Steppe and the Kirghiz Inner Horde of the guberniya of Astrakhan', and among the nomadic *inorodtsy* in Stavropol' guberniya.

2   Kadet ministers resign from the Government. Beginning of Government crisis.

3   Armed demonstrations in Petrograd under the Bolshevik slogan "All Power to the Soviets." Shooting in streets. Conference of Bolsheviks votes to support and lead the demonstration.

4   Kronstadt sailors arrive to join demonstration. Siege of Tauride Palace and the Soviet Central Committees. Prince L'vov orders the use of force to suppress the movement. Release, during the night, of evidence on German-Bolshevik financial collaboration. Lenin goes into hiding.

5   Bolshevik headquarters and newspapers raided and closed. Beginning of German counteroffensive. Finnish Sejm votes to assume state power. Second Universal of Ukrainian Central Rada.

6   Government orders arrest of Bolshevik and other leaders of the uprising. German breakthrough at Ternopol'. Arrival in Petrograd of troops ordered by the Government from the front.

7   Prince L'vov resigns. Government orders the disbandment of military units that participated in the July uprising.

8   Kerensky accepts Minister-Presidency, then leaves for the front. Publication of declaration by the Government.

10   Joint meeting of VTsIK and the Executive Committee of Peasants' Soviets declares Provisional Government the Government to Save the Revolution. Russian troops retreating on Southwestern Front.

12   Government restores the death penalty at the front. Government decides to convene the Moscow Conference. Law restricting transactions in land.

13   Kerensky begins reorganization of the Government.

14   Law on the freedom of conscience.

16   Secret conference of Kerensky and Tereshchenko with military commanders at Stavka. Chernov circular to land committees.

17   Circular of Acting Minister of the Interior Tseretelli to government commissars ordering firm measures against disorders and arbitrary seizures of land.

18   Appointment of General Kornilov as Supreme Commander replacing General Brusilov. Government orders dissolution of the Finnish Sejm and the holding of new elections on October 1–2. Savinkov appointed Assistant Minister of War.

19 Pope's peace proposal to Western Allies and Central Powers. Holy Synod schedules opening of the Church Sobor for August 15.

20 Chernov resigns from the Government.

21 Kerensky resigns from the Government because of his inability to form a new ministry. Conference of party and other political leaders on the crisis decides to give Kerensky a free hand to form a new Government.

22 Kerensky accepts task of reorganizing the Government and begins negotiations. Prosecutor of Petrograd Court of Appeals releases evidence from the inquest on the Bolsheviks and charges them with armed revolt and German collaboration.

23 Announcement of the composition of the second coalition Provisional Government.

26 Opening of the Sixth Congress of the Bolshevik Party in Petrograd.

27 Law on the freedom of the Roman Catholic Church in Russia.

28 Law granting the Ministers of War and Interior the right to close meetings and assemblies.

AUGUST

1 Departure of Nicholas II and family to Tobolsk.

3 Kornilov arrives in Petrograd to discuss his program with the Government and announces that the combat potential of the army is improving.

4 Government issues the Temporary Instruction to the Ukrainian General Secretariat.

5 Establishment of the Ministry of Confessions.

8 Opening in Moscow of the First Congress of Public Leaders.

9 Postponement of elections to the Constituent Assembly to November 12 and its convocation to November 28.

10 Conference of Kerensky, Nekrasov, and Tereshchenko with Kornilov on proposed army reforms.

12 Opening of the Moscow Conference.

15 All-Russian Church Sobor opens in Moscow. Moscow Conference ends.

16–19 Threatened railroad strike, which is eventually canceled.

19 Germans break through the front at Riga.

20 Kornilov orders the evacuation of Riga.

21 Germans occupy Riga. Government decides to put Petrograd Military District under the jurisdiction of the Supreme Commander and to dispatch a cavalry corps to the capital to be at its disposal.

24 Kornilov-Savinkov agreement at Stavka on the reorganization of the Northern Front and the sending of a cavalry detachment to Petrograd.

25 Provisional Government orders the evacuation from Petrograd and its environs of nonessential persons and institutions.

26 Resignation of Minister of Food Peshekhonov. Kerensky receives V. N. L'vov with demands from Kornilov.

27–30 Revolt of General Kornilov.

27 Organization of the Committee for the People's Struggle Against Counter-revolution. Savinkov appointed Governor General of Petrograd. Law doubling fixed prices on grain.

28 Kadet ministers submit their resignations.

29 Chief Navy Prosecutor Shablovskii appointed President of an Extraordinary Commission of Inquiry on the Kornilov Affair. Ukase on the arraignment of Kornilov and his associates.

30 Kerensky appointed Supreme Commander and General Alekseev Chief of Staff. Appointment of Admiral Verderevskii as Minister of the Navy and General Verkhovskii as Minister of War. Rescript of the Government extending the jurisdiction of the Finnish Senate.

31 Bolshevik resolution passed in the Petrograd Soviet.

SEPTEMBER

1 Arrest of Generals Kornilov, Lukomskii, and Romanovskii at Stavka. Proclamation of the Republic. Council of Five formed.

3 Senate refuses to publish Government's ukase proclaiming a Republic.

4 Kerensky orders the dissolution of organizations and committees formed to combat the Kornilov revolt.

5 Moscow Soviet passes Bolshevik resolution.

6 Appointment of Nekrasov as Governor General of Finland.

9 Petrograd Soviet reaffirms Bolshevik resolution. Presidium resigns.

10 General Dukhonin appointed Chief of Staff to the Supreme Commander, replacing General Alekseev.

11 Maslov appointed Minister of Agriculture.

12 Large-scale disorders in Tashkent. Outbreaks in Ufa, Tambov, and other provincial centers.

14 Introduction of the sugar monopoly. Opening of the Democratic Conference in Petrograd. Transformation of Petrograd workers' militia into Red Guards.

18–19 Elections to the Finnish Sejm.

19 Democratic Conference's vote on the composition of the new government is inconclusive. Moscow Soviet elects a Bolshevik Executive Committee.

20 German fleet begins operations to capture Gulf of Riga.

21 All-Russian Union of Railroadmen calls a strike to begin at midnight September 23–24.

24 Strike of railroad workers begins. Law to increase wages and improve food supplies for railroad workers. Victory of Bolsheviks in Moscow Municipal Duma elections.

25　Trotsky elected President of the Petrograd Soviet. New coalition government formed.

26　Railroad workers call off their strike.

OCTOBER

1　Germans occupy islands in the Gulf of Riga.

3　Senate refuses to accept the Instruction to the Ukrainian Secretariat General.

4　Naval battle with German fleet off Gulf of Riga; Russian fleet retreats to Gulf of Finland after losses.

6　Dissolution of the State Duma and the State Council.

7　Provisional Council of the Russian Republic opens. Bolsheviks withdraw after Trotsky reads their declaration opposing participation. Publication of VTsIK's Instructions to Skobelev, its delegate to the Allied Conference.

10　Meeting of the Central Committee of the Bolshevik Party attended by Lenin votes for an armed uprising to seize power.

12　Second Congress of Public Leaders opens in Moscow. Petrograd Soviet resolves to organize a Military Revolutionary Committee.

14　Tenth Kadet Party Congress opens.

22　Minister of War Verkhovskii released from duties following his report in the Provisional Council. Military Revolutionary Committee tells Petrograd Garrison to disregard orders of the District Military Staff.

24　Kerensky goes before the Provisional Council to report the beginning of a Bolshevik uprising and to request a vote of confidence. Council passes resolution late in the evening which recommends the transfer of all lands to the land committees and the initiation of peace negotiations.

25　Detachments of the Military Revolutionary Committee seize strategic points in Petrograd. Kerensky leaves for the front at noon. Other ministers arrested in the Winter Palace late in the evening. Second Congress of Soviets opens at Smol'yni. Provisional Government is declared deposed.

26　Formation of the Committee to Save the Fatherland and the Revolution.

27　Kerensky and General Krasnov's cavalry occupy Gatchina.

28　Kerensky's troops occupy Tsarskoe Selo.

29　Military cadets' uprising suppressed by Bolsheviks in Petrograd.

30　Engagement with Bolshevik units near Pulkovo. Kerensky's units retreat to Gatchina.

31　Kerensky and military and civilian advisers decide to suspend military operations and to seek an armistice.

NOVEMBER

1　Kerensky flees Gatchina in disguise on learning of Cossack intentions to turn him over to the Bolsheviks.

Bibliography

With some few exceptions the Bibliography includes only works used or cited in these volumes. As elsewhere, the abbreviations *ARR, KA,* and *PR* have been used for *Arkhiv Russkoi Revoliutsii, Krasnyi Arkhiv,* and *Proletarskaia Revoliutsiia.*

Adamov, E. A. (ed.). *Evropeiskie derzhavy i Gretsiia v epohku Mirovoi Voiny po sekretnym dokumentam b. ministerstva inostrannykh del.* Narodnyi Komissariat Inostrannykh Del. Moscow, 1922.

———. *Konstantinopol' i prolivy po sekretnym dokumentam b. ministerstva inostrannykh del.* Narodnyi Komissariat Inostrannykh Del. Moscow, 1925–26. 2 vols.

———. *Razdel Asiatskoi Turtsii po sekretnym dokumentam b. ministerstva inostrannykh del.* Narodnyi Komissariat Inostrannykh Del. Moscow, 1924.

Alexander, Grand Duke of Russia. *Once a Grand Duke.* New York, 1932.

America's Message to the Russian People: Addresses by the Members of the Special Diplomatic Mission of the United States to Russia in the Year 1917. Boston, 1918.

Antisferov, Alexis N., Alexander D. Bilimovich, Michael O. Batshev, and Dimitry N. Ivantsov. *Russian Agriculture During the War.* Social and Economic History of the World War: Russian Series. New Haven, 1930.

Arkhiv Russkoi Revoliutsii. Berlin, 1921–37. 22 vols.

Aronson, G. "Sud'ba professional'nogo soiuza sluzhashchikh v 1917–20 gg." Ms. in the Hoover Institution.

Avdeev, N. (ed.). "Vokrug 'Gatchiny.'" *KA,* IX (1925), 171–94.

Avdeev, N., and others (eds.). *Revoliutsiia 1917 goda (Khronika sobytii).* Moscow, 1923–30. 6 vols.

Benckendorff, Count Paul. *Last Days at Tsarskoe Selo.* London, 1927.

Bibliografiia russkoi revoliutsii i grazhdanskoi voiny (1917–1921). Yana Slavik, ed. Prague, 1938.

Bilmanis, Alfred. *A History of Latvia.* Princeton, 1951.

Bilyk, P. (ed.). "V tsarskoi armii nakanune fevral'skoi burzhuazo-demokraticheskoi revoliutsii." *KA,* LXXXI (1937), 105–20.

Birzhevyia Vedomosti. Daily newspaper. Petrograd, 1917.

Bronch-Bruevich, V. D. *Na boevykh postakh fevral'skoi i oktiabr'skoi revoliutsii.* 2nd ed. Moscow, 1931.

Buat, General. *L'Armée Allemande pendant la guerre de 1914–1918.* Paris, 1920.

Buchanan, Sir George. *My Mission to Russia and Other Diplomatic Memories.* London, 1923. 2 vols.

Buchanan, Meriel. *The Dissolution of an Empire.* London, 1932.

"Bukhara v 1917 godu." *KA,* XX (1927), 78–122.

Bukhbinder, N. "Na fronte v predoktiabr'skie dni: po sekretnym materialam Stavki." *Krasnaia Letopis',* VI (1923), 9–63.

Bulygin, Paul, and A. F. Kerensky. *The Murder of the Romanovs.* London, 1935.

Bunyan, James, and H. H. Fisher. *The Bolshevik Revolution, 1917–1918: Documents and Materials.* Stanford, 1934.

Bykov, P. M. *The Last Days of Tsardom.* London, 1937.

"Bylevskii Papers." Ms. in the Hoover Institution.

Byloe. Journal devoted to the history of the Russian revolution and social movement. New series. Petrograd, 1917–26. Irregular numeration. 35 nos.

Catalogue méthodique de fonds russe de la Bibliothèque. Alexandra Dumesnil, ed., avec la collaboration de Wilfred Lerat. Catalogues des "Bibliothèque et Musée de la Guerre." Paris, 1932.

Chaadaeva, O. (ed.). "Soiuz zemel'nykh sobstvennikov v 1917 godu." *KA*, XXI (1927), 97–121.

Chamberlin, William. *The Russian Revolution, 1917–1921.* New York, 1935. 2 vols.

Charques, Richard. *The Twilight of Imperial Russia.* London, 1958.

Chernov, V. "Ts. K-t P.S.R. na rubezhe dvukh revoliutsii." Ms. in the Hoover Institution.

Chernov, Victor. *The Great Russian Revolution.* New Haven, 1936.

La Chute du Régime Tsariste: Interrogatoires. Préface de B. Maklakoff. Paris, 1927.

Curtiss, John Sheldon. *The Russian Church and the Soviet State, 1917–1950.* Boston, 1953.

Czernin, Count Ottokar. *In the World War.* London, 1920.

Daily Review of the Foreign Press. Issued daily by the General Staff, War Office. London, 1917.

Daily Telegraph and Morning Post. London, 1956.

Dan, F. "K istorii poslednikh dnei Vremennogo Pravitel'stva." *Letopis' Revoliutsii,* I (1923), 161–76.

Danilov, Youri. *La Russie dans la guerre mondiale, 1914–1917.* Paris, 1927.

Delo Naroda. Daily newspaper. Organ of the Central Committee of the Socialist Revolutionary Party. Petrograd, 1917.

Dem'ianov, A. "Moi sluzhba pri Vremennom Pravitel'stve." *ARR*, IV (1922), 55–129.

Den'. Daily newspaper. Organ of socialist thought. Petrograd, 1917.

Denikin, General A. I. *Ocherki Russkoi Smuty.* Paris, 1921–26. 5 vols.

———. *The Russian Turmoil.* London, 1922.

Dimanshtein, S. M. (ed.). *Revoliutsiia i natsional'nyi vopros.* Moscow, 1930.

"Dokumenty k 'Vospominaniiam' gen. A. Lukomskago." *ARR*, III (1922), 247–71.

Ekonomicheskoe Polozhenie Rossii Nakanune Velikoi Oktiabr'skoi Sotsialisticheskoi Revoliutsii. Akademiia Hauk SSSR. Moscow, 1957. 2 vols.

Epstein, Klaus. *Matthias Erzberger and the Dilemma of German Democracy.* Princeton, 1959.

———. "The Development of German-Austrian War Aims in the Spring of 1917." *Journal of Central European Affairs,* XVII (1957), 24–47.

Erzberger, M. *Souvenirs de guerre.* Paris, 1921.

"Fevral'skaia revoliutsiia i okhrannoe otdelenie." *Byloe,* No. 1 (1918), 158–76.

"Fevral'skaia revoliutsiia 1917 goda." *KA*, XXI (1927), 3–78; XXII (1927), 3–70.

"Fevral'skaia revoliutsiia v Baltiiskom flote (Iz dnevnika I. I. Rengartena)." *KA*, XXXII (1929), 99–124.

"Fevral'skaia revoliutsiia v Petrograde." *KA*, XLI–XLII (1930), 62–102.

Fleier, M. (ed.). "Vremennoe Pravitel'stvo posle oktiabria." *KA*, VI (1924), 195–221.

Fleier, M. G. "Pen'sionnaia praktika Vremennogo Pravitel'stva." *KA*, VIII (1925), 246–50.

Florinsky, M. T. *The End of the Russian Empire.* New Haven, 1931.

Forster, Kent. *The Failures of Peace.* Washington, D.C., 1942.

Galuzo, P. (ed.). "Iz istorii natsional'noi politiki Vremennogo Pravitel'stva." *KA*, XXX (1928), 46–79.

Gankin, Olga Hess, and H. H. Fisher. *The Bolsheviks and the World War: The Origins of the Third International.* Stanford, 1940.

Garvi, P. "Profsoiuzy Rossii v pervye gody revoliutsii." Ms. in the Hoover Institution.

———. "Rabochaia Kooperatsiia v pervye gody russkoi revoliutsii 1917–1921." Ms. in the Hoover Institution.

Gelis, Iosif (ed.). "Revoliutsionnaia propaganda v armii v 1916–1917 gg." *KA*, XVII (1926), 36–50.

———. "Romanovy i soiuzniki v pervye dni revoliutsii." *KA*, XVI (1926), 44–52.

Gilliard, Pierre. *Imperator Nikolai i Ego Semia.* Vienna, n.d.

Glavnyi Zemel'nyi Komitet. *Trudy Komissii po podgotovke zemel'noi reformy.* Petrograd, 1917–18. 5 parts.

Golder, Frank Alfred. *Documents of Russian History.* New York, 1927.

Golos Minuvshago na Chuzhoi Storone. Literary and historical journal. 1926–28. Irregular numeration. 6 nos.

Golovine, Lieutenant-General Nicholas N. *The Russian Army in the World War.* Economic and Social History of the World War: Russian Series. New Haven, 1931.

Great Britain, House of Commons. *Parliamentary Debates.* 1917.

Grenard, Fernand. *La Révolution russe.* Paris, 1933.

Gronsky, Paul P., and Nicholas J. Astrov. *The War and the Russian Government.* Economic and Social History of the World War: Russian Series. New Haven, 1929.

Gurevich, V. "Vserossiiskii Krest'ianskii Sezd i pervaia koalitsiia." *Letopis' Revoliutsii,* I (1923), 176–96.

Gurko, V. I. *Features and Figures of the Past: Government and Opinion in the Reign of Nicholas II.* Stanford, 1939.

Hahlweg, Werner (ed.). *Lenins Rückkehr nach Russland, 1917: Die deutschen Akten.* Leiden, 1957.

Hanbury-Williams, Sir John. *The Emperor Nicholas II as I Knew Him.* London, 1922.

Ignatiev, Count Paul N., Dimitry M. Odinetz, and Paul J. Novgorodsev. *Russian Schools and Universities in the World War.* Economic and Social History of the World War: Russian Series. New Haven, 1929.

Istoriia grazhdanskoi voiny v SSSR. Edited by Maksim Gor'kii and others. Moscow, 1935—. 4 vols. to date.

Istorik i Sovremennik. Historical and literary journal. Berlin, 1922–24.

"Iz zapiskoi knizhki arkhivista." *KA*, X (1925), 300–304; XXXV (1929), 214; L (1932), 196–209.

Izvestiia. Daily newspaper. Organ of the Central Executive Committee of the Workers' and Soldiers' Deputies. Subtitle varies. Petrograd, 1917.

Izvestiia Glavnago Zemel'nago Komiteta. Petrograd, 1917. 8 nos.

Izvestiia Ministerstva Zemledeliia. Published weekly. Petrograd, 1917.

Izvestiia Osobago Soveshchaniia dlia izgotovleniia proekta polozheniia o vyborakh v Uchreditel'noe Sobranie. Petrograd, May 25–September 10, 1917. Nos. 1–100.

"Izvestiia" Revoliutsionnoi Nedeli. Published by the Committee of Petrograd Journalists. February 27–March 5, 1917.

Jessup, Philip C. *Elihu Root.* New York, 1938. 2 vols.

Johnson, William H. E. *Russia's Educational Heritage.* Pittsburgh, 1950.

Kayden, Eugene M., and Alexis N. Antsiferov. *The Cooperative Movement in Russia During the War.* Social and Economic History of the World War: Russian Series. New Haven, 1929.

Kazemzadeh, Firuz. *The Struggle for Transcaucasia, 1917–1921.* New York, 1951.

Kerenskii, A. *Izdaleka: Sbornik statei.* Paris, 1922.

Kerenskii, A. F. *Izbrannyia rechi: Rechi A. F. Kerenskago o revoliutsii.* C ocherkom V. V. Kir'iakova: "Kerenskii kak orator." Petrograd, 1917.

Kerensky, A. F. *The Crucifixion of Liberty.* New York, 1934.

———. *The Prelude to Bolshevism.* New York, 1919.

Kerensky, Alexander F. *The Catastrophe.* New York, 1927.

"Komissiia po inostrannym delam." *Byloe,* No. 6 (1918), 9–28.

Krasnaia Letopis'. Historical journal. Leningrad, 1922–37. 66 vols.

Krasnov, P. N. "Na vnutrennem fronte." *ARR,* I (1922), 97–190.

Krasnyi Arkhiv. Historical journal. Moscow, 1922–41. 106 vols.

Krupskaya, Nadezhda. *Memories of Lenin.* New York, n.d. 2 vols.

Kucherov, Samuel. *Courts, Lawyers, and Trials Under the Last Three Tsars.* New York, 1943.

Lapin, N. (ed.). "Kadety v dni Galitsiikogo razgroma." *KA,* LIX (1933), 117–22.

———. "Progressivnyi Blok v 1915–1917 gg." *KA,* L–LI (1932), 117–60; LII (1932), 143–96; LVI (1933), 80–135.

Lapinskii, N. M. *Russko-Polskie otnosheniia v period mirovoi voiny.* Moscow, 1926.

Lenin, V. I. *Collected Works of V. I. Lenin.* Vols. XVIII (1930), XX (1929), XXI (1932). New York.

———. *Sochineniia.* 2nd ed. Moscow-Leningrad, 1926–32. 30 vols.

Letopis' Revoliutsii. Berlin-Petrograd-Moscow, 1923. 1 vol.

Letters of the Tsar to the Tsaritsa, 1914–1917. New York, 1929.

Letters of the Tsaritsa to the Tsar, 1914–1916. London, 1923.

Levina, M. (ed.). "Pechat' v dni kerenshchiny." *KA,* LVIII (1933), 131–33.

L'homme Enchaîné. Daily newspaper edited by G. Clemenceau. Paris, 1917.

Lozinskii, Z. *Ekonomicheskaia Politika Vremennago Pravitel'stva.* Leningrad, 1929.

Ludendorff, General. *My War Memories, 1914–1918.* London, 1920.

Lukomskii, A. S. *Memoirs of the Russian Revolution by General Loukomsky.* Trans. by Mrs. Vitali. London, 1922.

Maksakov, Vladimir V. *Khronika grazhdanskoi voiny v Sibiri (1917–1918).* Moscow, 1926.

Maliantovich, P. N. *Revoliutsiia i pravosudie.* Moscow, 1918.

Maliutin, B. "Nakanune oktiabr'skago perevorota." *Byloe*, No. 6 (1918), 3–41.

Manteyer, G. de (ed.). *Austria's Peace Offer*. London, 1921.

Martynov, E. I. *Kornilov (Popytka voennogo perevorota)*. Leningrad, 1927.

Martynov, M. "Agrarnoe dvizhenie v 1917 godu po dokumentam Glavnogo Zemel'nogo Komiteta." *KA*, XIV (1926), 182–226.

Mazour, Anatole G. *Finland Between East and West*. Princeton, 1956.

Mel'gunov, S. *Na putiakh k dvortsovomu perevorotu*. Paris, 1931.

——. *Sud'ba Imperator Nikolaia II posle otrecheniia*. Paris, 1951.

Michelson, Alexander M., Paul N. Apostol, and Michael W. Bernatzky. *Russian Public Finance During the War*. Social and Economic History of the World War: Russian Series. New Haven, 1928.

Miliukov, P. N. *Istoriia vtoroi russkoi revoliutsii*. Sofia, 1921–23. 1 vol. in 3 parts.

——. *Vospominaniia, 1859–1917*. Edited by M. M. Karpovich and B. Elkin. New York, 1955. 2 vols.

Ministerstvo Yustitsii. *Sudebnye Ustavy 20 noiabria 1864 g. za piat'desiat let*. Petrograd, 1914. 2 vols.

Morokhovets, E. A. *Agrarnye programmy rossiiskikh politicheskikh partii v 1917 godu*. Leningrad, 1929.

M. P. (ed.). "Bor'ba za zemliu v 1917 g." *KA*, LXXVIII (1936), 85–97.

Mstislavskii, S. *Piat' dnei*. Moscow, 1922.

Nabokov, V. "Vremennoe Pravitel'stvo." *ARR*, I (1921), 9–96.

Naglovskii. "Zheleznodorozhniki v russkoi revoliutsii, 1917–1920 gg." Ms. in the Hoover Institution.

Narishkin-Kurakin, Elizabeth. *Under Three Tsars: The Memoirs of the Lady in Waiting*. New York, 1931.

Nekludoff, A. *Diplomatic Reminiscences Before and During the World War, 1911–1917*. New York, 1920.

Nevskii, V. I. (ed.). "Verkhovnoe komandovanie v pervye dni revoliutsii." *KA*, V (1924), 213–40.

Nikitine, Colonel B. V. *The Fatal Years: Fresh Revelations on a Chapter of Underground History*. London, 1938.

Nikolaevskii, B. I. "A Collection of Extracts from Menshevik Newspapers, 1917–1920." Ms. in the Hoover Institution.

Nolde, Baron Boris E. *Russia in the Economic War*. Social and Economic History of the World War: Russian Series. New Haven, 1928.

Novaia Zhizn'. Daily newspaper edited by Maksim Gor'kii. Petrograd, 1917.

Novoe Vremia. Daily conservative newspaper. Petrograd, 1917.

Novyi Zhurnal. Quarterly. New York, 1942—.

Ogonek. Weekly social-political and literary-artistic journal. Leningrad, 1927. No. 11.

"Oktiabr' na fronte." *KA*, XXIII (1927), 149–94; XXIV (1927), 71–107.

Osobyi Zhurnal Zasedaniia Vremennago Pravitel'stva 1917. Petrograd, 1917.

Padenie tsarskogo rezhima: Stenograficheskie otchety doprosov i pokazanii dannykh v 1917 g. v. Chrezvychainoi sledstvennoi komissii Vremennogo Pravitel'stva. P. E. Shchegolev, ed. Leningrad-Moscow, 1924–27. 7 vols.

Paléologue, Maurice. *An Ambassador's Memoirs*. London, 1923–25. 3 vols.

——. *La Russie des tsars pendant la grande guerre*. Paris, 1921–22. 3 vols.

Pares, Bernard. *The Fall of the Russian Monarchy*. London, 1939.

Pavlovsky, G. *Agricultural Russia on the Eve of the Revolution.* London, 1930.

Pipes, Richard. *The Formation of the Soviet Union: Communism and Nationalism, 1917–1923.* Cambridge, Mass., 1934.

"Pis'mo vel. kn. Aleksandra Mikhailovicha k Nikolaiu II ot 25 dekabria 1916–4 fevralia 1917 gg." *ARR,* V (1922), 333–36.

Poincaré, Raymond. *Au service de la France: Neuf années de souvenirs.* Paris, 1926–33. 10 vols.

Pokrovskii, M. N. *Oktiabr'skaia revoliutsiia i antanta.* Moscow, 1927.

———. *Vneshnaia politika rossii v XX veke.* Moscow, 1926.

Pokrovskii, M. N. (ed.). "Ekonomicheskoe polozhenie rossii pered revoliutsiei." *KA,* X (1925), 69–94.

———. "Iz dnevnika A. N. Kuropatkina." *KA,* XX (1927), 56–77.

———. *Ocherki po istorii oktiabr'skoi revoliutsii.* Moscow, 1927. 2 vols.

———. "Politicheskoe polozhenie rossii nakanune fevral'skoi revoliutsii v zhandarmskom osveshchenii." *KA,* XVII (1926), 3–35.

———. "Stavka i ministerstvo inostrannykh del." *KA,* XXVI (1928), 1–50; XXVII (1928), 2–57; XVIII (1928), 3–58; XXIX (1928), 1–54; XXX (1928), 5–45.

Pokrovskii, M. N., and Ya. A. Yakovlev (eds.). *1917 god v dokumentakh i materialakh.* Moscow, 1925–39. 10 vols.

    I. *Petrogradskii sovet rabochikh i soldatskikh deputatov.* 1925.

    II. *Pervyi i serossiiskii sezd sovetov rabochikh i soldatskikh deputatov.* 2 parts. 1930, 1931.

    III. *Vtoroi vserossiiskii sezd sovetov rabochikh i soldatskikh deputatov.* 1928.

    IV. *Vserossiiskoe soveshchanie sovetov rabochikh i soldatskikh deputatov.* 1928.

    V. *Krestianskoe dvizhenie v 1917 godu.* 1927.

    VI. *Razlozhenie armii v 1917 godu.* 1925.

    VII. *Rabochee dvizhenie v 1917 godu.* 1926.

    VIII. *Burzhuaziia nakanune fevral'skoi revoliutsii.* 1927.

    IX. *Gosudarstvennoe Soveshchanie.* 1939.

    X. *Vserossiiskoe Uchreditel'noe Sobranie.* 1930.

Polner, Tikhon J., and others. *Russian Local Government During the War and the Union of Zemstvos.* Economic and Social History of the World War: Russian Series. New Haven, 1930.

Popov, A. (ed.). "Diplomatiia Vremennogo Pravitel'stva v bor'be s revoliutsiei." *KA,* XX (1927), 3–38.

———. "Inostrannye diplomaty o revoliutsii 1917 g." *KA,* XXIV (1927), 108–63.

Posledniia Novosti. Daily newspaper edited by P. N. Miliukov. Paris, 1920–40.

Pravda. Daily newspaper. Organ of the Central Committee of the Bolshevik Party. March 5–July 5, 1917. Published subsequently in 1917 as: *Listok "Pravdy,"* July 6; *Rabochii i Soldat,* July 23–August 9; *Proletarii,* August 13–August 24; *Rabochii,* August 25–September 2; *Rabochii Put',* September 3–October 26; *Pravda,* October 27—.

"Prodovol'stvennoe polozhenie v Moskve v marte-iiune 1917 goda." *KA,* XXCI (1937), 128–46.

Proletarskaia Revoliutsiia. Historical journal on the history of the October Revolution and the Russian Communist Party published by the Central Committee of the Russian Communist Party. Moscow, 1921–36. 120 nos.

Protopopov, A. D. "Predsmertnaia zapiska. S predisloviem P. Ya. Ryssa." *Golos Minuvshago na Chuzhoi Storone*, II (1926), 167–93.

Prozhektor. Illustrated literary, artistic, and satirical journal edited by N. Bukharin and A. Voronskii. Moscow, 1923.

Rabinovich, S. (ed.). "Taktika vyshego komandovaniia v fevral'skuiu revoliutsiu." *KA*, XXXV (1929), 212–15.

Rabochaia Gazeta. Daily newspaper. Central Organ of the Russian Social Democratic Party (Menshevik). Petrograd, 1917.

Rabochii, Rabochii i Soldat, Rabochii Put'. See *Pravda.*

Radkey, Oliver H. *The Agrarian Foes of Bolshevism: Promise and Default of the Russian Socialist Revolutionaries, February to October 1917.* New York, 1958.

Radkey, Oliver Henry. *The Election to the Russian Constituent Assembly of 1917.* Cambridge, Mass., 1950.

Rakhmetov, V. (ed.). "Aprel'skie dni 1917 goda v Petrograde." *KA*, XXXIII (1929), 34–81.

"Rasporiazheniia Vremennago Pravitel'stva." *Zhurnal Ministerstva Narodnago Prosveshcheniia.* LXXI (1917), 3–48.

Rech'. Daily newspaper. Organ of the Constitutional Democratic Party. Petrograd, 1917.

"Records of the German Foreign Office received by the Department of State." Microfilm copy T-120. Serial No. 3107h. Rolls 1498, 1499. Auswärtiges Amt. Germany. 1917.

Reddaway, W. F., and others. *The Cambridge History of Poland.* Cambridge, Eng., 1941. 2 vols.

Report of the Seventeenth Annual Conference of the Labour Party. Nottingham and London, 1918.

Reshetar, John S., Jr. *The Ukrainian Revolution, 1917–1920: A Study in Nationalism.* Princeton, 1952.

Ribot, Alexandre. *Journal d'Alexandre Ribot et correspondances inédites, 1914–1922.* Paris, 1936.

Robinson, Geroid Tanquary. *Rural Russia Under the Old Regime: A History of the Landlord-Peasant World and a Prologue to the Peasant Revolution of 1917.* New York, 1932.

Rodzianko, M. V. "Gosudarstvennaia Duma i fevral'skaia 1917 goda revoliutsiia." *ARR*, VI (1922), 5–80.

———. "Memorandum." Ms. in the Hoover Institution. N.d.

———. "Poslednii vsepoddaneishii doklad." *ARR*, VI (1922), 335–38.

———. *The Reign of Rasputin: An Empire's Collapse.* London, 1927.

Romanov, B. (ed.). "Finansovoe polozhenie rossii pered oktiabr'skoi revoliutsiei." *KA*, XXV (1927), 3–33.

Royal Institute of International Affairs. *The Baltic States: A Survey of the Political and Economic Structure and the Foreign Relations of Estonia, Latvia, and Lithuania.* London, 1938.

Rubinshtein, N. (ed.). "Vremennoe Pravitel'stvo i Uchreditel'noe Sobranie." *KA*, XXVIII (1928), 107–41.

Russian Review. Quarterly. New York, 1941—.

"Russkaia armiia nakanune revoliutsii." *Byloe*, No. 1 (1918), 151–57.

Russkaia Volia. Daily newspaper. Petrograd, 1917.

Russkii Istoricheskii Arkhiv. Publication of the Russian Historical Archive Abroad. Prague, 1929. 1 vol.

Russkiia Vedomosti. Daily newspaper of liberal persuasion with high standards of reporting. Moscow, 1917.

Russkoe Slovo. Daily newspaper. Moscow, 1917.

Sack, A. J. *The Birth of the Russian Democracy.* New York, 1918.

Sadoul, Jacques. *Notes sur la révolution bolchévique.* Paris, 1919.

Samoilov, S. "Fevral'skaia revoliutsiia v Minusinskoi ssylke." *PR,* IX (1926), 193-98.

Sbornik sekretnykh dokumentov iz arkhive byvshago ministerstva inostrannykh del. Narodnyi Komissariat Inostrannykh Del. Petrograd, 1917–18.

Sbornik Tsirkuliarov Ministerstva Vnutrennikh Del za period Mart–Iiun' 1917 goda. Petrograd, 1917.

Sbornik Ukazov i Postanovlenii Vremennago Pravitel'stva. Petrograd, 1917. 2 parts.

Scheidemann, P. *The Making of New Germany.* New York, 1929. 2 vols.

Schwarz, S. M. *"Fabrichno-zavodskie komitety i profsoiuzy v pervye gody revoliutsii."* Ms. in the Hoover Institution.

———. "Sotsial'noe strakhovanie v rossii v 1917–1919 godakh." Ms. in the Hoover Institution.

Semennikov, V. P. *Monarkhiia pered krusheniem 1914–1917: Bumagi Nikolaia II i drugie dokumenty.* Moscow, 1927.

Semenov, G. "Vospominaniia byvshego esera." *Prozhektor,* Nos. 8–9 (1923), 28–31.

Semenov Tian'-Shanskii, V. P. "Glavnyi Zemel'nyi Komitet." *ARR,* XII (1923), 291–95.

Serebrennikov, I. I. "Vospominaniia (1917–1922)." Ms. in the Hoover Institution.

"Sezd gubernskikh komissarov: Protokoly zasedanii 22–24 aprelia 1917 g." Mimeographed. Hoover Institution.

Schapiro, Leonard. *The Communist Party of the Soviet Union.* New York, 1960.

Shavel'skii, Georgii, *Vospominaniia poslednego protopresviter russkoi armii i flota.* New York, 1954. 2 vols.

Shidlovskii, S. I. *Vospominaniia.* Berlin, 1923.

Shliapnikov, A. G. *Semnadtsatyi god.* Moscow, 1923–27. 3 vols.

Shub, David. *Lenin.* New York, 1948.

Shul'gin, V. V. *Dni.* Belgrad, 1925.

Slavik, Ya. Ya. "Iz dnevnika generala M. V. Alekseeva." *Russkii Istoricheskii Arkhiv,* I (1929), 11–56.

Smirnov, M. I. "Admiral A. V. Kolchak vo vremia revoliutsii v chernomorskom flote." *Istorik i Sovremennik,* IV (1923), 3–28.

Smith, C. Jay, Jr. *Finland and the Russian Revolution, 1917-1922.* Athens, Ga., 1958.

Sobranie Uzakonenii i Rasporiazhenii Pravitel'stva. Petrograd, 1917. 2 vols., each in 2 parts.

Sokolov, N. A. *Ubiistvo tsarskoi sem'i.* Berlin, 1925.

Sprawozdanie z dzialalnosci Komisji Likwidacyjnej do Spraw Krolestwa Polskiego za czas od 15-go czerwca do 1-go sierpnia 1917 r. Petrograd, 1917.

Stankevich, V. B. *Vospominaniia 1914–1919.* Berlin, 1920.

"Stavka 25–26 oktiabria 1917." *ARR*, VII (1922), 279–320.

Stenograficheskie otchety Gosudarstvennoi Dumy. Chetvertyi Sozyv. Sessia IV, Sessia V. Petrograd, 1914–17.

Stenograficheskii otchet Osobago Soveshchaniia dlia izgotovleniia proekta polozheniia o vyborakh v Uchreditel'noe Sobranie. Petrograd, 1917. 5 vols.

Struve, P. B., K. I. Zaitsev, N. V. Dolinsky, and S. S. Demosthenov. *Food Supply in Russia During the World War.* Social and Economic History of the World War: Russian Series. New Haven, 1930.

Sukhanov, N. N. *The Russian Revolution 1917.* Ed. and trans. by Joel Carmichael. London, 1955.

———. *Zapiski o revoliutsii.* Berlin, 1922–23. 7 vols.

Le Temps. Daily newspaper. Paris, 1917.

The Times. London, 1917.

Titlinov, B. V. *Tserkov' vo vremia revoliutsii.* Petrograd, 1924.

Tobolin, I. (ed.). "Iiul'skie dni v Petrograde." *KA*, XXIII (1927), 1–63; XIV (1927), 3–70.

———. "Iz arkhiva Shcheglovitova." *KA*, XV (1926), 104–17.

Trotskii, L. D. *Oktiabr'skaia revoliutsiia.* Moscow, 1918.

Trotsky, Leon. *The History of the Russian Revolution.* New York, 1932. 3 vols.

Tseretelli, I. "Nakanune iiul'skago vosstaniia." *Novyi Zhurnal*, L (1957), 198–219; LI (1957), 120–46; LII (1958), 162–98.

Tseretelli, Irakli. "Reminiscences of the February Revolution: The April Crisis." *The Russian Review*, XIV (1955), 93–108, 184–200, 301–21; XV (1956), 37–48.

U. S. Department of State. *Papers Relating to the Foreign Relations of the United States, 1917*, Supplement 1, *The World War.* Washington, D.C., 1931.

———. *Papers Relating to the Foreign Relations of the United States, Russia, 1918.* Washington, D.C., 1931–32. 3 vols.

"V yanvare i fevrale 1917 g.: Iz donesenii sekretnykh agentov A. D. Protopopova." *Byloe*, No. 13(7) (1918), 91–123.

Vakar, Nicholas P. *Belorussia: The Making of a Nation.* Cambridge, Mass., 1956.

Vandervelde, Emile. *Three Aspects of the Russian Revolution.* London, 1918.

Varneck, Elena, and H. H. Fisher. *The Testimony of Kolchak and Other Siberian Materials.* Stanford, 1935.

Veiger-Redemeister, V. A. "S Kerenskim v Gatchina." *PR*, IX (1923), 79–95.

Velikaia oktiabr'skaia sotsialisticheskaia revoliutsiia: Dokumenty i materialy. Moscow, 1957—.

Revoliutsionnoe dvizhenie v rossii posle sverzheniia samoderzhavia. 1957.

Revoliutsionnoe dvizhenie v rossii v aprele 1917 g.: Aprel'skii krizis. 1958.

Revoliutsionnoe dvizhenie v rossii v mae-iiune 1917 g.: Iiun'skaia demonstratsiia. 1959.

Revoliutsionnoe dvizhenie v rossii v iiule 1917 g.: Iiul'skii krizis. 1959.

Revoliutsionnoe dvizhenie v rossii v avguste 1917 g.: Razgrom Kornilovskogo miatezha. 1959.

Oktiabr'skoe vooruzhennoe vosstanie v Petrograde. 1957.

Velikaia oktiabr'skaia sotsialisticheskaia revoliutsiia: Khronika sobytii. Moscow, 1957—.

I. *27 fevralia–6 maia, 1917 goda.* 1957.

II. *7 maia–25 iiulia, 1917 goda.* 1959.

Verkhovskii, A. I. *Rossiia na Golgofe.* Petrograd, 1918.

Vestnik Vremennago Pravitel'stva. Daily official newspaper of the Provisional Government. Petrograd, 1917.

Victoroff-Toporoff, V. (ed.). *La Première année de la Révolution Russe (Mars 1917–Mars 1918): Faits—documents—appréciations.* Berne, 1918.

Vinberg, F. *V plenu u obez'ian: Zapiski kontr-revoliutsionera.* Kiev, 1918.

Vishniak, M. V. "K istorii fevral'skoi revoliutsii: Po povodu knigi Olivera Radki." *Novyi Zhurnal,* LIV (1958), 200–215.

————. *Vserossiiskoe Uchreditel'noe Sobranie.* Paris, 1932.

Vladimirova, Vera (ed.). "Bol'shevizatsiia fronta v prediiul'skie dni 1917 g." *KA,* LVIII (1933), 86–100.

Vlast' Naroda. Daily newspaper. Democratic and socialist viewpoint. Moscow, 1917.

Volia Naroda. Daily newspaper. Organ of the right Socialist Revolutionaries. Petrograd, 1917.

Volia Rossii. Weekly. Prague, 1921.

"Vospominaniia ob oktiabr'skom perevorote." *PR.* X (1922), 43–93.

Vozrozhdenie. Paris. XXIV (1952).

Vulliamy, C. E., and A. L. Hynes. *From the Red Archives: Russian State Papers and Other Documents Relating to the Years 1915–1918.* London, 1929.

Vvedenskii, A. I. *Tserkov' i gosudarstvo.* Moscow, 1923.

Warth, Robert D. *The Allies and the Russian Revolution: From the Fall of the Monarchy to the Peace of Brest-Litovsk.* Durham, N.C., 1954.

Winship, North. "U.S. Consulate Reports: Petrograd Revolution, Mar.–July 1917." Ms. in the Hoover Institution.

Witte, Graf Sergei Yu. *Vospominaniia: tsarstvovanie Nikolaia II,* Berlin, 1922. 2 vols.

Yakovlev, Ya. A. (ed.). "Mart–mai 1917." *KA,* XV (1926), 30–60.

Yashnov, E. *Dostatochno-li khleba v Rossii?* Petrograd, 1917.

Z Dokumentów Chwili. Underground publication of the Poles during the German occupation. Warsaw, 1917.

Zagorsky, S. O. *State Control of Industry in Russia During the War.* Social and Economic History of the World War: Russian Series. New Haven, 1928.

Zalezhskii, V. N. "Hel'singfors vesnoi i letom 1917 g." *PR,* XVII(5) (1923), 117–89.

"Zapiska, sostavlennaia v kruzhke Rimskago-Korsakova i peredannaia Nikolaiu II Kn. Golitsynym v noiabre 1916 g." *ARR,* V (1922), 337–43.

Zapiski Instituta Lenina. Moscow. II (1927).

Zeman, Z. A. B. (ed.). *Germany and the Revolution in Russia, 1915–1918.* London, 1958.

Zenkovsky, Serge A. *Pan-Turkism and Islam in Russia.* Cambridge, Mass., 1960.

Zenzinov, V. "Fevral'skie dni." *Novyi Zhurnal,* XXXIV (1953), 188–211; XXXV (1953), 208–40.

Zhurnal Ministerstva Narodnago Prosveshcheniia. New series. Petrograd, 1917.

"Zhurnal soedinennago zasedaniia komissii po oborone i po inostrannym delam." *Byloe,* No. 6 (1918), 28–41.

Zhurnaly Zasedanii Vremennago Pravitel'stva. Petrograd, 1917. 2 vols.

INDEX

Index

The List of Documents in each volume should be used together with this Index. Newspaper editorials have not been indexed but are identified in the lists of documents. Volume I contains pp. 1–478; Volume II, pp. 479–1194; Volume III, pp. 1195–1829.

and was member of Executive Committee), 1177–83

Grinevich [K. S. Schechter] (Menshevik-Internationalist; member, Petrograd Soviet Exec. Com., 1917), 31, 71ff, 76, 216

Grinevich, Ensign, 424

Grinevich, Viktor Petrovich [Mikhail Grigorevich Kogan] (Menshevik; Chairman, All-Russian Council of Trade Unions, 1917), 750, 1506–7, 1508

Groman, Vladimir Gustavovich (Menshevik; member, Supply Commission, Petrograd Soviet; Soviet planner; sentenced in Menshevik Trial, 1931), 75, 633, 738

Gronskii, Pavel Pavlovich (Kadet; member, 4th Duma), 67–68, 602, 1215

Grubbe, E. K., 1535

Grünau, Freiherr von, 1072–73

Gruzinov, A. E., 1496–97

Gruzinov, Lieutenant Colonel, 172, 174

Guberniya, *see* Agrarian disorders; Land committees; Local government; Zemstvos; *individual names of guberniyas*

Guchkov, Aleksandr Ivanovich (Octobrist; President, 3rd Duma; President, Central War Industry Committee; Minister of War and Navy, March–May 1917; emigrated), 18, 1085, 1135, 1232, 1237, 1241, 1456, 1587; and abdication of Tsar, 24, 99–102, 103–4, 105, 108, 115; activities as Minister of War and Navy, 841–42, 848, 853, 854–56, 875–77, 880, 919, 1014f, 1225, 1230; appointment as Minister, 121f, 125, 131; on attack on Straits and Constantinople, 1039, 1059; and Declaration of Soldiers' Rights, 880; and Kornilov affair, 1527f, 1530f, 1534, 1536, 1710; resignation as Minister, 1197, 1267–68, 1295, 1396, 1495; speech before Front Congress, 911–13; speech to meeting of four Dumas, 1259–61

Gukasov, A. O., 697

Gukasov, P. O., 697

Gul'kevich, K. N., 1073

Gurevich, Vissarion Yakovlevich (S.R.; Assistant Minister of the Interior, 1917; member, Constituent Assembly, 1918; later member, Siberian Regional Duma and Far Eastern People's Assembly; emigrated), 598–600, 1144, 1146, 1342

Gurevich, Ya. Ya., 773

Gurko, General Vasilii Iosifovich (Acting Chief of Staff to Supreme Commander, December 1916–February 1917; Commander in Chief, Western Front, April–May 1917; dismissed by Kerensky), 886–87, 903, 922, 991, 1004, 1270

Guzhon factory, 764–65

Gvozdev, Kos'ma Antonovich (Menshevik; Chairman, Labor Group, Central War Industry Committee; member, Petrograd Soviet Exec. Com.; Minister of Labor, September–October 1917; later served under Soviets), 71ff, 759, 762, 1271, 1714, 1778, 1790

Gymnasia, see Education, secondary

Haase, Hugo (a leading German S.D.), 1160, 1178

Hague Convention, 1155

Halifax, 1088

Hanbury-Williams, General Sir John (British Military Representative at Stavka, 1914–17), 89–90, 178

Hanecki, *see* Ganetskii

Hardinge, Sir Arthur, 1168

Helfand, *see* Parvus

Helsingfors, 1581, 1631f. *See also* Finland

Henderson, Arthur (British trade unionist; Secretary, British Labour Party for 23 years; member of cabinet during War until 1917; forced to resign over Stockholm Conference; later member, Labour government and active in disarmament conferences), 1050, 1106, 1115–16, 1173–74, 1183, 1185–86

Hensel, Professor, 495

Herzegovina, 1129, 1152

Herzen, Aleksandr Ivanovich (Russian revolutionary leader and writer of mid-19th century; had great influence on Russian non-Marxist socialism), 330, 382, 542

Hindenburg, Field Marshal Paul von (Commander in Chief, German Armies on Eastern Front, 1914–16; Chief of Staff and Supreme Commander, 1916–18; President of German Republic, 1925–34), 1158, 1178

Hoffmann, H. A. (member, Swiss Federal Council, 1914–17; resigned over Grimm affair), 1177–83

Holy Synod, 815f; appeal for support of Provisional Government, 803–4; change in membership of, 803, 806–7. *See also* Russian Orthodox Church; Sobor

Hospitals, army, 1001

Hrushevskii, Mikhail Sergeevich (Ukrainian historian and statesman; President, Ukrainian Central Rada, 1917; emigrated, then returned as President, Ukrainian Academy of Sciences; arrested and banished to North Russia, 1930), 370

Hungary, *see* Austria-Hungary

Huss, John (1369–1415; Bohemian religious reformer; burned at the stake), 1152

Ignat'ev, Count Pavel Nikolaevich (Minister of Education, 1915–16), 771

Il'in, I. A., 1748, 1754, 1761

Il'kevich, Lieutenant General, 974

Illarion, Archbishop, 830

Imperial family, disposition of, 153–54, 177, 178–79, 181–84, 187–88, 189–90. *See also names of individual members*

Imperiali di Francavilla, Marquis Guglielmo (Italian Ambassador at London, 1910–20), 1125

Independent Labour Party (Great Britain), 1171

Industry, 298–99; Chambers of Commerce and, 683–84; Congresses of Representatives of, 671, 682–83, 716–17, 1401, 1403–4; general conditions of, 668–77, 1463–64; joint stock companies, 666; production, 667, 679–81, 1706; proposals for regulation of, 672, 674–75, 679, 1483–84, 1709, 1715; supply, 667–68. *See also* Economic Council and Central Economic Committee; Fuel; Labor